MONEY AND BANKING

INTRODUCTION TO

THE ANALYTICS AND
INSTITUTIONS

OF MONEY AND BANKING

William J. Frazer, Jr.
University of Florida

and William P. Yohe
Duke University

D. VAN NOSTRAND COMPANY, INC.
Princeton, New Jersey
Toronto   New York   London

D. VAN NOSTRAND COMPANY, INC.
120 Alexander St., Princeton, New Jersey (*Principal office*)
24 West 40 Street, New York 18, New York

D. VAN NOSTRAND COMPANY, LTD.
358, Kensington High Street, London, W.14, England

D. VAN NOSTRAND COMPANY (CANADA), LTD.
25 Hollinger Road, Toronto 16, Canada

PRINTED IN THE UNITED STATES OF AMERICA

Preface

This book—an analytical and institutional approach to money and banking—represents a systematic application of mathematics over a broad range of both money and banking topics. The use of elementary mathematics, in combination with the extensive treatment of the institutional aspects of the subject, makes the approach more operational. The variables and parameters of the elementry models take on a more detailed meaning in terms of underlying conditions, expectations, the operations of the financial markets, and so on. The mathematics, in effect, forces a more explicit statement of detailed features of elementary models than has been achieved in the past with words and two-dimensional drawings alone, especially in a comparable amount of space. The net effect should be an improvement in the level of communication.

The mathematics enters in other worthwhile ways: e.g., (1) as a simplifying device for a subject of growing complexity, (2) and as a means of assuring a greater consistency in the treatment of topics throughout the book. It often affords original ways of viewing things, such as the definition of the income velocity of money balances in terms of Keynesian parameters, the assignment of probabilities to coordinates pertaining to the liquidity preference demand for money, and so on.

In addition to the use of mathematics, the present work is directed toward providing the appropriate balance of institutional, historical and theoretical materials needed to introduce the reader to the operations of the banking system, the role and formation of monetary policy, and the latter's effect upon the various sectors of the economy and the manner in which these effects are transmitted throughout the economic system. Money and banking, as presented in these pages, is thought to contribute to an introductory understanding of monetary phenomena generally, commercial and central banking proper, and their implications for household, public, and business finance. The approach to the subject proceeds from the macro, the whole, to the micro, the parts; that is, it proceeds from the perspective of the entire banking system to that for the individual banks, or similarly, from the whole economy to the individual, firms, and governmental units composing the respective sectors of the economy.

The first two parts of the text are intended to provide a first approximation to an understanding of monetary phenomena, in general, and fractional reserve banking. In the first part the reader is introduced to the definition of money, changes in the motives underlying the demand for money, the supply of money balances, the rate of interest, and the meaning of the quality called "moneyness" and "liquidity." In the second part, apart from additional contemporary monetary theory, the reader is introduced to basic notions of conventional monetary economics—the quantity theory of money, the gold standard, and the real bills doctrine. It is considered desirable to bring these notions into juxtaposition in order to reveal something of the view in which our monetary system was originally contemplated, especially at the time of the founding of the Federal Reserve System. Appropriate modifications of the original quantity theory, the gold standard, and the real bills doctrine are introduced and discussed in Part Two and in other sections, but the brief discussion of them in Part Two serves also as a basis for considering some aspects of money and banking history, the original Federal Reserve Act, international monetary operations, all prior to the more detailed consideration of the foreign side of monetary operations in Part Seven.

Part Four provides, among other things, a description of the reserve and money supply accounts, and some aspects of the formation of monetary policy, and the central and commercial banking structures. It is followed by a discussion of central banking in relationship to a somewhat broader range of financial institutions in Part Five. These involve the U.S. Treasury, and the money, credit, and capital markets.

Part Six contains additional monetary analysis. The national income model is introduced, and additional topics concerning monetary analysis and financial institutions are considered within the framework provided by that model. These additional topics include investment and other multipliers, price-level changes, investment demand by the business sectors, the consumption function, consumer credit, other determinants of expenditures by the consumer sector, fiscal policy, growth, and the determination of the rate of interest.

The above topics are followed in Part Seven by additional emphasis upon the foreign side of monetary operations. Various international institutions are covered as well as the United States balance of payments, short-term capital movements, exchange rates, interest arbitrage, and notions of international liquidity that gained increased importance in the early 1960's, both with respect to the position of the United States as a key-currency country and with respect to an understanding of monetary policy on the domestic side. In fact, for the latter reason the chapters on monetary policy over the post-World War II years and the principles of monetary policy have been placed in Part Eight at the end of the book.

The various developments contributing to the final form of this book were greatly accelerated by William P. Yohe's collaboration. His influence is reflected over the entire work with particular respect to the presentation of the deviations of the bank reserve and money supply accounts, the notion of a quantitative monetary policy, financial institutions, monetary theory, and financial multipliers.

Many have contributed to this work in one way or another. From among them—including readers, journal editors, the publisher, a few encouraging colleagues, and students—at least two must be mentioned: Professor Paul E. Koefod and Mary Ann B. Frazer. The former was in a crucial way responsible for getting together the two young individualists who collaborated in this work and shared a common philosophy about their subject, and the latter performed the tedious, repetitious, and frequently boring task for typing numerous drafts of the many chapters. The tediousness of the typing task was compounded by the presence of the mathematics, and it was matched only by Mary Ann's uncommon skill as a mathematical typist.

WILLIAM J. FRAZER, JR.

University of Florida
September 1965

Contents

The Methodology of
Money and Banking

> . . . Mathematical treatment is relatively useful as the relations
> become relatively complicated. The introduction of mathematical
> method marks a stage of growth . . . (Irving Fisher, *Mathemati-*
> *cal Investigations in the Theory of Value and Prices* [1892]).

The subject of money and banking is traditionally an applied area of economics, finance is a closely related study, and certain aspects of these areas become inseparable as one views monetary operations in the broader setting of the financial markets. Economics itself has classically been defined as the study of the allocation of scarce resources among competing alternative uses and the satisfaction of wants. However, in the light of the occasional inadequate demand in the midst of adequate supplies of goods and services (i.e., the modern recession), economics is concerned at times with the national economic goals of employment, production, and purchasing power—all in the context of a relatively free economy. In the former instance, money enters as a medium of exchange; in the latter, the so-called monetary and financial mechanism—our system of money, banks, and financial markets—is relied upon to effect generally an indirect type of control over economic behavior. Money is so basic in the latter instance, in fact, that such an economy is sometimes called a "monetary economy." In order, then, to better understand the economy, predict its level of performance, and effect appropriate regulations, a body of monetary, banking, and financial theory is needed, as well as systematic observations. This chapter, consequently, reviews the role of theory and, in relation to the role of theory, the role of mathematics, causation, and statics and dynamics.

1

1.1. Applied Study: The Role of Theory and the Role of Mathematics

In applied study, theory concerns our explanations of real world phenomena. A good theory serves the purpose of explanation, and it should meet empirical tests and tests of logical consistency. The mathematics enters in the latter instance.

The role of theory. A theory—at least, for the purpose of our study—consists essentially of the following:

(1) Explicit definitions of the more important terms, such as "money," "the rate of return," "a key currency," "interest arbitrage," and the "prime-loan rate";

(2) Undefined terms, such as "and," "if," "but," and a wide variety of connectives and everyday terms with which the reader is assumed to be familiar;

(3) Assumptions (i.e., axioms, postulates, premises, or hypotheses) that may pertain to the motives of participants in some social setting;

(4) A formal structure like that provided by mathematics or a logical approach; and

(5) A set of conclusions, also sometimes referred to as propositions, rules, or theorems.

All of these steps in a theory are not always spelled out. In extreme instances, discussion may proceed only in terms of conclusions, and, even in some less informal instances, the assumptions may only be implied by the content of the discussion.

A good theory in applied study is judged by the correspondence of the assumptions to reality. Of course, it must also meet tests of internal or logical consistency. Meeting these tests, the theory will provide accurate interpretations of the real world and facilitate predictions. A theory also may be rather general or more limited in its applicability and usefulness. In the former case, the assumptions and definitions would be less restrictive; in the latter case, they may be too restrictive to permit any interpretation of the broader picture. In the study of money, banking, and finance we are often more concerned with the broad picture, and the smaller segments that may, we hope, be consistently fitted into that picture. Sometimes the terms "theory" and "model" are used synonymously, and, at other times, the term "model" is used in a more restrictive sense. Some models are simply analogies or descriptions rather than explanations. They do not reveal causal relationships.

A good theory may also be judged by other criteria: (1) a minimum number of assumptions that result in fruitful conclusions for the purpose at hand or (2) a reasonably small and yet sufficient number of variables (quantities that vary over some interval).

Theories, as indicated by the criteria, are abstractions from reality. But even abstractions, to be useful, must be properly applied. This often requires some background in, and some awareness of, the institutional and physical setting in which the application is to be made.

The role of mathematics. A formal mathematical system consists of a list of basic symbols and formal (as contrasted with substantive) definitions, a set of axioms, theorems, and proofs. The theorems often take an "if . . . , then . . ." form. The "if" part of the statement is an hypothesis, and the "then" part is regarded as a follow-up to a logical connection that can be established by a proof in terms of the axioms of the system. A proof, through terms of a logical process, indicates that what is to be proved follows from the axioms or previously proved theorems. On the basis of different sets of axioms, different mathematical systems may be developed. Their use to us lies in their logical consistency.

Even in sound nonmathematical exposition, elements of the mathematical or axiomatic approach are present. With respect to such exposition, one could list the implicit or explicit assumptions and restate the salient conclusions as propositions, and then prove the propositions by invoking the assumptions and perhaps using a bit of existing mathematics. The approach would be axiomatic, though the exercise would not be precisely analogous to formal mathematics, since the symbols are usually given real world meanings and the system is less formal.

The latter exercise may prove to be exhaustive and too detailed. In any event, it should appear that a proper use of some mathematics would yield certain benefits. Over-all, one of these should be a greater consistency of statements and conclusions about the real world. Another benefit, as in the case of some basic monetary model, should be a more complete disclosure of the meaning and possible relevance of the model to the real world. In the latter instance, the mathematics, in effect, forces a careful investigation of the meaning of the model and its relevance. Especially, where the applied subject itself is both complex and deeply involved, the use of mathematics should aid in simplifying the exposition and statements about sequences of causation.

1.2. An Elementary Monetary Model

As indicated above, a model or theory concerns assumptions, logical structure, and so on. Such structures, in turn, usually involve statements of causal relationships, systems of equations, a distinction between stock and flow variables, and special references to the role of time. This section introduces these topics, and, in the process, it introduces an elementary monetary model. The model recurs on numerous occasions throughout the book so we do not attempt to develop its full meaning until later.

Causation. Causation is an important aspect of applied study. The notion of causation may be related to the study of functions, and functions are used frequently in the following pages.

A function is a set of ordered pairs (or tuples). In the case of the plane (or two-dimensional space), it is a set of coordinates (x,y)—the coordinate measured from the y-axis and parallel to the x-axis, and the coordinate measured from the x-axis and parallel to the y-axis. In the case of three-dimensional space, it is the set of three coordinates (x,y,z) —all measured parallel to their respective axes.

Functional relationships may be defined by equations, and the latter often appear as systems of equations. Such a system is determinate if it yields a unique solution. This precludes the other two possibilities in which there are no solutions or infinitely many.

An elementary model. To illustrate the solution to an equation system, we introduce an elementary monetary model:[1]

(1) $$M_d = \alpha Y + \beta, \quad \alpha > 0,$$
(2) $$M_s = \gamma$$

where M_d is the quantity of money (presently, undefined) demanded,

M_s is the quantity of money supplied,

Y is national income, and

α, β, and γ are parameters.

M_d and M_s are stock variables. The stock of money, as emphasized later (Chap. 2 and 3) and as a statistical matter, will be viewed as the stock of paper notes and coins outside of banks plus the stock of deposits payable on demand at the bank and adjusted for interbank deposits. We speak often of the stock of money. Y, on the other hand, is a flow variable. It is expressed below as a rate per unit of time (e.g., a year) at a moment (e.g., some calendar date) in time. The parameters, α (alpha) and β (beta), indicate, respectively, the slope and the intercept of the line [or locus of points (x,y)] in regard to the vertical axis; they reflect our reasoning and observations that the demand for money is an increasing function of income.

Equation (2) shows the quantity of money supplied as some constant γ (gamma). This constant function reflects a view set forth in subsequent chapters that the supply of money balances forthcoming from the monetary system need not be dependent on income in the short run or on changes in income. As we shall see, it is a controlled variable. This stock of money, of course, is an accumulated amount up to a given time. The parameters are called constants, but they too may vary, with the result that the functional relationship between the variables varies. In dealing with variables, the parameters represent other things. Often for us, they will represent the underlying conditions—the state of technology or the more volatile state of the outlook toward the future.

In the present instance, the parameter α ($\alpha > 0$) reflects an important behavioral assumption:

Postulate: *The stock of money demanded by the community varies directly with the flow of income (and presumably assets).* This statement and the presumption about assets may be shown to be consistent with empirical findings. If the reader will think about the statement in relation to the real world, he will likely be willing to proceed on the assumption.

The assumption, in combination with equation (2), assures us that a solution to the equation system exists. Solving for Y in terms of the parameters, therefore, $\gamma = \alpha Y + \beta$, and

$$(3) \qquad Y_t = \frac{\gamma - \beta}{\alpha}$$

Here we have a solution for income at some base time (call it zero, $t = 0$) in terms of the parameters. Clearly, income can change in the present model only by effecting some change in underlying conditions. In the present instance, let us illustrate a downward shift in the demand for money (i.e., a shift in β to β^*), possibly in response to an anticipation of a future rise in prices. Thus

$$(4) \qquad Y_{t+1} = \frac{\gamma - \beta^*}{\alpha}$$

where $\beta^* < \beta$, and $Y_{t+1} > Y_t$.

Where we accept the ratio Y/M (recall that $M = \gamma$) as a measure of the income velocity of money, we may state a proposition:

Proposition: *Given the stock of money, shifts in the demand for money (i.e., shifts in parameters underlying demand) correspond to changes in velocity of money, and vice versa.* The proposition follows from the condition on the stock of money, the definition of the velocity of money, and the solution to the model. We will deal to a great extent with the velocity of money.*

---

* The elementary function $f(Y)$ is subject to shifting in the short run as the proposition suggests. Understanding the phenomenon characterizing this instability is important, and the instability is a problem with which public officials must deal, as we show. Thus, we deal with it explicitly. On the other hand, in advancing economics as an empirical science one may seek a more stable function, one with more stable numerical constants. In the 1950's and early 1960's there has been evidence of advances along this line by adding variables such as "expected income" (Sect. 18.1) to explain the demand for money and changes in the velocity of money, where expected income may be defined in terms of average income over a reference cycle (Fig. 4-1). (See, for example, Milton Friedman, "The Demand for Money: Some Theoretical and Empirical Results," *Journal of Political Economy*, August 1959, pp. 327-351.) At the present stage of the work in question, however, we choose to emphasize the simpler and more unstable functions. Extra variables affecting the demand for money and other goods are dealt with without their being made a formal part of equations.

Geometrically, the model represented by equations (1) and (2) would appear as in Fig. 1-1. The independent variable (Y) is shown on the horizontal axis, and the dependent variable $f(Y)^*$ is shown on the vertical axis. Also, in the illustration, we have indicated the magnitude of the intercept parameters β and β^* referred to above. The difference between these two parameters (i.e., $\beta > \beta^*$) is the change that brought about the increase in the flow of income from an amount per annum at time zero (Y_t) to an amount per annum at another moment in time (Y_{t+1}).

In some instances, we refer to the variables in our model as endogenous variables, and we refer to variable parameters, such as β, as exogenous variables. The term "endogenous" is meant to imply that the

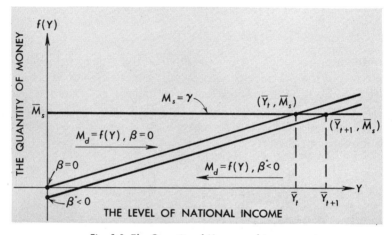

Fig. 1-1. The Quantity of Money and Income.

value of the variable is determined inside the system of equations or model, whereas the term "exogenous" is meant to imply that the value of the variable is determined outside of the model.

The flow of income. Representing some variables as flows is an important idealization which may be used considerably in subsequent analysis. An intuitive description of this process of idealization, consequently, helps emphasize the notion of a rate of change (velocity) and a change in velocity (acceleration), and it may improve our ability to intuit the meaning of certain data and interpret the ever-changing real world in other ways.

---

* In mathematics, the standard practice is to let the horizontal axis of the plane represent the independent variable, but due to a British influence the practice in economics is not carefully followed. Therefore, beware! In the present work, however, we will always indicate the axis representing the dependent variable by denoting that variable as a function of the independent variable. For example, in the present case the axis representing the variable M_d was indicated as $f(Y)$.

The mechanics of the idealization are straightforward. National income data are presented as quarterly rates per annum. In this form the data tell what the income would be for a year if the flow of income continued for a year at the average amount for a given quarter, and the data corresponding to the quarterly average of the rates of change per annum may be presented in the form of a histogram (see Fig. 1-2a). Now, if we idealize this form of presentation, we view the bars in the histogram as having smaller and smaller bases until they become only lines. In the ideal form we have the flow variable for income as a continuous function of time (see Fig. 1-2b), and change in the function then may be viewed as a rate of change in income. The notion of a flow

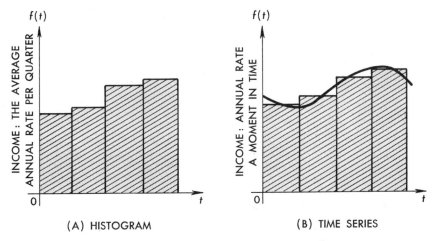

Fig. 1-2. Income: A Rate Per Annum at a Given Time.

is known in mathematics as well as in economics and other applied areas as velocity, and the rate of change in velocity, as when the slope of the tangent to the function increases and decreases, is known as acceleration.

Returning to equation (3), we note that the flow variable Y is itself a rate of change. So, using the quotient rule, $\partial Y/\partial \gamma = 1/\alpha^2$, and $\partial Y/\partial \gamma$, gives the rate of change in the variable Y (or acceleration in income) with respect to changes in γ. Similarly, changes in income velocity (i.e., changes in Y/M) are acceleration.

Statics and dynamics. The system consisting of equations (1) and (2) is static. The simple model as stated by those equations does not specify parametric changes, and its geometry may be regarded as providing a "time slice" of some portion of the economic process of continuous change. However, when time is introduced and the parameters and variables are in effect dated, we may call the model dynamic in the sense that time is introduced and we observe the process of change from one time to another.

An illustration of the notion of dynamics is presented in Fig. 1-3. There, the flat plane parallel to the Y,t plane represents the quantity of money supplied as a constant function of income and time. The surface intersecting this plane at an angle shows the quantity of money balances demanded as a function of income and time, and the plane slices the surface so as to provide a series of points in the form of one complete cycle of income from time zero to time four. Now, looking in from the left side of Fig. 1-3 and down the time axis and imagining the

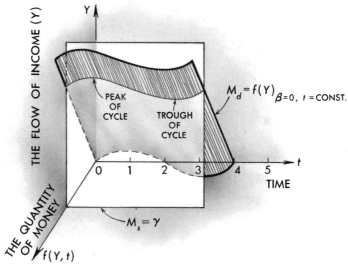

Fig. 1-3. The Demand for Money: A Dynamic Case.

plane $Y,f(Y,t)$ cutting through the time axis at zero, one should see Fig. 1-1 as if it were on its side and being viewed from behind. Maintaining the same points of view and imagining a plane parallel to the $Y,f(Y,t)$ plane and cutting the time axis at time one, one should see Fig. 1-1 after the parametric change from β to β^*. Indeed, parametric changes whereby the intercept parameter of Fig. 1-1 moves downward to time one, upward through time two, on to time three, and downward to time four are reflected along the line where the plane slices the surface. [Note: In Fig. 1-3 we could have shown the money supply increasing at some rate per annum with the effect that the cycle in question would have been about some increasing trend line. And somewhat more in accord with reality (Sect. 2.3 and 4.2), we could show the expansion phase to be of greater duration than the contraction phase.]

The term "static" with reference to the diagram does not mean, of course, that no change is taking place. Instead, it implies a "time slice" of our simple simulation of a continuous process, and we may, for example, simulate real world changes in the flow variable Y as the real world conditions corresponding to the parameters of equation (3) change. At times, in some discussions of mathematical economics, however, the term "dynamics" takes on a slightly different meaning from the present one. At those times, it means that a set of discontinuous changes, or changes that may be idealized into a discontinuous form, are being described and/or explained with the aid of difference equations.[3]

1.3. The Elementary Model Again: A Numerical Illustration

In applying mathematics, some have a strong urge to sense something as concrete as numbers from the real world. To satisfy such an urge in this introductory instance, such numbers are plugged into the earlier model—equations (1) and (2)—that corresponds to Fig. 1-1.

In proceeding, we denote the coordinates of an equilibrium point $(\overline{Y}_t, \gamma_t)$ or solution at one time, such as the trough of the 1960-1961 recession, and the coordinates of the equilibrium point $(\overline{Y}_{t+1}, \gamma_{t+1})$ at a subsequent time, such as year-end 1962:

(Dollar Amounts in Billions)

Y_{t+1} (seasonally adjusted, 4th quarter 1962, annual rate)	$= 565.2$
Y_t (seasonally adjusted, 1st quarter 1961, annual rate)	$= 500.8$
$Y_{t+1} - Y_t$ or $\Delta Y =$	64.4
γ_{t+1} (seasonally adjusted, daily averages 4th quarter 1962)	$= 147.0$
γ_t (seasonally adjusted, daily averages, 1st quarter 1961)	$= 141.8$
$\gamma_{t+1} - \gamma_t$ or $\Delta\gamma =$	5.2

Sources: U.S. Department of Commerce and Board of Governors of the Federal Reserve System.

Here, we have the facts at dates approximately corresponding to the coordinates of our points. We denote, too, the changes in income and the money supply over the period in question. We wish to note how the model generates these changes, but other questions may arise. For example, what portion of the rise in income is due to the change in the money supply and what portion is due to a change in some other condition?

Continuing, let us recall a few things. At the base time, $\beta = 0$, and therefore,

$$M_d = \alpha Y$$

or rearranging terms,

$$\alpha = \frac{M_d}{Y} = \frac{141.8}{500.8} = \frac{1}{3.53}$$

Now, we assume—with economists, a group of presently undefined bankers, and as discussed later (Sect. 2.2)—that the demand for money as a trend over time and as a function of income increases at approximately the same rate as income [i.e., $dM_d/dY = \alpha$ from equation (1)]. Also, from the solution,

$$Y = \frac{\gamma - \beta}{\alpha}$$

and

$$\frac{\partial Y}{\partial \gamma} = \frac{\alpha(1) - (\gamma - \beta)0}{\alpha^2}$$

$$= \frac{1}{\alpha} = 3.53$$

That is, the change in income with respect to the change in the stock of money is 3.53. Thus the portion of the change in income due to the change in the stock of money over the period in question was

$$3.53 \cdot 5.2 \text{ billion} = 18.36 \text{ billion}.$$

Since Y changed by 64.40 billion, and since 18.36 billion was due to the change in the money supply, the other 46.04 billion must have been due to the change in β. Since

$$\frac{\partial Y}{\partial \beta} = \frac{\alpha(-1) - (\gamma - \beta)(0)}{\alpha^2}$$

$$= -\frac{1}{\alpha}$$

the change in β required to effect a change of 46.04 billion in Y was $46.04/-3.53 = -13.0$ billion. In other words, what may be viewed as a change in the speculative motive for holding money by the business and financial sectors (Sect. 5.4) weakened to the extent of 13.0 billion and gave rise to 46.04 billion increase in income. Such a change could involve a change in the speculative motive or some combination of that motive and a change in expected income by the consumer sector (Sect. 18.1).

Viewing a blown-up sketch of the changes as if they occurred in the neighborhood of the point $(\overline{Y}_t, \overline{M}_s)$ in Fig. 1-1,

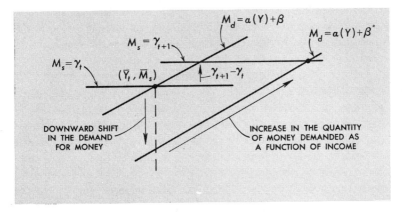

Again in words, the demand for money declined $(-\Delta\beta)$, the money supply increased $(\Delta\gamma)$, income increased (ΔY), and the quantity of money demanded increased as a function of income $[M_d = f(Y)]$.

1.4. Summary

One should beware of the dual role of such a term as "theory" in the pure and applied areas, respectively. In the first, it concerns only logical relationships (or mathematics). In the other, it concerns explanations of real world phenomena. In practice, these distinct usages sometimes become inextricably confused. As one is probably aware, the term "theory" has still an additional connotation. It is sometimes used to mean any statement of interpretation that is academic, useless, and far fetched. We shall try to avoid conveying any notion of that usage.

Mathematics finds its present use as a tool for monetary analysis. Our approach, one may say, is similar to that of any applied and systematic study, but it could proceed along more (or less) axiomatic lines. Definitions could be specified, and all the explicit and implicit assumptions could be presented as axioms along with the axioms of all other mathematical systems we wish to use. Then theorems or propositions corresponding to the conclusions of the more analytical portions of the book could be stated. We would then proceed to prove these theorems by reference to the definitions, axioms, and previously proved theorems. Perhaps someday our study will employ this approach extensively, but for the present we will use it sparingly.

To anticipate some aspects of the present approach to money and banking, an elementary model is introduced. It deals with the demand for money as a determinant of the level of income. Given the existence of a solution to the model, the definition of the income velocity of money, and the money supply, as a proposition we note that shifts in the demand for money are reflected in changes in income velocity. There is also a hint at the prospect of some control over the level of income through some indirect control over the stock of money.

The present uses of mathematics should help to achieve several things: (1) over-all logical consistency; (2) awareness of the complexity and vast number of interrelationships involved in the study of money and banking; (3) an operational statement of elementary monetary and banking models, and especially a distinction between stock and flow variables, and an awareness of the behavioral quality of the assumptions underlying our analyses; (4) a simplifying form of statement, and especially, explicit statements of causal relationships; and (5) a clearer view of the time dimension and the pattern of changes in variables and parameters over time.

References

1. William J. Frazer, Jr., "Monetary Analysis and the Postwar Rise in the Velocity of Money in the United States," *Schweizerische Zeitschrift für Volkswirtschaft und Statistik*, December 1964; and William J. Frazer, Jr., *The Liquidity Structure of Firms and Monetary Economics* (Gainesville, Fla.: University of Florida Press, 1965), Sect. 8.2.

2. For a statement and proof of the rule, see almost any calculus book. Two introductory books, however, may be cited: Paul H. Daus and William M. Whyburn, *Introduction to Mathematical Analysis with Applications to Problems of Economics* (Reading, Mass.: Addison-Wesley Publishing Company, Inc., 1958); and David S. Huang, *Introduction to the Use of Mathematics in Economic Analysis* (New York: John Wiley and Sons, Inc., 1964). These will be cited on other occasions.

3. See, e.g., David S. Huang, *Introduction to the Use of Mathematics in Economic Analysis* (New York: John Wiley and Sons, Inc., 1964), Chap. 7.

part one

Money, Other Assets, and the Rate of Interest

2

Money: Its Definition

> The history of the evolution of money, I could almost venture to suggest, is a strand in the history of the growth of civilization second in importance only to that of language. Money began as a commodity, and has ended as a system of recording transactions and bringing every act of purchase and sale, of borrowing and lending, of working and producing and consuming, that takes place anywhere in the whole world at any time, into some degree of relation with every other such act (G. L. S. Shackle, *Uncertainty in Economics and Other Reflections* [1955]).

Money is incapable of being meaningfully defined by saying that in the beginning there was barter—the exchange of one commodity for another—and that now there is money, something that may be exchanged for any number of commodities, other items, and obligations. Commodities, including gold, have most often served as money. In the pre-revolutionary days of the United States, money took such forms as wampum, furs, tobacco, cotton, whiskey, and iron nails, although accounts were reckoned in terms of the Spanish dollar and the British pound. In many instances, the early uses of money are not so different from the present ones. The latter simply appear to be made more complex by the widespread use of debt, a particular type of obligation, and the growth of accounting.

How, then, do we define money? The answer is that we define money by what it does, but, in that respect, our definition must be general enough to include the essential characteristics associated with the variety of items that have from time to time served as money.

2.1. The Definition of Money

The common and widely accepted definition follows: *Money is a (1) standard of value, (2) medium of exchange, and (3) store of value.* The three things that money does are discussed below. There is then the

15

additional step to be taken, namely, of identifying those items that serve as money in the real world.

The standard of value. The standard of value is not truly the property of any commodity, asset, or claim, although much of the problem of setting forth the accounting use of the monetary unit, such as the dollar in the United States, could be overcome if one could properly say it was a commodity. Traditionally some commonly accepted commodity, such as gold, was set by law in a fixed relationship to the monetary unit or unit of account. The government would declare that a certain quantity of that commodity was the monetary equal of the unit of account and that it met other qualities of a monetary standard. Though governments may still go through this act *de jure*, it was and continues to be devoid of substance. In the United States the dollar is said to be represented by a given quantity of gold, which happens to be 1/35 of the content of a gold ounce. "The dollar piece is a physical thing," however, and "the dollar has no physical existence." [1] The question then is how can the dollar in the United States, the pound in the United Kingdom, the franc in France, the Deutsche mark in Germany, the franc in Switzerland, the schilling in Austria, the lira in Italy, the guilder in Holland, the franc in Belgium, the dollar in Canada, the yen in Japan, the krona in Sweden, the peso in Argentina, and so on serve as a standard of value?

The answer is that a standard of value is nothing more than a written or verbal symbol referred to as the unit of account. The unit of account, or monetary unit, as it is variously called, is that unit in which people express the value of goods and services sold, reckon up wealth, and calculate credits (and debits).

A medium of exchange and a store of value. The properties identified with the holding of money include the medium of exchange and the store of value. The medium of exchange property is that identified with general acceptability or the demand for money for transactions purposes, and the general demand for money for these purposes may be referred to as the transactions demand for money. The acceptability results from moneys being easily identifiable, convenient to handle, and otherwise easily disposable as when it serves as an adequate store of value. This medium of exchange property consists of acquiring units of quantifiable items through a direct transaction and subsequently using them to acquire desired goods or services through another act of exchange. Money as a medium of exchange, in particular, permits an exchange of goods and services that need not be simultaneous—an immensely important property in a complex economy characterized by specialization and the division of labor.

The store of value property, on the other hand, is that which is identified with money as the asset of the highest degree of liquidity or

"moneyness" (Sect. 4.1). Money, in this sense, must be an item capable of being held without a prospective loss of principal or purchasing power. The holder of such items is in effect and, to some extent, frozen-in when their value declines and the class of items is said to lose its liquidity. An anticipated loss, identified with a particular class of items, consequently weakens the motive for holding them, and, conversely, an anticipated rise in value strengthens the motive for holding them. The absence of any anticipated change in the value of a given class of items serving as money neutralizes the strength of the motive for holding them as a means of experiencing a speculative loss or gain. At the same time, however, some portion of money balances may serve as a store of value for meeting anticipation and unforeseen developments. Later (Sect. 5.5) we identify these latter demands with both the speculative and precautionary motives for holding money, but, for the present, we shall emphasize changes in the speculative demand as it concerns the store of value property. We do this because such changes are of uppermost importance in the short run and are a source of economic problems—fluctuations in the level of employment, and so on.

2.2. The Motives Underlying the Demand for Money and a Restatement of the Definition

Three motives may be given for the demand for money balances. Upon stating these, and identifying the motives with various variables and parameters, our initial definition of money may be restated in equation form.

The motives underlying the demand for money. The three motives are the (1) transactions, (2) the precautionary, and (3) the speculative. The transactions motive is that which holds money for effecting transactions. It may be separated further into the income and the business motives. The former of these simply calls attention to a desire to hold more money as income increases in order to effect the greater volume of expenditures that accompany a larger income (Sect. 1.3), and the latter calls attention to the greater cash needs of business as business expands.

The precautionary motive is the desire for holding money as a precaution against unforeseen contingencies and as a means of taking advantage of unforeseen opportunities. In discussing such a motive for holding money, two writers point out that money "involves a minimum of commitment and provides a maximum of flexibility to meet emergencies and to take advantage of opportunities." Continuing, they note that "the more uncertain the future, the greater the value of such flexibility and hence the greater the demand for money. . . ."[2]

The precautionary motive also pertains to the proportion of assets held in money balances as a means of meeting such subsequent liabilities as bank loans. The quantity of balances demanded to satisfy this part of the precautionary motive depends on "the reliability of methods of obtaining cash," [3] and it may be related to the availability and/or ease of access to funds through bank borrowing and/or the disposition of liquid securities (Sect. 4.1).

The speculative motive, as emphasized on numerous occasions in subsequent chapters, has to do with an increase (decrease) in the demand for money balances in order to avoid probable losses (realize probable gains) from changes in the value of bonds or other assets. As we show later (Sect. 4.4), these probable changes concern changes in the rate of interest in the very short run. They also concern prospective changes in the average of prices for current output and other changes (Sect. 5.5).

Some alternative statements of the definition. There are two recurring equations defining the demand for money. One emphasizes the rate of interest, the other income. The two are interrelated.

Emphasizing the speculative motive and the rate of interest (i),

$$(1) \qquad\qquad g(i) = a + \frac{b}{i}, \quad b > 0$$

where $g(i)$ is the quantity of money demanded as a function of the rate of interest,

    a is the quantity of balances demanded in response to a given level of income, and

    b/i is the quantity demanded to satisfy speculative needs concerning probable changes in the rate of interest.

In this case, the parameter b is identified with the speculative motive. and changes in it relate entirely to the store of value function of money —all of which will be emphasized later (Sect. 4.4).

Re-emphasizing the relationship between the quantity of money demanded and income (Sect. 1.3),

$$(2) \qquad\qquad f(Y) = \alpha Y + \beta, \quad \alpha > 0$$

Here, the stock of balances needed to satisfy the precautionary motive, the transactions motive, and the speculative motive, as the latter concerns the rate of interest, is an increasing function of income. As the society becomes wealthier, given underlying conditions (i.e., α and β), quite generally it may be thought of as preferring money balances as a certain portion of wealth or income to satisfy the various motives. In this context, any change in the demand for money, such as may concern speculation with respect to prospective changes in the average of prices for current output, will come from variations in the proportion of balances held to meet unforeseen events, and so on, at a given level of income. Such changes, however, are simply an activation of balances, and we identify them with changes in β. Given income, the proportion of balances actually held is not altered. But changes in β, as shown earlier (Sect. 1.3), give rise to changes in income, and the balances as a proportion of income will decline, given the supply of balances available to the society. This is an activation of precautionary balances held for unforeseen developments.

In this latter context α, too, may change, but we view it as being associated with a more stable set of conditions. These would concern the transactions needs for balances and the precautionary needs, as they relate to the technology of bookkeeping, clearing and transferring systems, and routine practices regarding the management of money balances or cash from the users' point of view.

2.3. Some Dynamic Considerations: The Acceptance of Currency and Bank Deposits as Money

When we attempt to identify the class of items satisfying the above motives and the relationships defined by equations (1) and (2), we find that they may be different classes in different societies. One of the great accomplishments of modern society, as in the United States, and, in fact, one of the conditions for its being, has been the establishment of a system of banks (Chap. 3) and the success of efforts to make currency outside of banks and demand or check-transferable deposits (adjusted for interbank deposits)[4] acceptable as money. There are, however, special variations over time that concern the acceptance of given classes of items as money.

Secular and short-run variations. From among the different ways in which data for the stock of money are ordered in time, two are presently introduced: the secular (or long-run) trend and the cyclical (or short-run) variation.

A tendency for income ($=$GNP) and the stock of money (M) to exhibit about the same percentages of changes over the long run may be seen in Fig. 2-1. (Envision the smooth long-term tendencies implied by the two series.) As implied above, however, these movements are not entirely accidental. They probably resulted from the success of society's efforts to make currency outside of banks and demand deposits (adjusted) serve as money (Sect. 7.3 and 7.4), as well as accidental discoveries of gold (Sect. 6.3 and 7.4). Especially, in more recent years, there has been some explicit recognition of the desirability of having changes in the supply of money roughly approximate changes in income,[5] i.e.,

$$\frac{dM/M}{dY/Y} = 1, \quad \text{or} \frac{dM}{dY}\frac{Y}{M} = 1$$

as a secular matter. But the factor Y/M is nothing other than the velocity of money, and dM/dY $(=\alpha)$ is the change in the money stock with respect to income.

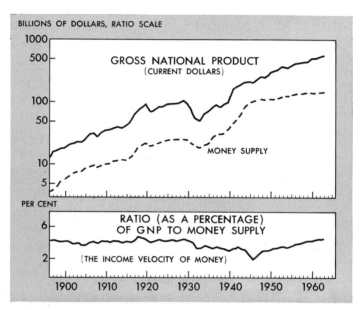

Fig. 2-1. Gross National Product and the Supply of Money. Source of data: Board of Governors of the Federal Reserve System and the U.S. Department of Commerce.

Now, recalling the solution to the earlier model (Sect. 1.3) and equation (3), $Y = (\gamma - \beta)/\alpha.$* Here, a decline (rise) in β is associated with a short-run increase (decrease) in income. Thus, identifying short-run shifts in the speculative demand for money balances, we would expect these shifts to give rise to short-run variations in income and velocity (the factor Y/M), given dM/dY, as a secular matter. Such fluctuations in the factor Y/M $(=GNP/M)$ are shown in Fig. 2-1 and in Table 2-1, with somewhat greater precision. Table 2-1 emphasizes the cyclical peaks and troughs for velocity over the post-World War II years.

Money and secular changes in its supply. We would not necessarily want to imply that the stock of supply should change at the same rate as income. For the present, we simply make several points about money and secular changes in its supply:

---

* If $\beta = 0$, then $Y = 1/\alpha(\gamma)$. Recalling (Sect. 1.3), Y ($=PO$), $1/\alpha = V_y$ and $\gamma = M$, $PO = MV$. We have an identity that will recur subsequently (Chap. 5 and 26).

Table 2-1. Income Velocity and Postwar Cyclical Peaks and Troughs

Year and Quarter	(1) GNP [1] $	(2) M [2] $	(3) Income Velocity (1) ÷ (2)
1948-4 (Peak)	265.9	109.4	2.43
1949-4 (Trough)	257.0	108.4	2.37
1953-2 (Peak)	368.8	125.9	2.93
1954-3 (Trough)	362.0	127.9	2.83
1957-3 (Peak)	448.3	134.7	3.33
1958-2 (Trough)	437.2	134.9	3.24
1960-2 (Peak)	506.4	138.6	3.65
1961-1 (Trough)	500.8	139.9	3.58
1963-4	600.1	153.0	3.92
1964-2	618.6	152.9	4.05

SOURCES: Board of Governors of the Federal Reserve System and U.S. Department of Commerce.

[1] Billions of dollars. Seasonally adjusted annual rates.

[2] Billions of dollars. Demand deposits adjusted plus currency outside banks, seasonally adjusted. Each quarter is an average for the period, computed by averaging four end-of-month figures.

(1) The quantity of money demanded is generally accepted as being some increasing function of income.

(2) An essential condition for a secular rise in income is having a stock of balances to accommodate the increase in income, given other conditions.

(3) Satisfying the increase in the quantity of balances demanded with a given class of items, such as currency outside of banks and demand deposits (adjusted), is a necessary condition for having that class of items serve as money.

2.4. Summary

Money is a medium of exchange, a store of value, and, indirectly, a standard of value. The medium of exchange characteristic permits an indirect exchange of goods. It consists of acquiring units of quantifiable objects through direct exchange and then using the units to acquire an object through a further act of exchange. In this sense, money serving as a medium of exchange facilitates the specialization and the division of labor-producing goods and services for a market rather than for a predetermined buyer. The store of value function of money pertains to the ease and convenience attached to its disposal without anticipated loss of principal or purchasing power. It is performed by the asset with perfect ease of disposal. The use of money as a standard of value is identical with the accounting use of the unit of account. Only in specific incidences, such as those pertaining to currency and demand deposits, does the unit of account become specifically identifiable with money.

The things money does are interrelated. The medium of exchange characteristic requires that money partly, at least, serve as a store of value, that is, before an asset is commonly accepted as a medium of exchange it must also be anticipated that the holder shall have the conveniences and security of money identified with its ease of disposal. And, in some incidences, such as the reckoning of the most liquid forms of credit, money is directly related to the unit of account.

The definition of money may be stated in equation form. One such equation relates the quantity of money demanded to the rate of interest. Another relates it to the flow of income. Both are interrelated, but the latter especially concerns shifts in the demand for money that give rise to short-run variations in income, and to other matters.

In stating the definition of money in equation form, the motives underlying the demand for money are identified with various variables and parameters. They also pertain to the functions performed by money. The motives are the transactions, precautionary, and speculative motives. The transactions motive emphasizes the use of money as a medium of exchange and concerns the routine use of balances for effecting expenditures. The precautionary motive emphasizes the store of value property and concerns the demand for balances to deal with unforeseen developments and unexpected opportunities. It also depends upon the ease of access to funds from banks and other sources. The speculative motive, too, emphasizes the store-of-value function of money. It concerns shifts in the demand for balances to avoid probable losses of principal or purchasing power and to realize probable gains.

Currency outside of banks and demand deposits (adjusted) have been accepted as classes of items serving as money in modern society, as in the United States. Their acceptance is an essential condition to the existence of that society. This acceptance, further, has been achieved partly by accident and partly as a result of conscious efforts. The acceptance of any given class of items as money balances, however, depends on their stock varying in such a way as to accommodate the needs for money for the various purposes, at least within rather broadly defined limits and in the long run.

References

1. Karl Olivecrona, *The Problem of the Monetary Unit* (New York: The Macmillan Company, 1957), p. 73. For a reference concerning the origin of

the term "dollar," see Arthur Nussbaum, *A History of the Dollar* (New York: Columbia University Press, 1957), p. 10.

2. Milton Friedman and Anna Jacobson Schwartz, *A Monetary History of the United States, 1867-1960* (Princeton, N.J.: Princeton University Press for the National Bureau of Economic Research, 1963), p. 673.

3. See John Maynard Keynes, *The General Theory of Employment, Interest and Money* (New York: Harcourt, Brace and World, 1936), p. 196. For general discussion of the motives, see also pp. 170-171 and 195-197.

4. Some would add time deposits to this list, as noted under subsequent topics. See also Friedman and Schwartz, *op. cit.,* pp. 629-630.

5. See Friedman and Schwartz, *op. cit.,* pp. 628-629.

3

Changes in the Supply of Money

John Law was one of the better-informed men of his day on the
subject of banking. He saw clearly that the amount of bank credit
is related to the cash held by the bank, stating that the Bank of
Scotland loaned its notes to the extent of four or five times the
amount of specie it had in vault and that it was by just this amount
that the money of the nation was increased (Lloyd W. Mints, *A
History of Banking Theory* [1945]).

The supply of money has been multiplied many times with the
growth of modern banking institutions. These began in Britain with the
goldsmiths. Indeed, the evolution of money from commodities, in this
instance gold, to a system of recording specific credit transactions—
namely, those involved in the processes of lending and investing by
modern banks—may be traced from their operations. These users of
precious metals learned initially that they could loan at interest units of
the material on hand, and subsequently that they could loan newly
mined and imported gold left with them for safekeeping as well. They
found that in both instances the depositors and borrowers were often
content with only the claim to gold rather than the gold itself. Thus
there evolved a reasonably safe operating ratio of the volume of this
commodity which should be kept on hand to the total of claims against
the lender. This practice of maintaining assets in the form of reserves of
only a fraction of bank liabilities or the total credits to depositors was
facilitated by the development of double-entry bookkeeping; in fact, it
gave banks the power to create the largest part of the supply of currency
and demand deposits.

The banking that evolved from the above practices is called fractional-
reserve banking. The claims by depositors against which a fractional
amount of reserves must be kept have at times consisted of both currency and deposits, with the emphasis shifting to deposits in modern
times. These claims in the form of currency and that portion of deposits

24

payable on demand we may call the supply of money balances, one being generally interchangeable for the other. The currency itself, furthermore, consists of coins and paper notes. The issuance of paper notes against a specie reserve by banks was of greater importance in the expansion of the supply of money in early years, and in the years since the Civil War (Sect. 7.4) the note issue function has been displaced by the growth of deposits payable on demand at the bank.

In the early stages of fractional-reserve banking, gold in the form of reserves served the purpose of protecting depositors and assuring the success of the banking business. An acceptable reserve ratio evolved from practice, and later, in the United States, the law required that banks maintain a reserve to meet possible withdrawals by depositors. The maintenance of separate reserves by independent banks, however, did not achieve the desired end, particularly in the post-Civil War years, as will be indicated later (Part III). Thus in 1913 the function of reserve balances and their form changed with the pooling of reserves in a single system of reserve banks called the Federal Reserve. The largest proportion of total bank reserves came to consist of credit balances with the Federal Reserve, and reserves in general came to be considered primarily as a medium through which the availability and cost of credit as well as the supply of money could be influenced. This chapter, however, illustrates only how fractional-reserve banking serves to bring about a multiple expansion or contraction of the supply of money in response to a corresponding expansion or contraction of reserves, and how the public's preference for combinations of currency and demand deposits and different classes of deposits affects changes in reserves and responses of the banking system to changes in reserves. The reference is to the multiple expansion or contraction of the money supply for the purpose of explanation, but, as we noted from Fig. 2-1, the supply is usually expanding. Consequently, *analyses pertaining to the real world will most frequently be concerned with changes in the rate of expansion as opposed to a contraction of the money supply.*

For the present we simply review the underlying principle of the expansion and contraction of bank credit as a first approximation to a fuller discussion of historical, institutional, and mechanical detail over a range of several chapters, and we introduce such complicating notions as that of currency drain and a time deposit drain. The underlying principle is related to developments during the entire period of the evolution of modern banking, but an introduction to the complicating notions permits us to deal with the processes of money and credit expansion and contraction in their realistic detail. In the first part of this period of modern banking, when claims against individual banks or bank liabilities included both demand deposits and paper currency, the relationship between changes in a bank's fractional reserves and changes in deposit and currency liabilities was more direct. In the period since the Civil War and including that since the founding of the Federal Reserve, on the other hand, the note issue function has been under a central control, paper currency has ceased to be the liability of individual banks, and different fractional requirements for reserves have come to be applied to demand and savings-type deposits, respectively. The first of these post-Civil War changes caused the currency holdings of commercial banks to become vault cash, and, as developments have taken place in recent times, vault cash has become a part of reserves. These developments, at the same time, along with the public's preference for relatively stable proportions of currency to demand deposits, have affected the banking system's capacity to expand or contract the supply of credit and deposits in relation to the reserve base. And the development of a distinction between demand and non-money savings-type deposits and their respective reserve requirements has similar effects on the processes of money and credit expansion and contraction.

The more general institutional conditions underlying the present illustrations include the fundamental accounting identity, profit optimizing behavior on the part of bankers, and a supply of creditworthy borrowers. On the basis of these, the supply of demand deposits may expand and contract in response to changes in reserves. The fundamental accounting identity for recording bank and other business conditions is as follows:

$$\text{Assets} = \text{Liabilities} + \text{Capital Accounts}$$

The items representing claims of the business unit, called assets, most often appear on the left-hand side of the balance sheet in the United States. The items representing claims against the business unit, consisting of liabilities and the capital account, appear on the right-hand side of the balance sheet. Furthermore, a comparison of a balance sheet for a given set of accounts at one date with that of a balance sheet for the same set of accounts at another date reveals changes in the respective accounts over the period that has lapsed between the one time and the other. Another of the institutional characteristics is that of profit motivation. The motivation is not necessarily that of greed, since profits may be thought of as a source of esteem for the operators of banking and other enterprises. Commercial banks, like other businesses, are run for profit, but in the case of such banks, the bulk of profits come from the flow of returns in the form of interest received from loans to customers and holdings of securities. Thus a bank should be expected to put into loans and investments as much as its reserves will permit, within the limit of prudence, for a bank must also maintain a certain amount of liquidity, apart from the reserve cover against deposits. Finally, there must be a supply of securities and some credit-worthy borrowers who have the will to engage in the various profitable enterprises.

3.1. The Banking System as a Whole

Gold may be thought of as being acceptable as reserves and currency, to illustrate the role of the banking system as a whole in the expansion and contraction of bank credit. Gold, in fact, served as reserves and still does in a modified form. It also circulated freely for many years, although it no longer does so, and other items have come to serve a similar function. The gold in the reserve form has been either the unminted gold of gold bricks or gold specie or coin, whereas gold circulating outside of banks has usually been in the form of specie. In any event, with modifications, the mechanics described are applicable not only to historical circumstances but also to the contemporary banking arrangement in which gold no longer circulates freely outside of banks.

To begin with, view the banking system as one big multiple-branch bank—a macro bank. This simplification facilitates subsequent explanations of the gold flows mechanism, factors affecting reserves, and financial developments generally. The role of individual banks and the movements of funds from one geographical region to another are also described later, with the introduction of several complicating factors.

Credit expansion. A simplified balance sheet for the whole banking system with a ratio of reserves to demand deposits of 15 per cent at time zero may be shown. That picture, excluding any references to the capital account and including the key accounts necessary to explain changes in bank assets and the money supply, is as follows:

Balance Sheet

The Macro Bank

(Time zero, 15 per cent actual
reserves, dollar amounts in billions)

Assets		Liabilities, etc.	
Reserves (R)	17	Deposits payable	
Earning assets—		on demand (D)	113
loans, etc. (L)	96		
	113		113

The total of demand deposits outstanding is 113 billion dollars, which is about the volume (other than interbank and United States government deposits) outstanding on the average in the early 1960s, some 40 times the volume outstanding in 1896 (periods for which data are available).

Suppose now that additional reserves come to the banking system. There are many reasons that this might happen. Later on, we shall be particularly interested in actions by the Federal Reserve to provide or extinguish reserves. At this point, however, we consider a simple instance of a primary deposit, i.e., deposits that add equally to a bank's reserves and deposits. Assume that there have been inflows of gold into the country from abroad or gold has been newly produced during the interval between time zero and time one, and that 10 billion dollars worth of this gold has been deposited in the bank. The balance sheet now appears as follows (where "+" indicates a change since time zero):

Balance Sheet

The Macro Bank

(Time one, 22 per cent actual
reserves, dollar amounts in billions)

Assets		Liabilities, etc.	
Reserves (R)	17	Deposits payable	
	+10	on demand (D)	113
Earning assets—			+10
loans, etc. (L)	96		
	123		123

The balance sheet reveals that the deposits were increased by crediting the accounts of the depositors, that the gold was set aside as an amount of reserves equal to the deposits, and that the actual reserve ratio is now roughly 22 per cent, which is in excess of the 15 per cent requirement. The bank is in a position to support greater deposits. Remember, it may increase earnings by expanding loans. The borrowers to whom the loans are extended do not necessarily want the gold itself. They may, instead, be perfectly satisfied with leaving it on deposit. The reader may now see why the banking system is referred to as a fractional-reserve banking. Even if no legal requirement for holding reserves relative to deposits were imposed, the bank, on the basis of custom or experience, would find that it needed to hold certain reserves representing only a fraction of deposits.

If the bank takes full advantage of its ability to support additional deposits as it expands its loans, the balance sheet at time two will be as follows:

Balance Sheet

The Macro Bank

(Time two, 15 per cent actual
reserves, dollar amounts in billions)

Assets		Liabilities	
Reserves (R)	17	Deposits payable	
	+10	on demand (D)	113
Earning assets—			+10
loans, etc. (L)	96		
	+57		+57
	180		180

On the basis of a 15 per cent reserve ratio, the 10 billion dollar increase in the gold supply had the effect of increasing the supply of money balances by nearly 67 billion dollars, six and two-thirds times the amount of gold placed on deposit. Most of this, nearly 57 billion dollars, came into existence because the bank responded to holdings of reserves in excess of requirements—an excess of $8\frac{1}{2}$ billion dollars worth of gold— by increasing loans. This is the sense in which a bank is sometimes described as creating money out of nothing more than a mode of expression (Sect. 2.1). The bank is said to be loaned up when all of its reserves are required to support its deposits.

In sum, the macro bank was able to expand the supply of credit (i.e., loans) and money balances after experiencing increased reserves by creating two different sets of obligations—(1) those obligations from borrowers to the bank in the form of loans and (2) those from the bank to the borrowers in the form of deposits. The latter may be transferred by check and used as a means of payment. The process in which (1) and (2) are intimately linked is an important instance of what is called debt monetization, i.e., the transformation of debt obligations into money. Commercial banks are unique among private financial institutions in being able to monetize debt. As we shall see in future chapters, the capacity to monetize debt carries many important implications. Also, as we shall see in those chapters, the government, including the Federal Reserve, is able to monetize debt. Furthermore, the government and commercial banks are able to monetize precious metals. For example, when the macro bank originally created deposits in payment for the unminted gold it actually monetized the gold.

At this point, four observations should be made: (1) We have been dealing with one large, economy-wide bank, thus there has been no problem of losing gold reserves to other banks as depositors transfer balances. (2) No portion of the bank's reserves has been drained away into the hands of the public. (3) Only demand deposits have been involved in the expansion process. (4) The bank has been assumed to utilize its potential for expanding loans and deposits. Eventually, we need to account for each of the complications suggested by these simplified assumptions.

Even in such a simple setting as the present one, however, a process of expansion of money and credit would most likely take place in a series of steps over time. Thus, to illustrate the more detailed expansion, assume that the bank calculates at each step a safe rule-of-thumb amount by which to expand its loans and deposits as the amount of its reserves over and above those needed to support existing deposits. As the expansion takes place, as one may see, this safe amount progressively diminishes toward zero. Further, a little reflection will make it clear that, with a 15 per cent reserve requirement, this amount at any step will be equal to 100 per cent minus 15 per cent (i.e., 85 per cent) of the amount by which loans and deposits were increased in the previous step. After three steps, including the original deposit of 10 as a step, demand deposits would have increased by the following sum:

$$10 + 10\,(1.00 - 0.15) + 10\,(1.00 - 0.15)\,(1.00 - 0.15)$$

After an n or undesignated number of steps, demand deposits would have increased by

$$10 + 10(0.85) + 10(0.85)^2 + 10(0.85)^3 + \ldots + 10(0.85)^{n-1}$$

Here, the increase in loans (ΔL), as well as the deposits (ΔD) created in making them, is the sum of this series less 10 billion dollars, i.e., to derive the increase the first item in the series must be omitted. The entire series as the number of terms goes from one to infinity is, of course, a geometric series whose successive terms are becoming smaller and smaller as the number of terms increases. If we added up an infinite number of such terms, we have

$$\sum_{n=1}^{\infty} 10(0.85)^{n-1} = \frac{10}{1.00 - 0.85} = 10\left(\frac{1}{0.15}\right) = 66.66\ldots$$

In this example, the reserve requirement is 15 per cent, and the product of the increase in reserves of 10 billion dollars and the reciprocal of the reserve requirement (i.e., $1/0.15$) yields the absolute increase in deposit liabilities. This reciprocal of the reserve requirement we call the money multiplier when it is used to indicate the magnitude of a change in deposits accompanying a change in reserves. We call it a credit multiplier when it is used to indicate the magnitude of a change in loans, and so on, accompanying a change in reserves.

More generally, if a is the amount of the original addition to reserves, or the amount of the primary deposits, and if r is the reserve ratio, then the sum, S_n, of the infinite series is given by the formula

$$S_n = \frac{a}{1 - (1 - r)}, \text{ or}$$

$$S_n = a\left(\frac{1}{r}\right)$$

Note that the smaller the reserve ratio, r, the larger will be the money or credit multiplier $(1/r)$ applied to a given initial change in reserves.

Credit contraction. The gold flows in our simple illustration may now be reversed to show a contraction in the supply of money balances. Suppose that instead of inflows there are outflows of gold summing to 5 billion dollars during the period beginning at time zero and resulting from purchases abroad by the economy in question. The loss is reflected on the balance sheet at time one relative to time zero by using minus signs to indicate the items which change.

Balance Sheet

The Macro Bank

(Time one, 11 per cent actual
reserves, dollar amounts in billions)

Assets		Liabilities	
Reserves (R)	17	Deposits payable	
	−5	on demand (D)	113
Earning assets—			−5
loans, etc. (L)	96		
	108		108

It is recorded as a 5 billion dollar credit* to the reserve account and by a corresponding debit to the account for demand deposits. The actual reserve ratio is now about 11 per cent, which is less than the required ratio of 15 per cent. The macro bank, therefore, must call in loans or allow outstanding ones to be repaid as they fall due without renewing or replacing them in order to increase the ratio. As the bank receives payments by check for the loans, demand deposits are correspondingly debited as loans are credited. At time two, the situation is again stable after the bank has contracted its loans by a little more than 28 billion dollars.

---

* A credit to assets is a decrease (−) in assets and a debit to the liabilities is a decrease. Conversely, a debit to assets is an increase (+) in assets and a credit to the liabilities side of the balance sheet is an increase in liabilities.

Balance Sheet

The Macro Bank

(Time two, 15 per cent actual
reserves, dollar amounts in billions)

Assets		Liabilities	
Reserves (R)	17	Deposits payable	
	−5	on demand (D)	113
Earning assets—			−5
loans, etc. (L)	96		
	−28		−28
	80		80

The actual reserve ratio is once again at 15 per cent, albeit the supply of money balances has contracted by 33 billion dollars or by the product of the money multiplier of 1/0.15 and the initial loss in reserves of 5 billion dollars brought about by outflows of gold.

Reserve dollars are sometimes referred to as high-powered dollars for reasons that are obvious. An increase in primary demand deposits, and therefore reserve dollars, provides the basis for a multiple expansion of loans and investments, and therefore demand deposits. The multiple expansion in deposits above the initial increment of primary deposits is sometimes referred to as secondary, derived, or borrowers' deposits. Unless banks can somehow replenish their reserves, a decrease in primary demand deposits, and therefore reserve dollars, precipitates a multiple contraction of loans and investments, and therefore demand deposits.

The process of credit contraction, like that of expansion, may be represented by an infinite geometrical series. In the present case, however,

$a = -5$, the initial decrease in reserves (and deposits),
$r = 0.15$, the reserve ratio, and
$S_n = -5(1/0.15) = -33.33$, the total decrease in deposits resulting from the initial withdrawal.

As a word of caution, we note that not all gains and losses of bank reserves are accompanied by initial gains and losses of deposits of equivalent amounts as when, e.g., a bank borrows reserves from the Federal Reserve banks (8.1). These changes operating through the Federal Reserve and inducing changes in loans and secondary deposits are based on the portion of an initial change in reserves that is in excess of (or deficient from) the reserve requirements. Thus the entire change in demand deposits may be independent of primary deposits and related only to the change in reserves, or to so-called excess reserves. In the simple examples used above the money multipliers and the credit multiplier are all of the same magnitude (namely, $1/0.15$). The multiplicand for the money multiplier is $+10$ billion dollars in the first example and -5 billion dollars in the second. The multiplicands for changes relating to the above examples and resulting from bank borrowing at the Federal Reserve and the repayment of such debt at the Federal Reserve, on the other hand, would be, respectively, the original reserve excess of $+8.5$ billion dollars in the first example and the deficit of -4.25 billion dollars in the second.

3.2. The Role of Individual Banks

The credit and monetary expansions and contractions above illustrated multiple changes in earning assets and deposits in response to changes in reserve and primary deposits for the banking system as a whole. Phenomena that are characteristic of the banking system as a whole, however, may not be characteristic of a single bank in the system. In fact, the discrepancy between the behavior of the banking system and a single bank in the system tends to widen at a given time with the number of banks composing the system. There may be at a given time, for example, a greater degree of discrepancy between the system of banks and the more than 13,000 individual banks in the United States at year-end 1963 than between the banking system in Canada and the eight individual banks in Canada at year-end 1963.

An individual bank experiencing an increase in primary deposits may more readily anticipate losses in reserves as its loans and deposits expand and as the number of banks composing a system increases. The reason for such a subjective and greater probable loss is the increase in the likelihood of a clearing drain as the number of banks increase. The clearing drain refers to the loss of reserves by one bank to another as the deposits expand through lending or investing and as they enter into the expenditure stream through their use in the purchase of goods and services. The loss of deposits results when the deposits are transferred by checks drawn against them and redeposited in other banks. Of course, there is also a greater likelihood that a single bank may be favored by a clearing drain operating to the disfavor of another bank as the number of banks in the system increases, but the probability of these favorable and unfavorable changes offsetting each other entirely at a given time is reduced as the total number of banks in the banking system increases. The net clearing drain, in a system consisting of a large number of banks, therefore, is more likely at any given time to limit the ability of an individual bank to expand loans and, therefore, deposits, or to diminish an individual bank's need to contract loans and, therefore, deposits. This net clearing drain or simply a clearing drain is external to a single bank and results in a net loss of reserves to that bank, but it is internal to the banking system as a whole and results in no net loss of reserves to the aggregate of banks.

In a banking system, such as that in the United States, special institutions arise in relation to clearing drains, and others arise to smooth out the effect of reserve changes from one bank to the system as a whole. These we will deal with in the present section after illustrating the effect of a clearing drain on individual banks, apart from these special institutions. Nevertheless, there remains for further consideration (Sect. 3.3) some other important drains. These are external to the banking system and have an effect on the banking system as a whole.

Loans and investments by individual banks. An expansion or contraction in reserves resulting, respectively, in a multiple expansion or contraction in loans and investments and consequently in demand deposits was illustrated earlier (Sect. 3.1) by reference to our macro bank. Now, in re-emphasizing the case of expansion with respect to the individual banks, let us note again that the borrower of funds will usually not want to leave the funds credited to his account indefinitely. He may withdraw the balances, or he may draw upon the balances to meet obligations to individuals or business units that have bank accounts elsewhere. Either way, the borrowed funds could eventually end up in another bank, and the individual banker cannot at all be assured that any of the funds loaned out will remain on deposit at the bank originating the loan.* In this instance, he will have to set aside a fraction of the initial increase in reserves if it resulted from a primary deposit, and he can safely expand his loans and deposits without risking a reserve deficiency only in an amount equal to that portion consisting of reserves in excess of the required amount. The balances created by additional loans, withdrawn and transferred elsewhere, become primary deposits to other banks, nevertheless. Thus a multiple expansion of deposits for the banking system as a whole is possible, depending on the reserve requirements and the initial increase in reserves for the system. This will be illustrated, after an aside on the mechanics of clearing.

The transfer of balances elsewhere may actually take place in either of two ways. The balances may have been withdrawn and deposited elsewhere. The balances, on the other hand, could have been transferred through the deposit of a check in a bank other than the one against which the check is drawn. This could result in the lending bank's meeting an unfavorable balance at a clearing house operated by an association of banks to facilitate the settlement of claims among the associated banks.**

* During periods of strong demand for loans and pressure on reserves, some bankers impose compensating balance requirements (Sect. 13.2) which specifically require customers to maintain certain minimal average balances. The effect of this is to reduce the magnitude of the clearing drain for the bank imposing such a requirement.

** The first clearing house in the United States was established in New York in 1853.

The debit at the clearing house would result in a decrease in reserves and deposits, and the credit to the receiving bank would result in an increase in reserves. Also, since 1914, it has been permissible for the deposit of the check in a different region of the country to be cleared through the regional clearing facilities of the Federal Reserve banks (Sect. 7.5). For example, a manufacturer of linens in Massachusetts may sell towels to a motel in Florida and receive in payment a check on a Florida bank. The Massachusetts bank then wants credit to its reserve account at the Federal Reserve Bank of Boston. Accordingly, the Massachusetts bank would send the check (together with other checks) to the Federal Reserve Bank of Boston, which in turn sends it to the Jacksonville branch of the Federal Reserve Bank of Atlanta. The Jacksonville branch would debit the reserve account of the Florida bank and forward the check. The Jacksonville branch would thereupon credit the Federal Reserve Bank of Boston, which in turn credits the account of the Massachusetts bank. The Florida bank, finally, would debit the account of the depositor who wrote the check.* The net effect of this regional clearing would be an increase in the deposits of the Boston bank, an increase by an equal amount of its reserves, and corresponding decreases in Florida.

Keeping in mind the mechanics of the process of borrowing and re-depositing in another bank, we may now illustrate the multiple expansion of loans and deposits through a group of individual banks. To do this and still be cognizant of developments, we must make two simplifying assumptions about the sequence of events that occur. These simplifications, however, do not affect the outcome for the whole banking system. The first is that expansion takes place in a single, nondiffused chain of events. That is, at each step only one bank has the excess reserves to expand its loans and deposits. In reality, however, an initial increase in reserves, particularly if it results from Federal Reserve action (Sect. 8.1), is spread over a number of banks. As these individual banks expand, their reserves quickly become diffused among a still greater number of banks of various types, sizes, and locations. The other simplifying assumption is that each bank expands on the basis of the expectation of a 100 per cent clearing drain. The reasonableness of this assumption, as

---

* In point of fact, the Massachusetts bank would probably give its customer an immediate credit for the check, while the bank would receive a deferred reserve credit at the Federal Reserve Bank of Boston based on the average length of time that should be involved before the Florida bank loses reserves. This gives rise to two kinds of so-called float. The first (Sect. 9.3) refers to the fact that the Massachusetts bank will probably receive its reserve credit slightly before the Florida bank loses reserves. At certain times in the year this may cause a rather large unintended advance of reserves by the Federal Reserve to commercial banks. The other, the interbank float, occurs because the Massachusetts bank adds to its customers' demand deposit before the Florida bank deducts from its customers' account. The money supply statistics for the United States are corrected for what would otherwise be double-counted demand deposits by subtracting such cash items in the process of collection.

actual developments take place, may even lend credence to the simple rule of thumb which holds that one bank can safely expand its loans and deposits in the amount of its excess reserves.

Apart from these simplifying assumptions, the other assumptions, for the present illustration, are the same as for the case of the macro bank— that the minimum reserve ratio is 15 per cent and a primary deposit of 10 billion dollars initiates the process. In reality (Sect. 8.1) all banks are not subject to the same reserve requirement, and legal reserve requirements apply only to averages for a given period. Consequently, this 15 per cent figure must be interpreted as some sort of weighted average ratio for all the banks involved in the process. For the present, then, we are dealing with banks that conform to the latter average.

Table 3-1 illustrates a process of expansion under these circumstances. In the illustration, Bank A receives a primary deposit of 10 billion dollars from some source outside the banking system, and of this amount 1.5 billion dollars is allocated to required reserves and the balance becomes the basis for expanding loans. The borrower from Bank A receives a checking account, against which he writes a check payable to a deposit customer of Bank B. Bank A sees its reserves reduced to the minimum fraction (15 per cent) of its deposits, since it loses all of its original excess reserves to Bank B in the clearing process. Thus Bank A's clearing loss is Bank B's gain, which is what permits expansion to continue. Bank B receives a primary deposit, i.e., one causing it to receive an equivalent amount of reserves. Again, the required portion is set aside, and loans are increased by the amount of excess reserves, and so on ad infinitum, until any remaining excess reserves have been used up in supporting increased demand deposits. The total potential increase in loans is 56.67 billion dollars, and in deposits it is 66.67 billion dollars. Actually, as the increments at each step are progressively declining, most of the process will have worked itself out after a relatively small number of steps.

The figures for the increases after a finite or an infinite number of steps, once again, are simply the terms of a geometrical progression (Sect. 3.1) and the nth partial sum of that progression. For example, the increases in demand deposits, where $a = 10$, $r = 0.15$, and the balance sheets of Banks A, B, C, ... yield the 1st, 2nd, 3rd, ... terms, respectively, are given by the formula

$$\sum_{n=1}^{\infty} a(1 - r)^{n-1} = 10 + 8.50 + 7.225 + 6.141 + \ldots$$

$$+ 10(0.85)^{n-1} + \ldots = \frac{10}{0.15} = 66.66 \ldots$$

The illustration demonstrates the important principle, stated earlier, that multiple expansion (or contraction) in a fractional-reserve banking sys-

Table 3-1. Multiple Expansion of Lending and Deposits Through the Banking System

(15 per cent reserves, no other drains)

(Amounts in billions of dollars)

Bank A

Required reserve	1.50	Demand deposit	10.00 ← Initial increase
Excess reserve	8.50		
Loans	8.50	Demand deposit	8.50 ⌐

Bank B

Required reserve	1.275	Demand deposit	8.50 ⤶
Excess reserve	7.225		
Loans	7.225 - ⊦-Demand deposit	7.225 ⌐

Bank C

Required reserve	1.084	Demand deposit	7.225 ⤶
Excess reserve	6.141		
Loans	6.141	Demand deposit	6.141 ⌐

Additional Banks

Required reserve	6.141	Demand deposit	40.942 ⤶
Excess reserve	-0-		
Loans	34.801		

All Banks

Required reserve	10.00	Demand deposit	(original)	10.00
Excess reserve	-0-	Demand deposit		56.67
Loans	56.67			

tem containing a large number of banks is a phenomenon associated with the system and not with an individual bank in it.

Extending the effects of changes in reserves of individual banks. There are operations by which the effect of a change in total demand deposits (and/or reserves) for the banking system as a whole may be passed throughout the banking system, until deposits have changed by a multiple of the initial change. These operations in effect, then, tend to overcome the discrepancy at a given time between the behavior of the system as a whole and that of individual banks in the system as changes take place over time. The effect of a change in deposits and/or reserves passed throughout the system from one or more banks by these operations would be the same as the effect of such changes described earlier

(Sect. 3.1), and the same mathematical descriptions would apply. The methods by which the results are achieved operationally, however, should be of interest. These consist of (1) the proper functioning of the correspondent banking arrangement within the geographical confines of the United States, (2) transactions in Federal funds, (3) the buyback technique or sale and repurchase agreement, and (4) the purchase or sale of government securities or other liquid assets. The first is more traditional and will be dealt with as a part of the history of banking in the United States (Part III). The others are also dealt with later (Sect. 13.2). Each is simply introduced for the present:

(1) A bank may experience an increase in reserves for varied reasons. It may also, at the time, not be faced with a ready demand for bank credit by creditworthy borrowers. In such a case there may be a demand in some other geographical area or in a financial center. The bank initially receiving the increase in reserves may, in such a case, transfer the reserves to its correspondent in the financial center which may, in turn, advance balances for speculative purposes in the form of loans secured by stock market collateral or for other purposes. The funds may have even entered the country through the financial center to begin with. Also, the funds may be transferred from the financial center when they are needed by the bank initially advancing them to its city correspondent. In any event, correspondent banking provided and continues to provide a means for employing excess reserves and for otherwise smoothing out the effect of a change in reserves at one bank to the banking system as a whole.

(2) Since the early 1950's especially, the Federal funds market has functioned as a means for smoothing out the effect of changes in the aggregate of bank reserves to the banking system as a whole. It is a market that facilitates the movement of the reserves of one bank to another through the debiting (−) and crediting (+) of claims against a central pool of reserves. More specifically, it is the market for borrowing and lending immediately available reserve balances at a pre-arranged interest cost to the borrower. Banks in need of reserves may purchase (borrow) them, and banks with an excess of reserves may sell (lend) them. Such transactions are usually of the straight Federal fund type or they may be of a modified type characterized by the use of repurchase agreements and buybacks. The more uniform Federal funds transactions involve an unsecured loan for one night or until the next working day. Usually the parties agree to the loan directly over the telephone, by bank wire, or through an agent. The transfer of reserves from one account to the other may then take place after a telephone or wire request to the Reserve bank where the reserves are centrally kept, but this request in turn must be followed by letters of confirmation from the lending and borrowing parties. The written statements confirm the re-

quest for the movement of funds from one account to the other and then back again, and the interest may be paid separately to avoid the charge on wire transfers of odd amounts. In New York City, in particular, however, the reserves may simply be purchased with a check drawn on the borrowing bank and in an amount adjusted for interest cost. The check in this case is cleared the day after the purchase and results in the reverse transfer of bank reserves.

(3) Either repurchase agreements or buybacks may be used to achieve the same smoothing out effect as the "straight" Federal funds transaction. The main differences are the generality of the two notions and the form of contracts. The repurchase agreements or buybacks would have the same economic effect on the movement of bank reserves independent of any present-day pool of bank reserves or so-called Federal funds. And contracts involving repurchase agreements and buybacks pertain to the purchase and sale of securities. Under the repurchase agreement there may be a single contract in which the bank with a possible excess of reserves offers to buy securities and the seller offers to repurchase the same securities at a future date. The selling bank receives a check drawn on another bank, and the clearing of the check has the effect of increasing the reserves of the selling bank while decreasing those of the bank against which the check is drawn. At the expiration of the agreement the process is reversed. Under the buyback, the economic effects of the purchase, sale, and repurchase are the same—only two separate contracts may be made at the same time. One of these may be for the sale (and purchase) of securities for immediate payment and the other may be for the purchase (and sale) of securities for delivery and payment at a later date.

(4) The final method of adjusting reserves is by the general purchase and sale of government or other securities. The sale of these securities would entitle the selling bank to reserves just as under the repurchase agreement. The difference would simply be the absence of an agreement to repurchase.

3.3. Multiple Expansion (or Contraction) Processes: Some Complicating Factors

We have considered thus far only two influences on the ability of the banking system, through the activities of individual banks, to bring about multiple changes in credit and demand deposits. These were the level of reserve ratios and the amount of initial changes in reserves. In dealing with these influences, the expansion process was viewed as the gradual absorption of excess reserves until reserves were at their required levels. The system as a whole, however, lost no reserves as individual banks expanded. The clearing drain was entirely internal to the system and external to an individual bank, and this phenomenon accounted in part for the difference between the behavior of the whole system and that of individual banks.

There are, however, factors other than reserve requirements which are external to the banking system and which work with reserve requirements in dissipating or reinforcing an initial change in reserves. These mainly include the cash drain and the time deposit drain. Both are allowed for in deducing general equations for changes in the money supply and general statements for money and credit multiplies. The resulting statements, however, must be further modified in order to deal with the processes of money and credit expansion (or contraction) in the more complex situations where different reserve ratios apply to different classes of banks. The reference, furthermore, has been made to both expansionary and contractionary processes. Still, in developing the present topics below, the discussion proceeds in terms of expansionary processes, but this should cause no great difficulty. The general results deduced are clearly applicable to contractionary processes, too.

The cash drain. In recent years the public has wanted to hold paper currency and coin in an amount equal to about 25 per cent of their demand deposits. This per cent we call the coefficient of average cash drain. Also this per cent implies that currency regularly comprises about 20 per cent of the money supply (i.e., currency plus demand deposits). The constancy of the coefficient of average cash drain at times when there are changes in the supply of cash balances implies, furthermore, a constancy in the ratio of a change in currency holdings to a change in demand deposits. This ratio (expressed as a per cent), in turn, we call the coefficient of the marginal cash drain. The underlying explanation for the existence of cash drain is simple. A general increase in bank lending and deposits tends to be the concomitant of an increase in economic activity. Thus with a larger volume of transactions (Sect. 2.2) arises a greater need for currency.

The term "cash drain" refers to a drain on a bank's till cash. The reference to cash in the present context, then, relates only to currency,* since a bank's till cash does not ordinarily include demand deposits. A cash drain and a reduction of till cash, then, may result from a withdrawal of currency from banks by the public, and this withdrawal is external to the banking system. This means that the cash drain reduces reserves by an equal amount, where we include vault cash as reserves. In other words, the currency drain absorbs the system's reserves by 100 per cent of the amount of the drain, as contrasted with demand deposits, which absorb reserves only fractionally. Thus either reserve requirements for deposits

---

* The term "cash" in other contexts may be synonymous with "money," as when we speak of a nonbanking institution's cash account (Sect. 17.1).

would have to be 100 per cent or the public would have to hold all of a money increase in currency in order for the money and credit multipliers (Sect. 3.2) for the banking system to be only equal to one.*

The effect of a 25 per cent cash drain on the expansion of deposits and lending throughout the banking system is illustrated in Table 3-2. The table proceeds from an initial increase in demand deposits at Bank A. The 15 per cent of required reserves are then set aside, and the remains of the deposit appear as excess reserves. This latter magnitude also appears as loans and as another increase in demand deposits. Then, assuming that the latter increase is in part drained off in the form of currency and in part transferred to another bank through a check used for some payment, the latter increase appears in part as a cash drain and in part as a demand deposit at Bank B. The process continues to work through additional transactions, until the consolidated set of changes for all banks appears at the bottom of the table. There the proportion of the increase in currency (i.e., 5.3125) to the bank-induced increase in demand deposits (i.e., 21.25) is approximately 25 per cent, and the ratio of the increase in reserves (i.e., 4.6875) to the increase in deposit liabilities (i.e., 31.25) is 15 per cent.

However, there are three other points to be noted particularly about the expansion process: (1) The reserve drains and cash drains are equal at each stage of the process. (2) There are now several different multiplier effects. Apart from the original primary deposit, demand deposits have increased by less than bank loans, and the difference is due to the drain of currency into the hands of the public. (3) The multiple expansion in all of the variables is considerably less than in the absence of a cash drain. This is, of course, due to the greater reserve absorbing power of a currency drain relative to an increase in demand deposits.

The ultimate effect of the initial increase in demand deposits and the cash drain upon the banking system as a whole may now be stated in general form in terms of a system of equations. Furthermore, the general solution of the equations for the change in the money supply may be found, and, upon substituting specific values for the parameters and values for the initial changes, a specific solution corresponding to the

---

* For many years there have been numerous advocates of 100 per cent reserve banking in order to restore to the government the direct constitutional power to create money (Sect. 7.2).

Also entire theories of changes in business and economic conditions have been built on the notion that a positive (negative) cash drain lags behind the expansion (or contraction) of bank lending and deposits. In the upswing of business activity, so the theories go, banks expand on the basis of fractional reserves; when, after some delay (e.g., because of the time involved before wage rates and incomes respond), the cash drain occurs, banks will be forced to contract loans and deposits, which precipitates a downswing in business activity. Eventually, cash flows into bank reserves again, and the upswing begins again. According to some individuals, 100 per cent reserves are supposed to eliminate this sort of disturbance.

Table 3-2. Multiple Expansion of Lending and Deposits Through the Banking System

(15 per cent reserves, 25 per cent cash drain)

(Amounts in billions of dollars)

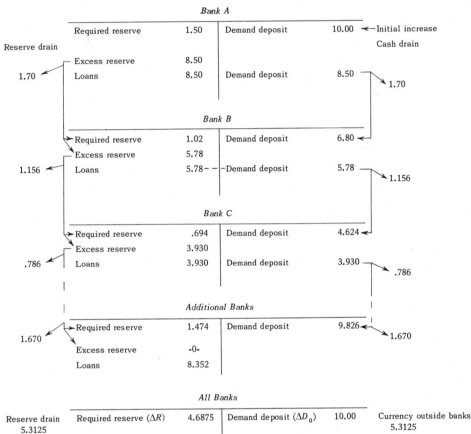

Bank A			
Required reserve	1.50	Demand deposit	10.00 ←Initial increase
			Cash drain
Excess reserve	8.50		
Loans	8.50	Demand deposit	8.50
Bank B			
Required reserve	1.02	Demand deposit	6.80
Excess reserve	5.78		
Loans	5.78	Demand deposit	5.78
Bank C			
Required reserve	.694	Demand deposit	4.624
Excess reserve	3.930		
Loans	3.930	Demand deposit	3.930
Additional Banks			
Required reserve	1.474	Demand deposit	9.826
Excess reserve	-0-		
Loans	8.352		

Reserve drain 1.70 / 1.70
Reserve drain 1.156 / 1.156
.786 / .786
1.670 / 1.670

All Banks

Reserve drain 5.3125 — Currency outside banks 5.3125

Required reserve (ΔR)	4.6875	Demand deposit (ΔD_0)	10.00
Excess reserve	-0-	Demand deposit (ΔD_1)	21.25
Loans (ΔL)	26.5625		
	31.25		31.25

results in Table 3-2 may be found. The general equation system is as follows:

$$(1) \quad \Delta M = \Delta D_0 + \Delta D_1 + \Delta C$$
$$(2) \quad \Delta C = c\Delta D_1$$
$$(3) \quad \Delta R = r\Delta D_0 + r\Delta D_1$$
$$(4) \quad \Delta R_0 = \Delta C + \Delta R$$
$$(5) \quad \Delta L = \Delta D_1 + \Delta C$$
$$(6') \quad \Delta D_0 = \Delta R_0 \quad \text{or } (6'')\Delta D_0 = 0.$$
$$(7) \quad \Delta R_0 = \text{known amount,}$$

where the seven variables are

ΔM, the increase in the supply of money,
ΔD_0, the initial primary deposit,
ΔD_1, the bank-induced increase in deposits,
ΔC, the increase in the public's currency holdings,
ΔR_0, the initial increase in reserves,
ΔR, the increase in required reserves, and
ΔL, the increase in bank loans, and so on.

The two parameters are

c, the proportion of currency to demand deposits preferred
 by the public (i.e., $\Delta C/\Delta D_1$), and
r, the minimum reserve requirement.

Equation (1) is simply definitional. It indicates the variables comprising a change in the money supply. Equations (2) and (3), however, are behavioral equations—the one indicating the public's preference for additional currency relative to additional deposits, and the other indicating the banks' minimal reserve requirements.* The next two equations, (4) and (5), are identities. Equation (4) simply states that an increase in reserves is ultimately used to fulfill reserve requirements or to satisfy the public preference for currency, and the other of these identities expresses the equality between the increase in bank lending and the induced increases in currency and demand deposits. Equation (6') or (6''), furthermore, simply specifies whether the initial increase in primary deposits exists or whether reserves possibly resulted from some means other than an increase in primary deposits. In the illustration presented in Table 3-2, there is a one-to-one relationship between the initial demand deposit (of 10 billion) and the increase in reserves (of $1.50 + 8.50$ billion), but in some other instances an increase in reserves may occur independent of an initial increase in deposits. And, finally, equation (7) simply defines the increase in reserves with reference to some unspecified amount.

Thus we have a simple linear system of n equations and n variables. We know that the solution to such a system is likely to exist by the theory of linear equations. Consequently, attempting a solution by the method of substitution, we find the general solution

$$\Delta M = \underbrace{\Delta D_0}_{\substack{\text{primary} \\ \text{deposit}}} + \underbrace{\frac{1+c}{r+c}(1-r)\Delta R_0}_{\substack{\text{initial excess} \\ \text{reserves}}}$$

$$= \Delta R_0 \qquad \underbrace{\Delta D_1 + \Delta C,}_{} \quad \text{where}$$

---

* Some people would rather refer to the reserve equation, (3), as a structural or institutional equation, where r may be specified by the central bank. However, banks have considerable leeway in determining the effective r, subject to a floor value for it set by the central bank.

$$\Delta L = \frac{1 + c}{r + c}(1 - r)\Delta R_0, \text{ and}$$

$$\Delta D_1 = \frac{1}{r + c}(1 - r)\Delta R_0, \text{ etc.}$$

Now, using these general results, and substituting the particular values for the variables and parameters in the above case, we have:

$$\Delta D_1 = \frac{1}{0.15 + 0.25}(1 - 0.15)10 \text{ billion dollars}$$

$$= 21.25 \text{ billion dollars,}$$

$$\Delta L = \frac{1 + 0.25}{0.15 + 0.25}(1 - 0.15)10 \text{ billion dollars}$$

$$= 26.5625 \text{ billion dollars, and}$$
$$\Delta M = 10 \text{ billion dollars} + 26.5625 \text{ billion dollars}$$
$$= 36.5625 \text{ billion dollars.}$$

But these numerical results correspond to the results in Table 3-2.

Note too, in terms of the general solution, that the earlier case (Sect. 3.2) with no cash drain may be derived by setting c equal to zero. Thus what was said in the earlier numerical illustration about the relative magnitudes of the various credit and monetary changes may also now be verified easily.

Given values for the parameters, the situation defined by the equations (1) through (7), and particular equilibrium values[*] for the variables may be sketched as Fig. 3-1. There we denote absolute changes in the independent variable (i.e., $|\Delta R|$) along the vertical axis, and absolute changes in the dependent variables appear along the horizontal axis. Equation (6') specifies a line through the origin, the general equations for ΔD_1 and ΔL specify other lines, and the coefficient $(1 - r)$ and changing levels for some initial deposit (ΔD_0) specify a fourth line. Now, to find equilibrium values for the various dependent variables one simply assigns a particular value $\Delta \bar{R}_0$ to the initial increase in reserves, draws a horizontal line through point a, and drops a vertical line at this point to find the initial increase in deposits ΔD_0. Starting from this latter equilibrium value, one then follows the arrows in the diagram to find other equilibrium values where the initial increase in deposits exists (i.e., $\Delta D_0 \neq 0$) as in equation (6'). In this case, the entire change in the money supply is the sum of the initial increase in deposits, the induced increase in deposits, and the currency drain (i.e., $\Delta M = \Delta \bar{D}_0 + \Delta \bar{D}_1 + \Delta \bar{C}$). Note too that the difference between the increase in loans

[*] The bar over a variable will at times be used to denote an equilibrium value for the variable.

and the induced increase in deposits is the magnitude of the cash drain (i.e., $\Delta \bar{L} - \Delta \bar{D}_1 = \Delta \bar{C}$).

If there is no initial primary deposit accompanying the reserve increase, the solution to the initial system of equations (1) through (7) relies upon equation (6″) instead of (6′). In this case, to find equilibrium values in Fig. 3-1, one would simply extend a horizontal line from the

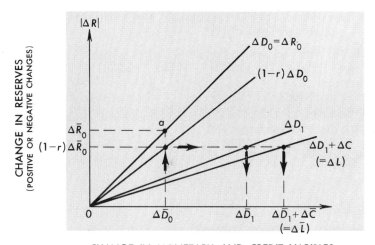

CHANGE IN MONETARY AND CREDIT VARIBLES
(POSITIVE OR NEGATIVE CHANGES)

Fig. 3-1. Financial Expansion with a Cash Drain.

initial change in reserves ($\Delta \bar{R}_0$). The coordinates of the points where this line intersected the lines corresponding to the various functions [other than $(1-r)\Delta D_0$, of course] would then correspond to the equilibrium values for the various variables, and so on. In this latter case, where the solution relied upon equation (6″) instead of (6′), all of the initial reserve increase is in excess of requirements, and the general solution to the equation system would be

$$\Delta M = \frac{1+c}{r+c} (\Delta R_0), \text{ where}$$

$$\Delta L = \frac{1+c}{r+c} (\Delta R_0), \text{ and}$$

$$\Delta D_1 = \frac{1}{r+c} (\Delta R_0), \text{ etc.}$$

As matters turn out, the coefficient [i.e.$(1+c)/(r+c)$] to the excess reserve variable, in the general solution to the latter money supply change, is the money or credit multiplier (Sect. 3.1). In the present case, if there is no currency drain, then we have $(1/r)$ ΔR_0, as at the outset (Sect. 3.1). To derive such multipliers more directly, *one simply takes the sum of the relevant drain coefficients and divides this by the sum of the products of all of the drain coefficients and their corresponding reserve absorption ratios.* In the present case, where

$1 + c$ is the sum of the money drain coefficients,

$1 \cdot r + c \cdot 1$ is the sum of the products of all of the drain coefficients
and their corresponding reserve absorption ratio (i.e., r
and 1, respectively),

the rule for deriving either the money or credit multipliers yields the following:

ratio of desired demand deposits to demand deposits (i.e., unity)

$$\frac{1 + c}{1 \cdot r + c \cdot 1}$$

coefficient of cash drain

reserve absorption by cash drain (100 per cent)

coefficient of cash drain

reserve ratio for demand deposits

As long as $r < 1$,

$$\frac{1 + c}{1 \cdot r + c \cdot 1} > 1$$

Other complicating factors. The basic form of the expression for the credit and money multipliers continues to recur. At times, however, further modifications of the basic form of the multipliers are called for, in addition to that for the currency drain. These are needed in order to obtain multipliers that are applicable to money and credit expansionary (and contractionary) processes that are complicated by the presence of time deposit drains and different reserve requirements for different classes of banks.

A time deposit drain results from the public's electing to allocate a part of the increase in bank liabilities into savings-type deposits instead of demand deposits, and from the characteristics of these savings-type deposits. For one thing they cannot directly enter into the expenditure stream in the form of a check, and, for another, their owner must be prepared to wait a certain period of time before withdrawing the deposit. The savings-type or time deposits, then, are less liquid than money and typically carry a lower reserve ratio either on the basis of regulation or experience. Thus a drain of reserves arises from simply holding time deposits in lieu of an increase in demand deposits working against the counter drain arising from the release of excess reserves at the lower requirement. Even so, where both currency holdings and time deposits increase along with demand deposits, and on the basis of the above rule for deriving such multipliers, one would state the money multiplier as follows:

$$\frac{1+c}{1 \cdot r + c \cdot 1 + t \cdot r'} \text{ or } \frac{1+c}{r+c+tr'}, \text{ where}$$

t is the ratio of the desired change in time deposits
to the change in demand deposits, and
r' is the reserve ratio for time deposits.

In the present application of the rule, the time deposit coefficient (t) does not appear in the numerator of the money multiplier, but it does appear in the denominator. In terms of the rule, this is because only money (i.e., currency and demand deposit) coefficients appear in the numerator, and the products of all drain coefficients and their corresponding absorption ratio appear in the denominator. The credit multiplier, however, would appear as

$$\frac{1+c+t}{1 \cdot r + c \cdot 1 + tr'},$$

since the expansion in credit is equal to the sum of the expansion in demand deposits, currency, and savings-type deposits. Setting the money and the credit multipliers with both currency and time deposit drain in juxtaposition,

$$\frac{1+c}{r+c+tr'} < \frac{1+c+t}{r+c+tr'}, \quad r' < 1$$

Clearly the credit multiplier with a currency and time deposit drain is greater than the money multiplier with a currency and time deposit drain. And clearly, too, the presence of the time deposit drain reduces the money multiplier, i.e.,

$$\frac{1+c}{r+c} > \frac{1+c}{r+c+tr'}$$

But the credit multiplier with both time deposit and currency drains is greater than the money multiplier with a currency drain and without a time deposit drain, i.e.,

$$\frac{1+c+t}{r+c+tr'} > \frac{1+c}{r+c}$$

The several types of banks with varying reserve requirements for demand deposits include those classified by the Federal Reserve (Sect. 8.1) as (1) country banks and (2) reserve city and central reserve city banks, as well as the selected groups of state-chartered banks (Sect. 11.5). The latter groups are especially difficult to deal with in a simple model for money and credit expansion, since some of their reserves include balances at other banks or securities of a short maturity date. The former classes of banks, nevertheless, may be dealt with, positing that the two groups in question share a change in deposits in such roughly fixed proportions as d and $1 - d$, respectively. These shares, of course, necessarily sum to 1 [i.e., $d + (1 - d) = 1$]. They are analogous to the other drain coefficients, only now instead of $1 \cdot r$, there will be $d \cdot r_{cm}$ and $(1 - d)r_{rm}$, where

r_{cm} is the reserve ratio for demand deposits of country banks and
r_{rm} is the reserve ratio for reserve city and central reserve city banks.

Thus, letting the same cash and time deposit drain coefficients apply to the two sets of banks, the money multiplier becomes

$$\frac{1 + c}{dr_{cm} + (1 - d)r_{rm} + c + tr}, \quad *$$

This kind of expression enables us to assess such things as the significance of changes in the differential between reserve ratios for various classes of banks, as well as the extent to which these different classes of banks participate in money expansion (or contraction) processes.

In subsequent topics we shall encounter financial multipliers again. At that time we will be examining the influence of nonbank financial institutions on the behavior of the banking system. At the present level at which multiple expansion and contraction processes are examined, however, we have obtained insights into the nature of the banking sector of the economy. Government policy actions and exogenous disturbances are both continually being transmitted to the entire economy through this sector.

3.4. Summary

Commercial banks can create money in payment for the debt instruments they acquire. They may also contract the supply of money and credit when the process that initially led to its expansion is reversed. Given an initial change in bank reserves, the actual operation of the processes depends on the prevalence of some basic institutions. These include a fractional-reserve banking system, some of its accouterments —such as a means of transferring excess reserve balances—and the will

---

* Note that in relationship to the earlier money multiplier with cash and time deposits drains, the earlier single product $(1 \cdot r)$ would correspond to two products $[dr_{cm} + (1 - d)r_{rm}]$. In fact, the plain r in the earlier discussion could be interpreted as a weighted average reserve requirement for changes in demand deposits for all banks subject to the Federal Reserve's reserve requirements, i.e.,

$$r = \frac{dr_{cm} + (1 - d)r_{rm}}{d + (1 - d)}$$

(A weighted average is defined as a weighted total divided by the sum of the weights.)

to engage in enterprise, both among bankers and creditworthy borrowers. As we shall see, banks are unique among nonfinancial and financial businesses in their capacity to create money.

The explanation of the expansion and contraction of the supply of money and credit may be given in terms of the banking system as a whole and in terms of the individual banks comprising the entire system. The total results of the explanations are the same, but the behavior of an individual bank is very different from the aggregate of banks. In tracing a process through separate banks, we must allow for operations that facilitate the transfer of deposits and the full utilization of reserve funds. Historically, these consist of the movement of specie reserves, and, more recently, the interbank clearing of checks. They consist of, in other instances, correspondent banking, the Federal funds market, the use of repurchase agreements (or the buyback technique), and the general purchase and sale of government or other securities.

The banking system's capacity to expand earning assets and money is constrained by factors which drain or absorb initial changes in reserves. Given the equation system of n equations and n variables underlying this process, general solutions may readily be found for changes in the money supply and earning assets. These general results contain coefficients allowing for the various drains on reserves and the supply of money and, moreover, are applicable to negative changes in the supply of money and contraction in the process that generated the supply of money and credit to begin with.

The need to maintain a minimal ratio of reserves to demand deposits is not the only factor limiting this potential expansion. A drain of currency into the hands of the public accompanying an expansion of demand deposits reduces the potential of the banking system. The reason is that currency absorbs bank reserves dollar for dollar, while demand deposits absorb reserves only fractionally with reserve requirements of less than 100 per cent. Induced increases in time deposits, since they typically carry lower reserve requirements, broaden the lending power of the banking system, although they restrict the system's capacity to expand the supply of money.

The general rule for finding the multiplier expression for the change in the money supply that results from an initial excess of reserves is as follows: the sum of the monetary drain coefficients is divided by the sum of the rates at which all of the currency and deposit variables absorb reserves, where each is multiplied by its own drain coefficient. Besides making it possible to incorporate various classes of deposits in explanations of expansion processes, this rule has numerous other applications, some of which will be encountered later. A specific application was to the expansion through two classes of banks with different reserve requirements.

4

The Rate of Interest, Liquidity, and Money Balances

> We cannot get rid of money even by abolishing gold and silver and legal tender instruments.* So long as there exists any durable asset, it is capable of possessing monetary attributes and, therefore, of giving rise to the characteristic problems of a monetary economy (J. M. Keynes, *The General Theory of Employment, Interest, and Money* [1936]).

In an economy not entirely regulated by other than market forces, some asset will arise to serve as money. In such an economy, the store of value quality of money (2.1) is of central importance. This is because shifts in the preference for money emanating from changes in the store of value quality of money concern two other sets of important changes. These, distinguished according to time dimensions, occur in the very short run and over the short cycle of income, employment, and output. These latter changes in employment, and so on, we refer to as characteristic problems of a monetary economy, since they noticeably arise in situations involving a preference for more or less money—all in a market economy and in relation to the stock of money. The changes in employment, and in other things, and the forces giving rise to them are introduced in the next chapter. A good portion of the book concerns them in one way or another.

This chapter, in part, in anticipation of subsequent chapters, deals with changes in the very short run. These would include changes in the preference for money relative to that for so-called near-money or safe assets, and changes in the interest rates and prices of the latter assets, all occurring in a single phase of the short cycle, or in an even shorter period. The first section of this chapter, consequently, describes the general

---

* Monetary assets become so-called legal tender or lawful money when the law gives creditors the right to settle their obligations by offering them as a means of payment.

characteristics of the latter assets, as well as a wider range of selected assets. It introduces a very general model concerning the preference for assets. Other sections introduce the rate of interest and the structure of rates, the rate of interest and security prices, notions about the switching of assets, and changes in the strength of the preference for money balances as opposed to some other assets.

4.1. The Preferred Combination of Alternative Assets

The holders of wealth,* or assets, may be thought of as preferring to hold their wealth or assets in various forms. These forms may include, in the broadest sense, human capital (18.1) as affected by training, education, and special individual skills; in a narrower sense, they may include only the more tangible and nonhuman forms. In either case, under two simplifying conditions, as initial steps, and under two assumptions listed below, the individual may be thought of as combining assets with the view to maximizing the flow of returns from holding the assets, rather than because of the assets themselves.

As one initial step, we will think of the prospective returns from each of m classes of assets as a perpetual stream. This stream of returns we denote as R, per some period. Later, after the introduction of the initial choice situation, these returns may be thought of as being of different magnitudes for different periods. Such returns per some period may then be denoted $R_1, R_2, R_3, \ldots$ where, for example, 1, 2, and 3 are the 1st, 2nd, and 3rd year in the future, and so on. The other initial step is that the absolute return per period (i.e., the flow) consist of the elements $Q, C,$ and L (i.e., $R = Q - C + L$), when

Q is generally some dollar return or yield,
C is some carrying cost, payment for storage, or wastage with the passage of time, and
L is some security or convenience associated with the holding of the asset

On some subsequent occasions, we will deal only with the dollar returns net of carrying costs. Liquidity elements, nevertheless, enter into all of the more general discussions concerning choice situations.

For the present, we consider only nonhuman forms of wealth: currency

* Our use of the term "wealth" as a stock of assets is consistent with the earlier meaning Irving Fisher gave to it. This is also true with respect to our use below of the terms "stock" (or "fund") as some accumulated amount of wealth, and of "flow" (or "stream") as an addition to wealth or the enjoyment of services. For an intuitive and still helpful approach to these meanings, then, see Irving Fisher, *The Nature of Capital and Income* (London: The Macmillan Company, Ltd., 1930), pp. 51-65.

and demand deposits, marketable United States government securities, and such assets as deposit-type savings, corporate bonds, corporate stocks, and instrumental capital.

Currency and demand deposits are considered as money. The series of prospective returns from holding such balances generally consist of substantial liquidity and virtually no yield or carrying cost. *Marketable government securities* are obligations of the Federal government. Their yield exceeds their carrying costs, generally in the form of tax payment on the yield, and they are generally regarded as low-risk, liquid assets. *Such assets as savings-type deposits* (Sect. 3.3) are so-called near-money, along with marketable obligations of the government. So-called near-money assets, as their name implies, are those that may be safely converted into money on short notice and with little prospective loss of principal. The yield on these assets may be above that on some issues of government securities—their carrying cost is usually negligible—and the magnitude of their liquidity element is near that of government bonds. *Corporate bonds* are debt instruments issued by private corporations. They are marketable, generally of higher risk, and therefore less liquid than government bonds. Their yield is characteristically higher than that on government bonds, and their carrying cost consists of a tax payment on the yield. *Stocks* represent claims of the owners against corporations. Their claim is subordinate to that of bondholders, and as such they represent a residual claim against earnings and assets of corporations. Their yield (dividends per share), less the carrying cost (consisting mainly of a tax payment), is generally higher than that for most other financial instruments. They are riskier and consequently less liquid than bonds. *Instrumental capital* consists of items that may be used to assist some process of production or supply a service. Its yield or output generally exceeds its carrying cost, and its liquidity is virtually zero.

The classes of alternative assets may be listed according to the characteristic order of the magnitude of the elements comprising the returns from some common dollars amount for each class:

Alternative Sets of Assets (*A common dollar amount*)	*Absolute Amounts* $(Q - C)$	L
Currency and demand deposits	0	+
Safe assets (including near-money assets and bonds)		
Stocks		
Instrumental capital	+	0

In particular, the classes are listed according to the increasing order of the magnitude of their yield less their carrying cost (i.e., $Q - C$) and the decreasing order of the magnitude of their liquidity (L). According to the order of these magnitudes and by our definition of money (Sect. 2.1), the asset serving as money includes currency and demand deposits. However, the relative importance of the elements entering into the streams of prospective returns R_n ($n = 1, \ldots, m$) for m different assets may vary from time to time, with the result that no asset persistently possesses a constant degree of liquidity (or moneyness). The characteristic whereby no asset persistently possesses a fixed degree of moneyness ultimately gives rise to particular problems in a monetary economy. These concern fluctuations in the value of assets and the respective levels of income, employment, and output (Sect. 5.4).

The model for the choice situations relies mainly upon two assumptions—the one about maximizing behavior and another about rationality. Assumption 1 is that the choice among available alternatives is viewed as being made so as to maximize satisfaction (or utility), and the individual or behavioral unit is viewed as having the capacity to rank preferences at a given time. If the decision-making unit prefers item x_1 to x_2, it is said to derive more utility from x_1. Assumption 2 is rather nominal: (1) The decision-making unit must know at a given time whether from among all possible pairs it prefers x_1 to x_2, or x_2 to x_1, or whether it is indifferent between them; (2) only one of these three possibilities must be true for any pair of alternatives; and (3) if the subject shows a preference for x_1 over x_2 and x_2 over x_3, at a given time, then there must also be a preference for x_1 over x_3.

Now, let us denote an optimal choice of assets and then generalize this statement to complete the description of the model for the general choice situation. Consider, to begin with, satisfaction or utility (U) as some function of money (M), safe assets or bonds (B), stocks (S), and instrumental capital (I). This function, to be maximized, we denote[1]

$$U = f(M, B, S, I)$$

Moreover, the constraint within which the choice must be made may be considered as the sum of the value of the assets in question. This constraint function, we denote as

$g(M, B, S, I) = P_M M + P_B B + P_S S + P_I I$, or in implicit form,
$g(M, B, S, I) - P_M M - P_B B - P_S S - P_I I = 0$, where
P_M is 1 (or the price per dollar),
P_B is the price per bond,
P_S is the price per stock, and
P_I is the price per unit of instrumental capital.

Thus, forming a Lagrangian function,

$L(M, B, S, I, r)$
$\qquad = f(M, B, S, I) + r[g(M, B, S, I) - P_M M - P_B B - P_S S - P_I I]$,

and r is the Lagrangian factor of proportionality.

Next, to denote the first-order conditions[2] for the constrained maximum, we set the first partial derivatives for each of the $n + 1$ variables in the Lagrangian function equal to zero and form a system of $n + 1$ equations and $n + 1$ variables (i.e., $M, B, S, I,$ and r):

$$\frac{\partial L}{\partial M} = \frac{\partial U}{\partial M} - rP_M = 0$$

$$\frac{\partial L}{\partial B} = \frac{\partial U}{\partial B} - rP_B = 0$$

$$\frac{\partial L}{\partial S} = \frac{\partial U}{\partial S} - rP_S = 0$$

$$\frac{\partial L}{\partial I} = \frac{\partial U}{\partial I} - rP_I = 0$$

$$\frac{\partial L}{\partial r} = g(M, B, S, I) - P_M M - P_B B - P_S S - P_I I$$

Dividing the first four of these equations by the respective prices, we see clearly

$$\frac{\frac{\partial U}{\partial M}}{P_M} = \frac{\frac{\partial U}{\partial B}}{P_B} = \frac{\frac{\partial U}{\partial S}}{P_S} = \frac{\frac{\partial U}{\partial I}}{P_I} = r$$

But the numerators of these ratios are nothing more than the respective flows of returns from acquiring additional assets in the form of money, bonds, stocks, and instrumental capital, i.e., $\partial U/\partial M = R$ and $R/P_M = r$, $\partial U/\partial B = R$ and $R/P_B = r$, and so on. A proposition follows:

Proposition 1: *The combination of assets yielding the maximum stream of returns follows from equating the rates of return (i.e., r's) from any further expenditures on the respective classes of assets.* If one ratio (or its corresponding rate of return) is higher than another, a better adjustment can be made within the restraints upon choice. A higher ratio (or rate) on a given asset may result from a greater return or a lower price or both. If this occurred, a better adjustment could be made by increasing the holdings of the given item. The increase in demand would, in turn, contribute to a rise in price and a decline in returns. At the same time, the disposition of other assets would contribute to a decline in the corresponding prices and an increase in the corresponding returns. The characteristic order of the magnitudes of the elements comprising returns may now be expressed as rates rather than absolute amounts, where the alternative assets can be expressed in any dollar amounts:

Alternative Sets of Assets	Rates	
	$(q-c)$	l
Currency and demand deposits	0	+
Safe assets (including near-money assets and bonds)		
Stocks		
Instrumental capital	+	0

As it turns out, in the case where total assets serve as a constraint, the factor of proportionality (r) is the rate of return for each of the n sets of assets whose value may be expressed in terms of the perpetuity form of the capital value formula. That is,

$$P = \frac{R}{r}$$

where R is the absolute return per annum, for example, for an infinite number of periods, and where

r is the rate of return for discounting the absolute return to make it equal to the supply price (P) or capital value. [*]

[*] The expression $P = R/r$ is a form of the general formula for the sum of a finite number of terms in a geometric progression where the last or mth term corresponds to prospects pertaining to the mth future time interval, $m \to \infty$.

For example, as denoted later (Sect. 4.3), the present value P of an amount R due n years from now, when P could be invested at compound interest rate r for n years in order to end up with R, is given by

$$P = \frac{R_n}{(1+r)^n}$$

But, in the case of a perpetuity yielding the same amount R each year from $n = 1$ until $n = m$, $m \to \infty$, we have for the total present value $P^{(s)}$, a simple geometric progression with an infinite number of terms:

$$P^{(s)} = \frac{R}{(1+r)^1} + \frac{R}{(1+r)^2} + \cdots + \frac{R}{(1+r)^m}, \quad m \to \infty$$

Now, multiplying both sides of the latter equation by $(1+r)$ and subtracting the latter equation from the result, we get

$$P^{(s)}[(1+r) - 1] = R - \frac{R}{(1+r)^m}$$

$$P^{(s)} = \frac{R - R\left(\frac{1}{1+r}\right)^m}{1+r-1}$$

From this last expression

$$P^{(s)} = \frac{R}{r} - \frac{R}{r}\left(\frac{1}{1+r}\right)^m$$

$$P^{(s)} = \frac{R}{r}$$

as $m \to \infty$, for $r > 0$ in the equation, since $\left(\frac{1}{1+r}\right)^m \to 0$.

Upon rearranging the terms of the latter expression, $r = R/P$. In this form, the ratio R/P serves only as an index to the rate of return (r) when the latter is derived by equating a finite stream (or flow) of returns (i.e., R_n, $n = 1, \ldots, m$) to the price. Nevertheless, the characteristic for an optimal adjustment whereby the rates of return for different items for a given subject are equal should be clear.

4.2. The Rate of Interest and the Structure of Rates

The rate of interest (i) is similar in its economic characteristics to the rate of return (r). In fact, we will view the two rates as different references to the same thing, apart from the distinction between the rate of return (r), as the rate for holding assets, and the rate of interest (i), as the fundamental cost of obtaining funds for asset expansion in some contexts (Sect. 5.5, 17.2, and 17.4). For the time being, however, we will refer to the rate of return on such financial instruments as bonds and, at times, stocks as the rate of interest (i). This rate, too, may include several elements, and, in discussing the structure of rates, we shall concern ourselves mainly with yield (expressed as a rate). In everyday discussion, the yield element as set forth by us is called the rate of interest. The rate is the price paid for credit if one is the user of funds. The absolute amount paid out is a source of income to the source of the borrowed funds.

The riskless rental element and the risk element. The reference has been to the rate of interest. There are actually many rates, all of which are interrelated.* For example, there are two distinguishable elements in any given yield or interest rate. These include the so-called riskless rental element and the risk element, and the rates on all financial assets of similar maturity may be said to include the same magnitude for the riskless element. In the monetary literature, the rate on long-term government securities is usually referred to as the riskless rental value of money. The riskless rental value is that providing the maximum assurance of the payment of interest and principal over a long period of time, and a change in it may be reflected in a movement in the structure of rates.

The portion of an interest rate net of the so-called riskless element is the risk element. The magnitudes for interest rates on securities of a similar maturity and carrying different risks and tax features tend to

---

* This general meaning is in keeping with Irving Fisher's use of the term. He observed the many kinds of interest rates that varied according to risk, and included "not only the implicit interest realized by the investor who buys a preferred stock." He said, "We may even include the rates realized on common stock" (Irving Fisher, *The Theory of Interest* [New York: Kelley and Millman, Inc., 1954], pp. 206-207). See also Fritz Machlup, *The Stock Market, Credit and Capital Formation* (London: William Hodge and Co., Ltd., 1940), pp. 22-23.

be differentiated at a given time according to the difference in the magnitude of the respective risk elements.

The yield curve. As implied above, the magnitudes for interest rates generally may be affected by the time-to-maturity feature. The curve relating yields (as rates) to the time to maturity for a given class of securities that differ only with respect to the time-to-maturity feature is called the yield curve. In any event, a change in the riskless element may be reflected in upward or downward movements in the entire structure of interest rates or a shift in the n yield curves [i.e., $i_j = f_j$ (time to maturity), $j = 1, \ldots, n$] corresponding to the n different financial assets, such as government securities, high-grade (i.e., Aaa) corporate bonds, and lower-grade (i.e., Baa) corporate bonds, after the change in the riskless rate has had time to work itself out.

Movement in the structure of rates. Evidence of movement in the structure of rates may be observed in Fig. 4-1. There the time series for interest rates on debt instruments of various risk and time to maturity reflect upward and downward movements: upward in 1953, downward in part of 1953 and 1954, upward in 1955 through 1957, downward in 1958, upward in 1959, downward in 1960-1961, and so on. There, too, the reader should gain some sense of the time dimension of what we refer to as the short cycle, the duration of a short cycle being measured from one upper turning point to a succeeding one, or from a lower turning point to a succeeding lower point.

Also, in the illustration, differences may be observed between the per cent per annum on high-grade corporate bonds (Aaa) and lower-grade corporate bonds (Baa). These are primarily differences in risk cost to borrowers, and payments (as rates) to lenders for accepting risk.

4.3. The Rate of Interest and Security Prices

In the next chapter a distinction is made between the first two and the last two classes of assets outlined above (Sect. 4.1). This distinction is extended to include the tendency for the yields (as rates) on the first and the last two classes to vary inversely over the short cycle of income, employment, and output. In the very short run, however, there is some tendency for yields (as rates) on the different assets to vary directly with one another. Given some change in the riskless rental value of money (Sect. 4.2), as may emanate from some sector of the financial markets, the change may be spread to other sectors of the market, along the mechanical lines set forth in the discussion of proposition 1 above. Whether the change will spread and what is the length of the time required for the spread of the change to other sectors, of course, depend upon the degree of competition and the absence of fric-

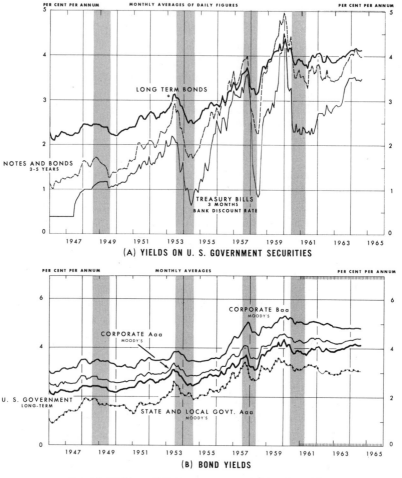

Fig. 4-1. Yields on U.S. Government and Other Securities.

* New series. Securities are classified according to maturity or first call date. Long-term bonds include bonds due or callable after eight years in the period January 1919–October 1925; after 12 years, November 1925–December 1934; after 15 years, January 1935–March 1952; after 12 years, April 1952–March 1953; and in ten years or more, beginning April 1953. Yields on bills are those for new issues through 1940; market yields thereafter. Bills included are 3-month issues except in the period March 1934–December 1937, when issues were somewhat longer term.   Note: The lines separating the gray from the more heavily shaded area are turning points of cyclical change as reported by the National Bureau of Economic Research. The turning points are November 1948 (peak), October 1949 (trough), July 1953 (peak), August 1954 (trough), July 1957 (peak), April 1958 (trough), May 1960 (peak), and February 1961 (trough). Source of data: Board of Governors of the Federal Reserve System.

tions inhibiting the proper functions of the markets. But, in the properly functioning and highly developed financial markets, the responsiveness of yield changes in one market to those in another is made more sensitive by the presence of a number of individuals and institutions that engage in switching and arbitrage transactions.

In the above markets, switching transactions refer to those changes in assets that occur when an individual or institution disposes of one asset—its price having risen (and yield declined)—and buys another, thereby transferring the rise in price (and decline in yield) from one market sector to another. And, more restrictively, arbitrage may be said to consist of this selling in one market for immediate purchase in another, when both the disposition and acquisition are confined to a similar set of assets, such as government securities. The result of switching, in the present instance, would be downward shifts in the other $n-1$ yield curves [i.e., $i_j = f_j$ (time to maturity), $j = 1, \ldots, n-1$] corresponding to the downward shift in the initial or nth yield curve. The result of the arbitrage would be to provide a smoother shape in the curves than would be present in the absence of arbitrage transactions.

As implied above, yields (as rates) tend to vary inversely with the values of securities, once they become outstanding issues. The yield on a new issue of marketable bonds as contrasted with an outstanding issue, for example, would be tailored to suit the market so that there is a correspondence of the yield on the new issue and the face value of the bond with the yields on similar bonds and their prevailing market values (Sect. 12.3). But after the initial distribution of the issue, its value and yield may change with the vicissitudes of the market, pronouncements about the success or failure of various political and economic ventures, and excursions into outer space. For the present, therefore, we mainly want to illustrate more specifically the interrelationships between market values, yields (as rates), and the prospective streams of returns with respect to marketable debt instruments and stocks.

Debt instruments. Interest on such debt instruments as bonds is generally in the form of contractual interest and/or a discount or premium. Contractual interest is usually represented by coupons attached to the bond. In this case, the coupon is usually tailored to suit the market at the time of issue. Bond prices may then decline or rise. If bond prices decline, the bonds outstanding go to a discount in the market. The fact that a bond may be purchased for less than its previous purchase price means that a new buyer will receive interest in excess of the returns from the coupons in the case of a coupon bond. This, in effect, means that the interest one may expect from purchasing the bond at the lower price has increased. It also means that the holder of similar-type bonds can now buy the same bonds at a discount or liquidate his present holding at a loss. If bond prices rise, on the other hand, the bond outstanding may go to a premium in the market. The fact that a bond must be purchased for more than its previous price means that the buyer will receive a smaller interest return on his principal. This also means that the holders of other bonds obtained at an earlier price may sell them, realizing capital gains. Capital values have, in other words, increased. Now, in the case of discount obligations (i.e., marketable debt instruments without coupons or other means of the serial payment of interest), the interest payment will be wholly in terms of the discount (i.e., the difference between the purchase price and the maturity value expressed as a rate of return on the purchase price). The discount will be large or small depending upon the rate of interest and the time to maturity.

What has been said in words about the prices and yields (as rates) of marketable bonds may be said more rigorously. We may express the price (P) of a bond as a function of time [i.e., $P = f(t)$], where the parameters are a 20-year contractual or serial payment of dividends (i.e., D_n, $n = 1, 2, \ldots, 20$), the rate of interest (i), and the separate return of the principal at maturity (R_{20}). To begin with, the equation defining the function involving only the prospective serial payment is

$$(1) \qquad P^{**} = \frac{D_1}{(1+i)^{1-t}} + \frac{D_2}{(1+i)^{2-t}} + \cdots + \frac{D_{20}}{(1+i)^{20-t}}$$

$n - t > 0,$* $n = 1, \ldots, 20$. The equation defining the function involving the face value (or value at maturity time 20) is

$$(2) \qquad P^{*} = \frac{R_{20}}{(1+i)^{20-t}}$$

The equation defining the function for the actual market or present value of both the prospective serial payments and the return at maturity would be the sum of equations (1) and (2):

$$(3) \qquad P = \frac{D_1}{(1+i)^{1-t}} + \frac{D_2}{(1+i)^{2-t}} + \ddots + \frac{D_{20} + R_{20}}{(1+i)^{20-t}}$$

$n - t > 0, (n = 1, \ldots, 20)$.

Two sets of parametric values for the equations (1), (2), and (3), input values for the variable (t), and the resulting values for the variable (P) are shown in Table 4-1. The first set of numbers includes selected input values for t, the corresponding output values $P[=f(t)]$, and the parameters, as shown in the table. The second set of numbers includes

---

* This notation means that the terms of the equation with exponential values less than zero (i.e., $n - t \leq 0$) are not a part of the definition of the function. Note that at $t = 1$, according to our notation, the first term drops out. At that time, the payment for the first coupon D_1 is due and we are beginning the second year. The number 1 is included in the second year.

some selected input and output values, after a change in the rate of interest to 6.5 per cent, as shown in the table. The result, of course, is that the initial coupon rate no longer corresponds to the actual market rate of interest, and the value of the bond too, as a function of time, has changed.

Table 4-1. The Market Price (P) of a Coupon Bond: Given the Periodic Dividends, the Face Value, and the Rate of Interest

Set 1.
$D_n = \$5.00$ $(n = 1, 2, \ldots, 20)$
$R_{20} = \$100.00$, and
$i = 0.05$

Set 2.
$D_n = \$5.00$ $(n = 10, 11, \ldots, 20)$
$R_{20} = \$100.00$, and
$i = 0.065$

Time in Years	P^{**} (1)	P^* (2)	$P^{**} + P^* = P$ (3)	Time in Years	P^{**} (1)	P^* (2)	$P^{**} + P^* = P$ (3)
0	62.31	37.69	100.00				
1	60.43	39.57	100.00				
2	58.45	41.55	100.00				
3	56.37	43.63	100.00				
4	54.19	45.81	100.00				
5	51.90	48.10	100.00				
6	49.49	50.51	100.00				
7	46.97	53.03	100.00				
8	44.32	55.68	100.00				
9	41.53	58.47	100.00				
10	38.61	61.39	100.00	10	35.94	53.27	89.21
11	35.04	64.46	100.00	11	32.28	56.74	89.02
12	32.32	67.68	100.00	12	30.44	60.42	90.86
13	28.93	71.07	100.00	13	27.42	64.35	91.77
14	25.38	74.62	100.00	14	24.21	68.53	92.74
15	21.65	78.35	100.00	15	20.78	72.99	93.77
16	17.73	82.27	100.00	16	17.13	77.73	94.86
17	13.62	86.38	100.00	17	13.24	82.78	96.02
18	9.30	90.70	100.00	18	9.10	88.17	97.27
19	4.76	95.24	100.00	19	4.70	93.90	98.60
20	0.00	100.00	100.00	20	0.00	100.00	100.00

The particular functions defined by the substitution of values in the more general equations are sketched in Fig. 4-2. The function defined by equation (3) with an interest rate parameter of 5 per cent, for example, is a continuous function over time intervals of one year—namely, $0 \leq t < 1$, $1 \leq t < 2$, $2 \leq t < 3$, $\ldots$, $19 \leq t < 20$, to correspond to the due dates for the serial payments of interest. The bond, as indicated in the illustration, has a higher market price just prior to the due date for a serial payment rather than immediately afterward. A properly functioning market will reflect this development with respect to a single bond issue.

The function defined by equation (3), after a change in the rate of interest to 6.5 per cent at time ten (i.e., $t = 10$) is also shown, as well as the other functions defined by equations (1) and (2). The broken lines represent the functions with the interest rate parameter of 6.5 per cent. Note that the increase in the interest rate at time ten results in a decline in the present value of the bond at that time and until maturity. A proposition follows:

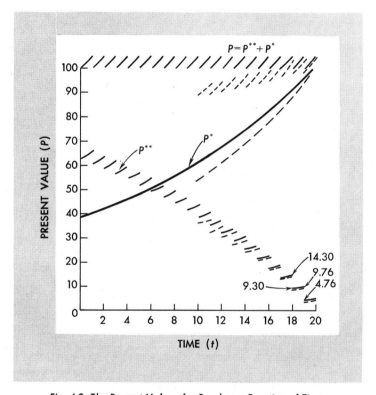

Fig. 4-2. The Present Value of a Bond as a Function of Time.

Proposition 2: *A given increase (decrease) in the rate of interest causes the value of a marketable bond to decline (rise) more, the longer the time to maturity.* This means that the longer the time to maturity, the greater is the extent to which a bondholder can be frozen-in as a result of a rise in the rate of interest, and the greater is the extent of a loss of liquidity.

Figure 4-2 provides only a single instance of the result of a change in the interest rate. Imagine, however, what would appear in that illustration if different rates in a single series in Fig. 4-1 were successively inserted in equation (3) as parametric values for the rate of interest. The result, of course, would be a changing series for the bond's price corresponding to the changes in the interest rate series. We would be, in effect, simulating the price of a given bond as it would occur over time in the real world. (*The reconstruction of the illustration along such lines is left as an exercise for the reader.*)

Stocks. The analysis of the interrelationships between stock prices, yields, and prospective returns is more complicated than that in the case of bonds and near-money assets. This follows from several features: the absence of contractual interest, the absence of a fixed maturity date, the role of retained earnings (i.e., earnings not paid in the form of dividends), and the prospect that a large portion of the returns to a shareholder may be in the form of appreciation in share price. The matter may be further complicated by the absence of an active market for a particular share and by the common identity between the shareholders and managers, particularly of small companies. Therefore, we must emphasize certain assumptions concerning particular illustrations.

One such illustration of the above interrelationships could deal with the most complicated possibility of a widely traded share in a large company. However, we would need to make a number of assumptions: (1) we would likely view management as being separate from ownership, prompting us to assume some prospective distribution of future earnings (after taxes) in the form of retained earnings and dividends. (2) We would need to assume some definite horizon concerning prospects about the realization of appreciation (or depreciation) in share value, and about the return of the principal investment in presenting any numerical illustration as in the above case of a bond. (3) And we would need to assume that there is shareholder satisfaction (or dissatisfaction) concerning the retention of earnings, whether the reinvested earning of the company will contribute to additional earnings per share, and whether the latter will in turn contribute to a return equal to that from the payout and reinvestment of retained earnings.

With the above assumptions, we would have two separate prospective returns at the horizon to evaluate, which would include the prospective appreciation and the return of the principal investment. And there would, as well, be the need to evaluate the stream of dividend payments. All of this would result in such an equation as (3) above, only there would be three separate returns in the numerator of the last term. There would, then, be an inverse relationship between share price and yields (as rates) for discounting the given prospects, all as in the case of the bond. Prospects may change and result in changes in share prices, and so on, but given the prospects there is still the inverse variation as in the case of the bond.

4.4. The Liquidity Preference Demand for Money and the Supply of Money

The model containing an equation for the supply of money balances and another defining the relationship between the quantity of money balances demanded and the rate of interest constitutes a basic monetary model. The rate of interest in the model may be solved in terms of the parameters—including one for the stock of money—and these parameters may be shown to correspond to certain conditions concerning expectations and the motives for holding money. The strength of the speculative motive in particular, as it enters into the model, may be shown to relate the rate of interest prevailing in the present to the prospective rate. The latter rate, as shown below, is intimately related to the use of money as a store of value (Sect. 2.1), because of the inverse relationship between prospective changes in the rate of interest and prospective changes in the values of other assets (Sect. 4.3). The presence of the stock of money in the model and the solution for the rate of interest in terms of the parameters, moreover, suggest the prospect of exercising some control over the rate of interest via the stock of money.

In introducing the above matters, this section draws upon an earlier list of the motives for holding money (Sect. 2.2), and considers the following:

(1) The speculative demand for money in relation to the rate of interest, (2) the liquidity preference model, (3) changes in the supply of money, and (4) the rate of interest and equilibrium in security prices.

The speculative demand for money. The demand for money balances is a decreasing function of the rate of interest. A common form, introduced earlier (Sect. 2.2), is

$$g(i) = a + \frac{b}{i}$$

As income increases and the stock of assets needed to serve the several motives (Sect. 2.2) increases, the parameter a increases, and so on, as mentioned earlier (Sect. 2.2). But the function derives its shape mainly from considerations concerning the speculative motive and the term b/i, as we shall show. The other motives are emphasized on other occasions.

Several explanations for the slope of the function at a given point abound: (1) the higher (lower) the rate of interest the larger (smaller) the interest payment is for parting with money balances, and (2) as the rate of interest declines (rises) there is greater and greater (smaller and smaller) likelihood of a decline (rise) in the value of securities. Actually, these two explanations reinforce each other, but the latter one emphasizes more strongly the speculative motive for holding balances.

In a world where interest rates (Sect. 4.2) and security values (Sect. 4.3) vary inversely, three possibilities may arise at a given time with respect to future changes in interest rates and, therefore, security values. The value of the securities may rise (R), decline (D), or undergo no change (N) with reference to prevailing values and interest rates. At any given time, consequently, there is certainty that at least one of these events will occur. That is, the sum of the probabilities for these three outcomes will always sum to one (i.e., $P_D + P_R + P_N = 1$). But individual expectations and/or the aggregate of the individual expectations comprising the market may be thought of as operating in an environment where interest rates usually vary over some domain over time—as from 2 per cent to 5 per cent in the case of government securities— where the recent past influences prospects and where some level of rates is considered normal. Thus one could reason that as the rate of interest varied over its historical range from its upper bound to its lower bound, individuals and markets assess varying probability weights from zero to one to the prospect of a decline in security values. Conversely, as the rate varied from its lower bound to its upper bound, the weight for the prospect of a rise in security values should vary from zero to one, and the probability of present rates prevailing in the future should vary from zero at the extremes to some maximum probability in the neighborhood of the normal rate of interest.

Figure 4-3 shows a sketch of the function relating the rate of interest (i) to the speculative demand for money balances (M_B), along with the assignment of probabilities. The dependent variable $g(i)$ is shown on the horizontal axis and the independent variable is shown on the vertical axis. At points A, B, and so on of equal distance along the curve the probabilities of a rise in value (P_R) and a decline in value (P_D) decrease and increase, respectively, in a progressive fashion. In fact, the nonlinear shape of the curve is attributed to the progressive nature of the probability of the prospect for a decline in values as one moves downward along the curve, and the progressive nature of the probability of the prospect of a rise in values as one moves upward along the curve. Also, note that the probability of no change from the normal rate reaches a maximum at point C, since

$$P_N = 1 - (P_R + P_D)$$

At this point, nevertheless, a positive quantity of speculative balances are held. The motive for holding these balances can be due only to uncertainty over the future rate of interest. Further, as the probability of a decline in security values (or a rise in values) increases, there is a demand for a larger (or smaller) quantity of speculative balances.

Of course, the precise location of such points as A and E, where one would subjectively assess the probability of a rise in value at one (i.e., $P_R = 1.0$) and the probability of a rise in value at zero (i.e., $P_R = 0.0$), is not precisely known. These points may lie at extreme distances along the i-axis and the $g(i)$-axis, respectively, or they may tend to be located in the neighborhood of the normal rate of interest. The point, too, may change where there is maximum uncertainty about a change in one direction or another. In any event, some conjectures about the location

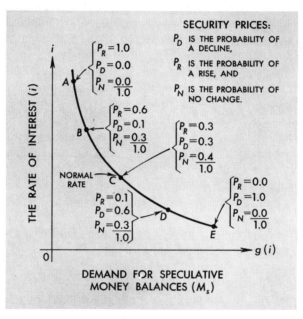

Fig. 4-3. The Demand for Speculative Money Balances as a Function of the Rate of Interest.

of the points corresponding to certainty of a rise or a fall in values reveal some interesting characteristics about individuals and markets as they give effect to their speculative needs for money.

Assume, for the moment, that as the rate of interest declines along our curve, each individual investor is certain at some point, such as E, of a rise in the rate and a decline in values (i.e., $P_D = 1.0$ and $P_R = 0$). Assume too that the opposite is true (i.e., $P_R = 1.0$ and $P_D = 0$) as soon as that point is reached. In other words, assume that such points as E and A get sent into the same point in such a way that each individual's speculative demand for money is only a point. At any rate at the height of the point or above, the individual in question is going to hold all securities, and at any rate below the point he is going to exchange all of his securities for cash. Thus aggregating individual demands of this type for different individual investors X, Y, Z, we get several coordinates to which we may fit a market demand curve for speculative balances, but characteristics of each investor and the resulting market demand reveal some important aspects of the sensitivity of the speculative demand for money to interest rate changes.

Figure 4-4 contains such individual demand situations and the resulting market demand. In the illustration, investors X, Y, and Z are timid, moderate, and aggressive speculators, respectively. Investor X, for example, is willing to exchange money for securities and the prospect of appreciation in values only at a relatively high rate, whereas investor Z appears willing to make the exchange of an even larger amount of money at a relatively low rate of interest. Also, the market demand is

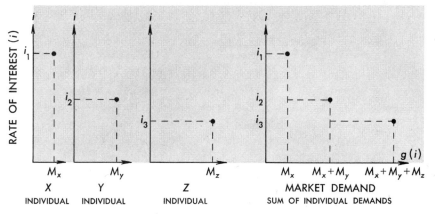

Fig. 4-4. The Certainty Hypothesis and the Speculative Demand for Money.

simply the horizontal sum of the individual demands. In the aggregate, for the rate (i) from i_1 down to i_2 (i.e., $i_1 \geqq i > i_2$) only X holds speculative balances. For the rate (i) from i_2 down to i_3 (i.e., $i_2 \geqq i > i_3$), both X and Y hold balances. And for the rate from i_3 downward (i.e., $i_3 \geqq i \geqq 0$), the entire market would attempt to exchange its securities for money balances.

Now observe from Fig. 4-4 that the larger the amount of money balances held by such aggressive speculators as Z, the flatter the slope of the curve through the resulting points within the domain of interest rates from i_3 to i_1, and that the larger the amount of money balances held by such timid speculators as X, the steeper the slope of the curve through the points. Also, given the amount of securities the market could convert to money, the narrower the domain of interest rates, the steeper the slope of the curve within the domain of interest rates. Our idealized assumptions about probability and interest rate changes help us to illustrate the rationale underlying the slope of our function for the speculative demand for money. Collectively, they are sometimes referred to as the certainty hypothesis,[3] but the same results would follow from the aggregation of individual demand curves independent of such restrictions.

However, the significance of the slope has to do with the response of the financial markets to interest rate changes, given the supply of securities and some rate of interest. If the slope of the curve in our construction is flat, the smaller the rise called for in the rate of interest in order to get the market to exchange money balances for a given volume of securities. In general terms the stock of speculative balances held in relation to the rate of interest was defined earlier (Sect. 2.2) as b/i ($=M^{(S)}$).* So, if we continue to deal only with the properties of the shape and location of the curve and rearrange terms, we find in this case that $i = b/M^s$,** and the slope in relation to the i-axis is, by the quotient rule,

$$\frac{di}{dM^{(S)}} = \frac{M^{(S)}(0) - b \cdot 1}{(M^{(S)})^2} = \frac{-b}{(M^{(S)})^2}$$

Thus, the smaller the parameter b is, the less is the slope (i.e., $di < dM^{(S)}$), given the speculative stock $M^{(S)}$. In other words, the smaller b is, the greater is the sensitivity of the financial markets (as represented by $dM^{(S)}$) to interest rate changes (as denoted by di) and, conversely, the less is the sensitivity† of interest rate changes (i.e., di) to changes in the speculative stock of money balances (i.e., $dM^{(S)}$).

---

* This aggregate speculative demand in relation to the rate of interest is the sum of n individual demands, i.e.,

$$\sum_{j=1}^{n} (M^{(S)})_j,$$

where $(M^{(s)})_j = b_j/i$, and $(M^{(s)})_j$ is the speculative balance sought by the jth individual, household, or business unit.

** In some instances, even in general terms, a more desirable shape and location for the demand curve over its domain of definition may result from the use of other equation forms for the equilateral hyperbola.

† Sometimes this sensitivity is expressed in terms of the interest elasticity of the speculative demand [denoted η(eta)] where the higher η is, the greater the sensitivity, is to a change in i. At a single point (i, $M^{(s)}$),

$$\eta = \left| \frac{dM^{(S)}}{di} \right| \frac{i}{M^{(S)}}$$

where $dM^{(s)}/di$ is the slope of the curve in relation to the M^s or $f(i)$-axis, and
$i/M^{(S)}$ represent the ratio of the coordinates of the point where the sensitivity is being evaluated.

In words, the interest elasticity is given by the absolute value of the proportional change in the demand for speculative balances called forth by a proportional change in the rate of interest, i.e.,

$$\left| \frac{\Delta M^{(S)}/M^{(S)}}{\Delta i/i} \right| = \left| \frac{\Delta M^{(S)}}{\Delta i} \right| \frac{i}{M^{(S)}}$$

and the definition for η follows by taking the limit as $\Delta i \to 0$.

The aggregate demand for and supply of money: changes in the underlying conditions. Upon combining the various demands for money balances into a single function of the rate of interest [i.e., $M_d = g(i)$], we may recall (Sect. 2.2)

$$M_d = a + \frac{b}{i}, \quad b > 0$$

where the variables and parameters retain their earlier meaning. We then refer to the set of ordered pairs (i, M_d) as i varies over its domain of definition as the schedule for the liquidity preference demand for money. In the equation, we have the demand for money as a decreasing function of the rate of interest, where the underlying conditions correspond to the parameters a and b. The most important of these conditions for purposes of analyzing and predicting the very short run and apart from $a = f(Y)$ is, as one may expect, the underlying state of market expectations about the future rate of interest. These correspond to b in the model.

Offhand, one may expect the views about market expectations to be so intangible as to defy any systematic treatment. We can, nevertheless, rely upon a bit of practical psychology. For one thing, expectations do not appear to change without cause; the changes, apparently, require a reorientation of thinking, usually dependent upon general political, economic, and social events. For another thing, observations seem to indicate that a change in the mass psychology that may at times prevail in the financial markets need not reflect an imitation of responses, but may result from many individuals reacting to the same change in the setting.

The simple model involving the liquidity preference demand for money may be written,

(4) $$M_d = a + \frac{b}{i}, \quad b > 0$$

(5) $$M_s = \gamma$$

(6) $$M_s = M_d$$

Equation (4) represents the aggregate of individual preferences for money (Sect. 4.1). Equation (5) defines the supply function. The constant in the equation would indicate that the supply of money is not affected by changes in the rate of interest in the very short run. This is because the supply of money may be thought of as depending upon such exogenous factors as those affecting the level of commercial bank reserves (Sect. 3.2 and 10.1) rather than the rate of interest per se. Equation (6) simply follows from our reasoning about the slopes of our functions. If we have selected significant relationships, our system is a well-determined one (i.e., $M_d = M_s$).

The solution for i in the above model is

$$(7) \qquad \bar{\imath} = \frac{b}{\gamma - a}$$

Now, from equation (7), an increase in γ would cause a decrease in the rate of interest.[*] A strengthening of the speculative motive for holding money balances (i.e., a change in b) would cause a rise in the rate of interest. This would occur, for example, in anticipation of a rise in the rate of interest (and, therefore, an anticipated decline in security values). Conversely, the reverse changes in the parameters γ and b, respectively, would cause a rise in the rate of interest in one instance, a decline in the other. Evidently a relationship exists between the rate of interest prevailing in the present and that expected to prevail in the future. We state this result as a proposition:

Proposition 3: *The prevailing rate of interest reflects the prospective rate of interest.* The model for the liquidity preference demand for money balances would appear as Fig. 4-5. There, the independent and dependent variables [i.e., i and $g(i)$] are represented by the vertical and horizontal axes, respectively. The initial schedule for liquidity preference is defined by equation (4) and the schedule for the supply of money is defined by equation (5). A schedule for liquidity preference, after an increase in the speculative demand for money, is denoted $M_d = a + b^*/i$. The increase in demand (the supply of money remaining constant) is such as would result from a prospective rise in the rate of interest, the ultimate effect in the model being an increase in the rate of interest (i.e., $\bar{\imath}_{t+1} - \bar{\imath}_t$).

Changes in the supply of money. The possibility of control over changes in the rate of interest is evident in the above model. The rise in the rate of interest ($\bar{\imath}_{t+1} - \bar{\imath}_t$) resulting from an increase in the speculative demand for money balances could be offset by an increment in the supply of money.

This increase in the money supply and its offsetting effect on a rise in the rate of interest would occur, for example, if the constant (γ) in the equation defining the supply function were to increase. In terms of earlier analysis (Sect. 3.3), such an increase in the supply of money as that from one time [$(\overline{M}_s)_t$] to another [$(\overline{M}_s)_{t+1}$] may be defined

---

[*] Actually, the rate of change in i with respect to γ would be, by the quotient rules,

$$\frac{\partial i}{\partial \gamma} = \frac{-b}{(\gamma - a)^2}$$

We could also differentiate i with respect to other parameters. For the rules pertaining to the differentiation, see David S. Huang, *Introduction to the Use of Mathematics in Economic Analysis* (New York: John Wiley and Sons, Inc., 1964); Paul H. Daus and William Whyburn, *Introduction to Mathematical Analysis with Applications to Problems of Economics* (Reading, Mass.: Addison-Wesley Publishing Company, Inc., 1958); or other sources.

$$\triangle M = \frac{1 + c}{r + c} (\triangle R_o)$$

Implicit in the relationships of the model, nevertheless, is a connecting link between factors affecting bank reserves, along with the possibility of control over interest rates, and the problems of a monetary economy to which changes in the rate of interest (and the value of financial assets) may give rise.

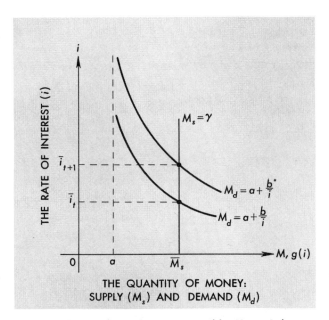

THE QUANTITY OF MONEY:
SUPPLY (M_s) AND DEMAND (M_d)

Fig. 4-5. The Liquidity Preference Demand for Money Balances.

The rate of interest and equilibrium in security values. As a final aside on the equilibrium rate of interest ($\bar{\imath}$), we state as a proposition the earlier inference that this rate yields an equilibrium value for securities:

Proposition 4: *If the rate of interest is in equilibrium at a moment in time, then security values too must be in equilibrium.* This would be true, because of the interrelationship between the rate of interest and security values and the tendency to adjust the former, through the demand for speculative balances, until the market obtains an equilibrium in the combination of assets (Sect. 4.1).

In deducing equation (7), several steps were given:

$$\gamma = a + \frac{b}{i} \quad \text{and} \quad \gamma - a = \frac{b}{i}$$

The first of these states that the equilibrium rate of interest, as in Fig. 4-5, is determined by the intersection of the aggregate supply-and-demand schedules for money. The second states the equilibrium in terms of the supply of and demand for speculative balances only. The model determining the equilibrium in the rate of interest in terms of speculative balances, then, is as follows:

(8) $$M^{(S)} = \frac{b}{i}$$

(9) $$M_s - a = \rho$$
(10) $$M^{(S)} = M_s - a \text{ (or } M_s = M^{(S)} + a)$$

where $M^{(s)}$ is the speculative demand for cash balances, with reference to the rate of interest and

$M_s - a$ is the supply of money balances (γ) less the quantity of balances a.

Equation (10) is again simply the condition for a solution to equations (8) and (9). The supply of speculative balances in equation (9) is

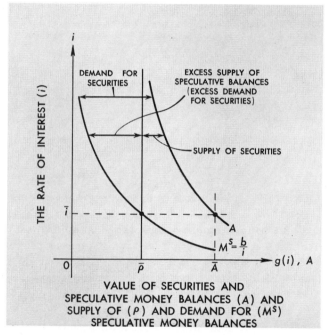

Fig. 4-6. Equilibria in the Rate of Interest and Security Values.

viewed as some constant ρ (rho). Note that a decrease in the supply of speculative balances causes an increase in the equilibrium rate of interest, and so on.

The geometric counterpart to the latter system of equations and their solution is shown in Fig. 4-6.[4] There also, however, is shown an additional curve (A) for the value of the total stock of speculative money balances, bonds, and other securities held by the public. Note that this value varies inversely with the rate of interest, which merely reflects the earlier proposition whereby the market value of a given stock of securities varies inversely with interest rates. At interest rate $\bar{\imath}$, the value of money and securities is $\bar{A}$. If the A-curve represents the total stock of financial assets held by the public and the M^s-curve represents the demand for the money portion of these assets, then the horizontal distance between the A- and $M^{(s)}$-curves represents the public's demand for securities at various interest rates. On the other hand, if the ρ-line represents the supply of speculative balances, then the horizontal distance between the A-curve and the ρ-line represents the supply of securities at various rates of interest. Note that, since the only options here are holding securities and/or speculative money balances, an excess supply of speculative balances is equivalent to an excess demand for securities—the state of affairs at all interest rates above $\bar{\imath}$ and thus the source of downward pressure on interest rates, i.e., upward pressure on securities prices. Only at interest rate $\bar{\imath}$ are the supply of and demand for both speculative money balances and securities in equilibrium. This is consistent with subsequent observations about the securities markets and the interpretation of the speculative demand for money balances. General equilibria in the rate of interest and security values do not exclude a routine volume of transactions for securities since the values and rates on individual securities comprising the aggregates vary so as to offset each other in the aggregate.

4.5. The Yield Curve, Expectations, and Some Switching of Assets: An Example Concerning the Banking Sector

Commercial banks are usually thought of as holding at least two classes of earning assets (Sect. 3.1)—loans and investments. Loans tend to be their main business, but they hold some securities as a secondary reserve. This is intended as a source of liquidity, but optimizing asset managers are expected to switch the composition of their investments with the view to maintaining adequate liquidity and additional earnings as well. Here we introduce this one aspect of the management of bank assets[5] with the view to revealing more about the yield curve, expectations, and the switching of assets.

The yield curve again. The yield curve, like the rate of interest (Sec. 4.3), reflects the outlook of investment portfolio managers and others in the market with respect to prospective future rates. It reveals an extra dimension of the expectations of the market and investor preferences at a given time.

The yield curve may take the shape of an upward sweeping, downward sweeping, or constant curve, such as the three curves sketched in Fig. 4-7b for times, 3, 2½, and 2, respectively.

An upward sweeping curve such as that at time 3 reflects the market expectation that rates will rise over time. The relatively stronger demand for short-dated issues in anticipation of a rise in yields accounts for their lower yields in per cent by earlier analysis and proposition 2. Similarly, the downward sweeping curve, such as that at time 2, reflects the prospect of a decline in yields over time, and the prospect that rates will decline and security values rise strengthens the preference for the longer-dated issues relative to shorter-dated ones. The constant curve, such as that at time 2½, simply represents a fairly balanced preference with respect to the demand for long- and short-dated issues, and reflects

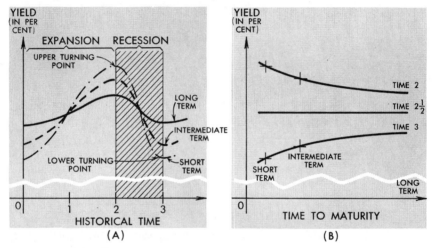

Fig. 4-7. A Hypothetical Structure of Yields (in Per Cent) Over Time: (A) Hypothetical changes in yields over time; (B) hypothetical yield curve.

the temporary prospect of constant yields over time with respect to time to maturity.

However, there is no pure logic about the shape of the yield curve and its behavior over the short cycle solely with respect to the expectations of the market and independent of basic institutional features, such as we allow for from time to time. For example, the declining yield curve exhibited itself at times in the 1920's,[6] before large nonfinancial corporations began making extensive liquidity adjustments through a portfolio of liquid assets (Chap. 17). Then, in late 1959 and early 1960, it exhibited itself again, partly in response to a monetary policy concerning international gold flows (Sect. 23.5). Nevertheless, changes in the yield curve—in its shifts and shape—and in the expectations reflected in it can still be meaningful.

The yield curve may be expected to shift downward in response to a prospective decline in the rate of interest (Sect. 4.2), and the yield on short-dated securities may be expected to decline more in response to a prospective rise in rates over time and the relatively stronger preference for short-dated issues as a source of liquidity at such times and with respect to the future. And, conversely, the entire curve may be expected to shift upward in response to a prospective rise in rates, and the rise in the yield on long-dated issues may be relatively less than that on short-dated issues when there is a relatively greater prospect of a decline in rates and appreciation in values when rates are high.

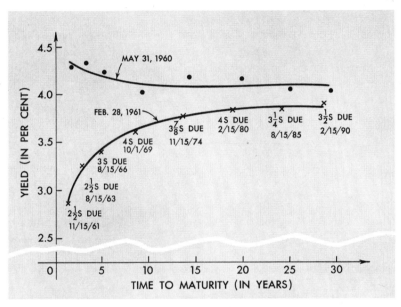

Fig. 4-8. Yield Curve for Taxable Treasury Securities. The market quotations are over-the-counter closing bid quotations on fixed maturity issues in the New York market, as reported to the Treasury by the Federal Reserve Bank of New York.

These latter notions with respect to shifts in the yield curve and simultaneous changes in its shape would be reflected in the yield curves in Fig. 4-8. The curves there are empirically derived from eight issues of United States government securities of different maturity. The curve for May 31, 1960, precedes the upper turning point of the 1960-1961 recession, and the curve for February 28, 1961, corresponds roughly to the lower turning point of that recession. Note that over the cycle in this example the yield spread between short-dated securities varies within a wider range than the yield spread on long-dated securities. This feature, in particular, is common to the general type of postwar cycle as may be seen from Fig. 4-1, where the yield on Treasury bills varies over a wider range than the yield on long-term government bonds. Also, the narrow

spread between the bill rate and the long-term bond rate at the upper
turning points indicates a constant yield curve at such times for most of
the cycles shown, and the wider spread at the lower turning points indicates an upward sweeping curve.

Expectations and some switching of investments. In view of what has
been said about the need for liquidity and earnings, bank asset management, expectations, and changes in the yield curve, we would expect
some switching of investments. One would expect to observe a decrease
in the relative emphasis on short-dated issues (of one-year maturity or
less) vis-à-vis longer-dated ones at the upper turning point of a cycle,
and to observe a converse pattern of emphasis at the lower turning point
of the cycle. These patterns of emphasis, however, are in fact what one
usually observes with respect to the preferences of portfolio managers
as illustrated by the following maturity distribution of United States
Government security holdings by banks in all leading cities (dollar
amounts in billions):

	Maturity Range			
	Within 1 Year (per cent of total)	*One to 5 Years* (per cent of total)	*After 5 Years* (per cent of total)	*Total Holdings* (per cent of total)
June 29, 1960 (near peak)	10.9	71.2	18.0	100.0
December 28, 1960	26.8	57.1	14.0	100.0
April 26, 1961 (near trough)	30.6	53.2	16.1	100.0

NOTE: The parts may not sum to totals due to rounding.
SOURCE OF DATA: Board of Governors of the Federal Reserve System.

4.6. Summary

The holders of wealth face alternative choices in selecting the combination of assets they prefer. The alternatives may include money balances, near-money assets, bonds or other so-called safe assets, stocks,
and instrumental capital. The preference is usually explained with reference to the prospective series of returns from the assets where, in the
present context, the streams of returns include yield net of carrying costs,
plus allowances for liquidity. The optimizing combination of assets,
however, is achieved by adjusting holdings of assets until the respective
rates of return from acquiring additional assets are equal. In this context, we begin by discussing wealth and a stock of assets, and end by

emphasizing changes in the various classes of assets. The various classes of assets, as proportions of the total, may vary in response to changes in the prospective series of returns (i.e., $R_m = Q_m - C_m + L_m$, $m = 1$, $\ldots$, n) and, therefore, in response to changes in the elements comprising the rates of return (i.e., $r_m = q_m - c_m + l_m$, $m = 1, \ldots, n$). The magnitude of these elements generally range from a high degree of liquidity and a negligible yield less a carrying cost on money balances to a negligible liquidity premium and a return in the form of a yield on instrumental capital.

The individuals comprising the market are motivated to hold smaller proportions of money balances for speculative purposes as their subjectively derived probabilities for the prospects of a rise in security values increase. The converse is also true. And the individuals as well are even shown to hold some positive amount of speculative balances at the level of interest rates corresponding to maximum uncertainty—the point of equal probabilities for a rise or a fall in security values. Over time, changes in underlying conditions correspond to changes in the collection of attitudes toward speculation and the subjective evaluations about the normal rate of interest and the domain of definition for the speculative demand for money. They do this in such a way as to affect the location and shape of the curve relating the rate of interest to the speculative demand for money, despite diversity among the expectations of individual investors. For one thing, changes in the underlying conditions favoring prospects for a rise in security values cause a downward shift in the speculative demand. For another, changes in those conditions contributing to the prospects of a decline in security values or the maximum of uncertainty over the direction of change in security values cause an upward shift in the speculative demand for money.

Aggregating individual preferences for money and viewing collective changes in expectations lead to an emphasis on the effect of very short-run changes in the speculative motive for holding money in relation to other assets. Changes in expectations and the demand for money in relation to other assets give rise to changes in the rate of interest.

We may speak of changes in the rate of interest and have in mind a movement in the structure of interest rates. A rise in the rate of interest corresponds to an upward movement, and a decline corresponds to a downward movement. All rates comprising the structure of interest rates are interrelated, and a change in one sector may be transmitted to another, depending upon the absence of monopoly and frictions and the proper functioning of the financial markets. Arbitrage transactions and the switching of assets by individual traders and institutions are means of transferring yield changes from one market sector to another.

Upward shift in liquidity preference demand for money balances accompanying a prospective decline in the value of securities (and a rise in the rate of interest) will result in a rise in the rate of interest, given a constant supply of money. Acting upon the latter change in expectations, holders of such assets as bonds will attempt to reduce the proportion of them in relation to their holdings of money. As they do so, bond prices decline and yields rise. The process continues until the rates (and values) adjust to those expected to prevail in the future. The prospect of an increase in security prices will have the reverse set of effects, given the stock of money, and so on.

Changes in the yield curve and its shape at a given time also reflect expectations. An upward sweeping yield curve reflects the market expectations of a rise in rates over time, a downward sweeping curve reflects the market expectations of a decline, and there is a variety of variations in the shape as the curve moves upward from an upward sweeping position to a constant or downward sweeping position, and vice versa. There is a rationale to these latter movements in the curve when one considers the prospects for gains (and losses), and the preference for liquidity. As the curve moves to an upward sweeping position, we are led to expect an increase in the proportion of assets in the shorter-dated issues, at least from the commercial banker's point of view. As the curve moves toward an upward sweeping position, we expect the reverse set of changes, and so on.

The above role of the stock of money in relation to other assets and the rate of interest suggest that changes in the supply of money are related to changes in the level of interest rates and changes in the shape of the yield curve. In this way, a connecting link is established between the supply of money and the rate of interest so as to suggest the prospect of influencing a monetary economy through changes in the stock of money and some control over factors affecting the demand for money and other assets.

References

1. It is possible for any single-valued increasing function to serve as a utility function because the postulate about ranking or preference implies only an ordinal measure—a more or less sort of thing as contrasted with the assignment of cardinal measure to utility. See, for example, Paul H. Daus and William Whyburn, *Introduction to Mathematical Analysis with Applications to Problems of Economics* (Reading, Mass.: Addison-Wesley Publishing Company, Inc., 1958), pp. 170-171.

2. For elementary discussions of the Lagrangian function, see David S. Huang, *Introduction to the Use of Mathematics in Economic Analysis* (New York: John Wiley and Sons, Inc., 1964), pp. 106-114; and Daus and Whyburn, *op. cit.*, pp. 164-176.

3. See Richard A. Musgrave, *The Theory of Public Finance* (New York: McGraw-Hill Book Company, 1959), p. 459.

4. For the source concerning this particular illustration, see Abba P. Lerner, *Essays in Economic Analysis* (London: The Macmillan Company, Ltd., 1953), p. 295; and John G. Gurley and Edward S. Shaw, "Financial Aspects of Economic Development," *American Economic Review,* September 1955, pp. 528-529.

5. For further reading on the subject, see Roland I. Robinson, *The Management of Bank Funds,* 2nd ed. (New York: McGraw-Hill Book Company, 1962).

6. *Ibid.,* pp. 353-360.

part two

Financial Orthodoxy: The Main Stream

5

The Quantity Theory of Money, the Price Level, and the Demand for Money

> The quantity theory of money is a term evocative of a general approach rather than a label for a well-defined theory. The exact content of this approach varies from a truism defining the term "velocity" to an allegedly rigid and unchanging ratio between the quantity of money—defined in one way or another—and the price level—also defined in one way or another (Milton Friedman, *Studies in the Quantity Theory of Money* [1956]).

This and the succeeding chapter include an introduction to some fundamental notions—(1) the quantity theory of money, (2) the automatic gold standard, and (3) the real bills doctrine. All have, at times, determined some of man's actions and shaped some of his institutions. Moreover, remnants of the institutions and the notions themselves linger on in modified garb. One in particular—the quantity theory—is quite alive. The way the latter attempted to explain price changes and the way it evolved constitute the subject matter of this chapter. The emphasis of the general approach is shown to have shifted from the effect of changes in the supply of money on prices to the effects of changes in the strength of the motives for holding money, changes in the rate at which money balances change hands, and changes in the supply of money on income.

Using an earlier classification of assets (Sect. 4.1), we shall show that changes in the prospective returns from holding stocks of instrumental capital, rather than money and so-called safe assets, give rise to opposite changes in the relative exchange value (or prices) of those assets. These changes, in turn, give rise to changes in the speculative demand for money and the flow variable Y ($=PO$) for income and there-

fore prices and/or output and employment. The belief that such a relationship existed between the demand for such liquid balances and the
level of output, however, was not generally held by economists before
1936. The theory of output and the theory of money were treated separately, with little tendency toward integration. On the output side, there
was J. B. Say's law of markets (Sect. 5.3). As a behavioral postulate, it
held the following:

Postulate: *"As a consequence of the view of money as a medium of
exchange only, and not as a store of value [Sect. 2.1]—the community's
excess demand to hold cash is zero under all circumstances"* (our italics).[1]

On the monetary side, there was the quantity theory of money. Stated
by Hume as early as 1752, and by Bodin as early as 1568, it held that
changes in the average of prices for current output were directly proportional to changes in the quantity of money in existence. Stated later by
Simon Newcomb and Irving Fisher, it held that the average of prices on
all transactions varied directly with changes in the money supply.
Changes in the supply of money were viewed as causing prices to change,
and the change in prices caused people to be satisfied with holding the
existing stock of money. The emphasis was primarily on the transactions
demand for money alone, rather than changes in the speculative demand,
and this emphasis did not lead to any explicit analysis of the changes in
output.

In introducing the role of money in relation to output, the evolution
of some monetary notions, and the interrelationships between the earlier
classes of assets, several topics follow: the quantity theory approach
(Sect. 5.1), general equilibrium and the quantity theory (Sect. 5.2), the
measurement and significance of price changes for goods and services
(Sect. 5.3), and the speculative demand for money, income velocity, and
the flow of income (Sect. 5.4).

The present topics require that we emphasize several distinctions with
respect to the various groups of prices and the determination of the price
level generally. For one thing, there is the average of prices for all the
items entering into (or being offered in) exchange during a given period,
where the number of transactions may be viewed as the average rate
per period at a moment in time. For another thing, given the total stock
of assets at some zero moment in time, the increment in the stock in the
immediately preceding period is the average rate of change per period
in the stock at the beginning (time zero minus one) of the period. That
is, the increment in the total stock is the flow of new assets—including
any changes in the respective stocks of money, safe assets, stocks (i.e.,
equities), and instrumental capital (including durable goods and the
value of real services)—and the prices of the new assets may be viewed as
being among those in the general price level for the total stock of assets.
But the changes in the latter set of real goods and services is the output

of goods and services. The product of this output (O) and the average of prices (P) for it are the flow variable Y ($=PO$) for income. As matters turn out, we have a measure for changes in this latter average of prices, and it is the most comprehensive of the available measures for price changes (Sect. 5.2). Clearly, then, even the most comprehensive of the measures for price changes is a measure only with respect to price changes for the total output of goods and services, and it pertains to only one of the several classes comprising the total stock of assets.

5.1. The Quantity Theory Approach

The label "the quantity theory" has implied a general approach to monetary analysis. Thus the term "theory," in the present context, should not be taken to imply the term's formal meaning (Sect. 1.1). The major statements of the early approaches are referred to as the simple quantity theory, the transactions approach, and the cash balance approach.

The simple quantity theory. The simple quantity theory that dominated much of economic thinking throughout most of the nineteenth century was a variation of the Hume version of the theory. In that version, average prices (P) were viewed as varying in direct proportion to the supply of currency or pocket money (M), i.e., in equation form,

$$P = \lambda M$$

where λ (lambda) is some constant of proportionality.

The variations of the theory were affected by focusing on an equation that included certain "real" purchases, as well as the rate (velocity) at which the money balances changed hands in generating the corresponding flow of expenditures. Using, for example,

$$(1) \qquad P = \frac{MV}{O}$$

it was pointed out (1) that output (O) rises with improvement in technology, accumulation of capital goods, and the growth of the labor force, and (2) that the rate at which money balances change hands (V) may be influenced by changing monetary institutions. The expression (1) implicitly defined a particular velocity, conventionally called income velocity (V_y):

$$(2) \qquad V_y = \frac{Y}{M}$$

where V_y is the income velocity,
- Y is the product of the average price for a period and the output [i.e., $Y = P(O)$], and
- M is the average supply of money balances for the period.

Even so, the average price (P) was regarded as varying in a fairly dependable relationship to changes in the money supply (M), after making qualifications about velocity and output. Such qualifications were made in the United States in the form of the transactions approach and in England in the form of the cash balances approach, where, in the latter sense, the terms "cash" and "money" are used interchangeably.

The transactions approach. The transactions or "money in flight" approach was largely developed by Professor Irving Fisher.[2] His approach included an expression for the two sides to all transactions in the form of an identity, called the equation of exchange. The total value of such transactions was viewed as the product of the average price (P) for a period and the total volume of transactions (T), on one side, and, on the other, the product of the average money supply (M) and the rate (V) at which the money supply changed hands in generating the expenditures in those transactions:

$$(3) \qquad\qquad MV = PT$$

Equation (3), nevertheless, served to focus attention on some important relationships.

It implied more than revealed by its tautological form, wherein MV and PT simply denoted two different sides of the total value of the item entering into exchange. In fact, Fisher rearranged the equation so as to imply a causal relationship between changes in the money supply and prices:

$$(4) \qquad\qquad P = \frac{MV}{T}$$

Also, his definition of velocity was for the total of transactions (T) and not income transactions only. It was a definition of transactions velocity (V_t) expressed as the ratio of the money receipts from total monetary transactions (PT) for the period to the average of the stock of money during that period (i.e., $V_t = PT/M$). Fisher and his early followers, however, tended to emphasize the rather mechanical underlying causes of changes in velocity—such things as payment habits and the technical structure of the mechanism for making transactions. Velocity and transactions were thought to be roughly stable in the short run, at least. The view was that a change in the money supply causes a change in the price level, while velocity and transactions remained sufficiently stable to permit forecasting the effect of changes in the money supply.

In a review of some portions of neoclassical monetary theory (including the work by Fisher), persuasive formulations of the theory have been described with references to the following tripartite thesis:

"[1] an increase in the quantity of money disturbs the optimum relation between the level of money balances and the individual's expenditures; [2] this disturbance generates an increase in the planned volume of these expenditures (the real-balance effect); and [3] this increase creates pressures on the price level which push it upwards until it has risen in the same proportion as the quantity of money." *

In the 1930's and thereafter, attention became directed more toward the volume of income or product transactions than the total volume of monetary transactions. There was also emphasis on variations in the statistical concept of "money" and the separate velocities of its components.[3] The concern was thus with income velocity, rather than transactions velocity, although there was important work reconciling the two. This narrower focus for the Fisher-type approach is sometimes separately classified as the income approach to the quantity theory. For years, work on the approach continued primarily at the University of Chicago, and in the late post-World War II years the approach was revitalized considerably. The income version of the quantity equation has been modified by the introduction of time lags, by the broadening of the statistical concept of "money" to include time and savings deposits in banks (and thus a narrowing of the scope of velocity), and by an emphasis on the relation between the change in the money stock and the level of output in constant prices, rather than between changes in money and in prices (Sect. 26.5).

Still another offshoot of the original Fisher approach is the work on velocity in various sectors in the economy.[4] In the effort to pinpoint the reasons for the post-World War II rise in aggregate transactions and income velocities, Professor Selden compares a variety of velocity estimates with each other, and analyzes modified transactions velocities for certain geographic areas, for certain sectors, and for business-size classes.

These latter studies, contrary to the original view, have revealed that

---

* Don Patinkin, *Money, Interest, and Prices: An Integration of Monetary and Value Theory*, 2nd edition (New York: Harper & Row, 1965), pp. 163-164. The real value of money balances is said to increase when the ratio M/P increases, where M is the nominal stock of money and P is the average of prices. Note that an increase in the money stock M increases the real value of money balances. The latter increase is, at the same time, supposed to effect increases in the demand for all other goods (the real-balance effect) and prices, since people feel that their stock of money is too large for their needs.

An effect somewhat similar (though not identical) to the real-balance effect is the "Pigou effect." The Pigou effect is supposed to work somewhat along these lines: a reduction in prices (note an increase in real balances) makes consumers feel wealthier, and as a consequence they increase expenditures. There are complications, however, depending on the relative size and distribution of debt. As we imply later (Sect. 5.3), a decrease in prices increases the burden of debt. This effect may or may not be offset by other over-all effects of a decrease in prices. Individuals who behave according to the real-balance and Pigou effects are said to be free of a money illusion.

the velocity of circulation of money is not constant over time, that it tends to conform positively with cyclical expansion and contraction in real income in the short run, and that it is, indeed, an indicator of changes in business conditions. Others also have emphasized changes in response to changes in the strength of the motives (Sect. 2.2) for holding money. In particular, the cash balances or "money at rest" approach to the quantity theory originally introduced this approach.

The cash balances approach. In the decade following World War I, the quantity theory of money as discussed in the lecture halls of Cambridge University by John Maynard Keynes (1883-1946) and his contemporaries included an embryonic form of the liquidity preference demand for money (Sect. 4.4). In that form changes in the average of prices for output resulted from the interaction of the supply of cash balances (considered as currency and demand deposits) and the desire of the public to hold cash balances. The product of the average of prices for output (P) and output (O) was equal to income (Y), and the product of income and a factor of proportionality (k) were equal to the money supply (i.e., $Yk = M$). Equation (1) implied by the simple quantity theory was, in effect, rewritten as

$$(5) \qquad\qquad Y = \frac{1}{k} M$$

In this form, the so-called Cambridge k stood for the public's desire to hold cash balances, and its reciprocal (i.e., $1/k$) was, in effect, substituted for V in equation (1). The result of this seemingly trivial rearrangement of the quantity equation was to change the emphasis from "money in flight" to "money at rest" and to concentrate attention directly on the motives for demanding cash balances to hold.

In the cash balance approach, a strengthening of the motive to hold cash balances would correspond to an increase in the public's demand for cash (k) and, consequently, a decrease in income ($Y = PO$). Conversely, a weakening of the motive to hold cash balances would correspond to a decrease in the public's demand for cash balances (k) and, consequently, an increase in income. This is analogous to the discussion of a particular case in a later section (Sect. 5.4) in which a prospective rise in the average of the prices for the output of goods and services weakens the motive for holding money[5] and government securities and strengthens the motive for holding instrumental capital.

5.2. General Equilibrium and the Quantity Theory

General equilibrium analysis emphasizes the interdependence of the parts of the economy, including the real goods sector and the monetary sector, and it may be applied to matters concerning current production and/or the exchanges of existing stocks. In addition, it emphasizes the determination of price levels, such as those entering into the various formulations in the previous section (Sect. 5.1). The system of equations for general equilibrium, as stated below, permits us to focus upon the distinguishing feature of a monetary economy whereby the demand for money influences the determination of both relative and absolute prices in the real goods sector.[*] Also it exposes the fallacy of viewing an equilibrium in the real goods sector vis-à-vis general equilibrium over the whole range of real and monetary items, including money, bonds, instrumental capital, and so on.

A general equilibrium. Earlier (Sect. 4.1), we noted an equilibrium resulting from a preferred combination of n items subject to the constraint imposed by total wealth. Now we wish to view general equilibrium in terms of the equality of the supply of and demand for n items. In doing this, we note, as earlier, that the quantity demanded (and therefore the quantity supplied) of a given item depends on the price of all items, and the stock of wealth. In the earlier instance we were concerned mainly with equilibrium asset conditions for individuals, households, and firms in relation to the various markets. In the present subsection we are concerned mainly with market clearing conditions.

Let S denote the supply function, and D the demand function, and then we may denote the supply-demand equality for each item and the general equilibrium of the economy as follows:[6]

$$S_1(P_1, P_2, \ldots, P_n, A, M) = D_1(P_1, P_2, \ldots, P_n, A, M)$$
$$S_2(P_1, P_2, \ldots, P_n, A, M) = D_2(P_1, P_2, \ldots, P_n, A, M)$$
$$\cdots\cdots\cdots\cdots\cdots\cdots\cdots\cdots\cdots\cdots\cdots\cdots\cdots\cdots\cdots$$
$$S_n(P_1, P_2, \ldots, P_n, A, M) = D_n(P_1, P_2, \ldots, P_n, A, M),$$

where $P_1, P_2, \ldots, P_n$ are the respective prices of the n items, including money as one item, and where

A in combination with the average stock of money (M) is an index of the nonhuman wealth of the economy.[**]

[*] Absolute prices are said to have been indeterminate in classical economic theory. See Don Patinkin, "The Indeterminacy of Absolute Prices in Classical Economic Theory," *Econometrica*, January 1949. See also Gary S. Becker and William J. Baumol, "The Classical Monetary Theory: The Outcome of the Discussion," *Economica*, November 1952, pp. 355-376.

[**] There is no explicit income variable (William Baumol, *Economic Theory and Operations Analysis* [Englewood Cliffs, N.J.: Prentice-Hall, Inc., 1961], p. 231), since income may be thought of as the product of the average of prices and the current output of goods and services, and since wage and salary rates are presumably reflected in the prices of goods and services. The human capital in this context would be the wealth component resulting from capitalizing the flow of wages and salary income (compare "human capital," Sect. 4.1). It would also be that part of wealth that is enhanced by education, training, and so forth.

The system could be expanded by including other variables and parameters (for taste, expectations, and so on). Given the values for the parameters A and M and the prices in the present instance, the system contains as many unknowns (the quantities) as equations, and presumably a solution exists.*

However, there is one complication, which also arose earlier (Sect. 4.1). One of the n items is money, and the price of a single unit of money is one dollar. Thus one of the prices in the system must be the number "1." In such a case, one would have a redundant equation, and, though this need not prohibit a solution, earlier economists were concerned that it might. Consequently, they excluded the equation for the demand for money in their statement of general equilibrium and spoke of a system of $n - 1$ equations and $n - 1$ unknowns. To them money was simply a *numeraire* or unit of account, but, to account for the demand for money, an identity (albeit one that can be extracted from the Walrasian system of nonidentical equations)[7] was used. In 1942, it was named Walras' Law.** It may be denoted as follows:

$$(1) \qquad \sum_{i=1}^{n} P_i Q_i^{(S)} = \sum_{i=1}^{n} P_i Q_i^{(D)}$$

where the left-hand member is the sum of all of the products for the respective prices $[P_i (i = 1, 2, \ldots, n)]$ and the corresponding quantities supplied $[Q_i^{(S)} \ (i = 1, 2, \ldots, n)]$, and the right-hand member is the sum of all the products for the prices $[P_i (i = 1, 2, \ldots, n)]$

---

* Earlier equilibrium theorists set great store in an equation system's having the same number of equations as unknowns as a guarantee of the existence of a solution. Today, however, we recognize the need to also assume the satisfaction of several types of additional conditions in order for a simultaneous solution in terms of the n variables to exist.

For a brief outline of one of the proofs of the existence of a solution and the assumptions involved, see Baumol, *op. cit.*, pp. 311-316. The proof outlined involves "activity analysis"—"the application of linear programming methods to general equilibrium theory." The latter methods are entirely a post-World War II development. The two assumptions underlying the proof include perfect competition and constant returns to scale (as in a homogeneous function of degree one). The former assumption need not be fully satisfied in order for the analysis to be applicable to the real world. Homogeneous functions of degree one, moreover, are basic to a significant part of economics—see e.g., Lawrence R. Klein, *An Introduction to Econometrics* (Englewood Cliffs, N.J.: Prentice-Hall, Inc., 1962), pp. 90-103; and David S. Huang, *Introduction to the Use of Mathematics in Economic Analysis* (New York: John Wiley and Sons, Inc., 1964), pp. 83-88.

On systems of n equations and n variables see also William S. Vickrey, *Microstatics* (New York: Harcourt, Brace & World, Inc., 1964), pp. 118-124; and R. G. D. Allen, *Mathematical Analysis for Economists.* (London: Macmillan & Co., Ltd., 1938), pp. 278-281.

** Leon Walras (1834-1910) is credited with the discovery of general economic equilibrium.

and the corresponding quantities demanded $[Q_i^{(D)}$ $(i = 1, 2, \ldots, n)]$.

The use of the law to refute the notion that money is simply a numeraire to be excluded from the determinant system of equations is straightforward. Those demanding commodities are prepared to exchange an amount of money (e.g., currency and demand deposits) or some other commodities of equal value, and those supplying goods are prepared to accept in exchange their equivalent value in money (e.g., currency and demand deposits) or other commodities. Note, in particular, that the exchange does not necessarily require the use of money in the specific sense of currency and demand deposits. The exchange may involve units of items other than currency and demand deposits, and the item chosen is independent of the item called money, although all values are expressed in terms of the unit of account (Sect. 2.1). In fact, Walras' Law tells us that the supply of and demand for any single item omitted from the n items must be equal and not just the supply of and demand for units of currency and demand deposits. That is, if the value of the goods supplied is equal to the value demanded for all but the first item as we may assume from a system of $n - 1$ items and $n - 1$ equations, then for the first item

$$P_1 Q_1^{(S)} = P_1 Q_1^{(D)}$$

or

$$P_1 Q_1^{(S)} - P_1 Q_1^{(D)} = 0,$$
$$P_1 (Q_1^{(S)} - Q_1^{(D)}) = 0$$

and

$$Q_1^{(S)} = Q_1^{(D)}.$$

It makes no difference which equation we choose to drop from the initial system of n equations and n unknowns. The first was simply a convenient one to pick.

It follows from the requirements imposed by Walras' Law, and the solution to the $n - 1$ system of equations, that the quantity and price of the first item are also determined by supply and demand conditions. Since $Q_1^{(S)} = Q_1^{(D)}$, the n prices and n quantities are determined. The redundant equation, therefore, is harmless and causes no difficulty in our initial statement of general economic equilibrium.

The quantity theory. As implied by the initial general equilibrium equations, the solution is n specific prices on n specific quantities, given the quantity of money M. Since the n prices relating to each other and their absolute values make up the price level, the equations must also determine the price level, and presumably this is determined whether prices are high or low (inflated or deflated), given M. There must be one price level at equilibrium, and others will produce disequilibrium. But this is also implied by the equation of exchange where the concern is with the respective prices on all transactions or it is implied by the cash balance approach to the quantity theory where the concern is primarily with current output alone. In the former case, for example,

$$M = \frac{T}{V} P$$

where T (= const.) is the number of transactions,
V (= const.) is the velocity of money balances with respect to the total number of transactions, and
P is the average of prices on all transactions. In the case of current output,

$$M = \frac{O}{V_y} P$$

where O (= const.) is current output,
V_y (= const.) is the income velocity of money, and
P is the average of prices on current output.

In both instances, the higher the price level the greater the amount of money balances needed for effecting expenditures. (*Note:* Here and elsewhere the average of the respective sets and prices in question should be judged from the context of the symbol P unless otherwise denoted.)

If the latter price level is high for M = constant, the demand for money will exceed the supply, since people will hold money in lieu of spending it (i.e., velocity will decline). The effective demand for other items will then decline, and presumably the prices and current output of those items will decline to equilibrium levels. The converse in the case of lower prices would also hold. The general equilibrium system would work the same way; if prices are above the equilibrium level, prices and/or output will be forced down, and vice versa.

Thus far, at a moment in time (or in terms of averages for a period), the price level is determined. This is true for the quantity theory approach and our statement of general equilibrium, given underlying conditions. However, if there are changes in the underlying conditions, such as would correspond to shifts in the demand for money as a consequence of its store of value function, the same results as in the immediately preceding paragraph may come about. We are left with a proposition.

Proposition: *A positive (negative) shift in the community's demand to hold money gives rise to a decline (rise) in velocity and/or output.*

The acceptance of this proposition would lead us to reject the earlier statement of Say's Law.

5.3. The Measurement and Significance of Price Changes for Goods and Services

Some prices may rise and some may fall, rapidly or slowly, by much or by little (or not at all), in response to the factors impinging upon the demand side and the supply side of the market for the respective goods, services, and other items. Such movements may occur when prices for goods and services in general are rising or falling. These latter changes, however, are of special interest to us because they may affect the various classes of assets (Sect. 4.1) differently. Moreover, the measurements of these broad movements in prices for goods and services are provided by index numbers that are quite useful in analyses of the whole economy. This section, then, outlines the key price indexes and indicates the significance of changes in certain groups of prices for several classes of assets.

The three indexes. The price index numbers of widest use include those for wholesale prices, consumer prices, and the implicit price deflator for the gross national production of goods and services.[8] Of these, the wholesale price index has been traditionally the most widely used to indicate changes in prices. Then, with the rise of the importance of wage negotiations and the increased concern of price increases by consumers, the consumer price index came to be a well-known abstraction of price changes. Even more recently, price changes have come to be reported for the entire output of goods and services.

The movements of the series based on these indexes are shown in Fig. 5-1 for the period since 1929. It may be observed that the series generally show movements in the same direction, although small differences arise between the changes in the indexes. Statistically, these differences arise for several apparent reasons: (1) the price deflator includes prices of construction, exports and imports, and hire of general government workers, which are omitted from the other indexes or covered only in part; (2) the price deflator reflects the relative importance of the various goods and services in the total economy rather than in selected segments of the economy; and (3) the wholesale price index has somewhat greater volatility due to the degree of competitive market pricing in the items covered.

The three indexes (continued): wholesale prices. The wholesale price index is a general purpose index showing price changes for all commodities sold in primary markets in the United States. It provides a continuous monthly series for major groups of commodities, as well as for the more comprehensive measure of changes in the direction of price movements in primary markets generally. Prices are collected for nearly two thousand commodities. "Wholesale" as used in the title of the index simply refers to prices on commodities at the first level at which they enter into transactions. The index is one hundred times the quotient of a sum of products (namely, the sum of the products of the price relatives

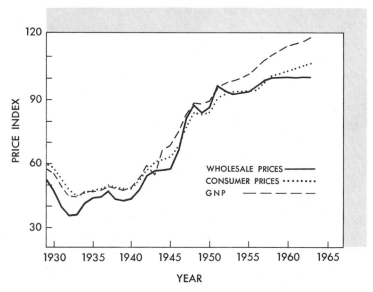

Fig. 5-1. *Wholesale and Consumer Price Indexes and the GNP Deflator, Since 1929. Source: Bureau of Labor Statistics, U.S. Department of Labor and Office of Business Economics and U.S. Department of Commerce.*

for each of the n commodities in the index and their value in the base period) and the total value of the n commodities traded in the base period. The one hundred causes the index to be equal to one hundred (per cent, with per cent sign omitted), instead of the one in the base year. The price relative simply states the relative price changes over a definite period of time for a given item, for example, p_1/p_0, when

p_0 is the price of a given commodity at time zero (0) and
p_1 is the price of the same commodity at time one (1).

And the weights are simply chosen to reflect the relative importance of the items in the index at the base period for comparing current prices. Thus we denote the wholesale price index (WPI) as the product of a weighted average of price relatives (i.e., the sum of the products of each weight and corresponding price relative divided by the sum of the weights) and 100:

a single price relative

value of the commodity
traded in the base period

$$\text{WPI} = \frac{\sum_{i=1}^{n} \left(\frac{p_1}{p_0} \cdot p_0 q_0 \right)_i}{\sum_{i=1}^{n} (p_0 q_0)_i} \cdot 100$$

total value of the n commodities
traded in the base period.

From this, we derive Laspeyres' formula for computing the index, simply by canceling out the base period prices (i.e., p_0) in the denominator:

$$\text{WPI (by Laspeyres)} = \frac{\sum_{i=1}^{n} (p_1 q_0)_i}{\sum_{i=1}^{n} (p_0 q_0)_i} \cdot 100$$

The method of computing the index may be said to give without equivocation the aggregate cost of a fixed bill of goods at one period in relation to cost at another period. The index, however, does not measure changes in the quality or proportions of the goods included in that "market basket," as the goods are sometimes called. For this reason careful use of the index requires that the span of time between the base period and the one for which the comparison is being made should not be too great.

The three indexes (continued): consumer prices. The consumer price index is designed to indicate changes in the price of a fixed market basket of goods and services purchased by urban wage-earner and clerical-worker families. These families comprise about 64 per cent of the urban population, and 40 per cent of the total population. The over-all consumer price index is published monthly, along with various sub-group indexes. It was initiated during World War I, when prices rose rapidly, for use in wage negotiations and first published in 1921, in roughly its present form.

The method of computing the index is somewhat similar to that for the wholesale price index. Only in this instance, the data are gathered by the sampling method. The sample consists of about 300 items consumed by urban wage-earner and clerical-worker families. Price relatives are computed for each item, and a system of weights is applied to represent the importance of each item in family budgets. The weights used until January 1964 were derived in the main from a comprehensive family expenditure survey made in 1950-1951; in 1964 a new weight structure and updated samples were introduced.

The three indexes (continued): the GNP deflator. The Department of Commerce publishes, regularly, data for the various national income aggregates and their components. The most comprehensive of these aggregates is that for gross national product (GNP). The data provided quarterly (at annual rates) and annually are in terms of both the prices that were in effect in those years and in terms of constant prices.

A time series for changes in the average of prices for the entire output of goods and services may be derived from the relationship between the current-prices series and the constant-prices series. This derived series is the implicit price deflator for gross national product. It is derived by dividing gross national product in current prices by the sum of the components of gross national product after each component has been deflated by a price index which approximates as closely as possible the price movements of that good or service.

Conceptually, the GNP deflator makes possible a discussion of real income or output in terms of constant prices. A doubling of the national output as measured by current prices, for instance, might not mean any increase in the well-being of the nation, if prices on the average and over the same period doubled and the physical volume of output remained unchanged. The GNP deflator, however, will permit a meaningful use of income data as a measure of changes in output. This can be accomplished by dividing the measures of income in current prices by the series for changes in the average of prices for the current output, with the result that changes in income will be measured in constant prices, i.e.,

$$\frac{Y}{P} =$$ income in constant prices (or payments for the output of goods and services as measured in constant prices),

when

Y is GNP in current prices, and

P is a price index for the output of goods and services.

Some significant aspects of price changes for goods and services generally. The broad changes in prices, such as those indicated by changes in the price indexes, are of special significance, because these changes (1) alter the distribution of income and wealth and (2) are closely related to changes in income, output, and employment (Sect. 5.4).

Price changes for the output of goods and services generally have a redistribution effect on the distribution of wealth through their impact on the values of the alternative forms of holding wealth. This effect is traceable to the distinction between the two broad categories of assets referred to in the last chapter: (I) money and safe assets, and (II) stocks and instrumental capital. The first group of claims are generally fixed in relation to their flows of returns and/or maturity value and consequently in terms of their absolute claim against future income.

The second group of claims, those of ownership, are claims against the residual portion of future income. As such, the latter claims automatically participate in rising incomes. And their values, as affected by prospective absolute returns, are not confined by a fixed maturity date. They are, in effect, free to rise as profit expectations become more buoyant. Consequently, a rising average of the prices for output benefits those whose wealth is more heavily concentrated in the various forms of ownership—stocks, real goods, instrumental capital, and the like—and it affects adversely those whose wealth is more heavily concentrated in

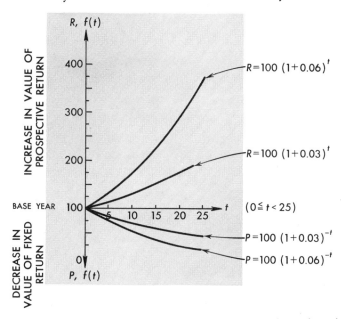

Fig. 5-2. Cumulative Effects of Price Increases for the Output of Goods and Services.

the form of cash balances and claims with a fixed maturity value. A declining average of prices for the output of goods and services has the reverse effect, benefiting the latter group at the expense of the former.

The effect of changes in the average of price for output on the value of variable prospective returns, as contrasted with fixed prospective returns, is illustrated in Fig. 5-2. The functions above the base-year axis are defined by

(1) $R = 100(1 + .06)^t$, and

(2) $R = 100(1 + .03)^t$, $0 \le t < 25$, and those below by

(3) $P = \dfrac{100}{(1 + .03)^t}$, and

(4) $P = \dfrac{100}{(1 + .06)^t}$, $0 \le t < 25$.

Those defined by equations (1) and (2) show what happens to a return, base = 100, when value varies with price increases for goods and services generally of 6 and 3 per cent per annum, respectively. The functions defined by equations (3) and (4) show what happens to the value of prospective returns, base = 100, when the returns are a fixed absolute amount. Observe that a 3 per cent rise in prices for 25 years will more than double the value of a variable return and reduce by more than one-half the value of a fixed return. A decline in the average of prices for output of 3 per cent per annum would simply reverse these latter effects, as if one were moving backward in the illustration through time, and so on.

The effects described imply an absence of change in the composition of asset holdings by individuals and institutions. The undesirable effects may be avoided and the desirable ones realized through appropriate changes in the composition of assets held by those who are aware of them. Actions directed toward avoiding the undesirable effects and experiencing the desirable effects, however, may themselves give rise to changes in demand for instrumental capital and classes of financial assets so as to have additional consequences for changes in income, output, and employment.

5.4. The Speculative Demand for Money, Income Velocity, and the Flow of Income

Having introduced notions with respect to a general economic equilibrium, interrelationships between the prices of all commodities, and an equilibrium price level, we may bring all of the notions together in slightly different form and see how changes in the strength of the motive for holding the various classes of assets contribute to disequilibrium and give rise to changes in income and other series. We will also illustrate the disequilibrium, the change in the flow of output, and the return to equilibrium with reference to a given number of units of instrumental capital. While we deal with a very elementary aggregative model involving a total of expenditures, the emphasis is on shifts in expenditures and changes in the velocity of money in response to the prospect of gains (or avoidance of losses). Shifts in expenditures by the business and financial sectors that give rise to changes in velocity are quite likely attributable to profit motives and forms of speculation. Shifts in consumer expenditures, as described later (Sect. 18.1), are likely attributable to these and other factors—including changes in "expected income."

Changes in the flow of income, income velocity, and other series. To observe the process whereby changes in the strength of the motive for holding the various classes of assets give rise to changes in income, and so on, we do several things: view the classes of assets as set forth earlier, recall the expression for the determination of income from an earlier model, restate the definition of income velocity, and state a hypothesis that causes our over-all system to generate changes over time in income, output, and velocity.

First, recall two (Sect. 4.1 and 5.3) sets of assets: (1) the first set of claims being generally fixed in terms of their maturity value and/or contractual returns and (2) the second set serving as a residual claim against future income, where in broad outline form, the assets in these two sets may appear as follows:

I $\begin{cases} \text{1. money} \\ \text{2. safe assets (including near-money assets and bonds)} \end{cases}$

II $\begin{cases} \text{1. stocks} \\ \text{2. instrumental capital} \end{cases}$

Next, from an earlier model (Sect. 1.3 and 2.2), recall

$$Y = \frac{\gamma - \beta}{\alpha},$$

where $M_s = \gamma$,

$M_d = \alpha Y + \beta$,

M_s is the supply of money,

M_d is the demand for money as a function of income,

Y is the flow of goods and services (i.e., GNP or income), and

α and β are the parameters with the earlier conditions attached to them.

Now, let us identify changes in β with shifts in the demand for money, and let us hypothesize that the prospective flows of returns from real goods and services, stocks, and so on rise (γ = constant), as may result from such influences on these flows as the prospect of a rise in prices on real goods and services during the expansion phase of a business cycle.

What then? Their values rise; the rates of return from additions to the stocks of instrumental capital (Sect. 4.1), real goods, and so on rise; and the speculative demand for money balances decreases (i.e., β decreases). Therefore, income rises, and so on. Money, with the prospect of a decline in value (i.e., decline in purchasing power and liquidity), is being disposed of at a faster rate in exchange for real goods and services. The strength of the motive for holding money as well as bonds and near-money assets is weakened. The sequence of switching is, for example, from bonds into money balances, and out-of-money balances into real goods and services. Bond prices fall, bond and near-money yields rise, stock yields decline, and the value of stocks and real goods and services rise. The converse set of relationships would also hold with the reverse set of prospects.

But look at our definition of the income velocity of money:

$$V_y = \frac{Y}{M}$$

Substituting the parameters for income into the definition of the income velocity of money, we get an expression for velocity in terms of parameters:

$$V_y = \frac{\dfrac{\gamma - \beta}{\alpha}}{\gamma} = \frac{1 - \dfrac{\beta}{\gamma}}{\alpha}.$$

We may simply view β as corresponding to the speculative demand for money and as a decreasing function of time in the expansion phase of the business cycle and an increasing function during the contraction phase—all in accordance with changes in the magnitude of prospective returns from stocks and instrumental capital. The result is a model explaining (1) changes in the volocity of money, (2) changes in the flow of income (and therefore output, since $Y = PO$), (3) changes in

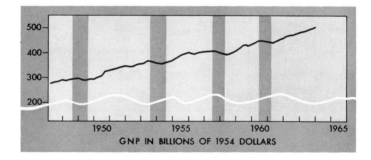

GNP IN BILLIONS OF 1954 DOLLARS

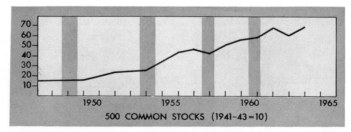

500 COMMON STOCKS (1941–43=10)

Fig. 5-3. *Stock Prices and Output in Constant Dollars. The series for GNP in constant dollars is based on seasonally adjusted quarterly totals at annual rates. The series for 500 common stocks is constructed from twelve-month moving verages of monthly data; the monthly data, themselves, are averages of daily figures. The shaded areas are the same as those in Fig. 4-1. Source of data: U.S. Department of Commerce and Standard and Poor's Corporation.*

yields on debt instruments, and (4) changes in stock prices (and therefore yields)—in accordance with observations such as those recorded
in earlier chapters (i.e., Table 2-1 and Fig. 4-1), and in Fig. 5-3.

We also note a number of secular changes in the various series, and
these too may be explained along the lines of the explanation for the
cyclical changes. One important secular change, the postwar rise in
the velocity of money (Table 2-1), in fact, has been attributed to a
relative decline in the precautionary motive (Sect. 2.2) as it concerns
less uncertainty about the future and, in the present context, a secular
decline in β.[9]

Imbalance, the flow of output, and equilibrium. The imbalance referred to above, when the prospective flow of returns from real goods
and services rises and when the flow of output expands, may be illustrated further with particular reference to a given number of units of
instrumental capital. For example, a change in the prospective flow of
returns R_n $(n = 1, \ldots, m)$ from a given number of units of instrumental capital at some initial time raises the value of such capital (CV),
i.e., it raises

$$CV = \sum_{n=1}^{m} \frac{R_n}{(1 + i)^n}, \quad i = \text{constant},$$

where i is the rate of interest (Sect. 4.3) for discounting the prospective
    returns.

But at this initial time, the supply price (C) or cost with respect to some
flow variable comprising a given number of new units of instrumental
capital of the same type is given,

$$C = \sum_{n=1}^{m} \frac{R_n}{(1 + r)^n}, \quad C = \text{constant},$$

where r is the rate of return that is necessary to equate the increased
    flow of returns $R_n(n = 1, \ldots, m)$ to the constan supply price.
Thus, comparing the value of existing instrumental capital with the
supply price of comparable capital,

$$CV > C = \text{constant},$$

or viewing the inequality another way,

$$r > i = \text{constant, where}$$

$$\sum_{n=1}^{m} R_n = CV[(1 + i)^1 + \ldots + (1 + i)^m] = C[(1 + r)^1 + \ldots + (1 + r)^m].$$

Consequently, a gain may be made from effecting an increase in the
flow of new capital, and, by the assumptions (Sect. 4.1), there is an
increase in the flow of new expenditures as we move from the initial
time. The increase in the flow of payments for current output, nevertheless, will contribute to a decrease in the flow of prospective returns

$R_n(n = 1, \ldots, m)$ as the stock of instrumental capital increases at a faster rate. The extra flow demand will raise the supply price, so that, as we move from the initial time, the latter changes brought about by the initial change in prospects will generate the new equilibrium (i.e., $CV = C$, $r = i$).

Also the same sort of process of imbalance (i.e., $CV > C$, $r > i$) and return to equilibrium (i.e., $r = i$) could result from a reduction in cost or supply prices (prospective returns constant), and these reductions in cost or economies could result from the use of special tax features (17.3) and/or technological developments (Sect. 15.2 and 15.3). In either case, whether cost change in response to economies or diseconomies and/or whether value changes in response to changes in the prospective flow of returns, the changing equilibrium corresponds to a rise in the rate of interest (= rate of return) in the expansion phase and a decline in the contraction phase. The presence of the rate of interest and the control exercised over it through the quantity of money (Sect. 4.3), however, indicate a connection between the practice of fractional-reserve banking, changes in the level of reserves, and changs in the flow of income (and, therefore, in prices, output, and employment).

The cost-value relationship (and thus the i-r relationship) introduced in this section is quite general. It anticipates a basic monetary model— the investment demand model (Sect. 17.2)—and a more detailed treatment of the analysis in question.

5.5. Summary

In Chapter 4 forces operating in the short run were viewed as being of a shorter time dimension than those operating over the short cycle of income, output, and prices—although there is a clear overlap between the time dimensions of the two sets of forces. The short-run changes introduced earlier—the shifts in the structure of interest rates (and therefore shifts in asset values) and the shifts in the liquidity preference demand for money—concerned, among other things, the prospect of exercising some control over the rate of interest (and therefore asset values) through changes in the stock of money. The present chapter, moreover, introduces notions about changes in the price level and continues to deal with changes in the demand for money and the stock of money. All prices have been shown to be interrelated and the price level has been shown to have some relation to the stock of money and the conditions underlying the latter relationship. The interrelationship between prices was indicated in part by a general equilibrium analysis and in part by a less general analysis involving classes of assets—namely, those with a fixed claim against future income and those with a residual claim against future income.

Several groups of prices have been distinguished in the present chapter:

(1) The average of prices on the goods and services entering into the total of transactions at a given time or for a given period, such as the universe of prices implied by the determinate system of equations for general economic equilibrium or by the Fisher-type equation of exchange;

(2) The average of prices on the current output of goods and services, such as the set of prices implied by the simple quantity theory, the cash-balances approach to the quantity theory, and the GNP deflator;

(3) The group of prices represented by the wholesale price index and the consumer's price index; and

(4) Other groups of prices, such as those on stocks and so-called safe assets (including near-money assets and bonds).

The notion of changes in some groups of prices in contrast to changes in prices on single items is of special interest. They introduce the prospect of realizing gains (and avoiding losses) through the switching of assets to accord with prospective price changes and the desire to realize gains (or avoid losses). Changes in the average of prices for current output or the prospect of such changes, further, are significant because (a) actual changes in the average redistribute wealth arbitrarily in favor of those with the less rigid incomes, the assets with a residual claim against future income, and the knowledge to take advantage of prospective changes in the average of prices; and (b) the prospect of changes in prices and the opportunity to realize gains (and avoid losses) may itself give rise to changes in the demand for certain classes of assets and, as shown, changes in income, output, employment, and prices.

The prospect of changes in the average of prices for current output may give rise to cyclical changes in output and so on. The inducement involved in the demand changes giving rise to the changes in output and so on, moreover, may be expressed in terms of the inequality of the capital value of some given amount of assets and the cost of acquiring additional assets of a similar amount and type. The inducement may also be expressed in terms of the inequality between the rate of return on existing assets and the rate of interest for relating the cost or supply price to the prospective stream of returns from the acquisition of additional assets.

In view of the latter inequalities, the emphasis on factors giving rise to changes in output and so on need not be entirely or even partially on changes in the average of prices for current output. Indeed, the inequality of capital value and cost or supply price could result from special tax features and technological and other developments tending to affect the flow of prospective returns from capital outlays and/or the cost or supply price. The latter factors would also affect the imbalance in the rate of return and the rate of interest. In the last instance, further, we are dealing with the prospect of control over income, output, employment, and the average of prices through control over the rate of interest and the stock of money.

Notions of control over the average of prices for current output (and, in turn, control over other economic measures) have evolved in terms of the quantity theory of money. Early versions of such an approach emphasized mainly the relationship between the price level—"defined in one way or another"—and the stock of money—"also defined in one way or another." There was the economy concerning output, on the one side, and there were the monetary trappings, on the other; the theory of output and the theory of money were separate. Later versions of the quantity theory approach, however, have dealt with changes in the demand for money, the determinants of income velocity, and the motives for holding money—all in terms of their relationship to income, the average of prices for current output, output, and employment. These later versions of the quantity theory approach have, accordingly, introduced the prospect of control over the latter measures through control over the stock of money.

References

1. E. J. Mishan, "Say's Law and Walras' Law Once More," *Quarterly Journal of Economics,* November 1963, p. 619. See also Robert E. Kuenne, "Say's Law and Walras' Law Once More: Comment," *Quarterly Journal of Economics,* August 1964, pp. 478-483; and E. J. Mishan's "Reply" in the same issue, pp. 484-487.

2. See *The Purchasing Power of Money,* rev. ed. (New York: The Macmillan Company, 1911, 1913).

3. For example, James W. Angell, *The Behavior of Money* (New York: McGraw-Hill Book Company, 1936).

4. Richard T. Selden, "The Postwar Rise in the Velocity of Money: A Sectoral Analysis," *Journal of Finance,* December 1961, pp. 483-545.

5. John M. Keynes, *A Tract on Monetary Reform* (London: The Macmillan Company, Ltd., 1923), pp. 74-78.

6. See William Baumol, *Economic Theory and Operations Analysis* (Englewood Cliffs, N.J.: Prentice-Hall, Inc., 1961, pp. 230-238). The works cited by Baumol and those cited by Mishan (*op. cit.,* pp. 617-625) comprise a large segment of the voluminous literature concerning the general subject of Sect. 5.2.

7. See Mishan, *op. cit.,* pp. 621-623.

8. For a broad discussion of the prices and the three indexes, see Willard L. Thorp and Richard E. Quandt, *The New Inflation* (New York: The McGraw-Hill Book Company, 1959), pp. 7-17; and U.S. Congress, Joint Economic Committee, *Government Price Statistics,* Parts 1 and 2 (Washington, D.C.: U.S. Government Printing Office, 1961.

9. See Milton Friedman and Anna Jacobson Schwartz, *A Monetary History of the United States, 1867-1960* (Princeton, N.J.: Princeton University Press, 1963), Chap. 12; and William J. Frazer, Jr., "The Postwar Rise in the Velocity of Money in the United States," *Schweizerische Zeitschrift für Volkswirtschaft und Statistik,* December 1964; and William J. Frazer, Jr., *The Liquidity Structure of Firms and Monetary Economics* (Gainesville, Fla.: The University of Florida Press, 1965), Chap. 8.

6

The Price Level, the Gold Standard, and the Gold Flows Mechanism

> Dr. Freud relates that there are peculiar reasons deep in our subconsciousness why gold in particular should satisfy strong instincts and serve as a symbol. The magical properties, with which Egyptian priestcraft anciently imbued the yellow metal, it has never altogether lost (John Maynard Keynes, *A Treatise on Money* [1930]).

The equations defining general economic equilibrium provided a determinate set of prices and quantities, given the money supply and other parameters (Sect. 5.2). These equations also called attention to the interrelationship between the prices of the various items and the quantities with respect to money and other items. Now, however, we wish to move to an even more Herculean level of generalization and note that the prices of one market economy are related to those of other such economies under the conditions of a properly functioning international gold standard. They are related because some of the goods and marketable financial instruments of one country are substitutes for those of the others, but they are related, too, because the values of the respective monetary units of the various countries are all tied to gold and related through the foreign exchange market and the gold flows mechanism. This chapter, consequently, deals briefly with some basic notions pertaining to the operations of the gold flows mechanism.

The objectives of the chapter are (1) to illustrate some interrelationships between countries operating under gold standard conditions, (2) to provide a foundation for the understanding of some historical developments in the United States prior to 1933 (Chap. 7), and (3) to provide an introduction to later topics concerning the mechanics of international payments (Sect. 21.1), short-term capital and gold flows, the United States balance of international payments (Sect. 21.2), and other international matters. The basic notions considered as pertaining to the operations of the gold flows mechanism are (1) the gold standard, (2) the quantity theory approach to price changes, and (3) the real bills doctrine. These notions come up in the process of setting forth the logic of the gold flows mechanism as it was originally viewed and as it operated over important intervals of history.

6.1. Gold, Gold Exchange, and Bimetallic Standards

Metals have enjoyed the quality of money over much of history, and gold in particular has occupied a pre-eminent position since the beginnings of modern banking. In fact, the practice of using currency notes and deposit liabilities of banks as money first gave rise to the concept of a "monetary standard," wherein, by various means, efforts are made to extend the monetary quality of some accepted money to the note issue and deposits. The initially accepted money in such a case provides the so-called standard, and the practice of having a standard in lieu of using the basic money itself as a circulating medium becomes a means of economizing the available supply of the monetary base. Where gold provided the monetary base and successful efforts were made to economize its supply through the use of note and deposit liabilities, the gold standard prevailed. The gold exchange and bimetallic standards have simply been extensions of the efforts to economize the gold base further in the process of enlarging the supply of money.

A monetary system could no doubt exist independently of any metallic base in a market type of economy, but no such system has arisen among the modern industrialized economies with relatively free markets. Even today, when gold is legally restricted from circulation in the United States (Sect. 7.5), gold plays a fundamental role with respect to international finance and the United States international role, in particular. Moreover, many of the basic aspects of the analysis with respect to the old gold standard mechanism are still applicable.

The gold standard. The classical form of the gold standard is based on three rules: (1) The first calls for the free coinage of gold. (2) The second requires that the price of gold (or its value in monetary units) be fixed by law. (3) The third requires that bank notes (paper currency), such subsidiary coin as may exist, and bank deposits be freely convertible into gold coin at some free market price.

The standard based on these rules has been said to be a "rough and ready way" of providing a currency. Under the standard, the currency issuing authority is the mint. It does nothing more than turn gold bullion into coins for all comers. Generally, the government runs the mint, and historically mints charged "brassage"—a small fee to cover the cost of minting. The gold coin then is a small ingot of gold, and its weight and quality (or fineness) is certified by the mint. Also, in order for the coin to pass as suitable coin, there must be freedom to melt and export pieces of metal. The fulfillment of this condition eliminates all discretion on the part of the currency issuing authority.

The requirement that the price of gold be fixed by law in monetary units determines the wealth value of the monetary unit itself. Once this legal price is fixed, the value of the monetary unit is no longer free to vary indefinitely in terms of the commodity. The actual value of gold as contrasted with its legal price, however, continues to be determined by free dealings in a market.

Gold, under the international standard (Sect. 6.3), moreover, is a commodity with a world market. It has a different price in terms of the monetary units of other countries, but the common acceptance of gold provides a means of expressing the relative wealth value of all those monetary units tied to gold. The pound, for example, is worth so much in terms of gold, the dollar is worth so much in terms of gold, and, therefore, the pound and the dollar are worth so much in terms of each other. Thus, if one pound $\rightarrow$ ($2.80) $\times$ 1/35 of an ounce of gold (where the symbol $\rightarrow$ means "implies"), and if one dollar $\rightarrow$ 1/35 of an ounce of gold, then one pound $\rightarrow$ $2.80, and the exchange rate for pounds in terms of dollars is 2.80. The rate at which one monetary unit expresses the value of another may be said to be relatively fixed at some par or parity value (such as $2.80 for the pound) on the basis of these conditions. We refer to such a "relatively fixed" rate as a "fixed" rate.

In effect, under the standard, gold coin is economized by being made freely substitutable for bank notes and bank deposits. The economizing is a way of using a given amount of gold to provide for a multiple amount of money balances (Sect. 3.1). Nevertheless, so long as these are all freely exchangeable for one another, without any prospective loss of value from holding either one, the public may be said to be indifferent as to whether or not they hold coin or bank notes.

Thus far, we have been discussing what is called a gold coin standard. When full weight gold coins are minted and allowed to circulate as money, a considerable attrition of the monetary base unavoidably occurs, due principally to wear, filing, and disappearance into small hoards. In order that countries might economize the gold stock more drastically, as well as facilitate the deliberate management of the operations of a gold standard, gold bullion standards came into being. Under such a standard, gold is only obtainable from the government in standard size bars (bullion), and gold coins are not permitted to circulate. The standard size bar in the United States at present contains $13,434.79 worth of gold and weighs nearly twenty-seven pounds.

The gold exchange standard. The gold exchange standard is a means of further economizing gold by using both gold and liquid claims against countries with gold convertible currencies as a base for the domestic money supply. Under such an arrangement, the gold convertible currency* is thought to be as good as gold itself. Usually, the gold convertible currency is the currency of some international leader, such as England in the 1920's and the United States in the 1960's, and its currency is called a "key currency." Under such a system, a key currency country has the paramount responsibility to maintain the acceptability of its currency as a reserve.

The monetary standard in most countries of the free world of post-World War II years is the gold exchange standard, which was also true of the 1920's (Sect. 7.5). The mechanism (Sect. 6.3) pertaining to the workings of such standards, however, was originally viewed like the gold standard as being fully automatic. Even in the post-World War II years where this view no longer prevails, the mechanics still apply with minor modifications.

A bimetallic standard. A bimetallic standard is one whereby the value of the monetary unit is expressed in terms of a fixed price for both gold and silver. Both the metals are coined freely under such a standard, and the use of silver is thought to broaden the monetary base.

Where the bimetallic standard has been adopted, the ratio of price of one metal to that of the other has been fixed by law to correspond to the ratio between the respective market prices at the time of the enactment of the law. Disturbances occur in the markets, however, and the relative market values do not remain fixed. Although a country may be *de jure* on a bimetallic standard, it is *de facto* on a single metallic standard when the metal that is overvalued in terms of the unit of account drives the relatively undervalued money out of circulation, with the effect that only one metal actually circulates as a medium of exchange.**

---

* In the jargon of international finance, the term "currency" carries a meaning different from that in national finance (Sect. 2.1 and 2.2). It refers to foreign-held money balances available as a substitute for gold for effecting international transactions.

** The phenomenon, whereby one so-called "bad" money drives "good" money out of circulation, has been called Gresham's Law, after Sir Thomas Gresham, adviser to Queen Elizabeth I of England. It is applicable to a variety of circumstances. A reformulation of the law may be stated as follows: when different forms of legal or valid tender money exist, the overvalued forms in terms of their relation to the unit of account tend to displace in circulation the undervalued or preferred forms. The "law" applies to the issue of full weight coins that are intended to circulate along with worn or debased coins (Gresham's actual case) as well as to the disappearance of gold or silver coins when the government overvalues silver or gold, respectively, relative to the market prices of the two metals.

Two contemporary authors point out that "cheap [i.e., overvalued forms in terms of their relation to the unit of account] money drives out dear money [i.e., undervalued] . . . only when there is a fixed rate of exchange between the two." They point out, too, that the dear money could still enter into circulation "by being

In some instances, bimetallism has been thought of as a device for achieving the advantages of silver for small transactions and gold for large ones. Though in fact it has worked imperfectly as a monetary standard, it may, nevertheless, be expected to function under highly limited conditions. These unlikely conditions would consist of a willing and able dealer who is prepared to hold a stock of metals in large enough proportion to the world demand and supply to govern the price of both.

Commodity standards. Strictly speaking, monetary standards involving reserves of gold or silver are special cases of commodity standards, wherein stocks of commodities are bought and sold by governments at fixed prices and are used as reserves for the money supply. It is conceivable and, indeed, has widely been advocated * that governments use "baskets" of basic storable commodities (e.g., grains, fibers, minerals, and fuels) in fixed proportions to define the standard monetary unit, rather than certain weights in gold or silver. Through sufficient government purchases, deflation and depression could allegedly be averted, while sales from the commodity reserves would prevent inflation. Such a scheme would present formidable technical problems in its administration, even if agreement could be reached on the proper composition of a standard "basket" of commodities.

United States monetary standards, 1792-1933. On the recommendation of Alexander Hamilton, the United States adopted a bimetallic standard in 1792,[1] following the colonial period in which such commodities as wampum and corn were, at times, actually made legal tender (i.e., legally acceptable as a means of paying debts). The Coinage Act of 1792 provided for the free coinage of both silver and gold in the ratio of 15 to 1. France, however, established a ratio of 15.5 to 1 in 1803. Gold was shipped to France where it would exchange for more units of silver. Silver was left to be coined and to circulate in the United States. In 1834 the mint ratio in the United States was changed to 16 to 1, with the result that silver was shipped abroad in exchange for gold. *De facto,* the United States may be said to have been on the gold standard from this date until 1933 (Sect. 7.5). With the Coinage Act of 1853 the gold standard was accepted *de jure.* The act abolished the free coinage of

---

accepted at its market rather than its nominal value. . . ." The requirement of a "fixed rate of exchange" is a necessary condition for the application of the law. See Milton Friedman and Anna Jacobson Schwartz, *A Monetary History of the United States, 1867-1960* (Princeton, N.J.: Princeton University Press for the National Bureau of Economic Research, 1963), p. 27.

* See, e.g., Benjamin Graham, *World Commodities and World Currency* (New York: McGraw-Hill Book Company, 1944). Graham's plea (p. viii) is representative: ". . . the gold-reserve system has meant stability, expansion, and full employment *for the gold-mining industry.* . . . An analogous reserve system for basic commodities can mean reasonable stability, balanced expansion, and high-level employment for all the primary industries of the world."

silver. Also, following the outbreak of the Civil War, the cheap money schemes (Sect. 7.4) were effected, with the result that paper currency exchanged for gold only at substantial discounts. The main form of paper money, called Greenbacks, issued during the war was made exchangeable at par for gold in 1879. Silver did not cease to be a political issue, but the gold standard operated *de facto*, even if somewhat imperfectly.

6.2. Exchange Rates and Gold Flows

Tying the value of the monetary unit to gold gives a world value to the monetary unit itself. This value can only be made effective, however, through the foreign exchange market (Sect. 21.1). In that market currencies may be exchanged for each other, or they may be exchanged for gold. Generally, two currencies in forms other than gold (i.e., bank deposits and paper currency) will exchange for each other as long as the rate at which one exchanges for the other moves within narrow limits. These limits were called gold points under the functioning of a more classical form of the gold standard, and, for most currencies since that time, they have come to be the buying and selling rates set by a central agency or government exchange stabilization fund. In either case, there is stimulus for gold itself to flow into (out of) the country whose currency is increasing (decreasing) in value in such a way as to re-establish a rate of exchange which moves within narrow limits (the limits may still be referred to as the gold points). How this adjustment mechanism works to effect gold flows and limit fluctuations in exchange rates will be introduced and subsequently dealt with in more detail (Sect. 21.3).

International payments and interbank balances. The majority of payments for business transactions between countries are made with bank credit. Generally, there will be banks in financial centers that will have "correspondent" relationships with banks in other centers. A foreign seller of goods and others items will want payment in the currency of his own country. The domestic purchaser of these items may obtain the means of payment through his bank. The bank will credit the account of its foreign correspondent, which will in effect make the payment to the foreign seller. As long as the purchases of goods, services, and other items in one country equal those purchases in another, the claims that arise between the correspondent banks cancel out. However, when country A begins to purchase more items from country B (or the rest of the world) than the latter purchases from A, then the supply of credits in country B available for exchange into A's currency decrease relative to the large supply of A's currency available for exchange into B's currency. B's currency may be said to be in short supply. Its price or exchange rate rises in terms of A's currency, and country A's exchange rate in terms of country B's monetary unit declines. These prices are made by dealers in the foreign exchange markets, which are generally the banks transacting in credit with one another.

The gold points and gold flows. Under practices pertaining to the more classical form of the gold standard, a move in the price of B's currency beyond the par exchange rate and the cost of shipping gold (the gold export points) would stimulate country A to export gold in order to replenish its foreign credits. And, again at the most general level of abstraction, the latter movement in B's price today would quite likely lead the managers of country B's exchange account to offer to sell their currency at the upper limit in such a way as to give effect to that limit. Then any resale of A's currency in exchange for A's gold would still cause gold to flow into the stronger currency country. This upper limit today would most likely be the par value of B's currency in terms of A's currency, plus one per cent of that value, as agreed upon with an international agency (Sect. 22.1). In either instance—the more classical case or the more contemporary one—gold has been used to offset the difference between the value of the imports of goods, services, and other items and the value of the exports of goods, services, and other items. The export of gold also tends to offset a rise in the price of country B's currency in terms of A's currency. Conversely, if the price of B's currency in terms of A's currency tends to decline below the lower limit on the price of B's currency, such as the par exchange rate less the shipping cost or the agreed-upon limit, then gold tends to flow into country A and offset the decline in the price of B's currency.

From the domestic or country A point of view, and in terms of the exchange rate for B's currency, the upper and lower limits on the price of B's currency in terms of A's currency are sketched in Fig. 6-1. The illustration is set up so that one can interpret it in general and in terms of the more classical or contemporary conditions, as well as in terms of a particular numerical example. The numbers used as an example pertain to the present-day par value of the pound in terms of dollars, and the limits at one per cent of either side of par value are those that the United Kingdom has agreed to maintain. The United Kingdom, for example, has a par value of $2.80 for the pound, and the Bank of England acting as an agent stands ready to effect an upper and lower limit on the dollar price of the pound at $2.82 and $2.78, respectively. They do this by buying all dollars offered to it at $2.82 and by selling dollars in exchange for pounds for authorized transactions when the price of the pound falls below $2.78.

The proper functioning of the gold flows mechanism or its modified present-day counterpart tends to confine fluctuations in the prices of foreign exchange within limits. Under the more classical conditions, these limits were set by the gold points—the gold export points, when the rate on exchange made the export of gold worthwhile, and the gold import points, when the rate favored the import of gold from the foreign country. Today, however, these rates are set for most countries engaging in monetary cooperation though agreement with an international agency (Sect. 22.1), although the points may still be called gold points. The majority of the cooperating countries have established par values for their currencies, and they have as well agreed to limit exchange rate fluctuations within one per cent of either side of par value. Under the old

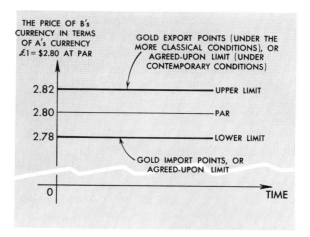

Fig. 6-1. *The Rate on Foreign Exchange Between Country A and Country B: The Domestic (or Country A) Point of View.*

system the spread between the limits was twice the shipping cost of gold, and under the contemporary system the spread is often 2 per cent of par value. In either case, a par or parity value is (was) determined by the relative quantity of gold in the two units of exchange.

6.3. The International Gold Standard and the Gold Flows Mechanism

When several important countries adopt the gold standard, the standard becomes international, in effect, and operations under the standard give rise to a foreign exchange market as a means of clearing claims and counterclaims between countries. The operations in the foreign exchange markets and the practice of confining exchange rate changes within the gold points, moreover, give rise to a somewhat mechanical system pertaining to gold flows and price level changes in the various countries. The system then seems to operate so as to regulate prices and generate price level changes as a means of correcting imbalances in a country's trade position.

The type of price level changes envisioned are those that result as some function of the stock of money, after allowance for changes in output. These would include those effected through the previous statements (Sect. 5.1) of the quantity theory approach that involved the average of all prices, as well as our more contemporary statement of general economic equilibrium (Sect. 5.2). This does not mean, however, that all supporters of the automatic gold standard accepted quantity theory views of the type outlined earlier and fixed exchange rates as set forth above (Sect. 6.2). All of the early quantity theorists endorsed the gold standard as a source of monetary discipline as set forth below, but among the so-called quantity theorists have been those with a variety of doctrinaire views about the gold standard. One, in fact, finds supporters of the gold standard as an institution among the following groups:

(1) Proponents of the real bills doctrine (Sect. 6.3) who favor the gold standard primarily as an institution because of the discipline it enforces.

(2) Commodity theorists, who believe that money has value only because of its actual or expected relation to gold and/or silver. These include the group of quantity theorists who, as described later (Sect. 7.5), predicted a rise in prices when the dollar price of gold was raised in the early 1930's.

(3) Those quantity theorists other than commodity theorists who happen to favor the automatic gold standard for its fiscal and monetary discipline. This group, of course, would not include quantity theorists who, for example, opposed the so-called fixed exchange rates pertaining to the operations of the gold standard vis-à-vis freely fluctuating exchange rates.

An alternative to operations under the international gold standard with so-called fixed exchange rates (i.e., fixed within limits) is freely fluctuating exchange rates. (In the absence of deliberate actions to fix exchange rates, freely fluctuating exchange rates are a characteristic of what is sometimes called a "paper" standard.) In such a case, the rates are allowed to fluctuate widely enough to compensate for price level changes in the various countries, presumably so as to bring about a balance of exports and imports. For example, under freely fluctuating rates, the cost of B's currency in terms of A's currency must rise so high as to restrict the purchase of imports from country B when A's price level rises relative to B's, and the rate must fall so low as to stimulate purchases when A's price level falls relative to B's. Under this system, there need be no residual in the balance of claims for exports by the respective countries to be met by a payment in gold. Instead, the exchange rates simply fluctuate to sufficient extremes to force the balance called for.[2] Here again, however, no such system has been tried by major industrial countries as a whole, and for the time being we will simply confine our present consideration of international adjustments to the more conventional mechanics with respect to adjustments through price level changes and gold flows.

Prices, the quantity theory, and the gold flows mechanism.[3] The acceptance of the gold standard and the adherence to the rules of the standard by several important countries provided an automatic regulator of the level of prices in the respective countries. Given some relationship between the levels of prices as implied by the average of prices on current output in country A (denoted $P^{(A)}$) and country B (denoted $P^{(B)}$), respectively, such as

$$P^{(A)} - P^{(B)} + \text{const.} = 0,$$

for example, gold was thought to be attracted toward country A when

(1) $P^{(A)} - P^{(B)} + \text{const.} < 0$ (flow toward country A),

and toward country B when

(2) $P^{(A)} - P^{(B)} + \text{const.} > 0$ (flow toward country B).

In effect, the relatively more favorable prices in country A as implied by inequality (1) was thought to attract gold to A because of an increase in A's exports to B and a decrease in A's imports from B, and the relatively more favorable prices in country B as implied by inequality (2) was thought to induce an outflow of gold from country A because of a decrease in A's exports to B and an increase in A's imports from B. Thus, where

$P^{(A)}$ is the average of prices on current output in country A (or more particularly the average of prices on exportable goods entering into foreign trade),

$P^{(B)}$ is the average of prices on current output in country B (or more particularly the average of prices on exportable goods entering into foreign trade),

$P^{(A)}$ is a function of the money supply in country A,

$P^{(B)}$ is a function of the money supply in country B,

ΔM is an increase in the money supply,

$\overline{M}$ is the equilibrium stock of money prior to the gold flow,

ΔR_0 is an initial increase in reserves,

r is a fraction of reserves to note and deposit liabilities,

c [$c = 0$ in the present use of an earlier formula (Sect. 3.3)] is some proportion of the money supply the public wishes to hold in the form of gold coin,

gold flows were viewed as regulating the respective levels of prices somewhat as follows:

PERIOD 1

$[P^{(A)} - P^{(B)} + \text{const.} < 0 \ (\text{flow toward Country A})]$

Country A
$\left(\begin{array}{c}\text{Inducement for}\\ \text{inflow}\end{array}\right)$

Country B
$\left(\begin{array}{c}\text{Inducement for}\\ \text{outflow}\end{array}\right)$

$$\Delta M = \left(\frac{1}{r}\right)(\Delta R_0) \quad \longleftarrow \quad (-\Delta R_0)\left(\frac{1}{r}\right) = (-\Delta M)$$

$$\Delta P^{(A)} = f(\overline{M} + \Delta M) \qquad\qquad\qquad f(-\Delta M + \overline{M}) = \Delta P^{(B)}$$

Terms of trade now favor Country B as shown at the outset of period 2.

PERIOD 2

$[P^{(A)} - P^{(B)} + \text{const.} > 0 \ (\text{flow toward Country B})]$

Country A
$\left(\begin{array}{c}\text{Inducement for}\\ \text{outflow}\end{array}\right)$

Country B
$\left(\begin{array}{c}\text{Inducement for}\\ \text{inflow}\end{array}\right)$

$$-\Delta M = \left(\frac{1}{r}\right)(-\Delta R_0) \quad \longrightarrow \quad \Delta R_0\left(\frac{1}{r}\right) = \Delta M$$

$$-\Delta P^{(A)} = f(\overline{M} - \Delta M) \qquad\qquad\qquad f(\Delta M + \overline{M}) = \Delta P^{(B)}$$

Terms of trade now favor Country A as shown at the outset of period 3.

PERIOD 3

$[P^{(A)} - P^{(B)} + \text{const.} < 0 \ (\text{flow toward Country A})]$

Country A
$\left(\begin{array}{c}\text{Inducement for}\\ \text{inflow}\end{array}\right)$

Country B
$\left(\begin{array}{c}\text{Inducement for}\\ \text{outflow}\end{array}\right)$

$$\Delta M = \left(\frac{1}{r}\right)(\Delta R_0) \quad \longleftarrow \quad (-\Delta R_0)\left(\frac{1}{r}\right) = -\Delta M$$

$$\Delta P^{(A)} = f(\overline{M} + \Delta M) \qquad\qquad\qquad f(-\Delta M + \overline{M}) = -\Delta P^{(B)}$$

Terms of trade now favor B.

The automatic regulation of price levels in relation to one another and the fulfillment of the implicit assumption that an inflow of gold was the inevitable consequence of a favorable balance of trade and an outflow the consequence of an unfavorable balance of trade, moreover, provided a certain discipline. For one thing, there was a premium on a country's being economically efficient in production, and, for another, there was a constraint on monetary and fiscal schemes designed to influence demand and prices through discretionary changes in money and credit in a given country. Indeed, some have viewed the automatic discipline of the gold standard as a desirable constraint upon the fiscal schemes available to overly ambitious politicians seeking excessive power.[4]

Gold flows and changes in short-term, self-liquidating, commercial paper ("real bills"). As we imply earlier (Sect. 3.1), a deposit of gold provided an opportunity for banks to expand loans and enlarge the money supply, and a withdrawal called for a contraction of loans and a reduction in the money supply. The latter eventuality, in fact, put a premium on the extension of loans to begin with that were of a more highly liquid character—i.e., loans that could mature or be liquidated in the process of contraction. The case for limiting bank lending to such loans has since been called the real bills doctrine or commercial loan theory of banking.

Under the doctrine, there was the view that loans extended for working capital purposes—e.g., the purchase of goods in shipment and inventory—would provide the needed liquidity. As the loans expanded, it would be possible to produce goods that could be sold to provide the means for the repayment of the loan. In this sense, there was something real behind the loan and it was "self liquidating." Further, bank loans (and the money supply) would be closely geared to changes in business activity.

The proponents of the real bills doctrine in its most doctrinaire form did not believe that price level changes would result from changes in the money supply, provided the practice of extending loans for working capital purposes only was adhered to. In this respect, the doctrine was at variance with the quantity theory approach to price level changes, particularly where a constant output was assumed. For the simpler advocates, the demand for loans was affected by factors outside of the banking system, and credit could be issued in excess only by the practice of extending loans for purposes other than working capital. They viewed the gold standard as an institutional force effecting a limit on this overextension of credit, i.e., credit other than that for short-term, self-liquidating commercial paper. The original Federal Reserve Act (Sect. 7.5) reflected this thinking.

The adherence to the doctrine in the extension of loans, however, would indeed present the opportunity to contract loans as they matured, provided the goods behind the loans yielded the means of repayment. There were some features about the extension of loans by banks in general and their contraction, however, that were to provide complications. Namely, all banks or even those located in a financial center could not dispose of a large portion of credit instruments of a so-called self-liquidating quality by selling them in the financial center as a means of contracting loans without depressing security prices (see financial markets and the mechanics of crisis [Sect. 7.2]), prior to the establishment of borrowing facilities at Federal Reserve Banks in 1914.

The gold standard and the self-regulating market (an over-all view). The gold standard worked reasonably well for many years throughout history. Not only did it serve to regulate markets, but also the necessary increase in the stock of gold seemed just right to accommodate the need for growth in the money supply as income and the volume of trade expanded. As one eminent writer said: "It happened that progress in the discovery of gold mines roughly kept pace with progress in other directions—a correspondence which was not altogether a matter of chance, because the progress of that period, since it was characterized by the gradual opening up and exploitation of the world's surface, not unnaturally brought to light *pari passu* the remote deposits of gold." [5]

Another writer has developed an argument for the sweeping historical generalization whereby the hundred years' peace, 1815-1914 (apart from the Crimean War, a more or less colonial event), was largely based on the proper functioning of the international gold standard.[6]

6.4. Summary

The international gold standard had the effect of relating the prices of one country to those of another, as does its present-day counterpart. Countries operating under the standard were expected to abide by certain rules, including the maintenance of a fixed price of gold in terms of its monetary unit. This latter practice gave a country's currency an international value in terms of gold and other currencies, as expressed by its par exchange rate. Moreover, the clearing of claims for exports and counter claims for imports among countries gives rise to a foreign exchange market, where exchange rates tended to fluctuate about the par rate and within limits initially determined by the shipping cost of gold. As a country's currency tended to increase in value in relation to its par value, its exchange rate tended to move toward the country's gold import points and the country received gold. Conversely, as a country's currency tended to decrease in value in relation to its par value, its exchange rate tended to move toward the country's gold export points and the country lost gold. In the first instance, the increase in the country's gold stock contributed to an upward pressure on the country's general price level, and, in the second, it contributed to a downward pressure.

The relationships between the general price levels of the various countries affected the trade position of the various countries. The less favorable price changes in some countries relative to those in others tended to curb exports and stimulate imports. The notion of favorable price changes in such a context simply reflected the preference for gold and a trade position whereby exports exeeded imports. On the basis of this preference, the international gold standard placed a premium or having an economically efficient productive setup, and it served as a regulator of excessive price changes in the various domestic markets.

Gold flows under the international gold standard, furthermore, exerted an effect on prices through the banking system in those instances where the extension of credit and money exceeded the change in output. An inflow of gold contributed to an expansion of bank credit and the money supply, and an outflow contributed to a contraction. The latter process placed a premium on having self-liquidating loans. There was the view, as embodied in the so-called real bills doctrine, that banks should confine a large portion of their lending to short-term, self-liquidating commercial paper. The more doctrinaire of the real bills advocates, however, did not believe that changes in the money supply would affect prices as long as the doctrine was rigidly adhered to in practice.

With respect to the emphasis under the real bills doctrine on bank liquidity, there were complications. Given time, short-term, commercial loans could be allowed to mature as loans were run off, but all of the banks in a financial center could not contract loans at once without depressing the value of much of the collateral behind the loans. As we shall see later, this business of maintaining adequate liquidity was to relate to two types of problems prior to 1933. One of these pertains to the illiquidity of loans based on securities traded in the stock market, and the other pertains to the illiquidity of banks after the establishment of the Federal Reserve System as a result of the failure of banks to adhere to the practice of maintaining a large portion of short-term, self-liquidating commercial paper.

The gold standard was not the only standard operating over the period of United States history, but it was the predominant one. Others have included the bimetallic and gold exchange standards. All were ways of attempting to economize a given stock of gold. Bimetallism was simply an unsuccessful attempt to place silver on an equal footing with gold as a monetary base. The gold exchange standard, on the other hand, was somewhat of a different matter.

The gold exchange-type of standard differs from the gold standard proper, mainly in that gold convertible claims against a key currency country may serve as the monetary base of other countries. From the point of view of individual countries, it was the type of standard prevailing in most countries in the 1920's, and it is the standard that has come to prevail in most Western countries since World War II. There are complications with respect to the operation of present-day gold exchange standards and the contemporary role of gold. These remain to be dealt with later.

References

1. See R. G. Hawtrey, *The Gold Standard in Theory and Practice* (New York: Longmans, Green and Co., 1927), pp. 65-91.

2. For a memorandum on the pros and cons of a system of fluctuating exchange rates as contrasted with an international payment system based on fixed exchange rates, see "A System of Fluctuating Exchange Rates: Pro and Con," *State of the Economy and Policies for Full Employment* (Washington, D.C.: U.S. Government Printing Office, 1962), pp. 648-661. See also George N. Halm, "Fixed or Flexible Exchange Rates?" *Factors Affecting the United States Balance of Payments* (Washington, D.C.: U.S. Government Printing Office, 1962), pp. 255-266; H. S. Houthakker, "Exchange Rate Adjustment," *Factors Affecting the United States Balance of Payments* (Washington, D.C.: U.S. Government Printing Office, 1962), pp. 292-293; and Egon Sohmen, *International Monetary Problems and the Foreign Exchanges,* Special Papers in Internal Economics, No. 4 (Princeton University: International Finance Section, Department of Economics, 1963).

Two other economists (see Milton Friedman and Anna Jacobson Schwartz, *A Monetary History of the United States, 1867-1960* [Princeton, N.J.: Princeton University Press for the National Bureau of Economic Research, 1963], Chap. 2) have viewed the United States as having a system of flexible exchange rates over the period from the Civil War until the return to the gold standard in the United States in 1879 (Sect. 6.1).

3. For a classical statement of price behavior under the gold standard, see John Stuart Mill, *Principles of Political Economy* (New York: Longmans, Green and Company, 1929), pp. 620-721. See also Jacob Viner, *Studies in the Theory of International Trade* (New York: Harper and Brothers, 1937), pp. 319-320.

4. For example, see James W. Bell and Walter E. Spahr (eds.), *A Proper Monetary and Banking System for the United States* (New York: Ronald Press, 1960). This volume was commissioned by the Economists National Committee on Monetary Policy, an organization of gold standard fundamentalists.

5. See John Maynard Keynes, *A Tract on Monetary Reform* (London: The Macmillan Company, Ltd., 1923), p. 165. Compare also the earlier discussion (Sect. 2.1) of the transaction demand for cash.

6. See Karl Polanyi, *The Great Transformation* (New York: Rinehart and Company, Inc., 1944).

For a collection of essays that relates gold to the foundations of Western civilization, at least in the nineteenth century, see Charles Rist, *The Triumph of Gold* (trans. by Philip Cortney) (New York: Philosophical Library, 1961).

part three

Money, Banking, and Financial Markets: A Historical Survey

7

Money and Banking in the United States through the Early 1930's

> Money *per se* was giving way to promises to pay money, most
> of which were never performed, in a primitive sense, but were can-
> celled by bookkeepers in the increasingly frequent offset of liabili-
> ties; and specie was dissolving into obligations to pay specie in a
> volume greatly exceeding the total that existed. These devices
> yielded fortunes and so had validity, but they were unsettling to
> society as were in their way the Newtonian physics, the senti-
> ments of the French Revolution, romanticism, or machinery driven
> by steam (Bray Hammond, *Banks and Politics in America, from the
> Revolution to the Civil War* [1957]).

The history of money and banks in the United States prior to 1933
readily falls into three distinct phases: (1) the American Revolution to
the Civil War (Sect. 7.1, 7.2, and 7.3), (2) the National Banking Act of
1863 to the Federal Reserve Act of 1913 (Sect. 7.4), and (3) the Federal
Reserve Act of 1913 to the Banking Act of 1933 (Sect. 7.5).

The first of these we identify with uncertainty over the legal responsibility for providing a currency, with only temporary successes in establishing some control over a multiplicity of note issues, with regional
differences in the practices of granting bank charters, and with regional
differences in the quality of the various note issues and the soundness
of banks. In this phase, and in the other two to come, the term "currency" was most often used to refer to the money supply generally and
not just the note issue and other money entering into hand-to-hand circulation. Historical works, other than the most very modern, and official
documents, as well, use the term in this sense. In part, it was a misuse of
the term, and, in some instances, it simply reflected an unawareness of

the role of bank deposits as a part of the money supply. Deposit liabilities, however, do not become a significant portion of the money supply until after the Civil War.

The second phase we identify with several national achievements and a mechanical flaw in the system. Among the achievements was a system of nationally chartered and supervised banks. There was, too, the ultimate achievement of a "sound currency" by which we mean a nationally acceptable note issue that was fully convertible at par into gold and other forms of reserves. The demand deposits of solvent banks became, as well, fully convertible at par into currency and other forms of hand-to-hand money. Along with these achievements, however, the several decades before the 1913 act have also been identified with a monetary system that precipitates crises and related problems because of its mechanical failure to defend against the effects of a seasonal "currency drain" (Sect. 3.3) on the level of monetary reserves. (The term "inelastic currency" has been used in various works and documents with reference to this latter phenomenon but, as we show, it has also been used as having a possibly less valid meaning.)

The third phase we identify with success in providing for a defense against the effects of seasonal shifts in the demand for currency. We identify it, further, with the inability of the then prevailing system to cope with economic stability more generally viewed, either because of a failure of "will" or of "power." Major developments of the period involved the stock market crash of 1929 and its aftermath. These are related to efforts to re-establish the international gold standard in the 1920's, an alleged struggle for power between New York and Washington officials to control the money and banking system, and the expansion of stock market credit.

7.1. Money and Banks Prior to 1863: An Over-All View

Modern banking does not begin in America until the Revolution. The Bank of Pennsylvania was established in 1780 by Robert Morris and a group of associates in order to afford credit facilities to the embarrassed Continental Congress. It continued operations until the latter part of 1781 and was fully liquidated in 1784. Morris described the institution as "nothing more than a patriotic subscription of continental money for the purpose of purchasing provisions for a starving army."[1] The subscribers were to execute bonds in the amount of their subscription to the stock of the bank. Upon the basis of this artificial capital structure the bank issued currency notes—called continentals, from which comes the expression "It ain't worth a continental." These currency notes could hardly be described as fulfilling the functions of money (Sect. 2.2). They circulated at considerable discount in terms of their relationship to the unit of account; the government was creditless. In the end, the supplying of the army depended upon the patriotic schemes of merchants and other men of substance. Consequently, in 1781, the Congress of the Confederation approved a plan for a new bank proposed by Robert Morris. With a capital to be paid in gold and silver, the bank was to issue notes acceptable by the government for the payment of duties and taxes; the Superintendent of Finances was to receive a daily statement of the bank's condition. On the last day of the year such a bank, the Bank of North America to be located in Philadelphia, was chartered by Congress. It was the "first real bank, in the modern sense on the North American continent." [2]

The doubt about the charter, characteristic of the ineffectiveness of the Confederation, clouded the act establishing the bank. The bank was submitted to charges of usury, favoritism, and interference with the state's prerogative of monetary issue. Controversy over the repeal of the bank's charter ensued. Fearful of losing its charter, the bank secured another from the state of Pennsylvania. Soon the government's shares in the bank were sold, and it became absorbed in private business: "Its directors wanted to make money. . . ." [3] By 1790, four such banks were in operation, or soon to be, in Philadelphia, New York, Boston, and Baltimore, respectively. The first of these, the Bank of North America, continued in business until 1929 when a younger competitor absorbed it. The Bank of New York, now the oldest in America, has been in business since 1784. The Massachusetts Bank took a national charter in 1865 and was absorbed by the First National Bank of Boston in 1903. The fourth, the Bank of Maryland, failed in 1834.

The rules and practices governing these first banks in North America constituted orthodoxy. Their founders were merchants, and the institutions were designed to render service to them. One may say they conformed to the real bills doctrine (Sect. 6.3). The loans, primarily short-term ones for the financing of actual sales of commodities, characteristically were extended to the local merchant directly so that he could pay drafts drawn on him rather than have the bank buy the draft. [4]

In the period of banking before the National Banking Act of 1863, the function of issuing currency notes was basic to banking. These notes would be issued by the respective institutions against a fractional amount of specie reserves (namely, gold coin before the issuance of a national currency). The notes outstanding appeared as bank liabilities in the same manner as the demand deposits (Sect. 3.1). The privilege to engage in this practice was a profitable one, and the early charters were extended by the states, generally in return for some other service needed by the community. [5] For example, in 1799 Aaron Burr obtained a corporate charter under which he started the Bank of the Manhattan Company by pledging at the same time to provide a needed water works for New

York City. The Manhattan merged with the Chase National Bank in 1955 and is now known as the Chase Manhattan Bank, with modern quarters in downtown Manhattan. It operated under the original charter given to Burr through the mid-1960's; the water works was short-lived.

The number of banking institutions grew more rapidly after 1800. At that date there were twenty-nine banks in business. They were mostly located in the North and as far south along the Atlantic seaboard as Charleston. Generally, they were most serviceable when they conducted their banking on sound commercial principles. Many of the institutions which sprang up as the country grew, particularly in the West and South, were not inaccurately described as "wildcat banking." The first failure, however, occurred in New England in 1809 and involved the Farmers Exchange of Glocester, Rhode Island.[6]

There are additional features which distinguished the beginning of banking in America. In Britain, for example, banking began with the goldsmiths who had a supply of gold for the expansion of loans. In America, it began because of a dearth of specie which circulated as money; needs were great, means were few. Individuals had to pool their scanty funds from which to further expand loans and, consequently, the supply of money. In Britain, partnerships and proprietorships characterized the business organization of banks. In America, banking started with governmental sanction and the corporate form of organization. This reflected the absence of large aggregates of closely held wealth with which to begin banking.

A perennial and pervasive need of the economic system of this early period, and to a large extent the subsequent period, could be viewed as one of establishing a currency (other than specie) and a system of demand deposits which would serve the functions of money to a high degree. In the early years attempts were made to satisfy the need by economizing specie through the use of a system of fractional reserves. To achieve the end, notes (or credit) of banks had to be created in just the right quantity and the bank assets had to be of just the right quality. As long as the notes issued on the basis of the specie reserve were freely substitutable for specie itself, they achieved the same status of money as the specie. When the notes were overissued or uncertainty as to their redemption existed, the notes would go to a discount. There would be, in a sense, a strengthening of the speculative motive for holding specie. Having to put the notes to a discount was frustrating to both banks and other business enterprises. It embarrassed the former and deprived the latter of needed credit. The notes would sometimes be gathered up at the low price and presented for payment at their initial value in specie. The effect would be a withdrawal of reserves to be hauled away. The supply of loans and circulating media would contract. Today, when the solution to the problem is no longer one of economizing specie or avoiding the consequences of strengthening the speculative and transactions demands for specie, it may nevertheless be said to consist, partly, of maintaining the money quality of currency and demand deposits and of effectively dealing with changes in the demand for money.

7.2. The Role of the Federal Government and Related Events

The institutions of the period with which the Federal government was associated included the Bank of the United States and the Independent Treasury System. The Bank of the United States operated under two distinct charters, the first running from 1791 to 1811 and the second from 1816 to 1836. The failure to extend the first charter was related to the suspension of specie payments in 1814, and the failure to extend the second was related to the panic of 1837, as was the specie circular of 1836. The operations of the Independent Treasury System, too, had their effect on events of the period, and there were other monetary events of less note in which the government had a hand.

The Constitution: Article I, Sec. 8. Related to the events of the period was the controversial subject of the constitutionality of banking. To complicate matters, there is nothing in the Constitution about banks and banking per se, but the banking powers of the Federal government have come to be covered by the monetary clauses of the Constitution. One is in the form of an authorization (Article I, Sec. 8), and four are in the form of prohibitions (Article I, Sec. 10). The authorization clause says: "The Congress shall have the power . . . to coin money, regulate the value thereof, and of foreign coin, . . ." The outstanding discourse on the monetary interpretation of this clause of the Constitution was first given by John C. Calhoun, Chairman of the Senate Finance Committee.[7] Speaking before Congress in February 1816, he emphasized that the power to regulate the currency of the United States was given to the Congress, but that the currency of the period was beyond the control of Congress under the arrangements of that time. He noticed that the authorization clause of the Constitution implied that Congress should have control over the steadiness and fixed value of the currency.

Over the years, judicial authority has had a tendency to interpret this authorization clause of the Constitution in its broader construction,[8] such as that given by Calhoun, and in this way the Federal government has assumed the business of printing money and viewing price level stability as a means of regulating its value. In the period before the Civil War, nevertheless, no decision on a case before the higher court was rendered on the grounds of the monetary clauses of the Constitution. On the one occasion when the constitutionality of banking was an issue before the Supreme Court, the decision was a more sweeping one of Federal power rather than of banking per se. It was at the time when the constitutionality of the Second Bank of the United States was being threatened in the case of *McCulloch* v. *Maryland*. The Supreme Court's unanimous opinion was in favor of McCulloch, a cashier in a branch of the Second Bank, and the opinion went beyond the status of the bank itself. It had "far greater significance for the development of federal powers in general than with the development of federal powers with respect to money and banking." [9]

The First Bank of the United States (1791-1811). Under the bill calling for a national bank, the First Bank of the United States received a charter that was to run for twenty years. The government reserved subscription to a proportion of the stock, and the remaining three-quarters was open to public subscription, one-fourth to be paid in specie, and three-fourths in government securities bearing 6 per cent interest. The capital was secured without difficulty. The bank opened at Philadelphia,[10] preceding the establishment of branches in Boston, New York, Baltimore, Washington, Norfolk, Charleston, Savannah, and New Orleans. The note issue of the bank was limited to the 10 million dollars of capital stock provided for by the charter, and they were receivable for all payments to the United States.

The lending operations of the bank were extensive; its operations were profitable.[11] The bank acted as fiscal agent and as a source of loans for the government, and its branches facilitated the transfer of government balances. Its loans, other than those to the government, were largely limited to commercial paper, customarily for sixty days, and its principal customers were the merchants, manufacturers, and, occasionally, wealthy landowners.

The bank provided many services. The note issue had wide acceptability. Through its branches it acted somewhat as a national clearing system for the notes of state banks. Moreover, by maintaining a general creditor position with the state banks, the bank was able to help check overexpansion by threatening to call for the payment of balances in specie.

The success of the bank foretold its downfall. Two features of the bank already referred to contributed to this, in combination with political factors:[12] (1) the successful commercial business of the bank, which attracted criticism from the numerous state banks established since 1790, and (2) the bank's method of control over the quality of bank notes. It was said, for instance, that by holding the notes of state banks for redemption in specie the state banks were kept in bondage to the Federal bank.

When the bank's charter expired in 1811 its life ended—the head office was sold, and the various branches were either liquidated or became local banks.

The suspension of specie payments in 1814. The refusal of Congress to recharter the Bank of the United States in 1811, in combination with the War of 1812, led to a suspension of specie payments in 1814. The Bank of the United States had followed a conservative policy, and, in the absence of its restraint, the general outlook for bank profits as well as the outlook associated with having the bank's specie reserve redistributed among state banks led to a rapid expansion of the number of state banks. In fact, the number of state banks increased from eighty-eight in 1811 to 206 in 1816,[13] under the speculative prospects for bank profits.

Moreover, the government, faced with the problem of financing the War of 1812, floated enormous loans. Some banks, consequently, found a tempting field for investment of their note issues in government securities. To make matters worse, the securities were used as the basis for a further expansion of the note issues. Between 1811 and 1816, bank note circulation increased from 28 million to 68 million dollars.

The expansion of the number of state banks and the bank note circulation coincided with a net withdrawal of specie from the country to pay for foreign purchases as well as with runs on the state banks for payment in specie at the time of the British raid on Washington in August 1814. The situation whereby the liabilities of the banks were increasing while the specie in their vaults was drawn down could not continue. The banks in New York and Philadelphia found themselves obliged to suspend specie payments in August 1814; the suspension became general, except in New England.

The suspension of specie payments was a new thing. The banks, however, remained open and otherwise transacted business as usual. Having suspended the payments, the banks were left free to further increase the note issue. Along with the general suspension and the uncertain outlook for resumption, the notes lost some of their quality of money; they went to a discount.[14]

The Second Bank of the United States (1816-1836). The condition of the currency notes and the finances of the government were in a sad state following specie suspension and the War of 1812. Many who had originally argued against the bank finally came to support it. Consequently, a bill providing for the Second Bank of the United States was passed and subsequently approved by President Madison on April 10, 1816.

Like its predecessor, the note issue by the bank was limited to the total capital, which in this instance was 35 million dollars. Its notes were receivable in all payments to the United States, and both notes and deposits were redeemable in specie, under a penalty of 12 per cent per annum in case of failure. Its relationship to the government was twofold: once again a proportion of the bank's capital was reserved for subscription by the government, and the remaining four-fifths was open to public subscription, part of which could be subscribed in the funded debt in the United States; and once again government deposits were to be made with the bank, while the bank was to transfer its funds without charge. Also, in keeping with the proportions of capital held by the respective subscribers, provision was made whereby five directors were appointed by the President and twenty by the stockholders residing in the United States. Branches were to be established wherever the directors thought desirable.

The Second Bank began operations in 1816 with a twenty-year charter. Its central office opened in Philadelphia, and by the end of 1817 there were eighteen branches in operation. The first year of operation was highly unsuccessful. But, after a few problems, including those concerning the case of *McCulloch* v. *Maryland* * and two changes in management, the bank came under its third president, Nicholas Biddle, to provide a currency that was more nearly uniform and sound than that of any period for years to come.

A member of a prominent Philadelphia family, Nicholas Biddle became president in 1823 at the age of 37 with a superfluity of social and economic advantage. He is interestingly described as having what experience alone could never give, lacking what it could give, and having "the untempered intellectual's preference for what ought to be. . . ." [15] But he has also been viewed as a pioneer in central banking since he directed the Second Bank's operations so as to achieve objectives similar to some of those of the present-day Federal Reserve System.[16]

The methods employed in exercising the bank's influence over credit and the quality of bank notes, however, were different from those possessed by present-day central banks. In the United States today, the central bank exerts its influence on commercial banks indirectly. Also it holds the reserves of commercial banks as a liability, and this practice contrasts with the earlier practice of holding note issues of commercial banks as assets. The Bank of the United States, at the earlier date, exerted its influence on state banks by constantly maintaining a creditor

---

* For a discussion of the case, see Bray Hammond, *Banks and Politics in America, from the Revolution to the Civil War* (Princeton, N.J.: Princeton University Press, 1957), pp. 264-266.

The bank's position in this case was ironical. While the government's plea was being made in the court in the name of James W. McCulloch, he and two of his colleagues were helping themselves to the bank's funds. One week after the Supreme Court's decision, it was disclosed that the bank's cashier was "an embezzler beyond the dreams of most contemporaries' avarice" (Hammond, *op. cit.*, p. 266).

position in relation to them, i.e., by holding as assets the note issue of the state banks. In this respect, the Second Bank was in a position to demand specie payment from a doubtful institution and thereby threaten its solvency if that institution failed to promptly redeem its notes.

There are also other features distinguishing the earlier and more contemporary institutions. One of these is the absence of direct competition between commercial banks and the present-day central bank. The Second Bank achieved much of its effect on credit ease or tightness through direct competition with state banks. Still another difference was the Second Bank's authority to certify whether a state institution's notes were redeemable in specie. Under the earlier law a state bank's notes were acceptable for the payment of government debts if its notes were redeemable in specie. Because the failure to certify the acceptability of a bank's notes was a serious blow to the prestige of a bank, this authority could be used somewhat as an implied threat to induce doubtful institutions to pursue sound policies.

In the period 1826-1832 the Second Bank was a conservative influence in the economy. Its notes became acceptable from Montreal to Mexico City, and the bank's accomplishments included the practical elimination of discounts on state bank notes. There were, nevertheless, objections, which concerned the conservative influence of the bank, the bank's potential power, its methods of exercising control, and the political conflicts of the time[17]

Whereas Biddle had managed the bank with skill and intelligence, he was no match for the popular hero, Andrew Jackson, in his efforts to save the bank. In Jackson's first administration (1829-1832), the bank was able to continue successful operations. Near the close of that administration, however, bitter conflict evolved. Biddle made the following frank statement to a Senate Committee in 1832: "There are few banks which might not have been destroyed by an exertion of the power of the bank. None have ever been injured. Many have been saved." [18] Following this, a bill rechartering the bank was vetoed by President Jackson. Although Jackson did not object to a central bank entirely,[19] he did object to this one.[20]

The popular verdict, in the Presidential election of 1832, left no doubt concerning the bank's charter, for it expired four years later, although the bank continued to operate under a Pennsylvania charter for several years. In the meantime, arrangements had to be made for the bank's expiration under its Federal charter. The government's funds were transferred to state banks, which were referred to as "Jackson's pets." The consequences were disturbing. These transfers in combination with the specie circular of 1836 brought about the suspension of specie payment in 1837.

The suspension of specie payments in 1837. Following the failure to

recharter the bank under a Federal charter and the announcement of
the plans to transfer government funds to state banks, the number of
state banks as well as the supply of note issues increased rapidly.[21] The
years were marked by an expansion in business activity and land speculation in the West. These excesses, then, in combination with several
other factors, brought the suspension of specie payments in 1837. One
of these other factors was the specie circular of 1836, an order stating
that agents for the sale of public lands should take only specie in payments. Another was accrual of surplus balances to the Treasury at a time
when it was unlawful for any bank to hold public funds in excess of
three-fourths of its capital.

The practice requiring that public lands be purchased in specie, and
the necessity of transferring balances in the form of specie from those
banks with excesses, had the effect of drawing millions of dollars from
reserves. To bring the adjustment required a contraction of loans in
some sections. As Dewey has said, "Millions upon millions of dollars
went on their travels North and South, East and West, being mere freight
for the time being, while the business from which the money was withdrawn gasped for breath in its struggle with a fearfully stringent money
market."

Developments on both the domestic and foreign sides combined to
place an excessive demand upon the market for liquid funds. The specie
reserves were inadequate to meet both the demands of the government
and of those presenting note issues for redemption. There was a general suspension of specie payments, notes went to a discount, and so on.

The Independent Treasury System. The maintenance of deposits with
the state banks was not altogether satisfactory. Thus to provide the
Treasury with facilities previously provided by the Second Bank of
the United States and to make the Treasury independent of state banks
and their unsatisfactory note issues, Congress adopted a sub-Treasury
act in 1840. It called for a number of independent treasuries throughout
the country in which government funds should be kept. Since payments
to the government were to be made in the form of specie or the government's own obligations, and since the Treasury accumulated surplus at
times, the sub-Treasury arrangement was such as to exercise, at times,
a contractionary or unstabilizing influence on bank reserves, bank notes,
and so on.

One writer describes the operations of the Independent Treasury
System and its effects on the availability of credit as follows: "The collection and disbursement of the Government funds alternately with-
drew funds from the banks and then restored them to banks; and the
fluctuations thus produced in the volume of bank funds caused fluctuations in the lending power of banks without reference to the credit
needs of agriculture, commerce and industry." [22]

The Independent Treasury System was discontinued in 1841, reestablished in 1846, and finally abolished in 1920. At that time the banks chartered under the Federal Reserve Act of 1913 became the principal fiscal agents of the Treasury.

7.3. Developments in the State and Private Sectors Prior to 1863

A number of significant developments with respect to money and banks took place in the period prior to the National Banking Act of 1863 that were independent of direct Federal authority and initiative. These pertained to the Suffolk System, the safety fund, the New York Free Banking Act of 1838, and the Louisiana Banking Act of 1842; some of the developments had a lasting influence. Also, private banks developed correspondent relationships with each other, and the financial markets evolved to complicate the arrangement of correspondent relationships between banks and the interdependence of banks and the economy. An outline of those features contributing to such crises as the panic of 1857 serves to illustrate, in particular, the interdependence between the money, banking, and financial market sectors that evolved in the later years prior to 1863.

The Suffolk System. The redemption of the bank notes of the country banks for specie became a problem as the geographical area in which the circulation of notes expanded. It was in reaction to such a problem that the Suffolk Bank of Boston provided the leadership for the establishment of an association of Boston banks for the redemption of country bank notes in 1824.

Under this association the various banks agreed to deposit a large sum, free, in the Suffolk Bank, and that bank undertook to be the clearinghouse for country bank notes. The large city banks stood ready at all times to redeem their bank notes, and the Suffolk Bank also offered to hold the deposits of country banks for the purpose of redeeming their bank notes. Those banks that failed to comply by redeeming their note issues regularly ran the risk of having the Suffolk Bank accumulate their note issue and present a large amount for redemption in specie at one time, no doubt to the distress of the country banks.

The Suffolk Bank, a state-chartered bank, was in operation until 1858. The plan for redeeming note issues implemented by it provided New England with notes that uniformly circulated at par and were held in good repute.

The safety fund. In 1829 New York adopted the Safety Fund Act. The act required that each bank pay 3 per cent of its capital stock to the Treasurer of the state, and the fund was used to redeem notes of any banks that failed, as well as to pay the other debts of insolvent banks. In addition, the act imposed certain limits: it restricted the issue of bank notes to twice a bank's paid-up capital, loans and discounts were not to exceed two and one-half times paid-up capital, and postdated notes were prohibited.

The fund existed for about forty years. The scope of its influence diminished, however, in response to the decline in the relative importance of the note issues of private banks (Sect. 7.4). Still, the idea behind the safety fund was the one revised a century later in the form of Federal deposit insurance (Sect. 12.6).[23]

The New York Free Banking Act. The New York Free Banking Act of 1838 opened the business of banking to anyone meeting the requirements of the act. At the same time, the act removed the chartering of banks from the legislature. Enterprise in banking became freer, and monopoly privilege diminished.

The act was also a landmark in the evolution of the currency system as a result of two important provisions pertaining to the issuance of notes. The first of these provisions provided for the issuance of notes by the state comptroller's office in return for depositing with the comptroller an equivalent amount of collateral. The notes carried the individual bank's name, but the requirement of an equivalent amount of collateral broadened the basis for a further expansion of notes and provided some security to the noteholders in the case of a bank failure. The collateral was to be equivalent to the full amount of the note issue and could consist of bonds of the United States and bonds of the state of New York and of certain other states, as well as such mortgages as were requested by the representatives of the agricultural districts. The second important feature of the act provided that every bank hold a specie reserve equivalent to $12\frac{1}{2}$ per cent of its note issue.

The first of the latter features set the precedent for the issuance of greenbacks secured by government securities under the national banking system (Sect. 7.4). The other feature, though repealed after several years, is similar in some respects to the gold certificate reserves required of the present-day Federal Reserve System (Sect. 10.2).

The note issue provided under the Free Banking Act contributed to the wide acceptance of the notes of New York banks in neighboring states. The widespread acceptance of the notes was also affected by the establishment in 1851 of a central system among New York City banks for the redemption of notes of other banks at par, and by the establishment in 1853 of a clearinghouse for the daily redemption of notes.

The Louisiana banking system. The Louisiana banking system provides another example of a sound currency and banking system. The state passed a banking act in 1842 that set forth, among others, the following requirements: (1) a minimum reserve in specie equal to one-third of total notes and deposits and (2) the backing of the remaining proportion of notes and deposits by commercial paper with a maturity date of ninety days or less.

The law is especially significant for the first requirement listed above. It was the first time a statute had specified a required reserve ratio of reserves to both deposits and notes.[24] This law, along with the abundance of short-term commercial paper and the rising favorable trading position at New Orleans, enabled the Louisiana banks to weather the panic of 1857 without suspending specie payments. The amount of specie held by Louisiana banks increased, until by 1860 their holdings were second only to those of the New York banks.

Correspondent banking. Correspondent banking (Sect. 3.2) within the domestic economy may be said to consist of a series of relationships between banks, whereby the large ones generally render services for the smaller ones in return for balances left on deposit. Such services have from time to time taken several forms: extending lines of credit upon which the smaller banks could draw or borrow from the city correspondents, facilitating foreign exchange transactions (Sect. 6.2), providing a liquid outlet for balances or excess reserves that the country bank may choose to leave on deposit in the city, and, in the period before the Civil War, redeeming a country bank's note issue. In addition to this list of services, however, the city banks paid interest on the reserve funds deposited with them, until the payment of interest on demand deposits was forbidden by law in 1933. Both state and, later, national banks (Sect. 7.4) outside of certain large cities were permitted to count balances on deposit with city correspondents as a proportion of their legal reserves.

This type of relationship between banks began with the development of banking and the means of communication in the period prior to 1863. As the financial markets developed, moreover, the correspondent arrangement became of greater importance. The New York market, in particular, provided a ready use of funds, and the balances began to accumulate very early in that city. Balances were accepted in New York at more favorable exchange rates, and these simply served to stimulate further the flow of bank balances to the city. The availability of balances, in turn, stimulated the development of the call-loan market,*

---

* The call-loan market is a market for loans payable on demand that are secured by stocks or bonds. The development of the market, however, depended on the availability of idle banker's balances that could be loaned to those wishing to temporarily finance the purchase of securities for others (as in the case of a broker), or to those wishing to trade in the securities market on their own account. The call loan is important in the study of money and banking because of the link it provides between the credit, money, and capital markets. In a sense, it was an indirect way of utilizing banker's balances in the development of a capital market. Indeed, it brought a new technique for financing the purchases of securities and carrying the burden of marginal sales of stock. Such loans were often obtainable at low rates and were, therefore, features attractive to speculators engaged in the purchase of stocks on margin.

which went hand in hand with the development of other financial markets.

Financial markets. The financial markets include the entire range of the credit, money, and capital markets. The credit market is the national market for bank credit (Chap. 3). The money market is the market for short-term liquid assets consisting of United States government securities, call loans, and other near-money assets (Sect. 4.1), such as commercial paper.* The capital market is that for longer-term funds and includes the market for new issues of stocks and bonds and trading in these securities once they have reached the market.

The activities of Wall Street were sufficient to produce specialists in stock trading as early as 1792. The New York capital market, however, was intimately related to the growth of the money market and the growth of the market for railroad and industrial shares.

The institutional developments and the mechanics of a crisis. As New York grew as a financial center and as correspondent banking developed, the institutional requirements on the domestic side were met for the typical monetary crisis of the years from about 1857-1907. The requirements on the international side were present even earlier and pertained to the automatic mechanism (Sect. 6.3), whereby imbalances in trade were settled in large part by gold flows.

The typical crisis depended on two facts and a sequence of developments, usually occurring in the fall of the year. The two facts were (1) that bank reserves consisted mostly of specie and (2) that the stock of specie could be varied on a large scale only by extreme changes concerning the gold flows mechanism (Sect. 6.3). Given these facts, the sequence of developments was as follows:

(1) In the fall of the year there would be an increase in the demand

---

* The two principal forms of commercial or business paper upon which banks made advances were the banker's acceptance and the promissory note. The acceptance, or draft, or bill of domestic exchange, as it was variously termed, was the standard instrument of trade credit in England and on the Continent. A banker's acceptance is a draft, often drawn by a seller of goods on a bank under a letter of credit issued by the bank at the instance of the buyer. When the bank "accepts" the draft, it becomes primarily liable for the instrument, in effect substituting its own credit for that of the buyer. In the United States, the acceptance generally originated in foreign trade transactions. A seller of cotton, for example, would draw a draft payable in ninety days covering a shipment to Liverpool. The buyer would have an arrangement with a bank in New York whereby the bank would accept the seller's draft on presentation and the buyer would provide funds to pay the acceptance at maturity. These instruments could readily be sold in the market by the seller of the goods who originally drew up the draft. They have usually been based on goods in the process of shipment and represented by the shipping documents. A promissory note, on the other hand, is based on the personal security of the maker. It has occupied a more prominent place in the United States, whereas the banker's acceptance has been the traditional instrument of trade credit in England.

for bank credit and currency (including specie), especially on the part of farmers needing to harvest their crops.

(2) The latter increase in the proportion of money consisting of specie would, in itself, bring about a cash drain (Sect. 3.3) and a contraction of reserves. The country banks would, as well, meet the needs of agriculture by withdrawing specie from their city correspondents.

(3) The latter withdrawal of specie from the city correspondents would force a contraction in the credit of city banks. This credit would be, in large part, in the form of call loans.

(4) The contraction in call loans would force the sale of securities and, therefore, precipitate a decline in the value of the collateral behind the call loans.

(5) The impact was bound to be uneven, considering the number of banks and their location, but the additional effects were to force some banks into the suspension of specie payments and to further intensify the demand for specie vis-à-vis deposits.

The above pattern of developments could place a strain on the banks and securities markets, but, at times, the strain could be compounded by an outflow of gold (Sect. 6.3). At such times, the unusual strain on city bank reserves and the contraction of call loans could result in the default on loans and an even more widespread suspension. The result would be a crisis or a "panic," as it was then called. The panic of 1857 was the result of such machinations, as were others to come on subsequent occasions until 1907.[25]

7.4. The National Banking System, Currency Controversies, and Crises, 1863-1913

An 1863 law, re-enacted in 1864 and entitled the National Banking Act, provided for several things, in very general terms: a system of nationally chartered banks, a national currency, and effective restrictions on insolvent banks with national charters. The system brought about by the legislation finally achieved a sound currency, in the sense that federally issued notes became generally convertible into other forms of currency in "hand-to-hand" circulation. In the period, as we shall see, currency in hand-to-hand circulation comes to consist "mainly of national bank notes, specie, U.S. notes, and silver certificates," and "these same items served also as till money for banks and as ultimate reserves against deposit liabilities. . . ."[26] The system, on the other hand, did not provide an elastic currency (Sect. 7.5)[27] as that term came to be used in its most valid sense—at least, in reference to the inadequacies of the monetary system of the pre-1913 period. In that most valid sense, "inelastic" referred to the inability of the system to meet a seasonal "cash drain" (Sect. 3.3). For example, as the demand for money increased and as the proportion of money in the form of currency vis-à-vis deposits increased in the fall of the year [i.e., an increase in the parameter c in the earlier context (Sect. 3.3)], the mechanics of the system called forth a contraction in the total money stock for the short run and prior to the import of specie from abroad.

An important difference under the act, apart from a sound note issue and sound banks, was that insolvent banks were more inclined to failure. Banks that could remain open in the past and simply suspend specie payments were, under the act, required to maintain reserves and the convertibility of the note issue.

Monetary crises recur over the decades following the Civil War, paralleling, at times, intense national controversies over the adequacy of the stock of money. The intensity of the currency controversies, as the latter controversies were called, waned after the national election of 1896. However, the last of the major monetary crises of the period—that of 1907—resulted in the establishment of a national monetary commission and soon thereafter in the Federal Reserve Act (Sect. 7.5). The act was to provide an "elastic currency," among other things.

A national currency and a system of national banks. The harsh necessities brought about by the Civil War required that the government and the economy partially reunite. To begin with, the Federal government resorted early in the war to two issues of paper currency, called greenbacks or United States notes. The Confederate successes, the failure of the Secretary of the Treasury to adopt a firm policy in support of taxation, the slow sale of government bonds, the withdrawal of gold from New York banks by depositors, and another instance of the suspension of specie payment as late as December 1861 led Congress, in February 1862, to provide for another issue of greenbacks and finally another.[28] Thus the weakened and embarrassed financial condition of the Treasury, in combination with the unsatisfactory note issues of state banks, gave Congress two motives for establishing a system of nationally chartered banks: (1) replace state banks with nationally chartered banks that would issue a sound and uniform currency and (2) provide a market for government bonds with which to finance the war.

The various provisions of the National Banking Act were taken from the New York Free Banking Act of 1838 (Sect. 7.3), the Louisiana Banking Act (Sect. 7.3), and the acts and practices of other states. Some of its principal features are as follows:

(1) The act provided for a separate bureau of the Treasury Department, (the Office of the Comptroller of the Currency) and the Comp-

troller was given the general power of supervision over the national banking system. To assure compliance with the act, all national banks were required to furnish statements of their financial condition, they were subject to examination by national bank examiners, and the Comptroller had certain powers of receivership in the case of failing or delinquent banks.

(2) It established criteria for the granting of bank charters and the issuance of notes. In the latter instance, the act prescribed that banks could obtain national bank notes against a required subscription of government bonds and by a transfer of government bonds to the Comptroller of the Currency. (This is the way the government helped to sell their bonds.) Also each national bank had to accept the notes of other national banks at par, in order to insure the par circulation of the notes.

(3) The act regulated bank loans in several respects: (a) it forbade banks from lending on their own stock; (b) it forbade the acceptance of loans collateraled by real estate, a provision modified by the Banking Act of 1935 and other legislation; and (c) it limited the loans a bank may extend to any one borrower to 10 per cent of the bank's capital.

(4) The act specified minimum cash reserves, varying according to the location of the banks (and, therefore, to the prevailing system of correspondent banks). These were to insure bank liquidity and limit the expansion of bank money to a given multiple of the reserve requirement. The required reserves were 25 per cent against all deposits for New York City banks as well as for other large city banks, although the latter group could allow deposits with national banks in New York City to count for half their reserves. National banks in smaller cities were required to maintain only 15 per cent against all deposits, and three-fifths of this sum might be deposited with other national banks maintaining reserves of 25 per cent.

(5) The act provided that national banks might be designated as depositories for Treasury funds and as a fiscal agent to the Federal government by the banks themselves providing a satisfactory security. [The Independent Treasury Act (Sect. 7.2) had in effect been suspended early in the war.]

The National Banking Act was not quick to realize one of its purposes: establishing a uniform currency. It had been hoped that state banks would take out Federal charters, but they did not immediately do this. As their position became evident, Congress acted and President Lincoln signed into law a bill providing for a tax of 10 per cent on the circulating notes of state banks. The tax effectively ended the circulation of state bank notes and greatly reduced the number of state banks, since the issuance of notes was quantitatively of more importance in the expansion of credit at the time. Even so, as deposits grew in importance in relationship to notes,* and as other advantages of state charters evolved, state banks again became important, in number at least.

The legislation of the period finally achieved a system of currency notes that circulated at par. The weaknesses of an inelastic currency in the more valid sense of the term, nevertheless, manifested themselves throughout the period in question. The currency in circulation and later the demand deposits did not vary sufficiently with the seasonal needs of agriculture, and so on, since no provision was made to counter the effect of a seasonal cash drain or to provide for the expansion of the reserve base.

Currency controversies. The so-called currency controversies of the period were, in essence, controversies over whether the stock of money should be more or less than the stock actually existing at any time over the period. They took the form, nevertheless, of controversies over currencies. The most prominent controversies were about the issuance of greenbacks[29] and the free and unlimited coinage of silver. The greenbacker's view was that the value of currency depended on its purchasing power which, they held, rested upon nothing but the laws of Congress. They favored the issuance of greenbacks without the resumption of their payment in specie as a means of stimulating improvements in economic conditions. The "hard" money advocates, however, won out in the 1870's in their efforts to resume specie payments for greenbacks. Under a Republican Secretary of the Treasury, John Sherman, greenbacks approached parity with gold, and gold payments were resumed in 1879.

---

* Bank notes outstanding and deposits as percentages of the total of bank notes plus deposits:

	Bank Notes as a per cent of total	Deposits as a per cent of total
1835-1839	0.56	0.44
1840-1844	0.55	0.45
1845-1849	0.54	0.46
1850-1854	0.53	0.47
1855-1859	0.47	0.53
1860-1864	0.39	0.61
1865-1869	0.31	0.69
1870-1874	0.28	0.72
1875-1879	0.25	0.75
1880-1884	0.19	0.81
1885-1889	0.12	0.88

NOTE: The percentages are based on averages of total dollar amounts on June 30 or nearest date.

SOURCE OF AVERAGES: Bray Hammond, "Historical Introduction," *Banking Studies* (Washington, D.C.: Board of Governors of the Federal Reserve System, 1941), p. 417.

The silverites' view was that prosperity depended on the free and unlimited coinage of silver. They pushed for legislation resulting in the Bland-Allison Act of 1878. The act restored the legal tender character of silver (Sect. 6.1) and authorized the Secretary of the Treasury to purchase silver bullion to be coined into dollars within limits set by an upper bound of 4 million dollars per month and a lower bound of 2 million. In addition, there was some provision for the issuance of silver certificates upon the deposit of silver dollars.

Against this background, the Republicans stood "unreservedly for sound money" in the election of 1896, and the Democrats were joined by the greenbackers and silverites in a platform for the free and unlimited coinage of both gold and silver. The issue was clear. William Jennings Bryan, the "boy orator of the Platte," closed the speech which won him the Democratic nomination:[30] "You shall not press down upon the brow of labor this crown of thorns; you shall not crucify mankind upon a cross of gold." The orator was never to be forgotten. He continued to run for President, but Friedman and Schwartz note that his failures were due more to the discoveries of gold "in South Africa and Alaska and the perfection of the cyanide process for extracting gold" than to "any waning in the effectiveness of his oratory or any shortcomings of his political organizations." [31]

The 1907 crisis and the Aldrich Commission. Crises that were typical of the period occurred in 1873, 1884, 1893, and 1907. The latter crisis, however, led to a re-examination of the monetary system and eventually to the Federal Reserve Act (Sect. 7.5).

The 1907 crisis had, among others,[32] the usual features of the crises of the period. These included their relationship to the corresponding banking arrangement, the autumnal demand for funds from the city correspondents, and the contraction of loans by the city banks. The latter, in turn, resulted in higher interest rates and a drop in prices of securities. Thus it was, in 1907, after a rise in share prices following a break in such prices in 1903. The Knickerbocker Trust Company, which had overexpanded its loans, closed in October when the crisis broke. This, followed by runs on several banks, produced a general feeling of uneasiness. The out-of-town banks continued to withdraw deposits, and the interest rate on call loans advanced—in some instances to 70 per cent. The crisis spread throughout the country. In the year 1908 alone, 153 banks failed, the largest number since 1893.

In the disturbing setting of the 1907 crisis and its resulting effects, in particular, Congress established the National Monetary Commission, chaired by Senator Nelson W. Aldrich, to recommend a more effective monetary organization for the nation. After several years of thorough consideration, the study of the commission along with those by other authorities resulted in legislation. This legislation was the Federal Reserve Act (Sect. 7.5).

7.5. Central Banking and Other Matters, 1913-1933

On December 23, 1913, President Woodrow Wilson signed the Federal Reserve Act into law.[33] It was the third attempt in United States history to establish a genuine central bank, the first two attempts relating to the first and second banks of the United States (Sect. 7.2). Classical lines of financial theory were followed, and the resulting central bank continued to operate upon conventional notions[34] for about twenty years. These concerned the quantity theory of money (Sect. 5.2 and 6.3), the gold standard (Sect. 6.1), and the real bills doctrine (Sect. 6.3), all in combination with the political tradition of regional autonomy. There was emphasis, especially, on the achievement of an elastic currency as a means of improving the workings of the monetary system.

With respect to political tradition, the act yielded to the popular, and sometimes justified, American prejudice toward centralized power. In this respect the act provided for the following: private ownership of the banks (as described in later chapters); twelve regional banks, each with a separate board of directors; and a central integrating and governing body—the Federal Reserve Board. The responsibilities of the new banks were largely defensive, and the initiative for policy changes, such as were expected, was given to the regional banks rather than the central governing board. All national banks were required to become members of the system, and other commercial banks were permitted to join. The member banks were required to maintain a prescribed ratio of reserves to demand deposits on deposit with the regional bank in their district. The reserves of the member banks could be increased by credits at the Federal Reserve and decreased by debits. The act also provided for a somewhat altered currency system. Initially, gold continued to circulate, and gold flows continued to have their prescribed effects.

Focusing for the present only on the "original" Federal Reserve Act, the first twenty years of Federal Reserve operations, and some related matters, this section contains four main topics. The first emphasizes the narrow goal of defense against the seasonal variations in the demand for currency and the broader goal of economic stability, all as implied in the original act. It also contains an outline of the means for achieving the goals and the philosophy and mechanics underlying the ends-means relationship. Other subtopics deal with the operations of the Reserve System in the first twenty years. These were, to a large extent, affected by the following: the System's initial role in financing World War I, apparent efforts to facilitate a return to the international gold standard following its abandonment in the war years, and, some would add, a struggle for power between the board and the Federal Reserve Bank of New York. Each of these is discussed below. The efforts to save the gold standard and the struggle for power are shown to involve the System in the stock market crash of the late 1920's. Together the various topics foretell the final topics—"the end of an era" and "epilogue."

The Federal Reserve Act: the first twenty years. Implicitly, the Federal Reserve was to overcome the various forms of mechanical failure, thought to be the root cause of economic instability to which the economy had periodically been subjected, and consequently achieve economic stability. These failures were sometimes seen as a general shortage of currency, sometimes as defaults in the collection of checks, sometimes as sharp regional shifts of currency or deposits, and sometimes as other seasonal, regional, or general manifestations of the inflexibility in the money and credit apparatus. To overcome them, the new legislation required that the Federal Reserve should (1) provide the country with an elastic currency, (2) provide facilities for discounting commercial paper, (3) provide an effective interregional check and currency clearing system, and (4) improve the supervision of banking.

The original Federal Reserve Act set forth the primary responsibilities of the Federal Reserve until the banking acts of 1933 and 1935 (Chap. 8). The check and currency clearing system along with bank supervision, and discount privileges, was to privide the base for a currency that would vary with the shorter-run seasonal needs of trade and with the longer-run and cyclical needs. The facilities for discounting or rediscounting commercial paper were to provide real bills with added liquidity on those occasions when the entire banking system sought to increase reserves by disposing of their liquid assets rather than allowing them to run off at maturity. The entire system was to work automatically, provided the rules of the real bills doctrine (Sect. 6.3) and the gold standard (Sect. 6.1) were adhered to.

As a routine matter the system was to defend against "cash drains" (Sect. 3.3) and provide an "elastic currency" in one sense of that term, as mentioned earlier. More generally, however, the founders of the Federal Reserve System as a group appeared to believe that the amount of currency and reserve bank credit would be just right, if issued against real bills or advances collateraled by government securities. In effect, a bank needing reserves could obtain them by discounting "eligible paper" or by advances collateraled by obligations of the United States. The advance was an outright loan differing somewhat in form from the discounts but not in substance. Eligible paper consisted of commercial paper representing loans of limited maturities to meet the current needs of commerce, industry, or agriculture vis-à-vis loans for investment or speculative purposes. It was thought by the Federal Reserve System's founders that this limitation of the System's lending authority would act as an automatic brake on the over-all expansion of the stock of money. The system, it was thought, would do this by placing a restraint on the expansion of Federal Reserve credit within the context of the automatic mechanism (Sect. 6.3). Under the law, moreover, each regional bank was to keep itself informed of the character and amount of its member-bank loans with a view to seeing that no undue use was made of bank credit. Then, as now (Sect. 8.1), an advance from the Federal Reserve was considered a recourse available to member banks to meet only temporary purposes. The policy of the Reserve banks, with respect to the cost of borrowing, was that discount rates charged for discounts at the Reserve banks should generally be above the cost of obtaining reserves from the sale of government securities and similar items from the member-bank's portfolio. When the Federal Reserve System was of the opinion that expansion should be encouraged, it would reduce its discount rates in relation to prevailing market rates.

The policy regarding rate changes and discounts provides an additional example of the regional autonomy of banks in the early decades of the Federal Reserve System. The law provided that each regional bank should determine the discount rate for its region, subject only to the approval and consent of the governing board in Washington. Thus the board could not initiate a change in policy. The discount rates were, moreover, the primary instrument over the control of bank credit in the early years of the System's operations.

The reserve requirements were prescribed by statute in the first years of the System, and there was no provision for changes in the requirements. The reserve balances of the member bank, by amendment to the Reserve Act in 1917, were required to be kept with the Federal Reserve banks. The reserve requirements, reflecting the structure of the correspondent banking system (Sect. 3.2 and 7.3), for the period 1917-1933 were:[35]

Demand deposits:	Percentage
Central reserve city banks	13
Reserve city banks	10
Country banks	7
Time deposits, all member banks	3

For purposes of determining reserve requirements, central Reserve cities were initially New York, Chicago, and St. Louis, with St. Louis later being reclassified as a Reserve city. Reserve cities were selected cities of intermediate size, and banks outside these cities were classified as country banks.

It was expected that excessive changes in the average of prices would be held in check automatically by the adherence to the gold standard, since reserve requirements were fixed. Inflows of gold could be expected to expand reserves (Sect. 3.1) and push prices up (Sect. 6.3) until an imbalance between domestic and foreign price levels reversed the flow of gold. Outflows would contribute to the reverse effects (Sect. 6.3). Under this arrangement there need be no "managed money." Given the "ubiquitous 'real bills' doctrine" and the extension of added liquidity to real bills, the system could be expected to provide automatically the volume of credit and the stock of money to satisfy the "needs of trade." In this sense, an "elastic currency" was to be provided, but this has been thought to be a less valid sense of the term, arising, in part, from "a failure to recognize fully the significance of deposits [as distinct from hand-to-hand currency] as money." [36]

In any event, the early duties of the system may be viewed as primarily "defensive" [37]—since it was to provide an elastic currency in the sense (Sect. 7.3) of serving as a defense against seasonal "cash drains," and since the system was to otherwise operate according to fixed rules and in the framework of "real bills," gold flows, and so on.

World War I financing. When the United States declared war on Germany in 1917, the Reserve banks were called upon to perform the service of supporting the wartime financing needs of the Treasury. This was done by accepting government securities from member banks as collateral for advances at a preferential rate, unlike the method of support in later years (Sect. 24.3). The advances, so secured, were known as "war paper." The arrangement was such that commercial banks could loan money to customers for the purchase of governments at a rate equivalent to the coupon rate on the bonds and then, in turn, the bank could discount the customer's note at the Federal Reserve at a lower rate. The spread between the two rates compensated the commercial banks for carrying the accounts. The consequences were an expansion of bank reserves and an expansion of bank credit by a multiple amount.

When the war ended in November 1918, the situation was inflationary. There was a shortage of goods, prices were almost double their prewar level, and the Federal Reserve banks could not restrict credit without affecting the success of the Treasury's Victory Loan in the fall of 1918. In this situation, the Reserve banks postponed a series of increases in discount rates until after the Victory Loan. Then some Reserve banks raised their rate on commercial paper to 7 per cent.[38] The commercial bankers became anxious to contract their indebtedness at the Federal Reserve, no doubt, partly in response to pressure from overenthusiastic Reserve bank offices.[39] Some loans collateraled by government securities were called; security prices declined. One of the Liberty Bond issues with a maturity of 100 sold below 82.[40] The higher rates, coming after imbalances in the price level and inventories had been effected, con-

tributed to a crisis in the spring of 1920, a time when prices through the
world collapsed. The decline in business activity, employment, and
prices continued until mid-1921.

The restoration of the gold standard and the Great Crash. After 1921
and apart from brief intervals in 1923-1924 and 1926-1927, the sectors
of the United States economy other than agriculture expanded, and the
price level remained relatively stable.[41] Nevertheless, there were problems concerning the restoration of the international gold standard following its abandonment in the war years. In this setting, the United
States monetary officials focused on the depressed state of agriculture
and the gold standard problem. Indeed, as we note below, they focused
on these problems at the expense of developments in the stock market
for which the Federal Reserve officials claimed no responsibility.

With respect to the international problem, the feeling existed among
United States and foreign banking officials that the future of international trade and cooperation lay in the restoration of the economies of
Europe to a properly functioning international gold standard,* and in
the restoration, in particular, of England's position of prestige and financial leadership. The latter, however, was thought to require the restoration of the pound to its old prewar price in terms of gold, but the
economic conditions abroad vis-à-vis the United States were unfavorable
to the restoration of the pound at this price. The old dollar price of the
pound tended to overvalue British goods at a time when high interest
rates and stable prices in America attracted gold from abroad. In order
to reverse the flows of gold, stimulate employment abroad, and facilitate
a functioning of the restored international gold standard, consequently,
easier credit and lower interest rates were called for in the United States.
To discuss the problem, the financial leaders of Europe were invited to a
conference in the United States in 1927.[42] Then, coincidentally or otherwise, came the now famous credit policy that provided credit for the
stock market boom. Broker's loans (i.e., loans made by banks to brokers
that enable them to expand credit to their trading customers) at weekly
reporting banks in New York City increased by 33 per cent over the
calendar year 1928. Stock prices rose rapidly. In the seventeen-month
period from April 1928 to September 1929 the percentage increase was
49 per cent in terms of Standard and Poor's monthly averages of 480
common stocks.[43]

Discount rates were belatedly raised in three steps from $3\frac{1}{2}$ per cent
to 5 per cent at most banks in August 1928. This, however, conflicted
with the Federal Reserve System's purchase of banker's acceptances to

---

* The gold standards established for the individual countries in this period were,
in large part, gold exchange standards, and the British pound was viewed as the key
currency (Sect. 6.1). In the 1920's, there was the view that England should fulfill
this role of the key currency country, but the economic strength required of such a
country (Sect. 23.3) resided elsewhere. The situation was not well understood.

help a depressed agriculture during the crop-moving season. The purchase of the acceptances merely enlarged the supply of credit. Since the majority of members on the Federal Reserve Board believed that stock market speculation was none of the System's business, they refused to take action.[44]

The additional credit contributed further to the exuberant rise in stock market prices and the increase in stock exchange credit. Even so, speculation was rampant; the average monthly interest rate on new call loans rose from 6.10 per cent in 1928 to 9.80 in March 1929. The high rates also attracted call money to the stock market from nonbanking sources. The high stock market prices and accompanying low yield on stocks made it possible for some companies to market stocks, upon which they had to pay 3 per cent at the prevailing stock yields, and then to turn about and lend this money on brokers' loans at the higher call-loan rates.[45]

Like other speculative booms, this one had taken off into a world where the only reality was advancing stock prices. They could continue to advance only as long as new money and new people were coming into the market, or only so long as traders' expectations contributed to a rise in the turnover of money balances. When the latter stopped, the boom broke. Thus, on Tuesday, October 29, 1929, the most devastating day in the history of the New York Stock Market came. The opening of the market on that day is described by Galbraith as follows: "Great blocks of stock were offered for what they would bring; in the first half hour sales were at a 33,000,000-a-day rate. . . . Repeatedly and in many issues there was a plethora of selling orders and no buyers at all."

The break came. Actually, it came some months after the midyear cyclical peak in business activity. The rise and fall of stock prices, and the ensuing wave of bank failures, however, were an important part of the wider range of economic developments of the 1920's and early 1930's.[46]

A struggle for power. Milton Friedman and his coauthor, Anna Jacobson Schwartz, view the discount rate policy of the months preceding the 1929 crisis as being somewhat different from the above view[47] (the one prevailing in the other works cited). They point out that the Federal Reserve System frequently cited foreign considerations as justification for the policies pursued, but they view these considerations as secondary. They do this, in part, because the Federal Reserve literature "contained almost no discussion of the policy measures appropriate to achieve the objective."[48] In the Friedman-Schwartz view, the discount rate policy preceding 1929 was the result of a struggle for power between the Federal Reserve Bank of New York and the board.

Friedman and Schwartz recognize that some concern existed over the control of bank credit expansion in the precrisis period. But the New

York bank wanted to control credit by raising the discount rate. However, the Federal Reserve Board was reluctant to permit increases in the
discount rate. Rather, it favored "direct pressure" to discourage member-
bank borrowing at the Federal Reserve, especially where banks were
extending loans for the purchase of securities. The board, by the latter
means of direct control, sought to avoid the effect of high discount rates
on buying for productive purposes. "The struggle for power within the
System," consequently, resulted in a "conflict centered on stock market
speculation only because that happened to be the most convenient and
immediate issue." [49]

The writers in question also recognize the presence of problems in
returning to the gold standard,[50] and the pre-eminence of the New York
bank in the "responsibility for international monetary relations." In the
first instance, they note that Britain "re-established a gold standard in
1925 at a rate that probably overvalued the pound." [51] Continuing, they
say: "There can be little doubt that Britain's problem would have been
vastly eased if the United States, and even more France, had permitted
a greater degree of monetary expansion—enough in this country [the
United States], for example, so that wholesale prices would have been
stable from 1925 to 1929 instead of falling about 8 per cent." In the
second instance, they note that "the Bank of England, the Bank of
France, and other central banks had always treated the New York
bank as their counterpart. . . . The Board had been kept informed
. . . but it had never had a major voice in forming policy." [52]

The end of an era. The immediate developments in the monetary and
financial sectors, following 1929, may be said to have challenged the
validity of the fundamental notions underlying its organization and
operation, and the soundness and/or the quality of the administration of
our system of money and banks. In their way, the existing system and
the notions symbolized the end of an era, which was over a century old.
These concerned the international gold standard, the quantity theory
of money, and the real bills doctrine. There were questions as to whether
the system could be expected to operate satisfactorily as a mechanical
regulator of economic activity.

Following the 1929 episode, banks were revealed as having overex-
tended credit on illiquid loans of a wide variety, including inadequately
margined call loans, mortgages, and other noncommercial loans. Bank
failures had been increasing in the 1920's, but in 1930, 1931, and in early
1933 there were increasing waves of failures.[53] In early 1933, the situation
became acute, and states began declaring bank holidays. When Franklin
Roosevelt took office as President in March 1933, bank holidays had
been proclaimed in about half of the states, and, after midnight on
March 6, he declared a holiday for banks throughout the country. It ex-

tended until March 13, 14, and 15, depending on the location of the bank. Congress was immediately summoned in special session and passed on the same day the Emergency Banking Bill.[54] Signed into law on March 9, it called for the surrender to the Federal Reserve banks of all gold coin and gold certificates. And, to clear up any uncertainty that gold would be paid out, a joint Congressional resolution was passed on June 5, 1933, "abrogating the gold clause in all public and private contracts." [55] This was preceded by the abandonment of the standard by Britain in September 1931, and then by twenty-five other countries within one year.[56] Thus there was an unequivocal break with notions about the automatic gold standard (Sect. 6.3).[57]

After having called in all the gold, the administration acted under the Thomas Amendment to the Agricultural Adjustment Act. The action was "explicitly directed at achieving a price rise through expansion of the money stock . . ." by a reduction in the gold content of the dollar. The intention was to permit the dollar to depreciate relative to foreign currencies, and also to become a "means of achieving a rise in domestic prices." Continuing, according to our source, "The dollar price of gold immediately started rising, which is to say that so also did the dollar price of foreign currencies, including both those like the French franc that remained on gold and those like the pound sterling that had gone off gold at an earlier date." It is also pointed out: "In the next three months, the market price of gold rose to $30 an ounce, and thereafter fluctuated erratically between a low of about $27 and a high of nearly $35 until January 30, 1934, when the Gold Reserve Act" [58] fixed the price of gold at $35 per ounce on January 31, 1934.*

The theory behind the action was a special form of the quantity theory of money (Sect. 6.3), but adequate demand for commodities was not forthcoming, and the money supply did not expand to the hoped-for extent. As one would expect from earlier analysis (Sect. 5.5) the expansion of the supply depended upon the successful use of the means for inducing additional expenditures (i.e., inducing appropriate changes in β and, therefore, in income and V_y, $\gamma = $ const., in the earlier analysis) so as to create demand for additional bank credit. Adequate demand for credit was not induced, even though the dollar value of monetary reserves was increased; the Thomas Amendment had provided the legal basis for such an increase. Even following the cyclical trough in February 1933, the revival was "initially erratic and uneven." The revival from the trough to the cyclical peak in April 1937 was itself incomplete. Money income was 17 per cent lower than in 1929. Per capita output was

---

* When the gold was revalued there accrued to the Treasury a revaluation "profit" of 2.8 billion dollars. Over the years this fund was used in an interesting variety of ways.

lower, too, although the following indicators of economic activity increased:[59] output in constant prices, money income, the average of prices for current output, the money stock, and the velocity of money.

The causes contributing to the failure of the money supply to expand to an adequate extent are complicated in their detail.[60] Nevertheless, there is a touch of truth, with respect to the thinking of monetary and banking circles of the time, in the reflections of Senator Ralph E. Flanders, a former President of the Federal Reserve Bank of Boston: ". . . The then Secretary of the Treasury and his advisers would devalue the dollar by a step and then go and look at the commodity ticker, and nothing happened. They went back and devalued it some more and went and looked at the commodity ticker, and still nothing happened. And they kept on doing it and still nothing happened, and finally they stopped." [61]

Senator Flanders continues:

> I am glad to see now that they have come around to recording velocity, and I am interested to see the significance that you [W. Randolph Burgess, former Undersecretary of the Treasury] have given it in your testimony to date, since I am a velocity fan [*laughter*].
>
> It seems to me that too little attention has been given to the question as to why money moves fast at some times and moves slowly at others. And it is the element of the *MV* side of the equation that is more or less mysterious. We find it, but so far as I have been able to observe, we do not endeavor to predict it or know what to do about it or whether we want to do anything about it, as we do about the *M*, we focus on the amount of money and then watch the V.[61]

Finally, with respect to the commercial banking developments in the early 1930's, the banks could have met the depositors' demands for currency and coin and avoided the widespread failures by rediscounting eligible paper at the Federal Reserve banks. This could have been the result if the banks had created an adequate supply of such paper in the extension of loans, but a tradition had developed against borrowing, other than temporary borrowing, and some banks had increased speculative loans in disproportionate amounts. They had extended credit and created larger proportions of notes and financial instruments that could not be rediscounted on the basis of the practices under the original Federal Reserve Act. There were questions about changing the criteria for eligible paper, as well as about the prevailing view of banking as primarily a commercial loan business.

Epilogue. A leading economist has taken a strong position about the acts and failures of the monetary officials concerning the 1929 episode, whereas we have only described some of the events leading up to and following the 1929 collapse. He believes that the severity of the ensuing recession was due primarily to "acts of commission and omission by the reserve authorities. . . ." It is emphasized that the Federal Reserve "should not have allowed the money stock to decline by nearly 3 per cent from August 1929 to October 1930 . . ." and there is further criticism of the subsequent contraction in the stock of money. This also centers upon the Federal Reserve's failure to deal with the recurrent liquidity crises and the bank failures beginning in November 1930. The failures were, he says, of "will, not of power." [62] And indeed, there is the view that the level of knowledge and the means to prevent the collapse were available to the authorities before the collapse.[63]

7.6. Summary

For forty of the forty-five years after 1791, the First Bank of the United States and the Second Bank of the United States served similar needs in the same way. They both served as the principal depository for the United States Treasury, and both directed their activities toward achieving a uniform and sound currency. Both had head offices in Philadelphia, and there were other similarities. The First Bank, however, had a capital of 10 million dollars, and the Second Bank had a capital of 35 million dollars. Because the latter developed central banking operations, such as those directed toward achieving orderly money-market and credit conditions to a high degree, it was a forerunner to modern central banking (as outlined in subsequent chapters). Its methods of control differed from those of modern central banking in several respects. It was not the only bank of issue. It engaged in direct competition with the banks over which it was to exert some control. Its control was largely maintained through its creditor relationship with the state banks. The suspension of specie payments following the expiration of the respective charters was evidence of the need for some type of central institution to perform regulatory functions for the monetary economy and to lessen the impact of intra- and international flows of specie.

The establishment of the Independent Treasury System, following the expiration of the charter for the Second Bank, reflected the need of the Federal government for a fiscal agent other than state banks. Even so, the Independent Treasury System was not too satisfactory. The operation of subtreasuries indicated the effect of the constantly increasing magnitude of Treasury transactions upon the money and credit markets. In a sense, it foretold of the need for some institution to smooth out or lessen the effect of these transactions upon the economy.

Apart from Federal institutions, in the country's earlier years, there was evidence of private and state efforts to achieve a more serviceable complex of financial institutions. For example, the Suffolk System arose to regulate the speculative excesses of note issues in New England, and the safety fund was another response to the same problem. There was also evidence of the growing interdependence between money, banking, and other areas of the economy. As the economy and the number of banks grew, other complementary developments took place. These consisted of correspondent banking and the related money market. The nature of these interrelationships was evidenced by the suspension of specie payments in 1857, a type of seasonal crisis which foreshadowed others to come.

During the fifty-year period beginning with the Civil War, economic instability was seen largely as a currency problem. At the outset of this period the National Banking Act was to serve the dual purpose of providing a market for government bonds and a sound and uniform currency. The system established by the act was slow to achieve a sound and uniform currency, and it failed to achieve an "elastic currency," especially as the latter concerned the seasonal demand for currency in hand-to-hand circulation. The system, nevertheless, partly reunited the government and the economy. There were continued crises.

The structural weakness, after the passage of the National Banking Act, was based upon the correspondent banking system, the autumnal demand for funds, and the fictitious liquidity provided by required reserves (reserves whose loss would result in bank failure). The over-all weakness of the arrangement centered around the tradition whereby country banks maintained some reserves with city banks which, in turn, expanded the volume of investment and call loans, often for speculative purposes. When, on occasion, the seasonal withdrawal of funds in combination with other factors caused a contraction in loans and investments in the city areas, the result was a combination of a violent contraction of loans, a collapse of security prices, and bank failures. Thus, following the panic of 1907, one with features common to others of the period, Congress appointed a commission to study the matter. A result was the passage of the Federal Reserve Act of 1913. Among other things, the central bank established by the act was to provide an elastic currency— as that term is used in both of its two senses, one a somewhat more valid use of the term than the other. For one thing, a defense was provided against the seasonal "cash drains" and short-run losses of reserves, and, in this respect, the Federal Reserve was quite successful. For another thing, however, the system was set up to operate automatically and according to rules, all within the context of "real bills," gold flows, and, lurking in the background, the quantity theory of money. In this latter context, the supply of credit and the stock of money was to vary with the needs of agriculture, commerce, and industry and, at the same time, constrain changes in the average of prices.

Ironically, in the latter respect, the advocates of a central bank for the United States triumphed on the eve of a new era. The international gold standard underlying the object of their triumph had broken down in the course of early operations. At the end of the 1920's and in the early 1930's the basic notions underlying the original Federal Reserve Act seemed less applicable to the conditions that existed. Features of the original act were soon to be measurably altered.

References

1. Also, for an account of the founding of the bank, see Bray Hammond, *Banks and Politics in America, from the Revolution to the Civil War* (Princeton, N.J.: Princeton University Press, 1957), pp. 49-55.

2. *Ibid.*, p. 50.   3. *Ibid.*, p. 63.   4. *Ibid.*, p. 77.   5. *Ibid.*, pp. 155-161.

6. *Ibid.*, pp. 172-176, for the interesting account of the failure of the Farmers Exchange Bank.

7. *Ibid.*, pp. 235-236.

8. See David Rich Dewey, *Financial History of the United States*, 17th edition (New York: Longmans, Green and Co., 1934), pp. 70-71; and Hammond, *op. cit.*, p. 103.

9. Hammond, *op. cit.*, p. 266.

10. For a discussion of the reasons behind locating the bank in Philadelphia, see Margaret G. Myers, *The New York Money Market*, Vol. I (New York: Columbia University Press, 1931), pp. 5-6.

11. See Dewey, *op. cit.*, p. 101.

12. For a discussion of the political factors, see Hammond, *op. cit.*, pp. 210-213 and 219-220.

13. Dewey, *op.cit.*, p. 144.

14. Those of Philadelphia banks, for example, were worth only from 20 to 50 per cent of their full value in terms of specie (Myers, *op. cit.*, p. 157).

15. Hammond, *op.cit.*, p. 295.   16. *Ibid.*, pp. 306-318.   17. *Ibid.*, pp. 443-444.   18. *Ibid.*, p. 297.   19. *Ibid.*, p. 381.

20. See the veto message (July 10, 1832) in William Letwin (ed.), *A Documentary History of American Economic Policy Since 1789* (Chicago: Aldine Publishing Company, 1962), pp. 114-134.

21. Hammond, *op.cit.*, p. 453.

22. Walter Wyatt, "Federal Banking Legislation," *Banking Studies* (Washington, D.C.: Board of Governors of the Federal Reserve System, 1941), p. 41.

23. Hammond. *op. cit.*, p. 445.   24. *Ibid.*, pp. 695-696.

25. For a detailed history of the monetary and banking factors contributing to the particular crises prior to 1914, see Milton Friedman and Anna Jacobson Schwartz, *A Monetary History of the United States, 1867-1960* (Princeton, N.J.: Princeton University Press for the National Bureau of Economic Research, 1963), Chap. 2-4.

26. *Ibid.*, p. 168.   27. *Ibid.*, pp. 168-169.

28. For a discussion of the suspension of specie payments and the three legal tender acts under which greenbacks were issued, see Wesley Clair Mitchell, *A History of the Greenbacks* (Chicago: University of Chicago Press, 1903), pp. 3-131.

29. The topics concerning greenbacks include the average of prices (Sect. 5.3), speculation, foreign exchange (Sect. 6.1), the role of gold, gold produc-

tion, the presence of a flexible exchange rate system (Sect. 6.3), and so on. For a comprehensive treatment of them, see the monumental volume by Friedman and Schwartz, *op.cit.*, Chap. 2.

30. See the Cross of Gold Speech (July 8, 1896) in Letwin, *op.cit.*, pp. 248-256.

31. See Friedman and Schwartz, *op.cit.*, pp. 8, 91-92, 118-119, 137, and 139.

32. For a comprehensive discussion of the 1907 panic and the subsequent developments, see Friedman and Schwartz, *op.cit.*, pp. 156-168.

33. There are numerous accounts concerning the founding of the system. See, for example, Carter Glass, *Adventures in Constructive Finance* (New York: Doubleday, Page and Company, 1927); Eustace C. Mullins, *A Study of the Federal Reserve* (New York: Kasper and Horton, 1952); Paul M. Warburg, *The Federal Reserve System* (New York: The Macmillan Company, 1930); H. Parker Willis, *The Federal Reserve System* (New York: Ronald Press, 1923); and Lester V. Chandler, *Benjamin Strong, Central Banker* (Washington, D. C.: The Brookings Institute, 1958).

34. For discussions of these matters, see Henry Parker Willis, *The Theory and Practice of Central Banking* (New York: Harper and Brothers, 1936), pp. 3-109; Lloyd W. Mints, *A History of Banking Theory* (Chicago: University of Chicago Press, 1945), pp. 223-271; and G. L. Bach, *Federal Reserve Policy-Making* (New York: Alfred A. Knopf, 1950), pp. 5-81.

35. For a note on the pre-1917 requirements, see Friedman and Schwartz, *op.cit.*, p. 194.

36. *Ibid.*, p. 169.

37. The term has been used in reference to the Federal Reserve's duties of "defending against those seasonal, regional, or perhaps accidental causes of sudden stringency that arise in the process of issuing currency, or clearing checks, on meeting net flow of funds among regions (or vis-à-vis other countries). . . ." See Robert V. Roosa, *Federal Reserve Operations in the Money and Government Securities Markets* (New York: Federal Reserve Bank of New York, 1956), p. 8.

38. For details on the discount rate episode of this period and some of the subsequent events, see Friedman and Schwartz, *op.cit.*, pp. 225-239 and 231-239, respectively.

39. See E. A. Goldenweiser, *American Monetary Policy* (New York: McGraw-Hill Book Company, 1951), p. 136.

40. See *Annual Report of the Secretary of the Treasury* (Washington, D.C.: U.S. Government Printing Office, 1951), p. 175.

41. On the economy of 1921-1929, see Friedman and Schwartz, *op.cit.*, Chap. 6.

42. Goldenweiser, *op.cit.*, p. 145; and Chandler, *op.cit.*, pp. 374-380 and 423-470.

43. See staff report, "Major Upward Movements in Stock Prices Since the Midtwenties," *Factors Affecting the Stock Market* (Washington, D.C.: U.S. Government Printing Office, 1955), p. 5.

44. Goldenweiser, *op.cit.*, p. 153. Also Friedman and Schwartz (*op.cit.*, p. 290) cite a famous 1929 statement in which the board assumed no right to serve as an arbiter of security speculation or values. They note, however, "that the desire to curb the stock market boom was a major factor in reserve actions during 1928 and 1929."

45. John Kenneth Galbraith, *The Great Crash* (Boston: Houghton Mifflin Company, 1955), pp. 36-37.

46. See, for example, Friedman and Schwartz, *op. cit.*, pp. 353-357, as well as the entire Chap. 7.

47. Their views are developed in *ibid.*, pp. 254-266.   48. *Ibid.*, p. 269.

49. *Ibid.*, p. 255.   50. *Ibid.*, pp. 279-284.   51. *Ibid.*, p. 284 and 279-284.   52. *Ibid.*, pp. 380-381.

53. For a detailed account of these failures and the holidays finally declared in early 1933, see *ibid.*, pp. 308-315 and 324-332.

54. On the Emergency Banking Act, see *ibid.*, pp. 421-422.

55. *Ibid.*, p. 469. These authors point out the following in their discussion (p. 468): "The clause, whose use dated back to the greenback period after the Civil War, required payment either in gold proper, or in a nominal amount of currency equal to the value of a specified weight of gold. It was designed precisely to protect lenders and others against currency depreciation. The clause, if honored, would have multiplied the nominal obligations of the federal government and of many private borrowers for interest and principal of debt by the ratio of the new price of gold to the old price of gold."

56. *Ibid.*, pp. 315-322.

57. On the domestic side, the type of monetary standard resulting from the developments in the early 1930's has been described as "a discretionary fiduciary standard." The term, as those who point it out (see Friedman and Schwartz, *op.cit.*, p. 474) suggest, "is vague and ambiguous" along with "the standard it denotes." This standard has the following characteristics: (1) gold continues to serve as a monetary base, at times, in a vague sense; (2) gold is sold in the form of bars of a certain minimum weight; and (3) the free coinage of gold is not permitted, but the government stands ready to buy gold at a fixed price and sell at such a price for legitimate purposes.

58. Friedman and Schwartz, *op.cit.*, pp. 464 ff.

59. *Ibid.*, pp. 493-499. The stock of money figure used by these authors is a seasonally adjusted total of currency held by the public plus demand and time deposits adjusted in commercial banks. Still, changes in it provide an indicator of changes in the stock of money as usually defined for statistical purposes in this work.

60. For the detail, see Friedman and Schwartz, *op.cit.*, pp. 462-483.

61. See *Investigation of the Financial Condition of the United States* (Washington, D.C.: U.S. Government Printing Office, 1957), p. 1121.

62. See Milton Friedman, *Capitalism and Freedom* (Chicago: University of Chicago Press, 1962), pp. 45-51. See also Friedman and Schwartz, *op.cit.*, Chap. 7.

63. *Ibid.*, pp. 407-408.

8

The Federal Reserve Act
Since 1933: Ends and Means

> The Congress hereby declares that it is the continuing policy and responsibility of the Federal Government to use all practical means consistent with its needs and obligations . . . in a manner calculated to foster and promote free competitive enterprise and the general welfare . . . to promote maximum employment, production, and purchasing power (Employment Act of 1946).

The consequences of the great crash (Sect. 7.5) and the apparent failures of the monetary officials to adequately mitigate them provided a setting for changes in the framework of central banking and in its responsibilities. The changes, as in the case of those following the crisis of 1907, were in response to problems concerning the adequacy of the monetary mechanism. Only in the early 1930's did the control over the monetary mechanism become considerably more centralized. The monetary officials were given a more explicit range of responsibilities, and events indicated that further emphasis would be placed upon the broad objectives of economic stabilization implicit in the original act.[1] This chapter, therefore, introduces in broad outline the goals of the Federal Reserve and the means of achieving them, both as they evolved out of the early 1930's. It also emphasizes the distinction between the general and selective means of controlling credit. A later chapter (Chap. 11) deals more fully with the structure of the Federal Reserve System. Still another (Chap. 25) deals, in a quantitative fashion, with the instruments at the disposal of the monetary officials, the ultimate goals, and intermediate goals, such as a given change in the stock of money, and their interrelationships. In the latter chapter, the looser reference to a goal will be replaced by a specific target variable. There will be intermediate target variables, ultimate target variables, and so on.

8.1. The Ends and Means: An Over-All View

The statement of the ultimate goals for the Federal Reserve's responsibilities evolving from the early 1930's took an explicit form in the Employment Act of 1946. This act, to which all government agencies subscribe,[2] held the goals to be the promotion of maximum employment, production, and purchasing power* within the context of a free-enterprise system. These same three national economic goals have been, on occasions in subsequent years, also stated unofficially in other phrases, such as low levels of unemployment, economic growth, reasonable price stability,[3] and a viable balance of short-term capital and gold flows.

Under the original Federal Reserve Act, in broad outline, an adequate degree of stability was to result from adherence to the rules (Sect. 7.5). In the context of the "real bills" doctrine (Sect. 7.5), there was the widespread feeling that this meant that the stock of bank credit [and presumably money (M)] should expand with the needs of trade[4] [and presumably income (Y)]—i.e.,

$$\frac{dM/M}{dY/Y} = 1 \quad \text{or} \quad \frac{dM}{dY}\frac{Y}{M} = 1.$$

After the early 1930's, however, a more aggressive role was attributed to the Federal Reserve. In terms of an intermediate goal, such as the stock of money, this apparently implied the following:

$$\frac{dM/M}{dY/Y} < 1$$

(or a rise in the velocity of money) in the expansion phase of business activity, and

$$\frac{dM/M}{dY/Y} > 1$$

(or a decline in velocity) in the contraction phase, as illustrated in Table 2-1. As a secular matter, of course, the explicit or implicit goal in question may continue to be

$$\frac{dM/M}{dY/Y} = 1.$$

Legislation giving the Federal Reserve broad new authorities, centralizing the system's control over credit policy, and changing the board's

---

* In a literal sense, the term "maximum purchasing power" in the Employment Act of 1946 implies an infinitely decreasing average for prices (P) over time (t). The usual meaning given the term "maximum purchasing power" and assumed throughout this work, however, is that purchasing power should be reasonably stable over time (i.e., on the average, $dP/dt = 0$).

name from the Federal Reserve Board to the Board of Governors of the
Federal Reserve System, was embodied in the Banking Act of 1933, the
Securities and Exchange Act of 1934, and the Banking Act of 1935.
The latter act clarified, added to, and consolidated the provisions of the
former banking act. These were the last acts representing broad changes
in the legislation pertaining to the Federal Reserve, although other legislation has on occasions brought about a temporary broadening of the Reserve System's control over consumer and real estate credit. Further, the
Federal Reserve Act has continued to be affected through amendments,
changes in the process of administration, interpretation, and gradual
acceptance of precedence.

The new authority referred to consisted largely of an extension of
controls over credit that may be classified as general credit controls (so-
called because of their effect on the quantity of credit in general), on
the one hand, and selective credit controls (so-called because of their
being directed at a particular kind of credit), on the other. The first
group of extensions included (1) the authority to make advances on
"satisfactory" as well as "eligible" paper to any member bank, (2) the
authority to vary legal reserve requirements between those previously
prescribed by statute and twice that amount, and (3) the statutory recog-
niton of Federal Reserve open market operations as a credit control instrument.

The second group included the authority to regulate credit terms for
the purpose of purchasing or carrying securities. Taken together these
extensions may be said to have given "a dynamic conception" to Federal
Reserve responsibilities as opposed to the largely defensive responsibilities identified with the original Federal Reserve Act.[5] Moreover, in arriving at policy decisions under the enlarged responsibilities, there was
the implication within the legal framework of an increased reliance upon
the exercise of "fallible human judgment." This was in contrast to the implications within the legal framework of the original act of a strict adherence to rules designed to effect the appropriate policy automatically.
The idea of spelling out the rules for the conduct of monetary operations,
nevertheless, is never entirely absent from discussions of monetary policy.
As we shall see, it recurs (Sect. 26.5). Even the later emphasis on a
quantitative monetary policy (Sect. 25.1) implies a formal use of logic as
a means of forcing a more careful examination of the relationships between goals and instruments and as a means of avoiding inconsistencies.

The centralization of the Federal Reserve System's control over credit
consisted primarily of centralizing the decision-making function in the
Board of Governors of the Federal Reserve System. This was achieved
largely by giving the board the authority to initiate changes in reserve
requirements and by giving the entire seven-man board, along with five
Reserve-bank presidents, membership on the new Federal Open Market

Committee, which, in turn, was given responsibility for the conduct of the Federal Reserve open market operations. Also the independence of the board was strengthened by removing its *ex officio* members—the Secretary of the Treasury and the Comptroller of the Currency.

8.2. General Methods of Regulation

The general methods of regulation are changes in the discount rate, changes in reserve requirements and the open market purchase, and sale of securities (usually government securities).[6] The importance of the discount rate as a control device, however, has been reduced by the presence of the more useful and potentially effective means of credit control; namely, changes in reserve requirements and, more particularly, open market operations. As one writer notes, the decline in the importance of the discounting (and/or borrowing) at the Federal Reserve as a source of reserves since the 1920's is indicated by the fact that the average for borrowing as a per cent of total reserves declined from 30 in the period 1922-1929 to 3.2 in 1951-1959.[7]

Discount operations. Initially, the discount rate occupied the key position as a control device, although its use was limited by the restrictions on the type of paper discounted (short-term, self-liquidating commercial paper) and by the tradition against borrowing.[8] Over the years, however, the relative importance of commercial paper has declined,[9] firms of increasing asset size have become suppliers of funds to the more liquid financial markets, and other traditional demands for funds have changed.[10] These changes, in turn, paralleled changes in the type of lending by commercial banks, since banks could not live on the interest returns from a truly commercial banking business. They also tended to hinder adequate assistance by the Federal Reserve to member banks in time of recession.

Reflecting the declining importance of commercial paper, the discount standards of the Federal Reserve were broadened in the early 1930's. And, thus, another of the guides to the central banker—the real bills doctrine (Sect. 7.5)—formally lost its former sway. The Banking Act of 1935 granted permanent authority to the Federal Reserve banks, subject to the regulations of the Board of Governors, to make advances on "satisfactory" as well as "eligible paper," whereas under the old law (except under certain extreme conditions prescribed by an amendment in 1932) Reserve banks could extend advances to menber banks only on "eligible paper." As the matter has evolved, member banks mostly use a part of their government securities as collateral in borrowing from the Federal Reserve. These securities are often already at the lending Federal Reserve bank where they are held in safekeeping for member banks. Of the three choices concerning collateral—(1) obligations of the United States, (2) "eligible" paper, and (3) "satisfactory" paper—however, a penalty rate of an additional one-half of one per cent is charged on advances secured by "satisfactory" paper. The discount rate as commonly reported, then, applies to advance collateral by obligations of the United States and "eligible" paper, but the collateral accepted as being "eligible" could, under some circumstances, be broadened to include municipal securities and other sound paper.

The discount window has continued to be important as a source of member-bank reserves to meet temporary requirements or unusual banking situations of a general or localized nature. The rate changes, nevertheless, are sometimes confusing as a guide to the intentions of monetary officials. Their possible effects are also conflicting, and the confusion and conflict have led to some suggestions for fundamental changes. The confusion centers around the role of the discount rate as a cost factor, and possible psychological effects of changes in the discount rate (sometimes called "announcement effects"). To begin with, the use of the discount rate as a cost factor relies upon the yield spreads between the discount rate and the money market rates, including those on Federal funds (Sect. 3.2) and short-term government securities (Sect. 4.2), respectively. In other words, the use of the discount as a cost factor depends upon its being a penalty rate. The Reserve authorities may want to discourage member-bank borrowing by maintaining the discount rate above the rates on Federal funds, other interbank loans, and short-term government securities. Adjustments in reserves brought about by the latter type of transactions simply redistribute the reserves among the commercial banks (Sect. 3.2), while borrowing from the Federal Reserve increases the reserves for the banking system as a whole. Under tight credit conditions, however, the money market rates may move above the discount rate and thus make borrowing from the Federal Reserve a least costly source of funds. Such a rate relationship may encourage member-bank borrowing and bring about an increase in reserve at a time when the borrowing constitutes an offset to the tight-money condition that brought it about. In order to maintain the desired yield spreads, therefore, the discount rate must be changed for the single purpose of bringing it in line with other rates, and changes in the rate for this purpose may interfere or conflict with the sometimes-intended psychological effect of the discount rate changes.

Psychological effects of changes in the discount rate are achieved through influencing the expectations of the policy-making groups of business firms and financial institutions. In this instance, the rate is said to have its effect by conveying the opinion of the informed Federal Reserve authorities to the policy-making groups outside of the system, such as those in nonfinancial business enterprises. "An advance in the rate," it has been said, "is commonly interpreted to mean that in Federal Reserve opinion there is danger of too rapid a pace of bank credit and monetary expansion, and a reduction in the rate to indicate that encouragement of expansion is in the public interest." [11]

Thus, from the banker's point of view, an increase in the rate may be interpreted as a warning about borrowing from the Federal Reserve, and a reduction in the rate may signal the Federal Reserve's approval of borrowing. From the nonfinancial firm's point of view, despite the complexity of the matter, an increase in the rate during a recession may convey an optimistic outlook for business, possibly reflecting an expected increase in earnings and a restrictive credit policy. A decrease in the rate at any time may convey a pessimistic outlook, possibly reflecting an expected decrease in earnings and the demand for bank credit. From the latter point of view, decreases would always seem undesirable, but they would, at times, be necessary as a matter of adjustment. In addition, it may be necessary to raise the discount rate, in order for it to serve as a deterrent to credit expansion. This increase may have a stimulating effect on business expectations that offsets the intended effect of the increase in the discount rate. In any event, the way in which a discount rate change should be interpreted is complex, and it is doubtlessly more satisfactory to read the announcement of the change and its explanation in trying to interpret the outlook and intentions of the monetary officials than to interpret the change alone.

The confusion over the effects of changes in the discount rate has led to several suggestions,[12] including the following: (1) that the rate be set in a fixed relationship to some selected rate in the market for the most liquid funds, such as the rate on short-dated government securities,[13] or (2) that changes in the discount rate be tied to changes in some such money market rate and that the yield spread between the two rates be varied on some discretionary basis.[14] It is suggested, in the first instance, that the discount rate be above the money market rate and varied automatically with the selected money market rate. This would permit the discount rate to serve solely as a cost factor, and other desired effects of monetary policy would be achieved through the use of other devices.* Through the adoption of such a discount rate technique, the importance of changes in the discount rate are minimized when compared with the power and flexibility of other credit policy instruments and other interest rate changes described later. In the second instance, the above ad-

---

* Such a "floating discount rate" was adopted by the Bank of Canada in 1956. It was abandoned in 1962, and the rate was raised to 6 per cent as an indication of Canada's determination to defend the value of the Canadian dollar in the foreign exchange markets (Sect. 6.2).

vantages would be gained and the monetary authorities could, in addition, vary the spread between the discount rate and the selected money market rate as a means of varying the degree of the penalty against borrowing at the Federal Reserve. In neither of the above instances, however, should the importance against borrowing at the Federal Reserve to meet general or localized emergencies be overlooked.

Changes in reserve requirements. Reserve requirements were originally viewed as protection for the depositor and as a basis for conducting sound banking. When they became prescribed by statute, however, they ceased to be protection for the depositor, in a sense. Instead, they became primarily a basis for credit expansion and a determinant of the limit of the multiple expansion of demand deposits and the stock of money, and since 1935, in particular, changes in the required ratio of reserves to deposit liabilities have been considered an instrument with which the central bank may influence the supply of credit and the stock of money. Also, since that time, new means of protecting depositors have been effected. Some of these, as described later (Sect. 11.4), include bank examinations, the function of insuring bank deposits and salvaging failing institutions, and the Federal Reserve's function as "a lender of last resort."

The Banking Act of 1935 extended to the Board of Governors the authority to prescribe reserve requirements for member banks and to vary the requirements within given bounds, whereas previously reserve requirements were rigidly set—except for limited authority granted in 1933. As the law stood from 1935 until 1959, the board had the authority to vary reserve requirements within the respective ranges provided for each of the board's earlier classification of commercial banks (Sect. 7.5), namely, central Reserve city banks, Reserve city banks, and country banks. The lower bounds for the ranges were the reserve requirement in effect in 1917, and the upper bounds were twice those respective amounts, except for a temporary broadening. Under the amended law leading up to 1959, the changes in reserve requirements were applicable to all or any of the bank groups. Also the changes were uniform for all banks in a group, except for the board's authority to permit individual banks in outlying Reserve or central Reserve cities to carry lower reserves than called for by their classification and to reclassify cities.

The 1959 Congress, however, made two modifying amendments to the Federal Reserve Act[15] in relation to the reserve requirements of member banks. In one of these amendments the authority to vary reserve requirements was unaffected, but the classification "central Reserve city" was to be determined, the upper bound for reserve requirements for Reserve cities was increased to 22 per cent, and, on December 1, 1960, the reserve requirements were made identical for banks formerly classified as central Reserve city banks and Reserve city banks. Thus, under the latter law, the board has the authority to vary reserve requirements within the following bounds for the following classes of banks:[*]

Lower and Upper Bounds	Percentage
Demand deposits:	
Reserve city banks	10 to 22
County banks	7 to 14
Time deposits:	
At all member banks	3 to 6

The predominant features distinguishing central Reserve city banks under the century-old corresponding banking arrangement (Sect. 7.3) were believed to prevail no longer. The board, furthermore, was given authority to reclassify banks, and to permit individual Reserve city banks to carry lower reserves than the full requirement whenever the unique character of a bank's business justified the permission. And, under the other 1959 amendment, the entire amount of a member-bank's currency and coin (i.e., vault cash) became countable by November 24, 1960, as a part of legal reserves, along with reserves on deposit at the Federal Reserve. This change was viewed as desirable since some banks in a given classification often have to carry larger amounts of vault cash. Further, there were believed to be other advantages, such as reductions in the cost of transporting and handling currency, and the maintenance of a larger stock of vault cash in the event of a national emergency.

Changes in reserve requirements, of course, do not directly alter the total of reserves. Instead, they change the proportion of bank deposits that must be kept on deposit as reserves with the Federal Reserve. These changes have their immediate incidence upon the liquidity positions of banks. An increase, for example, may immediately create a situation in which banks in general must borrow reserves through the discount window of Federal Reserve and subsequently contract loans and investments (and thus demand deposits) by a multiple amount of the change in reserve requirements, if there are no excess reserves to begin with. The immediate effect of such an increase would be higher loan rates and higher rates on other sources of money market funds. This

---

[*] It should be noted that reserve requirements do not have to be maintained in any direct relationship to demand deposits on a day-to-day basis. Instead, such requirements are computed by averaging daily deposits over a weekly period for Reserve city banks and over a semi-monthly period for country banks. For Reserve city banks, the week for maintaining a given average ends on Wednesday. The money market on that day is generally slightly easier, reflecting the efforts of the banks to do their borrowing for adjustment purposes during the first part of the statement week.

For a brief account of the origin of reserve settlement periods in the context of recommendations for changes in them, see Albert H. Cox, Jr., and Ralph F. Leach, "Defensive Open Market Operations and the Reserve Settlement Periods of Member Banks," *Journal of Finance,* March 1964, pp. 77-78.

would result from competitive banks, acting independently, trying to dispose of the more liquid assets—a feat incidentally which cannot be performed in the short run by the banking system as a whole without recourse to "the lender of last resort." The ultimate effects upon borrowers would be those brought about by higher interest rates and the reduced availability of funds (Sect. 25.2 and 25.3).

Conversely, a decrease in reserve requirements may result immediately in a situation whereby banks in general have excess reserves upon which they may expand loans and investments (and, therefore, demand deposits) by a multiple of the amount of the decrease. The immediate effect of such an increase would be lower loan rates as well as lower rates on money market funds, since each of the competitive banks, acting independently, would bid for money market assets. The ultimate effect upon borrowers would be that brought about by an increased availability of funds and lower rates of interest.

Changes in reserve requirements are a powerful credit control device, and, as such, even small changes are not used as a means of effecting day-to-day changes in credit conditions. It is believed that frequent changes in reserve requirements are disturbing to the credit and money markets. On the one hand, reserve requirements may be raised (1) to soak up excess reserves (or liquidity) in the system generally or (2) to bring about a more even distribution of excess reserves (or liquidity) among the various banks. These actions, in addition to their own effects, make the banking system more subject to the effects of the other credit control devices. On the other hand, reserve requirements may be lowered to increase bank liquidity and bring about an increased availability of funds and lower interest rates. Changes in reserve requirements, in any event, are unlikely to be used except in conjunction with other credit controls and, even then, only after full allowance for the other factors affecting member-bank reserves (Sect. 10.1).

Federal Reserve open-market operations. Open market purchases were contemplated in the original Federal Reserve Act, but the administrative situation was not such as to encourage them.[16] After the transition incidental to the ending of the World War I, open market transactions were engaged in, however, and control over them came to reside in the Federal Reserve Bank of New York. That bank's able governor, Benjamin Strong, described the reason for the initial transactions as follows:

> In the latter part of 1921 and early in 1922, the member banks had liquidated so large a portion of their discounts at the Reserve Banks that there was some concern felt by some of the Federal Reserve banks as to their earnings.
>
> . . . .
>
> So that in that period the Reserve Banks, being autonomous and having the power to invest money, were making considerable in-

vestments in the market, buying bills and buying Government securities.[17]

Purchases and sales of bills or government securities in the open market continued through the 1920's and the early 1930's,[18] though without statutory recognition and full understanding on the part of most of the officials of their effect. Specific statutory recognition was finally given to open market operations in the Banking Act of 1933, and later the Banking Act of 1935 re-emphasized this recognition while at the same time transferring increased control over open market operations to the board.

Today, open market operations constitute the primary means whereby the Federal Reserve effects day-to-day changes in the tone of the credit and money markets, apart from changes in the tone of the market originating elsewhere. The Federal Open Market Committee is responsible for the operation of the account from which the operations are conducted. The account, amounting to approximately 33.8 billion dollars at year-end 1963, is managed at the Federal Reserve Bank of New York, sometimes called "the big house" by other dealers in the market.

A purchase of securities for the open market account increases reserves for the banking system as a whole by the amount of the purchase. The increase then has a multiple effect on the expansion of credit and the money stock, depending on the reserve ratio, and the "cash" and time deposit drains (Sect. 3.3). The effect of a purchase on reserves of, let us say, some given amount from a group of government securities dealers may be simply illustrated. The purchase is made with a check drawn on the Federal Reserve. The dealers who sell the securities deposit the check (or checks) with commercial banks. The checks are then, in turn, presented to the Federal Reserve where reserve accounts are credited with an increase in reserves. Such increases are similar to those brought about by inflows of gold as indicated earlier (Sect. 3.1), and their effects, too, are similar. The steps leading to the increase in reserves would appear as follows:[19]

Federal Reserve Bank		Member Bank	
Assets	Liabilities	Assets	Liabilities
Government securities + (a)	Member-bank reserves + (c)	Member-bank reserves + (c)	Deposits + (b)

(a) Federal Reserve buys the securities and pays the dealer with a check,
(b) the dealer deposits the check in his bank, and
(c) the bank sends it to the Federal Reserve bank for credit to its reserve account.

A sale of securities from the open market account has the reverse set of effects. The steps involving the effects of a sale of some given amount may be illustrated. In this case, government securities dealers pay the Federal Reserve with a check drawn on a commercial bank. The Federal Reserve, in turn, debits the reserve account of the commercial bank against which checks are drawn. This decrease in reserves is similar to those brought about by outflows of gold (Sect. 3.1). Also accounts may be shown to reflect the effect of the sale on member-bank reserves, the basis for a multiple contraction of bank credit:

Federal Reserve Bank		Member Bank	
Assets	Liabilities	Assets	Liabilities
Government securities — (a)	Member-bank reserves — (b)	Member-bank reserves — (b)	Deposits — (c)

(a) Federal Reserve sells securities and receives a check in payment from a dealer,
(b) the Federal Reserve receives credit for the check by debiting member-bank reserves, and
(c) the member bank debits the demand deposit of the dealer.

Each of the above transactions in securities was between the Federal Reserve and government securities dealer, and yet the effect was described as being applicable to the banking system as a whole. The impact of the transactions, initially confined to one or a few banks, is spread over the entire banking system through transactions in Federal funds, other interbank loans, and United States government securities in the manner described earlier (Sect. 3.2).

In sum, through open market operations, credit can be made tight or easy in varying degrees. The Open Market Committee may call for operations to assure orderly conditions in the credit and money markets from day to day as those markets are effected by other factors. It may call for operations to tighten credit in preparation for an increase in reserve requirements or in preparation for a decrease in requirements. It may also influence credit conditions so that a change in the discount rate is nothing more than an action to bring that rate in line with other rates prevailing in the financial markets. One may say that open market operations are most symbolic of the "dynamic" responsibilities of the Federal Reserve and the initiative which the system takes to bring about maximum employment, production, and purchasing power.

8.3. Selective Methods of Regulation

General credit controls—discount operations, changes in reserve requirements, and open market operations—are directed toward affecting the availability and cost of credit. They leave the allocative or rationing function to the free market. Selective controls, on the other hand, are used to interfere with the allocative function of the free market and to deliberately affect the availability of specific kinds of credit. The selective controls used by the Federal Reserve from time to time have consisted of those over stock market credit, consumer credit, and real estate credit. In general, these controls have their impact through (1) specifying maximum loan values or down payments and (2) limiting the amount of time for the repayment of loans. Among the selective controls administered by the Federal Reserve from time to time, all have employed the first device, whereas only consumer and real estate credit controls have employed the second. The only selective form of credit over which the Federal Reserve has control today is stock market credit. The other forms of selective control are worthy of mention, nevertheless, if only because of their continued re-entry into discussions of credit control.

It may be noted, at the outset, that selective credit controls are often objected to because they are thought to discriminate arbitrarily against particular assets or businesses. For this reason, and because of the difficulty in administering them, the authority to control credit through their use has only occasionally been granted and, even then, only when a special emergency seemed to justify their use, with the exception of stock market credit.

It may be noted, too, that there has always been an element of selective control exerted through the Federal Reserve confining its discount operations to "eligible" or "satisfactory" paper and through statutes prohibiting the undue use of bank funds for purposes inconsistent with the maintenance of sound credit. These latter limitations upon credit, nevertheless, are of a different order from the selective controls referred to in this section, since they have generally been directed toward the maintenance of liquidity or the quality of credit.

Stock market credit. The Federal Reserve was given the authority to regulate stock market credit under a provision of the Securities and Exchange Act of 1934. The regulation of credit for the purchase of securities was introduced as a corrective of the kind of situation (Sect. 7.5) that developed in 1928 and 1929 when large numbers of people, lured by easy profits to be made by rising stock market prices, bought and sold large volumes of stock on the basis of a constantly growing volume of credit.

In regulating stock market credit the board prescribes minimum margin requirements under Regulations T and U. Regulation T applies to the amount of credit extended by brokers and dealers on securities listed on national security exchanges. They are prohibited from lending on unregistered securities except under certain limited circumstances, such as the temporary granting of credit for a cash transaction. Regulation U applies to the granting of credit by banks for the purpose of carrying stocks listed on national securities exchanges. It does not prohibit banks from making loans on securities other than stocks. Margin requirements, then, are the difference expressed as a percentage between the market value of the security (market value = 100 per cent) pledged as collateral and the maximum loan value of the security (expressed as a percentage of the market value). For example, if the market value of a stock is $10,000 (100 per cent) and the amount that may be lent is $7,500 (75 per cent), then the margin is $2,500 (25 per cent). Thus a higher margin requirement reduces the amount that a purchaser of securities can acquire with a given amount of collateral, and a lower margin requirement increases the amount that a purchaser of securities can acquire with a given amount of collateral.

An increase in margin requirements, though bearing directly on the lender, puts restraint upon the borrower and dampens demand for credit and securities. An increase can be used accordingly to keep down the volume of stock market credit even though lenders are able and eager to lend. Another effect of high margin requirements is to restrict the amount of pyramiding that can take place in a rising market. In other words, they limit the extent to which traders may add to their holdings, when the market is rising, by borrowing against the additional market value of securities already held in their accounts without putting up additional money or additional securities. Restriction of pyramiding exerts restraint on rising stock prices as well as on the growth of credit employed in the stock market. Conversely, other things being equal, a decrease in margin requirements releases the restraint upon the lender and stimulates demand for credit and securities.

Margin requirements and their relationship to the volume of stock market credit and the level of securities prices are discussed more fully later (Sect. 13.3).

Consumer credit. The regulation of consumer credit by the Federal Reserve was first established in 1941 by an Executive Order of the President under the so-called Trading with the Enemy Act of October 6, 1917, as amended. This authority was discontinued in 1947, temporarily reinstated in 1948, and then permitted to lapse in 1949. It was again reinstated under the Defense Production Act in early 1950 following the outbreak of the Korean War, and, in mid-1952, the authority was repealed for the final time by amendments to the Defense Production Act.

On those occasions when the board regulated consumer credit, it did so through the issuance of Regulation W and with the view to restricting the use of credit for selected items and consequently limiting the inflationary demand for such items. The regulation prescribed the terms upon which credit might be granted for such consumer items as automobiles, electric refrigerators, radios, washing machines, vacuum cleaners, and household furniture. At different times the regulation applies to different numbers of items. In the World War II years, it was broadened to include a larger number of items, charge accounts, and single payment loans as well as installment credit, although after World War II the regulation was relaxed and finally contracted to the area of installment credit. When it was applied to charge accounts, the accounts would be closed against further purchase for listed articles unless paid by a prescribed date. When it was applied to single payment loans for the purchase of selected items, the maturity date of the loan was limited and renewals of the loan were limited. When it was applied to installment credit, the minimum down payment and maximum maturity date of the credit were prescribed.

Real estate credit. The President, under the Defense Production Act of 1950, was also authorized (1) to regulate the terms on which real estate loans could be made, insured, or guaranteed by Federal agencies and (2) to regulate the terms on which credit could be extended on uninsured and nonguaranteed loans for the construction or improvement of real property. He delegated the first part of that authority to the Housing and Home Finance Administrator, a government agent responsible for coordinating the operations of Federal housing agencies, and he delegated the authority for restricting other kinds of real estate credit to the board. Thus the board, for a two-year period beginning in mid-September 1950, acted to restrict the use of real estate credit for the purpose of restraining its inflationary rise.

The board attempted its comprehensive control over real estate credit through the issuance of Regulation X. The Housing-and-Home-Finance Administrator concurred in the board's regulation and applied similar restraints to Federally aided loans. Regulation X, like Regulation W, specified the minimum down payment and the maximum maturity date of the loan as well as the minimum periodic amounts to be paid in amortizing the principal.

Real estate credit and the effects of Federal housing agencies and monetary policy generally upon the behavior and financing of the consumer sector are discussed further (Sect. 18.3), along with an additional discussion of consumer credit (Sect. 18.1).

8.4. Summary

In response to apparent shortcomings of the financial system, the Federal Reserve Act was drastically altered in the early 1930's. Over the years the act has been further modified by amendments, the process of administration, interpretation, and gradual acceptance of precedence. The principal changes in the act have extended to the Federal Reserve broader and more "dynamic" responsibilities for achieving economic goals. These have included the following: a broadening of the discount standards of the Federal Reserve to permit the extension of credit on "satisfactory" as well as "eligible paper," an extension of authority to vary reserve requirements within prescribed limits, the statutory recognition of open market operations as a credit control device, and an extension of authority to determine the terms upon which stock market credit may be granted.

With respect to discounting, an increase in the discount rate above other money market rates, such as those on Federal funds and short-dated government securities, is thought to have a restrictive effect on member-bank borrowing at the Federal Reserve. Conversely, a reduction in the rate below other money market rates is thought to encourage member-bank borrowing. Discount rate changes also, at times, have uncertain psychological effects. The confusion over the possible effectiveness of the discount rate has led to a recommendation that it be set in a fixed relationship to some selected money market rate, or that changes in the discount rate be tied to changes in some selected money market rate and that the yield spread between the two rates be varied on some discretionary basis. These recommendations suggest that the rate should always serve as a penalty rate by being constantly above the selected money market rate.

With respect to changes in reserve requirements, an increase enlarges the proportion of demand deposits that must be kept by member banks as reserves. It exerts some pressure on member banks to call in loans or allow them to run off in a multiple amount of the increase in the reserves required, if the banking system is fully loaned up and if other factors do not bring about offsetting changes. Conversely, a reduction in reserve requirements permits member banks to expand loans and investments (and, therefore, demand deposits) by a multiple of the amount of reserves freed by the reduced requirements, provided other factors do not bring about offsetting changes.

With respect to open market operations, a sale of securities from the open market account decreases reserves by the amount of the sale. In this instance, loans and investments (and, therefore, demand deposits) must be contracted by a multiple amount of the initial sale, if the member banks are fully loaned up and if other factors do not bring about offsetting changes. The sale contributes to credit tightness. A purchase of securities for the open market account, however, increases reserves by the amount of the purchase, and loans and investments (and, therefore, demand deposits) may be increased by a multiple amount of the purchase. The purchase contributes to credit ease.

With respect to stock market credit, an increase in margin requirements reduces the amount of new credit that may be extended for the purpose of purchasing or carrying securities listed on the national securities exchanges. A decrease in margin requirements increases this amount.

Other alternations in the authority of the monetary officials, in the early and mid-1930's, include the following: increased reliance upon judgment as opposed to rules, the shift of the initiative for effecting credit changes from the member banks to the Board of Governors, and the shift of the primary responsibility for conducting monetary policy from the regional banks to such central governing bodies as the Board of Governors and the Federal Open Market Committee.

Since the early 1930's, the Federal Reserve monetary operations have been conducted through the use of a combination of tools. One of the most powerful and, at the same time, the most flexible of these tools for day-to-day use is open market operations. Through these operations, a given tone in the money and credit markets may be achieved. The Federal Reserve may prepare the markets for the coordinated use of other credit controls, or it may simply give effect to the desired tone in the money and credit markets by inaction and reliance upon other market forces. By contrast, in the first two decades of the system, the discount rate constituted the focal point for Federal Reserve actions.

References

1. See Marriner S. Eccles, *Beckoning Frontiers* (New York: Alfred A. Knopf, 1951), p. 228.

2. See directives bearing upon economic objectives: *Monetary Policy and the Management of the Public Debt* (Washington, D.C.: U.S. Government Printing Office, 1952) pp. 209 and 213.

3. See Commission on Money and Credit, *Money and Credit: Their Influence on Jobs, Prices, and Growth* (Englewood Cliffs, N.J.: Prentice-Hall, Inc., 1961), pp. 9-45.

4. See Milton Friedman and Anna Jacobson Schwartz, *A Monetary History of the United States, 1867-1960* (Princeton, N.J.: Princeton University Press, 1963), pp. 169 and 253.

5. See Robert V. Roosa, *Federal Reserve Operations in the Money and Government Securities Markets* (New York: Federal Reserve Bank of New York, 1956), pp. 7-10. The embryonic form of "positive regulation" may,

however, be found as far back as 1921-1924, as reflected in Lester V. Chandler's discussion of "New Goals, New Methods": see his *Benjamin Strong, Central Banker* (Washington, D.C.: The Brookings Institution, 1958), pp. 188-246.

6. For references concerning these monetary controls, see Warren L. Smith, "The Instruments of General Monetary Control," *The National Banking Review*, September 1963, pp. 47-76.

7. *Ibid.*, p. 49.

8. For a discussion of the evolution of the tradition against borrowing, see Friedman and Schwartz, *op.cit.*, pp. 268-269.

9. See Eccles, *op.cit.*, p. 112.

10. See Friedman and Schwartz, *op.cit.*, pp. 244-249; and William J. Frazer, *The Liquidity Structure of Firms and Monetary Economics* (Gainesville, Fla.: University of Florida Press, 1965), Chap. 4.

11. *The Federal Reserve System: Purposes and Functions* (Washington, D.C.: Board of Governors of the Federal Reserve System, 1954), p. 36.

12. See Smith, *op.cit.*, pp. 64-68.

13. See Warren L. Smith, "The Discount Rate as a Credit-Control Weapon," *The Journal of Political Economy*, April 1958, pp. 171-177.

14. See, e.g., Commission on Money and Credit, *op.cit.*, pp. 64-66.

15. See "Implementation of the 1959 Act on Reserve Requirements," *Federal Reserve Bulletin*, December 1960, pp. 1326-1331.

16. Henry Parker Willis, *The Theory and Practice of Central Banking* (New York: Harper and Brothers, 1936), pp. 184-185.

17. See the statement by Benjamin Strong in W. Randolph Burgess (ed.), *Interpretations of Federal Reserve Policy in the Speeches and Writings of Benjamin Strong* (New York: Harper and Brothers, 1930), pp. 235-236. See also Chandler, *op.cit.*, pp. 208-221.

18. For a discussion of the evolution of the open market operations in the 1920's, see Willis, *op.cit.*, pp. 189-194; and Friedman and Schwartz, *op.cit.*, pp. 367-391.

19. *Exercises in the Debits and Credits of Bank Reserves* (Federal Reserve Bank of Philadelphia).

part four

Central Banking, Reserve and Money Supply Accounts, and the Banking Structure

9

The Federal Reserve, Reserve, and Money Supply Accounts

> Primary responsibility for regulating the flow of bank credit and money in the United States is vested in the Federal Reserve System. The discharge of this responsibility requires detailed, accurate, and current information concerning the economic situation in general and the workings of the banking and monetary system in particular (Board of Governors of the Federal Reserve System, "Banks and the Monetary System," *Supplement to Banking and Monetary Statistics* [1962]).

In accounting for member-bank reserves and the money supply, three statements of condition are needed: the consolidated balance sheet for the twelve Federal Reserve banks, the United States Treasury monetary accounts, and the balance sheet for the entire private banking system. The consolidated statement of condition for the twelve Federal Reserve banks is the most basic among these as a means of revealing the actions and inactions of the monetary authorities, as well as of revealing the Federal Reserve's position with respect to member-bank reserves, their own reserves, and so on. The others, nevertheless, are essential in accounting for member-bank reserves and the money supply.

In carrying out the objectives of accounting for member-bank reserves and the money supply, and for changes in the member-bank reserves and the money supply, we must first make some preliminary comments about double-entry bookkeeping, generally, and the unique way in which the banking sector effects cash settlements, in particular. We then proceed by introducing the statement of condition for the Federal Reserve banks and by reviewing the financial condition of the Federal Reserve. This statement is an important document from which one may learn much about the actions and inactions of the monetary authorities, the implementation of a given policy of credit ease of tightness, and the strategy

175

underlying the use of the various tools in giving effect to a particular policy in a given environment.

9.1. Double-Entry Bookkeeping: The Unique Position of the Banking Sector

In viewing the financial condition of the Federal Reserve banks and in accounting for member-banks reserves and the money supply, we deal with accounts as they exist at a moment in time in the context of an equation that states the fundamental accounting identity (i.e., assets = liabilities + capital accounts). This identity, of course, simply involves double-entry bookkeeping (Chap. 3) and balance sheets, wherein every entry involves either an offsetting entry on the same side of the equation or an entry of equal magnitude on the other side. In this respect, however, there are certain general statements we may make about the balance sheets and changes in balance sheets, and there are special statements to be made about balance sheets and changes in balance sheets for the banking sector.

Given the identity and its relation to financial statements in the form of balance sheets, generally, then one may perform the permissible algebraic operations of addition (subtraction), multiplication (division), and removal (or insertion) of parentheses, as well as additional operations that combine two equations: substitution and elimination by addition and subtraction. This means that the separate accounts relating to the two sides of the balance sheet may be regrouped in various ways so as to permit an expression of any one item in the equation in terms of all the other items.

Balance sheets, however, record stocks or a historical accumulation up to some moment in time. Often one wishes to view changes over time from one statement date to another, as in an earlier chapter (Sect. 3.1), in order to relate the changes to other changes with the same time dimension, such as output, employment, and expenditures. These discrete changes from one period to the next [called flows (Sect. 1.4)] are changes in stock. In viewing the changes, any increase (decrease) on the asset side is seen as a use (source) of funds, and any increase (decrease) on the liabilities side is seen as a source (use) of funds. In the context of the accounting identity, all this means is that the flows comprising the sources of funds will always equal those comprising the uses, where the term "funds" simply refers to bookkeeping entries.

Now, with respect to sources and uses of funds and the use of money as a medium of exchange (Sect. 2.1), a distinction must be made between the banking sector and other sectors. All other sectors effect a cash purchase or sale by decreasing or increasing cash balances, respectively. For example, all other sectors receive or give up money from a cash sale or purchase in such a way as to involve either an asset or a liability, such as a bond. In the case of a sale of an asset, the asset account goes down and cash goes up, and there is no change in total assets. In the case of a purchase of an asset, the asset account goes up and cash goes down. The banking sector, on the other hand, makes a cash sale or purchase of an asset, such as a security, by respectively decreasing or increasing its total assets and its currency and deposit liabilities. In other words, in the banking sector, the commercial banks may engage in a direct exchange of money in the process of purchasing or liquidating loans and investments by respectively expanding or contracting its liabilities. Further, the Federal Reserve may acquire or liquidate securities by respectively increasing or decreasing member-bank reserves. The operation of banks on the principle of fractional reserves are thus unique in this regard.

The import of all this for our purpose is simple. We wish to use the accounting identity in subsequently analyzing nonbanking sectors, in discussing the financial condition of the Federal Reserve banks, and in treating the derivation of member-bank reserves and money supply accounts. In the case of the money supply accounts, but contrary to the general case, an increase in the earning asset accounts of commercial banks simultaneously involves a source of funds and an increase in the money supply, even after allowance for possible currency and time deposit drains (Sect. 3.3) and other complications. Consequently, in the special cases of the member-bank reserve accounts and the money supply accounts, there will be a need to modify the usual references to the stock of assets and an increase in assets as a use of funds, and to the liabilities side and an increase in the liabilities side as a source of funds. In the special case of the member-bank reserve accounts, assets will be called a source of reserves (or "factors supplying reserve funds"). In the special case of the money supply accounts, assets will be referred to as expansive factors, and the accounts on the liabilities side will be referred to as contractive factors. The derivations of the latter sets of accounts and subsequent experience with other sets of accounts will make the present terminology more meaningful.

9.2. The Statement of Condition for the Federal Reserve Banks

Every Thursday a statement of the operations of the twelve Federal Reserve banks is released to the press. A consolidated statement of the twelve banks shows the condition of the Reserve banks at the close of business on Wednesday and appears in the daily press on Friday morning. A statement of condition for each Federal Reserve bank and a total (i.e., combined) column also appears. The present consolidated statement was published on a combined basis prior to February 1961. In general, the consolidated statement presents the data for the conditions after the elimination for duplications that would otherwise occur, as when a liability of one of the twelve banks appears as an asset for another.[1]

The release, known generally as the weekly statement of condition, also appears every month in the *Federal Reserve Bulletin*. The statement is very complete and informative to the reader. It is reviewed in this chapter to bring out technical points not elsewhere covered in the text, and to present those covered elsewhere in a different context, so as to give a more concrete meaning of bank operations to the nonspecialist and to introduce the prospective banker, or finance officer, to a useful source of current information. The statement is also needed for the derivation of the member-bank reserve and money supply accounts (Sect. 9.3 and 9.4).[2]

The first page of the statement released to the press shows the changes for the preceding year and for the preceding week in the bank reserve statement (Sect. 9.3). The second page shows the changes for corresponding periods in the consolidated balance sheet for the twelve Federal Reserve banks, and other pages show the statement for the individual Reserve banks. Other changes affecting the condition of the Federal Reserve banks, as well as the important changes affecting the bank reserve equation, such as those in Federal Reserve credit, monetary gold stock, and Federal Reserve notes in circulation, are also for the most part reflected by comparing the consolidated balance sheet at another statement date. The changes in the respective accounts are indicated by pluses and minuses on the weekly statement.

Table 9-1 shows the consolidated balance sheet of the Federal Reserve banks for the last statement week in June 1963. It also shows changes in the accounts presented for the statement week ended June 26, 1963, and for the period of June 27, 1962-June 26, 1963, as they appear on the Thursday press release. There is no particular significance attached to that period for this purpose; it is chosen merely to illustrate for the present a comparison of balance sheets accounts and, therefore, stock variables as a source of information pertaining to changes in the conditions of the Federal Reserve. For example, the first column shows data corresponding to the accounts as stock variables, the second column shows data for changes in the stock variables for the week ended June 26, and the third column shows data for changes in the stock variables for

Table 9-1. Consolidated Statement of Condition of the Twelve Federal Reserve Banks

(Dollar amounts in millions)

Assets		June 26, 1963	Change since June 19, 1963	Change since June 27, 1962
Gold certificate reserves		15,442	− 72	− 716
Cash	(344)	356	+ 8	− 16
Discounts and advances		612	− 142	+ 219
Industrial loans**		—	—	—
Acceptances		38	− 7	− 6
United States government securities:				
Bought outright		31,448	+ 108	+2,213
Held under repurchase agreement		149	− 97	+ 1
Cash items in process of collection	(1,176)	5,438	−1,471	+ 362
Other assets		485	+ 38	− 314
Total assets	(1,520)	53,968	−1,635	+1,743

Liabilities				
Federal Reserve notes	(344)	30,242	+ 12	+1,706
Deposits:				
Member-bank reserves		16,664	− 633	− 527
United States Treasurer— general account		1,054	+ 181	+ 476
Foreign		182	+ 15	− 160
Other		211	− 31	− 22
Deferred availability cash items	(1,176)	4,027	−1,198	+ 193
Other liabilities and accrued dividends		85	+ 4	+ 5
Total liabilities	(1,520)	52,465	−1,650	+1,671

Capital Accounts	1963	1963	1962
Capital paid in	481	—	+ 24
Surplus	934	—	+ 46
Other capital accounts	88	+ 15	+ 2
Total liabilities and capital accounts	53,968	−1,635	+1,743

The reserve ratio (i.e., the ratio of gold certificate reserves to deposit and Federal Reserve note liabilities as computed from nonconsolidated figures)†	31.7	0.1	− 2.5
Float	1,411	− 273	+ 169

SOURCE: Board of Governors of the Federal Reserve System.

* Figures in parentheses are the eliminations made in the consolidating process.

** The industrial loan program was discontinued on August 21, 1959.

† Legislation repealing the gold-certificate requirement for deposits as distinct from currency notes was signed into law on March 4, 1965.

the period of June 27, 1962-June 26, 1963. From the flow variable point of view, the data in the second column times the fifty-two weeks in a year give averages of rates of change per annum during the week, and the data in the third column give averages of rates of change per annum for the period of June 27, 1962, to June 26, 1963.

Each of the selected accounts from the balances shown in the table is discussed below in the descending order of appearance. This will be followed by a discussion of the gold certificate reserve ratio and Federal Reserve float, two important items which may be derived from the weekly balance sheet data.

The assets accounts. The assets accounts include such accounts as gold certificate reserves, cash, discounts and advances, and government securities.

The gold certificate reserves vary according to the net purchase or net sale of gold by the Federal Reserve Bank of New York, acting as agent for the United States Treasury, in the manner described below (Sect. 10.4). The Federal Reserve, for instance, is not permitted to hold gold, but a purchase of gold by the Treasury is paid for by a check against the Treasury's account at the Federal Reserve, and the Treasury replenishes its account by giving the Federal Reserve credit for gold certificates in an amount equal to the purchase. This arrangement may be said to give the Reserve banks an asset in the form of a claim on the Treasury.

Cash is currency in the vaults of the Reserve banks, other than Federal Reserve notes.

Discounts and advances represent credit extended largely to member banks through the discount window. The initiative for this form of credit expansion is taken by the member banks. The member banks secure reserves from the Federal Reserve banks by discounting eligible paper or, more commonly, by offering their own promissory notes secured by eligible paper, government securities, or other satisfactory collateral, as described earlier (Sect. 7.5 and 8.1).

Changes in this account represent relatively short-run adjustments on the part of member banks. Generally, the changes tend to move with changes in the tone (i.e., the ease or tightness) of the credit market, although the absence of change in the account may be accompanied by different banks alternately borrowing and repaying loans. In the general case, nevertheless, the account tends to increase as the tone of the market tightens and decrease as the tone eases in response to member-bank borrowing and repayment as the need arises and abates.*

---

* Another similar indicator dealt with at some length below (Sect. 24.2), and in part derived from the present account, is free reserves, i.e., excess reserves minus discounts and advances for (borrowings of) member banks. An increase in member-bank borrowing and a decrease in free reserves indicates a tight tone for the

Industrial loans, now only of historical interest, once included those loans extended to establish commercial and industrial enterprises for working capital purposes. The authority for such loans was granted as an emergency measure under an act signed into law in 1934. Under the law the board published Regulation S, setting out the ground rules for the lending under Section 13b of the Federal Reserve Act. In November 1935, loans and commitments outstanding under the program reached an all-time high of 60.6 million dollars. Thereafter, the volume of loans, with minor exceptions, became increasingly insignificant.* Almost a quarter of a century later, August 24, 1958, the Small Business Investment Act (Sect. 17.5) was signed into law, and, as a part of this action, Federal Reserve commercial lending—both direct and indirect—was revoked as of August 1959. The 13b program and the banks' asset account, "industrial loans," passed into history. The direct-loan business, such as that represented by the industrial loans account, has rarely been considered a proper function for a bank of issue.

Acceptances are bought outright or held by the Federal Reserve under repurchase agreement. Such assets may be acquired through open market operations (Sect. 8.1). In the 1920's these instruments were in the main channel for the release of Reserve bank credit to the money market (Sect. 7.3) and one of the Reserve System's main sources of income. Although this form of purchase has ceased to be of much quantitative significance as a means of extending Federal Reserve credit, the Federal Reserve has in recent years sought to revive the acceptance market. In fact, 44 million dollars worth of acceptances appear in the above statement of condition.

United States government securities comprise that portion of the Federal Reserve's portfolio consisting of Treasury bills, Treasury certificates of indebtedness, Treasury notes, and Treasury bonds. A breakdown of these holdings, by type of Federal debt instrument, is published in the regular weekly condition statement; for the statement corresponding to Table 9-1, the breakdown for securities bought outright would appear as follows:

---

market. Conversely, a decrease in member-bank borrowing and an increase in free reserves indicates an easy tone in the market.

* The decline in the lending activity, under Section 13b, may be explained by several factors: (1) In January 1935 business lending became a permanent part of the Reconstruction Finance Corporation (RFC)—a government agency whose charter expired in 1953—and the predecessor of the present Small Business Administration (Sect. 17.5). (2) Financial institutions showed an increasing willingness to part with funds to business under arrangements other than those specified by the real bills doctrine, such as (a) term loans—intermediate and long-term loans repayable in installments—and (b) accounts receivable financing (Sect. 17.5). See "The 13b Programs—An Experiment in Small Business Financing," *Monthly Review,* Federal Reserve Bank of St. Louis, March 1959, pp. 30-36.

(In millions of dollars)

	June 26, 1963	Change since	
		June 19, 1963	June 27, 1962
Bills	2,870	+ 64	+ 236
Certificates	14,443	0	+8,865
Notes	9,723	+ 24	−7,467
Bonds	4,412	+ 20	+ 579
Total	31,448	+108	+2,213

The weekly condition statement also presents a memorandum on the maturity distribution of loans and securities. The data for securities, including those held under repurchase agreement, for the statement week ended June 26 are as follows:

(In millions of dollars)

	June 26, 1963	Change since	
		June 19, 1963	June 27, 1962
Within 15 days	750	+ 39	+ 267
16 days to 90 days	5,421	−137	+ 313
91 days to 1 year	14,944	+ 65	+3,592
Over 1 year to 5 years	8,285	+ 44	−1,722
Over 5 years to ten years	2,032	0	− 187
Over 10 years	165	0	− 49
Total	31,597	+ 11	+2,214

The separate debt instruments are described later (Sect. 13.1), but for the present we may note that the data for both the breakdown by type of instrument and the time-to-maturity (Sect. 4.2) distribution of the Federal Reserve holdings are important in interpreting the Federal Reserve's open market position with respect to the type of debt instrument, and the maturity distribution of their holdings. Monetary policy has, at times (Sect. 24.3) in this respect, been directed primarily toward transactions in Treasury bills with the view that the effect of transactions in these bills would be spread elsewhere in the financial markets through switching and arbitrage transactions by traders and dealers in those markets. And, at other times (Sect. 24.3), it has been directed toward raising the yield on short-dated instruments relative to the yield on longer-dated ones, with the view to restraining outflows of gold and, at the same time, stimulating domestic investment (Sect. 5.4) in a period of recession by lower yields on long-term or capital funds.

Over-all changes in the total of the Federal Reserve's holdings of United States government securities as they appear in the weekly condition statement are of uppermost importance, nevertheless, in the earlier context of Federal open market operations (Sect. 9.1), irrespective of the type of securities or their maturity. In that context, a sale of securities effects a decrease in bank reserves, and a purchase effects an increase. The holdings are generally purchased outright, but some portion of them may be held under a repurchase agreement, as noted in Table 9-1. Those held under repurchase agreement represent assistance to securities' dealers (Sect. 13.2) in carrying their inventories of securities during periods of temporary credit stringency. In these instances, the Federal Reserve takes the initiative in making this type of credit available to the dealers, whereas the dealers themselves must initiate the transactions.

Special obligations are sometimes held in the Federal Reserve's portfolio. At such times they are represented separately on the weekly statement. They correspond to direct purchases of a special series of certificates from the Treasury for the purpose of permitting Treasury payments before tax receipts become available. The authority for this type of transaction has generally been extended for two-year periods; it permits the Treasury to carry a smaller cash balance than would otherwise be possible.

Cash items in process of collection represent checks deposited with the Federal Reserve banks that are in the process of collection at the time the weekly statement is made up. The account has a counterpart, *deferred availability cash items,* on the liability side described below. The difference between the two accounts is Federal Reserve float.

Other assets include bank premises, premium on securities owned, accrued interest and other accounts receivable, Federal Reserve deposits in foreign banks, and other items of small magnitude. Since the Federal Reserve's resumption of foreign exchange operations (Sect. 21.4 and 23.5) in February 1962, separate figures are provided for the Federal Reserve's assets which are denominated in foreign currencies.

The liability and capital accounts. The liability and capital accounts include those pertaining to Federal Reserve notes, member-bank deposits, paid-in capital, and surplus.

Federal Reserve notes are the principal part of currency in circulation (i.e., currency outside the Federal Reserve and Treasury). They are liabilities of the Federal Reserve banks and legal tender of the United States government. They are fully backed by eligible paper, government securities, and gold certificate reserves. Moreover, the notes have a first lien against all the assets of the originating bank of issue. Changes in the amount of Federal Reserve notes outstanding generally reflect seasonal and other variations in business activity, as described below (Sect. 10.1).

The account in the consolidated statement shows the notes of one Federal Reserve bank that are held by another Federal Reserve bank. The Federal Reserve notes of other Reserve banks are netted out in the process of consolidation and correspond to the figure of 344 million dollars in parentheses in Table 9-1. In a combined statement they would appear as an asset item. They represent notes being returned, or held for the purpose of being returned, to the bank originating the issue, or to the Treasury for retirement. The law requires the return of notes to the Federal Reserve banks originally issuing them, when they are received by another of the Federal Reserve banks. It also requires the return of unfit notes to the Treasury for retirement.

Deposits consist primarily of the reserve accounts of member banks and, to a much smaller extent, of the Treasury's general account, accounts of foreign central banks and treasuries, and others. The account is broken down into its component parts on the weekly statement. Changes in the reserve accounts of member banks would, of course, reflect a possible combination of changes in Reserve bank credit, gold flows, the demand for Federal Reserve notes, and so on. Changes in the Treasury's general account would reflect the interrelationship between the Treasury's revenues and disbursements (Sect. 13.2) and tax and loan accounts (Sect. 13.5) at commercial banks, in which the Treasury occasionally permits balances to accumulate before transferring them to their general account. Changes in the foreign accounts may reflect important factors affecting member-bank reserves, such as a transfer of funds by foreign central banks from the Federal Reserve to the commercial banks and vice versa. Also the changes in the foreign accounts may be associated with changes in other accounts, such as that for gold certificates. Changes in the other deposit account primarily reflects changes in the clearing accounts maintained by nonmember banks.

Deferred availability cash items arise from the Federal Reserve's practice of giving immediate credit for all checks deposited with them for collection. The credit appears as a liability other than a deposit until deposit credit is granted according to a time schedule that allows for the clearance of out-of-town checks through the mail. The time schedule is more generous than the actual time needed to collect the checks. Consequently, an imbalance is likely to occur between the magnitude of the *deferred availability cash items* and the *cash items in process of collection,* the former being smaller than the latter. The sum representing this imbalance is called the Federal Reserve float. It is described further, below.

Other liabilities and accrued dividends consist of unearned discounts on notes and securities and miscellaneous accounts payable, in addition to the accrued dividends.

Capital paid in represents the proportion of subscribed capital stock that has actually been paid in by the member banks. Member banks have been required to subscribe to capital stock of the Reserve bank in their district to the amount of 6 per cent of their own capital stock and surplus since the beginnings of the system (Sect. 7.5), although only one-half of the amount has actually been paid in and the other half remains subject to call.

Actually, the return on the member-bank's paid-in capital is a very favorable one, given the risk involved, and member banks are doubtlessly satisfied with the prevailing arrangement. But this arrangement of ownership has left the member banks and the Federal Reserve open to the charge that they have too direct an interest in each other's profits. The member banks, in fact, have been unique among nationally regulated industries in their ownership of the regulatory system, and the opinion, therefore, has been expressed that the stock subscriptions are no longer needed, that the Reserve banks are public service institutions, and that "the present form of capital stock should be retired." [3] The suggestion has been made then that instead of the present form of stock ownership, membership should be evidenced by the investment of a nominal sum of about 500 dollars by each member bank.

Surplus primarily represents that proportion of earnings, net of operating expenses, that is not paid out as dividends or to the Treasury in the form of an excise tax. The surplus may be drawn upon to pay dividends to meet deficits when such occur. Included in the surplus, however, was a small amount received from the Treasury in accordance with the law relating to the industrial loans account, prior to the discontinuance of the industrial loan program under section 13b of the Federal Reserve Act. In practice, surplus is now held at twice the year-end paid-in capital, with sufficient earnings retained to bring it to that figure. All of any additional earnings of the dividends are turned over to the Treasury.

Other capital accounts may comprise reserves for contingencies and net earnings for the year that have not been allocated at the time of the statement.

Other items. The other items referred to in Table 9-1 include the reserve ratio and Federal Reserve float. Neither is a part of the consolidated balance sheet of the Federal Reserve banks. Both, nevertheless, are important and may be derived from the balance sheet data shown in the statement of condition.

The reserve ratio has traditionally referred to the ratio of *gold certificate reserves* to *Federal Reserve notes* plus *deposits*, the first being an asset account and the last two liability accounts as they appear in the consolidated statement. It was thought to be important because the law prescribes that it must not be less than 25 per cent. The law, however, may be changed by legislative action, as it was in 1945 with the reduction of the minimum required ratio from 40 per cent for Federal Reserve notes and 35 per cent for deposits. In fact, legislation repealed the gold certificate entirely in early 1965. Accordingly, the reserve ratio refers only to the requirement against Federal Reserve notes. Since early 1965 the ratio only serves as a Congressional check upon the expansion of Federal Reserve notes. The legal limit is of little significance as a constraint on domestic monetary operations when the ratio is of sufficient magnitude to give the monetary authorities freedom of action, though its importance may arise in other contexts (Sect. 23.5).

Federal Reserve float is the excess of *cash items in the process of collection* over *deferred availability cash items* on a nonconsolidated basis. The data for deriving float, however, are included in the statement of condition in Table 9-1. The excess occurs because the time schedule for granting reserve credit for checks deposited with the Federal Reserve is less than the time actually required for the checks to clear. In effect, the bookkeeping works this way. The checks deposited at the Federal Reserve by member banks are first credited to deferred availability cash items, and on a fixed time schedule the credit is transferred to member-bank reserves. At the time the checks are initially deposited, the account for cash items in process of collection is debited simultaneously, and it is subsequently credited when the checks actually clear and the member-bank reserves are debited. However, the time lag between the granting of credit to the member-bank reserves, in the first instance, and the debiting of those reserves, in the latter instance, are such that there is a net balance in member-bank reserves. This net balance is measured by the excess of cash items in process of collection over deferred availability cash items. Consequently, changes in the Federal Reserve float primarily reflect changes in the volume of out-of-town checks and the weather, or in the seasonal volume of checks, which may affect the time required for the checks to go through the mail or in the sheer magnitude of the residual, respectively.

The significance of the imbalance between *cash items in the process of collection* and *deferred availability cash items* lies in the fact that the imbalance is a sum credited to member-bank reserves. Variations in Federal Reserve float, therefore, may affect the ease or tightness of credit. It is a variable to be reckoned with by the officers of the operating departments of the Federal Reserve and by their research staffs in the preparation of day-to-day projections of factors expected to affect Reserve bank credit. Depending upon the projections and the tone of the market desired, action may be taken to complement the projected effect or to neutralize or otherwise offset it.

9.3. The Treasury Monetary Accounts and the Derivation of Member-Bank Reserve Accounts

The legal reserves of member banks consist entirely of the deposits by the member banks in the Federal Reserve banks and vault cash (Sect. 8.1). The former are, of course, deposit liabilities of the Federal Reserve banks, while the latter are included among the currency liabilities of both Federal Reserve banks and the United States Treasury. As matters turn out, then, we need only to consolidate the balance sheets of all of the Federal Reserve banks with the appropriate balance sheet listings of the Treasury's monetary assets and currency liabilities, and then to perform permissible algebraic operations on the results until we have a statement for the total sources and total uses of member-bank reserves. This statement in a corresponding equation form, furthermore, turns out to be the member-bank reserve equation. Here we only derive a statement of the accounts in a form corresponding to the bank reserve equation, and we deal with the equation per se and its correspondence to real-world phenomena in the next chapter. As a practical matter, the derivation of the accounts in a form corresponding to the equation seems complicated, due simply to a conglomeration of items on the various balance sheets. We shall, consequently, simplify matters a bit by concentrating on the less trivial accounts for the purpose at hand.

The Treasury monetary accounts. The consolidated statement for the twelve Federal Reserve banks was previously introduced (Table 9-1). We wish now to consolidate this statement with a statement of the Treasury monetary accounts, following a statement of the latter accounts.

The Treasury accounts with which we wish to effect a consolidation are shown in Table 9-2. This statement of the accounts themselves is made up of several separate accounts—chiefly the gold and silver accounts and portions of the so-called general fund statement. Further, the statement relates only to the Treasury's own monetary liabilities (i.e., gold and silver certificates and coin), the monetary assets supporting them, and the Treasury's residual ownership of these monetary assets. This means that the Treasury's balances in the Federal Reserve banks and in private banks are excluded from the statement in Table 9-2.

Viewing the accounts in Table 9-2 more directly, there are five accounts to be explained. In this respect, *monetary gold stock* is the gold held by the United States Treasury that has given rise to bank reserves and paper currency. *Gold certificates* are certificates that have been issued or pledged against monetary gold. They may, for example, give rise to bank reserves in a manner similar to gold under the gold standard.

Silver certificates and coin consist primarily of (1) paper currency

Table 9-2. Treasury Monetary Accounts
(Dollar amounts in millions)

| | | Change since | |
Assets	June 26, 1963	June 19, 1963	June 27, 1962
Monetary gold stock	15,733	−65	−702
Treasury currency	5,582	0	− 18
Total monetary assets	21,315	−65	−720

Liabilities and Net Worth			
Gold certificates:			
Held by or pledged to Federal Reserve banks	15,442	−72	−716
Held by nonbank public	—	—	—
Silver certificates and coin: *			
Held by Federal Reserve banks	356	+ 8	− 16
Held by banks Held by nonbank public}	5,115	+ 7	+ 21
Total monetary liabilities	20,913	−57	−711
Treasury cash	402	− 8	− 9
Total liabilities and net worth	21,315	−65	−720

SOURCE: Board of Governors of the Federal Reserve System.
* Includes also other minor currency issues.

issued by the Treasury against silver bullion and silver dollars and (2) silver and minor coin. It also includes United States notes and small issues in the process of being retired.

Now, the other two accounts—*Treasury currency* and *Treasury cash* —are confusing because the terms themselves do not imply the substance of the accounts. The former reads as if it should be a liability of the Treasury, and the latter reads as if it should be an asset, whereas in fact the reverse is true. Treasury "currency," sometimes even more confusingly called "Treasury currency outstanding," really represents the assets or reserves held by the Treasury to support its silver certificate and coin liabilities. It is made up chiefly of monetized silver bullion, silver dollars held by the Treasury, old currency issues held as security against new issues, and a few other items. As a legal and practical matter, however, the Treasury has had some "free silver" * or an excess of silver

---

* The late President Kennedy directed the Treasury to halt the sale of silver from its "free" or "nonmonetized" stocks of silver in November 1961, and to retire some silver certificates. The purpose of the action was to assure an adequate stock of silver for the more immediate future growth in the need for coinage. The action came at a time when the consumption of silver by the arts and industry was expanding and

reserve over the reserves called for by law. This has been the case, since the law for years permits the Treasury to monetize silver above the pre-1963 statutory support price of 90.5 cents per fine ounce,* and since the Treasury chose in practice to monetize silver at its purchase price. Most meaningfully, then, one would simply think of the account, "Treasury currency," as corresponding to currency reserves or authorized currency, against which currency is issued on the liability side.**

Treasury cash is not cash at all. Instead of cash, the account "Treasury cash" represents the Treasury's net worth in its monetary assets. It is the residual account on the liabilities side that causes that side to balance against the total for assets. In other words, Treasury cash represents the Treasury's own claim to its monetary assets over and above the claims in the form of gold and silver certificates that the Treasury has distributed to holders (and other minor currency and coin creditors) outside of the Treasury. The unfortunate terminology, in the present instance, has

---

at a time when the price of silver was rising above the Treasury's selling price of 91 cents per fine ounce.

The time also appeared to be ripe for having the Treasury drop out of the market for silver, and, accordingly, the President recommended the repeal of the Silver Purchase Act. This was followed in 1963 by the elimination of provisions requiring the government to maintain a floor of 90.05 cents an ounce under newly mined domestic silver. One source has said that the silver purchase legislation in the United States has been motivated with the view to enlarging the money supply (Sect. 6.1) or raising the price of silver for the benefit of the producers (Sect. 7.14). Now, "with a minimum impact on silver prices, the Treasury was able to drop out and let the free market do the job of equating supply and demand" ("Free Market for Silver," *First National City Bank Monthly Letter*, December 1961, pp. 140-143).

* See preceding footnote.

** Through a combination of the 1961 directive (mentioned above) and legislation going into effect in June 1963, a gradual shift from silver certificates to additional Federal Reserve notes was set into effect. As with the directive halting the sale of "free silver," the purpose was to assure a substantial supply of silver for coinage. The 1963 legislation, however, expressly allowed for the disposal of silver by the Treasury at $1.2929 a fine ounce. Interestingly, the effect of this disposal price may have been to prevent the melting of silver dollars, because, at a higher price and disregarding the cost of melting and legal prohibitions, it becomes profitable to melt United States silver dollars for their silver content. Furthermore, following the actions in question and a widening of the gap between the total production and consumption of silver in the arts and industry, the market price of silver in New York and London reached $1.2930 in September 1963.

All of this raised interesting questions about the future of silver. An increase in the United States selling price could have subjected silver dollars with the silver content of 1963 to the prospect of being melted for silver. It could also have forced us to mint dollars and possibly subsidiary coins—half-dollars, quarters, and dimes—with lower silver content. (See "A New Chapter in Silver History," *The National City Bank Monthly Letter*, December 1963, pp. 137-140.) As matters turned out, silver continued in short supply, and in June 1965 President Johnson asked Congress to authorize large-scale reduction in the silver content of dimes, quarters, and half-dollars. Among other things, he also asked for authority to purchase domestically mined silver at not less than $1.25 per ounce.

arisen as a result of the close connection between the Treasury's net worth and particular monetary assets, as contrasted with the absence of any close connection between net worth and particular assets on the ordinary business balance sheet. Numerically, Treasury cash is equal to the portion of the gold stock against which no gold certificates have been issued or pledged plus the difference between the Treasury currency reserve and the currency issued against that reserve. Thus, the Treasury cash figure (or the net worth of the Treasury in terms of the present accounts) of 402 million dollars is equal to the 291 million excess of monetary gold stock over gold certificates, plus 111 million of Treasury currency (and coin).

The Treasury does maintain a cash account at the Federal Reserve, as well as balances at private banks, and we wish to deal with these balances (Sect. 13.5). Contrary to occasional assertions, however, these balances are exclusive of the above item for Treasury cash. The Federal Reserve itself has confounded confusion by grouping together Treasury cash and Treasury balances in Federal Reserve and private banks under the heading "U.S. Government deposits." Of importance to our present derivation of the accounts affecting member-bank reserves, however, is the certainty that Treasury cash and Treasury currency end up on the proper side(s) of our consolidated balance sheets.

The derivation of member-bank reserve accounts. The present derivation of the member-bank reserve accounts proceeds in two parts. The first part involves two steps: (1) a consolidation of the Federal Reserve and Treasury balance sheets (i.e., Table 9-1 and Table 9-2) and (2) a cancellation of common items found to appear on both sides of the balance sheet resulting from the first steps. The second part then involves a regrouping of the remaining items in two additional steps: (3) one causing two accounts to change sides and (4) another simply involving the rearrangement of accounts on the same side. The final result is a cumulative statement of sources and uses of member-bank reserves.

The two steps involving the first part of the derivation are outlined in Table 9-3. There, in the upper left-hand corner, are the Treasury monetary accounts (Table 9-2). In the lower left-hand corner are selected accounts for the consolidated statement for the twelve Federal Reserve banks (Table 9-1). There, too, we observe that the Treasury's gold certificate liability to the Federal Reserve offsets the Federal Reserve's assets account for gold certificates, and the Treasury's liability account for silver certificates and coin held by the Federal Reserve provides an offset to the Federal Reserve assets account for cash.

Next, as a third step, we simply reproduce the lower part of Table 9-3, in the form of Table 9-4, and perform permissible operations in the process. In this operation we subtract "other assets" and "deferred availability cash items" from both sides, and then cancel plus and minus values for the same items on given sides. In the result, as shown in Table 9-4, we are left with minus values for two items, and the items have in effect switched sides.

Finally, we record and rearrange the remaining accounts from Table

Table 9-3. Derivation [Steps (1) and (2)] of the Member-Bank Reserve Accounts

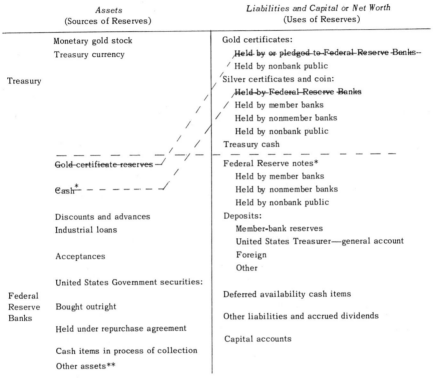

Assets (Sources of Reserves)	*Liabilities and Capital or Net Worth* (Uses of Reserves)
Monetary gold stock	Gold certificates:
Treasury currency	~~Held by or pledged to Federal Reserve Banks~~
	Held by nonbank public
Treasury	Silver certificates and coin:
	~~Held by Federal Reserve Banks~~
	Held by member banks
	Held by nonmember banks
	Held by nonbank public
	Treasury cash
~~Gold-certificate reserves~~	Federal Reserve notes*
	Held by member banks
~~Cash*~~	Held by nonmember banks
	Held by nonbank public
Discounts and advances	Deposits:
Industrial loans	Member-bank reserves
	United States Treasurer—general account
Acceptances	Foreign
	Other
United States Government securities:	
Federal	Deferred availability cash items
Reserve Bought outright	
Banks	Other liabilities and accrued dividends
Held under repurchase agreement	
	Capital accounts
Cash items in process of collection	
Other assets**	

* In the consolidated balance sheet for the twelve Federal Reserve banks, Federal Reserve notes held by other Federal Reserve banks than the bank of issue are deducted from cash and from Federal Reserve notes outstanding. Thus, the "cash" figure above is entirely Treasury silver certificates and coin, and the Federal Reserve notes figure represents notes held outside Federal Reserve banks.

** Includes the Federal Reserve's assets denominated in foreign currencies.

9-3 as well as from that portion of Table 9-3 that appears as Table 9-4. This combining of the results of steps (1) through (3) we denote as a fourth step, and record the results in Table 9-5. The reader should now be able to verify for himself that all the accounts remaining after steps (1) through (3) are accounted for in one of the eight categories in Table 9-5.

Table 9-4. Derivation [Step (3)] of the Member-Bank Reserve Accounts

(Treasury portion omitted)

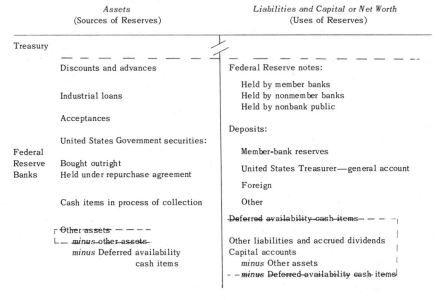

Assets (Sources of Reserves)	*Liabilities and Capital or Net Worth* (Uses of Reserves)
Treasury	
Discounts and advances	Federal Reserve notes:
	Held by member banks
Industrial loans	Held by nonmember banks
	Held by nonbank public
Acceptances	
	Deposits:
United States Government securities:	
Federal	Member-bank reserves
Reserve Bought outright	
Banks Held under repurchase agreement	United States Treasurer—general account
	Foreign
Cash items in process of collection	Other
	~~Deferred availability cash items~~
~~Other assets~~	
~~minus other assets~~	Other liabilities and accrued dividends
minus Deferred availability	Capital accounts
cash items	*minus* Other assets
	~~*minus* Deferred-availability cash items~~

Denoting in equation form the variables corresponding to the accounts in Table 9-5,

$$\underbrace{G + C_T + R}_{\substack{\text{sources of reserves} \\ \text{(``factors supplying} \\ \text{reserve funds'')}}} - \underbrace{(C_S + T_C + F + R_M)}_{\substack{\text{uses of reserves} \\ \text{(``factors absorbing} \\ \text{reserve funds'')}}} = 0$$

where sources always equal uses, and where

G corresponds to account (1),
C_T corresponds to account (2),
R corresponds to account (3),
C_S corresponds to account (4),
T_C corresponds to account (5),
F corresponds to accounts (6) and (7), and
R_M corresponds to account (8).

This, then, is the member-bank reserve equation. Note that we could express member-bank reserves as a stock variable (i.e., R_M) in terms of the remaining stock variables (i.e., G, C_T, R, C_S, T_C, and F).

Subsequently (Sect. 10.2), this equation is restated, and some real-world developments associated with changes in the variables are observed. In the meantime, however, other observations occupy our immediate interest. The member-bank reserve accounts, as published in the monthly *Federal Reserve Bulletin*, differ slightly from the accounts as

Table 9-5. Derivation [Step (4)] of the Member-Bank Reserve Accounts

Assets (Sources of Reserves)	*Liabilities and Capital or Net Worth* (Uses of Reserves)

(1) Monetary gold stock
(2) Treasury currency
(3) Federal Reserve credit:
    Discounts and advances
    Industrial loans
    Acceptances
    United States government
      securities:
      Bought outright
      Held under repurchase
      agreement
    Cash items in process of
      collection *minus* deferred
      availability cash items
      (Federal Reserve "float" *)
	(4) Currency in circulation: **
	    Gold certificates held by non-
	      bank public
	    Silver certificates and coin
	      held by nonmember banks
	    Silver certificates and coin
	      held by nonbank public
	    Federal Reserve notes held by
	      nonmember banks
	    Federal Reserve notes held by
	      nonbank public
	(5) Treasury cash
	(6) Federal Reserve deposits, other
	    than member-banks reserves
	    United States Treasurer—
	      general account
	    Foreign
	    Other
	(7) Other Federal Reserve accounts:
	    Other liabilities and accrued
	      dividends
	    Capital accounts
	      minus other assets
	(8) Member-bank reserves:
	    Silver certificates and coin
	      held by member banks
	    Federal Reserve notes held by
	      member banks
	    Member-bank reserve deposits
	      (in Federal Reserve banks)

* See Table 9-1.
** Net of member-bank vault cash.

presented in Table 9-5. One difference is merely in the order of presentation of the sources-and-uses categories. The present objective was simply to keep the order of the items as close as possible to the initial order in step (1). The other difference is in the "currency-in-circulation" category. We have netted out member-bank vault cash, while the Federal Reserve leaves it in "currency in circulation." This means that member-bank vault cash is double-counted in the Federal Reserve's published figures.

Alternative reserve measures. As we have seen above, the information contained on consolidated Federal Reserve balance sheets and the Treasury monetary accounts enables us to account for changes in total member-bank reserves. For policy-making purposes, the Federal Reserve is also interested in calculating various other reserve measures.[4] One of these, so-called nonborrowed reserves, could be calculated directly from the member-bank reserve accounts by a slight rearrangement of terms. This measure is defined as total member-bank reserves less member-bank borrowings from Federal Reserve banks, which are really "borrowed reserves." By deducting these borrowings from Federal Reserve credit on the "sources" side of the accounts and from total member-bank reserves themselves on the "uses" side, the accounts would be altered to yield this reserve measure.

All of the other reserve measures, however, require more information than is found on the Federal Reserve and Treasury balance sheets. We have already encountered the concepts of required reserves and excess reserves (Sect. 3.2). To calculate required reserves, it is necessary to know the amounts of net demand and time deposits of the two classes of member banks, as well as the appropriate percentage reserve requirements applicable for the period. With this additional information, the total reserve figure in the reserve accounts may be broken down into excess and required components, a breakdown which the Federal Reserve always provides in its published figures.

If then, in either the reserve accounts or the reserve equation, member-bank borrowings from Federal Reserve banks are deducted from Federal Reserve credit on the "sources" side and excess reserves on the "uses" side, it is possible to account for so-called net free (or net borrowed) reserves, defined as excess reserves minus member-bank borrowings from Federal Reserve banks.* We shall encounter this measure again, in connection with monetary policy (Sect. 24.2).

The Federal Reserve also regularly publishes data for two other reserve measures, which, with the necessary additional information and rearrangements of terms, could be incorporated into the framework of the member-bank reserve accounts:

(1) *Reserves available for private deposits.* This measure of reserves excludes from total reserves the reserves required behind the time and demand deposits of the Treasury in commercial banks. It is thus a measure of the reserves of member banks that could be used to support private (i.e., non-Treasury) demand and time deposits.

(2) *Reserves available for private demand deposits.* To set this measure, it is necessary to deduct the reserves required for existing private time deposits from reserves available for total private deposits. The result is a measure of the total reserves member banks could use to support their private demand deposits and is thus the reserve measure presumably most closely connected with the money supply.

---

* Note that nonborrowed reserves may also be defined as required reserves plus net free reserves.

9.4. The Money Supply Accounts and Alternative Measures of the Quantity of Money

A direct product of early flow of funds work (Sect. 15.1), the money supply accounts are technically known as the "consolidated condition statement for banks and the monetary system." They are derived from a consolidation of three balance sheets for the following groups that support monetary liabilities: the Treasury, the Federal Reserve banks, and the private banking system, including savings banks and the Postal Savings System.* Thus, in the derivation of the money supply accounts and a single account for the money supply, we may proceed from the previous. consolidation (Sect. 9.3) of the Treasury monetary accounts and the consolidated Federal Reserve statement. The resulting account for the money supply, however, corresponds specifically to but one of several closely related measures of the money supply. As was the case with alternative reserve measures, it becomes a simple matter to rearrange the accounts slightly in order to embrace other money supply concepts.

The derivation of the money supply accounts. As in the earlier derivation of the member-bank reserve accounts, the present derivation may be effected in two parts. The first part again involves two steps: (1) a consolidation of the bank reserve accounts with the balance sheet for the private banking system, including the Postal Savings System, and (2) a cancellation of common items found to appear on both sides of the balance sheet resulting from the first step. The second part also involves two further steps: (3) the regrouping of accounts by switching sides and (4) the rearrangement of accounts on the same side. The final result of the steps in the present consolidation is a statement of the accounts giving rise to the money supply and those accounting for the money supply and drains (Sect. 3.3) on the money supply.

* Beyond the accounting necessity for including in the consolidation the institutions responsible for monetary liabilities, the logic behind including still further ones is the presumption of high (positive or negative) correlations between their balance sheet items and money supply components. Thus the inclusion of mutual savings banks and the Postal Savings System, if meaningful, implies such correlations of changes in demand and time deposits in commercial banks, on the one hand, and savings deposits in mutual savings banks and postal savings accounts, on the other. On the same grounds, a case might be made for including other savings intermediaries (see Appendix to Chapter 15).

It might also be pointed out that, for similar reasons, the Treasury monetary accounts were included in the member-bank reserve accounts long before vault cash, in part a Treasury liability, could be counted as legal reserves. This implies that some member-bank reserve changes could be attributed meaningfully to Treasury monetary account changes and that many of the underlying details would be lost by confining the reserve accounts to the Federal Reserve's balance sheet.

Steps (1) and (2) of the present consolidation are shown in Table 9-6. With respect to the cancellations in step (2) in particular, all of the cash assets of private banks disappear—vault cash, deposits at the Federal Reserve banks, and interbank demand and time deposits. Federal Re-

Table 9-6. Derivation [Steps (1) and (2)] of the Money Supply Accounts

	Assets (Expansive Factors)	*Liabilities and Capital or Net Worth* (Contractive Factors)
Treasury and Federal Reserve Banks	Monetary gold stock Treasury currency Federal Reserve credit: - -Discounts and advances- - - - for member banks - - - Industrial loans Acceptances United States Government securities "Float"	Currency in circulation (net): - -Vault cash of nonmember banks- - - - - - Currency and coin held by nonbank public Treasury cash Federal Reserve deposits, other than member-bank reserves: United States Treasurer—general account Foreign (net) - -Nonmember banks- - - - - - - - Other Federal Reserve accounts Member-bank reserves: - -Vault cash- - - - - - - - - - Reserve deposits at Federal Reserve Banks -
Commercial and Mutual Savings Banks	Vault cash: - -Member banks- - - - - Nonmember banks- - Deposits at Federal Reserve banks - -Member banks- - - - - Nonmember banks- - - Deposits at other banks: - -Demand- - - - - - - - -Time- - - - - - - Loans and discounts United States Government securities Other securities Cash items in process of collection Other assets	Demand deposits: United States Treasurer - Other banks - - - - - - Foreign (net) All other Time deposits: United States Treasurer - Other banks - - - - - - Foreign (net) All other Borrowings: - Discounts and advances from Federal Reserve Banks All other Acceptances outstanding Other liabilities Capital accounts

serve discounts and advances for member banks (as well as occasional small amounts for nonmember banks) are also cancelled out, in order to end up with Federal Reserve and private bank loans on a completely net basis. The stock ownership of the member banks in the Federal Reserve could be cancelled too. Still, this is avoided as a means of conforming more nearly to the practice reflected in the Federal Reserve's published data.

The regrouping of accounts in step (3) involves a subtraction of various accounts from both sides of the consolidated balance sheet, along the lines set forth in Table 9-7. One of these subtractions—the one for "other assets" of private banks—is simply to build up a "catchall" group of

Table 9-7. Derivation [Step (3)] of the Money Supply Accounts

	Assets (Expansive Factors)	*Liabilities and Capital or Net Worth* (Contractive Factors)
Treasury and Federal Reserve Banks	Monetary gold stock Treasury currency Federal Reserve credit: Industrial loans Acceptances United States Government securities "Float"	Currency and coin held by nonbank public Treasury cash Federal Reserve deposits: United States Treasurer—general account Foreign (net) Other Federal Reserve accounts

Commercial
and
Federal
Reserve
Banks
	Loans and discounts
	United States government
	    securities
	Other securities
	Cash items in process of
	    collection
	Other assets
		Demand deposits:
		Unites States Treasurer
		Foreign (net)
		All other (except interbank)
		
		Time deposits:
		
		United States Treasurer
		Foreign (net)
		All other (except interbank)
		
		Borrowings:
		
		All other (except Federal Reserve advances)
		Acceptances outstanding
		
		Other liabilities
		Capital accounts

Subtrac-
tions
	minus Federal Reserve float
	minus Cash items in process of
	    collection (private banks)
	minus Other assets (private banks)
	minus All other borrowings
	    (private banks)
	minus Acceptances outstanding
		minus Federal Reserve float
		minus Cash items in process of collection
		    (private banks)
		minus All other borrowings (private banks)
		minus Acceptances outstanding

accounts that can be combined with the Federal Reserve "catchall" account: "other Federal Reserve accounts." Another leaves us with a minus account on the side opposite to that of its initial appearance, and all the subtractions, except the subtraction to build up a "catchall" account, are for the ultimate purpose of carrying loans and deposits as net figures.

All that remains in the derivation of the money supply accounts is the regrouping of the accounts. It is shown in Table 9-8. This final consolidated condition statement is exactly the same type of statement as that for the member-bank reserve accounts. In the present statement, however, the accounts on the two sides are referred to as expansive factors and contractive factors (Sect. 9.1), respectively. On the expansive

Table 9-8. Derivation [Step (4)] of the Money Supply Accounts

Assets (Expansive Factors)	*Liabilities and Capital or Net Worth* (Contractive Factors)
(1) Monetary gold stock	(4) Capital and miscellaneous accounts, net:
(2) Treasury currency	Other Federal Reserve accounts
	Other accounts or private banks:
(3) Bank credit	Other liabilities
	Capital accounts
Loans, net:	*minus* Other assets
Federal Reserve industrial loans, and	*minus* Federal Reserve float
acceptances	
Private bank loans and discounts	(5) Foreign bank deposits, net:
minus All other borrowings (except Federal	At Federal Reserve Banks (net)
Reserve discounts and advances)	Demand deposits at private banks (net)
minus Acceptances outstanding of private	Time deposits at private banks (net)
banks	
United States Government securities:	(6) United States Government deposits:
Held by Federal Reserve banks	
Held by private banks*	Treasury cash
Other securities:	Treasury deposits at Federal Reserves banks
Held by Federal Reserve banks	Treasury demand deposits at private banks
Held by private banks	Treasury time deposits at private banks
	(7) Time deposits—all other time deposits (except interbank) at private banks*
	(8) Money supply:
	Demand deposits adjusted:
	All other demand deposits (except interbank) at private banks
	minus Cash items in process of collection (private banks)
	Currency outside banks—currency and coin held by nonbank public

*Including the Postal Savings System.

side there are accounts that have given rise to the money supply, such as monetary gold, Treasury currency, and bank credit. On the contractive side, there are such accounts representing drains on the money supply as time deposits, bank capital, foreign deposits, and Treasury deposits at the Federal Reserve banks, as well as the account for the money supply itself. As in the previous case (Sect. 9.3), the accounts shown in Table 9-8 could be presented in equation form, with stock variables corresponding to the accounts. After rearranging the terms, the variable for the money supply could be expressed explicitly in terms of the variables corresponding to the accounts contributing to the money supply and those serving as drains on the money supply.

In the present instance, the demand deposit component of the money supply account is an adjusted account. The account is identical to the corresponding Federal Reserve data for "demand deposits other than interbank and U.S. Government deposits, less cash items reported in process of collection." In this respect, note in Table 9.8 that interbank deposits are canceled out, that United States Treasury and demand deposits net foreign demand deposits are put in other accounts, and that demand deposits adjusted includes a minus account for cash items in the process of collection from private banks.

The money supply account and alternative money supply series. The account for "demand deposits adjusted" and "currency outside of banks" in the money supply accounts corresponds to one money supply series. Another series reported in more recent years differs slightly from the money supply series, and still another relates to the so-called flow of funds accounts (Sect. 15.1).[5] In the order mentioned, one could designate these series for the quantity of money to accord with official references as follows: (1) the CCS series, which stands for Consolidated Condition Statement for Banks and the Monetary System; (2) the new money supply series; and (3) the flow of funds series.

The three series differ slightly as to coverage and statistical treatment. The primary significance of the quarterly flow of funds series lies in its eight-sector breakdown of money supply holdings. The new money supply series, reported semimonthly since 1960, differs from the monthly CCS series with respect to coverage in that it includes the demand deposits due to mutual savings banks and foreign banks and the vault cash of mutual savings banks. To eliminate some of the double-counting, Federal Reserve float (Table 9-1) is offset against demand deposits. Also the more recent series is the result of averages of daily figures, rather than figures for a single date. This difference in statistical treatment has the advantage of smoothing out some of the changes in the data, and it suffers from the disadvantage of having no clear conceptual meaning, such as a flow or a stock.

9.5. A Reconciliation of Changes: The Member-Bank Reserve and the Money Supply Accounts

Clearly, from prior discussion, interrelationships exist between the bank reserve (Sect. 9.3) and money supply accounts (Sect. 9.4) and the process of multiple expansion (or contraction) of earning assets and deposits (Sect. 3.3) through the banking system in response to increases (decreases) in reserves. Indeed, enough has been said to indicate that one could at least record with quantitative precision, as a historical matter, the changes in the member-bank reserve and money supply accounts and their interrelationships in terms of equations for changes in bank credit and the money supply (Sect. 3.3). Beyond this matter of the historical record and the interrelationships between the accounts, however, one could indicate in several other ways the interrelationships between changes in the accounts and the quantities of money and credit. These then are outlined below and one of them is used to indicate the interrelationships.

Changes in reserves, credit, and quantity of money: some alternative ways of indicating their interrelationships. The interrelationships among changes in the reserve accounts, the money supply accounts, bank credit, and the stock of money in response to a change in the bank reserve equation and within the context of the reserve and money accounts could be explored in three ways, in addition to that of comparing historical time series of the accounts. These would be in terms of (1) an explanation and prediction of the quantitative changes on the basis of detailed information; (2) an explanation and a qualitative prediction, or a simple prediction of the direction and order of change in bank credit and the money supply; and (3) an example based on relatively restricted assumptions.

The first two of these involve even more than an indication of interrelationships; they also involve a theory or an explanation of the interrelationships. In fact, indicating the interrelationships in terms of the first of these additional ways would be quite ambitious. The successful undertaking would involve explanations in terms of a theoretical structure and detailed assumptions of a quantitative nature that would subsequently agree with the predictions. The required assumptions would be those with respect to cash and time deposit drains (Sect. 3.3), reserve requirements (Sect. 8.1), reserve changes, and the willingness of bankers to lend and potential borrowers to borrow. Considerable information corresponding to the assumptions would be required with a greater detail and complexity than we have encountered thus far. It would deal with the alternative sources of funds for business (Chap. 17) and consumer (Chap. 18) expenditures, international financial and trade matters (Chap. 24), the management of bank loans and investments (Chap. 22), and so on.[6]

The second of the additional alternative means of indicating the interrelationships would be less ambitious than the first. It is the type that we could successfully handle on the basis of an introductory study of analysis and institutions and a feeling for short-run changes in banking, business, and financial conditions. Here we would be concerned with such matters as whether an increase (decrease) in reserves would lead to an increase (decrease) in the expansion (contraction) of bank credit and the quantity of money, whether the change in the expansion (or contraction) of credit would be more or less than the reserve and money supply changes, and so on. This type of forecast would be more simply based on relatively good and fairly general theories, on assumptions that lenders would prefer to lend rather than not lend, and so on.

The third of the additional alternatives will be presently carried out. In this instance, we specify some assumptions for the purpose of presenting an example and draw upon an earlier numerical example dealing with the multiple expansion (contraction) of bank credit and the quantity of money.

An example of the multiple expansion (contraction) of money and credit. In presenting this example of interrelationships between changes in member-bank reserves, bank credit, and the quantity of money, some numbers and specific assumptions are called for. The initial set of numbers involved is summarized in Table 3.2. The assumptions are as follows:

(1) The initial primary deposit represents a cash inflow. This, in turn, means that currency in circulation (net of member-bank reserves) and currency outside banks must decline by the amount of the initial deposit increase.

(2) Banks always maintain 20 per cent of their reserves in vault cash and 80 per cent in deposits at Federal Reserve banks.

(3) All banks participating in the expansion process belong to the Federal Reserve System.

(4) A 15 per cent reserve ratio prevails, and there is a 25 per cent cash drain, as in the initial set of numbers (Sect. 3.3). (As an exercise, the reader may wish to trace through the example using other alternative assumptions.)

Further, for simplicity and clarity, we will do several things. We will combine Bank C and "additional banks" from the initial illustration (Sect. 3.3). We will not separately record interbank clearing drains and losses (i.e., reserve losses by one bank that are exactly offset by another bank's reserve gains), nor will we separately record the mere transfers of demand deposits from one bank to another. We will, however, record net reserve losses resulting from the cash drain at each stage of the expansion process.

In carrying out the illustration, Table 9-9 combines the member-bank reserve accounts, the money supply accounts, the illustration initially associated with Table 3-2, and the additional assumptions and simplifications. The illustration starts with an initial demand deposit of $10 and a decrease in currency outside banks by a corresponding amount. It then proceeds with additional changes in reserves, currency in cir-

Table 9-9. Multiple Expansion Through the Banking System and the Bank Reserve and Money Supply Accounts

(15.0 per cent reserves, 20.0 per cent of reserves in vault cash, 25.0 per cent cash drain)

Bank A

Member-Bank Reserve Accts.		Reserve Change				Cash Drain		Money Supply Accounts	
Curr. in circ. (net)	−10.00	+10.00	Req. res.	1.50	Dem. dep. 10.00	−10.00		Dem. dep. adj.	+10.00
Mem.-bank res.:								Curr. outside banks	−10.00
Vault cash	+ 2.00		Excess res.	8.50			Bank credit + 8.50	Dem. dep. adj.	+ 8.50
Dep. at Fed. Res.	+ 8.00		Loans	8.50	Dem. dep. 8.50			Curr. outside banks	+ 1.70
Curr. in circ. (net)	+ 1.70	− 1.70				+ 1.70			
Mem.-bank res.:									
Vault cash	− .34								
Dep. at Fed. Res.	− 1.36								

Bank B

			Req. res.	1.02	Dem. dep. 6.80				
			Excess res.	5.78					
Curr. in circ. (net)	+ 1.16	− 1.16	Loans	5.78	Dem. dep. 5.78	+ 1.16	Bank credit + 5.78	Dem. dep. adj.	+ 5.78
Mem.-bank res.:								Dem. dep. adj.	− 1.16
Vault cash	− .23							Curr. outside banks	+ 1.16
Dep. at Fed. res.	− .92								

Bank C and Addit. Banks

(no entries)

			Req. res.	2.17	Dem. dep. 14.45				
Curr. in circ. (net)	+ 2.46	− 2.46	Excess res.	-0-		+ 2.46	Bank credit +12.28	Dem. dep. adj.	+12.28
Mem.-bank res.:			Loans	12.28	Dem. dep. 12.28			Dem. dep. adj.	− 2.46
Vault cash	− .49							Curr. outside banks	+ 2.46
Dep. at Fed. Res.	− 1.96								

All Banks

Mem.-Bank Res. Accts.—Cum. Total		Reserve Change				Cash Drain		Money Supply Accts.—Cum. Total	
Curr. in circ. (net)	−10.00	+10.00	Req. res.	4.69	Dem. dep. 10.00	−10.00		Dem. dep. adj.	+10.00
Mem.-bank res.:								Curr. outside banks	−10.00
Vault cash	+ 2.00		Excess res.	-0-	Dem. dep. 21.25	+ 5.31	Bank credit +26.56	Dem. dep. adj.	+26.56
Dep. at Fed. Res.	+ 8.00		Loans	26.56		− 4.69		Curr. outside banks	+ 5.31
Curr. in circ. (net)	+ 5.31	− 5.31		31.25	31.25				
Mem.-bank res.:		+ 4.69							
Vault cash	− 1.06								
Dep. at Fed. Res.	− 4.25							+26.56	
	−0−								

(no entries)

culation, member-bank reserves, and so on through the next set of changes. At each step of the expansion process, changes are recorded in the member-bank reserve accounts and the money supply accounts. All of the changes are then summarized at the bottom of Table 9-9, in terms of member-bank reserve accounts, accounts for member banks, and the money supply accounts. By reversing the sign for every number in Table 9-9, we could make the present example one for the multiple contraction of bank loans and the money supply.

This example involving the bank reserve accounts and other accounts should also help exemplify the point that the published accounts merely note changes in terms of accounting identities after they have occurred. The published accounts alone tell us nothing of the underlying causes of the changes; they do not explain the changes. More particularly, the money supply accounts can tell us nothing about the causes or future extent of changes in the quantity of money. This sort of thing requires a theory, assumptions, and information about reserve ratios, excess reserves, the actions and inactions of the monetary authorities, the willingness of bankers to extend credit, the public's demand for credit, and so forth. We still must define monetary policy and engage in more analysis. We must acquire additional information about the functioning of various institutions in the money and capital markets and about the mechanism which transmits changes in underlying conditions and financial variables into changes in aggregate expenditures, production, employment, and prices.

9.6. Summary

Accounts involving three groups—the Federal Reserve banks, the United States Treasury, and the private banking system—underlie the present derivation of the bank reserve accounts, the money supply accounts, and our understanding of the position of the Federal Reserve with respect to member-bank reserves and the quantity of money. The consolidated Federal Reserve balance sheet is the most important statement with respect to the member-bank reserve accounts, and it is essential to the derivation of the money supply accounts. This Federal Reserve statement is important in other respects, too.

The Federal Reserve statement, known publically as the weekly statement of condition, reveals more of the Reserve System's operations than is revealed for any comparable bank of issue in the world. The data that may be derived from the statement reflect details about the Federal Reserve's condition and certain financial situations and events in the economy, as well as the Federal Reserve's position in relationship to them. Changes in Federal Reserve notes outstanding, for example, reflect the public's demand for currency; changes in discounts and advances reflect changes in the tone of the credit and money markets; and changes in Federal Reserve credit generally (i.e., changes in government security holdings, discounts and advances, and float) reflect the Federal Reserve's actions to contribute to, neutralize, or otherwise offset the general tone prevailing in the financial markets. Moreover, the more detailed statement of condition reveals the debt instruments composing the Federal Reserve's open market purchases, as well as the maturity distribution of those debt instruments. On a weekly basis these data may reveal in considerable detail the Federal Reserve's short-run reaction to the market and their notion about credit ease or tightness. The latter type of information is important to specialists and government officials concerned with the sector of the market in which the Federal Reserve conducts its open market activities.

In the derivation of member-bank reserve and money supply accounts, as well as in the assessment of the uniqueness of banking sector accounts, special exceptions must be made with respect to the general notions of changes in balance sheet accounts. In general, with the exception of the banking sector, an increase (decrease) in an assets account is a use (source) of funds, and a cash transaction involving the sale (purchase) of an asset may be effected without changing total assets. Uniquely distinct from this general notion, however, an increase or decrease in particular assets, such as loans and investments and whatever may be carried out by the Federal Reserve in the form of a so-called cash settlement, involves a net expansion or contraction of assets, respectively. The same is true for commercial banks. Thus this unique position whereby the banking sector may create its own funds for cash settlements causes us to refer to an increase (decrease) in assets accounts in the bank reserve accounts as a source (use) of reserves. It also causes us to refer to an increase (decrease) in the assets accounts in the money supply accounts as expansive (contractive) factors. Further, this uniqueness distinguishes changes on the liabilities side of the accounts for the banking sector, as contrasted with all other sectors.

In any event, all of the accounts are presented in the context of the fundamental accounting identity, and permissible algebraic operations may be performed on the two sides of the identity to effect various arrangements of the accounts. In fact, equations containing the variables that correspond to the various accounts may be written, and there variables may be rearranged until we have an equation for member-bank reserves and a similar equation for the quantity of money. These various expressions then may be viewed as allowing for all of the accounting changes that possibly involve changes in member-bank reserves and the money supply. In this context, too, the variables may be interpreted as stock variables, and changes in them as flow variables. These are familiar concepts.

The derived expression for the quantity of money as "demand deposits adjusted," plus "currency outside of banks," however, does not yield the only series for the money supply. There are three: (1) our derived series —the monthly CCS or "single-date" series, (2) the new semimonthly or "daily-average" money supply series, and (3) the quarterly flow of funds series. These differ slightly as to coverage and statistical treatment. The new money supply series, reported since 1960, differs from the others with respect to timing and coverage. Most significantly, however, it provides data in the form of an average of daily figures rather than for a particular date. This form of statistical reporting provides a smoother series, but the series has no clear conceptual meaning as a stock or a flow.

The present review of the various accounts indicates the financial position of the Federal Reserve and its position with respect to member-bank reserves and the money supply. It also provides the opportunity to illustrate the interrelationships between member-bank reserves, the quantity of money, and the multiple expansion or contraction of credit through the banking system. In this respect, a great deal has been done toward illustrating the mechanics through which changes in underlying conditions and financial variables will reveal themselves. Even so, this illustration and the capacity to record and report such changes should not be misunderstood as an explanation in terms of causes and effects. These matters require a more comprehensive theoretical framework and additional familiarity with financial institutions and operations.

References

1. For an explanation of the necessary adjustments in the preparation of the consolidated statement, see *Federal Reserve Bulletin,* February 1961, pp. 164-165. They are chiefly in the Federal Reserve notes held by Federal Reserve banks other than the banks which issued them and in the cash items in process of collection and deferred availability cash items.

2. An introduction to these matters may be found in "Guides to Monetary Policy," in *Monetary Policy-Decision Making, Tools, and Objectives* (Federal Reserve Bank of Philadelphia, 1961), pp. 18-25.

In 1962 the Federal Reserve published, as supplements to its *Banking and Monetary Statistics* (1943), two pamphlets which would be useful companions to this chapter: "Member Bank Reserve and Related Items" and "Banks and the Monetary System." The former contains brief explanations of the member-bank reserve accounts and their data sources and provides statistics for the period 1917-1960. The latter contains comparable information for the money supply accounts, although statistics are available only for the period 1941-1960.

3. See Commission on Money and Credit, *Money and Credit: Their Influence on Jobs, Prices, and Growth* (Englewood Cliffs, N.J.: Prentice-Hall, Inc., 1961), pp. 91-92. Also, for discussion of a bill (H. R. 3783) to provide for the retirement of Federal Reserve Bank stock, and for other purposes, see *The Federal Reserve System after Fifty Years,* Hearings Before the Subcommittee on Domestic Finance of the Committee on Banking and Currency, House of Representatives, Vol. 1, 2, and 3 (Washington, D.C.: U.S. Government Printing Office, 1964).

4. "Measures of Member Bank Reserves," *Federal Reserve Bulletin,* July 1963, pp. 890-903; and "Reserves: Definitions," *Federal Reserve Bank of St. Louis Review,* September 1963, p. 6.

5. For a discussion of the three money supply series, see "Revision of Money Supply Series," *Federal Reserve Bulletin,* August 1962, pp. 941-951; and "A New Measure of the Money Supply," *Federal Reserve Bulletin,* October 1960, pp. 1102-1123.

6. A fairly modest example of such a study is A. J. Meigs, *Free Reserves and the Money Supply* (Chicago: University of Chicago Press, 1962).

10

The Member-Bank Reserve and Money Supply Accounts— Further Observations

SOCRATES: I see that your chief piece of money carries a legend affirming that it is a promise to pay the bearer the sum of one pound. What is this thing, a pound, of which payment is thus promised?

OECONOMIST: A pound is the British unit of account.

SOCRATES: So there is, I suppose, some concrete object which embodies more firmly that abstract unit of account than does this paper promise?

OECONOMIST: There is no such object, O Socrates.

SOCRATES: Indeed? Then what your Bank promises is to give the holder of this promise another promise stamped with a different number in case he regards the number stamped on this promise as in some way ill-omened?

OECONOMIST: It would seem—indeed—to be promising something of that kind.

SOCRATES: So that in order to be in a position to fulfill its promises all the Bank has to do is to keep a store of such promises stamped with all sorts of different numbers?

OECONOMIST: By no means, Socrates—that would make its balance-sheet a subject for mockery, and in the eyes of our people there resides in a balance-sheet a certain awe and holiness. The Bank has to keep a store of Government securities and a store of gold.

SOCRATES: What are Government securities?

OECONOMIST: Promises by the Government to pay certain sums of money at certain dates.

SOCRATES: What are sums of money? Do you mean Bank of England notes?

OECONOMIST: I suppose I do.

SOCRATES: So these promises to pay promises are thought to be in some way solider and more sacred than the promises themselves?

OECONOMIST: They are so thought, as it appears.

SOCRATES: I see. Now tell me about the gold. It has to be of a certain weight, I suppose?

OECONOMIST: Not of a certain weight, but of a certain value in terms of the promises.

SOCRATES: So that the less each of its promises is worth, the more promises the Bank can lawfully make?

OECONOMIST: There are complications, Socrates, but it seems to amount to something of that kind.

SOCRATES: Do you find that your monetary system works well?

OECONOMIST: Pretty well, thank you, Socrates, on the whole.

SOCRATES: That would be, I suppose, not because of the rather strange rules of which you have told me, but because it is administered by men of ability and wisdom?

OECONOMIST: It would seem that that must be the reason, rather than the rules themselves, O Socrates (D. H. Robertson, "British Monetary Policy," *Lloyds Bank Review*, May 1939).

In money and banking there are separate sets of accounts for member-bank reserves and the money supply (Sect. 9.3 and 9.4). They are quite basic in the study and operation of our money and banking system. One set represents all of the accounts contributing or absorbing member-bank reserves. It does this in terms of the historically accumulated amounts in the various accounts at a given time. A comparison of these accounts from one date to another reveals changes in the accounts and member-bank reserves over the period in question. The changes in all of the accounts other than the single account for member-bank reserves may, in turn, be viewed as giving rise to changes in reserves, the basis for changes in bank credit and the money supply. The other set of accounts, then, represents all of the accounts giving rise to the money supply. A comparison of these accounts from one date to another reveals the changes in the various accounts and the money supply.

The bank reserve and money supply accounts are fundamental, indeed, reporting, as they do, the bank reserve and money supply changes. The two changes are closely related, but, in a reconciliation of changes in reserves and the money supply (Sect. 9.5), such intervening factors as currency and time deposit drains (Sect. 3.3) must be allowed for.

The bank reserve and money supply accounts were shown earlier (Sect. 9.3 and 9.4) to be derived from other accounting statements, and changes in reserves were reconciled with the multiple expansion (or contraction) of credit and the money supply (Sect. 9.5). Earlier, too, the discussion emphasized that neither set of accounts tells why reserves or the money supply change. The accounts were described as simply revealing historical changes and their interrelationships in an accounting sense, independent of any fundamental explanation for the changes. Nevertheless, the accounts were said to reveal aspects of the implementation of monetary policy and the political and economic developments in the society. They were also said to have precise conceptual meanings in terms of the notions of a stock and a flow. In this chapter, consequently, we wish to relate the accounts more closely to bank operations, to reveal a little more of their conceptual meaning in mathematical terms, and to introduce in broad outline some of the political and economic developments in the years since the 1930's.

10.1. The Variables Affecting Member-Bank Reserves

The principal variables on the two sides of the bank reserve accounts (Sect. 9.3) are Federal Reserve credit, monetary gold stock, and currency in circulation. The other variables perform their role primarily by changing over time so as to have virtually no cumulative effect, even in the short run.

Federal Reserve credit. Federal Reserve credit includes credit extended to banks in the form of reserve balances at the Federal Reserve. It is extended through open market operations, the discount window, and Federal Reserve float. Open market operations consist of the purchase and sale of securities—usually government securities—in the open market (Sect. 8.1). They constitute the primary source of possible Federal Reserve credit expansion in the long run. They may be the source of an almost unlimited supply of bank reserves upon which the supply of currency notes and demand deposits may be further expanded. The other sources of Federal Reserve credit—discounts and advances and Federal Reserve float—are significant only in the short run. The tradition against borrowing allegedly limits the use of discounts and advances to transitory purposes. Federal Reserve float—described earlier (Sect. 9.2) as the excess of uncollected cash items over deferred availability cash items—is only a temporary, limited, seasonally volatile, and often unanticipated source of bank reserves. It is still a source to be reckoned with.

Monetary gold stock. The United States gold supply consists largely of the stock of monetary gold and, to a much smaller extent, of so-called free gold. Gold produced in the United States or flowing into the United States from abroad is usually monetized. Gold flowing out of the United States or into the Treasury's free-gold balances is demonetized. Therefore, the effect of gold movements are not essentially different from those under gold standard conditions, although no one would identify our currency system as a classical automatic gold standard (Sect. 6.3). In the Federal Reserve Act, the hint that something has happened to the gold standard is the use of the word "gold certificates," instead of the word "gold."

The essential differences between the role of gold today and in the era of the international gold standard consist of the absence of specie from circulation and the Treasury's position as the sole domestic holder of the precious metal. Gold ceased to circulate freely as specie when it was surrendered to the Federal Reserve banks under the Emergency Banking Act of 1933 (Sect. 7.5). It is illegal, since that time, for gold to be held by private United States citizens in monetary form. Gold may, nevertheless, be obtained from the Federal Reserve Bank of New York, acting as an agent for the Treasury. The United States Treasury, a principal holder of the free world's gold, stands ready to buy gold, as well as to sell it, at the fixed price of $35 per ounce* for the settlement of obligations to international banking institutions and foreign central banks and treasuries.

Gold, newly mined in the United States, is sold to dealers who are licensed by the Treasury to buy gold for use in industry and the arts. It is also sold to a United States assay office, or a United States mint, and the purchase and sale of foreign gold is handled by the Treasury's agent, the Federal Reserve Bank of New York. When the Treasury buys gold at the mint or through an agent, it generally pays for the gold with a check drawn against its account at the Federal Reserve. The seller of the gold will deposit or cash the check, which will ultimately be presented to the Federal Reserve for payment. Payment is made by crediting a commercial bank with reserves equal to the amount of the check, and the Federal Reserve will, at the same time, debit the Treasury's general account. The Treasury will generally, in turn, give the Federal Reserve credit for an equal amount of gold certificates, and the Federal Reserve will, at the same time, credit the Treasury's general account by an equal amount. In the end, the Federal Reserve has an increase in gold certificates on the asset side of its balance sheet and an identical increase in the reserves of commercial banks on the liabilities side. The monetary gold stock has increased, but the Treasury's cash balance at the Federal Reserve is unchanged, having only substituted credit for gold certificates for the debit incurred by the writing of the check. The transactions involving an inflow of gold and an increase in member-bank reserves may be briefly illustrated:[1]

---

* In practice, a one-fourth of one per cent handling charge is levied, so that the effective selling price is actually $35.0875 per ounce, and purchases are made at $34.9125.

Federal Reserve Bank		Member Bank	
Assets	Liabilities	Assets	Liabilities
Gold certificates + (d)	Treasury deposit − + (a) (d) Member-bank reserves at Federal + (c)	Member-bank reserves at Federal + (c)	Deposits + (b)

(a) Treasury draws a check against its deposit in the Federal Reserve bank to buy the gold from the importer,

(b) the importer deposits his check in his bank,

(c) the member bank sends the check to the Federal Reserve bank for credit to its reserve account, and

(d) the Treasury issues gold certificates to the Federal Reserve bank to replenish its deposit.

It should be emphasized, however, that reserve balances increase only if the check is cashed or deposited outside of the Federal Reserve. The Federal Reserve keeps accounts for other central banks that also act as fiscal agent for their respective governments, and it is not infrequent that dollar balances will be built up at the Federal Reserve. The increase in the reserves of commercial banks would increase, therefore, only when the balances were spent or placed in interest earning accounts outside of the Reserve System. This will most frequently be the case when market conditions favor the holding of dollar balances. The foreign central banks do not generally want to hold idle balances without interest, and they will accordingly instruct the Federal Reserve to buy government securities that yield an interest return.

Conversely, an outflow of gold and an increase in foreign dollar balances, generally at the Federal Reserve Bank of New York, will have the effect of contracting the reserve balances of commercial banks. The foreign central bank could, for example, instruct the Federal Reserve to sell some of its security holdings and purchase gold with the proceeds. The sale of securities would result in a contraction of bank reserves in the same manner as a sale of securities from the open market account, unless they were obtained directly from the open market account rather than the open market. The gold, in such a case, would be "earmarked," or segregated, for the foreign central bank's account at the Federal Reserve Bank of New York, where the gold is actually held. The Federal Reserve's gold certificate holdings would be reduced along with the Treasury's active gold account. The Treasury's account at the Federal Reserve would be credited with the amount of the sale. In effect, the Treasury would have exchanged gold for a deposit. Other effects could also result from a foreign purchase of gold. Foreign funds could be transferred from the "street" or from commercial banks to pay for the purchase, which would have the effect of reducing commercial bank reserves by the amount of the check used in payment for the gold. The transfer of the dollar balances from the "street" to the Federal Reserve may even precede the actual gold purchase, and, in this case, the actual effect on member-bank reserves would precede the gold purchase. Viewed most simply, the transactions involving an outflow of gold and a decrease in member-bank reserves would be as follows:

Federal Reserve Bank		Member Bank	
Assets	Liabilities	Assets	Liabilities
Gold certificate — (b)	Treasury deposit — + (b) (a)	Member-bank reserves at Federal — (c)	Deposits — (d)
	Member-bank reserves at Federal — (c)		

(a) The Treasury deposits a check drawn against a member bank in payment for gold,

(b) the Treasury reduces the Federal Reserve's gold certificate holdings and the Federal Reserve, in turn, reduces the Treasury's deposit,

(c) the Federal Reserve debits member-bank reserves by the amount of the check, and

(d) the member-bank debits the account of the purchaser of the gold.

As under the gold standard, movements of gold from one country to another, or, in some instances, the transfer of "earmarked" gold at the Federal Reserve from one country's account to another, are the ultimate means by which international obligations are settled.

Currency in circulation. Currency in circulation consists of Federal Reserve notes and Treasury currency outside the Federal Reserve banks and the Treasury. Treasury currency in circulation consists mostly of silver certificates, but it also includes United States notes of 1890, subsidiary coin, and remnants of obsolete issues not yet presented for retirement.[2] The primary form of currency is Federal Reserve notes, and we shall be mainly concerned with this.

Federal Reserve notes are liabilities of the Federal Reserve banks and obligations of the United States government. They are fully collateraled by eligible paper, government securities, and gold certificate reserves.

They are paid out to member banks on request, and the amount so paid out is charged to the member-bank's reserve account. They are paid out through the Federal Reserve agent, in the issuing Federal Reserve bank, who is also the chairman of the Board of Directors of the bank. The notes themselves are printed by the Federal government. It may be emphasized, however, that member-bank reserves can be replenished through open market purchases, which provide additional collateral for further expansion of the note issue. The ultimate expansion of note issue in this form is presently restricted through legislative action requiring the Federal Reserve to maintain a minimum reserve of 25 per cent in gold certificates against its note issue. The ratio, more fully described above (Sect. 9.2), has in the past been of little operational importance, since the prevailing ratio has usually been in substantial excess of the requirement. In the late 1950's and early 1960's, however, the prevailing ratio declined significantly because of United States gold losses.

Changes in the public's demand for currency has an effect upon member-bank reserves similar to that of open market operations and gold flows. Because a net withdrawal of currency has the effect of lowering member-bank reserves by the amount of the withdrawal, it may also precipitate a contraction of demand deposits by a multiple amount. The withdrawal since the inclusion of vault cash in reserves (Sect. 8.1) may come directly from vault cash or as a result of the replacement of vault cash through a reduction in member-bank deposits at the Federal Reserve. The effect of the withdrawal on member-bank reserves as it would operate through a reduction in member-bank deposits at the Federal Reserve may be illustrated:

Federal Reserve Bank		Member Bank	
Assets	Liabilities	Assets	Liabilities
	Member-bank reserves at Federal — (b)	Member-bank reserves at Federal — (b)	Deposits — (a)
	Federal Reserve notes + (c)		

(a) Currency is withdrawn from the member bank,
(b) the member bank replenishes its currency holdings by obtaining currency from the Federal Reserve, and
(c) the Federal Reserve substitutes its note issue liability for its member-bank reserve liability.

Conversely, where a net return of currency replenishes the reserves on deposit at the Federal Reserve: *

Federal Reserve Bank		Member Bank	
Assets	Liabilities	Assets	Liabilities
	Member-bank reserves at Federal + Federal (b) Reserve Notes — (c)	Member-bank reserves at Federal + (b)	Deposits + (a)

(a) Holder of currency deposits it in a member bank,
(b) the member bank sends the currency to the Federal Reserve bank for credit to its reserve account, and
(c) the Federal Reserve bank retires the notes.

In this case the people return currency, on balance, to their banks, and the banks return it to the Federal Reserve, where they receive credit to their reserve accounts. The Federal Reserve may, in turn, return the notes to the government representative and have them redeemed for the collateral previously pledged for the notes. A return of currency may have the effect of easing credit if offsetting action is not taken, such as a sale of government securities from the open market account.

Changes in the demand for currency must be allowed for in determining monetary policy or, in other words, in effecting the appropriate ease or tightness of credit. Generally, the demand varies for different days of the week and month as well as for different seasons and holidays. Perhaps the change in the need for currency can be dramatized, if one will envisage the array of Brinks, Wells Fargo, and other armored trucks entering a Federal Reserve bank on a Monday morning for the purpose of returning the money required to facilitate a "long weekend." Indeed, the regularity with which net withdrawals and net returns of currency occur enables the research department at the Federal Reserve Bank of New York to make more accurate projections of their effect of bank reserves and, to this extent, better enables the manager of the open market account to prepare to engage in open market transactions that will have an offsetting or counterbalancing effect.

* *Modern Money Mechanics: A Workbook on Deposits, Currency, and Bank Reserves* (Federal Reserve Bank of Chicago, 1961), pp. 16-17. A noteworthy result of the Vault Cash Act (1959) was to reduce substantially the volume of currency shipments to and from the Reserve banks, since member-bank vault cash became countable as legal reserves.

Other variables. Other variables in the member-bank reserves accounts are Treasury cash and its balances at Federal Reserve banks, foreign and other deposit and miscellaneous Federal Reserve accounts (other than member-bank reserves), and member-bank reserves themselves. Treasury cash has been explained above (Sect. 9.3). Changes in Treasury cash and Treasury deposits at Federal Reserve banks are likely to be of importance in the very short run. An increase in the Treasury and/or other deposits at the Federal Reserve tends to be accompanied by a decrease in member-bank reserves, other things being equal. Conversely, a decrease in the accounts tends to be accompanied by an increase in member-bank reserves, other things being equal. The management of the Treasury's balances at the Federal Reserve and their possible transitory effects are discussed later (Sect. 13.5). As shown in Table 9-5, foreign and other Federal Reserve accounts may vary directly with short-run changes in the gold certificate holdings of the Federal Reserve. Finally, member-bank reserves are a residual of cumulative changes in all of the accounts in the bank reserve accounts, other than member-bank reserves, after the vault cash of member banks is netted out of currency in circulation (Sect. 9.3). The effect of changes in the other accounts on member-bank reserves will tend to be reflected in the tone of the credit market.

10.2. The Member-Bank Reserve Accounts in the Form of an Equation

In the initial derivation of the member-bank reserve accounts (Sect. 9.3) from other accounting statements, the tautological nature of the accounts was emphasized. The emphasis was in part on the fundamental accounting identity (Sect. 9.1) underlying the accounts and on the operations of addition (subtraction), elimination, and so on that may be performed on the accounts. Now, however, we wish to view the same accounts as corresponding to variables in an equation—the bank reserve equation.

First, with respect to the principal accounts, it may be noted that changes in gold movements, the demand for currency, and Federal Reserve credit reflect numerous forces in the country's economic life. Gold flows are affected by official policies of foreign central banks and governments (Sect 23.2), by price-level and interest rate changes (Sect. 6.3 and 24.3), by political tension in both hot and cold wars, and so on (Sect. 23.1). Next, currency movements are influenced by the habits of the people, their holidays, and paydays, and by the level of business activity. And, finally, Federal Reserve credit is influenced primarily by the policy being effected at any given time by the monetary authorities. The policy may be reflected through direct action by the monetary authorities to change the cost and availability of credit, or it may be reflected in passivity by the monetary authorities at a time when gold, currency movements, and similar items are influencing the level of bank credit. Executing policy, in other words, may just as well be a matter of inaction as action.

Stock variables for sources and uses of bank reserves. In the form of the bank reserve equation, those variables that have, on a cumulative basis, contributed to member-bank reserve funds may be set opposite to those that have absorbed reserves, on a cumulative basis. In other words, the variables may be shown according to whether they fall on the supply side (sources) or the demand side (uses). Table 10-1 shows these

Table 10-1. Stock Variables for Sources and Uses of Bank Reserves, June 26, 1963, and Changes Since June 27, 1962

	Dollar Amounts (in billions)	Per Cent of Total	Change Since June 27, 1962 (in billions)
Sources of bank reserves (the supply side):			
Federal Reserve credit	33.7	61.2	+2.6
Monetary gold stock	15.7	28.6	−.7
Treasury currency	5.6	10.2	0.0
Total	55.0	100.0	+1.9
Uses of bank reserves (the demand side):			
Currency in circulation (net of 3.4 billion of currency and coin in member-bank reserves)	32.0	58.2	+1.5
Treasury cash	0.4	0.7	0.0
Treasury, foreign, and other deposits at Federal Reserve banks (excluding member-bank reserves)	1.4	2.6	+.3
Other Federal Reserve accounts	1.1	2.0	+.4
Member-bank reserves	20.1	36.5	−0.3
Total	55.0	100.0	+1.9

NOTE: Parts may not add to totals due to rounding.
SOURCE: Board of Governors of the Federal Reserve System.

balances as of mid-1963, in this form. On the sources side, sometimes called the "reserve base," and now officially "factors supplying reserve funds," is Federal Reserve credit that amounts to 33.7 billion dollars. Of this amount, the largest single source composing it is the Reserve System's government security holdings totaling 31.6 billion dollars at mid-1963. The monetary gold accounted for 15.7 billion of the bank reserves, and Treasury currency (caution!) amounting to 5.6 billion dollars accounted for the remainder. On the demand side, now officially called "factors absorbing reserve funds," the largest single variable accounting for the use of reserves is currency in circulation (net of member-bank vault cash). This accounts for 32 billion dollars. The other variable accounting for a large proportion of the use of reserves is member-bank reserves themselves, which total 20.1 billion dollars. The remaining variables correspond to balances other than member-bank reserves held at the Federal Reserve banks, as well as Treasury cash and the "catchall" of miscellaneous Federal Reserve accounts.

The bank reserve equation: stocks and flows. The bank reserve equation corresponding to the accounts in Table 10-1 could be denoted as follows:

$$(1) \qquad R + G + C_T - C_S - T_C - F - R_M = 0,$$

where R is Federal Reserve credit,

$\qquad G$ is monetary gold stock,

$\qquad C_T$ is Treasury currency,

$\qquad C_S$ is currency in circulation (net),

$\qquad T_C$ is Treasury cash,

$\qquad F$ is foreign and other Federal Reserve deposit and miscellaneous accounts, and

$\qquad R_M$ is member-bank reserves.

Also, equation (1) could be rewritten:

$$(2) \qquad R + G + C_T - C_S - T_C - F = R_M,$$

after adding R_M to both sides of the equation. Each of the variables in the equation, furthermore, is a quantity or stock accumulated over time, and a change in any one of the stocks may be thought of as a rate of change per unit of time. Equation (2), in other words, shows the supply of bank reserves on a cumulative basis, as of a particular date, and one may observe increases and decreases in the stock variables over given intervals of time. In this sense, the increments and decrements may be thought of as averages of rates for each year. And, more precisely, the limit of such an average (or increment), as the interval of time approaches a moment in time, is a flow or rate of change per interval at a moment in time. The flow of member-bank reserves is, e.g.,

$$\lim_{\Delta t \to 0} \frac{\Delta R_M}{\Delta t}$$

where ΔR is an increase in reserves, and

$\qquad \Delta t$ is an interval of time.

But, $\underset{\Delta t \to 0}{\text{limit}} \dfrac{\Delta R_M}{\Delta t}$ is simply the first derivative, i.e.,

$$\underset{\Delta t \to 0}{\text{limit}} \frac{\Delta R_M}{\Delta t} = \frac{dR_M}{dt}$$

Denoting, then, the changes in equation (2) in the flow form,

$$(3) \qquad \frac{dR}{dt} + \frac{dG}{dt} + \frac{dC_T}{dt} - \frac{dC_S}{dt} - \frac{dT_C}{dt} - \frac{dF}{dt} = \frac{dR_M}{dt}$$

Now, the area specified by an increment in reserves over an interval of time as it would appear in a bar chart or histogram is precisely equal

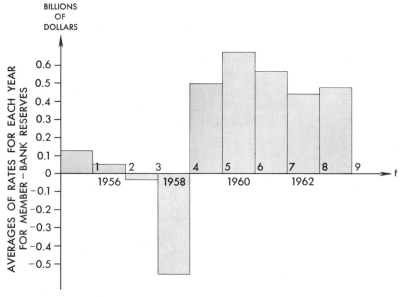

Fig. 10-1. Averages of Rates for Each Year for Member-Bank Reserves, 1955-1963. Reserves are adjusted to include all currency and coin held by member banks beginning November 24, 1960, and part of such holdings during the period December 1, 1959, to November 23, 1960. Before December 1959 reserves are those on deposit with the Federal Reserve banks. Source of data: Board of Governors of the Federal Reserve System.

to the amount of the change in the stock quantity. In the present case of member-bank reserves, the area over a definite interval of time, such as $\Delta t =$ Dec. 31, 1955, to Dec. 31, 1956, is the total addition to member-bank reserves in that interval of time, and the integral of the flow over that interval is precisely equal to the area. Particular changes, as implied by the incremental ratio in the case of member-bank reserves (i.e., $\Delta R_M/\Delta t$, where $\Delta R_M/\Delta t \approx dR_M/dt$), are sketched in Fig. 10-1. In that illustration, the dollar amounts (in billions) added to reserve are shown on the vertical axis, and time is shown on the horizontal axis. The area contained in the histogram for 1956 is 0.054 (billions of dollars), which we precisely denote

$$\int_1^2 \frac{dR_M}{dt}\, dt = 0.054 \text{ (billions of dollars)},$$

and the total change in member-bank reserves for the period December 31, 1954, to December 31, 1963, we denote as[*]

$$\int_0^1 \frac{dR_M}{dt}\, dt + \int_1^2 \frac{dR_M}{dt}\, dt + \ldots + \int_8^9 \frac{dR_M}{dt}\, dt = \int_0^9 \frac{dR_M}{dt}\, dt = 2.272$$

(billions of dollars)

Some changes in the principal variables. Flow data similar to that above and corresponding to semiannual averages of rates of change in the principal variables in the bank reserve equation could be presented. Such data would provide a broad outline of some general monetary developments for selected periods since the early 1930's. They would indicate in part the volatile nature of the changes in the bank reserve equation. The postwar data for gold flows in particular indicate in part the tendency for gold, prized by central banks as monetary reserves and hoarders as protection against currency depreciation, to respond increasingly to economic changes since the turmoil of the 1930's and the war years.

In the period mid-1933 to year-end 1941, it could be noticed that the major source of bank reserves was gold flows integrating to 18.7 billion dollars. These changes in the monetary gold stock reflected the increased dollar price of gold effected in 1934 (Sect. 7.5) and unsettled political conditions in the world at a time of world-wide depression when some foreign countries were adopting ideological systems other than capitalism. There were, in other words, flights of gold from abroad in this period. On the demand side, during the same period, the reserves were used to increase bank reserves and currency in circulation to a lesser extent.

During the period December 31, 1941, to December 31, 1945, corresponding roughly to World War II, the primary source of bank reserves was the expansion of Federal Reserve credit, largely through the purchase of government securities. Also, small amounts of gold flowed out of the country, chiefly as a result of large-scale purchases of goods from

---

[*] The result is precise, even though we denoted integrals for particular intervals and even if the curves over the respective intervals were defined by differential equations. One could, of course, approximate the continuous change in reserves (i.e., dR_M/dt) at any particular moment in time more closely by taking daily changes or quarterly changes in reserves. In the latter instance these would be multiplied by 4 to put them on a per annum basis, and histograms could be sketched. The bases of the histograms would become smaller, as the time interval became shorter. But, no matter how narrow the base of the histograms, the total area under the horizontal bars for the interval December 31, 1954, to December 31, 1963, would still sum to precisely 2.272 (billions of dollars).

South American countries. On the uses side of the equation, the increase in reserves was primarily used to support an increase in the volume of currency in circulation by 17.4 billion dollars. This increase in currency in circulation corresponded to the wartime increase in the utilization of resources and the rising income. Also, member-bank reserves were increased by 3.4 billion dollars, and, since reserve requirements did not increase for the remainder of the war after 1942, they were available to support an expansion of credit during the war years.

In the postwar period, year-end 1945 to October 31, 1949, the economy experienced substantial changes on both sides of the equation, though less in some instances than during the war years. On the supply side, Federal Reserve credit contracted by 7.2 billion dollars, but the contraction was partly offset by an inflow of gold amounting to 4.5 billion. On the demand side, member-bank reserves remained relatively unchanged with decreases in Treasury cash and currency in circulation contributing to reserves so as to offset the contracting effect of Federal Reserve credit.

In the years immediately following October 1949, there were several periods of relatively short duration in which gold flows had a substantial effect on member-bank reserves. Gold outflows began in September 1949, after devaluation of the pound and other foreign currencies in relationship to gold and the dollar. The outflows were, in other words, in response to increased purchasing power of gold abroad (Sect. 6.2, and 6.3). These outflows were intensified in 1950 when the outbreak of the Korean War touched off a scramble for raw materials. In the brief period of June 30, 1951, to August 31, 1952, gold returned as the United States export position improved along with the decline of raw material prices and a reduction of purchases for stockpiles. In the period of August 31, 1952, to March 31, 1955, postwar outflows of gold occurred again. They amounted to 1.6 billion dollars and reflected heavy military expenditures abroad by the United States at a time when foreign countries were reducing their import needs from the United States and strengthening their economies generally. In the period of March 31, 1955, to January 31, 1958, there were inflows of gold amounting to 1.1 billion dollars. These reflected mainly the foreign sale of gold to meet financial pressures and to facilitate foreign purchases in anticipation of shortages arising from the 1956 Suez Crisis. For some years after January 31, 1958, outflows continued, as indicated later (Sect. 23.1) in greater detail, in response to a strengthening of foreign currencies, a reduced incentive to hold dollar investments due to a fall in yields on short-term securities, and general improvements in the Western European economies.

Some conclusions. Even broad changes in the bank reserve equation since mid-1933 reflect a multiplicity of forces, and these changes tend to indicate the importance of the primary accounts corresponding to variables in the bank reserve equation. On the domestic side, Federal Reserve credit provides a good source for the long-run expansion of member-bank reserves from which a multiple increase in the money supply may be generated to satisfy the demand for currency and the short-term credit needs of business firms and consumers. On the foreign side, gold transactions promise to be an important means, as in the early 1960's, of facilitating adjustments in international payments. The possible impact of their effect upon reserve balances is well illustrated by the magnitude of the gold flows in the bank reserve equation.

Some reflection concerning the above developments should help in emphasizing a particular conclusion, namely, *changes in bank reserves and possibly in the tone of the market, or the cost and availability of credit, are not necessarily the result of action on the part of the monetary authorities.* Serious changes in bank reserve credit may be accompanied by deliberate inaction, or only partially offsetting action, on their part.

10.3. The Money Supply Accounts

The variables affecting the money supply may be viewed in a form and context similar to that for member-bank reserves. That is, the accounts may be viewed as accumulated amounts, and changes in the accounts from one time to another may be seen as flows. Furthermore, an equation could be written with variables corresponding to the various accounts, and the money supply could then be simply expressed in terms of either stock or flow variables. The procedures, however, would be similar to those above (Sect. 10.2), and the observed changes in the accounts over time would reflect developments in the economy and in the banking system similar to those above. In fact, two of the three accounts contributing to the supply of money on a cumulative basis are monetary gold stock and Treasury currency, which are identical to two of the three accounts on the supply side of bank reserves (Table 10-1). Consequently, for now, we only present the stock variables and data for the money supply accounts and changes in those accounts over a single annual period (Table 10-2) in a manner comparable to that for member-bank reserves (Table 10-1).

Table 10-2 shows that bank credit—of Federal Reserve, commercial, and mutual savings banks—is the major source of the money supply. On the other hand, time deposits are the major factor competing with the money supply in "using up," in the accounting sense, the money and credit base. The pronounced shift from demand to time deposits during the first half of 1963, as shown in the table, was partly seasonal, and partly in continued response to an increase in the interest ceilings on time

Table 10-2. Stock Variables for the Money Supply Accounts, June 29, 1963, and Change Since December 28, 1962

	Dollar Amounts (in billions)	Per Cent of Total	Change Since Dec. 28, 1962 (in billions)
Expansive factors (the supply side):			
Monetary gold stock	15.7	4.6	−0.2
Treasury currency	5.6	1.6	0.0
Bank credit	318.7	93.7	+9.3
Total	340.0	100.0	+9.1
Contractive factors (the demand side):			
Capital and miscellaneous accounts, net	29.7	8.7	+1.0
Foreign bank deposits, net	1.3	0.4	−0.2
United States Government balances	12.5	3.7	+4.4
Time deposits	149.3	43.9	+9.9
(subtotal)	(192.9)	(56.7)	(+15.1)
Money supply			
Demand deposits adjusted	115.3	33.9	−6.9
Currency outside banks	31.8	9.4	+0.9
Total	340.0	100.0	+9.1

NOTE: Parts may not add to totals due to rounding.
SOURCE: Board of Governors of the Federal Reserve System.

deposits in 1962. With respect to the money supply alone, if seasonally adjusted figures are used over the period in question,* then the money supply actually increased by 0.7 billion dollars, a combination of a fall of 0.4 billion in demand deposits adjusted and a rise of 1.1 billion dollars in currency outside banks.

The first half of 1963 embodied some unusual features and some less unusual ones. The large time deposit drain was unusual, but the contraction in the money supply was not unusual for a period of contraction in member-bank reserves, as we shall see later. Net loans during the period rose by 7.6 billion dollars, and the United States government securities held by Federal Reserve banks rose by 1.5 billion dollars. Also, the United States government securities held by commercial and mutual savings banks declined by 2.9 billion dollars, although the diverse movement between bank security holdings and loans is not unusual. The movement, in fact, anticipates some discussion of one recurrent Federal Reserve problem (Sec. 25.4) whereby bank loans and total expenditures

* Seasonally adjusted figures are available only for the money supply items in the accounts. The seasonal adjustment process is quite complex, since intramonth, as well as intermonth, factors are involved.

in the economy are able to increase at a time of restraint on the growth of total bank credit and the money supply. For the present we simply wish, from the operational point of view, to dramatize the potential impact of drains on the money supply and the divergent movement between changes in credit and the change in the money supply.

10.4. Summary

The bank reserve equation emphasizes the interrelationships between member-bank reserves and the other variables in the equation contributing to those reserves, either on a cumulative basis or during selected intervals of time. Member-bank reserves, in the context of the equation, are a residual of changes in the variables other than reserve bank credit. Treasury cash and foreign and other accounts, other than those corresponding to the principal variables, are relatively small and temporary in their impact on reserves. Nevertheless, they provide the additional variables to complete the equation.

Changes in the variables in the equation reflect political and economic developments in the society, and the interrelationships between the principal variables in the equation reveal some aspects of the implementation of a given credit policy by the monetary authorities. The changes in the gold holdings, for example, may reflect political instability in a given country as during the 1930's; it may reflect economic and military crises, such as the Suez Crisis or the Korean Conflict, or it may reflect a relative strengthening of the currencies of competing economies.

The interrelationship between the principal variables in the equation, in particular, dramatizes the way in which the Federal Reserve, in achieving its policy objectives, must adapt its operations so as to allow for the magnitude and direction of changes in currency in circulation and gold flows. In other words, the interrelationship calls attention to the policy effects of Federal Reserve action as well as inaction. For instance, the usual increase in the demand for currency during the Christmas season may result in a reduction in member-bank reserves and a tight tone in the credit market, if the monetary authorities do not intervene and provide an offsetting supply of Federal Reserve credit. The action to provide credit, in this instance, would not properly be viewed as a net contribution to credit ease. Also the monetary authorities may effect an easy tone in the credit market at a time when the monetary gold stock is expanding, if they do not take offsetting action in the form of a reduction in Federal Reserve credit. Increments and decrements in the level of member-bank reserves will not on all occasions correspond to credit ease or tightness, respectively. In such instances the demand side of the credit market must be considered. The most reliable guides to changes in credit policy as effected by the monetary authorities then become changes in the tone of the market itself, as reflected in the key money market indicators (Sect. 14.2) and other indicators of changes in credit conditions (Sect. 24.2).

The money supply accounts also reflect forces at work in the economy, and they reveal as well something of the complexity of the interrelationships among changes in member-bank reserves, changes in bank credit, and changes in the money supply. The supply side of the money supply accounts includes the monetary gold stock, and, consequently, the accounts will also reflect the forces giving rise to changes in the monetary gold stock in the bank reserve equation. Further, the money supply accounts, in combination with the bank reserve accounts, will reflect the possible parallel changes in Federal Reserve credit and bank credit. The demand side of the former set of accounts will reflect, as well, the possible parallel or divergent changes in bank credit and the money supply. The money supply accounts do this, in particular, by focusing on the possible parallel or divergent changes in time deposits. They also provide a clue to the probable impact of changes in the composition of bank earning assets.

References

1. *Modern Money Mechanics: A Workbook on Deposits, Currency, and Bank Reserves* (Federal Reserves Bank of Chicago, 1961), pp. 20-21.

2. See *Financial Condition of the United States* (Washington, D.C.: U.S. Government Printing Office, 1957), pp. 1506-1516.

11

The Structure of the Federal Reserve and Some Supervisory and Other Functions

. . . [The central bank proposed for the United States is] not a competitor in any sense with existing banks. It provides for an equality of privileges and advantages to all banks, great and small, wherever located. Its dominating principle is cooperation and not centralization. Its organization is of a form and character that will effectually prevent the control of its operations by political or other interests, local or national (National Monetary ["Aldrich"] Commission, *Report* [1912]).

Regional autonomy was a part of the philosophy underlying the original establishment of the Federal Reserve System with twelve regional banks and a Board of Governors in Washington (Sect. 7.5). Initially, the discount rate was the only control device in the hands of the policymakers of the system; the rest depended upon the automatic working of the system in response to the proper adherence to certain rules. The initiative for implementing changes in the discount rate rested with the regional banks, and whether a lowering of the rate had the desired effect, or indeed any effect, depended in turn on the initiative of the individual member banks. Since that time the control over the use of instruments for influencing credit and monetary conditions has drifted more toward the center, especially since the banking acts of 1933 and 1935 (Sect. 8.1). This chapter, therefore, includes a description of the structure of the more centralized Federal Reserve System since that time, with its more powerful Board of Governors and Federal Open Market Committee, as well as with its regional banks, their branches, the Federal Advisory Council, and the member banks. It deals with the appointment and election of the public and private members, respectively, of the major and minor policy-making groups. The chapter also describes, as well as the relationship of the Reserve System's structure to the instruments of credit policy (Sect. 8.2), the supervision of commercial banks and the other Federal agencies conducting supervisory functions. It also outlines structural and administrative changes recommended for improvements in the effectiveness of the nation's monetary and financial structure by the Commission on Money and Credit—a private group established in 1958 and supported by several foundations for the purpose of making such recommendations.[1]

Some of the important functions of the System in which the different groups participate in various degrees are, in sum,

(1) To influence credit conditions and the stock of money with the view to achieving maximum employment, production, and purchasing power within the context of free-enterprise institutions, which includes such functions as (a) the fixing, within limits, of member-bank reserve requirements, (b) the determination of the discount rates, (c) the determination of the activities whereby the system influences the cost and availability of credit through open market operations, and (d) the fixing of margin requirements for loans on stock exchange collateral; and

(2) To exercise supervision over commercial banks that are members of the system and to administer Federal Reserve, holding company, and other legislation.

Some of these functions have been dealt with previously. Others are introduced in this chapter.

Broadly, the Federal Reserve may be likened to a trusteeship created by Congress under the monetary powers given to that body by the Constitution. It is, on the one hand, partly independent within the structure of government so that, in its technical field at least, it shall be free to determine and carry out policy decisions; on the other hand, it is responsible to the Congress. Congress, however, makes no appointments to the Reserve System's policy-making boards and has only the right to give or deny its approval and consent in the case of the appointments made by the President of the United States to the Board of Governors of the Federal Reserve System. Perhaps a statement by the late Senator Kerr of Oklahoma is illustrative, in which he says that "the annual report of the Federal Reserve Board is worth studying for anybody who wants to find out how to become a creature of the Congress, be technically responsible to it, but practically independent of it."[2]

11.1. Policy-Making and Advisory Groups

The central policy-making groups within the Federal Reserve System are the Board of Governors and the Federal Open Market Committee, given the structure of the System growing out of the banking acts of 1933 and 1935. The former of these groups has also been assisted by an essentially advisory group—the Federal Advisory Council. Each is considered below.

The Board of Governors. The Board of Governors of the Federal Reserve System is located in Washington, D.C. Its seven members are appointed by the President of the United States, and they are removable only for cause. The appointments, made for fourteen years, are subject to the approval and consent of the Congress. They were purposely staggered so that one appointment should be made very two years, which would prevent a packing of the board by any single President. In appointing the members, the President is required to give due consideration to the representation of financial, agricultural, industrial, and commercial interests, as well as geographical divisions of the country. The President also appoints a chairman and vice chairman for terms of four years, from among the members of the board. The board's expenses are paid out of assessments levied upon the regional banks. The salaries of the board members are determined by the Congress in such a way as to correspond with those paid other high government officials. Consequently, the salaries of board members are on the average lower than those paid to the presidents of the regional banks.

Responsibilities of the board. The board is a policy-making and supervisory body, whereas the regional banks are primarily operating units. Among the board's policy-making responsibilities are those to approve or disapprove of discount rate changes, to initiate changes in reserve requirements, to initiate changes in margin requirements, and to formulate policy decisions along with other members of the Federal Open Market Committee. The notion of "policy" or "policy-making" in this context, however, concerns goals at the level of central bank operations—the ease (or tightness) of credit, and so on (Sect. 24.1). Later (Sect. 24.1), we re-emphasize the ultimate goals as set by the representatives of the people in the legislative branch of government. These include maximum employment, production, and so on (Sect 8.1).

Among the board's other statutory responsibilities are those carried out through the issuance and maintenance of regulations and by the direct examinations of the Reserve banks. The board appoints three of the nine directors of each Reserve bank, including the chairman and the deputy chairman. These are Class C directors, and they must not be officers, directors, or stockholders of any bank. Also the appointments (to be described subsequently) of the president and first vice-president of each regional bank are subject to the board's approval. The board issues regulations that interpret the provisions of the law relating to bank operations. It directs the Reserve System's activities in bank examination and supervision and coordinates economic research and publications. The annual budgets for each regional bank and their branches are submitted to the board; the salaries of Reserve bank officers and other employees are subject to the board's approval; and operating procedures and expenses generally are surveyed. Finally, the board submits an annual report to the Congress and publishes the weekly statement of the condition (Sect. 9.2) of the Federal Reserve banks.

The board: suggestions for organizational changes. In viewing the administrative arrangement in which the board functions and recalling its responsibilities, several suggestions for organizational changes to improve the responsiveness and general functioning of the board have been made.[3] Two of these relate to monetary policy directly, and another relates to administration. The first recognizes the claim for monetary stability within government and the need for a monetary authority independent of the more unstabilizing aspects of the political branches of the government. However, it also would strengthen the ties between the executive branch of the government and the Board of Governors with the view to strengthening the board with Presidential support and, at the same time, to increasing the degree of responsiveness of the board to particular conditions that arise from time to time. To achieve these ends, the proponents of this suggestion would reduce the number of board members from seven to five. They would then have ten-year terms of membership with one expiring every odd-numbered year, and they would have the chairman and vice-chairman of the board appointed from the members of the board to serve four-year terms coterminous with that of the President. The members would be eligibile for reappointment, and the expiration dates would permit the President to appoint a member shortly after inauguration. The reduction in the number of governors, furthermore, should enhance the prestige of membership.

The acceptance of the second suggestion with respect to the policy-making function, and closely aligned to the problem of responsiveness, would change the qualifications for membership. It would eliminate occupational and geographical qualifications for board members and emphasize instead the qualities of competence, independence, objectivity, experience, and/or education with respect to the broad responsibilities implied by the national economic goals (Sect. 8.1). There is the view that the listing of occupational qualifications produces claims for recognition from others to fill the small number of places. There is also the view that the status of the governors would be enhanced by the emphasis on personal qualifications. Perhaps then one may wish to emphasize the personal qualifications after due consideration for the geographical distribution of membership in order to avoid, at the same time, the hazards of a single parochial interest among the board members.

The third suggested change relating directly to administration would make the chairman the chief executive officer, which would empower him to handle administrative matters. The law would then explicitly authorize the board to delegate to other board members, senior staff officers, and committees those matters that concern the supervisory function (Sect. 11.4) and administration of the Bank Holding Company Act (Sect. 12.1) and other antitrust laws related to banking in the granting of bank charters. In addition, those delegated would handle the approval of applications for branches (Sect. 12.1), mergers (Sect. 12.3), and so on. There is with respect to this recommendation the view that the congestion of business detail at the top detracts from the time and energy board members should devote to the broad issues of credit policy.

The Federal Open Market Committee. The Federal Open Market Committee consists of the seven members of the Board of Governors and the presidents of five of the regional banks. The President of the Federal Reserve Bank of New York—because of both tradition and the location of the trading desk for open market operations (Sect. 8.2)—has always been a member of the committee, and the remaining memberships are rotated within four groupings of the other regional banks: (1) Boston, Philadelphia, Richmond; (2) Cleveland, Chicago; (3) Atlanta, Dallas, St. Louis; and (4) Minneapolis, Kansas City, San Francisco. Thus, the Chicago president serves every other year, the Atlanta president every third year, and so on. The Chairman of the Board of Governors is by statute the Chairman of the Federal Open Market Committee, and the President of the Federal Reserve Bank of New York is by tradition the Vice-Chairman. This is the committee described by Congressman Wright Patman, the ranking Democrat on the House Banking and Currency Committee at the time, as "the most powerful committee in the United States." He said, "It is more powerful than the Congress in many fields." [4]

Functions of the Open Market Committee. Following the abolition of its executive committee in June 1955, it became the practice of the Federal Open Market Committee to meet at three-week intervals, and, on some occasions, two-week intervals, to direct the sale and purchase of securities in the open market. At such meetings, the committee touches on all questions of policy, because of the overriding importance of open market operations and their interrelationhip with the other credit instruments. Indeed, according to the board's chairman in 1957, the committee has become "a clearing house for all of the aspects of policy determination in the System. . . ." [5] And, under the circumstances, all twelve of the presidents of the Federal Reserve, including seven nonvoting presidents and the voting members belonging to the Federal Open Market Committee, came to meet with the committee.

The Open Market Committee: suggestions for organizational changes. Despite the above developments, recommendations have been made by the Commission on Money and Credit to further recognize the centralization of authority and responsibility for credit and monetary policy.[6] One of these would abolish the Federal Open Market Committee and turn the responsibility for open market policies over to the Board of Governors entirely. In this respect, there has been the view that the distinction between the board and the committee is no longer useful, and that ambiguity about the responsibility for monetary policy should be avoided.

A bill (H.R. 9631), somewhat along these same lines, was introduced in January 1964. Sponsored by Congressman Patman at that time, it would have, among other things, abolished the Federal Open Market Committee, turned its functions over to the Board of Governors, changed the latter board's name back to the Federal Reserve Board (Sect. 8.1), increased the membership on the board, and place the enlarged twelve-man board under Treasury Department domination by making the Secretary of the Treasury its chairman.[7]

Another recommendation by the Commission on Money and Credit would also vest in the board the authority to determine the discount rate, with the possible additional provision that the board consult with the twelve regional bank presidents in the establishment of open market policy, reserve requirements, and the discount rate.

Federal Advisory Council. The Federal Advisory Council has consisted of twelve members who meet in Washington at least four times a year, as prescribed by the Federal Reserve Act. Each member, elected by one of the respective boards of directors of the regional banks, is chosen from representative and outstanding bankers in each district.

The council has been required to confer directly with the Board of Governors on general business conditions and to make recommendations concerning matters within the board's jurisdiction. A report of the House Committee on Banking and Currency on the original Federal Reserve Act outlines the nature of the council as follows:

> The functions of this board are wholly advisory and it would amount merely to a means of expressing banking opinion, informing the Reserve Board of conditions of credit in the several districts, and serving as a source of information upon which the board may draw in case of necessity. The desirability of such a body as a source of information and counsel is obvious, and it is believed that it gives to the banking interests of the several districts ample power to make their views known, and, so far as they deserve acceptance, to secure such acceptance.[8]

There has been the view, nevertheless, that the channels of outside advice to the board need broadening,[9] despite board authority to consult with *ad hoc* advisory committees in the furtherance of its work. To achieve this end some would replace the statutory Federal Advisory Council with a council of twelve members to be appointed by the board from nominations made by the directors of the regional Federal Reserve banks. They would, further, have the selected council members represent all aspects of the American economy and serve for three-year nonrenewable terms, and they would require the council to meet with the Board of Governors at least twice a year. They would have, as well, the law call for a conference of the twelve Federal Reserve bank presidents to meet with the governors at least four times a year.[10]

11.2. Federal Reserve Banks

The country has been divided into twelve districts with a Federal Reserve bank in each district and one or more branches in each of the districts, except those which include the Boston and Philadelphia banks. The map comprising Fig. 11-1 shows the boundaries of Federal Reserve districts and branch territories.

Form of organization and relative sizes. The twelve Federal Reserve banks have had corporate forms of organization. The banks are vested with a public interest, although the stock of each bank has been held by the member banks of the district. The member banks are required to subscribe to the Federal Reserve bank capital in an amount equal to 6 per cent of their own capital and surplus and to pay one-half of the subscription. The balance is subject to call by the Board of Governors.

Data on the paid-in capital for each Federal Reserve bank have been published by the Board of Governors. They serve as an indicator of the relative size of the various Reserve banks, and the latter data, along with data for deposits at the respective Reserve banks, serve as indicators of bank resources in the various districts. As of June 30, 1965, for example, we would judge the largest bank to be the New York bank with 26.2 and 29.5 per cent of the total for paid-in capital and deposits, respectively, for all twelve of the banks. Minneapolis would be the smallest at that time with 2.4 and 2.4 per cent, respectively.

The holders of Federal Reserve shares have not had the powers and privileges that customarily belong to stockholders of privately managed corporations. Neither has the stock had the normal financial attributes of corporate stock. It simply represents a required subscription to the capital of the Reserve bank, and its dividends have been fixed by law at 6 per cent.

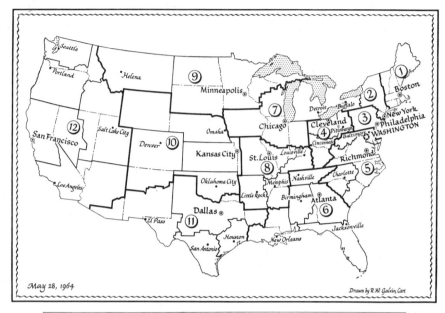

THE FEDERAL RESERVE SYSTEM

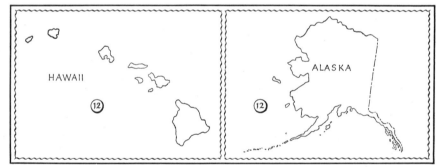

Legend

—— Boundaries of Federal Reserve Districts ——Boundaries of Federal Reserve Branch Territories

✪ Board of Governors of the Federal Reserve System

◉ Federal Reserve Bank Cities   • Federal Reserve Branch Cities

Fig. 11-1. Boundaries of the Federal Reserve Districts and Their Branch Territories.
Source: Board of Governors of the Federal Reserve System.

Earnings and governing structure. Apart from the earlier suggestion concerning the retirement of the above form of stock ownership (Sect. 9.2), there have apparently been no compelling reasons for changes with respect to earnings and the governing structure of the twelve Federal Reserve banks. Each Federal Reserve bank has derived its earnings primarily from its share of holdings in the open market account and, to a lesser extent, from its discounts and advances. Along with the growth of the open market account, these earnings have grown to a considerable amount. For example, the earnings on the 39,100 million dollars of government securities in the open market account at the close of business on June 30, 1965, at the nominal rate of 2 per cent, would be approximately 782 million dollars. The residual of earnings—after payment of operating expenses, the payment of dividends, and the retention of earnings—are syphoned off to the United States government under a provision that has given the Board of Governors itself authority to levy a tax upon the Federal Reserve's issue of notes.[11] Under this arrangement about 90 per cent of net earnings after dividends were paid to the Treasury in the post-World War II years. The rule in effect for some years has been that the Federal Reserve turns over to the Treasury any net earnings after dividends and over and above the amount necessary to keep its surplus equal to twice its paid-in capital. By this method of passing the earnings on to the Treasury, all of the people derive some benefit from these earnings and the government recoups some of the interest it pays on the Federal debt.

Each Federal Reserve bank has had nine directors of whom six are elected by the member banks and three have been appointed by the board as described above. Three of them have been known as Class-A directors, three as Class-B, and three as Class-C. Class-A and Class-B directors have been those elected by the member banks. The Class-A directors could have been bankers, one from a large, one from a medium, and one from a small bank. Bankers, however, have been excluded from serving as Class-B directors who have been selected from individuals actively engaged in the district in business, agriculture, or some other commercial pursuit. The directors of a Reserve bank have supervised its affairs, appointed the president and first vice-president for terms of five years (subject to the approval of the Board of Governors), and established the discount rates, subject to review and determination by the Board.

11.3. Member and Nonmember Banks

All banks with national charters have been required by law to be members of the Federal Reserve System, and all state banks could become members by meeting the prescribed requirements if they so desire, under the Federal Reserve Act, as it prevailed in the post-World War II years. At year-end 1964, the member banks accounted for only 45 per cent of the total number of commercial banks and 83.3 per cent of the total of deposits in all commercial banks. These figures represent some small decline in member banks and deposits relative to the respective total number of banks and total deposits since the post war and early war years. Even so, they indicate that in exercising control over member-bank deposits the Federal Reserve has directly controlled the greater portion of the total of deposits at all commercial banks.

Privileges and obligations of membership. Membership in the Federal Reserve System has carried certain privileges and obligations as well. On the one hand, each member bank been able to participate in the election of directors, to receive dividends, to share in the informational facilities provided by the System, to obtain currency as required, to borrow from its Reserve bank when in need of additional funds, and to use along with par nonmembers the Federal Reserve facilities for collecting checks, settling balances, and transferring funds. On the other hand, each member bank has been required to subscribe to the capital of its Reserve bank, comply with reserve requirements, keep its reserves other than till cash on deposit without interest at its Reserve bank, and to otherwise abide by certain rules prescribed by law or developed by regulation in accordance with the law. In the case of reserve requirements in particular, those for member banks have been frequently higher than those for nonmember banks. This latter difference in some instances, furthermore, weakens the incentive to join the Reserve System, and there has been the view that it may at times inhibit Federal Reserve action.[12]

Some problems concerning nonmember banks. Other problems with respect to nonmember banks include (1) their avoidance of the direct effects of the Federal's possibly more stringent reserve requirements, in some instances, and (2) the imperfection in the payments mechanism caused by the exchange charge by some nonmembers for the settlement of checks drawn on them. These problems, of course, are not overly serious, and restrictive credit conditions are felt by nonmember banks as the effective demand for bank funds increases relative to the capacity of the banks to expand loans, and as nonmember banks pay out and replace some of the vault-cash portion of their reserves. Even so, several proposals have been made to broaden membership in the Federal Reserve: All commercial banks would become members. (2) All banks insured by the Federal Deposit Insurance Corporation (Sect. 11.4) would become members. (3) All banks would be subject to the same reserve requirements. All three of these proposals, in fact, have been viewed as feasible and desirable.

The main recommendation of the Commission on Money and Credit would require membership by all insured commercial banks.[13] The adoption of this recommendation would bring into membership the bulk of nonmember banks. Data, at year-end 1964, would specifically indicate that the adoption would bring in an additional 52.8 per cent of the number of commercial banks, accounting for an additional 16.1 per cent of the total of deposits. The President's Committee on Financial Institutions, on the other hand, favored continuing the present practice of voluntary membership for state-chartered banks. They would, nevertheless, require that *all* commercial banks be subject to the same system of reserve requirements, with actual reserve ratios for demand deposits graduated with the size of bank.[14]

11.4. Supervisory Functions and the Insurance of Bank Deposits

Included among bank supervisory functions are bank examination, the issuance of regulations and rulings, the requirement of reports, the provision of counsel and advice, and supervision of bank liquidation. In addition, there is the granting of permits to exercise trust powers, the granting of voting permits to holding company affiliates, the granting of approval of consolidations and mergers, and the granting of approval prior to the acquisition of the voting shares of any bank by bank holding companies (Sect. 12.1). The latter of these functions was assumed by the Board of Governors under the Bank Holding Company Act of 1956, the purpose of the act being the maintenance of bank competition. The purpose of the other functions, briefly stated, is to aid in the maintenance of sound individual banks.

The statutory responsibility for bank supervision is divided among the respective states and three Federal agencies—the Comptroller of the Currency, the Federal Reserve, and the Federal Deposit Insurance Corporation (FDIC). As matters have evolved, the basic supervisory functions are performed within the framework of governing laws and regulations, but to a large extent the otherwise overlapping functions have been informally allocated among the regulatory agencies.

The functions performed by these agencies are said to contribute mostly to the successful conduct of credit policy by maintaining strong individual banks and a responsive banking system, i.e., one responsive to changes in reserves, required ratio constant. It is usually maintained that bank supervision as such cannot and should not be used to directly enforce credit policy, except insofar as sound banking contributes to that end.[15] There is the view, however, that the contribution to greater confidence in banking and the circulating medium, such as that brought about by the Federal insurance of deposits, has contributed to the attainment of a higher degree of monetary stability. Historical perspective (Chap. 7) and earlier analysis (e.g., Sect. 5.4) should provide some basis for this view.

The state agencies. The state agencies are among the oldest supervisory agencies, as indicated earlier (Sect. 7.3). They have the direct and primary responsibility for the supervision of state banks, so-called because of the source of their charters. These banks "operate under the supervision of State authorities, and, in the event of liquidation, have their activities terminated in accordance with provisions of state law." [16]

The Comptroller of the Currency. The Comptroller of the Currency is also among the older bank chartering and supervisory agencies. The National Banking Act (Sect. 7.4) provided there should be a Comptroller of the Currency responsible to the Secretary of the Treasury. The Comptroller has the responsibility for chartering and supervising national banks. Much of the Comptroller's previous responsibility for appointing and supervising receivers for closed banks has been in effect replaced by the responsibility of the FDIC.

The Federal Reserve. The Federal Reserve Act of 1913 gave the Federal Reserve authority to supervise all member banks. In practice, however, the Federal Reserve has limited its examination to state member banks and relied upon reports received from the Comptroller of the Currency on the other member banks. Apart from the Federal Reserve's supervisory activities carried out through the issuance of regulations, rulings, interpretations of statutes, and so on, the process of field examination is highly decentralized. It too, therefore, requires some effort at coordination within the system itself.

Contrary to the trend in the control over credit (Sect. 9.1), decentralization has been the capstone of Federal Reserve examination policy. The Federal Reserve's examinations are conducted by the various Federal Reserve banks. The field examiner makes his report to the chief Federal Reserve bank examiner, who, in turn, reviews the report and recommends action where it is called for. A copy of the report is then forwarded to the Board's Division of Examiners for review. The standardization, coordination, and implementation achieved in supervisory practices, therefore, come "primarily through annual staff conferences of board and Reserve bank personnel, through influence over general standards established for examinations, and in rare cases through board influence in the dismissal of Reserve Bank examiners deemed unsuited for their positions." [17]

The Federal Deposit Insurance Corporation. The Federal Deposit Insurance Corporation (FDIC) was another of the immediate consequences of the wave of bank failures in 1933 (Sect. 7.5). The Banking Act of 1933 superimposed this agency with some supplemental and duplicating functions on some other agencies, and the agency and its system of deposit insurance were made permanent under the Banking Act of 1935. Its main responsibilities were the administration of a system of deposit insurance and the supervision of insured banks. The insured banks include all banks that are members of the Federal Reserve System (including all national banks) and other banks approved for insurance by the Board of Directors of the Corporation.

The FDIC has supervisory powers over all insured banks, subject in some respects to permissive action by the other Federal supervisory agencies. They have also, in effect, extended deposit insurance to cover the full amount deposited by their practice of working out mergers and consolidations for failing banks so as to make them solvent institutions.

The insurance of bank deposits. The insurance provision of the 1935 act called for a maximum claim of $5,000 for each depositor of a bank that had been approved for insurance and subsequently closed on account of inability to meet the demands of its depositors. Later, under the Federal Deposit Insurance Act of 1950, the amount was raised to include a maximum claim of $10,000, and it has since been suggested that the maximum should be increased as a result of the increase in the average size of deposits.[18] Like the transactions demand for money itself (Sect. 2.1), the maximum doubtlessly should be some increasing function of income, if the maximum is to be considered significant as some constant degree of protection.

Insured banks, for their part, have paid insurance premiums at a flat rate assessed against average total deposits. It has been suggested, however, that the premiums banks pay should be based on rates depending upon the risk involved. In assessing risk, the magnitude of the risk element would vary with (1) the category of the loan, (2) the maturity of the loan, and (3) the capital surplus and reserves of the insured bank. In particular, in carrying out an audit, the examiner would be listing assets by type, and the amount of risk would be indicated by the products of the dollar volumes in each category and the corresponding risk elements. The insurance rate would vary with risk and would then be assessed against average total deposits. The effect of the acceptance of such a suggestion should be to make bank managers considerably more flexible in competing with other financial institutions and in accommodating the local need for loans.[19]

Deposit insurance does not assure complete liquidity in the face of a run on a bank lacking access to the Federal Reserve's discount privileges, but the insurance doubtlessly goes a long way toward contributing to confidence in banking and toward protecting the circulating medium from the consequences of bank failures. Two writers, in fact, have viewed Federal deposit insurance as the most important structural change in the banking system to result from the final banking crisis of the early 1930's: It is "the structural change most conducive to monetary stability since state bank notes were taxed out of existence [Sect. 7.3] immediately after the Civil War." [20]

Interagency coordination and proposals for the consolidation of regulatory functions. The various agencies perform some supervisory functions not shared by others, and, even where the statutory responsibility of the several agencies overlaps, they have cooperated in separating their efforts.[21] National bank examination and related duties, for example, are performed by the Comptroller's office; state member-bank examinations are performed by Federal Reserve examiners; and nonmember insured banks are examined by the FDIC in cooperation with state agencies which, nevertheless, are responsible for all state banks.

Despite the presence of cooperation among the supervisory agencies, some have recommended legislative changes leading to a single examining authority at the Federal level.[22] These would transfer the functions of the Comptroller of the Currency and the FDIC to the Federal Reserve. Others have pointed to the desirability of a consolidation of regulatory functions, but these would object to any further transfer of such functions to the Federal Reserve. They would wish to avoid imposing additional administrative responsibilities on the board that may interfere with the formation and execution of monetary policy. They would view as desirable instead the consolidation of functions, such as chartering, branching, insuring, and examining outside of the Federal Reserve. One of the most extreme of this latter groups of proposals has been made by James Louis Robertson, a member of the board.[23] He has suggested abolishing the Comptroller of the Currency and the FDIC and establishing a new Federal Banking Commission to assume the Competroller's, FDIC's, and Federal Reserve's supervisory functions.

11.5. Summary

The Federal Reserve System, through accident and design, gives representation to both public and private interest. The powerful Federal Open Market Committee, for instance, may have its policies determined by a majority vote consisting of the seven public members of the Board of Governors, or by five Reserve bank presidents and a minority of board members, or by some combination of the latter two groups. Also, the System appears to provide a reasonable degree of independence for its policy-makers within the framework of government. The members of the Board of Governors receive appointment for a fourteen-year term and cannot be removed without cause, whereas the directors of the respective Reserve banks, who recommend discount rate changes and appoint the president and vice-president of their banks, are elected or appointed for a shorter term. In the final analysis, the board itself is accountable to the Congress, which may amend the Federal Reserve Act when they think it necessary and in the public interest.

The adoption of recommended changes in the Federal Reserve System's structure and the assignment of policy and administrative responsibilities within the System, however, would change the above structural and administrative arrangements that have existed, for the most part, since the early 1930's. The adoption of some of the recommendations would reduce the membership on the board from seven to five members; abolish the Federal Open Market Committee and turn the responsibilities for open market policy over to the Board; change terms of membership on the Board from fourteen to ten years; alter the criteria for appointments to the Board to emphasize such qualities as competence, independence, experience, and/or education instead of occupation and geographical location; emphasize the executive-officer role of chairman to facilitate a delegation of administrative duties; and strengthen the tie between the executive branch of the government and the board by making the chairman's term of service coterminous with that of the President. The effect of these changes would be to further centralize authority and responsibility within the Reserve System. Perhaps, without weakening the independence of the monetary authority in the expression of its viewpoint and in trying to achieve the national economic goals, these changes would secure an improved coordination between the Federal Reserve's action (and inactions) and those of other agencies of government having effects on the levels of employment, production, and purchasing power. The adoption of some other recommendations would have some other effects: that of broadening membership in the Federal Reserve to include all insured commercial banks, and that of changing the form of stock ownership in the Federal Reserve.

Some recommendations concerning the Federal Reserve and other agencies would strengthen the coordination among the Federal agencies through legislation transferring those outside of the Federal Reserve to the Federal Reserve. Others would consolidate the functions of supervision, chartering, and so on in a single agency outside of the Federal Reserve to avoid detracting energies from the formation and execution of monetary policy. Over the years, overlapping statutory responsibilities of the several banking agencies have developed, in part as a result of historical accident and *ad hoc* banking legislation. Nevertheless, a reasonable degree of coordination has been achieved among these agencies through cooperation with the result of a reduction in the duplication of supervisory activities.

Among the supervisory agencies—the Comptroller of the Currency, the FDIC, and the Federal Reserve—the FDIC is unique in insuring deposits. In practice, however, they usually take over or merge failing institutions with sound ones and in effect increase the safety (and, therefore, liquidity) of the full amount of deposits. Still there are those who would presumably expand this maximum periodically as total deposits expand. And one imaginative individual would have banks pay premiums for this insurance on the basis of rates corresponding to the riskiness of their respective operations. This presumably could work to provide insurance for deposits, simultaneously free management to take on riskier loans, and, at least, favor the more conservative banker with lower premiums.

The supervisory functions should not directly concern the enforcement of credit policy, but supervision may contribute to sound, responsive, and competitive banks. Sound banks then, as earlier analysis would lead us to expect, contribute to monetary stability. Moreover, responsive banks and a competitive banking structure should improve upon the transmission of changes in reserves (required ratios constant) to changes in the stocks of credit and money and, therefore, interest rates.

References

1. See Commission on Money and Credit, *Money and Credit: Their Influence on Jobs, Prices, and Growth* (Englewood Cliffs, N.J.: Prentice-Hall, Inc., 1961), pp. 1-8. Also, for discussions concerning the latter document, see *Review of Report of the Commission on Money and Credit*, Hearings Before the Joint Economic Committee, Congress of the United States (Washington, D.C.: U.S. Government Printing Office, 1961). For an essay on the role of national commissions, see George J. Stigler, "The National Commission as an Instrument of Controlled Impartiality," *The Intellectual and the Market Place and Other Essays* (The Free Press of Glencoe, 1963), pp. 17-23.

2. See dialogue between Robert S. Kerr and W. Randolph Burgess, *Financial Condition of the United States* (Washington, D.C.: U.S. Government Printing Office, 1957), p. 767.

3. Commission on Money and Credit, *op. cit., pp.* 85-89.

4. See *United States Monetary Policy: Recent Thinking and Experience* (Washington, D.C.: U.S. Government Printing Office, 1954), pp. 94-95.

5. See the statement of William McChesney Martin, Jr., Chairman, Board of Governors of the Federal Reserve System, *Financial Condition of the United States* (Washington, D.C.: U.S. Government Printing Office, 1957), p. 1260. For a discussion of many unresolved issues surrounding Open Market Committee decision-making, see William P. Yohe, "The Open Market Committee Decision Process and the 1964 Patman *Hearings,*" *National Banking Review*, March 1965.

6. Commission on Money and Credit, *op.cit.*, p. 90.

7. For a copy and discussion of the bill (H.R. 9631), see *The Federal Reserve System after Fifty Years*, Hearings Before the Subcommittee on Domestic Finance of the Committee on Banking and Currency, House of Representatives, Vols. 1, 2, and 3 (Washington, D.C.: U.S. Government Printing Office, 1964).

8. Cited by William McChesney Martin, Jr., *op. cit.*, p. 1261.

9. Commission on Money and Credit, *op.cit.*, p. 89.

10. *Ibid.*, p. 89.

11. For a discussion of the legal authority which permits the board to do this, see *Financial Conditions of the United States* (Washington, D.C.: U.S. Government Printing Office, 1957), pp. 1580-1585.

12. Commission on Money and Credit, *op.cit.*, p. 76.

13. *Ibid.*, p. 77.

14. Committee on Financial Institutions, *Report to the President of the*

United States (Washington, D.C.: Government Printing Office, 1963), pp. 10-13. The proposal of the Committee on Financial Institutions is somewhat similar to a proposal made by the American Bankers Association in 1957, except that the latter body favored applying the same reserve ratios to all banks. See Economic Policy Commission, American Bankers Association, *Member Bank Reserve Requirements* (New York: A.B.A., 1957), esp. p. 152.

15. On this point of bank supervision, see, for instance, Henry Parker Willis, *The Theory and Practice of Central Banking* (New York: Harper and Brothers, 1936), pp. 85-87; R. F. Leonard, "Supervision of the Commercial Banking System," *Banking Studies* (Washington, D.C.: Board of Governors of the Federal Reserve System, 1941), pp. 191-193; and *Monetary Policy and the Management of the Public Debt*, Part 2 (Washington, D.C.: U.S. Government Printing Office, 1952), pp. 905-910 and 942.

16. Leonard, *op. cit.*, p. 194.

17. G. L. Bach, *Federal Reserve Policy-Making* (New York: Alfred A. Knopf, 1950), p. 108.

18. Commission on Money and Credit, *op.cit.*, pp. 170-171; and Committee on Financial Institutions, *op.cit.*, pp. 40-42.

19. See suggestion by Fred Lazarus, Jr., in Commission on Money and Credit, *op.cit.*, p. 171.

20. See Milton Friedman and Anna Jacobson Schwartz, *A Monetary History of the United States, 1867-1960* (Princeton, N.J.: Princeton University Press for the National Bureau of Economic Research, 1963, pp. 434-442.

21. For an outline of some arrangements for cooperation, see *Monetary Policy and the Management of the Public Debt* (Washington, D.C.: U.S. Government Printing Office, 1952), pp. 915-916.

22. Commission on Money and Credit, *op.cit.*, p. 174. The President's Committee on Financial Institutions recommends such changes only if further efforts "to achieve greater cooperation and coordination under common standards, regulations, and procedures" fail (*op.cit.*, p. 63).

23. See "Federal Bank Supervision," *Challenge*, October 1962, pp. 16-19.

12

The Structure of Commercial Banking in the United States

> I am sure that the days of small banks will before many years come to an end. . . . The detail of the business is augmenting with an overwhelming rapidity* (Walter Bagehot, *Lombard Street* [1873]).

There are features of the banking system in the United States that appear to have a striking contrast to those of countries possessing even relatively similar systems, such as the United Kingdom and Canada. Included among these distinguishing features are the presence of both state and nationally chartered banks (Sect. 7.4), the multiplicity of bank supervisory agencies (Sect. 11.4), and the partial separation of investment banking from commercial banking. In addition, there is the more striking contrast of the degree of consolidation among banks in the respective systems.

In the United Kingdom, structural simplification of the banking system has resulted from the gathering together of individual banks into a few undertakings, the principal among them being the so-called "big five" and the other six London clearing banks (or "joint stock" banks).[1] The "big five" ** alone account for about three-quarters of the banking resources of the United Kingdom and a similar proportion of branch offices. Alterations in this structure, however, have been relatively limited since 1918, when the banks agreed to submit proposals for further

---

* There were forty private banks (as distinct from joint stock banks) in Lombard Street admitted to the clearing house in 1810. The number was reduced to ten at the time of the first edition of *Lombard Street* (1873), and there was only one when the fourteenth edition of Bagehot's work appeared in 1915.

** The "big five" are Barclays, Lloyds, Midland, National Provincial, and Westminster.

amalgamations to the Treasury for approval, in order to remove anxieties concerning the possible emergence of a banking monopoly. In Canada, somewhat similar to the British experience, the commercial banking system has passed through periods of germination, proliferation, and consolidation, up until mid-1964 when their banking system consisted of the eight chartered banks, five of which have branches throughout the provinces. In the United States, by contrast, the tradition of so-called unit banking has persisted, though three types of multiple-office banking have prevailed. This chapter, then, describes the three types of banking organization—along with references to the provisions that govern them—and the institutional and cost factors contributing to the complex structure of commercial banking in the United States. It also deals briefly with bank merger regulations and the United States Justice Department's reaction to the tendency toward consolidation in the last post-World War II years. We are concerned with the subject as a part of our general background in banking, but we are also concerned with the structure of the credit market and the extent of competition. This is because the spread of credit ease or tightness to changes in the amount of bank credit and the stock of money are affected by the extent of the competition in the credit market.

12.1. Three Types of Multiple-Office Banking

The following are the three types of multiple-office banking that have prevailed: branch, group, and chain.[2] These are described below.

Branch banking. Branch banking is a type of multiple-office banking under which a bank as a single legal entity operates more than one banking office. The First and Second Banks of the United States (Sect. 7.1) were examples of this form of bank organization. Instances of this form were nearly extinct by the end of the nineteenth century, but, beginning in the twentieth century, and particularly since the 1920's, changes in Federal and state statutes have made further growth possible. The application of Federal and state laws and the duality of government chartering agencies (i.e., state banking agencies and the comptroller of the currency), moreover, have led some to refer to the commercial banking systems in the United States as a "dual banking system."

The growth of branch banking received its impetus on the legislative side in 1909 when California enacted a state-wide branch banking law. Since that time, there have been other acts and various provisions at both the state and national levels. But, in these terms, Federal legislation applicable to branch banking is never more liberal than state legislation applicable to the same area. As of 1963, eight states prohibited branch banking altogether, eight states permitted branches only under very special (usually local) circumstances, ten others permitted state-wide branch banking with no locational limitation, and twenty-four permitted varying degrees of local and/or state-wide branching.[3]

The postwar migration of people and industry to the suburbs has contributed to the increased importance of branches. Branches and additional offices as a proportion of total commercial banking offices increased from 16.3 per cent at year-end 1934, to 26.7 per cent at year-end 1951, to 51.2 per cent at year-end 1964.

Group banking. Group banking is a type of multiple-office banking consisting of two or more banks under the control of a holding company, which itself may or may not be a bank.* The holding company is referred to as the parent company and the controlled institutions as operating companies, though the parent company itself may also be an operating company. The operating companies (i.e., separately incorporated banks and their branches) may be controlled, directly or indirectly, through a business trust, association, or similar organization, but stock ownership is the usual form of control. To the extent that the parent organizations contribute efficiency to group banking operations, they do so by having the parent corporation or, in some instances, the service subsidiary of the holding company, provide such specialized services as research and advice on loan, investment, and legal matters. Present-day group banking, however, had to await the development of holding company charters. It was not until 1889 in New Jersey and thereafter in other states that the law provided for such a company other than through a special act of the state legislature; and the extensive development of group banking did not occur until the years 1927-1929. The major companies operating as late as the early 1960's were formed during these years. They survived the stock market crash of 1929 and the wave of bank failures in the early 1930's.

The holding company groups registered pursuant to the Bank Holding Company Act of 1956 accounted for approximately 5.7 per cent of the banking offices and 7.4 per cent of all commercial banks in the United States at year-end 1958. Their relative importance had increased moderately by year-end 1961.

Ever since the growth of group banking in the 1920's there has been some effort by independent bankers or others to increase regulations over bank holding companies. The Banking Act of 1933, following a study in 1930, brought group banking under Federal supervision in any case in which a member of the Federal Reserve System was involved as a constituent bank of such a group. The provisions of that act require

* Under the Bank Holding Company Act of 1956, the definition of the term "bank holding company" is based on the 25 per cent ownership or control of two or more banks, a provision long opposed by the Federal Reserve as too liberal. It has asked on numerous occasions for an amendment applying the 25 per cent test to *one* or more banks.

holding company affiliates (i.e., companies controlling member banks of the Federal Reserve System) to obtain voting permits before voting the stock of member banks. The holding company affiliates were also made subject to examination by the Federal Reserve authorities and were required to make regular reports of conditions. Other provisions established limits and collateral requirements for member-bank loans to affiliates, though these have since been superseded by the requirements of the Bank Holding Company Act of 1956.

The Bank Holding Company Act of 1956 is a complicated measure. It has been referred to by some as a "piece of class legislation," [4] and it is said to be "far from being a perfect piece of legislation." On the one hand, the act is said to give the holding company legislative approval, to make holding companies accepted as "full members of the banking family," and to remove the threat of dissolution. On the other hand, the act is said to make the independent bankers of the country breathe easier. In any event, the act places possible constraint on the growth of bank holding companies. No holding company may acquire additional banks outside of its own state, except in states that have passed laws explicitly welcoming such acquisitions by out-of-state holding companies. And the Federal Reserve's principal assignment under the act is to pass upon applications by bank holding companies to acquire additional bank stocks.[5] In carrying out this assignment, the act specifies that the Board of Governors of the Federal Reserve should consider the following criteria in approving applications to form new holding companies, acquire additional banks, and form new banks as a part of holding companies:

(1) The financial history and condition of the applicant and the bank or banks concerned;

(2) The prospects of the applicant and the bank or banks concerned;

(3) The character of the applicant and of the management of the bank or banks concerned;

(4) The convenience, needs, and welfare of the communities and the area concerned; and

(5) Whether or not the effect of the proposed transaction for which approval is desired would be to expand the size or extent of the bank holding company system involved beyond limits consistent with adequate and sound banking, the public interest, and the preservation of competition in the field of banking.

The passage of the Bank Holding Company Act of 1956 led some to refer to the banking system as "the triple banking system." [6] Under the so-called dual banking system, banks had been chartered by either the Comptroller of the Currency or the banking authorities of the respective states. Now the Federal Reserve has exclusive authority to charter, as well as to regulate, bank holding companies that own and control both national and state banks. Moreover, this overlapping of authority between state laws affecting bank holding companies and the Federal Reserve's responsibility (Sect. 11.6) has led some to note that in the issue of supremacy, Federal statutes have generally won out. It is fundamental in the American system that a state cannot nullify or modify an act of Congress in a field into which the government has moved.

Some observations may be summarized with respect to the above criteria (1) through (5). For one, the first three criteria seem to be readily satisfied, and the fourth criteria had a "controlling" effect only in connection with proposals to establish new banks. Meeting these criteria appeared to be necessary but not sufficient. Thus, for another observation, the more critical criteria to be met in obtaining the approval of applications is (5)—the competitive factor.

Chain banking. Chain banking is the most illusive form of multiple-office banking organization; it defies any precise definition. At one time, the term was restricted to cases where "the same individual or group of individuals controls two or more banks," [7] in contrast to control by a formal holding company. The term, however, has come to be broadened in scope to include "any community of interest or links among banks arising directly or indirectly from stock ownership."

Evidence of direct control by an individual or group of individuals would presumably be indicated by outright stock ownership in two or more banks. Since, except for bank holding companies, there are no requirements for reporting such stockholdings, there are no regular compilations of statistics. All we know results from special studies. One, using data for 1945, identified 115 bank chains involving 522 banks with seventy-four branches, and over half of the chains were in seven states where branch banking was either prohibited or severely restricted.[8] Another study in 1962 concerned the 200 largest member banks. It uncovered an intricate network of stockholder links, particularly among large banks in major metropolitan areas.[9]

In the major financial centers of New York, Philadelphia, Chicago, Detroit, and Cleveland, the most significant stockholder links involved the holdings of so-called bank nominees. In principle, the use of nominees is simply a legal device, mainly for facilitating transfers of property. For example, many of the stocks held by a bank for its trust customers, including common trust funds, are assigned to nominees in order to avoid delays in securing authorizations to sell. Dividends and voting rights are ostensibly passed on by the bank to the ultimate owner of the stock, rather than the nominee. While nominees may in principle be persons, the convention among banks is to incorporate special nominee companies.

The information about direct stockholder links among competing banks does not, in itself, provide any evidence of common control. It does, however, raise at least two sets of questions: (1) Who are the ultimate stockholders behind the nominees and who actually exercises the voting rights on nominee holdings of bank stocks? (2) But much more fundamental is, how much of a bank's stock must be owned in order to exercise effective control over its activities and how many banks must be so controlled before a chain may be said to exist?

Stockholder links among banks could be the basis for direct control of competing banks. The 1962 study of chain banking also investigated one possible source of indirect control, which it included in its broadened conception of chain banking. It would, of course, be difficult or impossible to enumerate or identify all of the possible ways for indirect control to exist. Even so, the study included a tabulation of all cases of loans by the 200 largest member banks which were secured by 10 per cent or more of the stock of other banks—cases of so-called loan links among banks. More than half of the 200 banks were found to have made such loans, involving the stock of nearly 1,200 banks. To cite an example, one Chicago bank (Illinois is a unit banking state) had loans secured by 50 per cent or more of the stock in twenty-seven banks.[10] Loan links among banks, according to the study, appear to cross state lines and to be more prevalent in states where greater restriction is placed on branching and bank holding companies.

As with stockholder links, the information on the existence of loan links among banks is not, in itself, evidence of common control. That so many links do exist raises the unanswered question of whether many of these links are really cases of banking chains.

12.2. Unit Banking vs. Multiple-Office Banking

The political strength of independent bankers and the American tradition of opposition to a centralized money power have operated so as to perpetuate the existence of the predominant structure of unit banking as opposed to the structure of branch banking predominant in other countries, namely, the United Kingdom and Canada. This early preference for local autonomy, furthermore, has been reflected in the evolution of the guiding principles of chartering new commercial banks and branches, and in the variety of arrangements reflecting the interdependence of the commercial banks. On other occasions, forces have contributed to a consolidation of the banking system. Economies in large-size operations appear to be among these forces.

Chartering new banks. American banking law was greatly influenced by the principle of free banking, beginning with legislation pertaining to free banking in Michigan in 1837, continuing with the more important New York Free Banking Act of 1838 (Sect. 7.3), and extending to the Banking Act of 1935 (Sect. 8.1). The former acts were intended to democratize commercial banking, and the New York act especially served as a model for other state banking laws. The principle of free banking, on the other hand, was modified by the Banking Act of 1935. In order to avoid an overbanking condition, the latter act provided a list of criteria that needed to be considered by the Comptroller of the Currency (Sect. 11.4), before chartering a new bank; by the Federal Reserve, before admitting a noninsured state bank to membership; and by the Federal Deposit Insurance Corporation (Sect. 11.4), before insuring a nonmember state bank. The criteria to be considered included the financial history and condition of the bank, the adequacy of its capital structure, its future earnings prospects, the general character of its management, the convenience and needs of the community to be served by the bank, and the consistency of its corporate powers with the criteria generally.

The policy of the authorities for the respective task of chartering and admitting new banks or bank offices is not defined clearly. It rests on the judgment of the supervisory officials, usually with respect to the convenience or need for additional banks or branches. At times, need can best be measured by the willingness of individuals to supply new capital. However, at other times, applications for charters as well as applications for branches have characteristically been rejected because of insufficient need. This apparent contradiction is explained, in the first instance, by the desirability for competition wherever possible, and, in the latter instance, by the apparent undesirability of too much competition resulting in the weakening of existing banks. In the latter respect, the Commission on Money and Credit—a private group selected to survey American financial institutions and make suggestions for changes— concluded in 1961 that "in evaluating the 'convenience and necessity' to the community of a new branch some tendency exists to stress the 'necessity' by permitting new offices only when the market can provide a profitable business for this office without reducing the business of existing offices." They further stated that "applications for unit banks take precedence over applications for branches." And they then suggested that "these policies on market entry may unduly restrict competition among banks" and that proper balance should be given to "the desirability of competition." [11]

Banking and economies of size (some general comments). A number of features of United States banking reflects the centralization of some service functions for banks, either through the Federal Reserve or on a cooperative basis. These features include collection and check clearing facilities provided by the Federal Reserve, local and regional clearing house associations, and the performance of services through correspondent banking (Sect. 3.2 and 7.3). Banks in outlying places and the smaller banking centers have found and continue to find advantages in the maintenance of balances in other financial and commercial centers through correspondent arrangements, although the importance of interbank deposits relative to total deposits is declining.* The city correspondents have facilitated domestic and foreign exchange operations and the clearing of checks for nonpar banks.** They have clipped and collected maturing coupons, and furnished safekeeping facilities, investment counsel, and credit information.†

The centralization of all of these services tends to make certain cost of banking independent of the size of individual bank operations. Questions, nevertheless, arise as to whether banks with branch operations or

* The decline in the relative importance of interbank deposits and the financial centers (Sect. 8.2) as a holder of these deposits is reflected in the following data:

Year-End	Total Deposits for All Banks		Total Interbank Deposits for All Banks		Interbank Deposits in Central Reserve City Member Banks	
	(dollar amount in billions)	(per cent)	(dollar amount in billions)	(per cent)	(dollar amount in billions)	(per cent)
1941	81.8	100	11.0	13.4	4.2	5.1
1945	165.6	100	14.1	8.5	4.7	2.8
1960	266.2	100	18.9	7.1	6.5	2.5

SOURCE: Board of Governors of the Federal Reserve System.

** Nonpar banks are those banks that do not remit at par checks drawn on them and sent through the mail, although the common law places the legal obligation to pay at full face value—up to the total of the drawer's account—all checks presented at a bank's counter or window. The non par banks referred to may discount the checks or charge "exchange," ostensibly on the ground that it cost something to send a remittance through the mail. This means that a $100 check might remit at, say, $99.75, the exchange amounting to $0.25. All checks collected and cleared through a Federal Reserve bank, however, must be paid in full (i.e., at par or without deduction of a fee or charge) by the banks on which they are drawn. The latter banks include those on the par list. They are member banks and nonmember banks that maintain clearing balances with a Reserve bank. On December 31, 1964, there were 12,128 banks on the par list, as compared with a total of 1,547 not on the par list.

† Of course, the correspondent or city banks themselves, on the other hand, benefit from the earnings derived from loans and investments made possible by the larger reserves that result from the transfer of balances to the financial center. Further, the business of maintaining balances in financial centers continues to be encouraged where some nonmember state banks are permitted to count interbank balances as legal reserves.

For a general discussion of correspondent banking services, see Leslie Waller, "Our Unique Correspondent Banking System," *Banking*, August 1961, pp. 39-42.

large banks generally may outperform the smaller banks and possess the capacity at least to provide more economical and serviceable banking. As the economy has grown more complex along with the task of bank management, small unit banks have faced such problems as those of inadequate capital and successor management, and there is the suggestion that they have not always been able to provide services at cost comparable to those of competing institutions. Branch and group banks, on the other hand, have been able to compete favorably with unit banks and grow when permitted to do so, probably in some instances at more favorable cost for capital funds, due in part to a wider market for their stocks. The larger branch banks have been able to provide both a training ground and managerial opportunities for bank personnel, as well as sufficient resources for handling loans to both the larger and smaller customers. The group banking systems, too, have apparently been able to provide these services, and they have certain additional advantages. These include the opportunity to operate in several states and thus to cut across state lines. They provide a vehicle for moving capital funds (and, therefore, bank reserves) from a part of the country where there is slower economic growth to parts where there is faster growth. The group systems, furthermore, provide an element of contact with the various communities through the local directors required on the boards of the operating banks, though this possible advantage may be offset by reduced control over operating companies by parent or holding companies.

Measures of economy and profitability. Among the bases for comparing the relative economies and profitability of the various unit and multiple-office bank organizations are the following: (1) the relationship between bank cost as a per cent of assets and bank size, (2) net current earnings as a return on assets, and (3) net current earnings as a return on capital. The relationship between total cost as a per cent of assets and bank size is analogous to the familiar average cost curve in economics. Since a bank's output in the form of loans and investments comprises most of a bank's assets, the ratio (as a per cent) of the total cost to assets is a measure of average cost. The relationship between average cost and size is usually discussed in terms of a U-shaped curve. Average cost as a function of size declines as economies of size are effected, and then they rise as diseconomies set in.

However, net current earnings as a return on total assets and as a return on the capital account, respectively, are measures of profitability. The first of these—the rate of return on total assets—should rise as assets increase, if economies of size are present and unless gross earnings as a per cent of assets decline faster than average total cost. The other of these measures of profitability—the return on bank capital—could indicate the relative attractiveness of bank stocks to present and prospective shareholders and, therefore, provide some clues to the future evolution of the banking structure.

But there are complications; differences in risk must be allowed for in assessing the desirability of larger bank profits. Consequently, to get at the matter, we state two propositions:

Proposition 1: *One would expect larger banks to have smaller rates of return on the capital accounts, if shares of large banks are less risky as a result of greater diversification and differences in quality of the loan and investment portfolios of large banks.*

Proposition 2: *One would expect the returns on capital accounts (as rates) to rise as banks increase in size, if the assumptions pertaining to the first of the above measures of profitability were satisfied and if one views the capital account as an offset to the accounts for plant and equipment (= some constant or decreasing proportion of asset size).*

Now, the fulfillment of the various assumptions—a decline in average cost in excess of the decline in gross revenue, relatively less risky portfolios, and a given correspondence between a bank's capital accounts and those for plant and equipment, as banks increase in size—would result in the two expectations described in propositions (1) and (2), respectively. Indeed, there would be a world with an unusual inducement for growth in the average-size bank, for as banks grow in size they would become more attractive investments for both the risk and profitability points of view. Below, we examine our various assumptions and find them to be relevant to the real world.

Economies of size and profitability (some data and statistical analysis). To indicate approaches to the answers to some of the above questions pertaining to economies of size, profitability, and bank capital, we review briefly some of the regularly reported Federal Reserve data in the form of operating ratios for all member banks and the results of a study in the early 1960's of a sample of approximately 270 unit banks in the Kansas City Federal Reserve District.[12] The latter study represents an initial use of regression analysis as a means of providing tentative answers to such questions.

Evidence from operating ratios (as percentages) with respect to economies of large-size bank operations and returns on assets and capital for firms by size of deposits are shown in Tables 12-1 and 12-2. The data in Table 12-1 would seem to indicate the presence of economies of size as firms increase in size. Total cost as shown in column (5), after netting out interest on time deposits [column (3)], declines steadily and sharply. This would appear to follow mainly from the decline in wages and salaries [column (2)] as percentages of assets and to the more modest decline in other expenses [column (4)], including net oc-

Table 12-1. Costs as Percentages of Assets for All Member Banks, 1962

Ratios (as Percentages)* of Cost Data to Total Assets

Bank Size (deposits in thousands of dollars)	Total Cost [approximately the sum of columns (2), (3), and (4)] (1)	Wages and Salaries** (2)	Interest on Deposits (3)	Other Expenses (4)	Total Cost Less Interest on Deposits [i.e., col. (1) −col. (3)] (5)
Less than 1,000	3.30	1.73	0.52	1.05	2.78
1,000-2,000	3.20	1.47	0.81	0.91	2.39
2,000-5,000	3.21	1.47	0.81	0.91	2.40
5,000-10,000	3.27	1.29	1.10	0.89	2.27
10,000-25,000	3.41	1.31	1.17	0.93	2.24
25,000-50,000	3.39	1.31	1.17	0.90	2.22
50,000-100,000	3.23	1.25	1.12	0.85	2.11
Over 100,000	3.04	1.26	0.94	0.81	2.00

* The ratios in each bank size group are averages of ratios for the individual banks in the group.

** Includes officer and employee benefits.

NOTE: The method of deriving the above percentages is described as follows (see "Relationship of Bank Size and Bank Costs," *Monthly Review,* Federal Reserve Bank of Kansas City, February 1961, p. 4): "Column 1 represents the difference between average ratios of gross and net earnings [before income taxes] to total assets for each size class. Columns (2), (3), and (4) are approximate ratios obtained by taking the product, for each size class, of the average ratio of gross earnings to assets and the average ratio of the relevant expense item to gross earnings [after proper adjustments for percentages]. A rough test of the reasonableness of this procedure may be made by comparing the sum of columns (2), (3), and (4) with column (1). . . ."

cupancy expenses and other current expenses. The data in Table 12-2 indicate a modest and irregular rise in net current earnings,* as percentages of assets [column (1)], as banks increase in size up to 100,000 thousands of dollars and over. This reflects, in part, the economies of size and, in part, a decline in gross earnings to assets. Nevertheless, the capital accounts of banks as percentages of assets [column (2)] decline regularly and sharply, and the net effect is regular and sharply rising returns as percentages of the capital accounts [column (3)]. This in-

* Net current earnings (before income taxes) are considered a good measure of profitability for banks because banks have often had latitude in making adjustments to earnings after taxes from year to year. To arrive at net income after taxes, adjustments must be made to net current earnings for net losses (or recoveries) on bad loans, the net change in valuation reserves, and taxes on income. See William P. Yohe, "Commercial Bank Earnings, the Strengthening of Capital Accounts, and Monetary Policy," *Southern Economic Journal,* October 1960, pp. 106-107.

**Table 12-2. Bank Earnings and Capital and the Net Current Earnings
on Bank Capital for All Member Banks, 1962**

Percentages* of Total Assets

Bank Size (deposits in thousands of dollars)	Net Current Earnings (before income taxes) (1)	Capital Accounts (2)	Net Current Earnings to Total Capital Accounts (in percentages)* (3)
Less than 1,000	1.16	13.2	9.5
1,000-2,000	1.21	11.1	11.2
2,000-5,000	1.20	9.7	12.7
5,000-10,000	1.20	8.7	14.1
10,000-25,000	1.17	8.1	14.9
25,000-50,000	1.17	7.8	15.4
50,000-100,000	1.18	7.6	15.8
Over 100,000	0.67	7.9	17.3

SOURCE: Board of Governors of the Federal Reserve System.
* The percentages are based on averages of ratios for individual banks.

crease in returns could reflect a greater risk resulting from the relatively smaller amounts of capital for the larger banks. It could also reflect the greater earning power of banks as they increase in size, on the basis of either or both of two assumptions: (1) that the larger banks have relatively less risk in their loan and investment portfolios and/or (2) that the smaller capital accounts as percentages of assets reflect economies in the use of plant and equipment.

Questions pertaining to the adequacy of bank capital and the presence of different degrees of risk for banks by size class are difficult to deal with, since many factors affect both. Even so, data on loan losses indicate that small banks face greater risk,[13] and the second assumption would be consistent with the descending order of the percentages in Table 12-1, column (4).

The regression analysis of the more detailed data on unit banks in the Kansas City Federal Reserve District are consistent with the data shown for all member banks in Tables 12-1 and 12-2. Figure 12-1 shows some of the results of the Kansas City Reserve Bank's study in the form of regression equations. The several equations were derived by fitting curves to data for net current earnings to capital accounts, net current earnings to assets, and total cost to assets, each with respect to banks by asset size.

The first upper curve in Fig. 12-1 portrays a declining segment of a U-shaped size-cost curve, and there is no evidence of a flattening out of the curve as banks increase in size. The tendency for this curve to decline was traced to several factors: (1) a higher degree of specialization among employees at larger banks (e.g., managing the portfolio of government securities is a specialized job, and the larger the volume the specialist can handle, the lower the unit cost of handling) and (2) reductions in transactions cost for securities purchased in large volume.

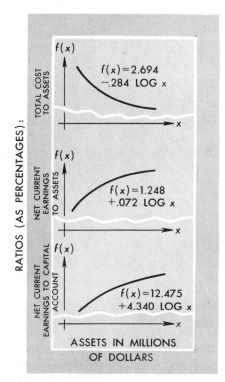

Another point pertained to the economies resulting from the use of mechanical and electronic equipment in facilitating bank handling and accounting cost, but the impact of mechanization resulting from innovations in modern electronic equipment were not felt to have been registered in the period 1956-1959. Even so, there has been the prospect of the smaller banks also participating in the benefits from the new technology—either because of the availability of small units of equipment or because of access to a service center.

Some have pointed out that the apparent economies of large banks could be due to the handling of the very large accounts rather than to costs of operation. This role of the large accounts should be recognized, but the total of the assets reflecting large accounts would still seem to be the best base for measuring economies due to increasing size.

Fig. 12-1. Average Cost and Returns on Assets and Capital for a Sample of Banks by Asset Size. The regression functions are based on cross-sectional data from a sample of approximately 270 unit banks in the Kansas City Federal Reserve District for the years 1956-1959. All are significantly different from zero slope at the 5 per cent level of significance. Source: Federal Reserve Bank of Kansas City.

12.3. Bank Mergers

Branch banks, group systems, and unit banks may grow through increases in the size of their operations, given the number of banking offices and separately chartered institutions. Branch and group banking systems may also grow through the establishment of new branches and newly chartered banks, respectively, as well as through the acquisition of existing unit banks as branches or as members of a group or chain system.

Unit banks, too, may grow along this latter route. The usual case is a bank merger, whereby one institution acquires the assets and assumes the liabilities of an existing institution.

The usual reasons given for absorbing an existing bank as a branch, a member of a group or chain system, or as a part of another unit bank include the following: the need for economies of size, the need to service customers with a growing demand for loans (given the limit on loans to a single customer of 10 per cent of a bank's capital and surplus), the uneven rate of growth of some banks vis-à-vis others, the need to effect a more complete line of banking services, the desirability of a wider market for a given bank's stock, management problems, and inadequate bank capital. Some of these reasons pertain to the motives of the acquired bank and others to the acquiring bank, but some could be satisfied by internal growth. Even so, merger and consolidation arrangements are usually thought to be mutually beneficial by the institutions involved, and banking regulations have required that the appropriate Federal regulatory agency consider various factors in approving of mergers, consolidations, new branches, and new banks. The traditional factors considered have been financial history, the condition of each bank, the adequacy of a bank's capital structure, the adequacy of management, the convenience and needs of the community, and the public's interest. However, in the decade of the 1950's over 1,500 banks were absorbed by others, a trend that led to a strengthening of merger regulations via Federal statute and a Supreme Court ruling.

The Bank Merger Act of 1960. An act of May 13, 1960—the Bank Merger Act of 1960—amended Section 18(c) of the Federal Deposit Insurance Act to require Federal approval of mergers and consolidations involving insured banks.[14] Under the act the appropriate regulatory agency must consider the traditional banking factors and, as an additional factor, the effect of any merger or consolidation on competition and any tendency toward monopoly. The appropriate agency is the Comptroller, if the acquiring, assuming, or resulting bank is a national bank or District of Columbia bank; the board, if such a bank is a state member bank; and the FDIC, if such a bank is a nonmember insured bank (except a District bank).[15] Furthermore, the agency responsible for approving a particular merger is to receive an advisory opinion from the other two banking agencies and the Department of Justice on the effect of the proposed merger on competition.

Bank mergers and the Department of Justice. In the early 1960's the Justice Department intervened in the proposed merger of the Philadelphia National Bank with the Girard Trust Corn Exchange Bank. It did so on the grounds that the proposed merger ran counter to antitrust laws, even after it had been approved by the appropriate banking authority, the Comptroller of the Currency. The result was a Supreme

Court ruling in June 1963 [16] in which the Court gave the Justice Department a powerful weapon with which to block some bank mergers.

The trust busters themselves had never attempted to block bank mergers in exactly the above way, but at the time of the June 1963 ruling the Court made clear its view that bank mergers may be challenged by the Justice Department under Section 7 of the Clayton Antitrust Act of 1914, together with the wide interpretation given that Section in June 1962, in the Brown Shoe Case.[17] Section 7 prohibits mergers whose effect "may be substantially to lessen competition, or to tend to create a monopoly," and the new policy—following the Celler-Kefauver Act of 1950 and the Court's ruling in the Brown Shoe Case—indicates mergers are likely to be held illegal unless it can be demonstrated that they might increase competition in the relevant markets.[18]

The Supreme Court opinions with respect to the June 1963 ruling indicated that the growth of banks may be desirable as a means of realizing economies of size. However, there was the view that growth by internal expansion was socially preferable to growth by acquisition except where the merger or consolidation increased competition in the relevant market.

The relevant market area in banking. Until the market area in which banking competition effectively takes place can be precisely identified and defined, a completely satisfactory policy toward bank mergers, in particular, and banking concentration, in general, cannot be forthcoming. The dilemma was stated by the President's Committee on Financial Institutions:[19] ". . . The market in which financial institutions, especially banks, operate is difficult to define. In some of their loan and deposit operations banks serve a local market which may be sheltered from competition. In other transactions, they deal in national markets which are highly competitive. The absence of a single well-defined market complicates the task of judging the impact on competition of mergers and other structural changes." There have been a number of attempts to specify the relevant market (or markets) and thus to assess tendencies toward monopoly in banking. It is useful to review the basic approaches underlying these attempts.

One general approach is in terms of the output markets in which banks participate. Thus, for example, Alhadeff singles out the business loan market, where banks are more predominant than in other loan or security markets, and divides this market into three submarkets based on the mobility of (or alternatives available to) large, medium, and small business borrowers.[20] He asserts that the large borrower submarket is a national (in some cases, international) market, and that the small borrower submarket is composed of many local markets, with the medium borrower submarket between these extremes. He then argues that the effects of a bank merger on competition must be assessed in terms of the effects on concentration in the submarkets in which the merging banks are active. It is interesting to note that in the Philadelphia National Bank-Girard Trust Corn Exchange case, the lawyers for the banks argued that the merger would enable the banks to enter the national (large borrower) loan market and, thus, increase competition there. But Justice Brennan, in his opinion, stressed the anticompetitive effects in the Philadelphia area.*

Another approach is in terms of the input or raw material markets in which banks participate. Studies employing various measures of change in deposit concentration in national, state, and local areas are based on this conception of the relevant market.** This approach, particularly as it relates to local areas, has been given additional support by the work of Donald R. Hodgman. His basic thesis is that the essence of commercial banking is in the provision of services, including loans, to deposit customers, and that it is misleading to conceive of banks merely as institutional lenders and investors. Thus he concludes that

> . . . the relevant market is that for bank services. The basic services of safekeeping and transfer of money which banks provide attract deposits which in turn exert a dominant influence upon the allocation of bank credit, particularly in a period of credit stringency. . . .
>
> . . . But a very substantial number of the consumers of banking services in any given area are effectively limited in their choice of banks to those available within a fairly restricted geographic region. In short, the relevant banking market for purposes of bank regulation has relatively narrow geographic limits. This is the vital fact which must guide public policy toward concentration of banking in a given geographic area.
>
> Any development of branch banking or any bank merger which appreciably decreases the alternatives open to consumers of banking services within a geographic area to choose among alternative banks will decrease the relative bargaining strength of these customers and thus the ability of competitive forces to maintain fair prices for such services.[21]

* "If anti-competitive effects in one market could be justified by pro-competitive consequences in another, the logical upshot would be that every firm in an industry could, without violating Section 7 [of the Clayton Act], embark on a series of mergers that would make it in the end as large as the industry leaders" (quoted in "Decline Possible in Bank Mergers," *The New York Times*, Financial Section, June 23, 1963, p. 11).

** See, for example, FDIC, *Annual Report*, 1960, pp. 49-61. The FDIC regularly computes the proportion of total bank deposits in the United States held by various numbers and percentages of banks, the proportion of deposits in each state held by the largest and the five largest banks, and the proportion of deposits in the leading counties of forty-eight metropolitan areas held by the largest and the five largest banks.

Professor Hodgman's view, one may note, is consistent with both the Federal Reserve's position in the 1953 Transamerica case* and the Supreme Court's decision in the Philadelphia National Bank-Girard Case, despite some confusion of loan and deposit concentration by both of the latter. In contrast and understandably, mergers among large banks are usually defended on the grounds of allegedly beneficial effects on competition in national loan markets. Future research and analysis should help to resolve the problems of market definition, as well as to determine at what level a bank's or bank group's market share becomes quantitatively substantial.**

12.4. Summary

. The commercial banking structure in the United States is without uniformity or symmetry. It consists principally of three types of organizations, a multiplicity of regulatory agencies, and the separate state and Federal laws governing the movement, establishment, and acquisition of banks or branches containing bases for possible conflicts of jurisdiction between regulatory agencies. The three types of organizations include unit banks and branch and group or chain banking systems, and they are unevenly located throughout the economy. The various regulatory and chartering agencies include the state agencies, the Comptroller of the Currency, the Federal Reserve, and the FDIC. Further, there are several examples of a possible source of conflict of jurisdiction between the regulatory agencies. For one, the Bank Holding Company Act of 1956 requires Federal Reserve approval of applications to acquire bank stocks in states where bank holding companies operate under state regulations. For another, the appropriate Federal regulatory agency—the Comptroller of the Currency, the Federal Reserve, or the FDIC—must approve of bank mergers under the Bank Merger Act of 1960 but, at the same time, the Justice Department also has jurisdiction over antitrust matters pertaining to bank mergers and consolidations.

* *Transamerica Corporation* v. *Board of Governors of the Federal Reserve System.* (The decision was reprinted in *Federal Reserve Bulletin,* August 1953, pp. 836-841.) In that case, the Federal Reserve argued (p. 839) that "commercial banks . . . draw their business largely from areas within which customers may conveniently visit the banks as occasion may require," so "commercial banks are largely local." The Federal Reserve, however, lost the Transamerica case since the empirical part of its argument was based on Transamerica's holding company control over banking in a whole five-state area and presented no evidence of control in specific localities, which the board itself had argued constituted the relevant market areas.

** "Quantitative substantiality" refers to the relative market shares the courts will accept as evidence of "substantial lessening of competition" under the Clayton Act. The decision in the Brown Shoe Case suggests that the courts will no longer require evidence of a large market share, although in the Philadelphia National Bank-Girard Case much was made of the fact that the merger would give one bank 30 per cent of the market in the Philadelphia area.

Regulations pertaining to the banking structure provide no clear guide to what the future structure of banking will be like. On the one hand, there appear to be inducements in the form of economies of size and greater returns on investment contributing to the growth of unit banks and branch and group banking systems. On the other, there has been an increased emphasis on competition in banking as indicated by the Justice Department's jurisdiction in bank mergers since 1963 and some aspects of the Bank Holding Company Act of 1956 and the Bank Merger Act of 1960. In this context, special problems arise pertaining to an unsatisfactory definition of "the relevant market" for a bank's products or services and the absence of agreement over the scope of a relevant market.

There are data in support of the view that banks enjoy economies of size and greater returns on capital accounts at a constant or possibly declining risk as they increase in size. Presumably branch and group systems enjoy these advantages, too, to the extent that they facilitate specialization among some employees, provide a training ground for successful management, enjoy other economies from centralized operations pertaining to automatic equipment, and enjoy the benefits of multiple offices. The larger unit banks and the group systems, especially, also have a wider market for their shares and consequently enjoy some cost advantages from this feature. Some of the smaller bank operations, of course, are doubtlessly well managed and have access to specialized services that are economically provided by city correspondents or other banks in a chain banking system.

References

1. See *United Kingdom Financial Institutions,* rev. ed. (London: Her Majesty's Stationery Office, 1960), pp. 7-10 (section on "The Commercial Banks").

2. For general discussions of multiple-office banking, see C. E. Cagle, "Branch, Chain, and Group Banking," *Banking Studies* (Washington, D.C.: Board of Governors of the Federal Reserve System, 1941), pp. 133-140; U.S. Senate, Joint Committee on the Economic Report, *Monetary Policy and the Management of the Public Debt,* Part I (Washington, D.C.: Superintendent of Documents, 1952), pp. 544-558; and Board of Governors of the Federal Reserve System, *Recent Developments in the Structure of Banking,* Staff Report Submitted to the Select Committee on Small Business, U.S. Senate, January 5, 1962 (Washington, D.C.: Superintendent of Documents, 1962), pp. 2-15.

For works that emphasize group banking, see Gerald C. Fisher, *Bank Holding Companies* (New York: Columbia University Press, 1961); W. Ralph Lamb, *Group Banking* (New Brunswick, N.J.: Rutgers University Press, 1961); and U.S. Congress, House of Representatives, Committee on Banking and Currency, *Bank Holding Companies, Scope of Operations and Stock Ownership* (Washington, D.C.: U.S. Government Printing Office, 1963).

3. *Report of the Committee on Financial Institutions to the President of the United States* (Washington, D.C.: Superintendent of Documents, 1963), p. 51.

4. See Benjamin J. Klebaner, "The Bank Holding Company Act of 1956," *The Southern Economic Journal,* January 1958, pp. 313-326; J. Brooke Willis, "United States," *Banking Systems* (Benjamin Haggott Beckhart, ed.) (New York: Columbia University Press, 1956), pp. 856-857; Marriner S. Eccles, *Beckoning Frontiers* (New York: Alfred A. Knopf, 1951), pp. 434-456; and *The Federal Reserve Bulletin,* September 1957, pp. 1014-1035.

5. For an outline of decisions of the Board of Governors of the Federal Reserve System pertaining to the acquisition of existing banks by holding company groups, the formation of new holding companies, and the establishment of new banks in group systems, see Jules Backman, "The Bank Holding Company Act," *The Bulletin,* C. J. Devine Institute of Finance, New York University, April-June 1963.

See also Fisher, *op. cit.,* pp. 160-166, for an outline of state legislation affecting bank holding companies.

6. See *The Triple Banking System: Impact and Significance of the Bank Holding Company Act of 1956* (New York: M. A. Schapiro and Co., Inc., 1956).

7. House of Representatives, Select Committee on Small Business, *Chain Banking: Stockholder and Loan Links of 200 Largest Member Banks* (Washington, D.C.: Superintendent of Documents, 1963), pp. iii and 6.

8. *Federal Reserve Bulletin,* April 1947, p. 463.

9. House of Representatives, Select Committee on Small Business, *op.cit.,* Chap. 3.

10. *Ibid.,* p. 85.

11. Commission on Money and Credit, *Money and Credit: Their Influence on Jobs, Prices, and Growth* (Englewood Cliffs, N.J.: Prentice-Hall, Inc., 1961), p. 165.

12. Lyle E. Gramley, *A Study of Scale Economies in Banking* (Kansas City, Mo.: Federal Reserve Bank of Kansas City, 1963). Similar results were obtained in a study of the Chicago city area: see Irving Schweiger and John S. McGee, "Chicago Banking," *The Journal of Business,* July 1961, esp. pp. 314-333. An earlier study of California banks is contained in David A. Alhadeff, *Monopoly and Competition in Banking* (Berkeley, Calif.: University of California Press, 1954), esp. Chap. VI and X.

13. See Gramley, *op. cit.,* pp. 47-50.

14. For a brief outline of the more limited measures pertaining to Federal control over mergers and consolidations prior to the early 1900's, see Lamb, *op.cit.,* pp. 70-73. See also Charlott P. Alhadeff and David A. Alhadeff, "Recent Bank Mergers," *Quarterly Journal of Economics,* November 1955, pp. 522-523.

15. See "Amendment to Federal Deposit Insurance Act," *Federal Reserve Bulletin,* June 1960, p. 611.

16. See "Comments on the Philadelphia-Girard Decision," *The National Banking Review,* September 1963, pp. 89-110; and *Annual Report of the Comptroller of the Currency—1961* (Washington, D.C.: U.S. Government Printing Office, 1962), pp. 18-19. For an account of the debate in the case, see *United States Law Week,* February 26, 1963, pp. 3267-3270.

17. *Brown Shoe Company* v. *United States.* See David Dale Martin, "The Brown Shoe Case and the New Antimerger Policy," *The American Economic Review,* June 1963, pp. 340-358.

18. For a discussion of competition versus the banking factors to be allowed for in considering applications for bank mergers, see David A. Alhadeff, "Bank Mergers: Competition versus Banking Factors," *Southern Economic Journal,* January 1963, pp. 218-230.

19. *Report of the Committee on Financial Institutions to the President of the United States* (Washington, D.C.: Superintendent of Documents, 1963), p. 46.

20. David A. Alhadeff, *Monopoly and Competition in Banking* (Berkeley: University of California Press, 1954), Chap. II; and "Bank Mergers: Competition versus Banking Factors," *Southern Economic Journal,* January 1963, p. 218.

21. Donald R. Hodgman, *Commercial Bank Loan and Investment Policy* (Champaign, Ill.: Bureau of Economic and Business Research, University of Illinois, 1963), esp. pp. 169-173.

part five

The Organization and Operation
of the Financial Markets

13

The Treasury, Debt Management, and the Government Securities and Credit Markets

> The Treasury's primary job is to finance the government at the lowest cost at which it can induce the public to buy and hold government securities over a long period. As an independent agency responsible to Congress, the Federal Reserve has the job of regulating money and credit in such a manner as to help maintain economic stability. Theoretically there should be no clash between these two objectives . . . (Marriner S. Eccles, *Beckoning Frontiers*, 1951).

A number of the Treasury's financial activities exert effects on the level of bank reserves and the money supply. Some of these were introduced earlier, as in the discussion of the monetization of gold (Sect. 10.1). There, the Treasury maintained deposits at the Federal Reserve, and these deposits could be debited at times to offset a credit to member-bank reserves and credited at times to offset a debit to member-bank reserves. In subsequent discussions of the derivation of the member-bank reserve accounts (Table 9-5) and the money supply accounts (Table 9-8), we noted that the United States Treasury general account at the Federal Reserve and the Treasury deposits at commercial banks appeared as a use of reserves and as a contractive factor in the money supply accounts, respectively. Also, as we note below, the Treasury has some influence over the structure of interest rates and the maturity distribution of outstanding debt instruments as it carries out the process of managing the Federal debt. Questions, therefore, arise:

(1) What are the implications of the Treasury's being able to influence the various accounts, term-to-maturity structure of interest rates, and the maturity distribution of the debt?

(2) How may the Treasury influence the structure of interest rates and the maturity distribution of the debt?

(3) How may the Treasury's activities influence the bank reserve and money supply accounts?

The answer to the first of these questions pertains to the possibility of a conflict in the goals of the respective agencies—the Federal Reserve and the Treasury. This chapter, then, not only introduces the possibility of this conflict but also provides answers to the other questions. It does so, however, in the process of describing the origin of the Federal debt, its composition, the techniques and problems pertaining to the marketing of the debt, the management of funds in trust to the Treasury, the management of the Treasury accounts at special depositories, and the government securities market.

13.1. The Possible Conflict Over Goals: An Over-All View

Taking a short and over-all view, there are two possible grounds for conflict between the Federal Reserve and the Treasury. First, as a means of short-run expediency, the Treasury may prefer to hold down or reduce the interest cost of the Federal debt at a time when the Federal Reserve prefers a more restrictive monetary policy. In other words, the Treasury may wish to float a new issue or roll over an old issue of securities at a lower rate than that consistent with the Federal Reserve's objectives. Second, and somewhat related, the Treasury may require the support of the Federal Reserve in the financing of a large block of new securities at a time when there is an insufficient market and when the latter agencies' objectives conflict with the Treasury's needs. It may be reasoned, for instance, that, for a new issue, there is no established market—there is all supply and no demand—and that the establishment of a fair market requires moderate stabilization of security prices for a short time. In the case of the Treasury's financing, this has been done over most of the post-World War II years by the central bank, since there was no private group to provide the benefit of underwriting support usually provided private issues.* In early 1963, however, the practice of underwriting sales by private groups was extended to smaller issues of long-term bonds. The support for other issues on occasion, nevertheless, may still take the form of an open market purchase of securities by the Federal Reserve during the underwriting phase and contribute to an expansion of bank reserves at a time when the monetary goals call for a reduc-

---

* It may be noted that the Securities and Exchange Commission has permitted limited price stabilization to facilitate the high-speed distribution of private issues, whereas, economically, price manipulation is condemned because it interferes with the natural equilibrating forces of supply and demand.

tion in the rate of expansion of bank reserves or even a contraction of bank reserves.

Taking a long view, there are no grounds for conflict between the Federal Reserve and the Treasury, and even in the short run there may be cooperation. The lowest feasible interest cost to the Treasury is doubtlessly that consistent with the fulfillment of the monetary objectives of maximum production, employment, and purchasing power. That is, the monetary policy that discourages the costly effect of inflation on the prices of debt instruments (Sect. 5.3), while at the same time maintaining a maximum level of employment (and, therefore, income and saving), is the policy most likely to result in the lowest feasible interest rates.

Allowing for both the short and long views, the possibility of conflict between the two agencies—the Federal Reserve and the Treasury— exist, not necessarily because of a basic conflict of objectives, but largely because of the Treasury's possibly having to compromise long-run objectives at times. At other times, the Treasury's goals with respect to tax policy in particular (Sect. 19.2) may be quite compatible with those of the Federal Reserve or outside the Federal Reserve's special bailiwick. The Treasury, nevertheless, is largely a political agency and as such it is susceptible to short-run expediency and more vulnerable to political pressures to achieve immediate objectives. Furthermore, there are numerous monetary effects that Treasury operations may exert, and these may be used to reinforce the Federal Reserve's policies or to nullify them. For this reason, a private commission—the Commission on Money and Credit —reporting in the early 1960's emphasized the need for a "measure of independence from the Treasury with respect to support of the Treasury securities market," [1] even after emphasizing the need for coordination and a stronger tie between the Federal Reserve and the Chief Executive (Sect. 11.1).

13.2. The Federal Debt and Its Composition

Changes in the size of the Federal debt reflect (1) budget surpluses or deficits, (2) the results of trust-fund transactions, (3) certain transactions of government-sponsored enterprises, (4) changes in government cash balances, and (5) changes in the amount of checks outstanding and other items in the process of clearing. The first of these factors is most often the major one giving rise to changes in the Federal debt. It refers to imbalances in revenues and expenditures in the conventional (or administrative) Federal budget, whereby an increase in the Federal debt arises when total budget expenditures exceed net budget receipts, and a decrease arises when the net revenues exceed the expenditures. Even when the budget is balanced over the fiscal year (i.e., the year ended

June 31), the net revenues and expenditures are never synchronized to avoid seasonal variations in the financial needs of the Treasury. Even so, expenditures tend to exceed net receipts over very long periods. Federal expenditures of the 1930's, the financing of World War II, and occasional financing since that time have resulted in an exceedingly large Federal debt. As a matter of fact, the growth of the debt, in combination with other factors, has given rise to government securities transactions as becoming the main business of the money market. The other factors are the decline in the importance of the call-money market centered at the money post at the New York Stock Exchange,* and the relative decline in the importance of commercial paper, including both promissory notes and bankers' acceptances, as a means of adjusting the short-term financial needs of nonfinancial businesses.

The effect of the second and third factors on the size of the debt, in combination with the first factor, corresponds roughly to imbalances in the so-called Federal cash budget, i.e., to imbalances in cash receipts from the public and cash payments to the public. Some, in fact, view changes in the cash budget with its greater comprehensiveness as a better indicator of the impact of the government's finances on the economy. The two budgets for fiscal year ended mid-1963, and the adjustments indicating their difference, are as follows:

FISCAL YEAR, 1963

	(Billions of dollars)		(Billions of dollars)	Surplus or Deficit (−)
Administrative Budget Receipts	86.4	Administrative Budget Expenditures	92.6	−6.3
Less: Intragovern- mental transactions	4.3	Less: Intragovern- mental transactions	4.3	
Receipts from ex- ercise of monetary authority	*	Accrued interest and other noncash expenditures (net)	1.1	
Plus: Trust fund receipts	27.7	Plus: Trust fund expenditures (including govern- ment-sponsored enterprise expen- ditures net)	26.5	
Equals: Cash budget— Federal receipts from the public	109.7	Equals: Cash budget— Federal payments to the public	113.8	−4.0

SOURCE OF DATA: Treasury Department and Bureau of the Budget.
* Less than 50 million dollars.

* The post was officially terminated in 1946, although there still remains a market for call loans.

Here we observe that trust fund and intergovernment transactions are the major difference between the two budgets. A third budget—the national income budget—is introduced later (Sect. 19.2).

The other two factors listed at the outset as affecting the debt contribute to imbalances mainly in the very short run. The more important of these, changes in Treasury's balances at the Federal Reserve, was introduced earlier (Table 9-5). Even so, all of the above factors operating over time affect in varying degrees the amount of Federal debt outstanding at any given time.

The composition of the Federal debt. The Federal debt is represented by interest-bearing securities classified as special issues, nonmarketable public debt, marketable public debt and a relatively small amount of noninterest bearing debt, and fully guaranteed securities of special government agencies. Its composition at mid-1963 was as follows:

	Billions of Dollars	Per Cent
Marketable public issues:		
Bills	47.2	15.6
Certificates of indebtedness	22.2	7.4
Notes	52.1	17.3
Bonds	82.0	27.2
Total	203.5	67.4
Nonmarketable public and other issues:		
Savings bonds*	48.3	16.0
Convertible bonds**	3.5	1.2
Other nonmarketable bonds	1.9	.6
Special issues†	44.8	14.8
Total	98.5	32.6
Total††	302.0	100.0

SOURCE: U.S. Treasury Department.

NOTE: The sum of the parts may not add to the total due to rounding.

* The fixed-interest, nonmarketable savings bonds have been sold on a discount basis since 1935. Their nonmarketable feature was intended to protect the small investor from the recurrence of market conditions, such as those following the Victory Loan of World War I (Sect. 7.5).

** The convertible bonds were of post-World War II innovation. They were tailored for institutional investors who plan long-term portfolios.

† These issues are generally sold to government trust funds (Sect. 13.5) and government agencies. Their features are generally controlled by legislative provision. For example, such a provision requires that the special obligations issued to the Federal Old-Age and Survivors Insurance (OASI) fund carry a yield equal to the average rate of interest on the entire interest-bearing Federal debt at the time of issuance.

†† Excludes approximately 0.37 billion dollars of debt not subject to statutory debt limit, fully guaranteed securities, and noninterest-bearing debt, not shown separately.

The marketable debt. The larger marketable portion of the debt is of particular importance, due to the marketability feature, as well as to its size. It is the outstanding debt whose prices (and, therefore, yields) fluctuate with changes in the tone of the market (Sect. 4.2), and through which the major effects of debt operations reach the economy.

The majority of the securities composing the marketable debt is fully taxable and distinguishable from one another mainly by the time-to-maturity feature (Sect. 4.2). In fact, at the time of issue the maturity feature largely distinguishes the four types of marketable issues: bills, certificates, notes, and bonds. Treasury bills are discount obligations with maturities ranging from ninety-one days up to one year. The discount feature implies that the purchaser receives an interest return by buying the obligations at less than their maturity or par value.* This feature distinguishes Treasury bills from other marketable issues that are sold at par and at rates stipulated by the Secretary of the Treasury, although the Treasury may sell any of the other issues at a discount on a competitive basis. The Treasury bills have been a standard part of the debt structure since 1929. They are regularly "rolled over" in cycles—a 13-week "bill cycle" for 3-month bills, a 26-week cycle for 6-month bills (usually 192 days), and so on. A bill issue is maturing every week, and there are weekly bill offerings.

Certificates of indebtedness are interest-bearing obligations limited to a maturity of one year. Customarily, certificates are issued at par by the Treasury, and the entire interest is payable at maturity.** Notes are usually issued at par with maturity between one and five years. Coupons covering the payment of interest semiannually are generally attached. Bonds are issued with an original maturity date of more than five years. They sometimes differ from the other government obligations by having a feature known as a "call date," which permits the Treasury to call in

---

* Once marketed, Treasury bills continue to be quoted in terms of a rate of discount from par. Thus, if a dealer's quotation for a particular bill issue was 1.80 per cent–1.75 per cent, the dealer would be willing to buy that issue at an annual rate of discount of 1.80 per cent from the face value or sell at a price equivalent to a rate of discount of 1.75 per cent.

The quotation of Treasury bills is referred to as being on a yield basis. The unit of quotation is called a "basis point"—1/100th of one per cent. For example, when the bid and asked quotations are 0.80 per cent–0.75 per cent, the spread is five basis points.

** Once issued, however, the practice is to quote Treasury certificates of indebtedness, notes, and bonds in terms of price—in 1/32nds, sometimes 1/64ths. For example, a quotation of 100.2–100.6 with respect to a particular bond means that $100 and 2/32nds ($100.0625) is bid by the dealer for each $100 par value of the bond, and $100 and 6/32nds ($100.1875) is asked by the dealer. In the pricing of certificates, notes, and bonds, the digits appearing after the decimal point are customarily 32nds; when these 32nds are translated into dollars and cents (an infrequent occurrence) a dollar sign is placed in front of the quotation, or there is some other special indication that the figure is in terms of dollars and cents.

the bonds for payment at par before the maturity date, and by having the name of the owner of the bond registered with the Treasury.

The marketable debt: the time to maturity. The time-to-maturity distribution of the marketable portion of the debt at mid-1963 is shown by maturity class as follows:

	Par Value in Billions of Dollars	Per Cent
Within 1 year	85.3	41.9
1-5 years	58.0	28.5
5-10 years	37.4	18.4
Over 10 years	22.8	11.2
Total	203.5	100.00

SOURCE: U.S. Treasury Department.
NOTE: The parts may not add to totals due to rounding.

Whether or not the debt is composed more of bills or bonds affects the time-to-maturity distribution of the debt, although this will not entirely be the case. A portion of the debt is generally maturing regularly, and this maturing portion will consist of bonds as well as Treasury bills, and others. In any event, by affecting the time-to-maturity distribution of the debt the Treasury may contribute to or reduce the effectiveness of monetary policy.

An increase of the portion of the debt in the long-maturity sector doubtlessly places an upward pressure on rates on long-term vis-à-vis short-term securities. It also contributes to the effectiveness of a tight-money policy. For instance, a given rise in interest rates generally is accompanied more by a greater price decline in the long- rather than in the short-term issues (Sect. 4.3). Consequently, the holders of long-term issues get frozen-in during the transition to a tight-money policy. At such times, the long-term issues lose liquidity, and the incentive is reduced for banks and others to liquidate governments and expand business and consumer loans to the extent that would otherwise be the case. Conversely, a decrease in the portion of the debt in the long-maturity sector places a downward pressure on the rates for long-term securities. It also reduces the effectiveness of a rise in interest rates, since the short-term securities decline less in price and provide an extra source of liquidity that reduces the effectiveness of monetary policy on the velocity circulation of money and the expansion of bank loans. The maturity distribution of the debt is of less significance during the transition to an easy-money policy. As interest rates in general decline, the prices of all securities rise, and both long- and short-term issues increase in liquidity.

13.3. The Government Securities Market and the Marketing of the Debt

The government securities market is the market for the marketable portion of the Federal debt. The market is said to be made by government securities dealers, and many other institutions purchase and sell securities in it. The business of the market consists of trading in old issues as well as new ones, such as those obtained from the Treasury in their refinancing and new financing operations. Thus in this section we describe briefly the institutions making the market, indicate the extent of participation in the market by various other institutions, and outline the procedures used in the marketing of the debt.

The government securities dealers. There were eighteen full-fledged government securities dealers—five banks and thirteen nonbank specialists —as of mid-1963, and such firms are especially adapted to handling large transactions. As dealers, these firms trade on their own account. To a large extent, they compete and trade among themselves, as well as with commercial banks and others. This is shown below by the dealer transactions in government securities by type of customer, week ending mid-1963:

(Dollar amounts: Averages of daily figures,
par value, in millions of dollars)

	Dollar Amount	Per Cent
United States Government securities dealers and brokers	391	26.9
Other dealers and brokers	17	1.2
Commercial banks	593	40.8
Others	454	31.2
Total	1,455	100.0

SOURCE: Board of Governors of the Federal Reserve System.
NOTE: Details may not add to totals due to rounding.

In normal times the dealers stand ready to negotiate and back up their price quotations on a large volume as either buyers or sellers. They quote bids and offers at so-called outside prices or prices at which they will buy and sell limited amounts; they will negotiate to handle other transactions of larger size.*

* Typical outside spreads during early 1959 were "4/32 to 8/32 ($1.25 to $250 per $1,000) for long-term bonds, 2/32 to 3/32 ($0.62½ to $1.25 per $1,000) for intermediate-term issue, 1/32 to 2/32 ($0.31¼ to $0.62½ per $1,000) on certificates or short-term bonds and notes, and 4 to 5 basis points ($0.10 to $0.12 per $1,000) on 91-day Treasury bills" (*Treasury-Federal Reserve Study of the Government Securities Market*, Part I [Washington, D.C.: Board of Governors of the Federal Reserve System, 1959], p. 82).

The ownership of the marketable debt. The extent of participation in the government securities market by institutions and others in general is indicated by the following data for the ownership of marketable government securities at mid-1963:

	Dollar Amount in Millions	Per Cent
Federal Reserve banks	32,027	15.7
United States Government agencies and trust funds*	11,120	5.5
Commercial banks	55,439	27.2
Nonfinancial corporations	10,144	5.0
Insurance companies	8,987	4.4
Mutual savings banks	5,852	2.9
Savings-and-loan associations	3,208	1.6
Others	76,730	37.7
Total	203,508	100.0

* The data are complete for United States government agencies and trust funds, but the other data are based on the Treasury's survey of ownership.

The general procedure in the marketing of the debt. The Treasury may use an auction technique in the marketing of the debt, or it may tailor an issue to suit the market and offer it for sale at a given price. The auction technique has usually been applied in the marketing of Treasury bills, and in 1963 (Sect. 13.4) it was extended to small issues of bonds in modified form.

In the case of Treasury bills, the sale is at a discount and on a competitive basis to the bidders paying the highest price for the bills. The Treasury invites tenders for a specified amount to be dated and issued the following Thursday. The tenders must be submitted up until a specified time on Monday. The tenders are made in even multiples of $1,000 on a maturity value basis, and bid prices are calculated to three decimal places. After the bids are received by a Reserve bank, acting as agent for the Treasury, the competitive tenders are arranged in sequence according to the bid price submitted in each bid. A tabulation of details regarding the tenders is then furnished the Treasury, and, late on Monday, the Treasury determines the extent to which tenders are accepted and gives the press a statement announcing the results for publication on Tuesday morning. The statement shows total bills applied for, total accepted, average price, high bid, low bid accepted and percentage of low bid accepted. The noncompetitive bids up to some set amount are automatically awarded at the average yield of accepted competitive bids, an arrangement helpful to country banks and others who do not keep in constant contact with the market.

In the case of those securities not offered on a competitive bid, the Treasury must "tailor" the debt instrument to suit the market and offer it for sale with certain interest and time-to-maturity features. The usual procedures in the marketing of the debt have involved final decisions by the Secretary of the Treasury with respect to the maturity and other features of an issue, while the market conditions themselves largely determine the magnitude of the yield. In getting the "feel" of the market for this purpose, the Secretary will usually rely in varying degrees on the opinions of others about the required features of the necessary financing. He will have the benefit of consultation by staff members and/or himself with a variety of sources. These will include the Federal Reserve, trade associations representing various segments of the financial industry as indicated by the institutions owning the debt, and others.

Once the Treasury has obtained information about the market and opinions as to its requirements, they may tailor the securities being issued to suit the market. That is, the Treasury may try to satisfy the preference of the institutions and individuals comprising the market for government securities in deciding upon the maturity features and similar matters that they attach to their obligations. The Treasury may, at other times, fix the maturity of new issues so as to have a particular effect on the market and other aspects of the financial system. It may, for instance, issue long-term securities rather than short-term ones with the view to increasing long-term yields relative to short-term ones and, by so doing, soak up liquidity. Further, it may issue more short-term issues and fewer long-term ones, with the effect of raising short-term rates and lowering long-term ones which would reduce the cost of long-term funds in the financial markets generally and increase liquidity at the same time.

At last, when the final decisions are made, the mechanical details of announcing an issue and placing it in the market are carried out. In the case of certificates of indebtedness, notes, and bonds, the sale is generally at par, with the Treasury fixing the yield to correspond to market conditions. The sale may be for new funds or in exchange for maturing securities other than Treasury bills. The orders are placed through the Federal Reserve banks. At times, the full amount of the respective orders will not be filled, and, at other times, the offering will not clear the market, depending in part on the yield set by the Treasury.

13.4. Supplementary Marketing Techniques

Marketing techniques—other than the straightforward tailoring of an issue to suit the market as the need for funds or the refunding of an issue arise and the outright tailoring of a new issue to alter the maturity distribution of the debt and the yield structure—may include (1) so-called cash refunding, (2) an underwritten sale of long-term issues, and (3) advance refunding. Also there have been other techniques that have been recommended as a means of improving the market for government securities.[2] The latter would include the use of a small number of issues of varying maturity to increase the homogeneity of the debt and thus encourage wider and more active trading, a regularization of Treasury offerings to reduce difficulty associated with refunding at erratic intervals, and a broadening of the use of the auction technique. It is viewed, in the latter instance, that an extension of the auction technique to longer time-to-maturity issues would relieve the Treasury of some of the responsibility for pricing decisions and avoid confusion and misplaced criticism of the Treasury.

Cash refunding. Among the marketing techniques outlined above, however, cash refunding refers to the refunding of an outstanding issue by offering the holders cash rather than the pre-emptive right to exchange for a new issue and the subsequent offering of a new exchange issue for sale for cash. The new issue in the latter case is in effect being exchanged for the old issue, but outside investors, as well as those currently holding the old issue, are permitted to purchase the new issue. There is the view that this form of refunding discourages speculation in new government issues to the extent that cash payment is required and outside investors participate in the purchase. There is also the view that this technique gives the Treasury greater opportunity to effect the maturity and ownership distribution of the debt. Along this line of reduced speculation, furthermore, the Treasury might require higher cash deposits with subscriptions for cash offerings, as well as evidence of a high margin requirement by those extending loans for the purchase of new issues (or, in other words, they may require a larger equity in the issue by the buyer). In fact, some have suggested that margin requirements along the lines of Regulations T and U, as applied to the stock market (Sect. 8.3), be applied to nonregulated lenders in the government securities market.[3]

An underwritten sale. An underwritten sale may be defined as one where new issues of securities are sold on an all-or-nothing basis to underwriters who assume the risk and responsibility for placing the securities with ultimate investors. More broadly, the term "underwriting" may apply to support operations for newly marketed issues. The practice of underwriting the sale and support of issues is quite widespread with respect to business financing (Sect. 14.1), and it takes various forms, even with respect to a central bank's support of its government's issues.[4] In this broader sense, underwriting of government issues could be provided by (1) commercial banks [especially through the use of tax and loan accounts (Sect. 13.5)], (2) securities dealers, (3) speculators, and (4) the central bank. Through the underwritten sale, in particular, the

Treasury may receive bids from groups of dealers or a syndicate under competitive bidding and sell the securities to the highest bidder.

As a means of broadening or maintaining the distribution of long-term Treasury obligations by enlisting the sales efforts of corporate and municipal bond dealers, the Treasury reinstituted, in January 1963, the technique of an underwritten sale for the first time in sixty-eight years. During that January 1963 episode, a seventy-five-member syndicate of government security dealers, banks, and investment houses submitted the highest bid on a quarter-of-a-million dollar offering of 30-year bonds with a 4 per cent coupon by bidding 99.851111 for a net interest cost to the Treasury of 4.008210 per cent. The total price bid by the high bidder was 275 dollars more than the bid by the next highest group, and the experiment was judged a success. However, the sum of 250 million dollars sought by the Treasury was the smallest on a cash offering of marketable bonds since 1937, and the size of the offering was thought to be close to the practical limit which could be sold competitively with the resources of the market as they stood in early 1963.

Advance refunding. Advance refunding is another supplementary technique. The debt managers may use it in special market situations, in an effort to achieve a longer average of the maturity of issues comprising the debt and lower interest cost.[5] It involves an offer by the Treasury to exchange new securities of longer maturity and at higher coupon yields for some outstanding securities of a shorter time to maturity. The offer by the Treasury is made in advance of the maturity date of the existing securities. It occurs in a market situation where the yield on government securities of a given time to maturity is above the yield prevailing at the time of the initial issue price of the old issue carrying the exchange right. Essentially, the Treasury, through the above technique, is trying to exploit a situation in which the same nonbank institutional investors want to show higher yields at a time when they are also hesitant to dispose of their lower yielding security and show losses on their books. In this situation, the Treasury officials are willing to offer securities carrying larger coupons per given par value and a relatively lower discount in exchange for older securities carrying smaller coupons and discounts in excess of those called for, in the present market, on new issues of comparable maturity. From the officials' point of view, they wish to reduce debt cost by exploiting the unwillingness of some investors to show losses and by avoiding any necessary additional cost to get the market to absorb a new issue comparable in maturity to the new issue in the refunding offer.

Advance refunding became a feasible means of taking advantage of the reluctance of some nonbank institutional investors to take capital losses following 1959 legislation that permitted postponement through exchanges of the tax consequences with respect to capital gains and losses.

Since that time, too, it has been used to contribute to a more adequate maturity distribution than may otherwise prevail under the existing conditions. These have involved a Treasury Department interpretation concerning the legal $4\frac{1}{4}$ per cent interest ceiling on new issues of government bonds and a combination of an upward trend in the structure of interest rates (Sect. 4.2) and a relentless increase in the short-term debt resulting from the passage of time. The $4\frac{1}{4}$ per cent interest rate ceiling on bonds was established by Congress in 1918 in connection with a World War I financial operation, but its effect was unfelt until the cost of long-term borrowing rose above $4\frac{1}{4}$ per cent in 1959 and part of 1960. The Treasury, at that time, interpreted the ceiling to apply to the coupon rate on new issues. Since then, however, the Treasury has announced an interpretation by the Attorney General that the sale of a new issue at a discount and at an effective rate in excess of a $4\frac{1}{4}$ per cent coupon yield would be permissible.

13.5. The Federal Investment Funds and Tax and Loan Accounts

Thus far, in describing the Treasury's marketing activities, we have emphasized how the Treasury may affect the yield structure in its marketing activities and the average time to maturity of the debt outstanding. We have indicated also that the average time to maturity has implications for the effectiveness of credit and monetary policy at the operational level and the liquidity of the government securities holdings of various sectors of the economy. In this respect, the Treasury may to some extent also influence the yield structure and the average time to maturity of the privately held debt by the type of securities purchased for the various Federal investment funds. But, in addition, they may influence the level of bank reserves as their balances are shifted from commercial banks to the Federal Reserve or maintained at the commercial banks. To deal with these latter activities, we introduce the Federal investment funds, the regulations governing their administration, and the Treasury tax and loan accounts.

Federal investment funds. The Treasury administers funds and accounts for the Federal Old-Age and Survivors Insurance (OASI), unemployment trust, civil service retirement and disability, national service life insurance, railroad retirement, postal savings system, FDIC (Sect. 11.4), government life insurance, and others. Of these, the (OASI) and the unemployment trust fund constitute the largest portion of the total investment funds.

The size of the funds and accounts administered by the Treasury has grown from 9.6 billion dollars at year-end 1941 to 58.4 billion at mid-year

1963, as shown by the United States government securities held by government agencies and trust funds:

(Par value in billions of dollars)

	Year-End 1941		Mid-Year 1963	
	(dollars)	(per cent)	(dollars)	(per cent)
Special issues	7.0	73	44.8	76.7
Public issues	2.6	27	13.6	23.3
Total	9.6	100	58.4	100.0

The funds represented by these totals are reserves accumulated for the payment of benefits. In this respect they are like the reserves of a life insurance company. In the management of the accounts, moreover, the Treasury has some margin of discretion in the investment of the proceeds despite statutory limitations, as may be illustrated by reference to the two largest funds. Legislative provision requires that the OASI funds be invested in special obligations only if the trustees (with the Secretary of the Treasury as managing trustee) determine that purchase of public issues was not in the public interest. The law also requires that the interest rates on these special obligations be equal to the average rate of interest on all marketable interest-bearing obligations of the United States not due or callable until after five years from the original date of issue. Investments of the unemployment trust fund may consist of either special or public issues, although the public issue purchase must not yield less than the yield on special obligations.

Finally, within the limitations provided, the Treasury has some discretion in the purchase of public issues for the trust funds. In exercising this discretion they may exert some occasional influence over the maturity of the marketable debt outstanding and over the time for scheduling new issues to reach the market, as well as provide occasional market support for a particularly weak issue.

The Treasury tax and loan accounts. In addition to the Treasury's accounts at the Federal Reserve banks, it maintains tax and loan accounts at roughly 11,000 special depositories. A bank becomes a special depository by pledging special securities as collateral and receiving the recommendation of the Federal Reserve bank in its district. The purpose of the accounts is to smooth out the random effect of changes in the Treasury's balances at the Federal Reserve upon the money and credit markets. But in marketing new issues the Treasury also takes advantage of the presence of these accounts to provide an extra incentive to the special depositories. They do this by permitting a credit to the tax and loan accounts upon subscription for some new issues by the depositories for their own account and for customers.

The present system of tax and loan accounts was first introduced in World War I when the Treasury was raising large sums of money that would have drained away bank reserves as the Treasury's balances at the Reserve banks increased. An increase in the Treasury's balances at the Reserve banks reduces bank reserves and has the same contractionary effect on bank reserves and bank credit as would a sale of securities from the open market account. And a decrease in those holdings increases bank reserves and has the same expansionary effect upon bank credit as would a purchase of securities for the open market account.

The banks that qualify as depositories may credit the tax and loan accounts of the Treasury with checks used in payment for the following taxes: personal income taxes, payroll taxes for the old-age insurance program, railroad retirement taxes, certain excise taxes, and corporate income taxes. In the case of the corporate income tax, the checks of over $10,000 drawn on the qualifying banks are returned to the banks even though they be submitted in payment at the Federal Reserve banks. These items are placed in special balances called X balances, however, and they are the first to be withdrawn when the Treasury makes a "call" (i.e., notifies the bank that at a certain date the balances will be withdrawn).

In the case of new Treasury issues carrying the tax and loan privilege, some extra incentive is provided for their initial purchase by the special deposit the depositories acquire prior to the time of payment or a drawing on tax and loan accounts. Several possibilities arise in practice. A customer's accounts may be debited and the tax and loan account credited, for one thing, with a net result of a reduction in the amount of reserves required against the deposit. During the time interval after the purchase and prior to a call on tax and loans accounts a bank retains reserves that would otherwise have been withdrawn by an immediate cash payment. This latter effect, for another thing, also results from a bank's subscription on its own account. This extra incentive, of course, is simply the benefit the banks would otherwise lose by making purchases for customers or their own account in the absence of the tax and loan privilege. Also there is no assurance the banks will hold the securities, but the incentive is thought to help with the initial distribution.

For the purpose of scheduling the withdrawal of funds, depositories are classified in three groups: Class A, Class B, Class C, in the increasing order of tax and loan balances at a given bench-mark date. The calls are less frequent in the case of Class-A depositories and more frequent in other classes. The depositories are notified in advance of a call date—the more frequent calls are on the B and C groups—the Treasury determines the amount of the call after consultation with representatives of the

Federal Reserve, and the respective Reserve banks handle the details of notification and the transfer of funds.

On the one hand, the net effect of the Treasury's tax and loan accounts is to increase the Treasury's potential control over the impact of the transfer of its balances. Consequently, this affects increments and decrements of bank reserves and, therefore, credit ease or tightness. On the other hand, the tax and loan accounts would smooth out the random effect that would otherwise exist from ignoring the impact of an imbalance of revenues and receipts on bank reserves and the money market. As a side effect, the presence of the accounts also provides the Treasury with the opportunity to attach a tax and loan privilege to some new issues and to thus provide some extra incentive for their purchase during the initial distribution period.

13.6. Summary

Taking a long view, there is no inconsistency between the Treasury's objective of maintaining low interest rates and at the same time contributing to the objectives to which all government agencies subscribe— maximum production, employment, and purchasing power. Taking a short view, the Treasury is, however, more vulnerable to political pressures to compromise long-run objectives: herein, along with the monetary effects of Treasury operations, lies the ground for possible conflict between the Treasury and the Federal Reserve.

The Treasury may contribute to, neutralize, or offset the effects of monetary operations by the Federal Reserve by altering the maturity distribution of the Federal debt, by issuing long-term securities rather than short-term ones, by managing Federal investment funds, and by managing Treasury tax and loan accounts. An increase in the proportion of the debt in the long-maturity sector contributes to the effectiveness of tight-money policy and, conversely, a decrease in the proportion of debt in the long-maturity sector reduces the effectiveness of tight-money policy. The issuance of long-term securities rather than short-term ones increases long-term rates relative to short-term ones. By so doing, it soaks up liquidity, while the issuance of short-term securities rather than long-term ones increases liquidity. The range of discretion in the management of Federal investment funds permits the Treasury to exert occasional influence over the maturity of the marketable debt outstanding and over the timing of the flotation of new issues, and occasionally permits the Treasury to provide support for particularly weak issues. The transfer of funds from the Treasury's tax and loan accounts and the disbursal of funds from the Treasury's account at the Federal Reserve are similar in their effects to open market sales and purchases; a transfer of funds from the tax and loan accounts contracts bank reserves by an equal amount, and a disbursement from the Treasury's Federal Reserve account expands reserves by an equal amount.

It would appear that in order for the central bank to discharge its obligations, the relations between the Treasury and the central bank must be continuous, intimate, and based upon mutual respect and understanding. In any event, the numerous monetary effects exerted by Treasury operations must be allowed for in the planning and implementation of monetary policy by the Federal Reserve.

References

1. Commission on Money and Credit, *Money and Credit: Their Influence on Jobs, Prices, and Growth* (Englewood Cliffs, N.J.: Prentice-Hall, Inc., 1961), p. 85.

2. Commission on Money and Credit, *op. cit.*, pp. 113-115; T. C. Gaines, *Techniques of Treasury Debt Management* (Glencoe, Ill.: The Free Press, 1962), pp. 153-196; and Warren L. Smith, "Debt Management in the United States," Study Paper No. 19, Joint Economic Committee, *Study of Employment, Growth, and Price Levels* (Washington, D.C.: U.S. Government Printing Office, 1960), pp. 142-153.

3. Commission on Money and Credit, *op.cit.*, pp. 116-117.

4. Smith, *op.cit.*, pp. 147-148.

5. *Debt Management and Advance Refunding* (Washington, D.C.: U.S. Treasury Department, September 1960); Commission on Money and Credit, *op.cit.*, pp. 113-115; and Smith, *op.cit.*, pp. 148-150.

14

The Money and Capital Markets

> Speculators may do no harm as bubbles on a steady stream of enterprise. But the position is serious when enterprise becomes the bubble on a whirlpool of speculation. When the capital development of a country becomes a by-product of the activities of a casino, the job is likely to be ill-done (John Maynard Keynes, *The General Theory of Employment, Interest and Money*, 1936).

The financial markets may be classified as the money, credit, and capital markets (Sect. 7.3). In this classification the government securities market would be a subsector of the money market, and the markets would be listed according to broad classes with respect to the degrees of liquidity of the financial instruments traded. They may also be classified, however, according to the form of market organization—either organized or negotiated markets. The organized markets are characterized as being "formally organized." They have standard procedures, formal arrangements for supervision, and central places for assembling bids and offers. The New York Stock Exchange is a prototoype of such markets. The negotiated markets, on the other hand, have flexible procedures, little formal supervision, and individual firms linked mainly by the telephone or other means of communication. They are also called over-the-counter markets, and the degrees of negotiation in these markets vary. Nevertheless, we may think of all the financial markets other than the organized exchanges as being over the counter.

The over-the-counter markets generally include the market for new issues of securities and the trading in securities other than those traded on the exchanges. Cutting across these various classifications, consequently, we see the money market as an informally organized and negotiated market for new and outstanding issues. Also we see the capital market as encompassing the organized exchanges and the sector of the over-the-counter market for the longer maturities of both new and outstanding issues of both stocks and bonds—excluding United States government bonds.

All of these markets are important in the study of the economy and in the study of the effectiveness of monetary controls, interest rates, and the availability of funds generally for effecting expenditures in the real sector of the economy. As we noted earlier in discussing equilibrium and the structure of interest rates (Sect. 4.1 and 4.2), as well as in discussing general economic equilibrium (Sect. 5.2), the prices on all items (and, therefore, yields) are interrelated. Price changes (and, therefore, yields) in one sector were described as influencing price changes in another. These changes, in turn, were described as influencing the demand for the various financial items, goods, and services in such a way as to give rise to the switching of assets and changes in the flow of income.

Now, however, we wish to outline briefly the organization and operation of the financial markets, exclusive of the credit market, in order to note their relevance to the Federal Reserve's control over credit. In particular, we wish to do two things: (1) describe the money market more fully, with the view to emphasizing selected yields in that market as sensitive indicators of change in credit conditions, and (2) focus some attention on the connection between the Federal Reserve's control over the availability and use of credit for purchasing and carrying securities and the level of activity on the organized exchanges and in the new issues markets. Later (Sect. 17.1) we wish to emphasize that smaller firms are more directly dependent than others, relative to their asset size, on banks for funds. We will also point out that larger firms are more directly dependent, in relation to asset size, on the broader range of financial markets for funds for expenditures on real goods and services. These latter differences and the attention given to the connection between credit conditions and the level of activity in the new issues market imply, as we shall note (Sect. 17.1), that credit conditions operate via somewhat different routes in exercising their effect on the cost and/or availability of funds to small vis-à-vis large firms. Presently, then, we introduce some institutional aspects of the route through which credit conditions influence the cost and/or availability of funds to those firms that rely most heavily on the broader range of financial markets for funds.

14.1. Over-the-Counter Markets: Their Organization and Operation

The over-the-counter markets comprise the new issues market and the resale market for securities other than those sold on the organized exchanges. The function performed by firms engaged in the new issues business is called investment banking. A highly specialized function, it involves the underwriting and marketing of new issues by firms acting as dealers. By contrast, the resale sector of the over-the-counter markets is distinguished by the prevalence of a large number of firms performing as both broker (i.e., on an agency basis) and dealer. The volume of transactions with individuals as opposed to institutions is relatively greater in the resale market. The large volume of small transactions by individuals in the higher risk securities are more naturally accommodated by the resale market, and the income to investment banking firms in this sector is primarily derived from underwriting secondary distributions and from customer and dealer differentials on transactions. The large transactions by institutions in bonds and other issues at a single price, on the other hand, are more naturally accommodated by the new issues market. Consequently, income on the new issues side is derived to a large extent from the underwriting of new issues and the service fees paid to investment bankers for their advisory work.

The new issues market. About 10 per cent of the 3,000-plus firms doing an over-the-counter business in the 1950's handled about 90 per cent of the new issues business, and even among this smaller group of firms there were large differences. Comparatively few have sufficient capital to handle all types of issues, and some consequently specialize in various types—government securities, municipal obligations, utilities, rails, and industrials. As with government securities dealers (Sect. 13.3), their capital is small, their profit margins are narrow, and they rely heavily upon commercial banks and other sources of funds with which to carry their inventory. In fact, the commercial banks themselves once engaged in the underwriting business, but since the Banking Act of 1933 they have been severed from their security affiliates to avoid their dealing with themselves as creditors, with the exception of those activities relating to the purchase and sale of certain state and municipal obligations and government securities.

The new issues market (competitive bidding and negotiation). A combination of procedures and variants of them are employed by investment bankers in the underwriting and marketing of a new issue to correspond to the diversity of risk involved, the various issues handled, and the varying requirements of the numerous units that rely upon the capital markets for new funds. Among these procedures, important to an understanding of the new issues market, are those of competitive bidding and negotiation by which the issuing firm may obtain a buyer and the various methods by which an issue may be offered for public sale. At any given time, issues characterized by low risk and a correspondingly wide market, such as high grade bonds, for which the probable yield can be easily estimated, may readily obtain a competitive bid, as in the case of Treasury bills (Sect 13.3).

Often groups of firms in the new issues market organize as a syndicate in order to obtain sufficient funds to submit bids, take up an issue, and at the same time diversify the risk. This method of bidding for new issues has been urged upon investment bankers by the Federal government, and required by states in the case of state and municipal issues. Moving along the scale, at any given time, however, there are issues characterized by a high risk and a correspondingly narrow market, such as common stocks of small and little known companies for which the task of pricing becomes increasingly difficult. In such instances there may be a buyer for an issue only after prolonged personal negotiation and even then at a price commensurate with the greater risk.* Also markets generally may be characterized as wide or thin in varying degrees at different times. Thus, apart from the conditions surrounding any particular issue at a given time, a selected issue may face a wider market and, therefore, more favorable market conditions at certain times rather than at others. The more favorable conditions may, in turn, affect the volume of financing.

The new issues market (methods of effecting a public sale). Several methods or combinations of them are possible in effecting a public sale through investment bankers. These methods, of course, exclude so-called private placement whereby some high-grade issues of well-known companies may be placed directly with a single public buyer, especially life insurance companies.** The methods include, however, (1) the purchase of an issue for immediate reoffering, (2) the acceptance of an issue on a best-effort basis, and (3) the guarantee of the sale of an issue.

In general, and apart from special circumstances, the selection from among the alternative methods for effecting public sales as well as for obtaining initial buyers is affected by the breadth or thinness of the markets for particular issues, at any given time, and by the width or thinness of the financial markets generally, at different times. The wider the markets the greater the probable frequency of the outright purchase of particular issues as opposed to their acceptance on a best-effort basis, apart from special cases such as that in which investment bankers may guarantee the sale of issues; and the wider the markets the greater the probable frequency of competitive bidding in comparison with personal negotiation as a method of obtaining buyers for given issues.

The resale market. The great bulk of the resale of securities, other than those traded on the exchanges, is handled by firms registered with the Securities and Exchange Commission, although dealer banks and other dealers limiting their activity to government and municipal securities are exempt from such registration. There is, furthermore, a tendency

---

* Reflecting the degrees of risk involved in the underwriting and marketing of various issues are the averages of compensation to investment bankers for the new issues registered with the general public for cash sale. For the years July 1947 to June 1950, these are reported in Irwin Friend *et al.*, *The Over-the-Counter Securities Markets* (New York: McGraw-Hill Book Company, 1958), p. 74.

** "Private placement" or "direct placement" refers to the placement of a new issue or loan directly with the lender (or purchaser of the security). Certain marketing costs may be avoided and greater flexibility in subsequent servicing of a firm's financial needs achieved by the procedure of private placement.

for a large proportion of the firms in the resale market to specialize in particular issues and different types of issues, although with considerable overlapping of the specialization by banks, specialists in government securities, and those who specialize in stocks and high-risk assets. Also transcending these relationships between broker-dealer firms and institutional and individual investors and their varying degrees of specialization are the activities of a significant number of professional traders employed on the resale side of the securities business generally. The firms and individuals represented by these employees make it their business to buy and sell either for or without a market position at frequent intervals with the objective of a net speculative gain. The interrelated and specialized activities of these traders and their contacts with each other make it possible for them to acquire a "feel" of the market with reference to its prices and general "tone." Indeed, the objectives of the dealers, the communication facilities connecting them, and their day-to-day contacts provide the financial markets with the depth, breadth, and resiliency needed to pass changes in one sector of the markets along to other sectors (Sect. 4.2). Therefore, they make the financial markets a more active and vital force in a market economy.

14.2. The Money Market: Instruments, Yields, and Sources of Funds

The money market is in fact the market for temporarily employing liquid balances and for obtaining their use on a temporary basis. Located in downtown Manhattan with a complex network of connections reaching other financial centers, it is the focal point of adjustments for the liquidity needs of the country, its financial institutions, nonfinancial businesses, and governmental units. As such, it is the first sector of the economy in which changes in credit ease or tightness are reflected.

A variety of financial instruments are traded in the money market, many institutions supply funds to it, and some of the rates of interest on the instruments traded in the money market are key rates in the structure of interest rates (Sect. 4.2).

The government securities market. Trading in government securities since the Federal deficits of the 1930's and World War II has become a large-volume business in the financial markets. Also since the mid-1920's and paralleling the rising importance of government securities in the money market has been a shift in the bulk of trading in government bonds from the New York Stock Exchange to the over-the-counter market.[1] The factors contributing to this shift include the growth in the relative importance of the short-term debt, the growth in the size of large institutional investors, and the tendency for large nonfinancial corporations to make liquidity adjustments through the money market, apart from the other factors giving rise to the Federal debt. Treasury bills (Sect. 13.3) were never listed on the New York Stock Exchange, and, as the amount outstanding grew, the volume of debt traded outside the exchange grew. And the growth of large institutional investors, such as insurance companies and nonfinancial corporations, has increased the emphasis upon transactions of the type most expeditiously handled through negotiation.

An organized exchange, by contrast, is well suited to handle the relatively small- and medium-size transactions of many individuals. Brokers acting as agents and trading on the exchanges for individuals match up individual bids and offers at varying prices and for a uniform charge. But the larger transactions on the New York Stock Exchange, for example, tend to be handled by specialists, in particular issues, who buy and sell large blocks at a discount or premium over the exchange price. The specialist in these cases must round up buying or selling orders and thus resort to techniques characteristic of over-the-counter trading. The government securities dealers apparently have been able to attract the business away from the New York Stock Exchange primarily because they were willing to handle large orders, in a short period of time, at a fixed price, and at relatively low cost for the large volume of trading.[2]

The Federal funds market.[3] The market for Federal funds (Sect. 3.2) was originated in the early 1920's, following the pooling of member-bank reserves (Sect. 7.5). Its early development, paralleling the post-World War I depression (Sect. 7.5), was the result of a combination of circumstances, including an excess of reserves at some New York banks, a deficit at others, and a penalty discount rate (Sect. 8.2). At such a time, the opportunity for optimizing bankers was clear. Banks with deficient reserves could minimize the cost of additional reserves by borrowing the excess reserves of other banks, and these others could also maximize revenue by lending reserves. In this setting, then, the bankers talked over the circumstances and began buying and selling Federal funds.

At first the transfer of funds was effected by an exchange of checks (Sect. 3.2), and then there were other developments. Firms dealing on their own account in acceptances, as well as in government and other securities, became active in the transfer of Federal funds through the use of repurchase agreements (Sect. 3.2). Some firms even had checking accounts at the Federal Reserve Bank of New York as a convenience to the bank in handling transactions in acceptances and government securities, and these firms could sell their own checks. In other cases, checks on Reserve balances could be acquired by settling security transactions with the New York bank before the funds reached the commercial banks. Soon, too, there were money brokers, or those acting as an agent, who came to arrange transactions in Federal funds between those banks with excess reserves and those with insufficient reserves.

At the outset of the 1930's, the soundness of the credit position of many banks was in doubt, and subsequently most banks had excess reserves along with the decline in the effective demand for bank loans.

However, as the government securities market came to reflect freer market conditions in the 1950's, and as yields on governments rose, the profitable opportunities giving rise to the initial market for Federal funds were again present. With yield on governments up, and with the discount rate serving as a penalty rate, the least-cost method of adjusting reserve positions more frequently involved Federal funds. And growth in the size of banks is a factor too. It becomes a factor, since the typical unit of trading in Federal funds is one million dollars, since the excesses and deficiencies of small banks are generally too small to be traded, and since there is a legal maximum on loans to a single borrower.[4]

As outlined above, the growth in the number of banks participating in the Federal funds market, the growth in the dealer apparatus, and the average daily volume of transactions in Federal funds are all reflected in transactions in Federal funds for selected periods as shown below:

Period	Average Daily Volume of Transactions (in millions of dollars)	Number of Participants	
		Banks*	Dealers in Acceptances and Government Securities
1925-1932	100-250	30-40	10
1950-1953	350-450	75-100	14
1955-1957	800-1,100	125-200	18

SOURCE: Parker B. Willis, *The Federal Funds Market: Its Origin and Development* (Boston: The Federal Reserve Bank of Boston, 1957), p. 15.
* Includes foreign agencies.

The selected periods shown above correspond to conditions that encouraged the growth of the market. The 1920's, for example, are represented, but in the 1930's activity in the market declined. Also, as shown above, both the number of banks and the volume of transactions in the market approximately doubled from the early 1950's through the mid-1950's.

From the beginning of the Federal funds market, the large New York City banks were the most active in the market. In subsequent years other banks have come into the market. Local markets, as well, have grown up in various other financial centers, and New York City banks have come to perform a brokerage function among their correspondents.[5] But, over-all, New York City continues to be the financial center.

The market for commercial and finance paper and bankers' acceptances. The market for commercial paper as broadly conceived consists of bankers' acceptances, finance paper, and promissory notes arising from the financing of trade. It has an important role in the history of banking, and promissory notes arising from commerce are among the oldest instruments traded in the money market in the United States. In viewing promissory notes so as to be identical with commercial and sales finance company paper, as distinct from bankers' acceptances, however, we may observe some separate influences operating upon the respective markets. The promissory notes, in the first instance, are secured only by the issuing firm and consequently originate with large concerns whose names would be easily recognized as creditworthy borrowers. The notes coming from this source have a date to maturity of three, four, or six months and they are discounted with dealers for resale, at times, to other financial institutions. Bankers' acceptances, in the other instance, are bills of a short maturity drawn by a buyer of goods, accepted by a bank, and sometimes by a third party, such as a dealer or another bank, with the creditworthiness of each standing behind the obligation as security. The credit risk, then, is in effect shifted to the bank accepting the bill, and such money market instruments attain a high quality. This source of credit, popular for a long time with European traders and investors, has, furthermore, received renewed interest in the United States market. It has a particular appeal to small traders, who may be less well known in the money market and to each other.

The volume of promissory notes outstanding declined in the 1920's as large firms found increasing convenience in the substitution of other means of short-term financial or liquidity adjustments, such as bank loans and short-term investments. In the 1950's, however, flexible credit conditions, the rise in the importance of consumer installment credit (Sect. 18.2), and sales finance companies (Sect. 17.5) paralleled a rise in the volume of commercial and sales finance company paper from about one-third of a billion dollars in 1950 to more than seven and one-half billion in 1963. The volume of bankers' acceptances, on the other hand, attained a peak in 1929, became nearly extinct in the war years, rose dramatically in the second half of the 1950's, and almost doubled in 1960 over 1959, while surpassing the previous 1929 peak. By 1963 they had increased nearly 50 per cent over 1960.* The circumstances giving rise to this rapid expansion are as dramatic as the expansion itself. They reflect an improvement in the trade relationships among free market economies, the increasing volume and importance of international trade, the achievement of convertibility of major European currencies since 1958, and other factors of fundamental importance to domestic and international monetary policy—all as outlined in Chapter

* Data are from the Board of Governors of the Federal Reserve System.

23. They also reflect Federal Reserve interest in emphasizing the international position of the dollar and in expanding the use of bankers' acceptances as a means of financing.

The Federal Reserve has actually acted to permit and subsequently to foster a market in bankers' acceptances in the United States. The Federal Reserve Act of 1913 authorized member banks to create acceptances under specific conditions and Federal Reserve banks to buy and sell them, subject to rules and regulations specified by the Board of Governors. The Federal Open Market Committee in 1955 authorized their purchase for the open market account. Under the latter authority the Federal Reserve has re-entered the acceptance market. Repurchase agreements have also been made at times to facilitate the financing of acceptance dealers, and the Federal Reserve Bank of New York purchases higher quality acceptances for the accounts of foreign correspondents.*

Under Regulation C, the Federal Reserve Act authorizes member banks to accept bankers' acceptances for four types of transactions: (1) the import of goods, (2) the export of goods, (3) dollar exchange, and (4) the storage and shipment of goods. At the end of World War II bankers' acceptances to finance imports and exports accounted for about 80 per cent of dollar acceptances outstanding, and these were predominantly used to finance imports. As conditions developed in the postwar period, however, the use of dollar acceptances by traders abroad to finance exports from the United States has risen substantially, and their use in dollar exchange and domestic trade has also risen.

The use of dollar acceptances to acquire dollar exchange is the relatively least important type of acceptance. Its use is unique, however, in that the bills do not arise from specific merchandise transactions. Instead, a foreign bank discounts its own bills with an accepting American bank in order to provide customers with dollars to finance imports when the importing country's exports are temporarily low. The acceptances then are repaid with dollars from a subsequent rise in exports to the United States. In this respect, banks of Latin American countries with such seasonal exports to the United States as coffee have been a frequent source of dollar exchange acceptances.

To illustrate the origin of a bankers' acceptance as it relates to its overwhelmingly important use in trade, we may imagine a transaction involving an import of goods from abroad. The importing firm, to begin with, would have its local bank issue a commercial letter of credit in favor of the foreign exporter. This letter would usually lead to the exercise of the right by the exporter to draw a so-called "time draft" on the American bank. The exporter would then discount the draft at his bank, and the latter would in turn forward the draft and accompanying documents to the bank in the United States. The exporter thus receives

* Data are available from the Board of Governors of the Federal Reserve System.

his funds upon discounting the bill, and the United States bank accepts the obligation to pay at maturity. For its part, the accepting bank usually receives a flat fee of a minimum of $1\frac{1}{2}$ per cent and the interest resulting from the discounting of the obligation, and the foreign bank receives the difference between the initial discount and a smaller discount by the accepting bank. The accepting bank, finally, may keep its own acceptance or sell it directly to a foreign buyer or a domestic bank or corporation. At other times they may sell their acceptance to a dealer, buy the acceptances of other banks, add their name to the latter acceptance, and sell the acceptance at a lower rate (and therefore higher price). The paper in this case has three names—the issuer, accepting bank, and another bank or dealer. It is of the quality usually obtained for bank customers and purchased for foreign accounts by the Federal Reserve.

The accepting banks in the United States, like government security dealers, are located mainly in New York City as are the small number of dealers in bankers' acceptances. The acceptance banks outside of New York City have been located in centers that reflect the relative importance of international trade. As in the case of other dealers in money market instruments, acceptance dealers obtain funds for financing their position from call loans from commercial banks and through repurchase agreements with nonfinancial corporations. They may also obtain funds from agencies of foreign banks and from repurchase agreements with the Federal Reserve Bank of New York, when the latter initiates the transaction.

As with the effect of credit conditions and yield changes on other forms of financing, so it is also with commercial and sales finance company paper and bankers' acceptances. The optimizing managers of sales finance companies may be expected to increase the sale of promissory notes when credit is tight and the relative cost of alternative forms of financing, such as bank credit, are high. And, indeed, individual banks may be expected to encourage the use of bankers' acceptances as a means of financing when their reserve positions are under pressure, since they may satisfy the customer and possibly minimize the strain on their individual resources by selling acceptances in the open market. Furthermore, the domestic holders of liquid assets, such as nonfinancial corporations and the international investors and speculators, respectively, may be expected to channel funds into the relatively higher yielding instruments, as yield on money market instruments rise in relationship to those on other forms of highly liquid securities and in relationship to the yields prevailing in other international financial centers. And, conversely, the reverse set of conditions too may prevail at other times. In fact, one may cite experiences that are consistent with all of these notions under conditions prevailing since the early 1950's.[6]

The market for call and dealer loans. Call and dealer loans are extended for the purpose of purchasing and carrying securities. Banks generally tend to extend these loans to individuals and brokers for purchasing and carrying securities (Sect. 14.3). But the extension of call loans to dealers is a more specialized business. The latter are extended by the big New York banks, and they are usually made on a preferential rate—a rate less than that on other security loans and greater than the Federal Reserve discount rate. This traditional means of dealer financing, however, has come at times to be supplemented and overshadowed— especially at times of credit tightness—by the use of repurchase agreements with nonfinancial corporations, banks outside of New York City, and others. The repurchase agreement is a means of enabling dealers to carry their portfolios, or maintain a position in money market securities, at more favorable terms than those available in New York.

At times also, the Federal Reserve itself will extend loans to dealers under repurchase agreements, especially in periods of stress. The rate charged for these loans, however, is usually above the discount rate, and the loan is extended only at the initiative of the Federal Reserve. This role of the Federal Reserve is viewed with approval, moreover, and there is the additional view that this source of funds should not be available to dealers at their own initiative due to the possibility of a conflict with a tight credit policy.[7]

Repurchase agreements with dealers may be viewed as a loan or an investment.[8] In either case, the agreements are a means for banks and nonfinancial corporations to employ funds in a liquid form, but for the dealer the longer maturity repurchase agreement arises when corporations seek an investment maturing at a specific date. The distinction between a loan and an investment would appear to be incidental, apart from the fact that some corporate treasurers are not empowered to make loans.

Certificates of deposit. Certificates of deposit have for the most part been of two types:[9] (1) savings-type time certificates and (2) time certificates of deposit as evidenced by a negotiable instrument in either registered or bearer form. The first of these came into use in the early 1950's and the other in the early 1960's. Only the more recent is clearly a money market instrument, but both types arose in response to the competitive desire on the part of individual banks to attract and maintain balances. The savings-type certificate was simply a means of offering depositors a higher interest rate for funds than could be offered on the more conventional savings-type deposit, since banks could afford to pay more for a certificate with a known maturity date as contrasted with savings deposits that could in practice be withdrawn on demand. The time certificate of deposit, however, was a competitive device on the part of the larger banks for attempting to attract some of the liquid balances of nonfinancial corporations from the government securities market and for achieving a use of the balances on a stable basis. Consequently, the time certificate of deposit assumed some of the marketable and maturity features of the short-term marketable government securities. Trading in the certificates became a part of the business of dealers in the money market, and like the United States Treasury's certificates of indebtedness (Sect. 13.2), the contracted interest is payable at maturity on the par amount of the certificate.

Closely related to these developments in the market for certificates of deposit and in the competive desire to maintain and attract balances have been developments in the use of certificates of deposit as a means of fulfilling the banking practice of requiring customers to maintain minimum or "compensating" balances as a condition for extending loans or, more commonly, lines of credit. A growing number of banks came to require in the 1950's the maintenance of an average deposit balance over a period of time of some portion, such as 10 to 20 per cent of the amount or line of credit that a bank has agreed to extend to a customer. This requirement in turn led to the growth of so-called "link financing" and the further use of a form of certificates of deposit.[10] The link financing itself referred quite simply to the linking of a third party to the requirement of maintaining a compensating balance. In such a case, certain types of firms with small balances on the average and in relationship to their borrowing needs may locate through a broker in the money market another party such as an insurance company or a pension fund that will itself maintain the necessary balance on deposit at the lending bank in exchange for a certificate of deposit. The certificate in such a case, however, may be for an average level of demand deposits, and the borrower of the funds pays the interest on the certificate either directly to the supplier of funds and/or indirectly as a part of the cost of the loan from the bank. Also there may be variations of the link financing technique that involve time deposits. In any event, certificates of deposit arise in either the negotiable or nonnegotiable form, depending on the compromise arrived at between the various parties to the initial arrangement. The investors for their part may prefer the liquidity of the negotiable form, and some banks may prefer the nonnegotiable certificate as a means of keeping track of the ownership of the certificate.

In the early development of certificates of deposit their dollar volume came to compare favorably with the volume of some other money market instruments, such as sale finance company paper and bankers' acceptances. There was, too, the prospect that the dollar volume of certificates would grow or at least continue in its relative importance.

Other money market instruments. Other money market instruments have evolved as a result of the entrance of the so-called quasi-government agencies into the short-term market for funds. Such agencies as the Federal Home Loan Banks and the Federal Intermediate Credit Banks have

294   MONEY AND BANKING

long been borrowers in the short-term or intermediate-term markets. And, in addition, other agencies have come into the market, such as the bank for cooperatives, the subdivisions of the Federal National Mortgage Association, and the local housing authorities.

The sources of money market funds. The money market is organized to handle large transactions on short notice, and on both the uses side and the supply side of the market large institutions engage in most of the operations. In the Federal funds sector of the money market the minimum-size transaction is in a single unit of one million dollars; in the market sector for commercial and finance company paper a firm must be sufficiently large and well known to place paper with its own name; the United States government is the single supplier to the government securities sector; and even in bankers' acceptances the large banks engage in the principal marketing activity for the smaller and less-well-known uses of funds. In the Federal funds market the large banks are both the major suppliers and users of the funds, but in the other instances the major suppliers of funds are a set of institutions that are distinct from the ultimate users of the funds. These net suppliers of funds include, for the most part, the Federal Reserve banks with their control over the availability of marginal funds and commercial banks, large nonfinancial corporations, insurance companies, and others.

The dealers too are net suppliers of a small amount of funds, but their significance is derived from their special role. They operate on a small amount of capital, borrow relatively large amounts of funds in the form of call loans and repurchase agreements to carry their position, and stand ready to conduct transactions as either buyers or sellers. They make their profits from narrow spreads between purchase and selling prices, from a large volume of business, and from appreciation in the values of the money market instruments they carry. The dealers are few in number— eighteen in the government securities sector, and five in bankers' acceptances at mid-1961—and quite specialized, although generally they make markets in all of the money market instruments except Federal funds. And even in this case a nonbank dealer may act as an agent.* Their number, however, is not so few as to cause a monopoly. Their market has been described as an "extremely active and 'a free higglers' market if there ever was one. . . ." [11]

The relative order of the importance of the various institutions as suppliers of funds to the money market on a cumulative basis at mid-year 1963 is shown in Table 14-1, and in the earlier data (Sect. 13.3) for holdings of government securities. From these data, one may observe in broad outline the dominant role of the Federal Reserve in the government securities market, and its role in the dollar acceptances sector of the

---

* The major firm specializing in this sort of thing in the postwar years has been Garvin, Bantel & Company.

**TABLE 14-1. The Ownership of Money Market Instruments
(Excluding Government Securities), Mid-1963
(Dollar Amounts in Millions)**

(1) Dollar Acceptances

	Dollar Amount	Per Cent
Federal Reserve banks		
Own account	43	1.6
Foreign accounts	83	3.1
Accepting banks	1,227	45.5
Others	1,344	49.8
Total	2,697	100.0

(2) The Financing of United States Government Security Dealers: Call Loans and Repurchase Agreements

	Dollar Amount*	Per Cent
Commercial banks		
New York City	1,022	27.8
Elsewhere	827	22.5
Corporations**	1,472	40.1
Other sources	353	9.6
Total	3,675	100.0

(3) Commercial and Finance Company Paper

	Dollar Amount	Per Cent
Placed through dealers	2,049	28.3
Placed directly (finance paper)	5,190	71.7
Total	7,239	100.0

* Data are seven-day averages of daily figures for the period ending mid-1963.

** All business corporations except commercial banks and insurance companies.

NOTE: Details may not add to totals due to rounding.

SOURCE: U.S. Treasury Department and the Board of Governors of the Federal Reserve System.

money market. One also observes from the various data that the large amounts of funds supplied by commercial banks in their purchase of government securities, dollar acceptances, and call loans to dealers are also shown. One finds, as well, the holdings of others and the significant role of corporations other than banks and insurance companies.

Some selected money market rates. Rates of interest are established by conditions underlying the various supply schedules for the sources of funds and the various demand schedules for the uses of funds, including the varying degrees of competition (or absence of it) in the various financial markets. The money market, however, has strong competitive elements in it. It is, in addition, a market for the temporary employment of large sums in anticipation of a stronger loan demand, better investment opportunities, tax payment dates, capital expenditures, and so on, and a market for such highly liquid uses as one-day reserves, goods in transit and storage, and the anticipation of Federal revenues from taxation. Consequently, the money market rates determined by these conditions and reflecting changes in them, in combination with gold flows, Federal Reserve actions (and inactions), and the investing public's willingness to hold varying quantities of money, and so on, are sensitive indicators of small changes in the tone of financial conditions. Among these rates in varying degrees of sensitivity are the Federal funds rate, the Treasury bill rate, and the rate on bankers' acceptances.

The Federal funds rate is a most sensitive rate as an indicator of day-to-day changes in the tone of the money and credit markets. This is due in part to bankers' attitudes toward the rate, and in part to the very short-term nature of a straight Federal funds transaction as a means of adjusting the level of bank reserves, but these explanations also account for some of the limitations we must attach to the rate as a money market indicator. In the first place, bankers' attitudes toward Federal funds may be said to depend on the precision with which they optimize returns and toward borrowing through the discount window at the Federal Reserve (Sect. 8.2). The optimizing manager of a large bank in a reasonably competitive market wishes to employ funds when they are idle even for one day, and this same banker should wish to adjust deficiencies in reserves at a minimum cost. Furthermore, banks of all sizes may have a tradition of avoiding indebtedness to the Federal Reserve, especially when there are less costly alternatives. Thus the Federal funds market provides a logical means for optimizing bankers to adjust and redistribute reserves at a rate below the discount rate at times of excess reserves, slack loan demand, and so-called credit ease. And, as a corollary to this proposition, as the pressure on reserves tightens and the Federal funds rate approaches or equals the discount rate, then the volume of transactions in Federal funds would fall and the effective means for adjusting reserve positions would be through the Federal Reserve.

The main limitations to the Federal funds rate as a money market indicator now become obvious. Due to the size of the transactions and varying size of the banks involved in the Federal funds market, the rate would fail to indicate more than variations in the residual employment of liquid funds through the larger institutions. Also during periods of credit ease the Federal funds rate is an indicator of day-to-day changes in the tone of the money and credit markets, but during those periods of increasing credit tightness the rate would be expected to reach the discount rate, hover about that rate, and fail to register day-to-day changes in the degree of credit tightness, apart from an unusual ease that sometimes appears on Wednesdays.* The general deductions from reasonable axioms, nevertheless, have an interesting correspondence to real-world phenomena, whereby the Federal funds rate tends to fluctuate below the discount during periods of credit ease and above it during periods of credit tightness as shown in Fig. 14-1.

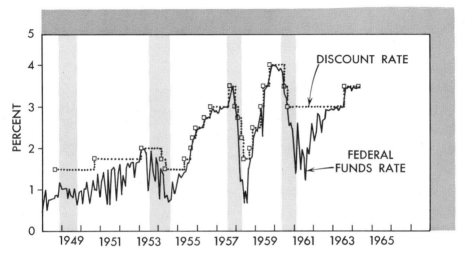

Fig. 14-1. The Discount Rate and the Federal Funds Rate. The discount rate is that for advances secured by U.S. Government securities and discounts of and advances secured by eligiple paper (Sect. 8.2). The Federal funds rate is from Garvin Bantel and Company's trading figures. The present series is constructed from monthly averages of daily "effective" rates being determined as that which most accurately represents the market for the day. More recently the company has been calculating a daily weighted average figure. The shaded areas are recessions as reported by the National Bureau of Economic Research (cf. Fig. 4-1).

The purchase and sale of government securities provide another means for adjusting reserve positions. Only the effect of such a transaction is slightly more lasting than the one for Federal funds, since the effect of the latter is reversed on the following business day. Consequently, the Treasury bill rate is another indicator of money market conditions. Changes in it, furthermore, operate to indicate changes in the degree of credit ease or tightness, and a broader set of institutions, including non-

* The decline in the rate on this last day of the reserve period or statement week reflects several things: a tendency for the principal banks to make more than an ample provision for an average reserve level for the statement week during the earlier part of the week, the fact that excess reserves cannot be carried into the succeeding reserve period, and the greater certainty about the necessary reserves due to the practice of basing reserves for Wednesdays on deposits as of the opening of business.

financial corporations and nonbank financial ones, becomes involved directly in government security transactions. This rate, then, along with the rate for dollar acceptances is shown in Fig. 14-2. The dollar acceptances do not provide the same broadly accepted means for adjusting

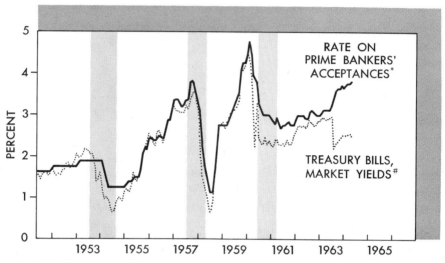

Fig. 14-2. The Treasury Bill Rate and the Rate on Bankers' Acceptances. * Averages of daily offering rates of dealers. # Yields are averages computed from daily closing bid prices. Source of data: Board of Governors of the Federal Reserve System.

bank reserve or corporate liquidity positions. They do, however, have an increasing international significance, and, from the borrower's point of view, they provide a means of obtaining funds when banks are fully loaned up. From the buyer's point of view, they provide employment for temporary funds and a relatively more worthwhile return at times.

14.3. The Organized Exchanges and Stock Market Credit

Most securities with which there is widespread familiarity on the part of individuals are traded on the organized exchanges—principally the New York Stock Exchange. The issues traded on the exchanges are outstanding issues, and, like other securities, their prices are the result of supply-and-demand factors and the discounting of a stream of prospective returns. Prices for the securities traded on the exchanges, however, are also related to the prices companies may obtain in exchange for the sale of new issues in the over-the-counter markets. In addition, they are affected by the various regulations, including margin requirements (Sect. 8.3). The conditions prevailing in the organized markets, consequently, are in part subject to Federal Reserve actions (and inactions), and they affect as well the cost and availability of funds to firms for liquidity needs and expenditures on real goods and services.

The organized exchanges. The New York Stock Exchange is the largest of the eighteen organized exchanges in the United States, and it has accounted for about 85 and 94 per cent of the trading in stocks and bonds, respectively. The next largest exchange, the American Stock Exchange, accounted for only about 8 and 6 per cent, with the emphasis in both instances upon trading in stocks, as indicated by the volume of trading shown in Table 14-2 for June 1963.

Table 14-2. Value of Securities Traded on the Organized Securities Exchanges, June 1963 Data (Dollar amounts in millions)

	Stocks		Bonds	
Registered Exchanges: °	Market Value	Per Cent of Total	Market Value	Per Cent of Total
New York Stock Exchange	4,278.5	84.9	119.5	94.4
American Stock Exchange	402.3	8.0	7.1	5.6
Other registered exchanges ° °	355.2	7.1	0.0†	0.0
All exempted exchanges††	2.0	0.0	0.0	0.0
Total	5,037.9	100.0	126.6	100.0

° The larger exchanges are required to register with the Securities and Exchange Commission.

° ° Other organized exchanges include Boston, Cincinnati, Detroit, Midwest, National, Pacific Coast, Philadelphia-Baltimore, Pittsburgh, Salt Lake, and Spokane Stock Exchanges; Chicago Board of Trade; and San Francisco Mining Exchange.

† Less than $100,000.

†† Exempted exchanges include Colorado Springs, Honolulu, Richmond, and Wheeling Stock Exchanges.

NOTE: Parts may not add to totals due to rounding.

SOURCE: Securities and Exchange Commission.

The New York Stock Exchange. The New York Stock Exchange is a voluntary unincorporated membership association. A membership is referred to as a "seat," a traditional figure of speech carried over from earlier days when the membership sat at tables during trading sessions. The number of seats on the exchange has been 1,325, and, representing privileges as they do, they may themselves be purchased and sold.

Most individuals who trade in securities do not do so as members of the exchange. Instead they usually conduct their business through a broker or one who serves as an agent for a customer in return for a charge called a commission. The largest among the brokerage firms and the most widely known in the United States is Merrill Lynch, Pierce, Fenner and Smith, Inc. This firm maintains offices in over one hundred cities in the United States. At its offices, as well as at those of some other

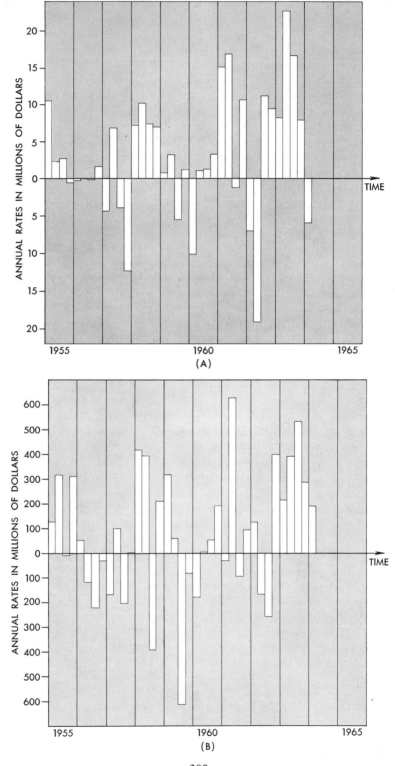

300

firms, there is usually a room which is called the customers' or board room, where the customer can watch a stock quotation board on which stock price quotations are recorded as they come in on the ticker.

Trading on the exchange is generally conducted in "round lots." A lot is generally 100 shares, but, in the case of the higher priced and less active shares, the exchange may designate ten shares as the unit of trading. In any event, the majority of middle-income individuals trading in securities are not likely to engage in trading in round lots. The broker doing a large business singly, or in conjunction with other brokers, may pool the orders from individuals until they are large enough to make up a unit of trading. In addition to commission brokers, however, there are others who perform various functions.

Stock market credit. One's interest in general monetary affairs and finance must in part be focused upon stock market credit for purchasing and carrying securities in view of the relevance of stock market yields, the Federal Reserve's control over stock market credit (Sect. 8.3), and the expectations prevailing in the stock market to the achievement of a maximum output for the economy as a whole and other goals of the monetary officials. The types of credit provided by banks and stock exchange firms reporting to the Federal Reserve include those types extended directly to customers and those extended to brokers and dealers.

On the customer's side there are two types, both of which are shown in Fig. 14-3. They are net debit balances and bank loans and are shown in the illustration as flows. Customer's net debit balances represent credit extended by stock exchange firms to their customers primarily for purchasing and carrying nongovernment securities, and loans to others represent credit advanced for the same purpose by reporting member banks to persons other than brokers and dealers. On the brokers' and dealers' side there are loans extended to the brokers and dealers and customers net free credit balances. These forms of credit are shown in Fig. 14-4 as flows. The free credit balances, in particular, are the balances of the customers at brokerage firms resulting from (1) balances deposited by the customers with the firms and (2) balances resulting from the sale by the broker of customers' securities.

The flows of stock market credit are affected by four somewhat overlapping factors: (1) The principal factor among these is the volume of stock exchange trading on margin. If the securities were purchased entirely by customers' unborrowed funds there would be virtually no demand for loans. (2) The second factor is the margin requirements pre-

---

Fig. 14-3. The Flow of Customer Credit. (A) Net debit balances (secured by other than Government securities) with New York Stock Exchange firms; (B) bank loans to other than brokers and dealers for purchasing and carrying securities other than Government securities. Source: Board of Governors of the Federal Reserve System.

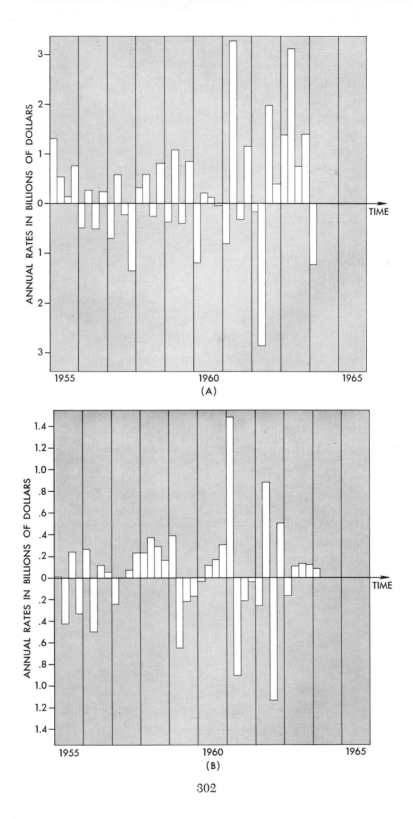

(A)

(B)

scribed by the Board of Governors of the Federal Reserve System. The lower the margin, the more traders requiring margin are permitted to borrow; the higher the margin, the less they are permitted to borrow. (3) The third factor is the level of security prices. A larger amount of credit is required for a margin transaction involving a given number of shares when stock prices are high. (4) The fourth factor is the volume of securities outstanding. As net new issues reach the market a larger volume of funds employed in the market is required to maintain a given level of stock market prices.

Of the four factors contributing to the volume of stock market credit outstanding, two of them—the volume of stock exchange trading on margin and the margin requirements—are among the responsibilities of the monetary authorities. And the remaining two—the level of security prices and the volume of securities outstanding—are indirectly related to their responsibility for the volume of credit. Through control over margin trading and credit generally, the monetary authorities may add to or reduce the volume of stock market credit outstanding and consequently affect the level of security prices.

14.4. Summary

The securities markets may be classified as the organized exchanges and the over-the-counter markets. The organized markets are characterized by formal procedures for bringing together buyers and sellers. In those markets the transactions are mainly facilitated by traders who act as agents in bringing together bids to buy and offers to sell. The organized markets are more impersonal. The over-the-counter markets, however, are conducted predominantly through informal negotiation. Thus they are particularly well suited for handling large transactions at a predetermined price, such as may characterize the market for new issues, and the highly liquid securities, such as those frequently purchased by large institutional investors. The negotiation procedure also lends itself well to small transactions in securities with a very high risk and a thin market that may be ineligible for listing under the requirements of the more formally organized markets.

The money market is a negotiated market. It is of central importance due, in part, to the large volume of liquid securities traded there, and due, in part, to its sensitive reflection of changes in credit conditions. It is a market conducted mainly over the telephone and by other means of

Fig. 14-4. The Flow of Brokers' and Dealers' Credit. (A) Flow of credit extended on securities other than Government securities; (B) flow resulting from customers' net free credit balance. Source of data: Board of Governors of the Federal Reserve System.

communication. Consequently, there is no central meeting place, but the market's primary business centers around downtown Manhattan. The market for the instruments traded is for the most part made by dealers who stand ready to buy or sell a large volume of instruments. In the process of making the market, they quote bid and ask prices at which they will handle transactions up to a certain size, and they will negotiate other deals as well.

The instruments to which the effective supply and demand for liquid funds give rise include Federal funds, United States government securities, commercial and sales finance company paper, dealers' loans, and certificates of deposit. Over the years, however, the forces shaping the various needs for short-term funds have caused the various instruments to appear in varying amounts. Commercial paper was the most prominent form of paper in the early years of United States banking. Call loans to dealers, too, were important. Still the establishment of the Federal Reserve in 1913 led to the development of a market for Federal funds, and refinements in the financial mechanism of the country have paralleled a highly developed system of trading in Federal funds. Furthermore, the decline in the use of commercial paper as a means of adjusting short-term liquidity positions of non-financial businesses in the 1920's, the subsequent rise in the size of the Federal debt, and the rise of United States Treasury bills in 1929 gave rise in turn to government securities becoming the main business of the money market.

In more recent years, the tendency for the larger nonfinancial firms to supply funds to the markets for the more liquid financial assets has in part affected the development of certificates of deposit. Also the large holdings of Federal debt instruments and the use of repurchase agreements as a substitute means of financing dealers have effectively reduced the relative importance of dealers' loans as a money market instrument. The rise in consumer credit in the post-World War II years and increased emphasis on international trade have contributed to a revival of the commercial paper sector of the market and a growth in the volume of bankers' acceptances.

The Federal funds rate, along with the Treasury bill rate, and other money market rates, reflects the conditions underlying the supply and demand for funds as well as the supply and demand for money balances, and all of the money market rates serve as indicators of credit ease and tightness. The Federal funds rate is a most sensitive indicator of changes in the degree of credit ease, and a less sensitive one for changes in the degree of credit ease and tightness. It also reflects responses from many quarters, due to the wide distribution of the ownership of Federal debt.

In contrast to the less informally organized markets are the organized exchanges—principally the New York Stock Exchange. Trading there is important to the study of the effects of monetary and credit conditions, nevertheless. This is due to the interrelationship between the securities traded on the organized exchanges and in the new issues sector of the over-the-counter markets, as well as to the control exercised by the monetary authorities over the cost and availability of funds for trading on credit in securities. Favorable cost conditions from the point of view of a user of capital funds are inducive to the issuance of new securities, and unfavorable ones are less inducive. The monetary authorities may in part restrict increases in securities prices by rasing margin requirements for borrowed funds for purchasing and carrying securities. Also they may in part affect price declines by lowering the margin requirement for borrowed funds for purchasing and carrying securities. In administering margin requirements, however, as in the control over credit generally, the monetary authorities have a tool for influencing the relationship between yields, rates of return from additional investment in real capital, expenditures on real capital, and the output of goods for the economy as a whole.

References

1. *Treasury-Federal Reserve Study of the Government Securities Market*, Part I (Washington, D.C.: Board of Governors of the Federal Reserve System, 1959), pp. 95-97.

2. *Ibid.*, pp. 76-84 pp. 98-101; and Commission on Money and Credit, *Money and Credit: Their Influence on Jobs, Prices, and Growth* (Englewood Cliffs, N.J.: Prentice-Hall, Inc., 1961), pp. 117-120.

3. See Parker B. Willis, *The Federal Funds Market: Its Origin and Development* (Boston: The Federal Reserve Bank of Boston, 1957); and *The Federal Funds Market—A Study by a Federal Reserve System Committee* (Washington, D.C.: Board of Governors of the Federal Reserve System, 1959).

4. The history of the limit is varied. But according to 1957 and 1958 regulations, the legal limit ranges upward from 10 per cent of a bank's capital and surplus for an unsecured loan, such as that involving a "straight" Federal funds transaction (Sect. 3.2), to no limit on a repurchase agreement involving short-term (18 months to maturity) government securities. See also *ibid.*, pp. 39-42.

5. *Ibid.*, pp. 35, 85-87, and 90-91.

6. See, for informal statements of some instances, "Bankers' Acceptances," *Money Market Instruments*, Federal Reserve Bank of Cleveland, 1962, pp. 24-29; and "Bankers' Acceptances," *Monthly Review*, Federal Reserve Bank of New York, June 1961, p. 97.

7. See Commission on Money and Credit, *op.cit.*, pp. 119-120.

8. *Treasury-Federal Reserve Study of the Government Securities Market*, Part I (Washington, D.C.: Board of Governors of the Federal Reserve System, 1959), pp. 30-40.

9. See Richard Fieldhouse, *Certificates of Deposit* (Boston, Mass.: The Bankers Publishing Company, 1962); and "Negotiable Time Certificates of Deposit," *Federal Reserve Bulletin*, April 1963, pp. 458-468.

10. See Fieldhouse, *op.cit.*, pp. 29-37; and Jack M. Guttentag and Richard G. Davis, "Compensating Balances," *Monthly Review,* Federal Reserve Bank of New York, December 1961, pp. 205-210.

11. See R. S. Sayers, "The New York Money Market Through London Eyes," *Central Banking After Bagehot* (Oxford: At the Clarendon Press, 1957), p. 139.

part six

The Behavior and Financing of the Business, Consumer, and Government Sectors

15

The Determination of the Level of National Income

A new *system*, that is what requires emphasis. Classical economics could withstand isolated criticism. . . . Inevitably, at the earliest opportunity, the mind slips back into the old grooves of thought, since analysis is utterly impossible without a frame of reference, a way of thinking about things, or, in short, a theory (Paul A. Samuelson, "The General Theory (3)," *The New Economics* [1948]).

Much of the theory of the determination of the level of national income is due to the work of John Maynard Keynes. The mode of thought, as introduced by Keynes, first appeared in the revolutionary work *The General Theory of Employment, Interest and Money* (1936). In essence, it displaced the latent belief in Say's law of markets. That law, as cited earlier (Chap. 5), held that "as a consequence of the view of money as a medium of exchange only, and not as a store of value—the community's excess demand to hold cash is zero under all circumstances." It was identified with general economic equilibrium at full employment, and only frictions could give rise to unemployment. Since there was no prospect of an inadequate volume of expenditures (or income) and employment resulting from a strengthened preference for money balances, a removal of any frictions thwarting the attainment of full employment would result in full employment.

As matters have evolved, there have been a variety of definitions of full employment. One views full employment as a condition where the number of involuntarily unemployed over the number of job vacancies is zero.[1] However, there are problems here of whether the skills, training, and education of the unemployed have an adequate correspondence to the types of jobs available. If they do not, the number of job vacancies and the number of jobs available as proportions of the total labor force could conceivably rise considerably. Some other definitions, on the

309

other hand, have implied goals for the maximum permissible level of unemployment, such as unemployment's being no more than 4 per cent of the total labor force. In these, the total labor force consists of the employed plus those actively seeking work or the involuntarily unemployed. These definitions imply the necessity for some unemployment as a result of the need for some mobility of labor—i.e., the need to have some workers moving from less productive to more productive jobs. This chapter, therefore, introduces a basic monetary model that determines the level of national income, and the level of employment in the short run.

The latter model, as presently introduced, is one of several implied by Keynes's original work and subsequent developments concerning that work. Another—the liquidity preference demand for money—was introduced earlier (Sect. 4.4). All of them, including a model for determining the flow of investment demand, are subsequently elaborated upon (Chap. 17-20). The present model is also related in this chapter to two additional models, concerning changes in income. One of these deals with economic growth and the other with the prospect of mechanical-like variations in income.

In dealing with some institutional facets concerning our basic model, the present chapter introduces the notion of a flow of a portion of the payments to the factors of production through financial intermediaries, and relates the income analysis to the two systems of national accounting—the older national income system, and the more recently available flow of funds accounts. The two systems of accounting are related to the model in question and to each other on a conceptual basis only as distinct from a precise integration of the accounting systems in terms of coverage and particular entries. The latter type of integration is not presently feasible because of the lack of correspondence between the coverage and particular entries in the accounting systems.

15.1. THE BASIC MODEL AND SOME ADDITIONAL DEFINITIONS AND CONCEPTS

The basic model and accounts concerning the flow of income and the flow of funds through financial intermediaries and between the various sectors of the economy are interrelated. First, both of the accounting systems are based on identities, and, conceptually, data for the many entries can be presented in both systems as stocks and as flows (e.g., Sect. 9.1). Second, the stocks or quantities in existence may be thought of as functions of time, and changes in the quantities thus become flows or rates of change with respect to time at a moment in time. These latter flows, then, can be combined by addition and netted by subtraction until some series of data are found to correspond to some crucial variables in the basic model.

The basic model. The basic model consists mainly of two equations and a behavioral postulate. The two equations are

(1) $$Y_d = C(Y) + I, \quad 0 < dC/dY < 1$$

(2) $$Y = C(Y) + S(Y)$$

where Y_d is aggregate demand,

$C(Y)$ is consumption (C) as some function of income (Y),

I is the flow of investment ($I = $ const.),

Y is the aggregate of payments received as income for current output (or supply), and

$S(Y)$ is saving (S) as some function of income.

The postulate is as follows:

Postulate: *As the flow of income changes, consumption changes directly by a smaller amount, i.e.,* $0 < dC/dY < 1$.

Given the latter postulate, the slope implied by equation (1) is less than one, and, by the rule for a derivative with respect to itself (i.e., $dY/dY = 1$), the slope implied by equation (2) is one. Clearly, a solution exists and this condition we may note at a moment in time:

(3) $$Y_d = Y, \text{ or}$$

(4) $$I_{const.} = S$$

Now, let us note some features of this model, some of which anticipate later topics:

(1) The postulate is a behavioral one; as such, it has frequently been studied with reference to empirical data.

(2) The constants may vary, and the functional relationships may shift. The hypothesis $dC/dY < 1$ holds only in the sense of a partial derivative (i.e., $\partial C/\partial Y < 1$) when the conditions underlying the consumption function change, as they frequently do (Chap. 18).

(3) The expenditures represented by the right-hand member of equation (1) may be broken down into various subclasses. This may be done, for example, so as to permit a special consideration of government expenditures and foreign expenditures for the net export of goods and services, or to permit a consideration of expenditures by the various sectors of the economy. Similarly, the right-hand member of equation (2) could be presented so as to reflect saving by the various sectors or groups. Later, with respect to expenditures in particular, we consider separately the nonfinancial business sectors (Chap. 17), the consumer sector (Chap. 18), and the public sector (Chap. 19).

The national income accounts. The national income accounts are reported by the United States Department of Commerce. In them, the gross national product (or GNP) represents the total of expenditures for consumption, government, and private investment in real capital, as well as foreign expenditures for the net exports of goods and services. The total of these expenditures may also be shown in terms of goods (durable and nondurable) and services. At times, the expenditures are called aggregate demand (Y_a). In the same accounts, the gross national product is primarily the value of all the factor services rendered for the goods and services produced. Sometimes this income generated for the factors of production is called aggregate income (Y), and it may be stated in both current and constant prices (Sect. 5.3). The data for these payments are published in different forms, such as wages, salaries, interest, rent, and profits, as gross income originating in manufacturing, agriculture, and so on. As one may say, the demand and supply sides of GNP are basically the same physical quantity in two different senses. In effect, there exists a double-entry bookkeeping system in which the total of expenditures is, except for certain nonincome charges, identical to the income generated. This we summarize, along with the several ways of viewing the income generated:

Demand		*Supply*	
Expenditures or for:	Expenditures for:	Gross income in the forms or of:	Gross income originating in:
Consumption	Goods output final sales	Wages and salaries	Agriculture
Investment (including additions to inventories)	Inventory change Construction	Profits, interest, and rent	Mining
Government	Services	Capital consumption allowances	Manufacturing
Net exports of goods and services		Sales and other indirect taxes	Trade, finance, insurance, real estate, transportation, etc.
Aggregate Demand	Aggregate Demand	Aggregate Supply	Aggregate Supply

SOURCE: U.S. Department of Commerce.

The flow of funds. The flow of funds accounts are reported by the Board of Governors of the Federal Reserve System.[2] The accounts record both the financial and nonfinancial aspects of transactions, whereas the national income accounts indicate the flow of the current output of goods and services and its distribution in the form of consumption and investment. They show sources and uses of funds for current transactions, as well as provide estimates of outstanding amounts of assets and liabilities. The accounts are comprehensive and show a standard classification of all transactions for five major sectors in the economy and for subsectors of these major sectors. The major sector classification consists of (1) the consumer and nonprofit sectors, (2) the nonfinancial business sectors, (3) the government sectors, (4) the financial institutions sectors, and (5) the rest of the world sector. The nonfinancial business sectors are further classified as farm, noncorporate, and corporate sectors. The government sectors are then shown separately, as the Federal and the state and local government sectors. And the financial institutions sectors include the commercial bank sector and separate sectors for savings institutions, insurance, and financial institutions not classified elsewhere.

Each transaction should, in effect, be viewed as being recorded on a balance sheet for the parties or sectors to the two sides of a transaction. Each payment by one unit is also a receipt of another: For the payment something is received, and for the receipt something is given up. In terms of the fundamental accounting identity (Chap. 3 and Sect. 9.1), there are four entries to every transaction—a debit and a credit to each of the two behavioral units to the transaction. The acquisition of an asset by one unit is a debit to an asset account and a credit to cash or a liability account, depending upon whether the payment is made in cash or by credit. Giving up the asset, on the other hand, results in a credit to an asset account of the other party and a debit to cash or some other asset account. As one may gather, a credit, whether to an asset account or a liabilities account, is a source of funds, and a debit, whether to an asset account or a liability account, is a use of funds. Hence, the terms "sources" and "uses" with reference to funds and the fundamental accounting identity carry over to an identity between sources and uses of funds.

What, then, are funds and what are flows in the present context? Funds are simply accounting entries. They correspond to our employment of the unit of account or monetary unit encountered earlier whereby one reckons wealth and calculates credits and debits (Sect. 2.1). The motion of funds is broader than that of money; funds are money only when bookkeeping entries involve the cash account and demand deposits of the commercial banking system (Chap. 3). A flow of funds, then, is a rate of change in any account at a moment in time where the historical accumulation of such flows simply constitute stocks (or assets and liabilities).

Sources of funds are always identical to uses of funds. Nevertheless, one can deal with particular groups of accounts, such as those for financial assets including stocks, bonds, and bank credit, or nonfinancial assets including inventories, plant, and equipment. One can thus observe the flows from the financial markets into the expansion of real capital assets, as well as observe the flows between different sectors. One can see where the funds arise and where they go.

The flows of expenditures, income, and funds. The aggregate of expenditures recorded in the national income accounts may be classified as consumption and investment. These expenditures may also include the services of the financial institutions sectors. The consumption expenditures may be interpreted to include purchases for private consumption and purchases for public consumption or government. Investment may be interpreted to mean effective expenditures for increases in inventory items, fixed capital goods, and the net export of goods and services. The precise classification is arbitrary, and it may be arranged to accommodate a particular analysis. In this same context, the portion of the aggregate income not consumed may be regarded as saving, by definition. In the national income identity, then, all counterparts correspond to equations (3) and (4). Today, however, saving and investment in the model are performed by different behavioral units, and a similar interpretation can be extended to the accounting identity. Capital outlays are primarily made by business units, and some funds are obtained outside of the units. In a similar sense, the portion of income not spent on consumption flows into insurance and other forms of institutionalized saving. In order to obtain funds externally, deficits are incurred. Financial claims or assets come into existence to represent these deficits in the form of bank notes, debt instrument, or shares of stock and the like. In this world the extent of such financing is indicated by the sum of the deficits incurred by spending units. For example, if GNP is 600 billion dollars and external financing totals 60 billion dollars, then 10 per cent of GNP is financed externally.

In a world where there is a separate identity between savers and investors, intermediaries have arisen to expedite the flows of portions of income into expenditures. In 1800, insurance companies were in their infancy, there were only a few commercial banks (Sect. 7.1), and other present-day financial intermediaries were nonexistent. After 1850, however, the assets of insurance companies increased on an average of 6.7 per cent a year. Banks, too, continued to grow, but after 1900 the assets of nonbanking institutions, such as life insurance companies, mutual savings banks, and savings-and-loan associations, grew somewhat more rapidly.[3] The point, then, is that in terms of the separate behavioral units, the units (i.e., the savers and investors) need not always formulate mutually complementary plans and act upon them at precisely the same time. Imbalances between aggregate demand and aggregate supply, or between saving and investment, occur. These imbalances give rise to changes in income and prices, and financial intermediaries play a crucial role.

The notion of partial flows of income through financial intermediaries is shown schematically in Fig. 15-1. The illustration is a time slice or a view of the flows at an instant in time:

$$\lim_{\Delta t \to 0} \frac{\Delta(\text{gnp})}{\Delta t} = \frac{d(\text{gnp})}{dt} = \text{GNP}$$

where gnp is a previously accumulated stock of gross national product, and GNP is the flow or gross national product per annum at a moment in time.

Moving clockwise and to the right of the vertical measure for GNP, flows are shown as payments to the factors of production. Then, the income

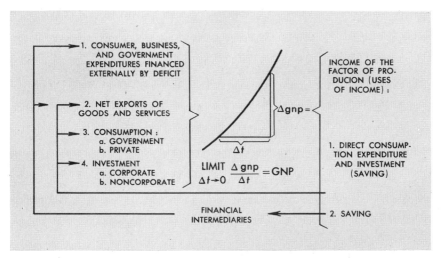

Fig. 15-1. The Circular Flow of Funds: A Cross-Sectional View.

received by the factors of production partly flows directly into consumption and investment outlays without external financing and partly into savings in the form of insurance payments, the purchase of savings-and-loan shares, funds extended to investment banks, savings bank deposits, and others. The institutions receiving these funds extend them to expenditure units that are, in turn, financing externally. These financial institutions have an intermediate position between savers, on the one hand, and investors and consumers financing externally, on the other. The monetary system, however, must be included as a special case in this context because of its capacity to expand the supply of credit (and thus add to the volume of expenditures financed externally) and contract the supply (and thus effect a contraction of the expenditures financed externally). The capacity of the monetary system to effect a balance or imbalance between the output of goods and services as aggregate expenditures then becomes of central importance (Chap. 16-20).

A distinction between commercial banks and nonbank intermediaries: an illustration. The above distinction between commercial banks and nonbank intermediaries may be illustrated. A manufacturer, for example, wants to expand his plant. He first goes to the manager of the local savings-and-loan association and requests a loan. The savings-and-loan manager declines, since income in the area has recently been inadequate, and he has received no new savings funds to lend. The manufacturer then goes to a bank that has sufficient reserves or access to reserves to support an increase in lending, and the bank makes the loan by creating a demand deposit in the manufacturer's name. The manufacturer then hires Jones for the construction job and pays Jones with a check. Jones will probably deposit the check in his own checking account, in order to be able to spend the funds conveniently at a later date. Or, somewhat less likely, he might deposit the check in a savings account at the bank or at the savings-and-loan association. If the latter occurs, the manager at the savings-and-loan association could now afford to take over the loan to the manufacturer from the bank.

The three lessons from this illustration are clear. Income and output have risen because the bank was able to provide the financing for an increase in expenditures before these expenditures added to income, while the savings-and-loan association was able to lend only as a result of new saving from an increase in income. Secondly, the original increase in the money supply might be entirely extinguished if the income recipient chose to add to his savings deposit (Sect. 3.3) or savings-and-loan shares. Thirdly, if we only looked at accounting statements drawn up at the end of the little episode, we might conclude that either the bank or the savings-and-loan association merely intermediates Jones' saving and the manufacturer's investment, and that neither institution really created any loan funds. We could thus come to the curious conclusion that Jones ultimately provided the financing for the manufacturer. However, we know the facts of the case. Independent of the initial creation of money and credit by the commercial bank, income would never have risen and, with it, deposits at intermediaries.

Now, the flow of funds accounts aid in providing data about flows of funds through the financial intermediaries. One can observe those institutions that receive more or less in the form of savings than they pass on to investors. The sources contributing to an imbalance in the financial markets can be observed, as well as the forms of financial instruments acquired in the use of funds. The flows in the flow of funds accounts are increases and decreases in the holdings of assets and liabilities, and as such they provide a view of the financing of the purchases of output, within the limits indicated by the third lesson from our example.

Imbalances in supply-demand relationships. The two types of imbalances referred to thus far give rise to valuation changes. The first of these—that between the aggregate supply and the aggregate demand for goods and services—gives rise to changes in the average of prices for current output. These were introduced earlier (Sect. 5.3), and they become the subject of a more intensive consideration later (Chap. 16). The other—the imbalance between the supply of funds and the demand for funds—gives rise to changes in the prices of financial instruments and, consequently, interest rates. These latter changes, too, were introduced earlier (Chap. 4), and they will receive further consideration. Also the interrelationship between the changes in the average of prices for current output and the interest rate changes was dealt with earlier (Sect. 5.4).

15.2. Aggregate Income and Aggregate Demand Again

Our basic model may be presented geometrically and considered more fully. In presenting the model geometrically, however, specifically defined functions are implied. We shall make these explicit and use simple linear relationships for the consumption and saving functions. We will deal first with the model in its static state (Sect. 1.2), and then we will introduce the time dimension.

The static state. Let the consumption function be defined by a simple linear equation: $C(Y) = \alpha Y + \beta$, $0 < dC/dY = \alpha < 1$. Thus, substituting for the function $C(Y)$ in equation (2), $Y = \alpha Y + \beta + S(Y)$, and $S(Y) = (1 - \alpha)Y - \beta$. The basic model then becomes

$$Y_d = \alpha Y + \beta + I$$
$$Y = Y$$

Given condition (3), for a solution,

$$Y = \alpha Y + \beta + I$$

or, at equilibrium,

(5)
$$\overline{Y} = \frac{\beta + I}{1 - \alpha}$$

These equations, the solution $\overline{Y}$, and the model in geometric form appear in Fig. 15-2.

A comparison of static equilibria. In economic analysis a special form of dynamic analysis consists of a comparison of static equilibria (Sect.

1.2)—an analysis of changes from one state of equilibrium to others. In the present context, these changes correspond to changes in the conditions underlying equations (1) and (2). By such comparisons we wish to make our analysis more flexible and intuitively plausible, since earlier analysis (Chap. 1-6) leads one to look for changes in the flow

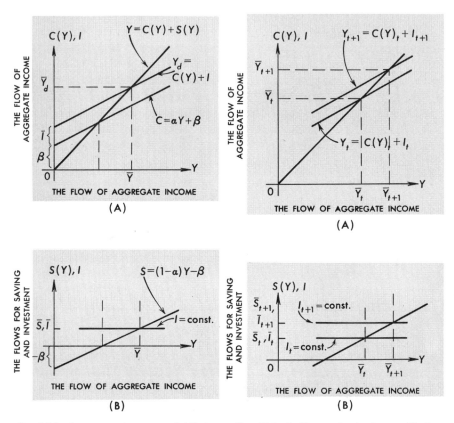

Fig. 15-2. Aggregate Income and (A) Aggregate Demand; (B) Saving and Investment.

Fig. 15-3. A Change in the Income Variable with Respect to a Change in the Investment Variable.

variable for income. The state toward which adjustments in the system tend may be a changing one.

Earlier (Sect. 5.4), an explanation was given for a change in the investment variable over time. There the change in the underlying condition was in response to a prospective rise in the average of prices, but, as we re-emphasize, it could have been a change in a tax or cost factor, or even a change in the psychological state concerning uncertainty about the future. Thus, introducing a change in investment and its effect on income, we have from equation (5) and by the quotient and other rules,

$$(6) \qquad \frac{dY}{dI} = \frac{1}{1 - \alpha}, \quad \alpha = dC/dY$$

In the general terms of equations (1) and (2) and condition (3), we have $Y = C(Y) + I$ and, using the composite function and other rules,

$$\frac{dY}{dI} = \frac{dC}{dY} \frac{dY}{dI} + 1$$

or, rearranging terms,

$$(6') \qquad \frac{dY}{dI} = \frac{1}{1 - dC/dY}$$

As matters turn out, equations (6) and (6') are simply formulas for the limit of an nth partial sum of a converging geometric series. The numerator 1, in the right-hand member, is the first term, and dC/dY is the common ratio: e.g.,

$$\sum_{n=1}^{\infty} 1 \left(\frac{dC}{dY}\right)^{n-1} = 1 + 1 \left(\frac{dC}{dY}\right) + 1 \left(\frac{dC}{dY}\right)^2 + \ldots + 1 \left(\frac{dC}{dY}\right)^{n-1} + \ldots$$

It is said to converge and have an nth partial sum where, in the latter case

$$\lim_{n \to \infty} \left(\frac{dC}{dY}\right)^n = 0$$

We have simply another way of saying that equations (1) and (2) have a solution. Equations (6) and (6') give the change in income for a given change in investment in the neighborhood of a point (i.e., Y, Y_d) as one moves over time.[4] Thus the rate of change in income with respect to a change in investment is equal to the reciprocal of the slope of the tangent to the saving function. The effect of a decrease in investment on income would simply be the negative of the right-hand member of equations (6) and (6').

A change in investment demand such as that implied by equation (6) is shown in Fig. 15-3. The illustration is similar to Fig. 15-2, only the flow variables at the initial time are denoted by subscript t, and those after the change in investment demand are denoted $t + 1$. Observe in Fig. 15-3, however, that the rate of change in the flow variable Y in response to a change in I depends upon the slope of the consumption function (dC/dY). If that slope had been greater, the effect on income would have been greater, as indicated by equations (6) and (6'). The effect of a decrease in investment could also be sketched (the reader may wish to do so as an exercise). In either case, the shifts in the aggregate in such an analysis are of course always effective shifts, and implicitly they are made subject to certain constraints.

The upward (downward) shift in investment must be effected by directly or indirectly activating (deactivating) money balances and/or by direct or indirect increases (decreases) in the money supply as may result when there is net borrowing (net repayment) at the bank. In other words, no shifts are possible in the absence of access to balances to activate (deactivate) by the parties desirous of effecting the shifts and/or in the absence of a change in bank credit. The extent of the presence of such balances in the proper hands and the degree of changes in bank credit provide varying degrees of constraint. Clearly, these changes in the money supply (M) and income (Y) involve the velocity of money (i.e., $V_y = Y/M$) as defined earlier (Sect. 2.2).

Thinking in terms of a period of time, the multiple increase (decrease) in income resulting from the upward (downward) shift in investment, as shown in Fig. 15-3, may be given as the quotient $\Delta Y/\Delta I$. That is,

$$\text{mult.} = \Delta Y/\Delta I \quad \text{or}$$
$$\Delta I \, (\text{mult.}) = \Delta Y \quad \text{or}$$
$$\Delta I + \Delta I \left(\frac{dc}{dy}\right) + \Delta I \left(\frac{dc}{dy}\right)^2 + \Delta I \left(\frac{dc}{dy}\right)^3 + \ldots = \Delta Y$$

Each of the terms in the left-hand member of the latter expression gives the change in expenditure for a period in which income turns over, and we sum these changes to get the multiple increase in income (i.e., ΔY). If the turnover is estimated from the income velocity of money (Sect. 2.2), then we note that most of the effect is worked out in about one to two years. A sketch of such changes may be shown by blowing up the movement in equilibrium from one point $(\overline{Y}_t, \overline{Y}_{d,\ t})$ to another $(\overline{Y}_{t+1}, \overline{Y}_{d,\ t+1})$ in the upper part of Fig. 15-3. This would appear as follows:

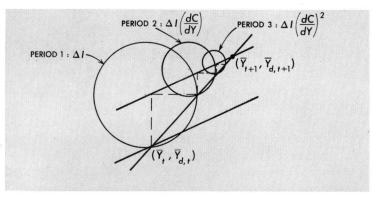

We could also denote the multiplier concerning a shift in the consumption function (i.e., a change in β) on income by differentiating equation (5). Such an increase in β would result in an upward shift in the aggregate demand relationship in the upper part of Fig. 15-3, just as the increase in investment, but the increase in β would result in a downward shift in the saving schedule in the lower part of Fig. 15-3. An upward (downward) shift in consumption would result in a positive (negative) change in the income variables and employment just as would an upward (downward) shift in investment. Similarly, such shifts would parallel either more (less) activity of money balances and/or increases (decreases) in the quantity of money. In this instance, however, a paradox occurs. The shift in the consumption function does not result in a lower level of saving as measured on the vertical axis in the lower part of Fig. 15-3, although the consumers may have planned to reduce saving at the prior level of income. Instead, the initial upward shift results in an increase in the flow of payments to the factors of production and a simultaneous increase in income through movement along the consumption function with which to increase the flow of expenditures and saving also. Conversely, if people planned to save more—an upward shift in the saving schedule—they end up saving less than planned as a result of the decline in their incomes. This is the well-known paradox of thrift.

Some dynamic considerations: price and output changes. What now would be the nature of the above increases in the flows of income $(Y = PO)$? A fuller response to the question comes later (Sect. 16.1). Briefly, however, only an increase in income resulting from an increase in prices would be forthcoming in the short run before production could be increased (i.e., ΔO) and new orders filled. To some extent, such a rise in income in current prices (Sect. 5.3) could be offset by two developments. For one, sales firms may meet some of the increased demand by reducing inventories without altering their prices. For another, the increase in demand could increase employment, and the higher level of employment and fuller utilization of resources could provide a larger flow of output or income in current prices.

Suppose, on the other hand, that the level of employment was given. What then? In the short run, only an inflated increase in income would probably occur, but, in the long run, technological advancement could cause income in constant prices to increase. The technological advances in this case would be labor saving. They may include the many innovations, each of relatively small significance, directed toward increasing output and expanding the use of automatic technology—i.e., the use of self-regulating devices.

15.3. Some Additional Dynamic Considerations

To re-emphasize the unlikely case of a constant equilibrium over time, two additional dynamic models are introduced. In both of these, the flow variables themselves are functions of time.

The first of these also anticipates a later topic on economic growth. It is the Domar macro model.[5] The model illustrates the necessity for parametric changes in the above national income model, where there are labor-saving advances in technology. It depends on the assumption that some constant rate of growth in income is a means of assuring a continuous and full utilization of resources under the impact of labor-saving technological advances. The model assumes an expanding flow of income in constant dollars, such as 4 per cent per annum. It then indicates the relationship that must exist among the flow variables and time to assure the full utilization of resources.

The other model is known as the acceleration principle. It focuses upon a possible source of rather mechanical changes in investment (and, therefore, income); it has little or no motivational content. But some modern methods of inventory control do employ mechanical techniques that tie inventory purchases to sales, as does the so-called acceleration principle.

The Domar macro model. The Domar model consists of three equations and three variables:

(1) $$S(t) = kY(t)$$

(2) $$I(t) = g\frac{dY(t)}{dt}$$

(3) $$S(t) = I(t), \quad k > 0, \quad g > 0$$

The variables S, I, and Y are in fact the same flow variables considered above for saving, investment, and income. Equation (1) simply expresses saving as some portion of income. Equation (2), along with the condition $g > 0$, implies that the flow of income is increasing at the initial moment in time. This is clearly seen by rewriting equation (2), $1/g\, I(t) = dY/dt$, where if $1/g\, I(t) > 0$, then $dY/dt > 0$ and the income flow is increasing. Equation (3) is the same as the earlier (Sect. 15.2) equation (4). The locus of equilibria, however, is now increasing over time as the present model implies.

In reducing the model to a single differential equation, one gets

(4) $$Y(t) = \frac{g}{k}\frac{dY}{dt}$$

This equation says that income $Y(t)$ is a constant multiple (i.e., k/g) of the change in the flow variable with respect to time (i.e., dY/dt).

Now, equation (4) is based on a function that is its own derivative. This is unique. Its solution becomes

(5) $$Y = ae^{k/g\ t}, \quad e \approx 2.718^{*}$$

and the flow of income is now expressed as an exponential function of time.

Permitting the analysis to begin at the initial moment in time $(t = 0)$, $Y = ae^{k/g\ 0} = a$. The value for a may be obtained from income at the initial time, and the values for parameters k and g could be obtained from initial conditions. Consequently, from this information $Y(t) = ae^{k/g\ t}$ may readily be sketched as t is permitted to vary, as in Fig. 15-4. A similar sketch could be made of all three of the variables in equation (1) and (2),

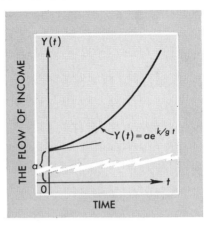

Fig. 15-4. The Equilibrium Flow of Income as an Increasing Function of Time.

where the interrelationship among the three is specified by

(6) $$I(t) = S(t) = kY(t) = kae^{k/g\ t}$$

Rewriting equation (5) of the previous section (Sect. 15.2),

$$\bar{Y} = \frac{\beta + kae^{k/g\ t}}{1 - \alpha}$$

Try to imagine how fantastically different the history of society would be if resources had been continuously and fully employed as represented by the flow of income in Fig. 15-4.

The acceleration principle. A simple version of the acceleration principle is a statement relating a so-called derived demand for investment goods to the acceleration of total sales, $dY(t)/dt$, where the flow variable $Y(t)$ corresponds to total sales or aggregate demand as a function of time. The flow of derived demand is increasing as long as the flow of

---

* There are several methods of solution, but we may solve equation (4) by the method of separation of the variables. For example, rearranging the terms, $\dfrac{1}{Y}\dfrac{dY}{dt} = \dfrac{k}{g}$.

Then integrating both sides of the latter expression, $\displaystyle\int \frac{1}{Y}\left(\frac{dY}{dt}\right) dt = \int \frac{k}{g}\, dt$, or $\displaystyle\int \frac{1}{Y}\, dY = \int \frac{k}{g}\, dt$. Continuing, $\log_e Y = \dfrac{k}{g} t + c$, c = constant of integration. Thus, by the definition of a logarithm, $Y = e^{k/g\ t+c}$, or $Y = e^c e^{k/g\ t}$, where e^c is some constant such as initial income (a). Therefore, $Y = ae^{k/g\ t}$, as in function (5).

sales is increasing at an increasing rate (i.e., $d^2Y(t)/dt^2 > 0$). As the rate of increase begins to decrease, the flow of derived investment decreases until it becomes zero as the flow of sales levels off and negative as the flow decreases.[6] Considering derived demand, for example, suppose that 100 machines valued at 10 million dollars are producing at a rate of output valued at 10 million dollars per year, and suppose further that the replacement demand for these machines is 5 per cent or 0.5 million dollars per annum. Now, let the demand for the output increase by 10 per cent to 11 million dollars per year. The new machines valued at one million dollars will be required in addition to replacement demand of five machines per year at 0.5 million dollars. There would be a 200 per cent increase in the demand for machines. Now, if sales only level off, the demand for machines would consist only of replacement demand. Derived demand would be zero. If demand then declined to the previous 10 million dollars per year, there would not even be the need for replacement demand. Derived demand would be negative.

The derivation of acceleration relationships is really quite simple, although there are many variations of the same basic theme. One of the most common forms of the acceleration relationship comes from two basic relationships:

(1)
$$I(t) = \frac{dK(t)}{dt}$$

where the flow of net investment at time t is equal to the rate of change in the total stock of capital goods (K) over time. And

(2)
$$g = \frac{K(t)}{Y(t)}$$

where the factor g is equal to the relationship that businessmen will strive to maintain between the total stock of capital goods (K) and their output or sales (Y) of both consumption and investment goods. Furthermore, in the latter instance, g is the proportion that businessmen try to maintain between their inventories and their sales of final goods, if our concern is only with net investment in inventories. It would also state the ratio that businessmen will try to maintain between total plant and equipment and the output or sale of final goods, if we are concerned with net investment in plant and equipment. In this event, the ratio g is sometimes referred to as the capital-to-output ratio or as the capital coefficient. In any event, the reliability of the relationship defined by (2) is affected in varying degrees, if businessmen at times passively allow their inventories to decline or accumulate, if they accommodate an increase in demand by using idle plant and equipment or by operating beyond the capacity defined by the equation, or if a linear equation inadequately explains the relationship between capital goods and sales (as a result, e.g., of certain economies accompanying the holding of larger inventories or greater plant capacity and equipment). But combining expressions (1) and (2) in one equation* defines one of the most common forms of the acceleration relationship. The equation, in fact, defines the net investment demand that is due entirely to the product of the factor g and the rate of change in the flow of total sales with respect to time (i.e., $dY(t)/dt$):

$$(3) \qquad\qquad I(t) = g\, \frac{dY(t)}{dt}$$

Clearly, from equation (3), a form of the acceleration principle is actually built into the Domar model by its second equation. In that model investment is simultaneously a constant proportion of the income flow variable by equations (1) and (3), and a function of the rate of change in the flow of income by equation (2). There, the accelerator only works for you, given the assumptions $k > 0$, $g > 0$ and $dY(t)/dt > 0$. Now, however, we wish to consider the effect of both an increasing and decreasing flow of income on so-called derived investment. We wish to do this independently of the requirement that investment is also some proportion of the flow of income, and with the view to understanding a possible source of instability in the economy.

The principle, as denoted by equation (2) in the Domar model, only without the restriction $dY(t)/dt > 0$, is shown in Fig. 15-5. The upper part of the illustration is simply a sketch of changes in the flow variable Y as a function of time. The slope of the tangent to the function $Y(t)$ times some constant is drawn in the lower part of the illustration. In fact, the latter part of the diagram shows derived investment. Compare, then, the two portions at $t = 1$, for $1 < t < 2$, at $t = 2$, for $2 < t < 3$, at $t = 3$, for $3 < t < 4$, at $t = 4$, and for $4 < t < 5$. At $t = 1$, $dY(t)/dt = 0$, and $g\, dY(t)/dt = 0$. For $1 < t < 2$, $dY(t)/dt < 1$ and $g\, dY(t)/dt < 0$. At $t = 2$, $d^2Y(t)/dt^2 = 0$, $dY(t)/dt < 0$ and $g\, dY(t)/dt =$ constant < 0; the flow of derived demand is a minimum. For $2 < t < 3$, $dY/(t)/dt < 0$, the flow of derived demand is negative (i.e., $g\, dY(t)/dt < 0$), but its rate of change is positive (i.e., $d^2Y(t)/dt^2 > 0$). At $t = 3$, $dY(t)/dt = 0$, and the flow of derived demand is zero (i.e., $g\, dY(t)/dt = 0$), but its rate of change is still positive (i.e., $d^2Y(t)/dt^2 > 0$). At $t = 4$, $dY(t)/dt$

---

* Multiplying the respective members of expression (1) by the opposite members of expression (2),

$$I(t)\, \frac{K(t)}{Y(t)} = g\, \frac{dK(t)}{dt}$$

Then dividing both sides by the factor $K(t)/Y(t)$, we get

$$I(t) = g\, \frac{dY(t)}{dt}$$

> 0, $g\, dY(t)/dt > 0$, and the flow of derived demand is a maximum (i.e., $d^2Y(t)/dt^2 = 0$). And so on. . . .

Thus there is a positive derived demand for investment goods as the flow of sales undergoes a positive acceleration, where derived demand is the product of some multiplier g and the change in the flow of sales.

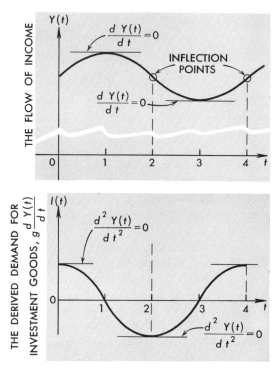

Fig. 15-5. The Acceleration Principle.

When the acceleration in sales is constant, derived demand is zero. And the flow of sales needs only to undergo deacceleration in order for derived demand to become negative.

Here it would appear, on the intuitive grounds, that the acceleration principle derives its name from the derivative of the flow of income with respect to time (i.e., $dY(t)/dt$), which is acceleration (Sect. 1.2). This appearance can be misleading, however, for in some contexts a factor such as that defined by expression (1) is called the accelerator.

15.4. Summary

In the complex world of modern financial institutions the link between aggregate income and aggregate demand is enjoined by a special group of financial institutions called financial intermediaries. There are flows of funds through the financial intermediaries between those who save and those who resort to external financing for their consumer and investment outlays. There is thus a separate identity for those who receive income and refrain from spending a portion of the income on consumption and those who employ the resulting saving in the form of investment. The analysis of the behavior of these consumers, in the former case, and investors, in the latter, leads to the formulation of separate functions for aggregate demand and aggregate output. The hypothesis that the slope of the consumption function is positive and less than one, then, assures the existence of a solution to the equations defining aggregate demand and aggregate payments to the factors of production for current output.

The condition underlying the functional relationship between consumption and income, on the one hand, and investment, on the other, is subject to change. The changes may give rise to changes in the level of national income. Changes in some of the conditions may give rise to changes in prices, and changes in some of the conditions may result in an equilibrium level of income at less than full employment. Indeed, some analysis concerning improvements in the technology of production, for example, would indicate the need to maintain persistently increasing flows of income just to assure full utilization of resources.

To complicate the matter of achieving a constant or persistently increasing flow of income, however, are changes in the state of underlying conditions. Expectations are among these. In addition, the acceleration principle indicates a possible mechanical source of instability once the level of total sales ceases to increase at an increasing rate. The principle indicates that derived demand may stimulate flows of expenditures and retard the flows. An increasing rate of sales supports the expansion of the flow of investment, and a decreasing rate dampens investment demand.

The changes in the underlying conditions, too, may give rise to changes in the income velocity of money via the definition of the income velocity of money. This suggests once again a relationship between the money supply and the levels of employment, output, and the average of prices.

References

1. See Joan Robinson, *Economic Philosophy* (Chicago: Aldine Publishing Company, 1963), esp. "The Keynesian Revolution," pp. 91-92.

2. For a discussion of these newer accounts and for further references, see "The Flow of Funds Accounts: A New Approach to Financial Markets Analysis," *The Journal of Finance*, May 1963, pp. 219-263.

3. See Raymond W. Goldsmith, *Financial Intermediaries in the American Economy Since 1900* (Princeton, N.J.: Princeton University Press, 1958).

Actually, the interpretation of the facts about the comparative growth of commercial banks and financial intermediaries since 1900 has been a subject for controversy. See Ezra Solomon, "The Issue of Financial Intermediaries," *Proceedings of the 1959 Conference on Savings and Residential Financing* (May 7 and 8, 1959), pp. 31-41.

4. Equations (6) and (6′) turn out to be of the same family as R. F. Kahn's famous employment multiplier. See R. F. Kahn, "The Relation of Home Investment to Unemployment," *Economic Journal*, June 1931, pp. 173-198.

5. E. D. Domar, "Capital Expansion, Rate of Growth, and Employment," *Econometrica*, April 1946, pp. 137-147.

6. For an early mathematical formulation of the principle, see Lloyd A. Metzler, "Nature and Stability of Inventory Cycles," *Review of Economic Statistics*, August 1941, pp. 113-129. For one of the first formulations, see John Maurice Clark, "Business Acceleration and the Law of Demand: A Technical Factor of Economic Cycles," *The Journal of Political Economy*, March 1917, pp. 217-235.

Appendix to Chapter 15

Financial Institutions: Some Taxonomic and Other Matters

There is a wide variety of financial institutions. Nearly all of them obtain funds from one group and dispense them to another; in this sense, they are all intermediaries of a type. Some, however, are more directly intermediate to the individual, on the one hand, who refrains from consumption and sets aside savings, and the investor, on the other, who makes a loan or places a new issue of securities in order to obtain funds for real capital outlays (Sect. 15.1). Others simply make markets and facilitate the exchange of financial assets that are already outstanding (Sect. 14.1 and 14.3). Still others, namely, commercial banks, may relate to both of these functions, and they may as well create funds for the investment process or absorb funds independently of their being in an intermediate position between savers and borrowers.

The matter of classifying financial institutions with respect to their position in relation to borrowers and savers is not without complications. In this appendix, nevertheless, we wish to review some classificatory schemes and settle upon a definition of financial intermediaries.

The classification of financial institutions (an over-all view). The financial system comprises the whole complex of financial institutions. These may be traditions and practices in finance or, in a more restricted sense, they may be thought of as financial enterprises. In this restricted sense, in which we presently consider financial institutions, a simple definition of "financial institutions" is "all enterprises, private and public, whose assets are predominantly claims and equities." [1] This definition is useful in describing an essential feature of such institutions, but it is of little help in drawing exact lines to facilitate the classification of many types of institutions. Still, three fairly standard classifications have arisen: (1) Raymond Goldsmith's enumeration of financial intermediaries, (2) that pertaining to the financial sectors in the flow-of-funds accounts, and

(3) the Commission on Money and Credit's breakdown of private financial institutions.

An examination of these classifications, however, suggests the prospect of a variety of ways of grouping or excluding financial institutions according to certain characteristics or specialties. Among others, we might cross-classify financial institutions in each of the following ways:

(1) By earning asset specialties—loans versus securities, business versus consumer loans, various maturities and degrees of risk versus others.

(2) By the nature of their liabilities and capital accounts—degrees of substitutability for money, fixed dollar amounts versus variable dollar amounts, deposits versus shares or equities, current versus deferred liabilities.

(3) By legal form of organization—stock versus mutual financial institutions, Federally versus state-chartered institutions, private versus public institutions.

(4) By regulatory status—regulated by Federal versus state authorities; regulated versus unregulated institutions; regulation of liquidity, lending and investment policies, liabilities and capital, payment of interest and dividends.

(5) By cyclical characteristics—stability of earnings from asset portfolios, stability of the structure of liabilities, stability of the amount of earning assets relative to the amount of deposits, stability of values or liquidity.

(6) By economic function—role in the payments mechanism, or by role in the saving-investment process.

From among these possible classifications our primary concern is with the fifth and sixth. The fifth is crucial to the operation of monetary policy and will be emphasized later (Sect. 25.4), and the sixth is crucial in the present appendix to the development of an understanding of the nature of savings intermediaries and savings intermediation. However, these possible classifications are not unrelated to the preceding classificatory schemes.

Savings intermediaries. The term "intermediaries" has been used in two quite distinct senses. These we wish to recognize, prior to accepting the more common usage for our purpose, and we wish to elaborate on what the definition of the term fails to suggest. We then proceed to outline the major financial intermediaries and to observe some of their similarities and differences.

Savings intermediaries (some terminology). Goldsmith has used the term "financial intermediary" to denote any sort of middleman or agent in the purchase and sale of financial assets (or financial claims, depending on the point of view). By this criterion, security brokers and dealers (Sect. 14.1) and mutual funds as outlined below are properly just as much intermediaries as are commercial banks or savings-and-loan associations. Most economists, on the other hand, use the term in a much more restricted sense. They use it, as we have (Sect. 15.1), to indicate certain financial institutions which stand between consumers, businesses, and governmental units having saving available out of present and past incomes and other consumers, businesses, and governmental units wishing to finance expenditures in excess of present income. Such institutions provide financial assets to the former and acquire financial claims against the latter.

Despite widespread controversy over some of the analysis and conclusions with respect to financial intermediaries, much of the terminology

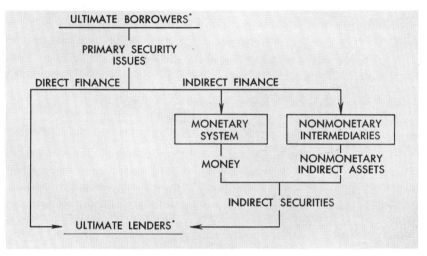

Fig. 15-A. Financial Intermediaries, Ex-Post and Gurley-Shaw Terminology. * Nonfinancial economic units, i.e., consumers, business firms, and government units. Adopted from John G. Gurley, "Liquidity and Financial Institutions in the Postwar Period" Study Paper No. 14, U.S. Congress, Joint Economic Committee, Study of Employment, Growth, and Price Levels (Washington, D.C.: Supt. of Documents, 1960), p. 21.

introduced by John G. Gurley and Edward S. Shaw[2] has gained acceptance in such contexts as the present one. Thus some of their terms are set forth in Fig. 15-A. There, financial intermediaries (including the monetary system—commercial banks and Federal Reserve banks) are conceived as buyers of primary securities (loan paper, stocks, and bonds) from ultimate borrowing units (consumers, business firms, and government) and issuers of indirect securities (money and savings deposits or shares) to ultimate lending units. This, then, is the sense in which certain institutions are financial intermediaries.

However, the view of financial intermediaries implied by the definition is necessarily an *ex post* picture of financial institutions, as we saw earlier (Sect. 15.1). It tells us little about the *ultimate* source of the lending power of financial institutions, and, in fact, it may mislead us into believing that the monetary system is limited in its activities to the funds supplied by depositors. This would seem, at times, to be the case when one looks backward over previous occurrences, but only nonmonetary intermediaries are so limited in the sources of their lending power, as contrasted with commercial banks that have the capacity to create a medium of payment (Sect. 3.3). Indeed, most of the money portion of the flow of funds emanating from the institutions outlined in Fig. 15-A is initially extended to ultimate borrowers in payment for primary securities rather than to ultimate lenders. Ultimate borrowers are the ones who spend funds for consumption, investment, or governmental purposes and thus generate income. This is how funds and money balances get into the hands of ultimate lenders (or savers).

Savings intermediaries (their classification). Let us now try to see what sorts of financial enterprises ought properly to be regarded as intermediaries. In doing this, let us simplify matters by excluding government lending agencies and government insurance and retirement funds and concentrating instead on private institutions.

What, then, shall we do with institutions performing as brokers and dealers in private and government securities, commercial paper, mortgages, receivables (factors), and other debt instruments? These institutions really serve primarily as agents in the purchase and sale of marketable debt, and they seldom are the repository for net new savings from outside sources. Their main function is to provide an efficient mechanism for the redistribution of holdings of old primary securities and use only temporarily their own capital and outside funds in the marketing of new primary securities. This group of firms, then, could be found as middlemen between groups involved in indirect means of financing, as well as between individual members of such a group.

In some respects, investment companies or so-called mutual funds are similar, although the turnover of the securities they handle is usually much lower than for brokers and dealers. Investment companies comprise financial institutions that, for the most part, purchase outstanding issues of securities with the proceeds obtained from the sale of securities. They are of two types: open-end companies and closed-end companies.[3] The open-end companies sell nonmarketable shares, although the shares may be resold to the company. The value of the shares in such a case is based on a proportion of the value of the investment company's own portfolio. When one resells the securities to the company, the company usually must liquidate a portion of its own shares. Conversely, when one buys securities in such a company, the company is then in a position to expand its portfolio. Such a fund, from the shareholders point of view, serves as a means of relegating the decision to invest in various securities to so-called expert managers, although the performance of mutual funds has been unimpressive by comparison with market averages.

The closed-end companies, on the other hand, have a fixed amount of marketable shares outstanding. Usually the value of these shares depends on the value of the securities held by the closed-end fund, but the total value of the securities outstanding has usually been below the total value of the securities held by the fund. Such funds simply provide the opportunity for the diversification of risk among a group of securities.

Clearly, investment companies are not intermediaries between the ultimate lenders and the ultimate borrowers in the purest sense. Still, the fact that open-end companies may issue new securities reveals some of the complexities in distinguishing financial intermediaries. These complexities are evidenced, too, by the variety of such terms used in attempts to distinguish intermediaries as thrift institutions, deposit-type financial institutions, and institutions with fixed-dollar obligations.

Savings intermediaries (the major ones). Despite the complexities in identifying intermediaries and partly on the grounds of expediency in securing statistics, the institutions most frequently listed as conforming to the financial intermediary type include commercial banks, mutual savings banks, savings-and-loan associations, credit unions, life insurance companies, and corporate pension funds. These may be shown along with the composition of the assets for the respective institutions in percentages for year-end 1961, as follows:

Per cent of Total Assets

	Cash Ac- counts	Real Estate Loans	U.S. Govt. Secur- ities	Other Loans	Other Secur- ities	Other Assets	Total
Commercial banks	20.3	10.9	23.9	34.0	8.6	2.4	100.0
Mutual savings banks	2.2	67.5	14.4	1.1	13.4	1.5	100.0
Savings-and- loan associations	4.0	83.8	6.4	—	5.8	—	100.0
Credit unions	°	6.5°°	°	69.1	°	24.4	100.0
Life insurance companies	1.1	34.9	4.8	4.5†	47.2	4.3	100.0 ·
Corporate pen- sion funds	1.5	2.8	6.4	°	85.1	4.2	100.0

NOTE: Components may not add to totals, due to rounding.

SOURCES: Board of Governors of the Federal Reserve System, Credit Union National Association, Institute of Life Insurance, and Securities and Exchange Commission.

° Unknown (residual included in other assets).

°° Assumes difference between total loans and installment loans represents real estate loans.

† Policy loans only. Other miscellaneous loans included in other assets.

Note that the latter data reveal the differences in the preferences of the various institutions for cash assets and various kinds of loans and investment in rather broad categories. The ratios (expressed as percentages) of cash to total assets and the predominance of shorter- or longer-term loans and investments are, of course, closely related to the nature of customers' deposits or shares in the institutions. For example, insurance companies are less likely than banks to have to adjust to a withdrawal of assets or a cash payment in exchange for a liability, and on this basis insurance companies would be expected to maintain low cash positions and to specialize in long-term loans and investments. In fact, at year-end 1961 life insurance companies held 1.1 per cent of their assets in cash. Also, at that time, over 60 per cent of their holdings of United States government securities had a maturity of over five years. Corporate pension funds on the same date held nearly half their assets in corporate bonds and more than one-third in common stock.

With respect to credit unions, only little is revealed of the details of their business. In principle, they make loans to members for a wide range of purposes from the savings provided by other members. The bulk of their earning assets and nearly 70 per cent of their total assets are in the form of installment loans to members, and these loans in turn would comprise about 10 per cent of total consumer installment credit in the United States at year-end 1961, as reported in the *Credit Union Yearbook* (1962). Somewhat over half of the number of credit unions is made up of groups of industrial, governmental, and communication and public utility employees. Nearly three-fourths of the credit unions held assets under $200,000, at year-end 1961.

Mutual savings banks and savings-and-loan associations are quite similar, in their investment activities, although their geographical distribution, mostly for historical reasons, is very different. As one writer emphasized in reference to their respective functions:

> . . . The savings banks were begun here out of a desire to provide working people with a place where they could keep their money with safety. On the other hand, savings [and loan] associations were started in this country in order to provide a means whereby people could borrow money with which to buy or build a home. . . . Thus, today we see savings banks primarily as savings institutions, but heavily invested in mortgages, and we consider the major function of our [savings and loan] associations to be the provision of home mortgage funds through a savings program not unlike that of the savings banks.[4]

As the above data show, savings-and-loan associations, sometimes called "building-and-loan associations," are highly specialized in mortgage lending, while mutual savings banks specialize primarily in mortgages and secondarily in United States government and other securities. In the early 1960's savings-and-loan assets were about twice the assets of mutual savings banks.

Further, with respect to savings banks and savings-and-loan associations, some rather crude estimates of annual deposit and share turnover (i.e., velocity, or the ratio of withdrawals to total deposits) show share turnover at 0.26 for savings bank deposits and at 0.30 for savings-and-loan shares for the period 1955-1959.[5] These estimates contrast with a 1957 estimate of 0.48 for time deposit turnover at commercial banks,[6] and a turnover in demand deposits of from 26 to 70 times, depending on location. All of this means that the average dollar of savings banks deposits, savings-and-loan shares, time deposits at commercial banks, and so on is withdrawn about once every four years, three years, and one-half year, respectively. Consequently, apart from regulatory differences, we would expect an increasing order of liquidity in the asset structure for savings banks, savings-and-loan associations, and commercial banks, respectively.

Summary. A financial institution is a business enterprise whose assets and, thus, sources of earnings are primarily in the form of claims and equities, rather than buildings and grounds, equipment, or inventories of goods. While there is no one universally accepted scheme for classifying financial institutions into various types, some of the differences are derived from two meanings given to the term "financial intermediary." To some, this denotes any middleman in a transaction involving the purchase and sale of financial assets. To others, "intermediary" denotes a middleman in the saving-investment process, one which accepts new saving for certain periods of time from ultimate lenders, and channels the funds into new investment when it purchases new claims against ultimate borrowers. Contrasted with an intermediary according to this interpretation is the possibility of a pure brokerage or agency function of other financial institutions. In principle, such institutions buy and resell financial assets for rapid resale to or for their customers. In practice, it is really impossible to find a "broker" or an "intermediary" in the purest sense of these terms. To be a pure broker, a financial institution would need both to engage simultaneously in purchases and resales and to deal only in previously existing financial assets, as contrasted with such new ones as new issues of securities. To be a pure intermediary, a financial institution would need to receive and retain only new savings and to buy and retain only new financial assets. A stock brokerage house, perhaps, comes close to the one extreme, and a savings-and-loan association, to the other. But even a stock brokerage firm may, for example, carry both a securities portfolio and credit balances in customers' accounts and may plow back into the business its own savings. Similarly, a savings-and-loan association may buy existing financial assets and merely channel new saving into the hands of dissavers or indirectly into the hands of ultimate borrowers.

Partly on principle and partly because of the availability of statistical information, certain private financial institutions are frequently singled out as being of the dominant intermediary type, although they are sometimes described as deposit-type or thrift institutions. These are commercial and savings banks, savings-and-loan associations, credit unions, life insurance companies, and corporate pension funds. There are, however, important differences among these institutions with regard to asset composition and, related to this, the turnover of deposits or savings shares.

References

1. Joseph Aschheim, *Techniques of Monetary Control* (Baltimore: Johns Hopkins Press, 1961), p. 112.

2. See, in particular, *Money in a Theory of Finance* (Washington, D.C.: The Brookings Institution, 1960), pp. 363-364.

3. On investment companies, see Securities Research Unit of the Wharton School of Finance and Commerce, *A Study of Mutual Funds* (Washington, D.C.: U.S. Government Printing Office, 1962). This study was done for the Securities and Exchange Commission.

4. W. O. DuVall, "Savings Associations and Savings Banks," *Directors Digest*, U.S. Savings and Loan League, August 1960, p. 1.

5. Stephen H. Axilrod, "Liquidity and Public Policy," *Federal Reserve Bulletin*, October 1961, p. 1166. The National Association of Mutual Savings Banks estimates the ratios for 1961 to be 0.28 and 0.27, respectively.

6. See George Garvy, *Debits and Clearings Statistics and Their Use* (Washington, D.C.: Board of Governors of the Federal Reserve System, 1959), p. 33, footnote 19.

16

The Price Level and Changes in Costs

> If money-rates of earnings were uniformly fixed in relation to output, being as it were piece-wages, so that they tended to increase or decrease automatically with every change in the coefficient of efficiency, then we should need to add nothing to what we have written above about the causation of price changes (John Maynard Keynes, *A Treatise on Money* [1930]).

We considered previously a variety of different sets of price averages (Chap. 5). In that instance, we described the general price level as the average of all prices including those in the financial markets, the market for the factors of production, the market for second-hand goods, and the market for the output of goods and services. In this chapter, however, we deal principally with the average of prices in the latter market—the market for the current output of goods and services. In accordance with popular usage, we presently refer to this average as the price level. We examine this price level in relation to several models, including the earlier national income model (Sect. 15.2), and in relation to inflation (deflation), various institutional arrangements, and business costs.

In the present instance, "inflation" ("deflation") is defined as a rise (decline) in the implicit GNP deflator (Sect. 5.4). The latter definition came to be a common one in the 1950's, but there are other possible definitions.[1]

The relevant institutional arrangements are those which, at times, affect particular (relative) prices and possibly the price level. An example of such arrangements is the collective wage agreements between labor and management as practiced in the 1950's. These often involve escalator clauses (Sect. 5.3) that provide for automatic wage changes and consequently a change in business costs in response to changes in a price index. They also involved other institutional arrangements that affect relative prices, such as automatic wage increases calling for a specific cents-per-hour or percentage increase in wages each year.

In the three decades following the 1920's there was a lapse of interest in price level changes, but in the 1950's there was a revival. The interest in the latter decade came to focus on a special type of inflation—namely, cost inflation, as defined below. In the late 1950's, too, there was an additional revival of interest in the role of prices with respects to equilibrium in the balance of international payments and the stability of gold flows (Sect. 6.3) and foreign exchange reserves. For the present, we consider domestic prices only without further reference to international considerations.

16.1. Monetary Analysis and Price Level Changes: The Main Stream

The main stream of analysis pertaining to price level changes, defined in one way or another, has been centered about the quantity theory of money (Sect. 5.1) and, in the recent generation, the quantity theory and the aggregate of expenditures (Sect. 15.2).

The quantity theory of money. Already much has been set forth about the quantity theory money, the related definition of the income velocity of money, and analyses pertaining to price level changes. We have, for example, reviewed the evolution of this approach. Also we noted how prices and/or output may vary in response to various combinations of changes in the money supply and, therefore, the velocity of the stock of money, as well as in response to changes in the demand for money and, therefore, the velocity of money.

Much still remains to be said about analyses pertaining to the quantity theory (e.g., Sect. 25.4 and 26.5) but, for the present, we develop more fully the aggregate expenditure analysis pertaining to price level changes.

Aggregate expenditures and demand inflation (deflation). To set forth more fully the earlier (Sect. 15.2) aggregate expenditure analysis of changes in the price level [i.e., the average of prices (P) for current output (O)], we proceed from some initial set of equilibrium conditions to a subsequent set of short-run equilibrium conditions. These we denote in Fig. 16-1 where

$\overline{Y}_t$ is the initial equilibrium level of income $(Y_t = P_t O_t)$,

$\overline{F}_t$ is the initial level of full employment (Sect. 15.1),

A_t is the initial equilibrium point,

$\overline{Y}_{t+1}$ is the subsequent equilibrium level of equilibrium following a shift in aggregate demand [i.e., $C + I$ as denoted earlier (Sect. 15.2)] from $C_t + I_t$ to $C_{t+1} + I_{t+1}$, and so on.

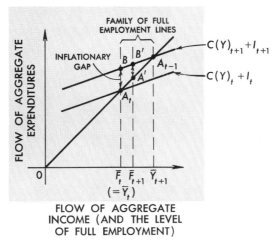

Fig. 16-1. National Aggregate Expenditure and Demand Inflation (Deflation).

Note, now, what happens following an upward shift in demand by an amount represented by the geometric distance $\overline{A_t B}$. This distance is the initial inflationary gap, and the extent of the inducement for price increases is the product of this gap and the earlier (Sect. 15.2) expenditure multiplier:

(1) $$\left(\text{i.e., } \overline{A_t B}\, \frac{1}{1 - dC/dY} = \overline{Y}_{t+1} - \overline{Y}_t\right)$$

The increase in the demand for output, however, need not go entirely into price increases. As prices and the demand for the factors of production, particularly labor, rise (i.e., as the job vacancies exceed the number of involuntary unemployed), the number of workers drawn into the labor force increases. Some may call this over-full employment. Housewives who may otherwise anticipate greater difficulties finding jobs enter the labor force, young girls are more likely to anticipate careers, possibly in combination with marriage, the number of students dropping out of school may increase, some prospective students become workers, others take on a second job, and so on until the labor force has increased from, e.g., $\overline{F}_t$ to $\overline{F}_{t+1}$.

Thus part of the initial inducement for price increases is met by an increase in output as the level of full employment rises. The extent of the inducement for a price increase, consequently is narrowed from that defined by equation (1); i.e.,

$$(\overline{A_t B} - \overline{A'B'})\, \frac{1}{1 - dC/dY} = \Delta O$$

and

$$\overline{A'B'}\, \frac{1}{1 - dC/dY} = \Delta Y - \Delta O,$$

where $\Delta Y - \Delta O$ is the rise in income in current prices that is due to the rise in the average of prices for output in constant prices.

Note that the level of full employment $\overline{OF}$ is some increasing function of aggregate demand $C + I$, just as the level of employment is a function of aggregate demand, i.e.,

$$\overline{OF} = \overline{OF}_t + f(C + I)$$

where, as an hypothesis,

$$0 < \frac{d\overline{OF}}{d(C + I)} < 1$$

Here we have illustrated the meaning of "demand inflation," which is a result of an increase in aggregate demand. The converse of the illustration would be demand deflation, and the inflationary gap would instead become a deflationary gap. As unemployment rises (i.e., as the job openings fall below the involuntarily unemployed), forces operate to reduce the size of the labor force and wages may or may not fall, depending on the stickiness of downward wage adjustments.

Given a demand level in current dollar terms in the above model, a number of additional economic phenomena may conceivably be illustrated—some pertaining to full employment, technological change, output, and prices in particular. For one, suppose there is a change in the capacity to produce as a result of labor-saving technological changes (Sect. 15.2). What then? The output level for full employment moves to the right, and it then becomes necessary for the demand in constant prices to increase, also as stated earlier (Sect. 15.3), just in order to maintain full employment. This could result from a lower average for prices (P) and an increase in output (O) such that income in constant prices increases. In such a case, the benefits of the technology would be passed on in the form of lower prices, increased demand for current output, and a rise in real income.

For another, suppose a change in wage rates effected by organized labor in mass production pursuits stimulates a wider use of technological devices of the labor-saving variety. What then? Unemployment could increase, and, in terms of the variables of the present model, this could take place without reducing income in current prices. The model will accommodate any variety of combinations of changes in the variables, including P, Y, O, F, C, I and dC/dY. The various combinations may follow from additional hypotheses, from the results of other models, including the subsequent notion of a cost push inflation (Sect. 16.3). The point is not to emphasize any overly extensive usefulness of the model for explaining such diverse phenomena. It is, instead, to emphasize the consistency of the model with any combination of changes pertaining to the variables in question.

A similar model to the above one may be stated such that the vertical and horizontal axes in Fig. 16-1 pertain only to aggregate expenditure and aggregate income, respectively, in constant prices. A difficulty, however, arises with respect to an equilibrium price level. For example, an upward shift in demand creates an inflationary gap, but there is no rise in the expenditure and income variables in current price terms to facilitate the attainment of the new equilibrium, such as A_{t+1} in Fig. 16-1. Presumably, "inflation continues indefinitely as long as the gap persists." [2]

Actually, we should expect three important differences between the extent of demand inflation and a simple multiplier increase in income where the analysis assumes only output changes, the average of prices constant: [3]

(1) An increase in expenditures at full employment which causes the price level to rise induces defensive reactions from those whose money incomes are fixed or lag behind price level increases. A so-called "inflationary spiral" is a popular conception for this process. A simple multiplier process primarily involves increases in output, rather than prices, so there are no induced defensive reactions.

(2) Multiplier changes in real output and income may proceed in either direction and are reversible; inflationary processes, at least in the short run, proceed only upward and tend to be irreversible. That is, once higher prices are attained, a fall in expenditures will cause little reduction in prices, with primary impact on output and employment.

(3) Multiplier processes are self-limiting, except in extreme cases of multiplier-accelerator interaction (Sect. 15.3). In other words, a change in expenditures leads to damped changes in income in the direction of a new equilibrium. Inflationary processes, on the other hand, may or may not be self-limiting.

16.2. Price Level Changes, Period Analysis, and "Guideposts" for Wage Changes

Demand inflation (deflation) as outlined above could also be illustrated in terms of saving and investment schedules (Sect. 15.2). But we introduce an identity from period analysis[4] instead. This permits us to deal quite explicitly with the relationship between changes in prices, wages, and output, as well as with that between price level changes, the notion of an imbalance in planned magnitudes for saving and investment, and output. Later, we relate changes in wages and the average productivity of labor to results deduced from this identity. And, finally, the latter changes are related to noninflationary guideposts for wage increases.

A Swedish identity. The identity[5] in terms of flow variables in current dollar terms follows:*

$$(1) \qquad I_0 - S_0 = (Y_1 - Y_0) + (I_0 - I_1),$$

where 0 and 1 are subscripts denoting *ex ante* (planned or expected before an event) and *ex post* (or after the event), respectively;

$I_0 - S_0$ are planned investment and planned saving, respectively;
$Y_1 - Y_0$ is unexpected income (or saving, i.e., $S_1 - S_0$, $S_1 > S_0$); and
$I_0 - I_1$ is unintended disinvestment ($I_0 > I_1$)—and, if negative ($I_0 < I_1$), it represents unintended investment.

Next, dividing both sides of the identity by output O:

$$(1a) \qquad \frac{I_0 - S_0}{O} = \frac{Y_1}{O} - \frac{Y_0}{O} + \frac{I_0 - I_1}{O},$$

where $\dfrac{Y_1}{O}$, the first term in the right-hand member, is the GNP deflator (Sect. 5.3) or price level.

Now we have

$$(1b) \qquad P_1 = \frac{Y_0}{O} - \frac{I_0 - I_1}{O} + \frac{I_0 - S_0}{O}$$

and rearrange this slightly

$$(1c) \qquad P_1 = \frac{Y_0 - I_0 + I_1}{O} + \frac{I_0 - S_0}{O}$$

Next, we work on the transformation, and recall the definition $Y_0 = C_0 + S_0$, and assume consumption plans are carried out, i.e., $C_0 = C_1$, so $Y_0 = C_1 + S_0$. Then making this substitution in equation (1c)

$$(1d) \qquad P_1 = \frac{C_1 + S_0 - I_0 + I_1}{O} + \frac{I_0 - S_0}{O}$$

Rearrange terms again

$$(1e) \qquad P_1 = \frac{C_1 + I_1 - (I_0 - S_0)}{O} + \frac{I_0 - S_0}{O}$$

By definition $Y_1 = C_1 + I_1$, so making this substitution in (1e) yields equation (2):[6]

$$(2) \qquad P_1 = \frac{Y_1 - (I_0 - S_0)}{O} + \frac{I_0 - S_0}{O}$$

* The simplest derivation of the identity in question from other identities is as follows:

If $Y_0 \equiv C_0 + S_0$, $Y_1 \equiv C_1 + S_1$, and $S_1 \equiv I_1$, then $Y_o \equiv Y_1 - I_1 + S_0$.

Adding I_0 to both sides of the latter expression and rearranging terms:

$$\underbrace{I_0 - S_0}_{\substack{ex\ ante\ \text{investment-}\\ \text{saving gap}}} = \underbrace{Y_1 - Y_0}_{\substack{\text{unexpected income}\\ \text{(or saving)}}} + \underbrace{I_0 - I_1}_{\substack{\text{unintended}\\ \text{disinvestment}}}$$

Note that, with respect to equation (2), the second term of the right-hand member deals with price level changes resulting from imbalances in planned investment and planned saving and from changes in output. Note, further, that the first term of that member deals with price level changes after a netting out of those due to the variables in the second terms. Finally, note that, if there are no imbalances in the equation (i.e., $I_0 = S_0$, $Y_1 = O$ or O_1), P_1 will be equal to unity (or, expressing prices for base year $= 100$, rather than unity, $P_1 = 1.00 \times 100$).

Below, we deal with each of the terms in the right-hand member of equation (2) and the price level changes associated with each.

Planned investment and planned saving. The inflationary situation is shown in Fig. 16-2. In that illustration the flows for planned investment and planned saving are shown on the vertical axis, and the flow of aggregate income (Y_0) is shown on the horizontal axis. Investment schedules are shown at time zero (t) and, following a shift in planned investment (Sect. 17.2), at time one ($t + 1$).

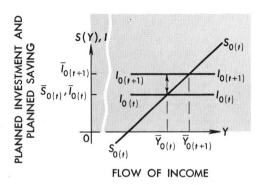

Fig. 16-2. *Planned Investment and Planned Saving: The Inflationary Situation.*

The shift in investment shows the increase in income $\overline{Y}_0$ following the upward shift in planned investment. Note that, through the term $(I_0 - S_0)/O$ in equation (2), planned investment exceeds planned saving (i.e., $I_0 > S_0$) by the amount of the heavy arrow, and the amount of the shift's contribution to a price level change in equation (2) depends on the change in output. If this is the only source of inflation, then the first term in the right-hand member of equation (2) is one, i.e., $[Y_1 - (I_0 - S_0)]/O = 1$ or 1.00×100, and the only rise in P_1 is due to the imbalance in planned investment after allowance for the change in output in real or constant price terms. However, price level changes resulting from the imbalance in planned investment and planned saving could cause Y_1 to rise in excess of the rise resulting from an imbalance in plans with respect to investment and saving. This could follow automatically from the demand inflation as a result of a widespread presence of escalator clauses in wage contracts.

The converse of the above shift in investment plans could be shown to illustrate a deflationary situation. Illustrating deflation is left as an exercise.

The wage bill and price level changes. To further illustrate the role of wages in inflation (deflation), we may focus on the major component of Y_1 in equation (2). It is the wage bill—WN, where

W is wages in current dollar or money terms, and
N is the number of employed workers.

We have the factor WN/O, or dividing both the numerator and denominator by N,

$$\frac{W}{O/N},$$

where O/N is the average productivity of labor.
Thus, from the ratio

$$\frac{W}{O/N},$$

an increase in wages in excess of an increase in the average productivity of labor contributes more to income in current dollars (i.e., Y_1) than to output. Consequently, the latter combination of changes causes the price level defined by equation (2) to rise. Here we simply emphasize the importance of the wage component in inflation. It could also contribute to deflation, or serve as an offset to other inflationary forces, where average productivity exceeded the increase in wages. This type of analysis becomes of special interest (Part VIII) when we recognize price stability or maximum purchasing power as a goal to be achieved by a policy of credit ease or tightness.

Changes in the average productivity of labor: a guide for wage changes. We have noted that an increase in wages in excess of the average productivity of labor could contribute to a rise in the price level. Over time, of course, technological changes (Sect. 15.2) could contribute to a rise in the average productivity of labor and, therefore, given wages, a decline in the price level. In this framework, wages may even rise and not contribute to a rise in the price level, if the average productivity of labor increases at the same rate.

In view of the relationship between wages, productivity, and the price level, and recognizing price stability or maximum purchasing power as an economic goal, several recommendations have been made from different quarters. The Committee for Economic Development concluded as follows:

> *Wage rates on the average should rise as fast as total (national) output per man-hour, which has been between 2 and 3 per cent a year.* The average rate of increase of wages could be higher if the average rate of increase of output per man-hour were higher. Wages should rise more than the average where labor is scarce, less where it is in surplus supply. Wage rate increases in particular industries should not be determined by increases in output per man-hour in those particular industries but should reflect the increase in *national* output per man-hour.[7]

Following this lead, the 1962 Economic Report of the President and the 1963 Report publicized guideposts for noninflationary wage behavior.[8] The general guide for wage increases in those reports is that "the rate of increase in wage rates (including fringe benefits) in each industry be equal to the trend rate of over-all productivity increase." Continuing, the 1963 Report said:

> Under these conditions the gain from increases in productivity throughout the economy would be shared between wage and nonwage incomes by allowing each to grow at the same percentage rate. Each sector of economic life would share in the gains of advancing productivity. The qualifications call for faster increases in wage rates in an industry that (a) would otherwise be unable to attract sufficient labor to meet demands for its products, or (b) currently pays wage rates exceptionally low compared with those earned elsewhere by labor of similar ability. Symmetrically, increases in wage rates would fall short of the general guide rate in an industry that (a) could not provide employment for its entire labor force even in generally prosperous times; or (b) currently pays wage rates exceptionally high compared with those earned elsewhere by labor of similar ability.

The Report also included similar guideposts for prices in the respective industries.

16.3. Cost (or Supply) Inflation

In the 1950's, economists and public officials reviewed some old ideas about inflationary price changes other than those ultimately resulting from demand forces, money supply changes, and so on (Sec. 16.1). Such terms as "the new inflation" and "cost push inflation" were used, and the discussions accompanying their use pointed to the widespread prevalence of economic pressure groups (including labor unions, trade associations, and others) and the results of "free collective bargaining" as being relevant to "the new inflation." A high point for such discussions followed experiences accompanying the 1957-1958 recession, viewed by some as "a classic case of wage-push inflation with its attendant unemployment effects." Output and income declined, at that time, and the GNP deflator increased somewhat. For example, from the fourth quarter of 1957 to the first quarter of 1958 the GNP deflator (1954 = 100) rose from 109.4 to 110.2, seasonally adjusted output in constant prices declined from 401.2 billion dollars per annum to 391, and seasonally adjusted income in current prices declined from 438.9 billion to 431—all indicating a rise in prices at a time of a decline in the effective demand for goods and services. (Of course, one would not wish to place too much emphasis on the preciseness of measures for output and income, but, where the errors in the estimates are likely to be constant, the directions of change revealed by the estimates warrant more confidence on the part of the investigator than the initial measures.) Also, in the 1957-1960 cycle, unemployment reached a cyclical high for the postwar years through 1960. Measuring from cyclical peak to peak, unemployment had averaged 4.2 per cent for the 1948-1953 cycle, 4.4 per cent for the 1953-1957 cycle, and 5.9 per cent for the 1957-1960 cycle. (The unemployment rates are shown later in Fig. 24-5.)

The inflation literature growing out of the period was described as being chaotic. The American Economic Association sponsored a survey of that literature by two writers who described their survey as "more of a guide through chaos."[9] According to the survey, analysts disagreed over the presence of a cost push phenomena,[10] and the reports by empiricists failed to settle many controversial issues pertaining to the existence and analysis of cost inflation.[11] Nevertheless, we shall review at the micro level the notion of such a thing as cost push inflation, examine some of its features at the macro level, and note the conclusions from one[12] of the many studies published in the late 1950's and early 1960's of the dilemma of rising prices and unemployment. The dilemma is important for the study of monetary policy, as emphasized later (Sect. 24.3 and 25.1), because of the prospect of the inconsistency of goals confronting the monetary officials—i.e., maximum employment and purchasing power, and a price level consistent with international objectives (Sect. 23.3 and 24.3). Preliminary to the more systematic study of monetary policy, however, we need to deal at greater length with the effects of, and the relationships between, monetary and fiscal policy (Chap. 17-19). We also need to understand more clearly the initial income model (Sect. 15.1), and the role of price changes in it, and some other models.

Cost push and demand pull (the micro level). The notions of a cost push and a demand pull on prices were not entirely absent from our earlier (Sect. 16.2) discussion of the price level defined by equation (2). In terms of equation (2), we could think of any price changes resulting from an imbalance in planned investment and planned saving in relation to output as being due to demand forces. The causes of the other price changes associated with the term $[Y_1 - (I_0 - S_0)]/O$ then could be thought of as being due to a cost push forward into higher prices or sticky prices and wages—i.e., a failure of prices to adjust downward in response to declining cost or the failure of cost to adjust downward in response to a declining demand for the factors of production.

To illustrate these price, cost, demand, and supply changes, let us state a few assumptions and definitions. First, think of an industry producing a single product with a single profit maximizing firm, and an industry-wide union. Next, let us define total revenue R and total Q (net of any allowance for the cost of funds for asset expansion) both as some function of the product x, such that

$$\frac{dR}{dx} = R'_t,$$

the marginal revenue curve at the initial time, and $R'' < 0$, R/x is average revenue or price per unit [and it may be shown that $d(R/x)/dx < 0$ since $R'' < 0$], and

$$\frac{dQ}{dx} = Q'_t,$$

the marginal cost or supply curve (including extra cost pertaining to the expansion of productive capacity) at the initial time. The maximum profit Π ($\Pi = R - Q$) output condition, consequently, becomes $\Pi' = R' - Q' = 0$, or $R' = Q'$, and we let the various curves and the initial equilibrium output $\bar{x}_t$ be denoted in Fig. 16-3. Thus, if labor costs per unit of output rise, marginal cost rises so as to effect a parallel shift in the curve from Q'_t to Q'_{t+1}. Under the conditions, the rise in labor cost will effect a higher price or average revenue (i.e., R/x) since the value for marginal revenue rises as sales or production decline from $\bar{x}_t$ to $\bar{x}_{t+1}$. This would be one form of a cost push forward into prices.

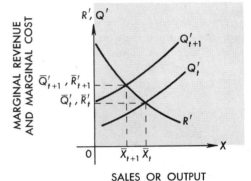

Fig. 16-3. A Hypothetical Example of Cost Push at the Micro Level.

The forward shift could be offset by an improvement in technology that reduced the cost of producing output x and therefore shifts the supply curve downward. For some, this combination of changes and offsetting change would not be an example of a cost push, but in a partial derivative sense (i.e., change in cost with respect to a change in the unit cost of labor) it would be such anyway. The forward shift could be accompanied by a similar forward shift in demand (or the average revenue curve) and, therefore, the marginal revenue curve, if demand conditions were improving from the firm's point of view. In this case, we would have a mixed demand, cost push type of inflation. And, further, if we view profit as a part of the means for effecting the payment for funds for asset expansion and as a cost affecting the marginal cost curve, then we could also think of a profit push[13] as the latter cost increased.

To sum up, the notion of the push is that prices rise because of an upward shift in the curve Q', and the notion of a pull, as in demand pull, is

that prices rise because of a forward shift in the average revenue curve
(i.e., R/x) or, in the present case, the marginal revenue curve (i.e., R').
In this framework, the Federal Reserve exerts a restraining effect via
tight credit and the riskless rental value of money (Sect. 4.2) by contributing to a cost or "profit" push in the above instance where the
marginal cost curve also reflects the cost of funds for asset expansion.
The Federal Reserve in its efforts, however, could be attempting to shift
the demand curve downward at the same time it raised the cost curve,
possibly with the view to restricting expansion in plant capacity and
output (and, therefore, employment), and weakening the bargaining
position of labor unions seeking higher wages. These analytical results,
of course, should clearly not be taken as conclusions about the real world
or even as definitive analytical results. They should, nevertheless, help
place the dilemma of rising prices and increasing unemployment before
the reader and serve to illustrate the meaning of "cost push" at the individual firm and industry level.

Cost push and demand pull (the macro level). There are problems of
aggregation pertaining to the transitions from micro relationships to
macro ones. Even so, "macro-economic models can be set up in their
own right . . . on the assumption that at least approximately aggregate
variables are directly and simply re-
lated." [14] We proceed on this assumption to a consideration of one
of several inflation models.[15]

In the model in question, as
shown in Fig. 16-4, the price level
is measured along the vertical axis
and output or real income along
the horizontal axis. Supply curves,
as for example S_0S, are shown to be
an increasing function of the price
level up to some full employment
output O_0 where the curve moves
vertically. Three such curves (i.e.,
S_0S, S_1S, S_2S) are shown in the illustration for three different cost positions. Aggregate demand curves,
on the other hand, are shown as de-

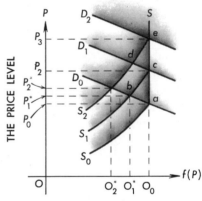

Fig. 16-4. Cost Inflation and a Government
Commitment to Full Employment.

creasing functions of the price level for three different demand situations
—D_0, D_1, and D_2—and with a given supply of money for each of the three
alternative demand situations.

Starting with the initial demand conditions and the curve D_0, the
supply curve may be viewed as shifting from S_0 to S_2 in response to the
cost-inducing pressures of oligopolies, unions, and other groups. The re-

sult is a series of equilibria—(O_0, P_0), (O^*_1, P^*_1), and (O^*_2, P^*_2)—reflecting rising prices from P_0 to P^*_2, declining output from O^*_0 to O^*_2, and, therefore, increasing unemployment. This is the cost push, and its initial effects.

But, assuming a government commitment to the maintenance of full employment, there is more. The Federal Reserve, for example, may supply the credit for additional expenditures with the view to achieving full employment. The results of a successful expansion of such credit and its flow into expenditures are the upward shifting demand curves, and further increases in the price level. With each demand shift following some corresponding shift in supply, the movement of the equilibrium point will be $a \rightarrow b \rightarrow c \rightarrow d \rightarrow e$. Given the achievement of the goal of full employment, in this case, there would have been an abandonment of the goal of price stability.

The labor market mechanism, unemployment, and inflation. The above analyses of inflation suggest two alternative explanations of the tendency toward a rising rate of unemployment in the late 1950's and early 1960's, or some combination of the two. It suggests that the increased unemployment is the result of (1) an inadequate aggregate demand or (2) a failure of the labor market mechanism. The mechanism in question is the one for adjusting the price of labor so as to clear the market of unemployed labor and for allocating resources from one geographical area or from one occupation to another. As suggested above and as we wish to show later (Sect. 24.3), the first alternative implies a more aggressive use of the conventional tools of monetary and fiscal policy (Chap. 19) as a means of increasing employment. On the other hand, the second alternative implies some sort of special policy position with respect to labor market institutions. Following the second alternative, the use of the monetary mechanism to achieve full employment simply aggravates further increase in the price level.

After studying the theory of the labor market mechanism and conducting empirical tests of the function of the mechanism as a basis for explaining the trend of increasing unemployment, one writer[16] arrived at several relevant conclusions with respect to the above policy dilemma and the various means of attaining a lower level of unemployment. They are summarized here:

(1) "The labor market is a reasonably efficient allocator of labor between regional sectors of that market."

(2) "There are apparently barriers to the mobility of workers between occupations and industries. . . ."

(3) Certain unionized industrial sectors "benefited in terms of income at the expense of other sectors. . . ."

The argument goes this way: "Unions practice restrictions to protect their wage gains, and as a result the level of employment is reduced in the union sector. The impact of this is to shift workers from the union to the nonunion sector with a resultant depression of nonunion wage rates." The net result, however, is a generally rising wage level, assuming a "downward 'stickiness' of relative sectoral wage rates in the nonunion areas."

(4) A net result of the latter conclusions is that "the post-1957 experience in the United States represents a classic case of wage-push inflation with its attendant unemployment effects."

With respect to the dilemma of rising prices and unemployment, and conclusion (2) above, the Congress passed the Manpower and Development Training Act of 1962. An intention of the act was to help "bring employee skills into better balance with employers' job requirements and to improve the geographical balance of labor supply and demand." According to the *President's 1963 Economic Report*,[17] "we can steadily improve the fit of available manpower to available jobs." We can do this, he suggests, "by correctly anticipating the economy's needs for upgrading knowledge and skills, and aiming our education and training efforts to meet them." Some economists, moreover, have recognized the need to enlarge upon the program effected by the Manpower Development and Training Act of 1962. The latter act has been, in fact, a forerunner to 1965 legislation dealing with manpower training.

16.4. Summary

Demand inflation (and deflation) may be explained in terms of the basic model pertaining to the determination of aggregate income and aggregate expenditures. In that model an upward shift in demand at full employment creates an initial inflationary gap whereby the extent of the inducement for inflation is the product of the gap and the expenditure multiplier. This initial inducement, however, may be met partly by an increase in the average of prices for current output and partly by an increase in the full employment level of output as an excess of job vacancies over the number of involuntarily unemployed draws new workers into the labor force. A downward shift in demand, proceeding from the initial full employment output, on the other hand, would have the converse set of effects—a deflationary gap, an inducement for deflation, a decline in the price level, a decline in the level of full employment, and a rise in unemployment (i.e., an increase in the number seeking jobs in excess of the unfilled vacancies).

The variables in the national income model may also vary so as to simulate various combinations of chances in output, employment, the price level, and so on—including cost-inflation as well as demand inflation. Cost inflation, however, is not readily explained by the basic national income model. In the case of price level changes in excess of those resulting from demand forces, an equation from Swedish period analysis helps us to consider demand inflation separately, at the analytical level at least. In that equation we view demand inflation (deflation) as being the result of imbalances in planned investment and planned saving. Other price level changes then are isolated in the term $[Y_1 - (I_0 - S_0)]/O$.

Since the wage bill is the major component of income in the latter term, we are able through this term to relate an imbalance in wages and the average productivity of labor to changes in the price level. In fact, the changes in the average productivity of labor may serve as guideposts for noninflationary wage changes in the various industries along with considerations of the scarcity or surplus of workers in the industry in question.

An often recognized type of inflation other than demand inflation is cost or supply inflation. It is defined as a net shift in the conditions underlying an industry or aggregate supply curve. Cost inflation with respect to changes in the GNP deflator is defined as a shift in the aggregate supply curve (i.e., aggregate supply as a function of the GNP deflator).

Inflation may also be mixed as when price level changes reflect upward shifts in both aggregate supply and demand (both as functions of the GNP deflator). The prospect or existence of such a thing as cost inflation poses a dilemma for the Federal Reserve officials. The question arises as to whether to stabilize prices with the view to maximizing purchasing power and permitting an increase in unemployment or whether to attempt maximum employment and permit rising prices.

The existence at times of cost inflation is denied by some. But others claim that their analyses of data support the likely existence of such an inflation at times, particularly with respect to the post-1957 experience in the United States. Given, then, the prospect of the existence of such an inflation, some suggest that the state of affairs "argues strongly for a rethinking of our policy position with respect to labor-market institutions." The Manpower and Development Training Act of 1962 is intended as a means of improving the labor market as a device for allocating and reallocating labor.

References

1. See Martin Bronfenbrenner and Franklyn D. Holzman, "Survey of Inflation Theory," *The American Economic Review*, September 1963, pp. 593-661.

2. For a representative statement of such a model, see *ibid.* pp. 600-602.

3. A. C. L. Day, *Outline of Monetary Economics* (Oxford: At the Clarendon Press, 1957), pp. 253-256.

4. Period analysis concerns the use of difference equations and the division of time into periods of equal length. In such an analysis one attempts to generate the events of one period with reference to those of one or more preceding periods and without any allowance for exogenous changes or changes in underlying conditions in the meantime. For a brief discussion, see William J. Baumol, *Economic Dynamics*, 2nd ed. (New York: The Macmillan Company, 1959), pp. 127-141.

5. See William P. Yohe, "An Analysis of Professor Lindahl's Sequence Model," *L'industria*, Milan, 1959, No. 2, pp. 10-12. The use of the identity in question is consistent with the widely used approach of Bent Hansen. See Bent Hansen, *A Study in the Theory of Inflation* (London: Allen & Unwin, 1951).

6. This identity is similar to Keynes' so-called second fundamental equation from his *Treatise on Money*. See Lawrence R. Klein, *The Keynesian Revolution* (New York: The Macmillan Company, 1950), pp. 15-30; and William J. Frazer, Jr., "Inflation: A Theoretical Note," *Southern Economic Journal*, January 1959.

However, the present identity permits us to avoid the Keynesian identity. Some say that "no one . . . has ever been able to understand precisely what Keynes' second fundamental equation means."

7. See *Defense Against Inflation* (New York: Committee for Economic Development, 1958), p. 58.

8. See "Wage and Price 'Guideposts'," *Economic Report of the President Transmitted to the Congress, January 1963*, together with the *Annual Report of the Council of Economic Advisers* (Washington, D.C.: U.S. Government Printing Office, 1963), pp. 85-86.

9. See Bronfenbrenner and Holzman, *op.cit.*, p. 594. Also, for a bibliography of the voluminous literature, see their work.

10. Bronfenbrenner and Holzman, *op.cit.*, pp. 628-639.

11. *Ibid.*, pp. 630-639.

12. Lowell E. Gallaway, "Labor Mobility, Resource Allocation, and Structural Unemployment," *The American Economic Review*, September 1963, pp. 694-716.

13. *Ibid.*, pp. 622-623.

14. See R. G. D. Allen, *Mathematical Economics*, 2nd ed. (London: The Macmillan Company, Ltd., 1959), pp. 694-724.

15. See Bronfenbrenner and Holzman, *op.cit.*, pp. 594-597.

16. Gallaway, *op.cit.*

17. See pp. 41-42 in the reference of footnote 8. See that reference also for an outline of the Development Training Act of 1962 in Appendix A, pp. 140-141.

17

The Nonfinancial Business Sectors: Their Behavior and Financing

> The various descriptions of securities which represent corporate capital are quotable on the market and are subject to market fluctuations; whereby it comes about that the aggregate effective magnitude of the corporate capital varies with the tone of the market, with the manoeuvres of the businessmen to whom is delegated the management of the companies, and with accidents of the seasons and the chances of peace and war (Thorstein Veblen, *The Theory of Business Enterprise* [1904]).

This chapter deals with the determination of investment expenditures by the business sectors and the alternative sources of funds available for such expenditures. From one point of view, the chapter focuses upon the third of the three basic building blocks of the Keynesian system (Sect. 15.1) and, from another, it examines one of the three major portions of aggregate demand Y_d [$Y_d = C(Y) + I + G$ where $C(Y)$ is the consumption function, $I(= \text{const.})$ is the flow of investment, and $G(= \text{const.})$ is the flow of government expenditures].

The model presented in this chapter is essentially Keynesian with some modifications and additions, and with emphasis on shifts in expectations with respect to future returns. The modifications result from developments since Keynes's time. The additions to the usual treatment are intended to emphasize the operational quality of the model. For example, several new relationships are established: time series for the backlog of planned capital outlays are viewed in relation to changes in the flow of investment; corporate liquidity is viewed as a source of funds for effecting future expenditures and in relation to planned capital outlays. In addition, the basic ingredients of the investment demand model have become so prominent a part of developments in the 1950's and early 1960's in the area of financial management that our approach points out the presence of a relationship between developments in the normative

353

theory and practice of management and the investment demand model. This interrelationship between the respective areas of financial management and income analysis should not be surprising. Both areas of inquiry find their origin in the work of Irving Fisher (Sect. 4.1).

The emphasis on the operational quality of the investment demand model leads us to recognize differences between firms as a function of asset size. Firms maintaining capital budgets as defined below and having wide access to alternative sources are distinguished from firms with more limited access to the entire range of the financial markets and with greater reliance on bank credit as a source of funds relative to their asset size. Allowances for such differences are important in an assessment of the differential effects of credit conditions on business firms by asset size.

To introduce our complex subject this chapter is organized into five parts: financial structure and firms by asset size (Sect. 17.1), financial management, expenditure plans, and the aggregate investment model (Sect. 17.2); the investment demand model and investment incentives (Sect. 17.3), an equilibrium structure, sources and uses of funds, and some effects of credit conditions (Sect. 17.4); and other business sectors (Sect. 17.5).

17.1. Financial Structure and Firms by Asset Size

In the analysis of the investment behavior of firms and the effects of credit ease or tightness on the expenditures of firms, we are led into an examination of the more generally recognizable financial differences in firms by asset size. In the analysis of these differences, we are concerned with the key sources of funds for asset expansion over which the policy-making unit of a firm may exercise control, and with the means of effecting liquidity adjustments. These key sources are the retention of earnings, bank borrowing, other debt financing (such as mortgages and bonds), and external equity financing. The principal means over which management exercises control in effecting changes in liquidity are changes in cash (i.e., money balances or demand deposits plus currency outside of banks), the purchase or sale of government securities or other liquid investments (Sect. 14.2), and bank loans or the repayment of bank debt.

The emphasis on the above accounts leads us to focus on corporate liquidity and near moneyness as indicators of the differences in the way in which firms effect adjustments in their cash accounts, on changes in selected balance sheet accounts as a proportion of total assets, and on the question of whether firms vary significantly in the distribution of income (net of taxes), all in relation to asset size. Our present interest in liquidity is conditioned by a later emphasis (Sect. 17.2) on liquidity as a source of cash for effecting expenditures.

Corporate liquidity. The net result of changes in the principal accounts for effecting liquidity adjustments are indicated by the liquidity ratio, broadly defined as

$$\text{Corporate liquidity} = \frac{\text{Cash} + \text{government securities (or similar liquid investments)}}{\text{Total current liabilities (including bank loans)}}$$

This particular ratio is a rather comprehensive indicator, but it permits us to focus on near-cash assets as well as bank loans as a means of obtaining funds on short notice for effecting subsequent expenditures. Focusing only on the accounts for government securities and bank loans, however,

$$\text{Near moneyness} = \frac{\text{Government securities}}{\text{Total bank loans}}$$

In both instances—liquidity or the index of near moneyness—the left-hand members are a decreasing function of bank indebtedness and an increasing function of government securities.

To indicate the meaning of our indexes for liquidity and near-moneyness, respectively, and their relationship to financial management and accounting detail, we may set forth some accounts and indicate the order of the magnitudes of selected elements in the flow of returns per some common unit. To do this, let us recognize that a flow of returns from holding most assets consists of three elements (Sect. 4.1)—a yield (Q) or dollar flow of returns, less some carrying cost (C) or wastage over time, plus a liquidity element (L). In the case of the liquidity element, there is nothing tangible to show for it, but it represents a security and convenience associated with holding an asset. Thus, from the point of view of these elements and selected balance sheet accounts, there are inflows to be maximized for the asset accounts and illiquidity to be minimized for accounts on the liabilities side, as follows:

	Inflows			Outflows
	$Q - C$	L		L
Cash (i.e., money balances)	0	+	Bank Loans	−
Government securities and similar noncash liquid assets	↓	↑	Bonds and mortgages	↓
Instrumental capital (inventories and plant and equipment)	+	0	Capital stock	0

On the one side, the dollar inflows ($Q - C$) and liquidity (L) are in the order of increasing returns and decreasing liquidity, respectively, as the accounts are listed. And, on the other, the liquidity outflows are in the order of a decreasing liquidity drain on the firm as the accounts are listed. This schematically presents the conflicting objectives of maximizing the aggregate dollar flows of return subject to the desire to maintain liquidity. Some refer to these conflicting objectives as the basic conflict to be reconciled by management. Within the constraint imposed by the total of assets (and the corresponding total for liabilities and net worth) the management may increase risk and the flow of dollar returns at the expense of liquidity and vice versa. In terms of some combination of assets and claims against the firm, management must find the level of liquidity that satisfies its present and prospective transactions needs as well as the propensity (or aversion) to risk.

An outline of analytical foundations. Given the axioms concerning rationality and the preference for more assets rather than less, and total assets as a constraint (Sect. 4-1), it may be shown that the flow of returns from holding assets in general is a maximum when the rates of return from the acquisition of additional assets of the various types are equal (Sect. 4.1 and 17.4). Similarly, given the same axioms, and some other total for a combination of liabilities or some combination of accounts serving as a source of funds, it may be shown that the cost of obtaining a given amount of funds is a minimum when the rate of interest from obtaining given amounts of additional funds from any of the several sources are equal (Sect. 17.4). Further, given the axioms and proceeding from a condition of equilibrium, it may be shown that a direct change will occur in a given class of assets whenever the rate of return from acquiring additional assets in that class changes, other rates remaining momentarily unchanged (Sect. 17.4). Here, we view the flows of returns as including both expected net dollar amounts (i.e., net of all cost except the cost of funds) and psychological returns associated in varying degrees with the convenience and security in holding certain assets (Sect. 4.1).

Now, as firms increase in size, and if we attribute the optimizing quality (and its dual, economizing, where costs are concerned) to their managers[1] (in accordance with our axiom about preference), we make an additional assumption. Namely, economies (or convenience for which managers are willing to pay something) result from holding a stock of government securities (or similar types of noncash liquid assets) and effecting adjustments in the need for (or excess of) cash through them rather than through bank loans. This we can put in a form that will permit empirical tests of data:

Assumption: *Beyond some minimum size, as firms increase in size, the ratio (as a percentage) of government securities to bank loans increases.* Tests of cross-sectional data concerning the assumption, moreover, have provided strong evidence that it is true.[2] The minimum in question may be thought of as occurring when financial managers become specialists, or, at least, when it is sufficiently early enough to allow the assumption to hold over the predominant portion of the scale for asset size.

Next, recall one aspect of the definition of the precautionary motive (Sect. 2.2) for holding cash: "The precautionary motive relates to the demand for cash as a proportion of assets for meeting unforeseen costs and expenses and/or as an asset whose 'value is fixed in terms of money to meet a subsequent liability fixed in terms of money [such as bank loans].'" [3]

Then, given the assumption about government securities, the above analysis, and the definition of the precautionary motive, we may state a principal proposition:

Proposition: ". . . *the precautionary demand does not increase proportionally with wealth (or total assets in the present instance) as wealth rises, and presumably income with it* [our italics]." [4] For instance, as firms increase in size, the ratio (as a percentage) of government securities to bank loans increases. This parallels a weakening of the precautionary motive relative to other motives (Sect. 2.2), and we expect cash to decline as a proportion of assets. Thus, we have a corollary to our principal proposition:

Corollary: *The turnover of cash balances increases as firms increase in size beyond some minimum size, as in a preceding assumption.* In this instance, balances affected by the precautionary motive, in effect, get drawn into the more active transactions sphere as firms increase in size. Here, the change in the turnover of balances would be indicated by some substitute measure for the income velocity of money (i.e., the ratio of income to the stock of money), such as the ratio of sales to cash.

Once again, tests of cross-sectional data have provided strong empirical support for the corollary,[5] and other relevant statements have been supported by empirical evidence. These include such statements as the following:[6]

(1) Corporate liquidity (as a percentage) is directly related to asset size.

(2) Government securities as a percentage óf assets is directly related to asset size.

(3) Cash as a percentage of assets is inversely related to asset size.

(4) Total bank loans as a percentage of assets is inversely related to asset size.

(5) Cash plus government securities as a percentage of assets is independent of asset size.

The changes in financial structure implied by these statements as firms increase in size, moreover, have been shown to be the main way in which financial structure changes as firms increase in size.[7] Other measures—retained earnings as a percentage of profits after taxes, long-term debt as a percentage of total assets, and owners' equity as a percentage of total assets—have been shown to be somewhat less dependent on firms by asset size.

One net result of the above analysis should be clear. Smaller firms are more directly dependent on banks as a source of funds in relation to asset size. Larger firms, by the same analysis, are more independent of banks and, consequently, the availability (or lack of availability) of bank credit (Sect. 25.3) during periods of credit ease (or credit tightness). There is the suggestion that credit policy must affect the larger firms that dominate the behavior of the aggregate investment variable (I) differently, or at least by a different route, such as through the financial markets generally. In allowing for these differences, the relatively smaller firms and some other business sectors are given special consideration at the end of the chapter (Sect. 17.5).

Changes in money balances and liquidity adjustments: some dynamic considerations. The above statements about firms permit us to conjecture about certain aspects of firms' behavior over time. For example, liquidity increases as funds are withdrawn from the capital market in the form of a sale of new stock and then are used to increase liquid assets or reduce bank loans. It may also increase as fund flow in from increases in earned surplus and depreciation as noted later (Sect. 17.3).

In any event, with respect to many firms, the net flow of funds between firms and the financial markets may be from the financial markets at times of rapid asset expansion, and there are times, too, when it may be into the financial markets. Such times as these may occur when there are no new stock issues, a repayment of bank loans, and/or purchases of noncash liquid assets as may in part be made possible by the flow of funds from internal sources—depreciation and retained earnings. The larger firms in general make the adjustments in their liquidity needs primarily through the purchase or sale of noncash liquid assets as shown above, and occasionally they may make these adjustments through the sale of new issues in the capital markets. The small firms are more inclined to make their liquidity adjustments through loans and the repayment of debt.

There are other sources for liquidity for some firms, in particular the smaller ones. One of these is accounts receivable as collateral for loans, and thus an unencumbered set of accounts is a potential source of funds. Also, in connection with bank loans, the smaller firms may get others, such as life insurance companies, to use relatively inactive balances as compensating balances (Sect. 14.2) at banks in exchange for a line of credit at the bank. The net effect of this arrangement is to transfer inactive balances into active balances as the borrowing firms draw on their lines of credit. Certificates of deposit (Sect. 14.2) arise in this connection, too, and they provide still an additional type of noncash liquid asset for liquidity adjustments. The roles of compensating balances, link financing, and the intense use of bank credit by smaller firms are consistent with the above statements about financial structure and liquidity adjustments.

17.2. Financial Management, Expenditure Plans, and the Aggregative Investment Model

Earlier (Sect. 5.4) we introduced the notion whereby a change in the rate of return in relation to the rate of interest at a given flow of expenditures led to a change in the flow of expenditures. Presently, we wish to develop this notion more fully as the third of the basic Keynesian models —i.e., the investment demand model. In doing so, we wish to introduce some notions about practices and the normative theory of financial management (i.e., theory about the way the financial manager ought to practice), and add a few of the analytical modifications necessary to our development of the investment demand model. There are interrelationships between the concepts of the rate of return and the cost of capital as set forth in the financial management literature and as presented in analyses of aggregate investment demand. In addition, the concepts as dealt with in both the management literature and in the analyses of investment demand have a common origin in the work of Irving Fisher (Sect. 4.1).

Financial management and expenditure plans. In the post-World War II years, there was an increasing emphasis on the notion and use of a capital budget at the level of the individual firm.[8] There the notion of a budget has usually meant to imply the planning of expenditures, and the term "capital" has usually referred to assets whose returns flow in beyond a one-year interval. The function of maintaining a capital budget at the firm level, moreover, and the major decisions pertaining to the composition of the investment in assets and the financial structure have been viewed as falling within the bailiwick of financing management.[9] The results of (1)—the selection of the various projects for asset expansion—and (2)—establishing criteria for limiting the extent of expenditures on additional assets—furthermore, have come to be viewed as a demand schedule for capital, in the first instance; in the second instance, the results are seen as a cost of capital (expressed as a rate), a cutoff rate, the "minimum required rate of return on proposals using capital funds," and so on.

In the latter two instances lies our present interest. For one thing, the evaluation of the worth of alternative projects and their selection utilize analysis of the kind set forth earlier (Sect. 4.1), and the concept of a cost of capital, as an interest cost reflecting the costs on alternative forms of financing and allowing for risk, is quite similar in many respects and plays a somewhat similar role to the earlier concept of a rate of interest (Sect. 4.1).[10] Consequently, there is something present in the literature about the way financial managers should behave and in the operations of individual firms that we may draw upon in developing explanations of the behavior and financing of business firms generally. This is true despite the presence of analytical and operational problems pertaining to the selection of a particular rate for the cost of capital by individual firms.

For another thing, data on the actual capital budgets of individual firms as reported by the National Industrial Conference Board in advance of actual expenditures and other similar types of data provide a leading indicator of the level of future capital expenditures.[11] In particular, they help in forecasting the level of future expenditures and, therefore, in planning, effecting, and timing the use of general credit controls so as to achieve the ultimate goals with respect to employment, output, and prices.

The above interrelationships are shown in Fig. 17-1. In the illustration,

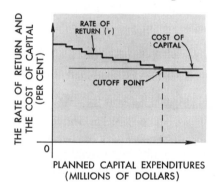

PLANNED CAPITAL EXPENDITURES
(MILLIONS OF DOLLARS)

Fig. 17-1. The Rate of Return, Cost of Capital, and the Level of Planned Capital Expenditures.

one views the various projects according to the order of decreasing rates of return after allowances for risk in the realization of the various returns and with the total level of planned expenditures increasing for additional projects. However, we note irregular steps or breaks in the demand schedule for capital as projects are added. There, also we see a rate for the cost of capital (rate = const.) that may shift, depending on the risk involved and the cost as affected by conditions in the financial markets.[12] Some may even show the latter rate to vary directly with the use of different sources of funds with the volume of funds needed for effecting the planned expenditures. But, in either case, there is a cutoff point at which the rate of return no longer exceeds the cost of capital, and the use of this point as a limit on the level of expenditures implies some sort of optimal profit goal.

The aggregate investment demand model. There are special conceptual distinctions to be made in the transition from schedules of the type set forth in Fig. 17-1 to the aggregate investment functions below, and there is the additional problem of the identification of the goals of financial managers. In the first instance, the rates for both the returns and the cost of alternative sources of funds are not independent of one another. For example, the returns from a new building may depend on the purchase of equipment for the building, and the returns from improvements in existing plant may depend on additions to the plant. Similarly, the cost of alternative sources of funds are interdependent. The cost of funds from bank loans or the sale of bonds depend on the amount of equity in a business and the amount of liquid assets.[13] In the second instance, some managers are reluctant to view their goal as a strict profit maximization one. Clearly, there is at least the necessity of reconciling profit criteria in the strictest dollar and cents sense with the managers' and shareholders' attitudes toward risk. Thus, as we move to the aggregates and the consideration of the above notions, we abstract from the above problems and attempt, at the same time, to maintain some degree of correspondence between our more abstract concepts and those of the normative theory and practice of financial management.

To do this, in the case of the rate of return, we define the rate as being the rate for relating the series of prospective returns (i.e., R_1, R_2, . . . , R_n) from the entire batch of expenditures to the cost or supply price of the projects in question, where the expected flow of returns reflects utility or benefit in some subjective sense after allowance for all cost except the cost of capital and after allowance for liquidity (the converse of risk). In this sense, then, we are thinking of a rate of return (r) from a flow of planned (or actual) expenditures, and the rate may be viewed as a decreasing function of the level of the flow of expenditures. The decreasing function would be due to the need to reduce the price per unit of output in order to dispose of a larger output or as a result of a higher cost per unit of output as the flow of expenditures increased.

In the case of the cost of capital, or the rate of interest (i) in our aggregative analysis, we speak of the rate of interest as a subjective rate. It allows for the risk involved in realizing the returns from the investment of the funds, and for any given financial structure. It will also shift with changing conditions in the financial markets.[14]

As for the goal pertaining to the level of expenditures, we retain the notion of profits being maximized after special allowances for risk. Thus we view equilibrium as existing at the point (I_t, r_t), where $I_t =$ flow of investment, and $i = r$. This assumption implies another, however, about the interest elasticity of the investment demand function in question and the rate of interest, but we relegate the treatment of the latter to an appendix (see Chap. 17). Also, in a conceptual sense, our formal model includes expenditures on instrumental capital in general, including inventories, plant, and equipment. (Note empirical measures for planned capital expenditures do not pertain to inventories.)

As indicated earlier (Sect. 5.4), the latter framework implies an expansion of the flow of expenditures when the rate of return exceeds the rate of interest (i.e., $r > i$) or, in other words, when the capital value of a given flow of expenditures exceeds the supply price of the instrumental capital in question (i.e., $CV > C$). Conversely, it implies a contraction in the flow of expenditures when the rate of interest exceeds the rate of return (i.e., $i > r$) or, in other words, when the supply price exceeds the capital value (i.e., $C > CV$).

The model deduced above is essentially the basic Keynesian model for investment demand.[15]

Effective expenditures and planned expenditures. We wish to present the model for investment demand, indicate changes in investment demand over time, and specify a relationship between changes in actual investment and the level or backlog of planned capital expenditures at the aggregate level, or at least for an aggregate of large firms. As in the above model, the rate of return (r) presently remains a decreasing function of the investment flow variable I; i.e.,

$$r = \mu I + \nu, \quad \mu < 0$$

where μ (mu) is the slope parameter and
      ν (nu) is the intercept parameter.

Also, we regard the rate of interest i as a constant [i.e., $i = \kappa$ (kappa)], and the equilibrium flow of investment is determined by underlying conditions [i.e., $I = (\kappa - \nu)/\mu$].

We wish, next, to think of different values for I as corresponding to different values for r [i.e., $I = (r - \nu)/\mu$ or the inverse $r = \mu I + \nu$] at a given time. However, we think of these other levels as those that are planned at difference values for r, since there is only one equilibrium level of expenditures $\bar{I}$ at a given time. The level of plans to be acted upon at a given time, then, is dependent upon the equilibrium value $\bar{r}_t$ (i.e., $\bar{r} = i$) at that time (e.g., $t = 0$), given the underlying conditions. Consequently, if the prospects for investment change so as to appear more rewarding (i.e., ν increases, $\nu^{(t+1)} > \nu^{(t)}$, then at the old equilibrium level of investment (i.e., $\bar{I}_t$) the rate of return is greater than the rate of interest (i.e., $r > i$), the level of planned outlays expands, and business activity expands as the equilibrium moves from $\bar{I}_t$ to $\bar{I}_{t+1}$. Conversely, a change to less rewarding prospects has the reverse set of effects. Viewing some cyclical movement in $\nu^{(t)}$, then, we get a cyclical change in the flow of effective investment I_t [$= (\kappa - \nu^{(t)}/\mu, \mu < 0$].

However, planned investment serves as a leading indicator, at times, and we wish to introduce how the backlog of plans may vary in relation to effective investment. To begin with, the backlog of plans may be thought of as leading the contraction in the flow of investment by a relatively short interval up to one year, and it may be thought of as lagging or leading the expansion in the flow of expenditures by a relatively shorter time at the lower turning point. The lag in the expenditures series behind the contraction in the backlog may be thought of as due to continued action upon prior commitments, as well as the advanced stage of some plans. This then is our explicit reference to involuntary expenditures. The interval between the downturn in the backlog and the upper turning point of actual expenditures may be singled out as a transition phase, a phase during which we are subsequently lead to expect unique financial changes. Approaching the upturn, however, the backlog does not lead or lead significantly; there is no interval of transition comparable to that preceding the upper turning point in actual outlays. This absence of transition results because the more favorable outlook must be translated into a backlog containing some new plans. In the meantime, the increase in outlays is more likely to be effected from earlier plans included in the backlog.

Planned financing and speculative shifts in the financial structure. In view of what has been said earlier (Sect. 17.1) about corporate liquidity as an indicator of the means of effecting expenditures, and about the relationship between the planned expenditures and the cycle of effective expenditures (Sect. 17.2), we are led to expect the earlier ratio for corporate liquidity (Sect. 17.1) to rise in the early expansion phase of the cycle and decline during the rest of the cycle. But there is the additional need to allow for this relationship in combination with speculative shifts in the financial structure. Thus we deal with both the relationship and the speculative shifts.

An expansion in the volume of planned outlays should cause an expansion in corporate liquidity and vice versa. This does not exclude other factors from affecting liquidity, but the present functional relationship has been shown to be significant on the basis of tests of cross-sectional data. The test provided evidence of the truth of the following statement: "The indicator (i.e., corporate (liquidity) for the planned level of desired money balances is directly related to the backlog of planned capital expenditures." [16]

Apart from the latter relationship and in view of earlier statements (Sect. 5.4) about a speculative demand for money and so-called safe securities (including noncash liquid assets) as opposed to instrumental capital, we would be led to expect a decline in the liquidity ratio in the expansion phase and a rise in the recession phase. In the earlier context, for example, a shift into more liquid assets (cash, safe securities, and so on) as opposed to the less liquid instrumental capital gave rise to a recession of expenditures, and we would now also expect this shift to give rise to an increase in the liquidity ratio. In the earlier context, too, the converse set of relationships would hold in the expansion phase.

Now, in applying the two notions above to the real-world sector for large firms as their liquidity structures change over time, they must be combined. Thus, for these firms, in the expansion phase there is a weakening of the speculative demand for liquidity and strengthening of the demand for liquidity as a means of effecting planned expenditures. With a strong upturn in planned expenditures in the early expansion phase, however, the transactions demand for liquidity should increase to some extent even though the potential increase is in part offset by a weakened speculative demand. In the contraction phase, then, there is a reduced need for liquidity as a means of effecting planned expenditures. Nevertheless, funds continue to flow into the firm in larger amounts from depreciation, and in reduced amounts from other sources. They will be more than adequate for the reduced volume of expenditures, given a relatively small or marginal dependence on external funds as a general rule, and the funds consequently should go to satisfy the increase in the speculative demand for liquidity.

Therefore, combining the analytical conclusions about the various phases of cyclical change, we are led to expect a changing relationship between liquidity and the backlog of planned outlays for plant and equipment. The prospects are that the indicator of planned financing leads the cyclical upturn in planned expenditures since liquidity rises in the recession and early expansion phases, and that liquidity may decline somewhat in advance of the decline in planned expenditures, depending upon the strength of the upturn in liquidity in the recession and early expansion phases.

17.3. The Investment Demand Model and Investment Incentives

Later (Sect. 19.3) we consider the government's tax and expenditure measures in general as means of achieving national economic goals—full employment, and so on. For the present, however, two specific tax measures are considered: accelerated depreciation and the tax credit. They are introduced as an exercise pertaining to changes in the investment demand model (Sect. 17.2), and as a means of indicating the likely impact of such measures on business costs.

Investment incentive: accelerated depreciation. Business firms have traditionally viewed annual allowances for the wear and tear and effects of obsolescence on their capital equipment as costs. These are referred to as depreciation allowances. Furthermore, the United States tax laws permit "reasonable allowances" for depreciation for the purposes of arriving at a tax base—the corporate income tax base in the case of corporations. Thus, as a deduction for determining the taxable income of a business, changes in the amount and timing of depreciation affect the rate of recovery of the initial outlay on capital goods, as well as the level of tax payments. Accelerated depreciation then refers to the more rapid write-off of the cost of a capital good for purposes of arriving at taxable income. It permits a larger portion of the cost of an asset to be recovered from income in the early life of the asset. In the case of corporations, this tends to reduce corporate income tax payments in the early life of the asset. The deductible cost becomes an internal source of funds along with retained earnings (Sect. 17.1).

Prior to the Internal Revenue Code of 1954 the straight-line method of depreciation was the most common. Under this method an asset for $1,500 with a life of five years, for example, would simply be depreciated at a straight-line rate of 20 per cent per annum or $300 per annum for five years. Since 1954, however, as permitted under the code, the double-declining balance method and the sum-of-the-years digits method have become the more common. Both permit a faster write-off of assets in their early life. The result, as shown in an example,* is a larger amount of depreciation in the early life of the asset.

The faster write-off permitted for capital assets including plant and equipment in their early life can be made even faster. It could be permitted by Congressional action or by the Treasury Department's interpretation of "reasonable allowances" and by their rules and guidelines for depreciating assets.

A more rapid write-off of assets should have significant effects on business profits. To begin with, the respective effects of accelerated depreciation for the ith firm with a persistently increasing flow of investment and the jth firm with a persistently declining flow of investments are increasing and decreasing amounts of deferred-tax payments, given the ith and jth firms with positive profits and given changing costs and revenues. Next, the deferred-tax payment may be viewed as an interest-free loan in its effect and the significance of accelerated depreciation from this point of view is the greater premium on a rising flow of capital expenditures in the form of an interest-free loan of increasing size. Con-

---

* In the case of the declining balance method, for example, the percentage of the original cost permitted for depreciation per annum on a straight-line basis is doubled (e.g., .20 × 2 = .40), and this doubled percentage is then applied to the undepreciated and declining balance of the cost of the asset. This example would appear as follows:

Year	Declining Balance (in dollars)		Rate per annum		Annual Depreciation (in dollars)
1	1,500.00	×	40	=	600.00
2	900.00	×	40	=	360.00
3	540.00	×	40	=	216.00
4	324.00	×	40	=	129.60
5	194.40	×	40	=	(194.40)

Note that the entire undepreciated balance after the fourth year is depreciated in the fifth year.

sequently, greater profits should result from the investment of the interest-free loans of sizes depending upon the growth of assets.

In the context of our analytical framework (Sect. 17.2), there are several interrelated effects of accelerated depreciation. One apparent effect is to increase the charges against income in the early years and to reduce them in the latter years, but, more fundamentally, this apparent effect does two things. It reduces the tax payment on income in the early years and increases it in the latter, and, at the same time, it provides a larger source of funds for early reinvestment. The returns in the early years, then, actually rise as a result of the reduced tax payment in those years.

Investment incentive: the tax credit and accelerated depreciation. The tax credit differs from accelerated depreciation in that depreciation continues to apply and is deductible from income for tax purposes whereas the tax credit is a direct credit for the payment of taxes. The one affects the size of the tax base, and the other is simply a credit against the tax revenue to be paid to the Treasury. A 7 per cent tax credit, for example, provides a credit against the current year's taxes amounting to 7 per cent of the expenditures on capital goods. Such a credit was adopted by the United States government in 1962, following its adoption in some other countries.

The effect of a credit of 7 per cent is to increase the return on the investment in the first year by 7 per cent of the investment. This, in turn and in the above model (Sect. 17.2), increases the value of the capital investment and the rate of return equating the prospective returns to their supply price. As in the case of accelerated depreciation, it provides the incentive for an increase in the flow of expenditures.

To re-emphasize the effects of accelerated depreciation and a 7 per cent tax credit on the rate of return, we may reproduce some United States Treasury Department illustrations.[17] In presenting the calculations in their illustrations thay make three assumptions: "(1) The applicable tax rate is 50.0 per cent, (2) the rate of return after taxes obtained under present law and straight-line depreciation methods is 5.0 per cent, and (3) the amount of revenue that an investment yields tapers off, so that net revenues in later years are smaller than net revenues in early years."

As they explain, the declining net revenue assumption reflects observations about cost and market demand. They view maintenance cost as rising with the age of the asset, and they view the demand for the asset's contribution to output as declining with the passage of time. Thus, in their example, a $1,000 investment with a ten-year life must produce $1,242 after taxes (i.e., $R_1 + R_2 + \ldots, + R_{10} = 1,242$) in order to yield a rate of return of 5 per cent under straight-line depreciation:

$$1,000 = \frac{184}{(1 + 0.05)^1} + \frac{171}{(1 + 0.05)^2} + \cdots + \frac{46}{(1 + 0.05)^{10}}$$

where the flow of returns sums to $1,242. A switch to accelerated depreciation under the double-dealing balance method then raises the rate of return from 5 per cent to 5.6 per cent, i.e.,

$$1,000 = \frac{234}{(1 + 0.056)^1} + \frac{202}{(1 + 0.056)^2} + \cdots + \frac{46}{(1 + 0.056)^{10}}$$

Note that by comparing the prospective returns under the two alternative methods of depreciation, the investment's return is higher in the early years and lower in the latter years under accelerated depreciation. Now, a 7 per cent tax credit increase the first year's cash return by $70, and this raises the rate of return for equating the prospective returns to the $1,000 investment outlay to 7.6 per cent, i.e.,

$$1,000 = \frac{304}{(1 + 0.076)^1} + \frac{202}{(1 + 0.076)^2} + \cdots + \frac{46}{(1 + 0.076)^{10}}$$

The accelerated depreciation has raised the rate of return by 12 per cent (or from 5 to 5.6 per cent), and the tax credit has raised the initial rate of return by an additional 40 per cent for a total increase of 52 per cent in the present illustration. The net effect of these changes in the context of our model (Sect. 17.2) is an upward shift in the investment demand schedule.

There are several frequently mentioned points in favor of the tax credit as an incentive device. For one thing, a greater incentive is provided to investment for a given loss of revenue to the Treasury, since the tax credit need not apply to the existing stock of assets. For another thing, the credit is simple to understand and could be changed by legislation to provide the desired amount of incentive for faster growth independent of fixing the return of the cost of an asset over its useful life. The latter is an aspect of accelerated depreciation that some believe deserves special attention. And, for a third thing, the credit is not viewed in corporate records as a cost; it is, consequently, less likely to distort pricing based on costs as costs appear in accounting records.

17.4. A Equilibrium Structure, Sources and Uses of Funds, and Some Effects of Credit Conditions

Earlier (Sect. 5.2) we introduced a general economic equilibrium that was also consistent with our equilibrium pertaining to the equality of the rates of returns from alternative assets (Sect. 4.1). Consequently, our aggregate investment demand model involves a less general type of equilibrium but, as matters turn out, its reconciliation with the earlier and more general equilibrium may be illustrated. To do this we simply apply the same mathematical methods to a more restricted number of accounts.

There are certain advantages in the present application of the earlier method. It permits us to view the structure of assets as an asset type of equilibrium, and it permits us to arrive at a few conclusions about the timing of the use of alternative sources of funds over the cycle of expenditures, output, and employment. Against this background, moreover, and, at the same time, allowing for other things, we may suggest some effects of credit conditions. The other things pertain to the role of internal funds, the earlier relationship between corporate liquidity and planned capital outlays, and the relationship between planned capital outlays and capital expenditures.

The optimal combination of assets. In emphasizing the results of managerial decisions in terms of the optimal combination of assets, we may isolate for consideration those asset accounts that are most likely to reflect the results of nonroutine decisions. As contrasted with the accounts for receivables and cash, we view the accounts resulting from nonroutine decisions as those for government securities and short-term investments, inventories, and plant and equipment. Accounts receivable may be viewed simply as a function of sales. A large firm will have a steady group of customers, or infrequent customers with an established credit, or finally, established criteria for the extension of the trade credit represented by the receivables. Generally, when the criteria for lines of trade credit and discounts for prompt payments are established they do not change erratically in the short run. Also, variation in the size of the cash account, in the short run, will depend on the degree of control over cash flows and the skill of the management of that account. No conscious decision is necessarily required to increase or decrease the size of these accounts, as would be the case, for example, in formalizing into the capital budget the plans for additional expenditure and also the plans for financing the capital expansion.

The account for government and other securities may be thought of, in part, as an indication of planned financing and partially the result of obtaining the means of payment for a backlog of planned expenditures. The inventory account could be thought of as a result of rather routine decisions and largely as a function of sales (Sect. 15.3), but we shall isolate it for consideration anyway, due to an occasional speculative demand for inventories and our earlier consideration of inventories as a part of instrumental capital in the national income framework. Further, the account for plant and equipment may be thought of as reflecting the results of the most conscious decisions of the decision-makers with respect to the most important outlays undertaken by the firm.

Viewing the flow of returns to be maximized as some function of governments (G), inventories (I), and plant and equipment (P) then, we may denote

$$U = f(G, I, P)$$

Furthermore, the constraint within which choice may be made is some function g of the respective assets. This we denote

$$g(G, I, P) = P_G(G) + P_I(I) + P_P(P),$$

where P_G is the price per unit of governments,

$\quad\quad P_I$ is the price per unit of inventories,

$\quad\quad P_P$ is the price per unit of plant and equipment.

Thus, forming the Lagrangian function,

$$L(G, I, P, r) = f(G, I, P) + r[g(G, I, P) - P_G(G) - P_I(I) - P_P(P)]$$

Now, the first order conditions for the constrained maximum are

$$\frac{\partial L}{\partial G} = \frac{\partial U}{\partial G} - rP_G = 0$$

$$\frac{\partial L}{\partial I} = \frac{\partial U}{\partial I} - rP_I = 0$$

$$\frac{\partial L}{\partial P} = \frac{\partial U}{\partial P} - rP_P = 0$$

$$\frac{\partial L}{\partial r} = g(G, I, P) - P_G(G) - P_I(I) - P_P(P) = 0$$

These equations then imply the equality of the ratios for the marginal utilities of the several assets to their respective prices, since the equations are set equal to zero. Moreover, upon dividing the first three equations by the respective prices

$$\frac{\frac{\partial U}{\partial G}}{P_G} = \frac{\frac{\partial U}{\partial I}}{P_I} = \frac{\frac{\partial U}{\partial P}}{P_P} = r,$$

where r is the rate of return (Sect. 4.1) on the acquisition of additional assets.

The marginal changes in the size of the accounts correspond to increases and decreases in the flows of returns from the respective accounts, and they are the adjustments to bring the respective rates or return into equality, apart from an occasional involuntary accumulation of such assets as inventories. This equality of the rates of return from holding assets may be stated in terms of the three elements comprising the rate of return:

$$q_G - c_G + l_G =$$
$$q_I - c_I + l_I =$$
$$q_P - c_P + l_P$$

Now, it does not matter where we draw the line between q, c, and l for assets other than government securities, since we shall be exclusively concerned with the sum of the elements comprising the rates, of return in those instances. However, in the case of government securities, let $q_G =$ interest payment received from holding them, $c_G =$ tax which must be paid on the received interest payment, and $l_G =$ liquidity premium.

Equilibrium and some other accounts. In order to deduce the rate of interest paid on the sources of funds that have been used in the purchase of assets in support of earnings, we now consider the purely financial accounts other than United States government and short-term securities through which funds may be withdrawn from the financial markets. These we consider to be the accounts for bank loans, bonds, and stocks.*

Viewing the ouflows of funds to be minimized as some function of short-term bank loans (T), bonds (B), and stocks (S), we have

$$U = f(T, B, S), \text{ and}$$

the constraining function becomes

$$g(T, B, S) = P_T(T) + P_B(B) + P_S(S),$$

where P_T is the price per unit of short-term borrowing,
P_B is the price per unit of bonds, and
P_S is the price per unit of stocks.

Thus, forming the Lagrangian function,

$$L(T, B, S, i) = f(T, B, S) + i[g(T, B, S) - P_T(T) - P_B(B) - P_S(S)],$$

and, this time, i denotes the Lagrangian multiplier. The necessary conditions for the constrained minimum then become

$$\frac{\partial L}{\partial T} = \frac{\partial U}{\partial T} - iP_T = 0$$

$$\frac{\partial L}{\partial B} = \frac{\partial U}{\partial B} - iP_B = 0$$

$$\frac{\partial L}{\partial S} = \frac{\partial U}{\partial S} - iP_S = 0$$

$$\frac{\partial L}{\partial i} = g(T, B, S) - P_T(T) - P_B(B) - P_S(S) = 0$$

Upon dividing the first four equations of the latter system by their respective prices,

---

* The use of only the three accounts is considered sufficient to illustrate the present equilibrium. If others are included, such as long-term bank loans or preferred stocks (as a separate category from common stock) or mortgages, the same analysis would be applicable.

$$\frac{\dfrac{\partial U}{\partial T}}{P_T} = \frac{\dfrac{\partial U}{\partial B}}{P_B} = \frac{\dfrac{\partial U}{\partial S}}{P_S} = i,$$

and i is the rate of interest or the fundamental cost of obtaining funds from the financial markets. The necessary condition says in words that the outflows to the various sources of financial markets funds are a minimum when the rates of interest for the respective sources are equal.

Moreover, the latter set of rates consists of the ratios of the marginal disutilities for the alternative forms of financing to the respective prices per unit of the forms of financing. If one form of financing is less expensive, in terms of the rate, than the others (e.g., that corresponding to the second ratio), then that form will be used more intensely. As the latter form is used, the absolute interest cost expressed as a flow (i.e., $\partial U/\partial T$) will rise, and the discounted price (P_T) will decline until the cost of that form of financing, expressed as a rate, is brought into line with the cost of financing on the other alternative forms of financing.

Once again, however, the flows consist of several elements, and the costs of financing through the alternative methods of financing are equal at equilibrium. The changes in the alternative methods of financing may be expected to reflect factors affecting the alternative costs of financing as they are reflected in the varying magnitudes of the elements comprising the cost of funds. The equality of the alternative costs of financing through the various means at a given time may be stated as follows:

$$\begin{aligned}
q_T{}^* - c_T{}^* + l_T{}^* = \\
q_B{}^* - c_B{}^* + l_B{}^* = \\
q_S{}^* - c_S{}^* + l_S{}^*
\end{aligned}$$

An equilibrium structure. In sum, we have noted several things: (1) equilibrium in our asset structure occurs when the rates of return from additions to the various classes of assets are equal; (2) interest costs are minimized when the rates for the interest costs of the alternative sources of funds are equal; and (3), in terms of our Keynesian model, equilibrium occurs under the condition $r = i$. Thus an equilibrium system may be stated upon recognizing the presence of the various elements comprising our various rates. It is as follows:

$$r = i;$$
$$\begin{aligned}
q_P - c_P + l_P = \\
q_I - c_I + l_I = \\
q_G - c_G + l_G = q_T{}^* - c_T{}^* + l_T{}^* = \\
q_B{}^* - c_B{}^* + l_B{}^* = \\
q_S{}^* - c_S{}^* + l_S{}^*
\end{aligned}$$

Stating the system in this way permits us to focus on the order of the magnitude of the various elements entering into the costs of alternative sources of funds from the financial markets, given certain market and tax information. It also permits us to focus upon some effects of changing the magnitude of particular elements.

To begin with, let the distribution of corporate earnings (E) be

	Per Cent
Corporate income taxes (T)	50
Dividends (D)	25
Retained earnings $[E - (D + T)]$	25
	100

approximately in accordance with observations since World War II, think of earnings of 20 per cent per some average share value (V) of $100 such that

	Per Cent
$D/V = 5/100 =$	05
$T/V = 10/100 =$	10
$[E - (D + T)]/V = 5/100 =$	05;

let the yields on stocks, bonds, short-term bank loans, and government securities be 5, 6, 4, and 3 per cent, respectively.

Also, let us recognize some results of the given facts. For one, 50 per cent of the income from government bonds must be paid to the government as a tax on income. For another, about 50 per cent of yield cost on all forms of debt financing may be deducted from gross corporate income for tax purposes. For still another, the yield on stocks is also a payment for a flow of retained earnings of a value equal to the funds from the sale of one stock (i.e.,

$$\text{Value} = 100 = \frac{\$5}{.05},$$

where 5 per cent is the yield from the firm's point of view and
$5 is the flow of retained earnings per share).

This in turn implies an effective yield outflow of 2.5 per cent on the funds from the sale of a single extra share of stock, as well as a payment in taxes of 10 per cent per share or four times (i.e., 10.0 per cent/2.5 per cent $= 4$) the yield of 2.5 per cent for the funds in order to make the yield on the funds an effective rate.

Thus, from our given information and its results, the order of magnitude of the variables is as follows:

	q^*	c^*	l^*	$i = 12.5$
Financial markets transactions (other than government securities):				
Stocks	2.5	10.0	0	12.5
Bonds	6.0	3.0	9.5	12.5
Bank loans, short-term	4.0	2.0	10.5	12.5
	q	c	l	$r = 12.5$
Other selected transactions:				
Government securities	3.0	−1.5	11.0	12.5
Inventories				12.5
Plant and equipment				12.5

The basic explanations following from the above considerations are those dealing with the form taken by the flow of funds in response to changes within the structure of the yield, carrying cost (or tax), and liquidity elements. For example, changes within the yield structure, such as a reduction in the yield element on bonds, would call forth an expansion in the use of bonds to obtain additional funds in order to raise the yields on bonds and re-establish equilibrium. Similarly, changes within the structure of liquidity elements in response to such factors as those causing disorderly market conditions in one sector of the financial markets as opposed to another may be expected to operate unfavorably upon financing in the disorderly sector. These changes become more a historical matter of describing or observing cause-and-effect relationships. Even so, they are important for explaining the prevalence of certain types of new issues at such times as may result in changes in the relative proportions of debt and equity financing.

The above considerations also bring such phenomena to the forefront as the higher rate of return required to effect a given amount of investment because of the taxation of corporate income. It points up the lessened degree of effectiveness of yield changes upon the decision to undergo real capital investment under the impact of corporation taxation. In other words, an increase in corporate tax rates has a damping effect on decisions to undertake capital investment, by increasing the fundamental rate for capitalizing the value of capital goods. At the same time, such an increase in corporate tax rates reduces the effectiveness of changes in yields. Conversely, a decrease in corporate income tax rates has an exhilarating effect on decisions to undertake capital investment by lowering the fundamental rate for capitalizing the value of capital goods, but simultaneously it increases the effectiveness of changes in yields.

Some further conclusions about the effects of credit conditions. In view of the availability of funds for expenditures on instrumental capital from depreciation and retained earnings, some individuals and groups have questioned whether monetary policy could contribute to greater stability in the level of employment and the flows of investment and production. As so often is the case in economics and business, however, we must look for the effects at the margin. In the present context we must look for the effects of changes in the tone of the financial markets on the internal and external flows of funds at the margin.

The funds for investment outlays may be thought of as flowing through the cash account from depreciation, retained earnings, and the financial markets. These funds from the financial markets may come from the sale of noncash liquid assets, bank loans, bonds, stocks, and so on.

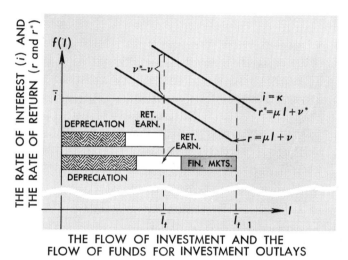

THE FLOW OF INVESTMENT AND THE
FLOW OF FUNDS FOR INVESTMENT OUTLAYS

Fig. 17-2. The Determination of the Flow of Investment and Sources of Funds for Investment Outlays.

However, given the earlier notion of a relationship between financial plans, as indicated by the liquidity ratio (Sect. 17.2) and planned capital expenditures as a leading indicator of cyclical change, we view some of the means of payment as going first into government securities and so on, and then as being withdrawn from the financial markets at the time of the expenditure. We are led, in this event, to view the more immediate sources of cash at the time of the actual expenditures, as in Fig. 17-2. In the illustration, an increase in investment demand corresponds to an expansion in the withdrawal of funds from the financial markets, retained earnings, and depreciation. The increased withdrawal of funds from the market we view as a result of an increase in the value of investment in relationship to cost conditions (i.e., $CV > C$, $r^* > i$ or $v^* > v$) at some immediately preceding level of investment. The increase in the flow of retained earnings, too, may result from this, since the retention of earnings becomes worth more at the rate of return r^* than their payout for reinvestment elsewhere at the rate i.

Now, in this context, an increase in the rate of interest would work toward contracting the flow of investment by reducing the profitability of the flow at the margin. It would do this in part by providing the incentive to reduce the withdrawal of funds from the market and possibly to return funds to the market through the purchase of noncash liquid assets. It would also contribute to an increase in the proportion of earnings paid out as dividends. This could be due to a premium on the payout of earnings under such conditions.

A fundamental relationship resulting from the above (Sect. 17.2) analysis is that between corporate liquidity and planned capital outlays (Sect. 17.2). The relationship, too, was shown to be consistent with tests of cross-sectional data. Thus we are moved to suggest that monetary policy may operate upon the level of investment outlays by affecting liquidity and the preference for utilizing the marginal flows of funds in varying amounts for security purchases, dividend payments, capital expenditures, and so on.

17.5. Other Business Sectors

The other business sectors are the nonfinancial corporate sector (excluding large manufacturing corporations), the nonfinancial noncorporate business sector, and the farm sector. The present consideration of these sectors, however, requires a modification in one of our implicit assumptions about the larger firms, namely, that of a separate identity for owners and managers. The smaller the firm the greater the likelihood of a common identity between sources of equity funds and the policy-making unit of the firm. Further, in applying the analysis to firms organized as individual proprietorships and partnerships, the personal income tax becomes related to them as the corporate income tax is related to corporate income. The emphasis is simply that the cost of the debt financing of a noncorporate business is also deductible as a cost in the taxation of personal income.

The nonfinancial corporate and nonfinancial noncorporate business sectors. The nonfinancial corporate (exclusive of large manufacturing corporations) and the nonfinancial noncorporate business sectors may, for convenience, be combined. The convenience, as it turns out, is simply that which permits a more common comparison between the financing of large, medium, and small businesses.[18] The primary difference between large and small firms, with medium size in between, may be thought of in terms of varying degrees of access to funds over the entire range of financial markets for the purpose at hand.[19]

To say that small firms lack access to the entire range of financial markets does not mean that such a firm is lacking in credit resources. An established firm with a good earnings record, good management, and a strong equity position undoubtedly has a good bank connection. Also there is the added collateral in the form of the owner's personal liability under the noncorporate forms of business organization. In addition, the bulk of the small business population is engaged in routine and repetitive activities that frequently have enough permanent or long-term investment without further recourse to the financial markets. There are, nevertheless, small firms whose needs are unjustified, and there are others of promising growth potential with unsatisfied financial needs because of unwillingness to broaden control or because of the excessive cost of or lack of access to funds.

Sources of funds and small businesses. Sources of funds to small firms may be classified as follows:

(1) Financing intermediaries, such as banks and insurance companies;

(2) Individuals and specialized lending and investing firms, including commercial finance companies and factors;

(3) Other business firms who extend liberal trade credit or provide other special credit arrangements that substitute for the working capital of small firms;

(4) Government loan programs for small business.

The primary source of financial markets funds to small businesses is in the form of commercial bank credit. Banks are generally local institutions with special community interest including the well-being of local business. These institutions extend short-term (maturity up to one year) loans as well as term and other long-term loans to small businesses, although they have a responsibility to maintain a relatively high degree of liquid loans to their portfolio. These loans are often backed by collateral or otherwise secured in order to reduce the risk in granting the loan. Because real estate ranks high among acceptable collateral, mortgage loans are frequent. Life insurance companies, too, are a source of intermediate- or long-term loans to small firms, and arrangements may even be made to have them maintain compensating balances for a smaller firm's line of credit. These companies, however, generally invest in government securities (including Federal, state, and local), corporate bonds, and mortgages. As a result, small business financing from this source generally represents a minor portion of investments of life insurance companies.

In addition to the sources mentioned, there are individuals and groups of concerns which enter more directly into the investment process. Sometimes, however, there will be an intermediary with the individual providing the funds offering a finder's fee for a good prospect. These individuals or groups are generally interested in concerns with unusual growth potential—especially those producing or distributing products or services that are based on advanced technological developments, or mining and oil companies with a promise of a rapid recovery of investment as well as a high profit return. Stocks of such enterprises may be purchased to be held for a short period with the hope of a substantial capital gain. After all, capital gains are taxed at more favorable rates than income.

Commercial finance companies (including sales finance companies and personal finance companies) and factors are sources of funds that have been developed to meet financial needs that have arisen in recent years. Their business is concentrated in the East and in the large metropolitan centers. They have developed techniques for supplying credit to businesses that cannot qualify for ordinary bank loans. The sales finance companies finance business as well as consumers. They finance inventories of dealers in automobiles and in other consumer durable goods. The companies also finance dealers' sales, though this is the subject matter of consumer credit. They sometimes, however, own factoring or commercial financing subsidiaries. Factoring, on the one hand, consists of purchasing accounts receivable. It is sometimes called "notification financing" because the trade customers are notified that their accounts have been purchased and are payable to the factor. Loans on receivables, on the other hand, may result with the receivables simply being assigned to commercial finance companies. These loans are sometimes referred to as "nonnotification financing" because the lender does not collect the accounts nor does he assume the risk of credit loss on the accounts. Such lenders also provide warehouse and "on-the-premises" financing of inventories.

Other means of financing small business include the financing of equipment sold to the smaller firms by larger manufacturers, the routine extension of trade credit, and the more liberal extension of such credit at times. Manufacturers sometimes provide installment financing of store fixtures, varied equipment, and industrial machinery. Furthermore, there is generally an excess of accounts payable over accounts receivable for nonfinancial businesses in the smaller asset size. At times, when funds are less available, this type of credit may be relied upon to a greater extent than at other times. Indeed, as a sales promotion device, the maximum number of days permitted for payment may, at times, be extended at no penalty to the debtor.

Small businesses (continued) and the Small Business Administration. The Small Business Administration (SBA) is the primary Federal government agency with a loan program designed specifically to promote the welfare of small business since 1953.[20] The SBA provides small business concerns with needed credit up to a limited amount through participating in loans with private sources or through direct loans when such financing is not otherwise available on a reasonable basis from banks and other private lenders. Other functions performed by the SBA include help to small firms in obtaining a fair share of government procurement and assistance in management and technical production problems. Other government agencies authorized to furnish loans or help businesses obtain credit include those acting under the Defense Production Act of 1950. The agencies acting under the authority of this act simply guarantee loans to expedite defense production.

Also the SBA is responsible for carrying out the provisions of the Small Business Investment Act (Sect. 9.2), an act intended to stimulate flows of private equity capital to small businesses. Essentially, this 1958 act[21] provided for making Federal money available to specialized investment companies—called small business investment companies or SBIC's[22] and the authority to grant Federal charters for such companies in the absence of state chartiering facilities. In any event, the SBA issues the licenses to obtain the government funds, and by 1961 over 200 SBIC's were licensed to operate under the 1958 act.

Sources of funds and small businesses (summary). In sum, the short- and intermediate-term needs of small business firms are reasonably well met with such diverse sources as commercial banks, insurance companies, larger nonfinancial corporations, finance companies, and the Small Business Administration. The long-term needs are only partly met by individuals and groups of concerns for firms with unusual growth potential whose policy-making units are not unwilling to have the control broadened through wider ownership. Beyond these sources, small business investment companies offer a source of long-term funds to small business. The unwillingness to share control is not only a characteristic of small firms but it is, at times, a costly problem as well. Almost all of the sources of funds to small firms are more costly than they would be if the equity position of such firms (or the personal wealth of owners in the case of noncorporate businesses) were stronger and if they could maintain portfolios of noncash liquid assets. It may be said that the higher cost of funds to small firms is due to the greater risk involved in extending loans to them as well as the cost of ascertaining the creditworthiness of such borrowers and the higher cost of processing small loans.

The farm-business sector. Much that has been said about the financing of small business may also be said of farm business. There are numerous farms, only a small proportion of which operate under a corporate form of organization. The primary means of outside financing are bank credit other than that secured by mortgages and mortgage financing. In some instances, businesses doing business with farm units provide trade credit and means of equipment financing. The small size of the production units limits the access of farm business to the wider financial market for funds.

Most farm proprietors are doubtlessly reluctant to dilute control through widening ownership and expanding the size of the production units.

In addition to these similarities to other small business units, however, the farm business sector is characterized by features that have led to a multiple expansion of government credit agencies to facilitate its financing since World War I. The features contributing to the growth of credit agencies may be thought of as those associated with technological changes in the industry, on the one hand, and those identified with its special nature, on the other. In the first instance, before World War I, land was cheap and the use of fertilizers and other improvements of land were infrequent, and the use of expensive power machinery was in its infancy. The efficiency of the production unit has tended to increase with size. In the second instance, the industry is characterized by the following: (1) many units producing similar products which adds to its competitive nature, (2) generally inelastic demands for its products, (3) the association of greater risk with small units and the possible effects of natural adversities (i.e., "acts of God," in fundamentalist thought), and (4) the excessive strength of the farm bloc in Congress.

The extensive public and quasi-public credit services to agriculture as of mid-1959 consists of (1) those operating within the Farm Credit Administration (FCA) and (2) those provided by the more specialized programs of the direct agencies of the Federal government.[23] The first group includes the land bank system, the production credit system and the banks for cooperatives. The first two of these are separate systems of cooperatively organized district banks and local lending associations. The latter is a set of quasi-public district banks extending credit to private cooperative associations marketing farm products or purchasing farm supplies, although these activities are excluded from the farm-business sector.

17.6. Summary

The principal changes in financial structure as firms increase in size pertain to the cash account, bank loans, and noncash liquid assets. As a proportion of assets, bank loans decline; this weakens the motive for holding cash as a precaution against meeting a subsequent liability, and noncash liquid assets increase. These differences between firms by asset size, moreover, have certain implications for assessing the effects of credit conditions. The smaller firms, for instance, rely more heavily on banks relative to their size for funds and, consequently, they are more subject to the availability of credit at the bank as a constraint on spending. The larger firms, on the other hand, have a more direct access to the financial markets generally relative to their size. Namely, they hold a larger proportion of liquid assets in noncash form, and these may readily be disposed of as a means of obtaining funds. Given the holdings of noncash liquid assets, then, the larger firms have a relatively stronger tie with credit conditions via the rate of interest or "cost of capital" for capitalizing the value of additional assets as contrasted with the availability of credit.

The latter rate (= const.) becomes one of the equations in our investment demand model. It allows for risk, and the rate (= const.) may shift in response to certain credit conditions. The other equation is that defining the rate of return from additional assets. Thus we have a solution, or equilibrium, under the condition whereby the rate of return is equal to the rate of interest. Such a model has features similar to those employed in capital budgeting at the individual firm level. However, we abstract some of the operational difficulties encountered in arriving at the rates in question at the firm level, and we recognize the interdependence of the profitability of separate projects entering into the capital budget, as well as the interdependence of the cost of alternative forms of financing. We denote the rate of return as the rate that would equate the flow of returns from the entire flow of capital expenditures to the cost of the flow of expenditures, and so on.

Recognizing capital budgeting practices and the resulting existence of series for the backlog of planned capital expenditures for large firms, we deal with the latter series as leading indicators, particularly of a decline in expenditures. We also note the presence of a relationship between corporate liquidity (as an indicator of the availability of funds for effecting expenditures) and planned capital outlays. This relationship, in combination with an earlier view about speculative shifts in liquidity, leads us to conclude that liquidity increases both in anticipation of expenditures and as a means of storing value.

The notion of equilibrium in our aggregative model is less general than general equilibrium (Sect. 5.2). Even so, using the methods of an earlier equilibrium analysis and recognizing the Keynesian equilibrium, we present an equilibrium structure for the business sector or large firms in particular. This structure permits us to focus on yields in the various financial markets and to arrive, for example, at conclusions about how firms may react in response to rising yields in the bond market and declining yields in the stock market. In fact, to the extent that there is external financing under the latter conditions, we anticipate a rise in the use of equity funds vis-à-vis debt funds, and so on.

Most of our emphasis on the investment and financial behavior of firms is in terms of a rather refined analysis. Some of its assumptions—implicit and otherwise—are strenuous. Clearly, they are inapplicable to the smaller type of firms that lack access to the entire range of financial markets. Such firms may lack access to the necessary funds for asset expansion, at times, even to banks and insurance companies. Under average credit conditions, and especially under stringent credit conditions, they may seek funds from commercial finance companies, through special credit arrangements, from small business investment companies, and from government loan program.

References

1. For a discussion of the motives of managers, see William L. Baldwin, "The Motives of Managers, Environmental Restraints, and the Theory of Managerial Enterprise," *The Quarterly Journal of Economics,* May 1964, pp. 238-256.

2. See William J. Frazer, Jr., *The Liquidity Structure of Firms and Monetary Economics* (Gainesville, Fla.: University of Florida Press, 1965), Sect. 7.2.

3. William J. Frazer, "The Financial Structure of Manufacturing Corporations and the Demand for Money: Some Empirical Findings," *The Journal of Political Economy,* April 1964, p. 177.

4. *Ibid.,* p. 177; and *The Liquidity Structure of Firms and Monetary Economics,* Chap. 7.

5. William J. Frazer, Jr., "Monetary Analysis and the Postwar Rise in the Velocity of Money in the United States," *Schweizerische Zeitschrift für Volkswirtschaft und Statistik,* December 1964, pp. 591-595.

6. William J. Frazer, Jr., "Financial Structure of Manufacturing Corporations and the Demand for Money: Some Empirical Findings, *The Journal of Political Economy,* April 1964, p. 178.

7. *Ibid.,* p. 179; and *The Liquidity Structure of Firms and Monetary Economics,* Chap. 3.

8. See, e.g., Joel Dean, *Managerial Economic* (Englewood Cliffs, N.J.: Prentice-Hall, Inc.), pp. 551-610; Executives, Armstrong Cork Company, "Capital Expenditure Policies and Procedures," *Variability of Private Investment in Plant and Equipment* (Washington, D.C.: U.S. Government Printing Office, 1962), pp. 25-29; and William H. White, "The Changing Criteria in Investment Planning," in the immediately preceding work, pp. 1-24.

9. See Ezra Solomon, *The Theory of Financial Management* (New York: Columbia University Press, 1963).

10. The literature on these concepts underwent rapid developments in the late 1950's and early 1960's, and the writers from both the financial management and monetary points of view have not settled on the operational detail and precise content pertaining to the concepts. See, e.g., Solomon, *op.cit.;* Alexander Barges, *The Effect of Capital Structure on the Cost of Capital* (Englewood Cliffs, N.J.: Prentice-Hall, Inc., 1963); and the works cited in the latter volume.

11. One series for planned capital outlays is that provided quarterly by the National Industrial Conference Board. See Morris Cohen and Martin R. Gainsbrugh, "A New Survey of Capital Appropriations," *The Conference Board Business Record,* October 1956. pp. 418-434. The survey is reported quarterly in *Newsweek* magazine and the *Conference Board Business Record.* Other important and useful surveys of plant and equipment expenditure expectations are conducted by the McGraw-Hill Department of Economics and

jointly by the Department of Commerce and the Securities and Exchange Commission. The latter surveys are reported for the coming year in a fall issue of *Business Week* and in the March issue of the *Survey of Current Business.*

12. See Solomon, *op.cit.*, p. 32.

13. See Solomon, *op.cit.*, p. 10; Arthur Smithies, "Economic Fluctuations and Growth," *Econometrica,* January 1957, pp. 13-14.

14. Solomon, *op.cit.*, p. 32.

15. For an exposition of investment demand in the orthodox Keynesian literature, see Alvin H. Hansen, *A Guide to Keynes* (New York: McGraw-Hill Book Company, 1953), pp. 117-125; and Smithies, *op.cit.*, pp. 10-15.

16. William J. Frazer, Jr., "The Financial Structure of Manufacturing Corporations and the Demand for Money: Some Empirical Findings," *The Journal of Political Economy,* April 1964, p. 182.

17. *Revenue Act of 1962, Hearings Before the Committee on Finance,* United States Senate (Washington, D.C.: U.S. Government Printing Office, 1962), pp. 114-116.

18. Actually, the attempts at defining business sizes are somewhat arbitrary. Some may be according to the absolute size of assets. Others may be according to the given proportion of total assets for a whole industry. See Eleanor J. Stockwell, "What Is 'Small' Business?" *Financing Small Business* (Washington, D.C.: U.S. Government Printing Office, 1958), pp. 150-171.

19. George W. Mitchell, "Review of Survey Findings," *Financing Small Business* (Washington, D.C.: U.S. Government Printing Office, 1958), pp. 359-370.

20. See Carl Arlt, "Government Loan Programs for Small Business," *Financing Small Business* (Washington, D.C.: U.S. Government Printing Office, 1958), pp. 253-281.

21. The 1958 Congress reached a "high-water mark for legislation benefiting the nation's small business concerns." The acts passed by Congress in that year included, in addition to the Small Business Investment Act, the Small Business Act, the Technical Amendments Act, and the Small Business Tax Revision Act—all extended some form of special favor, tax or otherwise, to small business. The acts apparently recognized small business as a vital institution, worthy of government subsidy, since there was little evidence to support the notion about the unavailability of capital for small business. See Eugene A. Myers and Randall S. Stoute, "New Federal Aids for Small Businesses," *Michigan Business Review,* March 1959, pp. 11-15; and Irving Schweiger, "Adequacy of Financing for Small Business Since World War II," *The Journal of Finance,* September 1958, pp. 323-347.

For a more recent SBA-sponsored report on the effects of tight credit on small business and for additional bibliography pertaining to the financing of small business, see Deane Carson, *The Effect of Tight Money on Small Business Financing* (Providence, R.I.: Prepared by Brown University for the Small Business Administration, 1963).

22. See "Small Business Investment Companies," *Monthly Review,* Federal Reserve Bank of Chicago, October 1958, pp. 13-16; and "Small Business Investment Companies, A Progress Report," *Monthly Review,* Federal Reserve Bank of Chicago, May 1961, pp. 11-16.

23. See R. J. Saulnier, Harold G. Halcrow, and Neil H. Jacoby, *Federal Lending and Loan Insurance* (Princeton, N.J.: Princeton University Press, 1958), pp. 151-233.

Appendix to Chapter 17

Competition and the Interest
Elasticity of Investment Demand

The question arises from time to time as to whether changes in credit conditions have any effect on business expenditures, and discussions pertaining to the question may take the form of the effect of the availability (or the lack of availability) of credit (Sect. 25.3), or the effect of a change in the rate of interest on investment expenditures, as in the investment demand framework (Sect. 17.2). In the latter instance, moreover, one may encounter denials of the presence of any effects from changes in the cost of credit, given its availability. The conclusion, in such instances, is that investment demand is interest inelastic. This is usually loosely taken to mean that changes in the rate of interest have little or no effect on investment outlays by business firms.*

Special problems arise, however, in measuring the effects of changes in the rate of interest on investment. For example, if investment demand (Sect. 17.2) is shifting upward faster than the rate of interest, then we still expect in such a period of rising demand and rising interest rates

---

* The notion of a high inelastic investment demand ($\to 0$) has also been dealt with in terms of the so-called "liquidity trap," by some writers and in other contexts. These have concerned the demand for money—the quantity theory (Sect. 5.1) or the liquidity preference demand for money (Sect. 4.4). In the first instance, "if the money stock rises, velocity will not rise as much or may even fall." In the second and more common instance, the liquidity trap has been discussed with reference to that portion of the liquidity preference curve, such as point E in Fig. 4-3, where a small change in the rate of interest calls forth an infinitely large change in the demand for money, i.e.,

$$\left| \frac{dM/M}{di/i} \right| \to \infty$$

Although probability has not been explicitly introduced in these discussions, note that at point E, in Figure 4-3, there is virtual certainty that bond prices will decline (and interest rates rise).

383

an expansion in investment expenditures, and a rise in the activity of money balances (Sect. 5.4). Conversely, if investment demand is shifting downward faster than shifts in the rate of interest, we still expect a contraction in investment demand and a decline in the activity of money balances.

The question of whether investment demand is inelastic, in other words, is not simply one of whether changes in the rate of interest vary indirectly with changes in the flow of investment over time. The existence of a solution to our investment demand model and its usefulness in analyzing changes in investment, nevertheless, do depend in some measure on the hypothesis of interest elasticity of investment demand, at a moment in time, or in some measure on the freedom of entry of new firms to participate in greater than normal profits, as we wish to demonstrate.

Formally, the hypothesis of the interest elasticity of investment demand is as follows:

$$\left| \frac{dI/I}{dr/r} \right| = \left| \frac{dI}{dr} \right| \frac{r}{I} > 1,$$

where a percentage change in the rate of interest (i.e., $\Delta r/r$) is said to call forth a greater percentage change in the flow of real capital investment [i.e., $(\Delta r/r) < (\Delta I/I)$]. The hypothesis keeps recurring, although evidence from business attitude surveys of the prewar years seemed to support the opposite notion of interest inelasticity.[1] Perhaps the recurrences demonstrate both the lack of a better alternative and the difficulty of obtaining reliable information from the possibly misleading utterances of respondents. As one well-known professor re-emphasizes for us: "It is arrogant to doubt data, but one should also use common sense as evidence."[2] Consequently, let us further examine the hypothesis concerning interest elasticity as it relates to our investment demand model. We wish in particular to show the following: (1) the implicitness of the hypothesis in the solution of our fundamental Keynesian model (Sect. 17.2), assuming an absence of competition for greater than normal profits as defined below, and (2) the consistency of the existence of a solution with the familiar freedom of entry axiom from economics.

The elasticity of investment demand. The assumption of profit maximization (Sect. 17.1) is, at the outset, a part of our model. The primal assumption of profit maximization, however, has a dual side—the assumption of cost minimization. One implies the other. And in the context of our aggregative model, we view the aggregate of decision-making units of the respective firms as maximizing absolute returns (i.e., rI) net of all cost except the cost of funds, on the primal side, and minimizing the absolute cost of funds (i.e., iI), on the dual side. We assume they do this independently of investment opportunities evidenced by greater than normal profits for other firms (i.e., $rI > iI$). We relax this strenuous assumption below, but, for the present, we want to illustrate, using numbers, the point that the assumption of the elasticity of investment demand is implicit in the existence of a solution to our investment model.

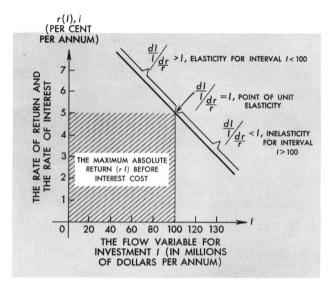

Fig. 17-A. Interest Elasticity of Investment Demand: An Example.

To begin with, the particular example is set forth in Fig. 17-A. It is as follows:

(1) $$r = \mu I + \nu, \quad \nu < 0$$
(2) $$i = \kappa,$$

where $\mu = 1/20$, and $\nu = 10$.

There, in the illustration, we have a schedule relating the level of the flow variable I to the rate of return (r) on the flow. Also we have denoted there the elasticity (or inelasticity) of investment demand for different intervals for the flow variable. For example, for $I > 100$, demand is inelastic (i.e.,

$$\left| \frac{dI/I}{dr/r} \right| < 1),$$

for $I < 100$, demand is elastic (i.e.,

$$\left| \frac{dI/I}{dr/r} \right| > 1),$$

and for $I = 100$, demand is unit elastic (i.e.,

$$\left|\frac{dI/I}{dr/r}\right| = 1).^{*}$$

Considering only the primal assumption, the flow of investment would be increased until $I = 100$. At that level the absolute return on the flow net of all cost except interest is a maximum. Note, for example, if $I = 60$, then $r = 7$, and the absolute return is 420 (million) dollars, and so on:

I	$\times$	r	$=$	absolute return[**]
80		6.0		480
100		5.0		500 (max.)
120		4.0		480
140		3.0		420

The maximum absolute return then is at $I = 100$, independent of any constraint other than that afforded by the profit maximization assumption.

Next, continuing with the particular example and moving on to Fig. 17-B, let us impose the rate of interest at 3 per cent. At this rate the coordinates for a solution to the model at the initial time specify the equilibrium point E_t (140, 3), where the coordinates are the flow variable and the rate, respectively. The equilibrium level for the flow variables is $I_t^{(E)}$, but the maximum profit level for the flow variable is I_t. The level of investment falls short of that determined by the model. Further, the level of investment is unchanged by the introduction of the particular rate of interest (i.e., $i = 3$). And at the level of investment I_t, there is excess or greater than normal profit (i.e., $rI_t > iI_t$) after allowance for risk. On the other hand, suppose the rate of interest is raised to 6 per cent. At the old level of investment (I_t), the rate of interest is greater than the rate of return (i.e., $i > r$), and the absolute interest cost exceeds the absolute return. There are less than normal profits (i.e., $rI_t < iI_t$) for $I = 100$, the maximum profit equilibrium is at the point (80, 6), and the level of flow consistent with our assumption would be 80 million dollars per annum at the new moment in time. In this instance, the flow of investment and the level of the flow determined by a solution are the same. Consequently, we see that the assumption of elasticity of

---

[*] An important property of the elasticity of a function is its independence of the units in which the variables are given, since it deals with percentage changes. We could quote I, in other words, in hundreds of dollars or millions of dollars, as long as we confined ourselves to the product of the derivative $|dI/dr|$ and the factor r/I.

[**] Actually our I is the supply price of the flow of investment and r is the rate for discounting the stream of prospective returns from the flow. The product Ir therefore suggests the form of a perpetuity (i.e., $I = R/r$), and as a consequence the *absolute returns* in question serve mainly as an index of profits per annum on I rather than a flow of profits themselves (see Sect. 4.1 and compare with Sect. 5.4) unless the discounted stream approximates a perpetual flow.

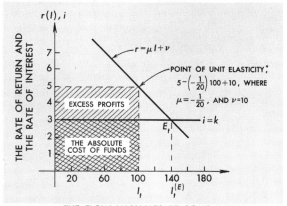

THE FLOW VARIABLES AT SOME INITIAL
TIME FOR INVESTMENT (I_t) AND THE
EQUILIBRIUM LEVEL OF INVESTMENT $(I_t^{(E)})$

*Fig. 17-B. Interest Elasticity of Investment Demand: An Example. * In this particular example the point of unit elasticity in the schedule defined by the equation (1) is the point (100, 5), where $\mu = -1/20$, and $\nu = 10$. To check this, first solve equation (1) for the flow variable I. Then differentiating both sides of the result (i.e., $I = [r - \nu]/\mu$, with respect to r, $dI/dr = 1/\mu$. Next, substituting this result in the definition of elasticity, and then substituting $r = 5$, $\mu = -1/20$, $I = 100$ we get, in sum*

$$\frac{dI}{dr} \frac{r}{i} = \frac{1}{-1/20} \frac{5.0}{100} = 1.$$

investment demand is implied by the existence of a solution to our particular model under the assumption of an absence of any competitive interest by existing firms or potential firms in the greater than normal profits of other firms.

As a proposition, we may conclude that under the latter assumption, the hypothesis of the interest elasticity of investment demand is implicit in the solution to the Keynesian investment demand model.

Freedom of entry: another hypothesis. One way to cause the above model to generate a flow of investment corresponding to the equilibrium conditions (i.e., $r = i$) is to make some assumption about the presence of competition. Indeed, some make the point that Keynes assumed perfect competition,[3] but we need not assume all of the axioms of perfect competition. Freedom of entry is enough. Even less strenuously, this axiom could be interpreted to mean simply that some existing firms will expand investment in the various industries with the view to exploiting the presence of greater than normal profits in the operations of other firms.

In either case, the fulfillment of the conditions in question may be viewed as pushing investment to a level consistent with the solution to the investment demand model, even in a neighborhood of inelastic demand. Attracted by the greater than normal profits (i.e., $rI_t > iI_t$), such as appear in Fig. 17-B, new firms may enter into business. At the same time, they may increase the flow of investment expenditures and reduce the rate of return until the solution to the model in fact determines the level of investment, even under conditions of an inelastic investment demand.

The freedom of entry axiom causes investment to behave in the model as if investment was interest elastic. At least, that is, a decline in the rate of interest causes investment to expand in the partial derivative sense.

References

1. William H. White, "Interest Inelasticity of Investment Demand—The Case from Business Attitude Surveys Re-examined," *The American Economic Review*, September 1956, pp. 565-587; and William H. White, "The Changing Criteria in Investment Planning," *Variability of Private Investment in Plant and Equipment* (Washington, D.C.: U.S. Government Printing Office, 1962), pp. 1-24. See also Executives, Armstrong Cork Company, "Capital Expenditure Policies and Procedures," *Variability of Private Investment in Plant and Equipment* (Washington, D.C.: U.S. Government Printing Office, 1962), pp. 25-29.

2. Paul A. Samuelson, "The Current State of the Theory of Interest Rates, with Special Reference to Mortgage Rates," *Conference on Savings and Residential Financing*, 1960 Proceedings, pp. 23-26. With respect to the relationship between the rate of interest and the demand for money by business firms, results from more recent empirical studies indicate a further denial of the relevance of the liquidity-trap hypothesis as an explanation of observed economic behavior. See Allan H. Meltzer, "The Demand for Money: A Cross-Section Study of Business Firms," *Quarterly Journal of Economics*, August 1963, p. 415.

3. See Arthur Smithies, "Economic Fluctuations and Growth," *Econometrica*, January 1957, pp. 10-11.

18

The Consumer Sector: Factors Affecting Consumer Expenditures

> In the Protestant Ethic, morality was identified with savings because of the idea that man, rather than society, was ultimately responsible for his destiny, and that, considering the way things were stacked, he'd better well attend to it. As our society has grown more beneficent, external forces, like the corporation personnel department, have assumed much of the protective job, and it is this defensive alliance, not a slackening of moral fiber, that has robbed saving of its moral imperative (William H. Whyte, Jr., *The Organization Man* [1956]).

The consumer has become a complex figure in economics—due, in part, to the accumulation of more detailed observations of his behavior, and due, in part, to the development of a more complicated way of life. In the main line of economic thought, he was seen by Jeremy Bentham (1748-1832) and the devotees of classical economics and their followers as responding in receipt of units of pleasure and pain. This view has been referred to by some as that of economic man. However, with the passage of time, the consumer has been viewed as maximizing something loosely called satisfaction and still as having some freedom of choice in our partly free society. His essential social nature has been recognized without sacrificing the most essential notions of economics. And since 1936, in particular, further importance has been given to his behavior in economics by J. M. Keynes's psychological law and related studies in psychological economics.[1] Keynes's observations led him, in fact, to formulate his consumption function (Sect. 15.2). He held the following: "The fundamental psychological law, upon which we are entitled to depend with great confidence both *a priori* from our knowledge of human nature and from the detailed facts of experience, is that men are disposed, as a rule and on the average, to increase their consumption as their income increases, but not so much as the increase in their income.[2]

In the instance pertaining to the consumer's way of life, a complicating aspect has been the growth of financial institutions in the intermediate position between the flows of saving and investing (Sect. 15.1) or spending generally, and the accompanying "automatizing" or "contractualizing" of saving (e.g., payroll saving plans, pension deductions, life insurance premiums, and so on). In this setting, the consumer has acquired a stock of liquid assets. Furthermore, there has been a psychological acceptance and widespread development of the practice of making available and granting large amounts of installment credit [i.e., credit to be repaid in a number of installments (Sect. 8.3)] to consumers with which to finance purchases of an expanding volume of consumer durable goods, housing, and even trips to the Bahamas and a weekend in Miami. The effect here has been to broaden the range within which the consumer may effect transactions for current output in the short run by drawing, in effect, upon his future income. But, perhaps more striking, as noted below (Sect. 18.1), is the fact that consumers' views about their expected incomes change and these changes give rise to an expansion (and, alternately, a contraction) of credit in the short run, and to the changes in their actual income in the environment of modern credit practices and institutions. We must, then, derive some orderly view out of the details about consumers' economic behavior in this complex environment. In doing this, several topics follow: the consumption function in perspective (Sect. 18.1), expenditures (exclusive of those on housing and nondurable goods) and some effects of monetary policy and credit conditions (Sect. 18.2), and housing expenditures, government-sponsored programs, and the effects of credit conditions (Sect. 18.3).

These topics do not constitute a survey of the voluminous amount of theoretical and empirical work on the consumption function.[3] Instead, we wish to show (1) that the consumption function $C(Y)$ exhibits instability in the short run, (2) that its instability is influenced by the growth of savings and the practice of granting installment credit, (3) that consumption may be expressed as a function of a number of important variables other than income, and (4) that consumer expenditures may be affected in the short run by credit conditions and monetary policy. In the process of showing the above, we also introduce some institutions and practice affecting the extension of credit to consumers, and emphasize major classes of expenditures, such as those on automobiles and housing.

18.1. Some Perspectives on the Consumption Function(s), Consumers' Expenditures, and Factors Affecting the Expenditures

The consumption function hypothesis (i.e., $0 < dC/dY < 1$) has been stated above as a fundamental psychological law. There is, then, the implication of a behavioral group like the consumer sector, and there are other implications. There are those pertaining to how the function fits in with the earlier (Sect. 15.1) aggregate demand function (i.e., $Y_d = C(Y) + I$) and the more general equilibrium analyses (Sect. 5.2 and 15.1). Given the notion of a behavioral group, there are questions about the identification of particular classes of expenditures with those by the consumer sector vis-à-vis others—the business sector(s), the government sector(s), and so on. There are also some unsettled issues about the definition of consumer expenditures vis-à-vis investment expenditures.

Thus, to deal with the implications above and the latter problems of classification, we simply introduce the controversial issues pertaining to the definition, treat the problem as an arbitrary matter for our purposes, view the original consumption function as the sum of functions for several classes of expenditures, and treat the consumption function for the consumer sector in the perspective of our earlier and more general analyses (Sect. 4.1 and 5.2). Then we shall present some specific equations from empirical study as a means of providing some introductory perspective on the various factors affecting consumer expenditures.

Some problems of classification. The consumption function has been discussed as the consumer sector's demand for goods and services as a function of income. But some would classify consumers' durables, as well as housing, as investment. They would, for the most part, view the durability of the item in question as the distinguishing feature. Others, however, would question this practice. One writer, for example, questions "giving up the threshold of the household as the dividing line between investment and consumption of commodities." He points out that business expenditures for coal are investment, and that "durability of goods is no criterion for investment." [4]

The consumption function(s). Earlier, the consumption function was generally denoted $C(Y)$ (Sect 15.1). Now we re-emphasize this function as the sum of a number of separate functions, i.e.,

$$C(Y) = C_n(Y) + C_s(Y) + C_d(Y) + I_h(Y) + G,$$

where C_n is consumption expenditures on nondurable goods (i.e., only tangible goods of the nondurable quality),

C_s is consumption expenditures on services,

C_d is consumption expenditures on durable goods,

I_h is consumption expenditures on housing,

G (= const.) is collective expenditures by the public in the form of government purchases of goods and services, and

Y is the aggregate of income received by wage and salary
earners and the owners of other factors of production.

This separation of expenditures anticipates the subsequent chapter
pertaining to the government sector. At the same time, it provides a set
of expenditures corresponding to classes of purchases by the consumer
sector, but we wish to emphasize a discussion of consumer behavior in
terms of a behavioral unit—the consumer sector.*

Keynes, and early Keynesians, viewed the aggregate consumption
function as a very stable function of income (i.e., constant underlying
parameters over time), although he dealt with other factors under the
headings "objective" and "subjective." [5] He was especially concerned
with the determination of income, and he treated consumption as its
dependent variable. As matters have turned out, however, the function
has been shown to shift in the short run under conditions of modern
society. In the present setting for our society, the aggregate of the flow
of consumer expenditures will include some infrequent expenditures by
individuals and households for goods that would cost more, save work,
produce pleasure, and enhance prestige. These goods could be extra
bathtubs, automobiles, television, air conditioning units, or washing machines. Also the aggregate will include expenditures for recreation, travel,
education, and medical expenses. In both instances, modern credit facilities and stocks of widely distributed liquid assets will permit the consumption of these various goods and services without the consumers
having to wait, at times. Many of the outlays for durable and less durable
goods and services can, at times, be postponed. Thus, at a given time,
we will want to view these large and less frequent expenditures as tending to balance out so as to effect a smooth stream of expenditures when
seeing them as a function of income. But, over time, we will wish to view
the function as a shifting one when a number of individuals and households reacting to a common change in the setting, a news event, or some
other stimuli outside of the immediate environment tend as a group to
increase (or decrease) the flow of expenditures. We will want, furthermore, to recognize below the wider range within which these shifts may
occur (1) as a result of the psychological acceptance of credit buying
and the availability of installment credit and (2) as a result of the availability and backlog of liquid assets as savings media.

Had Keynes anticipated the likely sources of instability in his function
under modern credit and savings arrangements, he may or may not have

---

* The consumer sector in the flow-of-funds accounts (Sect. 15.1) comprises individuals in their capacity as members of households. See references in an earlier
section (Sect. 15.1).

stated his function otherwise. On the one hand, there is the need to view consumption in response to the parametric shifts or as functions of other variables, and, on the other, there is the need for a general framework of the type he presented. It is not as general as it could be (e.g., compare Sect. 5.2), but it is sufficiently general to permit practical policy recommendations pertaining to the use of credit, tax, and expenditure measures as a means of maximizing employment, output, and so on (e.g., Sect. 17.3 and 19.3). Thus we continue to work within the framework of the initial model (Sect. 15.1), even while taking the subsequent and more general view of consumption expenditures and the subsequent and more detailed view of the determinants of consumption.

The analytical perspective. In putting the consumption function in the perspective of our earlier analyses (Sect. 4.1 and 5.2), we proceed from the initial analysis (Sect 4.1) by thinking of consumers as maximizing utility subject to a constraint in the form of total assets, or as equating the rates of return for the respective flows of outlays on categories of items including net saving. In this instance, we ask: what is the total value of the flow of income to consumers, the group that ultimately receives all of the returns from the factors of production either in the form of salaries and wages or interest, dividends, rent, and retained earnings? Clearly, in terms of income received, this total value must be the discounted value of the flow of GNP (viewed as payments to the factors of production). Note that this total value concept would include the discounting of income from all forms of labor, and the total value would, consequently, include the value of human capital. Further, in terms of expenditures, the total discounted value of GNP must include stock variables, exclusive of the stock of money (Sect. 5.2), such as those for (1) durable goods, (2) nondurable goods (i.e., only tangible goods of the nondurable quality), (3) services, (4) housing, and (5) net savings [i.e., dollar savings (Sect. 15.1) less borrowings where savings are in such forms as savings deposits, time certificates of deposits, savings-and-loan shares, credit union shares, insurance, bonds, and equities]. In sum, viewing income received as income spent for goods and services and net savings, we have a form of total asset constraint where

$$\text{Total assets in dollar units as the discounted value of income to the factors of production} = \begin{cases} \text{Stocks in dollar units of} \\ (1)\ \text{durable goods} \\ (2)\ \text{nondurable goods} \\ (3)\ \text{services} \\ (4)\ \text{housing} \\ (5)\ \text{net savings} \end{cases}$$

Now, changes in prospective income change total assets, and this change is necessarily accompanied by changes in the various stock variables comprising expenditures as proportions of the total. Indeed, our earlier analysis (Sect. 15.2) would indicate this prospect. For one thing, as long as the stocks are all changing at constant rates, there are no changes in the stocks as proportions of the total. In terms of earlier analysis, however, the only way we can change income to the factors of production is in terms of changes in aggregate demand—namely, a shift in the consumption function (and, therefore, the saving function) and/or investment. If the shift is in terms of investment, income changes and consumption and saving change as functions of the change in income. Depending on the slope of the consumption function, the proportions may or may not change. On the other hand, if the shift is in terms of the consumption function the proportions clearly change. For example, an upward shift in the consumption function (and, therefore, a downward shift in the saving function) increases income and saving. Viewing investment as constant ($I = $ const.), the flow for stock variables (1) through (4) increases more than the flow for (5). [Conversely, a downward shift in the function $C(Y)$ would have the reverse set of results.] But in addition we may even wish to specify other hypotheses and note other changes in proportions. For example, where

$$C(Y) = C_n(Y) + C_s(Y) + C_d(Y) + I_h(Y),$$

we may wish to hypothesize, in accordance with widely recognized facts, that

$$dC_n/dY < d(C_s + C_d + I_h)/dY$$

That is, as wealth grows, a larger proportion of expenditures goes to durable goods, services, and the quality and quantity of housing.

The two main propositions we wish to state on the basis of the above analysis are these:

Proposition 1: *A change in the expected flow of income alters the rate of change in wealth, and, at the same time, it parallels changes in the flow of income.*

Proposition 2: *If consumers expect income to rise (decline) and use consumer credit (repay debt) or attempt to reduce (increase) saving as a means of altering expenditures on the bases of this prospect, they will in fact bring about their expectation of a rise (decline) in income.*

The two possible factors permitting these shifts in the consumption function that bring about the fulfillment of the expectations, as previously mentioned and as subsequently discussed, are (1) the modern practice of granting consumer credit for consumer expenditures and (2) the backlog of accumulated savings. Note that we treat these factors as *permissive* and *enabling* rather than *causal*.[6] If consumption varies as a result of income, the expenditures are effected out of income by our statement of a consumption function. The availability of consumer credit per se will not shift the function, but it may permit such shifts. As we note later (Sect. 18.2), changes (i.e., extensions less repayments) in the volume of consumer credit are indicative of shifts in the consumption functions. Empirically, the question would be resolved by noting whether the credit was available before an upward shift in the function. The evidence would be the unused resources of consumer credit institutions, and the extra resources or excess of liquid assets held by commercial banks. Usually an upward shift in consumer expenditures is accompanied by a reduction in the availability of consumer credit as the volume of credit expands (Sect. 18.2). The lack of availability of consumer credit, however, is subsequently viewed as an upper bound on the shift in the consumption function.

Just as the absence of indebtedness is a potential source of funds for effecting expenditures, so, too, are the cash and noncash liquid assets of the consumer sector,[7] as in the business sector (Sect. 17.1). This is what occurs: If the shift with respect to the consumer sector's demand for goods and services is upward, then savings may be drawn upon or consumer credit utilized to effect the shift and increase the income velocity of money (money supply = const.). If the shift is downward, then consumer debt must contract and income velocity decline (money supply = const.). In this instance, attempts to increase the flow of net saving simply result in a decline in income and income velocity (money supply = const.).

Some factors affecting consumer expenditures. As the consumption function hypothesis states, consumer expenditures are an increasing function of income. In addition, as the above introductory discussion indicates, a number of other factors operating through changes in conditions underlying the function may affect consumer expenditures. Those already explicitly stated or implied would include expectations, the rate of interest, the liquidity position of consumers, the modern practice of granting installment credit, prices, and the durability of the items in question. Later, we deal in somewhat greater detail with the financial factors involved and shifts in the consumption function in particular. However, to set forth in perspective some of the crucial factors affecting consumer expenditures in the short run, we introduce a few equations defining consumer demand in terms of an expanded number of independent variables. These extra variables come, one may say, from treating variable parameters as variables. The equations in question define the earlier (Sect. 18.1) variables (i.e., C_n, C_s, C_d, and I_h), all in 1954 dollars (i.e., constant dollars with a 1954 base) for one quarter. They are the consumption equations from Lawrence Klein's quarterly forecasting model.[8] They are as follows:

$$(1) \quad C_n = 27.7 + 0.259 \underbrace{\frac{Y-T}{p_n}} + 8.88 \underbrace{\frac{P}{W}} + 0.191 \underbrace{\frac{1}{8}\sum_{i=1}^{8}(C_d)_{-i}} + 0.0056 \underbrace{\left(\frac{L}{p_n}\right)_{-1}}$$

disposable income deflated by implicit deflator for nondurables | ratio of nonlabor personal income (i.e., distribution variable) | average of previous 8 quarters nondurables expenditures | end of previous quarter liquid assets of consumers deflated by price of nondurables (L = cash balances)

$$(2) \quad C_s = -152.0 + 0.103 \frac{Y-T}{p_s} + 41.1 \frac{P}{W} + 0.0188 \frac{1}{8}\sum_{i=1}^{8}(C_s)_{-i} + 0.0596 \underbrace{\left(\frac{L}{p_s}\right)_{-1}} + 1.13 \underbrace{N}$$

[similar to equation for C_n] | population (millions)

$$(3) \quad C_d = -67.1 + 0.363 \underbrace{\frac{Y-T}{p_d}} + 58.4 \underbrace{\frac{P}{W}} - 1.14 \underbrace{\frac{1}{8}\sum_{i=1}^{8}(C_d)_{-i}} + 0.174(C_d^{(e)})$$

disposable income deflated by implicit deflator for durables | ratio of nonlabor personal income (i.e., distribution variable) | average of previous 8 quarters durable expenditures | Federal Reserve index of consumer buying intentions for durables

$$(4) \quad I_h = -11.3 + 0.0764 \underbrace{\frac{Y-T}{p_h}} - 0.776 i_L + 0.0011F + 0.00812(I_h^{(s)})_{-1}$$

disposable income deflated by implicit deflator for nonfarm residential construction | average yield or corporate bonds (per cent) | number of marriages (thousands) | previous quarter's number of housing starts

The endogenous variables, in addition to those defined above, are

$Y - T$ (i.e., income less taxes), a measure of disposable income;

W labor income;

P nonlabor personal income;

$C_d{}^{(e)}$ Federal Reserve index of consumer buying intentions for durables;

L cash balances;

p_n, p_s, p_d, p_h averages of prices for durables, nondurables, services, and housing, respectively;

i_L a function of rates on ninety-day commercial paper (denoted i_S) and the previous quarter's i_L; and

i_S a function of last quarter's per cent of total bank reserves held in excess of requirements and of the average of current Federal Reserve discount rates.

Note that each of the four classes of expenditures is increasing functions of disposable income, decreasing functions of their respective averages of prices, and so on. Note, too, that cash balances (L) are used in equations (2) and (3) as a liquid asset variable of strategic importance, that housing demand in particular is an increasing function of the number of marriages, and so on.

18.2. Consumer Expenditures (Exclusive of Housing and Nondurable Goods) and Some Effects of Monetary Policy and Credit Conditions

This section deals with consumer expenditures for durable goods from the demand side of the market, on the one hand, and from the sources of credit side, on the other. On the demand side, it proceeds by further developing the rationale underlying a fundamental notion—namely, the increase in the durable portion of consumer expenditures contributes to the potential increase in the instability of consumer demand. In doing this it re-emphasizes the role of prospective price-level changes on demand and introduces attitudes of consumers toward price changes as relevant variable. It then proceeds to deal with the effects of the monetary authorities' policy with respect to price level changes on consumer expenditures, all within the analytical framework set forth.

On the credit side, this section deals with the question of durability, reasons underlying the increased availability of funds for durable expenditures, and the resulting increase in the potential instability of consumer expenditures. Within the framework developed, it then deals with some effects of credit conditions on the sources of credit side of the market. Also, and again within that framework, it deals with the effects of credit conditions on the spread between the limits within which the consumption function may shift, at least as such shifts pertain to the practice of granting installment credit.

Most of the present discussion would also apply to housing expenditures and shifts in the expenditures, after allowing for the operations of special governmental agencies pertaining to housing. Housing expenditures, shifts in those expenditures, sources of funds for home expenditures, and certain effects of credit conditions on those expenditures are dealt with in a separate section (Sect. 18.3), however, partly because of the effects of the agency operations in question.

Durability and the instability of expenditures (the demand side). As another proposition:

Proposition 3: *The increase in the proportion of total expenditures for durable goods and services in modern times and the related hypothesis* $dC_n/dY < d(C_s + C_d)/dY$ *imply some increase in the potential instability of the consumption function, in the framework of earlier analysis* (*Sect. 5.4*). This proposition follows because of (1) the increased durability of goods and the durability of the flow of prospective psychic returns or utility from expenditures, even on such intangible items as medical services and travel; and because of (2) the effects of prospective price changes and attitudes toward inflation on the value vis-à-vis the cost attached to the goods and services in question.

To illustrate the above proposition, let us denote the prospective stream of returns from our several classes of expenditures, and the respective rates of return needed to equate the future expenditures to their present costs [denoted $C_n (= \text{const.})$, and $(C_s + C_d)(= \text{const.})$]:

$$C_n(= \text{const.}) = \frac{R_1}{(1 + r)}$$

$$(C_s + C_d)(= \text{const.}) = \frac{R_1}{(1 + r)} + \ldots + \frac{R_n}{(1 + r)^n}$$

Now, suppose consumers expect prices to rise, and that they are disposed to take advantage of the prospect. What then? Clearly, from earlier analysis (Sect. 5.4) the returns (i.e., $R_1, \ldots, R_n$) more distant from the initial time rise more in value. Consequently, the rate of return rises more for the latter set of expenditures. The changes needed to bring about the new equilibrium are as follows: (1) a rise in the proportion of expenditures on services and durable goods and (2) a rise in the aggregate of expenditures since, by hypothesis, $dC_n/dY < d(C_s + C_d)/dY$, and the consumption of nondurables increases as income increases. (The converse set of expectations and a different attitude toward the prospective price rise could bring about different changes.)

In introducing attitudes as a variable, i.e.,

(prospects and news about $\to$ (attitudes toward $\to$ (consumer behavior),
changes in p_n, p_s, and p_d) the price changes)

we are recognizing certain principles about the psychological behavior of consumers:[9]

Principle 1: "People get accustomed to a certain type of news, do not notice it, and do not react to it."

Principle 2: Small price advances, initial perceptions of price advances, or large price advances stimulate advance buying.

Principle 3: When price advances persist, as during so-called "creeping inflation," consumers may react by reducing the flow of their discretionary purchases. In extreme form this is a "buyers' strike."

Principle 4: Consumers' attitudes toward and perceptions of price changes are subject to change.

A study of consumers' behavior and attitudes in the postwar United States, however, supports the above principles and the view that American consumers react negatively to persistent price increases, "particularly, in the crucial periods from the spring of 1951 to mid-1952 and in 1957. . . ."

Of course, on practical grounds, there is another reason for expecting consumer expenditures for durables and certain services to be less stable than those for nondurable goods. Namely, the purchases of durables and many services, including some medical and dental services and travel, are easier to postpone than expenditures on such nondurable items as food. An old washing machine, an automobile, a pair of glasses, or some given state of physical condition can be made to provide service a bit longer.

Some effects of monetary policy (the buyer's side).

Proposition 4: *Monetary policy may have a stabilizing effect on consumer expenditures, in the preceding framework.* In this case, by "monetary policy" we have in mind the monetary authorities' goals as actually attained with respect to the average of prices for the output of goods and services.

In the case of factors contributing to an increase in expenditures, monetary policy may have an offsetting or constraining effect by damping any prospect of rising future returns, and/or by raising the prospective returns on saving. In the case of an inadequate level of employment of resources, monetary policy may have a stimulating effect in the short run by bringing about the expectation of a rise in the magnitude of the prospective flow of returns from durable goods and services and/or by lowering the value of the prospective returns on saving.

These effects presently attributed to monetary policy are pretty generally recognizable. There remains the additional need to deal further with the effects pertaining to the cost and availability of funds for expenditures on durable goods and housing as well as with the institutional characteristics of these respective markets.

Durability and the instability of expenditures (the sources of credit size). The modern institution of consumer installment credit provides the consumer with a wider range within which to effect shifts in the flow of his expenditures relative to his income over time. This is due in part to the practice of extending such credit for some services, such as travel, usually on the basis of a steady salary and a satisfactory credit standing. But it is due more so to the rule of thumb for granting credit on many durable goods. The rule is that installment credit may be granted for the purchase of a durable good and repaid over the life of the good. The common condition is that the unpaid balance of credit does not exceed the value of the good. For example, thirty-six-month sales contracts on automobiles became common in 1955. Later, with the introduction of the five-year warranty on automobiles as an indication of their durability, there were instances of forty-two-month and even forty-eight-month contracts. These latter contracts meant that a larger total volume of credit could be extended upon the introduction of the contract. They also meant that consumers could effect a larger shift in their flow of expenditures for a given monthly payment. And, if consumers chose to repay their credit before extending it again, the longer contracts imply, furthermore, a potentially larger drop in subsequent expenditures.

The following proposition follows from the above:

Proposition 5: *The flow of installment credit corresponding to shifts in the consumption function is the new extensions of installment credit net of the repayments.* At least with respect to the credit side, as contrasted with the direct use and liquidation of accumulated savings, the function is shifting upward and the flow of credit is positive when the new extensions exceed the payments. Conversely, in this same respect, the function is shifting downward and the flow is negative when the repayments exceed the new extensions.

Figure 18-1 shows flows (extensions net of repayments) expressed as average rates per annum for the years including the recessions of 1953-1954, 1957-1958, and 1960-1961. The flows are shown for the major components of installment credit: automobile paper, other consumer goods paper, repair and modernization loans, and personal loans. Automobile paper, of course, corresponds to credit for the purchase of automobiles, other consumer goods paper represents a general type of credit other than that for automobiles, repair and modernization loans pertain to credit for repairing and improving owner-occupied dwelling units (Sect. 18.3), and personal loans include those for medical expenses, education, travel, and possibly any of the above items (for example, some may find it feasible and less expensive to finance an automobile through a renewable ninety-day note, with stock as security and with some schedule for reducing the principal every ninety days over a thirty-six-month period). In the illustration, the decreases in the flows correspond to the recession phases, and the increases correspond to the expansion phases, as would be anticipated from our analysis.

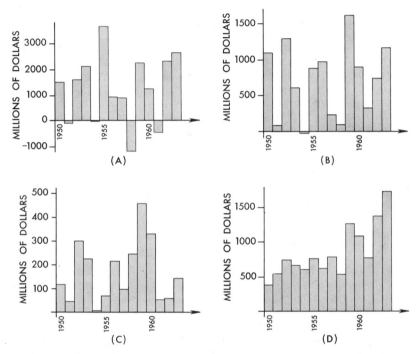

Fig. 18-1. Installment Credit by Major Parts: (A) automobile paper; (B) other consumer goods paper; (C) repair and modernization loans; (D) personal loans.

Figure 18-2 shows flows of installment credit from the installment credit sources. The most active sources in this field as shown in the illustration are sales finance companies and commercial banks. The diagram indicates the extent to which consumers deal directly with both credit-granting institutions, but there are other indirect relationships. Some involve businesses and relate to sales finance companies (Sect. 17.5). And with respect to banking, there are two special plans relating to installment credit: (1) charge-account banking and (2) the check-credit system. The charge-account plan permits an individual under the plan with a participating bank to make a purchase from a local merchant under the plan who, in turn, receives a cash payment from the bank for a fee, which in its turn bills the customer. If the buyer's payment is delayed beyond a certain period, his credit account at the bank is placed on an installment basis. The check-credit system, on the other hand, is

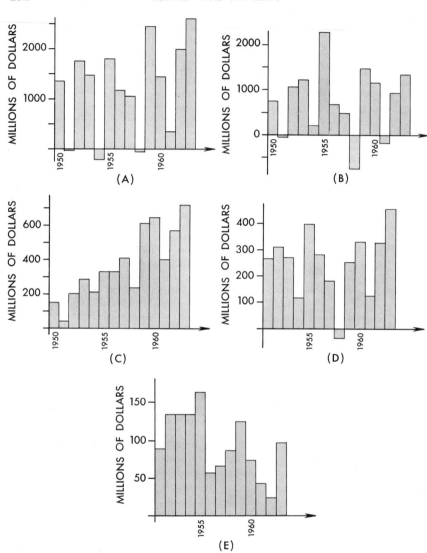

Fig. 18-2. Installment Credit by Granting Institutions: (A) commercial banks flow; (B) sales finance companies flow; (C) credit unions flow; (D) consumer finance companies flow; (E) other flow.

similar to the English "overdraft" system and permits one to draw against a line of credit previously extended by his bank through the use of a book of specially coded checks. As the checks are cashed, the borrowing customer is obliged to make monthly payments to his bank on previously agreed-upon terms.

Automobiles: an instance of the demand for durable goods. The automobile is a durable good of principal economic importance. In the early 1960's, its sales comprised a proportion of GNP approximately equal to that for housing expenditures and, like housing (Sect. 18.3), the sales of many other industries depend upon the sale of automobiles for their own sales. Their demand, moreover, has been extensively studied and shown to depend on a number of factors operating over both the long and short runs.[10] As above, and in addition to the prior importance attached to income, however, we mainly emphasize the permissive and causal factors pertaining to short-run shifts.

As implied in the more general analysis (Sect. 18.1), the spread between the limits to the extent of fluctuations in auto sales, and, therefore, in some portion of the sale of other materials, is clearly affected by the practice of financing a large portion of auto purchases with installment credit. Changes in auto sales, as reflected in the changes in the volume of installment credit, have contributed to all of the recessions and business expansions shown in Fig. 18-1. These shifts, furthermore, have apparently been substantially affected by other than purely economic considerations.

As indicative of one predominant aspect of the consumers' reaction to a major portion of Detroit's products and the various foreign imports, one finds such expressions as "a new variety of ego-stirring expensive cars," and Detroit's "insolent chariots." [11] With the record United States auto production in 1955 of 7.9 million cars,[12] as reflected in terms of the volume of credit, this record year was not again surpassed until the introduction of radical style and quality changes in the early 1960's.

Some effects of credit conditions (the sources of credit side).

Proposition 6: *Credit ease (tightness) as effected by the Federal Reserve officials may broaden (narrow) the limits within which consumption function shifts may be effected, within the above framework.* It may do this by operating through the availability and cost of funds to the credit-granting intermediaries and, consequently, by affecting the capacity of the credit-granting intermediaries to expand credit. They may broaden (narrow) the spread between the limits by easing (tightening) credit and reducing (increasing) its cost to credit-granting intermediaries.

The credit-granting intermediaries depend upon the spread between their buying rate and selling rate for profits, and when their costs rise above the returns they expect, they make less funds available at less favorable terms with respect to both the maturity of a loan and the initial down payment. Assuming easy credit conditions in the recession and early expansion phases of the business cycle, sales finance companies, for instance, may profit from obtaining funds at low cost and making them available to credit-worthy borrowers at relatively favorable cost and on favorable terms with respect to down payments and the length of the maturity of the installment loan. The longer maturity for loans, the lower down payment, and a favorable liquidity position spell out a high upper bound to the credit facilities upon which consumers may draw. As the expansion phase progresses, however, and assuming tighter credit conditions as it progresses, sales finance companies costs for long-term funds rise above the more economical costs they may expect in the future. Prepayment options permitting the refinancing of long-term debt issues are available, but these are at higher costs. The shorter-term credit and money markets must then be called upon to supply the funds for further credit expansion. Limits upon these sources are set by: (1) the need to maintain the most profitable level of liquidity; (2) the variation in the seasonal and cyclical supply of funds available to sales finance companies through the direct placement (Sect. 17.2) of commercial paper with nonfinancial corporations; and (3) the provision of the National Banking Act of 1863 (Sect. 7.4), as well as a similar provision in many state banking laws, which limits the maximum amount a bank may loan to one borrower to 10 per cent of the bank's capital and surplus.[13] The previously high upper bound upon the credit facilities available to the consumer then becomes an effective constraint. The sales finance companies ration credit to the more carefully selected borrowers, and even then on less favorable terms. The positive flow of installment credit ceases (extensions of credit no longer exceed repayments); the consumption function for expenditures financed from this source shifts downward.

18.3. Housing Expenditures, Government-Sponsored Programs, and the Effects of Credit Conditions

Expenditures on the purchase of new housing have been estimated to have been about 4 per cent of GNP over the postwar years. And viewing housing expenditures in relation to the equipment, furnishings, services, and so on accompanying them, the broader class of expenditures rises to about 12 per cent of GNP according to the estimates of one expert.[14] Changes in the expenditures for housing, and the effects of credit conditions on these expenditures, consequently, are important determinants of changes in GNP, the level of employment, and so on. The determinants of the demand for housing, including credit conditions, however, are not simply set forth. For one reason, governmental institutions have arisen to affect the expenditures on housing and, at times, cushion the effect of credit tightness on the liquidity of the debt instruments for extending housing credit—namely, mortgages. These have been due primarily to welfare views about the relationship of housing to our health and security. For another reason, expenditures on housing are an increasing function of income; we look less favorably on the quality of our old stock of housing as we become more affluent as a society (i.e., as average income rises in constant dollars). For still another reason, and in addition to the latter relationship to income and the credit and other institutional factors, the demand for housing is greatly affected by demographic factors. These refer to all of the things affecting net household formations and the age composition of the population. These latter factors we must allow for, therefore, especially in analyzing the trend of the demand for housing. Even so, we confine our discussion primarily to the conventional type of housing financing, government housing agencies, and the effects of credit conditions, since our present interests are primarily in changes in expenditures in the short run and in the effects of credit conditions on housing. We do this following a brief reference to some demographic factors.

The "life cycle" in housing. The life cycle in housing may be briefly set forth. To begin with, newlyweds may typically move into apartments or in with the in-laws. Continuing:

> As income rises, this undesirable state changes quickly or is avoided. Next, the interest in individual housing rises very sharply in the year or two years preceding the date when the first child enters kindergarten. Then, except for mobility of employment and other considerations, there is an element of stability as far as housing is concerned until the children reach early teen-age. At this point there is a new demand for housing, more specifically in terms of space and also quality . . . [because] queuing up for the bathroom behind several daughters is a bit of a problem.[15]

As a consequence of the life cycle in housing, the number of marriages is a factor affecting expenditures on housing, as shown in equation (1) above, as well as age distribution. An increase in the proportion of the population, between the ages 22 and 44, becomes a more important factor than the growth of the total population. On this basis, population was expected to increase by 18 per cent in the 1960's, but in the ages where housing demand was strongest the increase was estimated at only about 3 per cent.[16]

Housing expenditures, conventional financing, and credit ease (or tightness). Home financing involves obtaining credit through the sale of a mortgage or lien against the property being financed. It is of three types: FHA, VA, or conventional financing. Here we simply outline some common features of all forms of home financing, introduce sources of funds for conventional financing, and deal with the effects of credit ease or tightness on home expenditures, independent of government programs.

The purchase of a house typically involves a large initial cost and down payment to buyers relative to most of their incomes and daily expenditures. The credit represented by the mortgage and the interest on the unpaid balance of the loan is then repaid in installments. These installments historically ran over a short period of time but, in response to the competitive stimulus from government programs, mortgages with thirty years to maturity and smaller installment payments have been common in the postwar years. Also, housing expenditures under this type of financing (i.e., exclusive of government participation in the mortgage market and the effect of long-run factors as the growth and composition by age group of the population) would react to cyclical changes in income and general credit conditions so as to conform positively with the short cycle of expenditures generally. For example, the intermediate suppliers of funds other than commercial banks for home financing are primarily insurance companies, mutual savings banks, and savings-and-loan associations. These institutions (Sect. 23.2) would react to easy credit conditions in order to supply credit at a lower interest rate, lower down payment, and longer maturity in the recession and early expansion phases and on less favorable terms in the later expansion phase. On the consumer side, the easier credit would have a stimulating effect on expenditures, after a sufficient lapse in time to plan and effect expenditures. The lower rates would increase the value of a prospective purchase relative to its cost or supply price, and the easier credit condition may, at the same time, contribute to the prospect of inflation and raise the flow of returns or utility expected from the project in question. This prospect would be such that it would further increase the value of the project in relation to its supply price. The effects of general credit tightness would be the converse of the latter effects. And, again there would be some lag in the effect on expenditures, since previously effected plans would continue to be carried out.

In assessing the probable effects of interest rate changes on consumers' demand for credit for housing expenditures, however, it is important to recognize a purely numerical phenomenon. Aside from net income tax advantages associated with various amounts of interest payments, the mere fact that the typical mortgagor makes constant monthly payments on a very long-term mortgage means (1) that small changes in contractual interest rates have relatively little effect on the monthly payment and (2) that, in turn, this latter change itself is likely to have only a small direct effect on consumers' demand for credit. The former of these effects—that of a change in the interest rate on monthly payments—as applied to a $10,000 mortgage for twenty and thirty years, alternatively, is illustrated as follows:

Interest Rate (per cent)	Monthly Payment*	
	Twenty-year Loan	Thirty-year Loan
$4\frac{1}{2}$	$63	$51
5	66	54
$5\frac{1}{2}$	69	57
6	72	60
$6\frac{1}{2}$	75	63

SOURCE: Calculated from *Constant Annual Percent Loan Amortization Schedules: Monthly and Quarterly Payments*, 2nd ed. (Boston: Financial Publishing Co., 1954).

* Monthly payments approximated to closest dollar. Amount of mortgage should be regarded as net of closing costs and any other initial charges. Interest rates should be interpreted as effective rates, i.e., contract rates plus any additional monthly charges (for example, the additional $\frac{1}{2}$ per cent insurance charge on FHA-insured loans).

Note, in this example, that a $\frac{1}{2}$ per cent change in either case changes the monthly payment by only about $3. Thus, when the FHA, a government agency described below, lowered the interest ceiling on its insured mortgages from $5\frac{3}{4}$ per cent to $5\frac{1}{4}$ in 1961 (and, because of a $\frac{1}{2}$ per cent insurance charge, the effective ceiling rate was reduced from $6\frac{1}{4}$ per cent to $5\frac{3}{4}$ per cent), a family considering a $10,000 mortgage for twenty years would find its monthly payments reduced from about $73.50 to $70.50. This would contrast with the greater effect of the term of a loan on the monthly payment, also as shown in the example. One notes in that case that a twenty-year loan at $4\frac{1}{2}$ per cent can be carried with the same monthly payment ($63) as a thirty-year loan at $6\frac{1}{2}$ per cent.

Federal agencies (VA and FHA). Governmental agencies affecting the market for housing include the Veterans Administration (VA) and the Federal Housing Administration (FHA). They also include the government-sponsored, subsequently discussed, Federal National Mortgage Association (FNMA), sometimes called "Fannie Mae." * The programs of

* The operations of other Federal housing agencies, including the FHA, are coordinated through the Housing and Home Finance Agency (HHFA). The three major subdivisions consist of the Home Loan Bank Board (FHLBB), the Public Housing Administration (PHA), and the Federal Housing Administration (FHA). The FHLBB is a part of the Home Loan Banking System which also consists of eleven Home Loan Banks, the Federal Savings-and-Loan Insurance Corporation (FSLIC), and member savings-and-loan associations. It provides credit to home financing institutions on a plan similar in some respects to that by which commercial banks obtain credit through the Federal Reserve banks. Savings-and-loan associations may turn to the Home Loan Banks and augment their normal cash flow through borrowing; the associations may be said to create credit (but not money and not by a multiple of any increase in their savings capital—Sect. 23.2). The FSLIC is a corporation which provides insurance of shares in member savings-and-loan associations. The PHA's activities have been primarily directed toward the development of low-rent housing facilities for lower-income groups. The FHA's activities are discussed below.

the three agencies have been expected to increase the flow of credit into housing by insuring the lenders of funds against loss or by otherwise providing liquidity to the holders of VA-guaranteed * or FHA-insured ** mortgages. One of the effects of the VA- and FHA-underwritten mortgages, however, has been to cause housing expenditures to vary, at times, counter to the short cycle of income, output, and employment.

The feature causing VA-guaranteed and FHA-insured mortgages to have an unusual effect is the legal limitation upon the interest rate on these forms of financing. In the recession when rates on other debt instruments are low, the rates on VA and FHA forms of financing are relatively favorable from the lender's point of view, and such credit institutions as savings-and-loan associations and insurance companies operating through local mortgage companies† tend to make more funds available for the construction of new homes than would otherwise be the case. On the other hand, as the expansion phase progresses, interest rate on other debt instruments may rise so that there is a strengthened preference for the other types of debt instruments by financial intermediaries relative to the preference for VA-guaranteed and FHA-insured mortgages at their previous rates. As such times, regulatory changes, such as a small

---

For a history of these and other institutions in the Federal lending and loan insurance fields, as well as a review of their performance and impact on production, prices, and financing, see R. J. Saulnier, Harold G. Halcrow, and Neil H. Jacoby, *Federal Lending and Loan Insurance* (Princeton, N.J.: Princeton University Press, 1958), pp. 286-361.

* The Veterans Administration's program has provided a plan whereby approved lenders could be guaranteed at no cost up to 60 per cent of the amount of the loan to an eligible veteran of World War II. The guaranteed portion has been limited to $7,500, being designed to take the place of the usual cash down payment. The VA program was last scheduled to expire in June 1958. It has, however, been extended from time to time.

** The FHA program dates from the passage of the National Housing Act of 1934. Under that act, approved lenders are insured for the full amount of their mortgage loans in return for a premium paid into an insurance fund that may be supplemented by government funds if necessary.

† Mortgage companies act as correspondents in originating and servicing mortgages, mostly government-insured ones. They trade on their own account and operate with substantial turnover in their inventory. Over the second half of the 1950's, they increased the share of the volume of VA- and FHA-underwritten mortgages originated from about one-third to over one-half; this parallel declines in the proportions originated by commercial banks and insurance companies. Their expanded role illustrates the specialization in real estate financing since the development of Fannie Mae's operations.

The growth of mortgage companies has reportedly also reflected the emergence of the practice of "warehousing" mortgages. Under this practice the companies accumulate mortgages until their volume is large enough to place elsewhere, such as with life insurance companies and mutal savings banks, often in other parts of the country. The companies carry the mortgages largely by obtaining short-term funds from commercial banks and by using the mortgages as security for the loans.

See "Postwar Patterns of Homebuilding and Financing," *Monthly Business Review*, Federal Reserve Bank of Cleveland, August 1961, pp. 5-8.

one in the rate ceiling, may be made, and the practice of discounting*—
limited by law until 1958—can cause effective rates on VA and FHA
loans to rise above the rate ceiling on such loans. These effects, however, have been limited since a large increase in the rate ceiling may de-

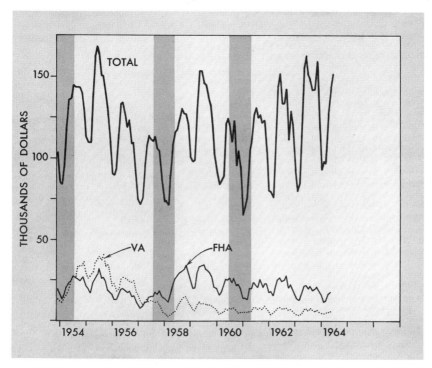

Fig. 18-3. Nonfarm Private Housing Starts by Type of Mortgage (in Thousands of Units).
The series for total nonfarm housing starts is the revised series for monthly housing
starts (see "Revised Monthly Housing Starts," Construction Review, July 1964). The
cyclical turning points are those reported by the National Bureau of Economic Research
(see Fig. 4-1). Source of data: Bureau of the Census, Veterans Administration, and Federal Housing Administration.

feat the purpose of regulation, and some lenders and borrowers dislike
dealing with each other on the discount basis.

The countercyclical consequences of the VA and FHA programs are
shown, at least during the 1953-1954 recession, in Fig. 18-3. In the late
1950's, however, the VA and FHA financing began to decline in impor-

* The practice of discounting refers to cases where the borrower in effect receives less than the face value of the mortgage (and usually a less expensive house),
but nevertheless he is expected to repay the face value of the mortgage plus the interest accruing on the unpaid balance. The practice has at times taken on a disguise;
some mortgage brokers and savings-and-loan officials—unaware of the underlying cost
in builders' supply schedules—insist that the builder pay the discount rather than
the buyer.

tance relative to conventional financing, and changes in the age distribution of the population contributed to a weakening of housing expenditures. Indeed, the rates on FHA-insured mortgages, contrary to the previous pattern, led the cyclical downturn. In 1961 and 1962, moreover, housing expenditures were procyclical—residential construction and its financing parallel general business conditions. This latter behavior reflected the relative increase in conventional financing and the tendency for credit to remain relatively easy during the cyclical expansion following the 1960-1961 recession, as shown later (Sect. 24.2) in terms of the volume of free reserves.

"Fannie Mae." The Federal National Mortgage Association (i.e., "Fannie Mae") was intended as a supporting agency for the government housing programs in its early stages.[17] After being reorganized under the Housing Act of 1954, however, it had as its principal objective the provision of a secondary market facility as a means of widening the market for government-insured mortgages and increasing their liquidity. As a secondary facility it was to provide a market for previously originated, government-underwritten mortgages at times when mortgage funds were scarce, although the purchases are for a fee and in exchange for the purchase of a small amount of stock in Fannie Mae. Alternatively, they were to sell mortgages when credit conditions eased. Further, Fannie Mae's operations are supposed to be self-supporting. This, in turn, means that they cannot afford excessive losses on their sales when market yields (as rates) are rising, nor can they carry a larger inventory without its affecting their costs, since their funds for carrying mortgages are from the sale of common stock, notes, and bonds.*

Since 1955 Fannie Mae has contributed to the developing of a secondary mortgage market.[18] Except for a short while when credit eased in 1958, it was a net buyer of mortgages, but during the post-1960 period of relatively easy credit it was a net seller on more frequent occasions. It has, in addition, served to widen the market for government-underwritten mortgages by buying them in scarce-credit areas (such as some places in the South and West) and selling them in abundant credit areas (e.g., areas in the Northeastern section of the country).

Fannie Mae's sources and buyers* of mortgages, as of December

---

* At mid-1963 the United States Treasury held about two-thirds of the equity in Fannie Mae; the other one-third was issued to sellers of mortgages to that agency. The relatively small amount of liquidity, however, serves as the risk capital and as a basis for sale of bonds in the private capital markets up to ten times the amount of its capital and surplus. Ultimately, the entire equity of Fannie Mae is to become privately held as the private equity increases with the mortgage purchases effected by Fannie Mae. See " 'Fannie Mae' in the Secondary Mortgage Market," *Monthly Business Review*, Federal Reserve Bank of Cleveland, August 1963, pp. 7-8.

* Fannie Mae does not know the identity of the ultimate purchasers of the mortgages it sells, since it sells to numerous private distributors or "mortgage dealers" who in turn resell the mortgages to their customers. See *ibid.*, p. 4.

1962, are shown in Fig. 18-4. There, one may note that mortgage companies are a principal source of mortgages for the secondary market, and mutual savings banks and insurance companies are principal buyers of these mortgages. The illustration reflects the relatively expanded role of mortgage companies in the late 1950's, as originators of VA- and FHA-underwritten mortgages vis-à-vis commercial banks.

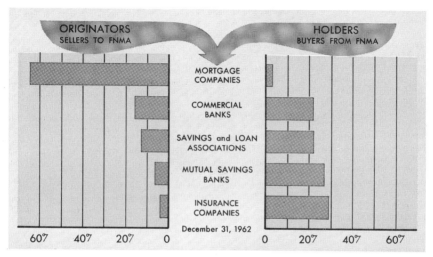

Fig. 18-4. Fannie Mae's Sources and Buyers of Mortgages. * "The percentage distribution of originators of government-insured mortgages is the same as the percentage distribution of sellers of mortgages to the FNMA. Alhough there is no distribution available of mortgage buyers from the agents of FNMA, it is assumed that this distribution is the same as the percentage distribuion of holders of government-insured mortgages, as reported by FHA and VA." (See " 'Fannie Mae' in the Secondary Mortgage Market," Monthly Business Review, Federal Reserve Bank of Cleveland, August 1963). Source: Federal Housing Administration, Veterans Administration, and Federal National Mortgage Association.

Now, our interest in Fannie Mae, in the present context, stems from two sources. One, the transmission of credit ease or tightness throughout the system is facilitated by the development of more perfectly functioning markets, as when facilities are provided for the movement of surplus funds from one area of the country for use elsewhere. But, most importantly, its purchases of mortgages during periods of rising interest rates tend to smooth out the impact of credit tightness on local mortgage markets. Here, the originators of mortgages may sell mortgages to Fannie Mae and obtain funds for originating more mortgages, but they may do so only at increasing interest rates, since Fannie Mae can make changes in the schedules of prices to accord with local conditions, and since its operations must be self-supporting.[19] Fannie Mae, too, may have to obtain additional funds to carry a larger stock of mortgages. This can be done only at an increasing interest cost on its notes and bonds, but, presumably, the bonds and notes it sells, and particularly the shorter maturities, are more liquid than the mortgages. In the latter case, the net effect is somewhat of an offset to the effectiveness of tight credit on housing expenditures.

18.4. Summary

The consumption function, denoted $C(Y)$, was originally viewed by Keynes and early Keynesians as being stable. It constituted a basic function of Keynes' equilibrium system; indeed, the consumption function hypothesis, $0 < dC/dY < 1$, permitted a solution to his aggregate supply-aggregate demand model. By stating the hypothesis in words as a fundamental psychological law, however, Keynes emphasized the behavioral quality of the hypothesis.

As time passed, the potentiality of shifts in the consumption function has come to be recognized as a possible source of instability in aggregate demand, and, therefore, in income. This increase in potential instability results from a number of sources that pertain mainly to the following: (1) the wider range within which the function may shift in the short run as affected by the backlog of liquid savings and the modern practice of granting consumer installment credit and (2) the increase in the proportion of expenditures for services (C_s) and housing (I_h) and the decline in the proportion of expenditures for nondurable goods (C_n), i.e., $dC_n/dY < d(C_s + C_d + I_h)/dY$.

The accumulation of the savings and the practice of granting installment credit are simply permissive conditions. They broaden the range within which the function may shift. The relative increase in the importance of durable goods and services in the consumer budget, on the other hand, mean that the subjective evaluation of the goods and services are more subject to shift in relation to their supply prices. This follows because returns expected in the more distant future are more greatly affected by a prospective rise (or decline) in prices, for example, and consequently their value rises (or declines) more for a given rate of interest.

As the above evaluations of goods and services change in relation to their supply prices, they give rise to shifts in the demand for the flow of goods and services. If the shift with respect to the consumer demand for goods and services is upward, then savings may be drawn upon or consumer credit utilized to effect the shift and increase the income velocity of money (money supply = const.). If the shift is downward, then consumer debt must contract and income velocity decline (money supply = const.). In the latter instance, attempts to increase the flow of net saving simply result in a decline in income and income velocity (money supply = const.). Over-all changes in the volume of consumer debt itself simply reflect shifts in the consumption function. These latter shifts can possibly be offset by attempts to liquidate past savings, but, in the partial derivative sense, there is no way to change the volume of consumer debt except by shifting the consumption function.

The latter relationship between consumer credit and shifts in the consumption function lead to the conclusion that the modern practice of extending credit for consumer expenditures widens the range within which the function may potentially shift. The interrelationships between the credit-granting companies and banks, the availability of credit at those institutions, and the conditions of easy and tight credit, however, lead us to conclude that the Federal Reserve has some influence over the spread between limits pertaining to shifts in the consumption function through their control over credit conditions in the short run.

With respect to each of the several categories of consumer expenditures, exclusive of housing, we are led to emphasize many factors affecting the various classes of expenditures other than income, even after limiting our interest to the short run. In the case of consumer durables, for instance, varables were introduced, at one point or another, such as the average of prices, expectations about future prices, attitudes toward price changes, credit conditions, the stock of liquid savings, public reactions to style and quality changes, and durability.

The relationship between consumer expenditures and expected prices lead to emphasis upon the effect of the Federal Reserve's policy with respect to price level changes within the given analytical framework. There, we noted that, subject to various psychological principles, a policy leading to an expected rise in prices stimulated expenditures and that actions contributing to the prospect of stable or declining prices stabilized expenditures. In particular, in this framework, allowance was made for the psychological principles governing the attitudes toward price changes. These included, for instance, the principle whereby a persistent price advance may cause consumers to react by reducing their discretionary purchases.

We could expect housing expenditures in the short run to be governed by factors and conditions affecting the demand for consumer durable goods. Indeed, independently of government-underwriting programs for mortgages—namely, VA-guaranteed and FHA-insured mortgages—we would expect credit demand for housing expenditures and the demand for housing to behave procyclically. The presence of the latter programs, however, modifies our views about these procyclical effects. For one, there is the interest ceiling on mortgages guaranteed by the VA or insured by the FHA to discourage the use of these government supports at times of tight credit when lenders face relatively more attractive earnings on alternative investment opportunities. For another, the operations of Fannie Mae tend to smooth out the effects of changes in credit conditions on local mortgage markets.

Viewing the two sets of government-sponsored programs together, we note that Fannie Mae is likely to be a net seller of mortgages mainly when credit in general is easy, in relation to the interest ceilings (as rates) on VA- and FHA-underwritten mortgages. Under the persistent fulfillment of the latter conditions, housing expenditures behave procyclically. On the other hand, when yields (as per cents) are rising and when market yields on other investments relatively more attractive to suppliers of funds, Fannie Mae cannot afford the losses from the sale of its inventory. Under these conditions its inventory builds up, and it must obtain funds to carry the inventory. The instruments it sells to obtain funds at such times are likely to be more liquid than the mortgages it buys, and the net effect is somewhat of an offset to the effects of credit tightness. When the credit becomes very tight relative to the interest ceilings on VA-guaranteed and FHA-insured mortgages, furthermore, and given the existing institutions outlined above, housing expenditures are likely to behave countercyclically.

References

1. Characteristic of these studies has been George Katona, *The Powerful Consumer: Psychological Studies of the American Economy* (New York: McGraw-Hill Book Company, 1960).

2. See John M. Keynes, *The General Theory of Employment, Interest and Money* (New York: Harcourt, Brace and Company, 1936), p. 96.

3. For an example of a survey of theoretical and empirical work on the consumption function and for references to a voluminous literature, see Gardner Ackley, *Macroeconomic Theory* (New York: The Macmillan Company, 1961), pp. 208-307. See also, Robert Ferber, "A Study of Aggregate Consumption Functions," National Bureau of Economic Research Technical Paper No. 8, 1953; Robert Ferber, "Research and Household Behavior," *American Economic Review*, March 1962, pp. 19-63; and H. S. Houthakker, "The Present State of Consumption Theory," *Econometrica*, October 1961, pp. 704-740.

4. See Frederick A. Lutz, "Comment," *Consumer Installment Credit* Part II, Vol. V (Washington, D.C.: U.S. Government Printing Office, 1957), p. 234. This volume is one of six resulting from an extensive National Bureau of Economic Research–Federal Reserve study of consumer installment credit. The study followed the widespread use of installment credit to finance a record volume of auto sales (Sect. 18.3) in 1955.

5. Ackley, *op.cit.*, pp. 267-307, expands on the discussion of these two classes of factors.

6. Ackley deals succinctly with this question and, contrary to our own conclusion, concludes as follows: "We do not know to what extent consumer

credit operates as a *causal* as opposed to a permissive factor in consumer spending" (*op.cit.*, pp. 286-287).

7. See Stephen H. Axilrod, "Liquidity and Public Policy," *Federal Reserve Bulletin*, October 1961, pp. 1161-1177.

8. See Lawrence R. Klein, "A Postwar Quarterly Model: Description and Applications," *Conference on Models of Income Determination*, Income and Wealth series (Princeton, N.J.: Princeton University Press, 1964).

9. See George Katona, "Consumer Investment and Business Investment," *Michigan Business Review*, July 1961, pp. 18-19; and Eva Mueller, "Consumer Reactions to Inflation," *The Quarterly Journal of Economics*, May 1951, pp. 246-262.

10. See, e.g., Milton H. Spencer, Colin G. Clark, and Peter W. Hoguet, *Business and Economic Forecasting: An Econometric Approach* (Homewood, Ill.: Richard D. Irwin, Inc., 1961), pp. 244-252; and the references cited therein.

11. "Three Years Back-to-Back," *Monthly Review*, Federal Reserve Bank of San Francisco, September 1963, pp. 133-137.

12. Actually the total sales figure, including imports, was 7.6 million in 1963 as compared with 7.5 million in 1955. Data are from *Ward's Automotive Reports* and R. L. Polk and Co. See "A Seven-Million Car Market?" *Monthly Economic Letter*, National City Bank of New York, November 1963, pp. 124-127.

13. See Donald P. Jacobs, "Sources and Costs of Funds of Large Sales Finance Companies," *Consumer Installment Credit*, Part II, Vol. I (Washington, D.C.: U.S. Government Printing Office, 1957), pp. 341-345.

14. See Walter E. Hoadley, "The Housing Market in the 1960's," *Conference on Savings and Residential Financing, 1961 Proceedings*, Sponsored by United States Savings and Loan League, p. 136.

15. *Ibid.*, pp. 137-138.

16. *Ibid.*, p. 140

17. "'Fannie Mae' in the Secondary Mortgage Market," *Monthly Business Review*, Federal Reserve Bank of Cleveland, August 1963, pp. 2-3.

18. *Ibid.*, pp. 3-5.

19. *Ibid.*, p. 6.

19

The Public Sector: Fiscal Policy, Economic Stabilization, and Growth

> The concept of stabilization previously directed at achieving and maintaining a stationary level of full-employment income at stable prices must be replaced by one of securing a growing level of capacity income at stable prices. Moreover, there is the further problem of choosing between various rates of growth (Richard A. Musgrave, *The Theory of Public Finance* [1959]).

Earlier, the effects of various taxes on business expenditures and the level of employment (Sect. 17.3) were mentioned, as well as government debt (Sect. 13.2) as a response to excesses in government expenditures over revenues. Earlier, too, we mentioned the goals set out for the monetary authorities (Sect. 8.1). In the present chapter, however, we wish to make some allowances for the actions and inactions in the public sector as they relate to these same goals, as they relate to other fiscal responsibilities of the government (Sect. 19.1), and as they may combine with changes in the tone of the money and credit markets (Sect. 19.4). We also wish to indicate specific budget variables (Sect. 19.2) and their multiplier effects (Sect. 19.3) in the context of this broad discussion of the government sector, since most of the prominent budget variables pertaining to a fiscal policy have multiplier effects, such as those for investment and consumption in our earlier model (Sect. 15.2).

Government is said to be effecting a fiscal policy when it shapes the magnitude and composition of expenditures and taxes so as to contribute to economic stabilization, a predetermined rate for economic growth or other national economic goals. The role of shaping expenditures and revenues in economic stabilization and analogously as a means of providing adequate growth to assure the achievement of the national economic goals of maximum employment, production, and purchasing power is not new. In fact, in the 1930's and the early post-World War II years economic growth itself was viewed as a means of assuring the full utiliza-

416

tion of resources—the employment of an expanding labor force and those temporarily out of work as a result of technological advances (Sect. 15.3 and 16.2). Later, in the late 1950's, the emphasis shifted to allow, also, for the possibility of faster economic growth. Though subsequently supported for other reasons (Sect. 19.4), the initial shift in emphasis was in response to the increased burden of national security from 36 per cent of Federal expenditures for the current output of goods and services in 1940 to 86 per cent in 1960, and in response to such comparative growth estimates as those made by the Central Intelligence Agency. That agency estimated that GNP in the United States in constant prices increased at an average of 3.25 per cent per annum in the 1950's, in comparison with a 7 per cent average in the USSR.

There have been variations in the mix of fiscal and monetary policies. In the early post-World War II years, the emphasis was on the notion of a rather rigid countercyclical fiscal policy, in combination with a neutral (Sect. 24.3) or a countercyclical monetary policy at the operational level (Sect. 24.1). Later the postwar experiences revealed problems with respect to the timing of a countercyclical fiscal policy, and, still later, the shift in the emphasis to include the prospect of faster growth as a fiscal goal complicated matters pertaining to the coordination of fiscal and monetary policies. Thus we note an increase in the reliance on monetary controls vis-à-vis fiscal measures as means of achieving stability (Sect. 19.4). These experiences, it would seem, suggest a warning against drawing rigid conclusions about the necessity of any single mix of policies. As we note later, even in broad qualitative terms, there are twenty-seven different policy mixes at the operational level for fiscal, debt, and monetary policy. Situations may change, making it necessary to call for any one of the twenty-seven.

19.1. Fiscal Policy and Economic Stabilization

As often viewed by economists, fiscal policy as a stabilization device would result in budget surpluses in the expansion phases of business activity and budget deficits in the contraction phase. The surpluses could result from increases in tax rates and/or increases in tax revenues and decreases in expenditures. In the most general sense, the increase in revenues in the expansion phase would be viewed as indirectly damping demand by the other sectors, and the decline in the expenditures would directly reduce demand. Conversely, the deficits could result from the reverse set of changes and have the reverse set of effects. Nevertheless, the sole objective of the revenue system and government is not the conduct of countercyclical fiscal policy. Some expenditures, such as those for national security—Marshal Plan aid in the early postwar period, the

Korean War mobilization in 1950-1952, and the post-Sputnik defense programs—become necessary, independent of the need to make expenditures in the expansion phase of the cycle. In addition, the urgency of the programs may not be appropriately timed to achieve the desired fiscal effect.

Still other complications in effecting a countercyclical fiscal policy pertain to the proper timing of the political actions of Congress and the President and to the presence of a budget balancing philosophy. With respect to the first, crucial timing difficulties are inherent in democratic processes and our system of checks and balances; with respect to the second, the constraint on Congressional expenditures resulting from the presence of a budget balancing philosophy serves to provide some economic discipline in government in lieu of the absence of the constraint usually imposed by competition among private enterprises. To a large extent, the public and those seeking balanced budgets may accept the notion of a balanced budget over the entire cycle rather than in each given fiscal year, and they may even accept changes in government debt (D) less than or equal to proportional changes in income—i.e.,

$$\frac{\Delta D/D}{\Delta Y/Y} = \lim_{\Delta Y \to 0} \frac{\Delta D}{\Delta Y} \frac{Y}{D} = \frac{dD}{dY} \frac{Y}{D} \lessgtr 1.$$

But taxes once levied have a way of continuing in effect, and even the acceptance of an ever-increasing public debt may not assure well-timed fiscal actions.

Usually, fiscal policy measures are divided into those which are (1) automatic and those which are (2) discretionary. The above obstacles to appropriate timing do not apply so significantly to the automatic stabilizers, which include those taxes whose tax yields change automatically in the same direction as income and those outlays that change automatically in the opposite direction from income, given the tax and expenditure structure. And the discretionary features of fiscal policy are those that require changes in the tax and expenditure structure as a result of legislative or administrative action. The tax yield and outlay changes in the first group relate to the shorter-run goal of stabilization by definition, but a discretionary fiscal policy is complicated by the possibility of its relating to the shorter-run stabilization goal and to the attainment of a predetermined growth rate. The problem of the appropriate timing of a fiscal policy is less crucial in the latter case.

The conduct and timing of an appropriate fiscal policy is also further complicated by the presence of a consciously or unconsciously determined fiscal policy on any of the three levels of government—Federal, state, and local. The role of the Federal government in providing national defense, the reliance on the personal and corporate income taxes as the primary sources of revenue, and the need for central planning in such matters as a national system of superhighways assure a primary role for the Federal government in matters of fiscal policy. Despite this, however, state and local government expenditures have shown a stabilizing response to changes in monetary policy, and they have grown almost as rapidly in the post-World War II period as Federal expenditures.

Some fiscal actions over the postwar years. Fiscal actions revealed in the imbalances of the Federal sector's receipts and expenditures have tended to serve as a stabilizing force in the postwar years, apart from lags in timing. Data from the national flow of funds accounts (Sect. 15.1), for example, show that the net withdrawal (a source) and the net return (a use) of funds from and to the financial markets would appear reasonably stabilizing through most of the postwar years through 1960, apart from a net withdrawal of funds in 1952 and in part of 1953.

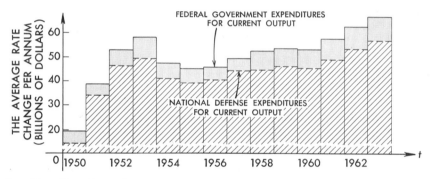

Fig. 19-1. Flows for Federal Government and National Defense Expenditures. Source of data: U.S. Department of Commerce.

In 1955-1957—years of cyclical expansion—the excesses of receipts of funds over expenditures net of changes in cash holdings were returned to the financial markets through the purchase of securities. In response to the recession of 1957-1958 and the slow recovery of 1958-1959, there were excesses of expenditures over receipts, net of changes in cash holdings. The automatic stabilizers, however, were mainly the cause of these results and carried part of the burden of destabilizing discretionary actions. Except during the early phase of the Korean War, increases in statutory tax rates usually accompanied increases in expenditures, the high taxes were usually retained during recessions, and tax rate decreases were in part offset by declines in expenditures. For the most part, changes in expenditures for a portion of the current output of goods and services simply reflected changes in expenditures for national defense, as indicated in Fig. 19-1. These changes in average flows for Federal expenditures on the current output of goods and services and the national defense portion of them (the shaded areas) are shown.

Automatic ("built-in") stabilizers. The most sensitive automatic stabilizers are the corporate and personal income taxes and the payroll taxes in combination with unemployment compensation. The first group is particularly sensitive because the tax base (i.e., the incomes subject to the tax) varies more than in proportion to income, since firms and individuals move into higher tax brackets as their incomes increase. The second group is particularly sensitive because revenue from the payroll taxes varies directly with income and employment, and unemployment compensation varies indirectly with income and employment. In some measure, the revenue from the most important taxes will vary with cyclical changes in income, output, and employment. These may even include sales taxes (i.e., specific taxes on cost per unit of output and ad valorem taxes in terms of a percentage of sales prices) and, in a decreasing order of sensitivity, property taxes.

Briefly, the extent of automatic stability may be viewed as depending on three related and overlapping features of the economy: (1) the progressiveness of the tax structure (i.e., the tendency for the taxes in the structure to take a larger proportion of high incomes and a smaller proportion of low incomes), (2) the degree to which the respective tax bases and outlays fluctuate with national income, and (3) the relative size of the government. The first applies mainly to taxes as they bear directly on individuals, or after a shifting of taxes to individuals. In this case, the more progressive the tax structure, the greater the tendency for a change in personal incomes to cause a greater proportional change in revenues to the government sector. The second feature relates to particular tax bases like the more volatile corporate income. Also, in terms of payroll taxes, changes in the tax base are a compound of changes in individual incomes and the level of unemployment (and the latter requires greater outlays as well). And, finally, given these first two features, the larger the government sector's claim to GNP, the greater a given change in GNP will effect the size of revenues to the government sector. The conclusions, however, likely apply only up to a point in the growth of the relative size of the government. That point would be reached when the government's economic activities predominate the system. Up to that point, the business cycle arises in response to the many decisions by individuals and firms reacting to changes in the general economic setting of relatively free enterprise. Beyond that point the cycle would doubtlessly be of a different nature, due mainly to the inability of the government in its control over production to anticipate the needed structure of production and effectively implement its economic plans.

Formula flexibility and tax-rate changes. Formula flexibility is an approach sometimes suggested for overcoming the problems of timing in discretionary fiscal matters with respect to economic stabilization.[1] It usually implies provision for automatic changes in tax rates in response to prescribed changes in selected economic indicators. For instance, a given decrease (or increase, as the case may be) in the rate of increase in GNP or some leading cyclical indicator, such as planned capital expenditures (Sect. 17.2), would automatically call forth an across-the-board cut (increase) in the personal income tax or some other selected tax. Such changes of course may have uncertain effects on the granting of installment credit and the defaults on the repayment of the resulting debt (Sect. 18.2), but formula flexibility could strengthen automatic stabilizers. In fact, automatic changes under formula flexibility could become so strong as to become destabilizing. Also the conditions and economic setting may change so as to require a constant review of any selected indicator relating to such automatic changes, and then the problem arises as to whether the President should properly be granted such discretionary authority. Even so, formula flexibility would avoid the possible bias of discretionary action, and, appropriately effected, it could insure a better timing of some fiscal changes than could result from strictly discretionary action.

Discretionary changes in expenditures. Discretionary changes in expenditures have often been the source of instability in the postwar years, and the shifts in priorities and politics motivating these expenditure changes are likely to continue at the Federal level at least. Even independently of these shifts, however, the immediate difficulty with these discretionary expenditures as countercyclical measures for short cycles of the postwar variety is that of timing. Some long-range projects, like national highway programs, can be advanced or retarded as cyclical conditions warrant, but most projects usually require completion, especially if the long-run requirements of the economy call for the projects to begin with. Proposals, nevertheless, have been made to improve the countercyclical effectiveness of changes in discretionary expenditures. On the local level, in particular, interest rate changes tend to call forth desirable expenditure changes.

A backlog of plans for public expenditures and the consideration of advanced appropriations by the government analogous to those of enterprises in the private sector (Sect. 17.2) have been proposed as a means of improving the timing of discretionary expenditures.[2] A backlog of up-to-date plans with respect to public projects would presumably shorten the necessary time to effect expenditures as in the business sector (Sect. 17.2), and the extension of greater flexibility to the Chief Executive with respect to the timing of projects may be feasible.

At the state and local levels of government, projects are often approved at a given rate of interest, and a decline in interest rates below the maximum rate on approved projects results in an increase in the flow of new issues to the market and a corresponding increase in expenditures. Conversely, a rise in interest rates above the maximum approved rate results in a postponement of issues scheduled to reach the market and a re-evaluation of the urgency of the projects to be financed externally.

19.2. Federal Budgets and the Budget Variables

Several notions have been recognized: (1) a countercyclical fiscal policy, (2) a balanced budget as a net result of deficits in periods when income is below some trend line and surpluses in periods when income is above some trend line, and (3) an equal or smaller proportional change in the Federal debt than in income as a long-run constraint on the growth of the Federal debt. Still, there are three alternative sets of accounts for the measurement of a surplus or a deficit for specific analyses. In this section, consequently, we list the three budgets and indicate the accounts corresponding to the variables with which we work in the next section (Sect. 19.3).

The alternative budget selected is somewhat arbitrary and relates to other questions, although being consistent in the use of one set of accounts for a given purpose is important in any event. Accepting one form and operating in the context of countercyclical fiscal policy—apart from the questions of the effect of taxation on incentive, expenditures, and growth—changes in accounts that have a less repressing (and, therefore, more stimulating) effect on expenditures for the current output of goods and services should be effected as income declines below some trend line. The reverse set of changes should be effected as income rises above some trend line.

The three budget forms. The three different budget forms are as follows: (1) the administrative or conventional budget, that records the receipts and expenditures of the Federal government as authorized by legislative enactment; (2) the cash budget that is designed to show the flow of funds between the Federal government and the public; and (3) the national income budget that records Federal receipts and expenditures in conformity with Department of Commerce calculations with respect to the national income accounts (Sect. 14.1). In the first two budgets, receipts tend to be recorded at the time of payment, whereas, by contrast, receipts are recorded on an accrual basis in the third budget form. Similarly, on the expenditure side, in the first two budgets, purchases of goods are recorded at the time of payment, whereas in the national income budget they are more nearly recorded according to the time of delivery.

The three budgets may be reconciled in an accounting sense, as in earlier discussion (Sect. 13.1). There, the cash budget was derived from the conventional budget, and one could equally well outline the adjustments required to derive estimates of the national income budget from the accounting totals in the cash budget.[3] Given these adjustments, then, the receipts and expenditures for a Federal budget on a national income accounts basis would appear as follows:

(Billions of dollars)

Receipts (or tax revenues, T)—national income accounts:

Personal tax and nontax receipts
Corporate profits tax accruals
Indirect business tax and nontax accruals
Contributions to social insurance

Expenditures (or expenditures, G, and transfer payments, U)
—national income accounts:
Purchases of goods and services
Transfer payments in conceptual sense (including accounts for transfer payments, grants to state and local governments, net interest paid, and subsidies less current surplus of government enterprises)

Surplus or deficit $(-)$ (i.e., Receipts − Expenditures)

The uses of the various budgets. Each of the three budgets has a somewhat specialized role. For example, the administrative budget is primarily a control over taxing and spending activities (Sect. 19.1), the cash budget has some advantage in assessing the impact of Federal financing on the financial markets and the liquidity of the private sector (Sect. 13.1), and the national income budget complements other data in the national income accounts. We continue (Sect. 19.3) our analysis in terms of aggregate income (Y) and disposable income as these measures relate to the national income accounts.

The national income accounts budget is balanced when there is no surplus or deficit as shown above. But, as implied by the accounts in the national income budget, a balance does not necessarily mean a neutral effect on the economy and national income Y. Taxes, as listed under receipts, may be taken from various groups and dispensed to others in the form of goods and services expenditures or grants. There may be effects resulting from such a structural means of redistributing income, and changes in this means of redistributing income may have additional effects, as noted later (Sect. 19.3). In this instance, we are still left with the prospect of viewing the expenditures of each sector as a demand function and analyzing the effect of receipts, transfer payments, and so on on the demand functions of other sectors. As even more clearly shown later (Sect. 19.3), changes in tax revenues resulting from changes in the tax structure and changes in goods and services expenditures of equal magnitude—so-called marginal balanced budget changes —especially will not have a neutral effect on income, output, and employment (Sect. 19.3).

19.3. Multiplier Effects and Government Budget Variables

Multiplier effects of changes in the flow of government expenditures and other budget variables on aggregate demand immediately follow from earlier analyses (Sect. 19.1 and 15.2). In these respective analyses, a distinction was made between the consumption as a function of disposable income Y^d and consumption as a function of aggregate income Y. The multiplier effects of the budget variables in the two analyses are similar in direction, but there are some significant differences that warrant emphasis. The relevant policy discussions in the early 1960's, in particular, were couched in terms of aggregate income rather than disposable income, and our discussions of the demand for money include aggregate income and/or total assets as independent variables (Sect. 1.2, 5.4, and 15.1). In addition to setting forth these various multiplier effects and emphasizing some of their differences, this section contains some qualifications pertaining to the use of multiplier analysis as a basis for policy recommendations and actions.

Multiplier effects (and disposable income). The multiplier effects of changes in government budget variables, such as government expenditures (G), taxes (T), and transfer payments (U), may each be considered and compared with each other in a modification of the earlier national income (Y) framework (Sect. 15.2). In this modified framework, we view consumption (C) as a function of disposable income $(Y^{(d)})$, i.e.,

$$C = f(Y^{(d)}),$$

where, by definition,

$$Y^{(d)} = Y - T + U,$$

and where we define the aggregate demand function

$$Y = C(Y^{(d)}) + I + G,$$

as contrasted with the earlier analysis (Sect. 15.2) where income Y consisted of $C(Y)$, government expenditures (a constant function of income), and I (a constant function of income). (Note that actual consumption is the same in any event, with only the slope of the consumption function being different, depending on the independent variable $Y^{(d)}$ or Y.).

In this framework, then,

$$Y = f(Y - T + U) + I + G,$$

and we may differentiate with respect to the three budget variables G, T, and U. First, with respect to government expenditures,

$$\frac{\partial Y}{\partial G} = \frac{\partial C}{\partial Y^{(d)}} \frac{\partial Y^{(d)}}{\partial G} + 1,$$

by the chain rule and rearranging terms,

$$(1) \qquad \frac{\partial Y}{\partial G} = \frac{1}{1 - \partial C/\partial Y^{(d)}},$$

the government goods and services expenditure multiplier.

Next, with respect to taxes,

$$\frac{\partial Y}{\partial T} = \frac{\partial C}{\partial Y^{(d)}} \frac{\partial Y^{(d)}}{\partial T},$$

and by the definition of disposable income, transfer payments constant in the partial derivative sense,

$$\frac{\partial Y^{(d)}}{\partial T} = \frac{\partial Y}{\partial T} - \frac{\partial T}{\partial T};$$

thus substituting the result of the definition into the differentiation,

$$\frac{\partial Y}{\partial T} = \frac{\partial C}{\partial Y^{(d)}} \left(\frac{\partial Y}{\partial T} - \frac{\partial T}{\partial T} \right)$$

Upon carrying out the multiplication in the right-hand member of the latter expression and further rearranging terms,

$$(2) \qquad \frac{\partial Y}{\partial T} = - \frac{\partial C}{\partial Y^{(d)}} \frac{1}{1 - \partial C/\partial Y^{(d)}},$$

the tax yield multiplier.

Third, with respect to transfer payments,

$$\frac{\partial Y}{\partial U} = \frac{\partial C}{\partial Y^{(d)}} \frac{\partial Y^{(d)}}{\partial U},$$

where, by the definition of disposable income, taxes are constant in the partial derivative sense, and, by substituting,

$$\frac{\partial Y}{\partial U} = \frac{\partial C}{\partial Y^{(d)}} \left(\frac{\partial Y}{\partial U} + \frac{\partial U}{\partial U} \right)$$

Upon rearranging terms,

$$(3) \qquad \frac{\partial Y}{\partial U} = \frac{\partial C}{\partial Y^{(d)}} \frac{1}{1 - \partial C/\partial Y^{(d)}},$$

the transfer payments multiplier.

Now, we may observe several things. For one, the government expenditure multiplier, as defined by equation (1), is similar to the earlier investment multiplier (Sect. 15.2), except for the difference in the slope of the consumption function. For another, the tax yield and transfer payments multipliers, as defined by equations (2) and (3), are identical except for opposite sign. In principle, transfer payments are negative taxes and they affect disposable income in the opposite direction from taxes. Both taxes and transfer payments, however, affect aggregate demand (Y) in equations (2) and (3) only indirectly, insofar as they induce changes in consumption expenditures through the coefficients $-\partial C/\partial Y^{(d)}$ and $\partial C/Y^{(d)}$, respectively. This is because they are subject to saving leakage through the marginal propensity to save (Sect. 15.2). This leakage, as we re-emphasize later, distinguishes the absolute value of the latter multipliers from the expenditure multiplier. The absolute values for both are smaller than the expenditure multiplier, since $0 < \partial C/\partial Y^{(d)} < 1$; hence, the leverage is greater with goods and services expenditures than with equal tax yield and transfer payment changes.

Multiplier effects (and aggregate income). Multiplier effects and government budget variables operating in the unmodified framework of earlier analysis (Sect. 15.2) are not extremely different from those involving disposable income. The main difference pertains to the slope of the consumption function and the conditions surrounding it. The similarities and this difference are easily emphasized.

Given aggregate demand and consumption as a function of aggregate income, as in earlier analysis (Sect. 15.2),

$$(4) \qquad Y = C(Y) + I + G,$$

where

$$\frac{dC}{dY} < \frac{dC}{dY^d},$$

$$\frac{dY}{dG} = \frac{1}{1 - dC/dY} < \frac{dY}{dG} = \frac{1}{1 - dC/dY^{(d)}},$$

$$(5) \qquad \frac{\Delta Y}{\Delta G} = 1 + 1\left(\frac{dC}{dY}\right) + 1\left(\frac{dC}{dY}\right)^2 + 1\left(\frac{dC}{dY}\right)^3 + \dots,$$

$$\Delta Y = \Delta G + \Delta G\left(\frac{dC}{dY}\right) + \Delta G\left(\frac{dC}{dY}\right)^2 + \dots$$

and each term of the right-hand member of the latter expression represents the addition to aggregate demand in each succeeding period. As noted earlier (Sect. 15.2), most of the effect of the change in expenditures works itself out in the first few periods.

The difference in the magnitude of the multipliers for aggregate and disposable incomes, respectively, results from the presence of the given tax structure (including "built-in" stabilizers) as one of the conditions along with habits, underlying the original function, and other contractual payments as set forth earlier (Sect. 18.1). In the original function, for example, as income declines, consumption declines less than would be the case for disposable income as the independent variable with tax yields built into it. This is true because the taxes paid and tax rates confronting the consumers decline and the receipt of transfer payments increase. This difference in the slope of the consumption function is readily illustrated. For example, given an income tax at a constant rate t, the tax yield T will be

$$T = tY,$$

and consumption before the tax rate t as some linear function will be

$$C = aY + b$$

Then after the tax

(6) $$C = a(1 - t)Y + b,$$

and the tax in effect reduces the slope of the function. If the rate increases, as indeed it does in the setting of the progressive income tax, then the slope is even less. Thus, given the existing tax structure, we simply restate the earlier (Sect. 15.2) consumption function,

$$C = \alpha Y + \beta$$

Other government budget variables take the form of a change in business taxes, or a tax credit for business, and, therefore, a shift in investment demand (Sect. 17.3). But they may take the form of an equal across-the-board statutory tax change for consumers (i.e., a tax change affecting the tax liabilities of all groups by the same percentage) and/or a tax change that affects either lower or higher groups and not those at the other extreme. In the case of these statutory tax changes we simply have a parallel shift in the consumption function. Denoting consumption in terms of our earlier linear equation (i.e., $C = \alpha Y + \beta$), or

$$Y = \alpha Y + \beta + I + G,$$

and by the chain rule,

(7) $$\frac{\partial Y}{\partial \beta} = \frac{1}{1 - \alpha},$$

the simple multiplier. But, in the case of the statutory tax change, all of the initial change does not enter into or detract from expenditures. In terms of equation (5) what we really have is the sum of the terms in the right-hand member of the equation, beginning with the second term, but with negative sign for an increase in taxes. That is,

(8) $$\frac{\Delta Y}{\Delta \text{ Tax revenues}} = -\left[1 \left(\frac{dC}{dY} \right) + 1 \left(\frac{dC}{dY} \right)^2 + 1 \left(\frac{dC}{dY} \right)^3 + \cdots \right]$$
resulting from
statutory tax
change

This result would follow from multiplying both sides of equation (5) by the marginal propensity to consume with respect to aggregate income and attaching the correct sign. It would be analogous to equation (2) above.

One of the results of the above multipliers pertains to the effect on income of so-called marginal balanced budget changes—i.e., in the present context, balanced changes in the flow of government goods and services expenditures and the flow of tax revenues resulting from changes in the tax structure, tax rates, and so on, as symbolized by t. In this case, we set the multipliers in equations (5) and (8) in opposition to one another. Clearly, from the latter set of equations,

$$(9) \qquad \frac{\Delta Y}{\Delta G} > \frac{\Delta Y}{\Delta T}, \quad \text{and} \quad \frac{\Delta Y}{\Delta G} + \frac{\Delta Y}{\Delta T} = 1,$$

where T is tax revenues resulting from changes in the tax structure. Thus, a balanced increase (or decrease) in the budget in this way will actually increase (or decrease) the flow of income by the amount of the budget increase. [A similar result, as opposed to an identical one, could be shown by setting equations (1) and (2) in opposition to one another.] The present result (9), furthermore, is one of the simplest versions of the unitary balanced budget multiplier, so-called since the combined multipliers sum to unity. From this kind of analysis follows an important conclusion: the sheer size of government budgets, even though balanced, may exert an important influence on the levels of income, output, and employment.

A tax cut proposal: a case study. The analysis pertaining to statutory tax changes and the multiplier, given consumption as dependent on aggregate income, underlay a tax cut proposal in President Kennedy's 1963 budget.[4] On that occasion, the weight and authority of formal analysis was brought to support the proposal.[5] The proposed cut of about 11 billion dollars was largely for consumers and a means of achieving a fuller utilization of resources, faster economic growth, and an increase in consumption expenditures. The latter was to result in a "feed-back" in the form of higher revenues to the United States Treasury and state and local governments as well. Aggregate demand was discussed largely with respect to aggregate income.

The proposal was supported in discussion, subsequently modified, and then written into law—the Revenue Act of 1964. In the discussions, the estimates ranged from those of a "primary multiplier" of approximately 2, implying a marginal propensity to consume of 0.5,[*] to estimates of the interacting multiplier and accelerator effect of approximately 3.5.

Multiplier analysis as a basis for effecting policy: some qualifications.

---

[*] More explicitly, for a statutory tax cut the "primary multiplier" (i.e., with $(dC/dY) =$ const. and no accelerator) was 2, and

$$2 = \frac{1}{1 - dC/dY}, \quad \frac{dC}{dY} = \frac{1}{2}$$

By the method of equation (8), we would have come up with $dC/dY = 2/3$.

The analytical results in the form of the above equations require some qualifications before serving as a basis for policy actions and recommendations. The qualifications we shall emphasize pertain to the kind of analysis (continuous or discrete), the prospect of offsetting side effects of the actions taken, income redistribution effects, a distinction between purely mechanical and behavioral changes, the prospect of conflicting goals, leakage, and the extent of government control over the various budget variables.

Some qualifications (continuous vs. discrete changes). Multipliers appear in various forms, often dependent on whether the analysis relates to rates of change at a moment in time (i.e., flows) with special allowances for changes over time as in equation (4), or to fixed periods of time and discrete rather than continuous changes. The multipliers in our analyses pertaining to comparative statics (Sect. 15.2) are not of the same mathematical nature as the multiplier interacting with the accelerator; they operate in the context of separate and distinct models.

Some qualifications (offsetting side effects). The expenditure multipliers in equations (1) and (5), as with the other multipliers discussed above, give precise effects, other things being equal in the partial derivative sense. There may be, however, offsetting or reinforcing side effects in addition to those specified by the multipliers. An increase (decrease) in the flow of government expenditures, for example, may affect adversely (favorably) the business sectors, prospects for streams of returns. This, in turn, may cause a decrease (increase) in the flow of expenditures by that sector and, therefore, in the levels for income, output, and employment.

Some qualifications (income redistribution). In the case of any portion of a statutory tax change that results in different percentage changes in the tax liabilities of different income groups, there may be a need to allow for some special effects on expenditures for some groups with special marginal propensities to consume.[6] Also altering the tax and transfer payments structure as a means of affecting the apparatus for distributing income may change the consumption function and, therefore, income, output, and employment.

In allowing for the latter prospect, we deal with several notions. The first is stated for a tax cut, but the case for an increase in tax rates could also be stated. It is purely logical:

(Part 1) *A reduction in the percentages* (i.e., tax liabilities expressed as percentages of income) *that decreases to zero as we move to higher income groups decreases the slope of the consumption function (and, therefore, the multiplier).* (Part 2) *A reduction in the percentages that increase from zero as we move to higher income groups increases the slope of the function (and, therefore, the multiplier).* These statements follow from the reasoning pertaining to equation (5) and the way the tax structure affects the slope of the consumption function. Note that we have the change in the percentages decreasing to zero or increasing from zero. This is because percentage changes common to all groups concern parallel shifts in the function entirely. The decreasing percentage changes as we move to higher income groups, on the other hand, have the effect of raising the values of the function for lower levels of income and of leaving the values of the function relatively less changed at higher levels of income. One net effect of these changes is a decline in the slope of the function. A reduction in percentages (i.e., tax liabilities as percentages of income) that increases as we move to higher income groups has the converse set of effects.

Another possibility is that the statutory tax change of the type referred to may result in a larger (smaller) proportion of funds for lower income groups up to and including 50 per cent of the population with higher consumption to income ratios. The result here could be an increase (decrease) in the ratio of aggregate consumption to aggregate income (i.e., C/Y) and consequently greater spending. On the other hand, one may recognize a dependency of spending on the frequency of "invidious comparisons"—so-called "conspicious consumption"—and other characteristics pertaining to our culture.[7] Then, recognizing such characteristics, one may argue that a more (less) equal distribution of income will decrease (increase) the ratio of consumption to income (i.e., C/Y). In other words, a more (less) equal distribution of income may decrease (increase) the strength of the motive for consuming additional goods and services.

Some qualifications (behavioral vs. mechanical changes). A behavioral change as implied in some of our models is one where the underlying setting or conditions pertaining to the psychological state of things change. A change in expenditure behavior is such a change when it results from a change in the tax and government outlay mechanism for redistributing income. Similarly, changes in β in our earlier money demand function (Sect. 1.2 and 5.4) and shifts in the consumption function (Sect. 18.1) are examples of such a change, but all behavioral changes are not as simply and directly handled in the operational sense as the change in the quantity of money demanded with respect to a change in β. By contrast, a more purely mechanical effect is one that results from a change in some quantifiable variable, such as income, government expenditures, or tax revenues from a change in the tax structure.

In the use of multiplier analysis as a basis for policy recommendations, efforts should be made to distinguish the purely mechanical aspects of change from the behavioral, as most may agree. The effect of a more purely mechanical type of change (such as the multiplier effect resulting from a change in the tax structure), given the consumption function, is readily predictable in the partial derivative sense. The effect of an action depending on an underlying psychological type of change (such as may be associated with a change in the mechanism for redistributing income), on the other hand, is less likely to be predictable on simple mechanical grounds alone, even in the partial derivative sense.

Some qualifications (conflicting goals). In discussions pertaining to equation (1), on the one hand, and equations (2) and (3), on the other, we noted a difference. Namely, a certain amount of deficit from increasing goods and services expenditures would be more effective in increasing income per dollar of deficit than cutting tax revenues or increasing transfer payments. This would seem to place a priority on the use of expenditures in order to, for example, achieve a goal of faster economic growth (Sect. 19.4), possibly as a means of bearing the burden of growing national defense requirements, educational needs, and so on. The use of expenditures, however, may conflict with other predetermined goals, such as that of limiting the growth of the relative importance of the role of the government sector in our economic lives (i.e., the proportion of government expenditures in aggregate income, or the ratio G/Y).

The latter goal, then, would place a premium on the use of statutory tax changes as emphasized above and on various other occasions (Sect. 17.3), as a means of achieving a full utilization of resources or a predetermined pattern of growth. A greater increase per annum in the flow variable Y, of course, would be consistent with larger expenditures for national defense and social overhead, such as spending on hospitals, schools, and the beautification of the countryside. As the flow variable Y increased, the variable G could also increase without increasing the relative importance of the government sector (i.e., G/Y).

Some qualifications ("leakage"). In forecasting the multiplier effect of a change in government budget variable, allowing for the distribution of leakage over time is important. With respect to equation (5), there is no leakage in the first period. Thereafter, leakage increases rapidly in each period, depending on the factor (dC/dY) and its exponential power, with the result that the multiplier effect has largely worked itself out in a few periods. The leakage is said to vary inversely with the size of the multiplier. In the case of changes in the budget variables for tax cuts, or its negative—a transfer payment—the amount of leakage is even greater, as indicated by the coefficients $-\partial C/\partial Y^{(d)}$ and $\partial C/\partial Y^{(d)}$, respectively, in equations (2) and (3). In these cases, there is the implication that the leakage is spread out over the entire amount of the multiplier effect. Such extra leakage occurs, however, at the initial time of the change in the budget variable. Then the second term in a progression, such as that denoted by the right-hand member of equation (5), becomes the first term in the right-hand member of an expression like (8). The leakage here refers to the loss of the entire effect of the first term of the right-hand member of an expression like (5).

Some qualifications (the extent of government control). With respect to the actual control by government over the various budget variables, some have argued that governments can really exercise much discretion only over goods and services expenditures and tax rates. Continuing, they argue that only "educated guesses" may be made about tax revenues, with the frequent result that unintended deficits or surpluses may occur. Nevertheless, changes in expenditures have become recognized as being subject to considerations having little or nothing to do with economic stabilization (Sect. 19.1), and the net result has been an increase in the amount of attention devoted to the effects of changes in the tax structure.

19.4. Policy Mixes, Economic Stability, and Growth

"Economic growth" refers to an increase in GNP in constant prices, GNP per capita (i.e., the ratio of GNP in constant prices to the given population), industrial production, or some other measure pertaining to national production or output. And "faster economic growth" may refer to a growth rate in excess of the one that would prevail in the absence of measures taken to raise the growth rate. Of course, in strict analytical terms, faster growth simply means an acceleration of the growth rate.

Here, we merely introduce the broad subject of growth along with the various policy mixes pertaining to our monetary and fiscal systems and the management of the public debt. Growth and monetary, fiscal, and debt policies are somewhat diverse subjects in most respects. Their treatment under the one subtopic in the present context is called for, however, largely on the grounds that the use of tax and expenditure measures to achieve a predetermined growth rate partially restricts their countercyclical use. A predetermined growth rate in excess of that resulting from countercyclical fiscal and monetary policies is usually viewed as a trend about which the shorter-run cyclical changes occur. Thus to use tax and expenditure measures to stimulate faster growth in a period of cyclical expansion is inconsistent with their use to dampen the cycle at such times.

Possible policy mixes. Three kinds of policy have been recognized: monetary, fiscal, and debt policy. In addition, in broad qualitative terms, we have recognized that each may be carried out in three different ways. With respect to the tone of the money and credit market (Sect. 14.2), for example, monetary policy (m) could be easy (m_1), neutral (m_2), or tight (m_3). With respect to fiscal policy (f), it could be expansive (f_1), neutral (f_2) in the sense that expenditures and revenues change at the same rate and in the same direction as income,* and contractive (f_3). With respect to the time-to-maturity structure of the Federal debt (Sect. 13.2), debt policy (d), could be expansive (d_1) in the event of a shortening of the average time to maturity, neutral (d_2) in the sense of no change, and restrictive (d_3) in the sense of a lengthening of the average time to maturity.

Using a bit of mathematical notation, we may simply denote the three kinds of policy, and the number of ways each can be conducted:

$$m = \begin{pmatrix} m_1 \\ m_2 \\ m_3 \end{pmatrix}, \quad f = \begin{pmatrix} f_1 \\ f_2 \\ f_3 \end{pmatrix}, \quad d = \begin{pmatrix} d_1 \\ d_2 \\ d_3 \end{pmatrix}$$

Now, recalling a fundamental principle from mathematics, we may note the number of different ways the policies may be pursued together. That is, if one kind of policy (or thing) can be done in p different ways, and, if after it has been done in any one of these ways, a second kind of policy can be done in q different ways, and so on, then the policies may be carried out, in the order stated, in $p \cdot q \cdot \ldots$ different ways. In the present instances $3 \cdot 3 \cdot 3 = 27$ different ways.

There are indeed a large number of alternative ways of combining fiscal, debt, and monetary policies. If the fiscal and debt management policies were only used so as always to complement and reinforce each other, then by vector multiplication,

$$(f_1, f_2, f_3) \begin{pmatrix} d_1 \\ d_2 \\ d_3 \end{pmatrix} = (f_1 d_1 + f_2 d_2 + f_3 d_3),$$

and the feasible policy mixes would be represented by the three terms of the vector product, although only one of the mixes could be pursued at a given time. Combining these with monetary policy, by scalar multiplication

$$(f_1 d_1 + f_2 d_2 + f_3 d_3) \begin{pmatrix} m_1 \\ m_2 \\ m_3 \end{pmatrix} = \begin{pmatrix} m_1 f_1 d_1 + m_1 f_2 d_2 + m_1 f_3 d_3 \\ m_2 f_1 d_1 + m_2 f_2 d_2 + m_2 f_3 d_3 \\ m_3 f_1 d_1 + m_3 f_2 d_2 + m_3 f_3 d_3 \end{pmatrix}$$

The resulting vector shows nine different ways that monetary policy may combine with debt and fiscal policies that complement and reinforce each other. It shows only three different ways if we require mone-

---

* With respect to the criteria for neutral policies (and, therefore, the related expansive and restrictive policies), we are implying that as income changes other things change by the same proportion. This is consistent with an absence of change in the various rates of return, yields, the tax and expenditure structure for redistributing income, etc. It is also consistent with monetary analysis that pertains to a homogeneous demand function for output of degree one.

tary policy also to be complementary. (In this event, all but three of the terms in the last vector vanish.)

There are still eighteen other possibilities, and any one could happen, depending in some instances on restrictions imposed on the uses of the instruments for carrying out a policy by political and institutional considerations (Sect. 25.1). Taking, for illustrative purposes, a rather complicated combination, such as $m_2f_1d_1$, what sort of combination do we have? Expansive, except with respect to m_2, and this was roughly what we had following the 1960-1961 recession (Sect. 24.3) and the inadequate rate of recovery from that recession. Fiscal policy was expansive, with the view to stimulating growth and reducing unemployment, the averaged maturity of the debt was shortened with the view to placing upward pressure on short-term rates relative to the long-term ones. And by way of the expansion of credit, the monetary authorities were attempting to lessen the restrictive rise in interest rates historically accompanying economic expansion. The debt policy, particularly as effected in combination with the switching of maturities within the Federal Reserve's holdings of government securities (Sect. 24.3), was to stabilize an outflow of gold and liquid balances on deposit in the United States, while at the same time counteracting the more restrictive pressures operating through the long-term rate and on domestic investment and employment.

The particular policy mix $m_2f_1d_1$ emphasizes one of the points made at the outset of this section. Namely, the use of tax and expenditure measures to attain faster growth will, at times, be inconsistent with their countercyclical use. Here, for instance, fiscal policy in its discretionary aspects, at last, is more clearly involved with the trend of growth than with constraining cyclical expansion, and monetary policy is at least neutral (m_2) or even restrictive (m_3) as it should be in a period of cyclical expansion. The debt management part of this mix is not counter to the cycle, and we consider its role in the above context later (Sect. 24.3).

Economic growth. Analyses pertaining to economic growth are broad, important, and many dimensional.[8] To merely place the subject in perspective with respect to our policy mixes, therefore, we simply touch upon some of the most general aspects of it. These pertain to (1) the purposes of faster growth, (2) the means of attaining faster growth, and (3) the cost of faster growth—all within the broad framework of political, social, and economic institutions in the United States.

The purposes cited in defense of faster economic growth have been varied and somewhat related. One of these was the traditional one of assuring a full utilization of resources—mainly, full employment. Another was that of strengthening the economy as a means of reducing the outflow of gold from the United States following a widespread move toward the convertibility of foreign currencies in 1958 (Sect. 23.1). Still another purpose was simply to improve the social welfare, in the sense that the social benefits to be gained exceeded the social cost. And, as another, faster growth has been cited as a means of lessening the burden of national defense by increasing our capacity to pay taxes without involuntarily foregoing consumption expenditures.[9] As the world came to be organized at the outset of the 1960's, a country's ability to allocate materials and talent to scientific achievements and influence other countries was believed to depend in large measure on economic performance. There was the view, too, that, among less developed countries, the reputation of an economic system and the desire to emulate it depend in large measure on the system's growth performance—its ability to effect scientific achievements, to acquire the benefits of technological innovation, and to provide military defense.

The detailed list of measures mentioned as a means of increasing growth is extensive.[10] Most of them, nevertheless, fall in a few groups:

(1) Those that would achieve greater stability with respect to the business cycle,

(2) Those that would increase investment and incentive for longer hours and a more innovational and entrepreneurial type of activity,

(3) Those that would remove barriers to the attainment of full employment and the greater mobility of resources from the less productive to the more productive employments, and

(4) Those that would increase the work force.

With respect to the first group we need no new policy goals, and no one has suggested any new instruments as such for achieving greater stability. There are lags, as we later discover (Sect. 26.2), to be overcome in the recognition of situations calling for changes in credit and monetary controls and in the implementation of effective actions. However, minimizing these lags has not been mentioned as a source of faster growth per se. As to the second, most of the more basic measures that relate to our present policy mixes pertain to changes in the tax structure. These would simply encourage better performance by encouraging risk taking, particularly with respect to investment. The tax measures would include the use of faster write-off for capital goods, the tax credit (Sect. 17.3), and less progressive income tax rates, such as those contained in the Revenue Act of 1964 (Sect. 19.3). Here in this category is where we encounter changes in the tax structure that may on occasion be at variance with the notion of strictly complementary fiscal and monetary policies. As to the third category, there are many prospects: actions against monopoly in the product and labor markets, actions to improve communication between those seeking jobs and those hiring workers, actions to improve programs for the retraining and relocation of workers, and so on. And we will leave the growth of the work force to economic law, the immigration officials, and marriage and the family for a while.

For most of the measures that may be effected as a means of attaining faster growth, there are some social costs that vary with the rate of growth sought. An increase in economic growth tends to accelerate the displacement and relocation of workers as their present employment becomes unprofitable in a given industry or occupation. In some instances social costs are evident from the need to rehabilitate workers with obsolete skills and to facilitate their movement to new localities. There are also strains on managers of firms whose products become obsolete and less in demand. The above, and other costs, consequently, must be balanced against the gains, and the optimal rate of growth should be one where the benefits from growth are greater than or at least equal to the above cost of growth. In an operational sense, this must mean that the optimal rate of growth is the maximum rate politically acceptable to a society that is reasonably well informed about the likely consequences of the alternative choices.

19.5. Summary

The early notion of a fiscal policy was that of a countercyclical fiscal policy, such as may be effected by automatic or discretionary measures. Economic growth was implied as a result of greater economic stability, full employment, and so on, but faster economic growth was not a goal in itself. The notion of faster growth did not attract wide attention in the United States until the late 1950's.

After recognizing the two types of countercyclical fiscal policy measures—automatic and discretionary—we may summarize some results of earlier discussion:

(1) The sole objective of the revenue system and government is not the conduct of a countercyclical fiscal policy.

(2) Crucial timing difficulties in using the discretionary measures are inherent in our system of government.

(3) Automatic stabilizers are effective means of stabilizing economic activity.

(4) The extent of stability resulting from the automatic stabilizers depends on the progressiveness of the tax structure, the degree to which the tax bases and government outlays fluctuate automatically with income, and the relative size of the government.

(5) Formula flexibility and the maintenance of a backlog of planned capital expenditures are means of shortening the time lag in effecting a discretionary fiscal policy.

(6) The formula flexibility could strengthen the effectiveness of automatic stabilizers, but there are side effects that may be undesirable. Raising tax rates may, for example, force low and middle income wage earners to default on heavy installment debt, and a constant review may be required to assure that the appropriate indicator was triggering the changes in tax rates.

With respect to countercyclical stabilization and faster economic growth, most of the more concrete measures for attaining either must operate through the government budget variables—tax revenues, government purchases of goods and services, and transfer payments. Changes in each of these have multiple effects on aggregate income, given the slope of the consumption function. The multiplier for government goods and service expenditures, however, is the largest of the multipliers. The others, in effect, may be derived from this multiplier by making allowances for extra leakage. In the case of an increase in taxes, the multiplier is simply the negative of the product of the slope of the consumption function and the multiplier for goods and services expenditures; in the case of an increase in transfer payments, it is the positive of the latter product. In the cases for decreases in all three instances, the signs should simply be reversed.

The extra leakage resulting from an increase in taxes as contrasted with an increase in expenditures leads us to the so-called unitary balanced budget multiplier. That is, increases in expenditures and taxes of the same amount balance the budget, but the flow of income is increased by the amount of the balanced budget increase. This may also be viewed as the result of setting two multiplier processes in opposition to one another.

The multipliers for the government budget variables may be stated in terms of the earlier national income model and a modification of this model with disposable income as the dependent variable. In these two instances, the net results of changes in the budget variables are not different, but the important difference pertains to the slope of the consumption function and the treatment of underlying conditions. Consumption as a function of disposable income has a greater slope than consumption as a function of aggregate income, and this results from the treatment of the tax structure as a condition underlying the consumption function in the latter instance. Mostly, our macro analyses have been in terms of aggregate income as the dependent variable.

The purely logical results implied by the use of budget variable multipliers for simple analysis or as a basis for recommendations and governmental actions require some qualifications. One must make allowance for the prospect of offsetting or supporting effects elsewhere, in part of a psychological nature. Also, in the case of any portion of statutory tax changes that result in different percentage changes in the tax liabilities of different income groups and alter the income redistribution structure, allowances must be made for possible effects resulting from the redistribution of income. The possible effects do not follow entirely from the applications of logic.

Still other qualifications apply to the use of budget equation multipliers. These pertain to leakage, the extent of government control, behavioral versus mechanical changes, models containing continuous variables as opposed to discrete variables with fixed time periods, changes that follow on purely logical grounds as contrasted with those involving institutional and psychological phenomena, and the prospect of conflicting goals.

With respect to the presence of conflicting goals, a proposed policy may not be feasible due to its conflicting with some other policy. Most notably in the early 1960's, the emphasis on tax measures to achieve a change in the growth rate conflicted with their use in support of a countercyclical fiscal policy. Although these developments revealed no unusual difficulty in the use of measures for effecting policies, they did, on the other hand, illustrate the possibility of using one set of measures to achieve one goal and another set to achieve another goal.

Even in broad qualitative terms, there are twenty-seven possible policy mixes for monetary, fiscal, and debt management policies. Doubtlessly, a variety of these may find application from time to time, and under various circumstances. In such a framework, nevertheless, an increase in the emphasis on some predetermined growth implies a greater reliance on monetary and credit variables as means of achieving economic stability. Shifting a trend line upward with discretionary tax measures during a period of cyclical expansion does not release the same measures for countercyclical use.

References

1. Commission on Money and Credit, *Money and Credit: Their Influence on Jobs, Prices and Growth* (Englewood Cliffs, N.J.: Prentice-Hall, Inc., 1961), pp. 129-130. See also Richard Musgrave, *The Theory of Public Finance* (New York: McGraw-Hill Book Company, 1959), pp. 512-515.

2. Commission on Money and Credit, *op.cit.*, pp. 138-141.

3. See, e.g., "Federal Budgets and Fiscal Policy," *Monthly Review*, Federal Reserve Bank of Minneapolis, September 1962, pp. 2-6.

4. See *President's 1963 Tax Message* (Washington, D.C.: U.S. Government Printing Office; and *Economic Report of the President* together with the *Annual Report of the Council of Economic Advisers* (Washington, D.C.: U.S. Government Printing Office, 1963), pp. 38-52.

5. See *Hearings, January 1963 Economic Report of the President*, Part I (Washington, D.C.: U.S. Government Printing Office, 1963); and *Report of the Joint Economic Committee on the January 1963 Economic Report of the President* (Washington, D.C.: U.S. Government Printing Office, 1963), pp. 45-55.

6. See Musgrave, *op.cit.*, pp. 439-441.

7. See, e.g., James S. Duesenberry, *Income, Saving, and the Theory of Consumer Behavior* (Cambridge, Mass.: Harvard University Press, 1952), pp. 17-46.

8. See, in particular, Edward F. Denison, *The Sources of Economic Growth in the United States and the Alternatives Before Us,* Supplementary Paper No. 13 (New York: Committee for Economic Development); and Klaus Knorr and William J. Baumol (eds.), *What Price Economic Growth?* (Englewood Cliffs, N.J.: Prentice-Hall, Inc., 1961).

9. *Ibid.,* pp. 143-153.

10. Denison's partial list contains thirty-eight items. See Denison, *op. cit.,* pp. 276-279.

20

The Determination of
the Rate of Interest

> But the quantity of money is only one determinant of income and the rate of interest. Other determinants are (1) the investment-demand schedule, (2) the consumption function, and (3) the liquidity preference schedule. These three, together with the quantity of money as fixed by the monetary authorities, determine together the level of income and the rate of interest (Alvin H. Hansen, *Monetary Theory and Fiscal Policy* [1949]).

Earlier (Sect. 4.4) we discussed the liquidity preference demand for money, and the supply of money in combination with the rate of interest (Sect. 4.2). We now, however, wish to combine this discussion with other determinants of the rate of interest—the saving (or similarly, the consumption) function (Sect. 18.1) and the investment demand function (Sect. 17.2)—and the classical theory of interest. We wish also to indicate other, more complicating, factors that may influence changes in the rate of interest within the resulting analytical framework. The formal results are a more general theory of the rate of interest that includes the so-called classical and the liquidity preference views as determinants, and several propositions about the growth of income, the money supply, and the composition of financial claims as these relate to the rate of interest. The particular financial claims dealt with are those involving commercial banks, nonbank financial intermediaries (Sect. 15.1), and the Federal debt (Sect. 13.2).

The more general theory permits us to focus upon the actual flows of funds to and from the financial markets where the rate of interest is effected, and to say that these flows give rise to the rate of interest as explained by our theory. Both the data for the flows and our general theory of interest focus upon the banking system's control over the supply of money (Sect. 3.1) and the possible use that may be made of this control to give effect to the level of interest rates, after allowance for complicating factors. The theory and the description of the flows are intended to complement one another so as to provide a more operational meaning for the theory. The introduction of the complicating factors should provide further insights into the complexities to be allowed for in the understanding of monetary developments and the conduct of monetary policy.

20.1. The General Theory of the Rate of Interest

As we shall show in this section, the rate of interest is determined by the interaction of (1) the liquidity preference demand for money and the supply of money, (2) the volume of saving out of current income, and (3) investment demand, all in combination with the classical view of the theory of interest. The theory consisting of these determinants calls attention in particular to the point of entry for the monetary authorities in their efforts to achieve the national economic goals with respect to income, output, prices, employment, and economic growth.

In classical economic theory, and in terms of national income concepts (Sect. 15.1), the rate of interest may be viewed as determined by investment demand as denoted earlier (Sect. 5.4 and 17.2) and by a schedule relating the volume of saving to the rate of interest. The latter shows saving as some increasing function of the rate of interest. Thus, given investment demand (i.e., $i = \mu I + v$, $\mu < 0$) from the earlier discussion (17.2), investment demand as a function of the rate of interest is denoted

$$(1) \qquad I = \frac{i - v}{\mu}, \quad \mu < 0, \quad v > i,$$

and saving (S) as a function of the rate of interest may be approximated by

$$(2) \qquad S = \frac{i - \beta}{\alpha}, \quad \alpha > 0, \quad \beta < i$$

Recognizing the condition for a solution to equations (1) and (2) whereby $I = S$, we have

$$(3) \qquad i = \frac{\mu\beta - \alpha v}{\mu - \alpha}$$

This, then, is an approximation to the rate of interest as presented in the classical theory.

However, in the broader aggregate demand framework (Sect. 15.2), the solution (3) to the rate of interest is inadequate, for in that framework saving is an increasing function of income. There will be different saving schedules (2) for different levels of income. Consequently, we express this relationship between saving and income by denoting the parameter β as some decreasing function of income, i.e.,

$$\beta_y = f(Y_y), \quad d\beta/dY < 0,$$

and, for example, for four different and increasing levels of income (i.e., $y = 1, 2, 3, 4$), we have a family of four saving schedules. These schedules along with the investment demand schedule are sketched in Fig.

$$S_y = \frac{i - \beta_y}{a}, \quad a > 0, \quad i > \beta_y = f(Y_y), \quad d\beta/dY < 0$$

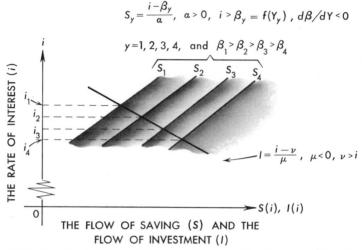

$y = 1, 2, 3, 4,$ and $\beta_1 > \beta_2 > \beta_3 > \beta_4$

$S_1 \quad S_2 \quad S_3 \quad S_4$

$I = \frac{i - \nu}{\mu}, \quad \mu < 0, \quad \nu > i$

THE RATE OF INTEREST (i)

$S(i), I(i)$

THE FLOW OF SAVING (S) AND THE
FLOW OF INVESTMENT (I)

Fig. 20-1. The Classical View: Interest as Determined by Saving and Investment.

20-1. Allowing for a more continuous change in income in terms of the solution (3), we show the rate of interest (3) as a decreasing function of income in the illustration (Fig. 20-3) for the determination of the rate of interest in the national income framework.

Now, at the outset (Sect. 4.4) the rate of interest was viewed as being determined by the liquidity preference demand for money (i.e., $M_d = a + b/i$) and the supply of money (i.e., $M_s = \gamma$). We also noted the demand for money as a linearly increasing function of income (Sect. 5.4). This we viewed in terms of an increase in the parameter a, or, in terms of the solution

$$(4) \qquad\qquad i = \frac{b}{\gamma - a},$$

where we view the parameter a as some linearly increasing function of income [i.e., $a_y = f(Y_y)$]. The solution in terms of equation (4) is sketched in Fig. 20-2 for four increasing levels of income (i.e., $y = 1, 2, 3, 4$), along with the schedule for money (i.e., $M_s = \gamma$), and the liquidity preference demand for money (i.e., $M_d = a + b/i$). Allowing, finally, for a continuous change in income, we have

$$i = \frac{b}{\gamma - a}, \quad a = f(Y),$$

and this is sketched in Fig. 20-3,* along with the solution to the classical model.**

As the analysis turns out, both the liquidity preference model and the classical model tell us what the rate of interest will be, given income.

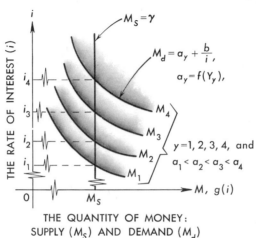

THE QUANTITY OF MONEY:
SUPPLY (M_s) AND DEMAND (M_d)

Fig. 20-2. The Liquidity Preference Demand for Money Balances, the Supply of Money Balances, and the Rate of Interest.

Thus, for varying levels of income, we observe the sets of solutions (4) and (3) to the two models, respectively,† in Fig. 20-3. These two sets of solutions together determine the rate of interest and income as indicated

* Viewing i as a function of Y involves the function-of-a-function rule, and thus the slope is denoted

$$\frac{\partial i}{\partial Y} = \frac{b}{(\gamma - a)^2} \frac{\partial a}{\partial Y},$$

where $b/(\gamma - a)^2$ is $\partial i / \partial a$, by the quotient rule, and $\partial a / \partial Y$ is a positive constant by assumption. Since the parameter a in the denominator of the latter equation increases as income increases, the curve for $i = g[f(Y)]$ is increasing at an increasing rate.

** Viewing i in the classical model as a function of income, the slope by the function-of-a-function rule is denoted

$$\frac{\partial i}{\partial Y} = \frac{\mu}{\mu - \alpha} \frac{\partial \beta}{\partial Y},$$

where $\mu / (\mu - \alpha)$ is $\partial i / \partial \beta$ by the quotient rule, and $\partial \beta / \partial Y$ is a negative constant by assumption. Since $\mu < 0$ and $\alpha > 0$, the function has a constant slope.

† The curves defined by equations (3) and (4) are commonly referred to elsewhere in the literature as the *IS* curve and *LM* curves, respectively, because of the relationship between saving (*S*) and investment (*I*) in the first instance and liquidity and the supply of money in the second.

by the intersection of the lines defined by equations (4) and (3) in Fig.
20-3. They do it in a manner suitable to our broad framework of aggregate demand (Chap. 15). Referring to Fig. 20-3, for example, an increase in the money supply (γ) shifts the corresponding function in the
illustration downward, decreases the rate of interest ($i_t > i_{t+1}$), and increases income ($Y_t < y_{t+1}$).* Also, an increase in investment demand
resulting from a more optimistic outlook for returns corresponds to an
upward shift in the schedule defined by equation (3), a higher rate of
interest, and a higher income. These and other changes, too, may be illustrated, as an exercise by the reader.

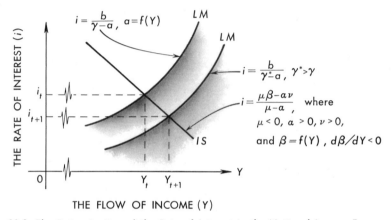

THE FLOW OF INCOME (Y)

Fig. 20-3. *The Determination of the Rate of Interest in the National Income Framework.*

The rate of interest in the classical model and the liquidity preference
model is, of course, the same rate of interest, given income. Combining
the two, as in Fig. 20-3, then simply allows us to discuss the supply of
saving and investment demand as determinants of the rate of interest
at varying levels of income. At the same time the combination permits
a simultaneous recognition of the all important role of the supply of
money balances and the liquidity preference demand for these balances
as cofactors affecting the rate of interest. The combined model has practical appeal, too, for, without abandoning the notion of liquidity preference as a determinant of the rate of interest, we can literally observe the
residual portions of flows of saving and flows of investment funds
through the financial markets as they determine the rate of interest at a
given level of income.

* This sequence of causation could also be illustrated with reference to the three
separate models for liquidity preference (Sect. 4.4), investment demand (Sect.
17.2), and the saving investment relationship (Sect. 15.2). The sequence of causation would be $\Delta M \to \Delta i \to \Delta I \to \Delta Y$.

20.2. The Rate of Interest, Flows of Funds, Proportions, and Changes Over Time

The general theory of the rate of interest related the rate to flows for saving and investment, to the stock of money and the liquidity preference demand for money, and to the level of income. Earlier in the book, too, we noted that this rate was an abstraction referring to the structure of rates (Sect. 4.2), that the flows for saving and investment had financial counterparts (Sect. 15.1), that the financial flows were in part expedited by the presence of financial intermediaries, and that the banking system could influence these flows. Also, observing the structure of the theory as set forth in the earlier illustrations for this chapter we may note some other phenomena:

(1) That the rate of interest and income will change if there is a change in either the flow of saving, the flow of investment, the liquidity preference demand for money, or the stock of money, and

(2) That the rate of interest will not change if equilibrium values for all of the other variables, including the money supply ($M_s = \gamma$), change in the same direction and as some constant proportion of income.*

Against this background, we wish to denote and describe the flows of funds to and from the financial markets (including the money, credit, and capital markets) that give effect to the general level of interest rates prevailing in those markets at any given time. This should enlarge upon

---

* The proof of the latter proposition follows from the assumptions that all variables change by the same proportion. In terms of the equation

$$i = \frac{b}{\gamma - a},$$

in Fig. 20-3, where, by the assumptions and earlier conditions,
$$\gamma = f(Y), \text{ and}$$
$$a = f(Y), \text{ respectively.}$$

Thus, $i = g[\gamma, a]$, and by the chain rule,

$$\frac{\partial i}{\partial Y} = \frac{\partial i}{\partial \gamma} \frac{\partial \gamma}{\partial Y} + \frac{\partial i}{\partial a} \frac{\partial a}{\partial Y}$$

Therefore, differentiating the equation, we get

$$\frac{\partial i}{\partial Y} = \frac{-b}{(\gamma - a)^2} \frac{\partial \gamma}{\partial Y} + \frac{b}{(\gamma - a)^2} \frac{\partial a}{\partial Y} = 0, \quad \text{since} \quad \frac{\partial \gamma}{\partial Y} = \frac{\partial a}{\partial Y}$$

by assumption. In this case the LM-line in Fig. 20-3 is a constant function of income, and, as I and S change as constant proportions of income, the rate of interest in the illustration does not change.

the meaning of the theory in an operational sense and emphasize the unique role of the banking system as well. We wish next to recall previous discussions about money as a constant proportion of income, saving as a porportion of income, and so on and to formalize certain notions about these various proportions, the rate of interest, and changes over time. Such formal results should be of significance in broadening our view of the complexity of the banking system's role in the achievement of maximum employment, production, purchasing power, and faster economic growth.

Flows of funds. The present description of the flows of funds to and from the financial markets supplements what has been said above about the determination of the rate of interest and the money supply as a factor entering into that analysis. It focuses further upon the relationship between the flow of saving into investment as the flows are effected in the financial markets and emphasizes the way in which the contraction or changes in the rate of expansion of bank funds may affect that relationship.

The level of interest rates prevailing at any given time is, on the one hand, the result of the supply of funds from current income, the changes in the money supply as generated by the banking system, and the strength of the motives in the various sectors of the economy for holding idle balances (i.e., the conditions underlying the liquidity preference schedule) at that time, and the demand for funds, on the other. The entire volume of funds comprising the supply and the entire volume satisfying the demand need not consist of flows through the financial markets. Nevertheless, a portion of the supply enters the markets either directly or through financial intermediaries, and a portion of the demand for funds is financed externally. These residual or extra amounts reflect supply and demand forces generally: they are the ones that give effect to the level of interest rates. A rise in rates is an indication of a short supply of funds relative to the strengthened demand for funds and a strengthening of the speculative motive for holding money rather than bonds and other near-money assets. A decline in the rate is an indication of a weakened demand for funds relative to the supply of funds and a weakening of the speculative motive for holding money, and so on. Consequently, data showing the net advances of funds from the respective sectors of the economy to the financial markets and the net withdrawal of funds from those markets by the respective sectors of the economy will give some indication of the origin of the supply or withdrawal of those financial markets funds effecting changes in interest rates.

Such data in the form of annual averages of flows to and from the financial markets could be shown. They would portray an average of net flows of funds into the financial markets in some instances and an average of net flows out of the financial markets in others. The sum of the integrals (Sect. 10.3) for the average flows into the markets and the sum of the integrals for the average flows from the markets for a given time interval would be equal, of course, and the sum of these sums is zero. This is analogous to the identity between saving and investment (i.e., $S = I, S - I = 0$).

The data could be broken down to show the average net advance or withdrawal of funds by the respective sectors of the economy—the consumer sector (C), the business sector (I), the government sector (G), the rest of the world sector (W), the financial institutions sector (F), and the banking sector (B). Therefore, in accordance with $S - I = 0$,

$$\int_0^1 \frac{dC}{dt}\, dt + \int_0^1 \frac{dI}{dt}\, dt +$$

$$\int_0^1 \frac{dG}{dt}\, dt + \int_0^1 \frac{dW}{dt}\, dt +$$

$$\int_0^1 \frac{dF}{dt}\, dt + \int_0^1 \frac{dB}{dt}\, dt = 0$$

and so on, for each time interval we would wish to show, since the net positive and negative flows will sum to zero.

Among the sectors that would be represented in such an illustration as we have outlined, special attention could be called to the banking sector. The banking sector, as could be seen, is in a position to supply, vary the rate of supply, or withdraw a certain amount of funds in order to affect the supply-and-demand relationship generally in such a way as to give effect to changes in the rate of interest. It should be recalled (Sect. 3.1 and 9.1), however, that banks may create their own assets and expand liabilities, independently of their expansion being a source of funds and in contrast to the case of other types of business, household or governmental units. This distinguishes the banking sector from other sectors for which sources-and-uses-of-funds statements may be constructed. In other instances, an increase in assets is conventionally described as a use of funds by the firm or sector represented and a decrease as a source. An increase in liabilities is usually described as a source of funds to the firm or sector represented and a decrease as a use.

Proportions and changes over time. As early as Chapter 2, we alluded to the possible need, as seen by some, for the money supply to grow as a constant proportion of income. In the Domar macro model (Sect. 15.3), saving and investment were shown as a constant proportion of income [i.e., $S(t) = I(t) = gY(t)$], and the need for income to grow exponentially [i.e., $Y(t) = ae^{k/g\, t}$] in order for resources to stay fully and continuously employed was shown as well. In a later chapter, too, reference was made to a possibly acceptable maximum for the Federal debt as some constant proportion of income (Sect. 19.1). On most occasions, in fact, the parts of asset or debt structures (e.g., Sect. 17.1) were shown as proportions of some total.

However, we now wish to restate one proportion about these proportions from earlier analysis and to add another. The first of these, along with its underlying rationale, was set forth in Chapter 4 (Sect. 4.1 and 4.4).

Proposition 1: *If the monetary authorities lower the rate of return on bonds through an increase in the money supply as a proportion of the total for the value of bonds and the money supply (or more generally as a proportion of the total for all assets), then they will lower the return on all assets.* This follows from the optimization assumption and switching between money and bonds (or, more generally, other assets).

Proposition 2: *If we view an increase in the scale of the operation of our society (i.e., an increase or doubling of population, stocks of goods productive equipment, and so on), then (a) the various proportions of the total of all assets remain unchanged and (b) the rates of return from the respective assets remain unchanged.* This would follow from earlier assumptions and some mathematics concerning homogeneous functions of degree one and Euler's Theorem.[2]

Now the implication of an increasing income [e.g., $Y(t) = ae^{k/g\ t}$, k, $g > 0$] and proposition (2) is that the money supply must grow as some constant proportion of the total income just to assure constant rates of return and to accommodate changes in the scale of operation. There is the further implication through proposition (1) that the changes in the flow of money (i.e., changes in additions to the money supply) may be used to offset the effect on interest rates and rates of return that may result from changing proportions over time.

Both of these latter implications then complicate the way in which we must view the conduct of a satisfactory monetary policy. There must be increases in money and credit just to accommodate the growth of income as a long-run matter, and there must be changes to offset and alter the varying proportions that may occur over time as a result of *exogenous* factors.

20.3. The Liquidity Preference Demand for Money and Changes in the Composition of Assets

From prior discussion (Sect. 15.3), the growth in income is unlikely to follow the smooth path of a continuous exponential curve. Many of the stocks of financial assets and flows as a proportion of some total, such as income, are likely to change too. Historically, for example, financial intermediaries and the claims against them have grown relative to the growth of commercial banks and claims against them (Sect. 15.1), and the composition of the Federal debt (Sect. 13.2) has changed. Relating these changes in proportions to the rate of interest (= rate of return) and the liquidity preference demand for money balances (Sect. 20.1) should sharpen our insight into the complexities and requirements for the conduct of monetary policy.

The liquidity preference demand for money vs. other financial assets. Preliminary to indicating some of the implications of shifts in the strength of the preference for alternative assets and other changes over time for the conduct of monetary policy, the liquidity preference demand for money balances (Sect. 4.4 and 20.1) is reveiewed in its relationship to the total value of financial assets in the hands of the nonfinancial public (i.e., excluding banks and other financial institutions).[3] This relationship and some shifts over time are presently viewed as they would appear in Fig. 20-4. The money supply as a proportion of total financial assets is then seen with respect to two alternative means of expanding the money supply—one through the purchase of securities from the nonfinancial public and another through the purchase of new issues of securities (Sect. 14.1)—and with respect to a growth in financial claims against nonbank financial institutions in excess of the growth of other financial assets.

In both parts of the illustration, the variable for the rate of interest (4) is represented by the vertical axis, and the variables for the money supply ($M_s = \gamma$), the quantity of money demanded ($M_d = a + b/r$), and the total value of the stock of financial assets (including money balances) in the hands of the nonfinancial public are represented on the horizontal axis. Both parts of the diagram show the point of equilibrium $g(\bar{r}, \overline{M}_s)$ between the supply of money balances (M_s) and the liquidity preference demand for such balances (M_d). They also show an increase in the stock of money balances from $\overline{M}_s$ to $\overline{M}^*_s$ (i.e., $\Delta M = \overline{M}^*_s - \overline{M}_s$) and a new equilibrium point $i(\bar{r}^*, \overline{M}^*_s)$, after some allowance for the effect of a lower rate of interest on investment demand and therefore upon income and the transactions demand for money balances. In other words, the new equilibrium point allows first for a tendency toward the equilibrium

$$\gamma^* = a + \frac{b}{r},$$

or

$$r = \frac{b}{\gamma^* - a},$$

and then it allows for an increase in the transactions demand for money balances from a to a^* so that the liquidity preference curve shifts rightward.

Beyond the shifts shown in both parts of the illustration, the total assets or A-curve of values for the total of assets held by the nonfinancial public is shown on the basis of two possibly exclusive ways of effecting changes in the money supply. One of these is shown in the upper part of the diagram and another in the lower part. In both instances, the A-curve

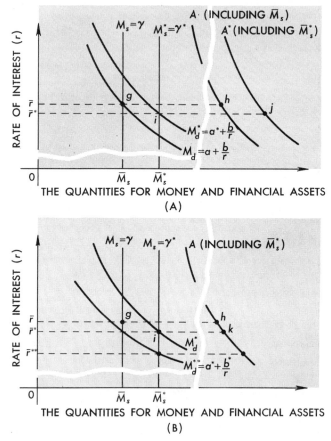

Fig. 20-4. *Equilibria for the Rate of Interest and the Value of Financial Assets Held by the Nonfinancial Public under Alternative Means of Effecting Money-Supply Changes: (A) Alternative 1: an exchange of new money balances for newly issued bonds; (B) Alternative 2: an exchange of new money balances for old bonds held by the non-financial public.*

represents the total absolute value of assets [as contrasted with the earlier reference (Sect. 4.4) to an index of value] as some decreasing function of the rate of interest. The A-curve in the upper part is shown to shift as the money supply shifts, and it is shown to shift by the same amount. In this particular instance, the banks are viewed as purchasing newly issued bonds so that there is no offsetting shift as would occur from the purchase of bonds from the nonfinancial public. The equilibrium point for the total value of the bonds then is shown to move from point h to j as the money supply and, therefore, total value of financial assets increases.

The A-curve in the lower part of the diagram is shown to remain in the same position as the initial A-curve in the upper part as the money supply increases. This occurs because the bonds acquired by the commercial banks as they expand the money supply are viewed as being purchased from the nonfinancial public. There is simply an exchange of new money balances for an equal dollar amount of bonds. In this instance, the new equilibrium for the value of bonds occurs at point k.

Proposition 3: *Where the commercial banks acquire additional bonds from the total holdings of financial assets by the nonfinancial public rather than from a new issue of securities, and where they do this so as to reduce the public's holdings of financial assets other than money, then there is a greater degree of drag on the total demand for money as income rises.* In the first instance, as in Fig. 20-4A, the lower rate of interest may account for an increase in the preference for a larger proportion of money balances. But in the second instance, as in Fig. 20-4B, the public is left with a much larger proportion of money balances. Clearly, $\overline{r^*i}/\overline{r^*j}$ is money balances held as a proportion of total assets, in Fig. 20-4A; $\overline{r^*i}/\overline{r^*p}$ is money balances held as a proportion of total assets in Fig. 20-4B; and

$$\frac{\overline{r^*i}}{\overline{r^*p}} > \frac{\overline{r^*i}}{\overline{r^*j}}$$

Thus, where the public is left with a proportion of money balances in excess of those that would result from an adjustment of preference to lower rates of interest alone, there would be a weakening of the preference for money. In Fig. 20-4B, in particular, we would expect a weakening of the speculative demand for money (i.e., a decrease in the parameter b) and a downward shift and change in the slope of the liquidity preference demand for money balances. The resulting liquidity preference demand we would denote as

$$M_d^{**} = a^* + \frac{b^*}{r}$$

In this case, especially, there would be a greater drag on the induced increase in the demand for money as income rises.

Proposition 4: *If the nonfinancial public regards intermediary claims as close money substitutes, then a growth of financial claims against nonbank financial institutions in excess of the growth of other financial assets of the nonfinancial public weakens the growth in the strength of the public's preference for money.* The hypothesis whereby the public regards such intermediary claims as savings-and-loan shares as close money substitutes is likely to have some validity in the real world. Such claims are quite liquid, relatively riskless, and involve no capital gains or losses [other than those that may result from changes in the purchasing power of the dollar (Sect. 5.3)]. Given this condition, in any event, an increase in the proportion of intermediary claims held by the public will weaken their preference for some constant proportion of money balances. The claims yield a flow of dollar returns and satisfy in part the speculative motive for holding liquid balances. Thus where we denote the demand for money and the equilibrium rate of interest respectively as

$$M_d = a + \frac{b}{r},$$

and

$$r = \frac{b}{\gamma - a},$$

a decrease in b provides some offset to the rise in the demand for money (M_d) and the rate of interest (r) that results for other reasons. The analytical support for this proposition then is analogous to that for proposition (3).

An immediate corollary to this proposition is that a given change in the money supply would have less effect on the rate of interest, given the faster growth of intermediaries. The rate of change in the interest rate with respect to a change in the money supply (Sect. 4.4) would be

$$\frac{dr}{d\gamma} = \frac{-b}{(\gamma - a)^2},$$

and a smaller value for b flattens the slope of the liquidity preference curve in the neighborhood of a given point. The implications of this for monetary policy are obvious. The monetary authorities should bring about much larger money supply changes in order to achieve given changes in interest rates.

The reader should be warned that this general discussion of changes in proportions is conducted in terms of changes in the public's total assets. Over-all, this is satisfactory, since someone's claim is someone else's liability. But for the analysis of a particular sector, such as the business sector (Sect. 17.1) or the consumer sector (Sect. 18.1), the claims and counterclaims may not be completely offsetting in terms of their contribution to liquidity as indicated earlier (Sect. 17.1). The problem of the financial analysis of particular sectors is a bit more complicated.

The composition of the Federal debt. As we have noted on various occasions (e.g., Sect. 17.1), the marketable portion of the Federal debt (Sect. 13.3) comprises a large portion of the assets held by various sectors of the economy. Also its composition consists of various maturities of debt instruments. Consequently, in varying the composition of the marketable debt with respect to more liquid or less liquid maturities, the securities available to satisfy various preferences may be altered. The availability of a larger proportion of short-term securities and a smaller proportion of long-term securities (Sect. 13.3) with a greater prospect for valuation changes may weaken the speculative demand for money balances, along the same line of reasoning as that underlying propositions (3) and (4). And, conversely, a larger proportion of long-term securities may have the reverse effect on the preference for money balances. Moreover, the securities could be sold to the nonbank public (ignoring nonbank financial intermediaries) or to the banks, with differing implications for interest rate changes.

Thus we could work out a large number of possible degrees of effect on interest rates by assuming various combinations of the composition and distribution of the marketable portion of the Federal debt. In order to simplify the analysis, however, let us outline only the four extreme cases and their implications. The implications of other cases would then simply be combinations of those for the extreme cases. The extreme cases include the following:

(1) The sale of the marketable Federal debt (consisting entirely of short-term securities) to banks only,

(2) The sale of this debt (consisting entirely of long-term securities) to banks only,

(3) The sale of the marketable Federal debt (consisting entirely of short-term securities) to the nonbank public only, and

(4) The sale of this debt (consisting entirely of long-term securities) to the nonbank public only.

With respect to the first two cases, banks could acquire the short- or long-term securities only by disposing of marketable securities other than governments through sales to the public, if they held no excess reserves. This would initially shift the M_s-line to the left and raise interest rates (and therefore depress security prices), since the increase in the government's deposits from the sale of securities decreases bank reserves. The money supply would then be restored as the government spent the deposits, but the public's increased holdings of marketable securities would strengthen their speculative demand for money (i.e., an increase in the parameter b) and raise interest rates. The greater slope (i.e., $\partial r/\partial \gamma$) would also increase the effect on the rate of interest of money supply changes in the neighborhood of the new equilibrium.

If, in these cases, the central bank provided the commercial banks with sufficient reserves to acquire the securities, then the money supply would increase. There would also be a reduction in interest rates, and then a rise in investment expenditures and thus income, and the rise in the demand for money balances resulting from the larger transaction demand (i.e., an increase in a) would offset some of the downward pressure on interest rates.

With respect to the sale of short-term government securities to the nonbank public (the third case), the result would be analogous to the relatively rapid growth of intermediary claims held by the public [proposition (4)]. But if the public were sold new long-term securities (the fourth case), there would be a stronger demand for money than in the case of short-term securities. Quite likely, the demand for money balances would reinforce the upward pressure on interest rates that would result from the sale of the government securities in the first place. On the other hand, the public might well regard its holdings of long-term governments as highly liquid assets, and this would lead to the opposite results by offsetting some of the preference for holding money balances.[4]

In the first two of these cases and in a change from one to the other of the remaining cases, there may be a need for central bank actions to offset the effects of the cases on the rate of interest. The need for action (or inaction), of course, would depend on other developments. Nevertheless, we note that an increase in the speculative demand for money by the public, as in the first two cases, makes the resulting interest rate more sensitive to changes in the money supply. Thus

$$\frac{dr}{d\gamma} = \frac{-b}{(\gamma - a)^2},$$

and an increase in the parameter b increases the slope of the demand curve in the neighborhood of a given point so that a given money supply change affects the rate of interest more than previously (i.e., prior to the increase in b). A switch in the composition of the debt from short-dated securities (the third case) to long-dated securities (the fourth case) would have a similar effect. Further, if the circumstances were reversed, the converse set of changes would result.

20.4. Summary

The rate of interest may be viewed as being determined by the supply of saving and the demand for saving (i.e., investment demand). It may also be viewed as being determined by the liquidity preference demand for money balances and the supply of money balances. Both views, however, pertain to the same rate of interest at any given time, and both also depend upon the level of income at any given time. For example, saving is a function of income, and the liquidity preference demand for money is also dependent on income. As these matters appear, a more general expression for the rate of interest is desirable.

The more general theory for the rate of interest is achieved by (1) finding the equation for the set of solutions to the classical model at different levels of income, (2) finding the equation for the set of solutions to the liquidity preference model at different levels of income, and by (3) combining the latter two equations into another and more general model. In the more general model, the classical and liquidity preference models enter as determinants of both the rate of interest and income. The resulting model, then, is a sufficiently general one permitting us to observe the effects of changes in the supply of money, and changes underlying investment demand and saving (and therefore consumption) on both the rate of interest and income.

The rate of interest (= rate of return) and income will change if there is a change in either the flow of saving, the flow of investment, the liquidity preference demand for money, or the stock of money. This, one may note from the illustrations relating to the general theory of interest and on other grounds. By the same reasoning, the rate of interest will not change if equilibrium values for all of the other variables change in the same direction and as some constant proportion of income. The implications here are interesting in that the central bank must provide for a growth in the money supply to accommodate growth in income. They are also of interest in that changes in the composition of the public's assets as a result of bank action or other outside factors will change the rate of interest. The general discussion of changes in proportions is conducted in terms of changes in the composition of assets. In general this is satisfactory, for someone's claim is someone else's liability, but, for the analysis of particular sectors of the nonfinancial public, the sector's attitude toward liquidity is affected by the illiquidity of the claims against the sector as well.

Through the banking system, some control is exercised over the rate of interest. This exercise of control operates through the system's capacity to alter the money supply as a proportion of total assets, and through its capacity to alter the flow of new money in relation to the flow of income. In this context, the system may take action to effect changes in the rate of interest or to offset changes resulting from other sources.

The growth of the public's claims against nonbank financial intermediaries relative to the growth of those against banks, and the changes in the composition of the Federal debt, are among the important outside sources affecting the rate of interest. Where the public regards changes in its composition of financial assets as being less liquid, they strengthen their preference for money balances. Given the money supply, this means that a given change in the supply of money will have a greater effect on the rate of interest, in the neighborhood of an equilibrium point for the supply of money and the liquidity preference demand for money. On the other hand, when the public regards changes in its composition of financial assets as being more liquid, it weakens its preference for money balances. Given the money supply in this case, a given change in the supply of money will have a smaller effect on the rate of interest.

The general relationships that we have focused upon permit us to associate the rate of interest as an abstraction with the structure of rates prevailing at any given level of income. The rate of interest may be viewed as the result of the residual portion of funds flowing into the financial markets from current income, the new money generated (or withdrawn) by the banking system, and changes in the strength of the motive for holding idle balances, on the one hand, and the residual portion of the demand for funds satisfied by drawing upon the financial markets, on the other. These residual or extra flows reflect supply and demand forces generally, and they are the ones that cause changes in the structure of rates—an upward movement in the structure of interest rates corresponding to an increase in the rate of interest and a downward movement corresponding to a decline in the rate of interest. Furthermore, the net residual flows to and from the financial markets for the respective sectors may be integrated for a given interval of time, and the results of the integration may be summed and set equal to zero, in a manner analogous to the identity between saving and investment ($S = I$, or $S - I = 0$). And the data corresponding to annual (or quarterly, and so on) averages of the net residual flows permit us to observe changes in the supply of funds and their sources in terms of sectors and changes in the demand for funds and their users by sectors.

The banking system enters into both the analytical model of the rate of interest and the financial markets in its capacity to supply or withdraw funds and consequently affect the rate of interest, as well as the availability of funds. On the analytical side, the banking system affects the rate of interest by increasing (or decreasing) the quantity of money and by supplying (or withdrawing) investable funds. On the financial markets side, the banking system may effect net flows of funds into the financial markets or it may, in effect, withdraw net flows from the financial markets. The role of the system may be observed from actual data in both instances.

References

1. See Alvin H. Hansen, *A Guide to Keynes* (New York: McGraw-Hill Book Company, 1953), pp. 140-153, and *Monetary Theory and Fiscal Policy* (New York: (McGraw-Hill Book Company, 1949), pp. 71-82; and Harry G. Johnson, "Monetary Theory and Keynesian Economics," *Money Trade and Economic Growth* (Cambridge, Mass.: Harvard University Press, 1962), pp. 107-125.

For a bibliography and a survey of some interest, theories and related matters, see G. L. S. Shackle, "Recent Theories Concerning the Nature and Role of Interest," *Economic Journal*, June 1961, pp. 209-254.

2. See David S. Huang, *Introduction to the Use of Mathematics in Economic Analysis* (New York: John Wiley and Sons, Inc., 1964), pp. 83-88.

3. The exposition is based partly on Don Patinkin, "Financial Intermediaries and the Logical Structure of Monetary Theory," *American Economic Review*, March 1961, esp. pp. 109-111; John G. Gurley, "Liquidity and Financial Institutions in the Postwar Period," Study Paper No. 14, Joint Economic Committee, *Study of Employment, Growth, and Price Levels*, 1960, pp. 52-57; Richard A. Musgrave, *The Theory of Public Finance* (New York: McGraw-Hill Book Company, 1959), Chap. 22 and 24; John G. Gurley and Edward S. Shaw, "Financial Aspects of Economic Development," *American Economic Review*, September 1955, pp. 528-529, note 16; and J. J. Polak and W. H. White, "The Effect of Income Expansion on the Quantity of Money," *International Monetary Fund Staff Papers*, August 1955, pp. 398-433.

4. The difficult empirical problem of determining the "savings component" from the "liquidity component" of various financial assets is discussed by Stephen H. Axilrod, "Liquidity and Public Policy," *Federal Reserve Bulletin*, October 1961, pp. 1164-1169.

Another possibly small effect relating to the application of the analysis is the so-called "wealth effect." It refers to the effect on consumer behavior resulting from valuation changes and to the effect of changes in the amount of the public's holdings of financial assets on their expenditure decisions.

Appendix A to Chapter 20

Banks, Interest Rates, and the Price Level—The Wicksell Model

A model synthesizing some interest theory (Sect. 20.1), the quantity theory of money (Sect. 5.1), notions pertaining to aggregate supply and aggregate demand (Sect. 15.2), and the functioning of a modern banking system (Sect. 3.1) was formulated as early as 1898 by Knut Wicksell, an outstanding Swedish economist.[1] The model, in fact, anticipates and predates some of the more recent and current notions found in monetary analysis. These, as we shall see, included a loanable funds theory of interest, the notion of an historical equality between aggregate saving and aggregate investment (Sect. 15.2), and the notion whereby price level changes arise in response to an imbalance between planned saving and planned investment (Sect. 16.2). The model, moreover, is formulated as a difference equation model,[2] and a review of some current notions in this form should be instructive.[3] In the present review of a simplified version of the model, we only outline the assumptions in words and present the model largely in geometric terms. The mathematical formulation of the model as a first-order linear difference equation system and the system's solution have not been reproduced here.[4]

The assumptions of the simplified version of the present Wicksellian model are as follows:

Assumption 1: The economy is operating at full employment. This, then, permits us to view output (O^*) in constant prices as a constant (i.e, $O^* =$ const.) over a short interval of time.

Assumption 2: Investment in constant prices (I^*) is a decreasing function of the rate of interest (r) due to reasons that were previously outlined (Sect. 22.2). Linearly, $I^* = a - br$, or, rearranging terms $r = (a/b) - (1/b)I^*$, where a and b are positive constants and r is the rate of interest charged by banks.

Assumption 3: The supply of saving in constant prices (S^*) from

458

income in constant prices is an increasing function of the rate of interest. Linearly, $S^* = c + dr$, or $r = (1/d)S^* - (c/d)$, where c and d are positive constants. [Of course, this assumption could also be stated in terms of consumption in current prices (C^*) as a decreasing function of the rate of interest.]

Assumption 4: Investment demand in current prices (i.e., I^*P) and planned saving in current prices (i.e., S^*P) also depend on the level of prices expected for the period.

Assumption 5: The price level that is expected for a period (i.e., $P_{0(t)}$) is viewed as being equal to the actual price level that was realized in the immediately preceding period (i.e., $P_{1(t+1)}$), where

P_0 is the expected (*ex ante*) price level and
P_1 is the actual (*ex post*) price level.

In addition to the symbols already emphasized,

$\bar{r}$ is the "normal" (i.e., equilibrium) rate of interest as distinct from the bank rate (r),

$\overline{D}$ is the equilibrium level of aggregate demand as distinct from aggregate demand (D) generally, and

$0,1,(t)$, as subscripts, are planned or expected (*ex ante*), actual (*ex post*), and time period, respectively.

Portions of the model are sketched in Fig. 20-A. Variables for the equilibrium rate of interest and the bank rate are shown on the vertical

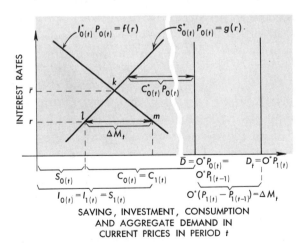

Fig. 20-A. A Wicksellian View: Interest Rates, the Ex Post Equality of Saving and Investment, Price Level Changes, and Changes in the Quantity of Money.

axis, and variables for saving, investment, consumption, and aggregate demand are shown on the horizontal axis. The diagram shows schedules for investment and saving as decreasing and increasing functions of the rate of interest, respectively [i.e., $I^*_{0(t)}P_{0(t)} = f(r)$, and $S^*_{0(t)}P_{0(t)} = g(r)$]. The vertical line $\overline{D} = $ const. corresponds to output in current prices and aggregate demand in current prices at the initial time when there is no expected price level change, and the vertical line $D_t = $ const. corresponds to aggregate demand in current prices when there is an actual price level change.

In fact, in the illustration, one may observe a complex of monetary relationships: (1) a form of the classical view of the rate of interest, (2) the actual equality of saving and investment at a given time, and (3) changes in aggregate demand in current prices in response to a change in the quantity of money. In the first instance, we view the intersection of the schedules for the supply of saving (i.e., $S^*_{0(t)}P_{0(t)}$) and the investment demand for funds (i.e., $I^*_{0(t)}P_{0(t)}$) at the point k. This intersection also yields the equilibrium rate of interest $\overline{r}$, or "normal" rate as Wicksell called it. Moreover, if this rate is attained by the banking system (i.e., $r = \overline{r}$), then ex ante saving and investment are equal [i.e., $S_{0(t)} = I_{0(t)}$]. There is no price level change [i.e., $P_{1(t)} = P_{1(t-1)}$], and the actual investment demand plus the consumer demand is equal to the equilibrium level of aggregate demand (i.e., $I_{1(t)} + C_{1(t)} = \overline{D}$). In this case, too, actual expenditures are equal to output so that aggregate demand cannot be blamed for any price changes. In fact, this is a simple illustration of J. B. Say's law of markets (Sect. 5.2).

What, then, happens when the equilibrium rate $\overline{r}$ is above the bank rate r as may occur when banks continue to expand credit and the money supply at a rate below the equilibrium rate? This takes us to the third instance above. In this case there is an imbalance between planned saving and planned investment (i.e., $S_{0(t)} < I_{0(t)}$, or in terms of geometric distances, $\overline{rl} < \overline{rm}$), and the additional loanable funds (i.e., ΔM_t or $\overline{lm}$) are forthcoming from the banking system. Similarly, since income in the form of output remains unchanged (i.e., $\overline{D} = O^*P_{0(t)} = S_{0(t)} + C_{0(t)}$), aggregate demand exceeds aggregate output by the amount ΔM_t (i.e., $D_t - \overline{D} = \Delta M_t$). But in the diagram, the higher aggregate demand (i.e., $D_t = O^*P_{1(t)}$) depends on a change in the price level. Indeed, the change in aggregate demand is the distance denoted by the product of the output in constant prices and the change in prices [i.e., $O^* (P_{1(t)} - P_{1(t-1)})$]. We see, as in an earlier analysis involving Say's law, the price level change was initiated by a change in the money supply rather than a shift in aggregate demand. Consequently, we have here, too, a form of the quantity theory of money (Sect. 5.1).

This relationship between the expansion of bank credit and the price level change may also be seen if we combine the equations of the model and eliminate all variables but the price level, expressd in period t as a function of itself in the preceding period:

$$P_{1(t)} = \frac{a - br}{c + dr} P_{1(t-1)}$$

This equation is a simple first-order (one period lag) linear difference equation, which has the general solution:

$$P_{1(t)} = \alpha \left(\frac{a - br}{c + dr}\right)^t$$

where α is a constant whose value depends on the initial price level (before any change occurred), on whether $r < \bar{r}$ ($\alpha > 0$) or $r > \bar{r}$ ($\alpha < 0$), and the units in which price changes are to be expressed. If $r < \bar{r}$, then $(a - br) > (c + dr)$, and any $P_{1(t)}$ will always be higher than $P_{1(t-1)}$ by a constant proportion, i.e., over time $P_{1(t)}$ will rise exponentially. (Now work through the case where $r > \bar{r}$.)

Wicksell, himself, believed that aggregate demand might at least temporarily become effective in an amount exceeding or falling short of supply at last period's prices, thus causing prices to rise and fall, respectively. He also believed that the price increases or decreases might continue at about the same rate for some time, and, when a new equilibrium price level is established (e.g., as a result of some exogenous factor), it could be considerably above or below the original price level. He attributed the cause of this phenomenon to the ability of a modern fractional reserve banking system to create money in the process of financing planned investment expenditures in excess of *ex ante* saving.[5] (This could also work in the opposite direction if banks offset *ex ante* saving by destroying previously created money and credit.) The extent of this action by banks, further, tends to be enhanced by the fact that banks, for relatively long periods, may "freeze" their loan rates at certain levels and keep right on lending at these rates so long as their absolute reserves do not reach what they regard as a dangerously low level. With money expanding to finance expenditures and not disappearing into idle balances and with real output fixed, the equation of exchange (Sect. 5.1) implicit in Wicksell's model tells us that the price level is the only variable left in the equation to respond.

How does a process of price increases get started? Well, there are various possibilities. The simplest, and perhaps the most likely of these, we shall examine. Suppose, for example, our hypothetical economy was initially in equilibrium at point l, a point of intersection between planned saving in current prices and an initial investment demand function. Now suppose the investment function shifts to the position it occupies in the diagram. The shift—contrary to Say's Law and the equation of exchange in its purest form—could be due to such things as an improvement in business confidence or opportunities opened up by innovations. Then there would now be an excess demand for saving at the old rate of interest r amounting to $\overline{lm}$ which could cause the rate of interest to adjust to the new equilibrium level $\bar{r}$, if investment expenditures had to rely on *ex ante* saving in order to be carried out. On the other hand, the upward pressure on the interest rate (and, thus, downward pressure and demand for funds) would not be forthcoming, and demand would be "effective" at D_t, if banks were able to finance the excess demand for investment at the old interest rate r. Aggregate demand would increase along the horizontal axis as prices were bid up (necessarily in proportion to the money supply change).

Point m is an important one. It represents a temporary (single period) loanable funds equilibrium, i.e., an intersection between the demand for loanable funds (investment) and the supply of loanable funds (*ex ante* saving plus new money created by banks in the process of lending).* In fact, Wicksell's analysis, appearing as it did in 1898, was the first presentation of what we call today a loanable funds theory of interest. The analysis, too, was the first to demonstrate the effect on demand in current prices of a discrepancy between *ex ante* saving and investment and to show, at the same time, that *ex post* saving and investment are always equal.

The price level changes can even be viewed as cumulative, in the present model. So long as the underlying real functions do not shift, banks do not raise their loan rates and curtail lending, and people keep on thinking at the beginning of each period that prices are going to remain constant at their just-realized level, the situation, relatively speaking, will be the same in each succeeding period, with prices rising at a constant rate each period (but exponentially over time, as compared with some beginning level). Thus the diagram may be used to represent any period in the so-called "cumulative process" by plugging in the real function and the price level for the previous period. The model is also one of the earliest examples of a fully determinate dynamic process or period analysis.

The model may be used to depict cumulative downward movements in prices, but we encounter difficulty in adhering to the assumption of fixed real output in the face of declining money demand and the high probability of downward movements in all prices that are less than perfectly parallel.

---

* Note that the supply of new bank-created funds may be thought of as a horizontal line through l and m. This is a perfectly interest elastic supply function.

Wicksell stated three alternatives and identical conditions for what was later called "monetary equilibrium" in his model.* These are (1) the equality between the equilibrium rate of interest and the bank rate, (2) equality of *ex ante* saving and investment, and (3) a constant price level. That these are identical conditions should be obvious from Fig. 20-A.

Wicksell (1851-1926) stands chronologically in a line from Thomas Tooke (1774-1858) to Lord Keynes (1883-1946) in attributing the ultimate cause of price level changes to discrepancies between aggregate demand and supply Yet, in this portion of his work at least, he was also a quantity theorist, which should be apparent from the illustration. The model, with not very drastic qualifications, is still of considerable significance in analyzing the link between the banking system and short-run periods of substantial inflation. For example, money in the hyper-inflation case studies in *Studies in the Quantity Theory of Money* (Friedman, ed.) can be interpreted as cases of a Wicksellian inflation. The United States in World War II and over the postwar years 1945-1951 (Sect. 24.3) could be described as a case of suppressed Wicksellian inflation. In World War II in particular, the suppressed inflation was in part the result of the Treasury borrowing from banks at a time when the Federal Reserve pegged money rates.

References

1. *Geldzins und Güterpreise* (Jena: Gustav Fischer, 1898), translated as *Interest and Prices* (London: The Macmillan Company, Ltd., 1936).

2. See David Huang, *Introduction to the Use of Mathematics in Economic Analysis* (New York: John Wiley and Sons, Inc., 1964), Chap. 7.

3. A simplified version of the model, on which the present exposition is based, appears in Wicksell's *Lectures on Political Economy*, Vol. II (London: Routledge and Kegan Paul, 1935), pp. 190-208.

4. For the analysis of such systems, see Huang, *op.cit.*, pp. 142-151.

5. The case we are examining here approximates Wicksell's "pure credit" economy, in which banks maintain no reserves. Thus their supply of new money and credit may be taken as perfectly elastic over a certain range, so long as banks try merely to maintain a certain minimal *amount* of reserves, rather than a certain *ratio* of reserves to deposits. See Don Patinkin, *Money, Interest, and Prices* (Evanston, Ill.: Row, Peterson and Company, 1956), pp. 428-430.

* The term was coined by Gunnar Myrdal; see his *Monetary Equilibrium* (London: William Hodge and Co., 1939).

Appendix B to Chapter 20

Two Theories of the Term Structure
of Interest Rates

One topic that we have not dealt with earlier in the discussions of monetary theory concerns the term or time-to-maturity structure of interest rates (Sect. 4.2). In that structure we find all kinds of differences among interest rates at one time and over time. These differences, for example, occur in interest rates or effective yields on public versus private debt instruments, corporate versus noncorporate debt, debt instruments versus equities, customer versus open market debt, domestic versus foreign debt, marketable versus nonmarketable debt, and old debt versus new debt. They occur as well as a result of market imperfections, including interregional differences deriving from the immobility of funds. Some of these differences we have observed or shall encounter later. Still, some review of the essential structure of the two leading theories of the term structure of interest rates is a useful addition to the subject matter of Chapter 20.[1] In reviewing the broader outlines of the theories, then, we shall not consider the numerous variations of the two aproaches that incorporate explicit types of financial investors and specific real world constraints on the working out of the predictions of the respective theories.

The two theories are the expected short-rate theory and the arbitrage theory.* In setting them forth we will consider all interest rates as

* Some would add an entire class of theories, sometimes referred to as institutional theories of the rate structure. These would deal with the maturity structure of the existing *stock* of debt instruments and the specialized asset preferences of various groups of institutional investors. These, however, are actually institutional factors influencing the actual structure of rates, and they are not a part of a theoretical structure. Culbertson's theory (see reference 1), for example, is an arbitrage theory incorporating particlar institutional constraints. Also, Axilrod and Young list four "influences" on maturity relationships in a popular article, thereby mixing up the theories and the institutional constraints. See Stephen H. Axilrod and Ralph A Young, "Interest Rates and Monetary Policy," *Federal Reserve Bulletin,* September 1962, pp. 1122-1127.

falling in either of two groups—short-term rates and long-term rates. In addition, we will assume (1) that the two sets of rates have been adjusted for any differences due to risk and liquidity (Sect. 4.1), and (2) that there are properly functioning financial markets as would result from the presence of optimizing buyers and sellers in a relatively free market [see reference 21 (Chap. 24) for a definition]. The problem, then, remains to explain any differences in the structure of rates that still exist and to predict certain future courses of movements from given conditions. As we shall see, these theoretical matters are of more than purely academic interest. Each theory in fact has implications for the conduct of monetary policy.

The expected short-rate approach. The expected short-rate approach to the time-to-maturity structure of interest rates is sometimes called the neoclassical theory of the rate structure, where the latter reference implies that the origin of the theory falls chronologically between the economic writings of the late 1800's and the appearance of Keynes' *General Theory* (1936). While not originated by him, the theory is nevertheless closely identified with Friedrich Lutz.

The main point of the theory is simply stated:

Proposition: *At any particular time, long-term rates represent an average of prospective short-term rates.* In other words, a positively sloping yield curve (Sect. 4.2 and 4.5) corresponds to a consensus of opinions prevailing in the financial markets whereby short-term rates will rise in the future, and a negatively sloping yield curve reflects the expectation that short-term rates will fall in the future. The link between short- and long-term rates is in the fact that a long-term loan may be effected either by a single contract of long duration or by a series of periodically renegotiated, short-term contracts. Thus, for example, if the current rate on a two-year loan is not equivalent to the average that one may expect to pay on two one-year loans, with the yield on the second loan renegotiated at the end of the first year, then the actions by optimizing lenders to take advantage of the higher yielding alternative would soon establish a temporary equilibrium in the rate structure. Finally, a horizontal yield curve reflects the expected constancy of future short-term rates, and presumably this kind of yield curve represents a long-run vis-à-vis a temporary equilibrium in the structure of rates.

So far, the reference has been to a consensus of opinions in the financial markets. Suppose, for the sake of greater detail, that there is still a common feeling as to the direction of interest rate changes but a diversity of expectations with respect to the degree to which interest rates will change. What then? The same general relationship holds between short and long rates, but the explanation becomes a bit more complicated. To illustrate this case, Professor Lutz introduces a sketch similar to that in Fig. 20-B.

With reference to the diagram,

$\overline{OO}{}^*$, a geometric distance, corresponds to a fixed total supply of funds to be allocated between the markets for short-term and long-term funds respectively,

$D_L = f(r)$ is the quantity of long-term funds demanded as a function f of interest rates on long-term funds,

$D_S = g(r)$ is the quantity of short-term funds demanded as a function g of interest rates on short-term funds,

r_eA is the expectations curve when the entire market expects no future change in interest rates and where point p is the only point equating the supply of and demand for funds in both markets at the same rate of interest, and

$r_eA{}^*$ is the expectations curve when the market expects short-term rates to be higher in the future.

In this particular illustration, the vertical distances measure prevailing rates and expected short rates, while the horizontal distance measures the demands for short- [i.e., $g(r)$] and long-dated [i.e., $f(r)$] funds, respectively; a total fixed quantity of funds; and equilibrium quantities for long- and short-term funds. These various horizontal measures are set off separately to facilitate reading, but they should all be read as all being measured along the common line segment $\overline{OO}{}^*$. Note, too, that, if the expectations curve r_eA were horizontal at some rate rather than r_e, then neither the short-term nor the long-term market would be in equilibrium, and changes would result to bring about equilibrium. For example, if the horizontal line moved parallel upward to the point q, then borrowers would be demanding less of both types of funds than lenders are willing to lend and rates would again decline to equilibrium as security prices rose in response to purchases by lenders.

Professor Lutz refers to the expectations line as a "line-up of 'subjective' long rates," but what we have done in drawing such a line is to view an accumulation of lenders and the volume of loanable funds according to their expectations about future short rates as embodied in the long rate. Moving from left to right on a rising curve, we would view an accumulation of lenders who think rates will be at a certain point or higher. Therefore, they would prefer to lend less on long-term contracts in the present. Moving from left to right on a falling curve, we would view an accumulation of lenders who think short rates will be at a certain point or lower in the future. Therefore, they prefer to lend more on long-term contracts in the present. Equilibrium, nevertheless, is established in the diagram (1) when the quantity of long-term funds demanded is equal to the quantity of long-term funds supplied, (2) when the quantity of short-term funds demanded is equal to the quantity of short-term funds supplied, and (3) when lenders are fully loaned up (i.e., when the fixed total supply of funds is entirely committed).

Now, with further reference to Fig. 20-B, let the expectations line change from r_eA to r_eA^* as suppliers come to expect higher short rates in the future. In this case, equilibrium in the long-term market will be at point $Q(r_L, D_L)$ where the coordinates of the point are the equilibrium rate $\bar{r}_L$ and the equilibrium quantity of long-term funds $\bar{D}_L$. And the

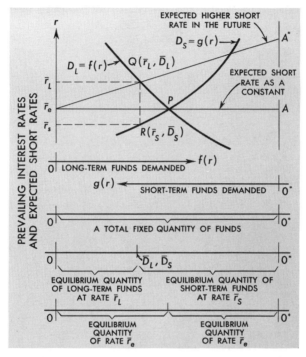

Fig. 20-B. Expected Short Rates, Prevailing Interest Rates, and Quantities for the Respective Supplies of (and Demands for) Long- and Short-Term Funds.

equilibrium in the short-term market is at point $R(r_S, D_S)$, where the coodinates of the point are the equilibrium rate $\bar{r}_S(\bar{r}_S < \bar{r}_L)$ and the equilibrium quantity of short-term funds $\bar{D}_S(\bar{D}_S =$ Fixed Total Quantity of Funds—less $\bar{D}_L)$. In this case, too, everyone represented by that segment of the expectations line r_eA^* to the right of point Q is in the short-term market; i.e., all the lenders whose subjective long rates exceed the market long rate r_L are suppliers of funds to the short-term market. In other words, the lenders who expect short rates to rise in the future will lend a more restricted amount of funds on long-term contracts at a high rate of interest r_L, and they will place the remaining quantity of funds in the short-term markets for the time being. Had they expected short rates to decline in the future they would be willing to lend a larger amount on long-term contracts and a smaller amount on short-term contracts at rates in excess of those on long-term contracts; they would be willing to loan funds on more favorable terms while they could lend on such contracts.

In brief, any rising expectations line through the initial equilibrium rate level $\bar{r}_e$ will always involve long rates in excess of the short rate; conversely, a declining line through the same point will involve short rates in excess of long rates. This, indeed, is the link with the simplest version of the expected short-rate theory. Lutz thinks there may be subsequently induced upward or downward shifts in the expectations line which further change the long and short rates.

Note, moreover, that throughout the discussion the expectations line was related to the expectations of the suppliers of funds. Although they were restricted to a fixed total volume of funds to lend, they were still free to switch their loans from the short- to the long-term market or vice versa. By contrast, the users of funds were represented by functions relating the various rates of interest to their demand for short- and long-term funds, respectively. The exposition did not deal explicitly with any shifts in the demand for funds in relation to changes in borrowers' expectations concerning the future course of interest rates. This has been one of the sources of criticism of Lutz' exposition of the theory. Professor Luckett, for example, criticizes Lutz for assuming a mobility of lenders between the short- and long-term markets but complete immobility of borrowers as may be due to a limited access to the entire range of the financial markets. There is no a priori reason, however, as the theory is set forth above, why the demand curves could not shift to simulate the actual market behavior of the borrowers. If borrowers or a sufficient number of them are free to finance long-term needs through a series of short-term contracts and vice versa, then there would be a tendency to move the rates in the respective markets toward equality and an equilibrium at point P in the diagram. Point P would be subject to changes in response to shifts in the borrowers' respective demand curves.

The arbitrage theory. The arbitrage theory is usually associated with those models that emphasize the determination of a single rate of interest and changes in such a rate that can be taken as an accurate indicator of changes in the level of all interest rates. Thus, it tends, among others, to be associated with the models containing the liquidity preference demand for money (Sect. 4.4 and 20.1) as one of the determinants of the rate of interest, since these models generally focus upon changes in a long-term, low-risk rate, such as that on United States government or high-grade corporate bonds, as an indicator of shifts in the structure of interest rates in the short run. The arbitrage theory, of course, is not alone in its reliance on the presence of arbitrage operations in removing various rate discrepancies, but it does place a special emphasis on the occurrence of arbitrage and switching operations (Sect. 4.2) with sufficient rapidity to eliminate discrepancies between long- and short-term rate movements in the very short run. In fact, both of the present theories rely upon assumptions about the presence of optimizing behavior and relatively free markets, and it is such behavior and market conditions that we associate with arbitrage and switching operations. As in the case of the expected short-rate theory, too, its most vociferous advocates have written extensively on a plethora of institutional restraints on, and requirements for, the operation of the financial market forces that are called for by the assumptions of the theory.

The main point of the present theory is most simply stated:

Proposition: *Interest rates in the short run undergo a coincidental or parallel movement.* The forces contributing to this movement and linking changes in one sector of the markets to those in others relate (1) to the substitutability of the alternative investment opportunities on the part of lenders and the alternative means of financing on the part of borrowers, and (2) to the tendency for changes in business, credit, and monetary conditions to have a simultaneous impact in the various financial markets. The working out of the forces, moreover, depends on the presence of optimizing participants in relatively free markets.

The particular implication of this theory for the carrying out of a Federal Reserve policy of credit ease or tightness should be clear. It is that the effects of changes in member-bank reserves may be transmitted to financial markets generally in the form of a tone of ease or tightness and that the effects of open market operations solely in the short-term sector of the government securities market on the availability and cost of bank credit on the yields of short-dated securities may be transmitted throughout the financial markets.[2]

As we shall see later (Sect. 24.3), the Federal Reserve endorsed the arbitrage view in the decade following March 1951, and, in substance, it continued to endorse it, though possibly not always in its purest form. At times during the recession of 1960-1961, for example, the monetary officials attempted to effect upward pressure on short-term rates and downward pressure on long-term ones with minor evidence of success. Possibly, the most widely held view among monetary writers and spokesmen on market aspects of the arbitrage theory is that expressed in a 1961 study by the Morgan Guaranty Trust Company:

> . . . When attention is turned to the relationship between the cyclical movements of short-term and long-term rates—the movements with which monetary policy is most fundamentally concerned—a deeply rooted tendency toward covariation is apparent.

On the basis of the refined statistics that have been presented, in fact, the linkage between short and long rates appears so powerful as to make discouraging the task of trying to force their movements appreciably apart for any prolonged period. The linkage also suggests that frictions in the money market are minimal under normal circumstances, as indicated by the effectiveness with which cyclical movement originating in one sector spreads through the others.[3]

An assessment of the theories. The two theories outlined above depend on essentially the same set of assumptions. They should not, therefore, contain inconsistent propositions. Still, on the one hand, the statement of the pure arbitrage theory need not involve any particular view of the role of expectations in the interest rate structure, and, on the other, the association of the arbitrage theory with the liquidity preference demand for money would involve some such view. Consequently, some may emphasize elements in one of the theories at the expense of those in the other. For example, advocates of the expected short-rate approach may be pessimistic about the effectiveness of certain Federal Reserve actions for reasons related to the interest rate structure.[4] (Advocates of the arbitrage theory may be pessimistic for other reasons.)

The expected short-rate advocates are dubious, first, about the ability of changes in the central bank discount rates to influence long-term interest rates and thus long-term investment. For example, a reduction in the discount rates will cause long-term rates to fall only if the expectation is generated that short-term rates will remain low, and this in turn implies that the discount rates cannot be changed very often. Further, as we have seen (Sect. 8.1), a reduction in the discount rate may have a damping effect on expenditures via the pessimistic expectations the rate change may engender for potential borrowers.

Second, advocates of the expected short-rate theory may be skeptical of open market operations that are used to alter the slope of the yield curve. The argument, briefly, is that the central bank will succeed in achieving a particular slope in the yield curve only if the market thinks it cannot succeed. Suppose, for example, that the Federal Reserve tries to maintain a positively sloped curve (i.e., long-term rates higher than short-term rates). If the market believes it will succeed over a relatively long period so that the link between the long-term and expected short-term rates is believed to be broken, then the suppliers of funds to the market would shift some of their holdings from the short-term sector to the long-term sector. This would tend to equalize the rates in the two sectors, unless the central bank is willing to take over the business of supplying the short-term market with funds in large amounts. Conversely, if the central bank were to attempt the opposite pattern as the Federal Reserve did for a brief period in 1961-1962 (24.2), then the shift from long- to short-dated securities would force them to absorb large quantities of long-term securities to accomplish its purpose.

The main criticisms of the expected short-rate theory, other than that mentioned earlier in this appendix about the immobility of borrowers, are several as advanced by Luckett:

(1) Lenders may have expectations about long-term rates that are in turn completely independent of their expectations about short-term rates.

(2) The theory requires "rational" investors to make extremely long-term predictions of short-term rates, for which most investors would not believe they had any grounds for doing accurately.

(3) Empirical studies have generally not borne out the theory, particularly for the 1930's. As matters are, there is no empirical evidence for accepting the first of these criticisms. The second criticism is of no special significance, since the beliefs of investors as revealed by what they say need not be of the same order of acceptability as their beliefs as revealed by what they do. And, finally, some of the axioms of the theory were likely to have been inoperative under the unusual conditions of the 1930's.

In fact, as we noted earlier (Sect. 4.5), a downward sloping yield curve is very likely to be associated with a subsequent shift toward a larger proportion of short-term maturities, and a rising yield curve is quite likely to foretell a shift toward a larger proportion of relatively longer-term maturities on the part of bank portfolio managers at least. The expected short-rate theory may very well provide one explanation of the investment behavior of lenders over the postwar type of short cycles, although we may wish to relate this behavior to liquidity preference notions (Sect. 4.4). The question of accepting the theory or some alternative theory, then, may not turn on the agreement of the resulting predictions of the theory with data at all. It may, instead, turn on the grounds of whether one theory has more or less intuitive appeal and whether the other offends the senses more or less. The question may even be raised by the practitioners and outside observers of central banking of whether the one theory as opposed to the other seems to embody more of the actual conscious and subconscious thought processes of the participants in the financial markets.

As matters turn out (Sect. 4.5) one may attach some significance to a particular slope for the yield curve as a means of predicting the behavior of portfolio managers; this, in turn, may have significance for conducting a monetary policy. Also the special emphasis in the arbitrage theory on arbitrage and switching operations as a means of transmitting changes in one market sector to others gives the latter theory special importance for the conduct of monetary policy. Thus the most meaningful elements of both of the present theories find a place among our theories and analyses of monetary, banking, and financial operations.

References

1. A much more detailed discussion of the theory of rate structure is contained in Joseph W. Conard, *Introduction to the Theory of Interest* (Berkeley: University of California Press, 1959), Chap. 14-17. The exposition here is based primarily on Friedrich A. Lutz, "The Structure of Interest Rates," *Quarterly Journal of Economics,* November 1940, reprinted in American Economic Association, *Readings in the Theory of Income Distribution* (Philadelphia: The Blakiston Co., 1949), pp. 499-532; Dudley G. Luckett, "Professor Lutz and the Structure of Interest Rates," *Quarterly Journal of Economics,* February 1959, pp. 131-144; and John M. Culbertson, "The Term Structure of Interest Rates," *Quarterly Journal of Economics,* November 1957, pp. 485-517.

2. See Winfield W. Riefler, "Open Market Operations in Long-Term Securities," *Federal Reserve Bulletin,* November 1958, esp. pp. 1264-1266. These pages contain a discussion of the "fluidity" (substitution and arbitrage) in debt markets that facilitates a transmission of the effects of open market transactions in the short-dated sector of the market for government securities to other sectors.

3. "A Closer Look at Interest-Rate Relationships," *The Morgan Guaranty Survey,* April 1961, p. 9. This study, using monthly data from January 1951 to March 1961 for three-month Treasury bills and twenty-year Treasury bonds, seeks to isolate four kinds of rate movements: cyclical, seasonal, and secular movements and those due to "the natural difference in the volatility of short-term and long-term rates." For a study utilizing six interest rate series and covering the period 1919-1958, see Herbert R. Runyon, "The Behavior of Selected Interest Rates in the Business Cycle," *Monthly Review,* Federal Reserve Bank of San Francisco, October 1959, pp. 146-150.

4. See, in particular, Charls Walker, "Federal Reserve Policy and the Structure of Interest Rates on Government Securities," *Quarterly Journal of Economics,* February 1954, pp. 19-42.

part seven

Monetary and Other Financial Operations: The Foreign Side

21

Some Mechanics of International Payments, Economic Adjustments, and Flows of Short-Term Capital and Gold

A pound sterling had at one time been a pound of *silver*. The effect of successive devaluations is reflected in the fact that the pound sterling of 1955 is equal to but one two-hundredth of a pound of gold (Seymour E. Harris, *International and Interregional Economics* [1957]).

The prior description of the domestic monetary apparatus involved a brief introduction to gold flows and foreign exchange (Sect. 6.2, 6.3, 7.5, 10.1, and 10.2). It was indicated that under the proper functioning of the automatic gold standard an imbalance between a country's exports and imports other than gold would be adjusted through a combination of gold flows and short-term financial claims. The imbalance was shown to relate to exchange rate changes and gold flows as the respective exchange rates approached their gold points. An exchange rate was said to be fixed within the limits set by the gold points, and the primary factor contributing to the imbalance to begin with and to the subsequent adjustment was a change in the relationship between the price levels (Sect. 6.3) of the respective countries. In this very broad framework, a country on the side of this price relationship that would experience such phenomena as a decline or less of a rise in prices relative to those of another country (or, in general, the rest of the world) would find foreign exchange dealers adjusting exchange rates in its favor. They would, in turn, experience an inflow of gold as its exchange rate reached gold import points. Conversely, the country operating on the reverse side of these price and exchange rate conditions would experience an outflow of gold as its exchange rate reached gold export points. The adjustments through changes in the respective stocks of gold called for an expansion of bank credit and a rise in the general price level of the country receiving the gold, and a contraction of bank credit and a decline in the general price level of the country giving up the gold.

We then noted a breakdown in the automatic gold standard prior to World War I, and attempts to return to this earlier mode of operation in the 1920's (Sect. 7.5). Many of the countries involved, in fact, returned to gold exchange standards (Sect. 7.5), since their central banks used both gold and liquid claims against other countries as backing for their domestic money supplies. The use of these liquid claims was to economize gold, but there were problems with respect to the operations under such a system. The par values of important currencies were unrealistic, and there was inadequate financial leadership for an international system that included the use of gold exchange standards by some countries. Indeed, the financial arrangements of the period were viewed as being more fully automatic than they actually were. Thus, in the 1930's, following a period of difficulties in effecting satisfactory operations under the standard, countries abandoned the arrangements of the 1920's in favor of exchange restrictions and autonomy in effecting greater control over the internal workings of their respective economies.

Since that time a combination of exchange controls and fixed exchange rates (Sect. 6.3) have been more heavily relied upon to facilitate adjustments in the international economy. The emphasis has increasingly shifted in the post-World War II years from complicated currency controls toward a greater interdependence and the operation of a gold flows mechanism that reflects the freer interplay of the market forces of the respective economies. By the early 1960's, the international monetary system of the Western economies, Japan, and others included:

(1) Arrangements for international cooperation,
(2) A successfully functioning institution whose charter specifies criteria for effecting changes in the par values of currencies,
(3) A set of exchange rates that fluctuate within limits set by gold points (Sect. 6.2),
(4) A large number of externally convertible currencies (i.e., currencies that are freely convertible into other currencies), and
(5) Properly functioning financial markets that facilitate the switching of funds in liquid investments in response to yield differentials in the respective financial centers.

The present group of chapters (21-23), consequently, enlarges upon the outline of these developments. It also introduces additional complexities relating to the gold flows mechanism and monetary operations under the conditions that had evolved by the early 1960's. Under these conditions some countries may be said to be on gold exchange standards.

These chapters will treat these subjects as a means of facilitating a better understanding of post-World War II financial developments, their relevance to domestic developments in the United States, and their significance in the conduct of monetary policy. The initial introduction to the gold flows mechanism (Chap. 6) was abstracted from details about the more contemporary institutions, including the functioning of the international payments system, and the way the system responds to basic imbalances and shifts of short-term funds from one financial center to the other. So the present chapter describes in greater detail the balance of international payments, short-term capital movements, spot and forward exchange rates, interest arbitrage, arbitrage in foreign exchange, and free gold markets and speculation in gold. The next chapter outlines the goals, operations, and arrangements provided by the post-World War II institutions for the cooperation of sovereign countries on monetary matters. These include the so-called Bretton Woods Institutions—the International Monetary Fund (IMF) and the World Bank. Chapter 23, finally, deals briefly with post-World War II developments in the United States balance of payments, the impact of these developments on the United States and the role of the United States in monetary developments in the postwar world, the role of the United States as a key currency country, and the significance of the these developments for monetary policy in the United States.

21.1. International Payments and Foreign Exchange Markets, Instruments, and Rates

International payments (and receipts) are made in exchange for imports (and exports). The payments (receipts) usually involve the conversion of one currency into another by banks, and the price of one currency in terms of another at which the conversion takes place is a foreign exchange rate (Sect. 6.2). The maintenance of inventories of such currencies and trading in them by banks and others give rise to foreign exchange markets. For the most part, the currencies provided by the markets are for the purpose of effecting transactions, but the proper functioning of these markets also involves the speculative motive for acquiring and disposing of balances. Shifts in the strength of this motive with respect to a particular currency, furthermore, affect the international system of payments that gives rise to the need for the trading in currencies to begin with. Thus, to help understand these interrelationships as they develop in this chapter, this section reviews some features of the mechanics of international payments, foreign exchange markets, market instruments, and foreign exchange rates.

International payments. From the domestic point of view, a country receives payments for exports of merchandise, sales of services, investment income, and the sale of United States securities, money balances, and gold holdings. The receipts may be in the form of claims against foreign banks or they may be in the form of domestic money balances. In the latter case, the foreign importer must convert his local currency into the exporter's local currency. The payments, on the other hand, are for merchandise imports, travel expenditures and other purchases of foreign services, government aid, and the acquisition of foreign securities, money balances, and gold. In this instance, the payments to the foreign exporter may be in the foreign currency or the currency of the domestic importer. If, for example, the terms of an agreement between a United States importer and a German exporter require payment in marks, then the importer may acquire mark balances from a New York bank, and the payment in marks will in effect contribute to a reduction in the balances held by New York banks in German banks. If the terms of the latter agreement called for payments in dollars, then the settlement of the transaction would contribute to an increase in dollar balances held by German banks, and the German exporter may then wish to sell his dollar balances to his local bank in exchange for marks.

In all of these instances, the distinctive feature of making payment is the conversion of one currency into another, and this conversion is primarily a banking function.

Foreign exchange markets and the market instruments. The conversion of currencies by banks gives rise to foreign exchange markets where currencies are traded, and the means of transferring balances are the instruments of the foreign exchange markets. The primary instruments include cable and mail transfers, bank drafts, and bills of exchange. From the domestic point of view, the cable transfer is an order in the form of a cable that instructs a foreign bank holding an account for the seller of a currency to transfer the account to the buyer of the currency. The buyer of the foreign currency may spend it in the foreign country or trade it. The mail transfer is very similar except that the order for the transfer of the account is sent by mail instead of cable.

A bank draft is a special form of a bill of exchange. It is called a sight bill, since it is payable on presentation. It arises when a New York bank, for example, sells its own foreign-held balances directly to a person or firm wishing to make payment abroad. The draft is like a check calling for payment to a specified person abroad. The foreign recipient of the draft may cash it as he would any good check.

A bank dealing in foreign exchange may also sell bills of exchange that are payable at some future time—30, 60, 90, or 180 days after presentation. They may be in dollars or a foreign currency, but the latter would usually be of most interest to the New York exchange market. A domestic seller, for example (Sect. 7.3), would draw a draft covering a shipment of goods abroad. The seller of the goods would subsequently present the draft to a New York bank with which arrangements had previously been made by the foreign buyer of the goods. The bank, then, extents its own backing or assurance of payment to the bill, and the bill becomes a marketable money market instrument. It may be discounted before payment at maturity with a check drawn by the foreigner in his own currency.

Foreign exchange markets and foreign exchange rates. Commercial banks and some institutions, such as central banks, may acquire foreign bank balances by buying exporters' claims on foreign banks, by selling their own balances in the foreign exchange market, and by other methods. The commercial institutions may also sell foreign balances to importers or others who wish to make payment in foreign currency. Through the trading of such institutions and their willingness to buy or sell balances, the institutions make and maintain foreign exchange markets in a manner similar to that whereby government security dealers make and maintain markets (Sect. 13.3). The trading in bank balances in the various foreign exchange markets of the world takes place at prices that are called foreign exchange rates (Sect. 6.2).

Usually, the trading in a given country takes place in a financial center —New York, London, Frankfort, or Zurich—and trading within the center takes place over the telephone. An integral part of the trading by dealers and others, however, involves arbitrage transactions. The most common of these transactions involves a purchase of currency for immediate resale in another market. Such transactions are not themselves speculative, but they are effected in order to take advantage of discrepancies that may exist in the structure of exchange rates at a given time. Those engaging in arbitrage make the price on a given type of exchange in one market roughly equivalent to that on the same type of exchange in another market. They make a world market for various types of foreign exchange.

For an example of arbitrage in the foreign exchange markets, think of the following rates in the respective markets: (1) the pound bid at $2.80 in New York, (2) the Deutsche mark offered at $0.2500 in Frankfort, and (3) the pound offered in London at 11.18 Deutsche marks. Now, these first two rates are par rates, and at these rates there are four Deutsche marks in a dollar (and, therefore, $4 \times 2.80 = 11.20$ in a pound). Clearly the pound is undervalued in London at 11.18 Deutsche marks in terms of these market conditions. Consequently, an alert and optimizing trader would buy marks in Frankfort for dollars, buy pounds in England for marks, and sell the pounds in New York. If the trader had purchased 1,000,000 marks in Frankfort to begin with at $250,000, then he could have purchased approximately 89,445 pounds (i.e., 1,000,000 ÷ 11.18) in London and sold the pounds in New York at approximately $250,446. In this case, he would have made about $446 (i.e., $250,446 − $250,000) from a sure thing. In the process of carrying out the transactions, however, supply-demand forces would be exerted to remove any exchange rate differentials on the same type of exchange in the various markets. This, in turn, would give effect to a single world price for a given type of currency in all foreign exchange markets.

Currencies are sought for purchases of merchandise imports, travel expenditures, and so on, and they are received from exports of merchandise, sales of services, and so on. They are sought and offered for speculative reasons. Shifts in the demand for currencies may give rise to gold flows, and the switching of short-term capital from one country to another. This is what we wish to deal with (Sect. 21.3 and 23.2) after considering the balance of payments, but for the present let us simply recall the following: for most currencies there is an officially declared parity, the rates on these currencies fluctuate within limits (Sect. 6.2), and a given rate, such as the dollar rate on pounds for cable transfers for immediate delivery, is determined by the quantity of the given currency offered and the quantity demanded. In this sense, the quantity forthcoming of this type of exchange is expressed by offers to sell in both the domestic and foreign markets; the quantity demanded is expressed by offers to buy in both domestic and foreign markets.

The rate of exchange and supply and demand. Earlier we denoted the price of pounds in terms of dollars on the vertical axis of Fig. 6-1 and time on the horizontal axis. Also in the illustration we showed the so-called gold export and import points as being three-quarters of one per cent above and below the par value of the British pound. Now, however, we wish to denote the quantity of pounds demanded and the quantity supplied as a function of the exchange rate.

We wish to do this while keeping in mind that changes in the market rate as determined by these conditions will be confined under contemporary arrangements within the limits set by the gold points. Once the gold standard set these limits, but today they are an integral part of the exchange rate agreements of the International Monetary Fund (Sect. 22.1). The responsibility for confining rate fluctuations to these limits is that of the central bank or a government stabilization fund. In the postwar years prior to 1961, the United States role in achieving these limits was passive, except that the United States Treasury maintained a relationship between gold and the dollar (Sect. 10.1) by setting the price of gold at $35 per fine ounce (or at $1 per 1/35 ounce). Dollar rate changes were effectively limited by this and the interventions of other members of the International Monetary Fund in the market to establish the limits on their own currency in terms of dollars. In February 1962, however, the Federal Reserve System announced its decision to enter the exchange market for its own account (Sect. 24.3); it had even begun limited operations as agent for the United States Treasury as early as March 1961.

The demand and supply curves for a given currency as functions of the exchange rate can be sketched in the usual way, as shown in Fig. 21-1. We see the demand for pounds as a monotonically decreasing func-

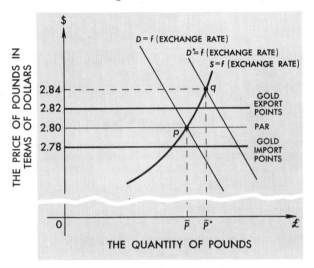

Fig. 21-1. The Dollar Exchange Rate and the Supply of and Demand for Pounds.

tion of the dollar exchange for pounds and the supply curve as a monotonically increasing function. The initial supply-demand equilibrium is at the point p ($\overline{P}$, 2.80). There are, however, some complexities when B's currency is expressed in terms of A's, and vice versa, and when one wishes to draw a set of demand and supply curves for each currency in order to show the interrelationships between their shapes and position.* Still, in the present instance we may introduce an increase in the dollar demand for pounds as in Fig. 21-1 so that there is a tendency for the dollar rate on pounds to increase as the value of the dollar depreciates in accordance with the equilibrium point q ($\overline{P}^*$, 2.84). To limit

* These complications result,

(1) since the price of B's currency in terms of A's currency is the reciprocal of the price of A's currency in terms of B's currency and vice versa (e.g., if the price of $1.00 is £.35, then 1/£.35 = $2.80 and 1/$2.80 = £.35), and

(2) since the product of quantity of B's currency demanded by A and the price of B's currency in terms of A's must equal the supply of A's currency as a function of the price of A's currency in terms of B's. (See Albert Gailord Hart and Peter B. Kenen, *Money, Debt, and Economic Activity*, 3rd ed. [Englewood Cliffs, N.J.: Prentice-Hall, Inc., 1961], pp. 313-319.)

the exchange rate, however, at the upper limit agreed upon, the Bank of England would enter the foreign exchange market to sell pounds for dollars. They would in effect shift the supply schedule to the right until the equilibrium point fell within the gold points, and, in the process, there would be other possible adjustments. For example, as the Bank of England acquired dollars in exchange for pounds, it may elect to exchange the dollars for United States gold at the price of $35 per ounce. This exchange would, in turn, contribute to an outflow of gold from the United States. As we will see later, this example has interesting implications for short-term capital flows as reported in the balance of payments (Sect. 21.2), and for the speculative demand for pounds in anticipation of depreciation in the value of the dollar (Sect. 21.3 and 21.4). Later too (Sect. 23.2), the analysis is related to critical monetary developments of the early 1960's.

21.2. The Balance of Payments

The balance of payments is a record of international payments (and receipts) in the form of an accounting statement. The statement presents payments to foreign countries and receipts from foreign countries, from the domestic point of view. The receipts are mainly for exports of merchandise, sales of services, investment income, and the sale of securities, money balances, and gold. The payments are mainly for merchandise imports, travel expenditures and other purchases of foreign services, government aid, and the acquisition of foreign securities, money balances, and gold. The United States statement, however, is not the result of a strict accounting of every purchase or sale, and neither are the statements for other countries whose data collections depend on sources other than exchange control records. The United States statement, instead, is constructed from many alternative sources of data,[1] each source collecting the data according to its own standards and principles. The Bureau of the Census collects the data on merchandise trade, data on various types of capital movements are collected by the Federal Reserve banks as agents for the Treasury, and so on.

Still, the international accounts are important in formulating domestic and foreign policies. One must also rely upon the accounts in the analysis of American trade and financial position with respect to the rest of the world. In this latter respect, the errors and omissions in the data are more serious from the accounting point of view than from the analytical point of view. As long as the procedures for collecting and reporting the data are fairly repetitious and routine, the real-world changes are still reflected in the data with sufficient reliability for the broader analytical purposes.

Balance of payments statements provide helpful information, and the accounting concept of double-entry bookkeeping (Sect. 9.1) facilitates the recording of transactions on both sides of the accounts, even when original data are available for only one side of the accounts. The data also take on increased analytical significance when arranged to reflect the balance of trade, capital movements, balance of payments disequilibria, payments surpluses and deficits, and the financing of the deficits.

The United States balance of payments. The balance of payments statement of the United States for the year 1963 is shown in Table 21-1. In that table the country's receipts may be seen as credits for exports, and payments to the rest of the world may be seen as debits for imports. The two sides—the credit and the debit side—of course, always balance as in the fundamental accounting equation (Sect. 9.1). The transactions may be arranged in particular categories, however, and, for any given period, a particular category may show a net balance of either credits or debits.

The current account and unilateral transfers. The first item in Table 21-1 reflects transactions for goods and services, along with unilateral transfers. A part of this, the difference between the value of a nation's merchandise exports (credits) and merchandise imports (debits), is called the balance of trade. A country is said to have a favorable* balance of trade when its merchandise exports exceed its merchandise imports.

Some of the mechandise exports as well as the exports of other goods and services may be disposed of in the special form of unilateral transfers. These receive a special accounting treatment. The net unilateral transfers shown on the present statement for the United States, for example, are gifts or grants by the United States in excess of those received from private pensions or remittances. The net unilateral transfers are shown as net debits or claims against the United States, and these debits may be offset by credits received for exported merchandise.

Capital movements. The second and third items in Table 21-1 are short- and long-term private capital movements. They arise from changes in private financial claims on foreigners (in effect, an import of foreign bank balances and securities) and changes in some financial liabilities to foreigners (in effect, an export of domestic deposit balances and short-term investments). United States short-term capital under item 3, for example, reflects bank deposits and purchases of other financial assets with a short maturity. These claims have been viewed as being highly liquid, since a widespread convertibility of foreign currencies in 1958, and probably are held as a store of future transactions balances and as a means of taking advantage of interest rate differentials (Sect. 21.3). Even so, there has been a tendency to treat them as if they were long-term capital for certain balance of payments analyses since they are

---

* The use of the term "favorable" implies a preference for gold or capital investment required to bring about a balance in the over-all statement. It is a traditional usage reflecting the preference of societies in the sixteenth and seventeenth centuries for gold.

Table 21-1. Balance of International Payments of the United States, Year-End 1963

(In millions of dollars)

Items	Credit (Receipts of funds for exports)	Debits (Payments of funds for imports)	Net Credits (+'s) or Debits (−'s)
1. Goods and services (i.e., the current account): *			
Merchandise	21,902	16,962	
Services**	9,701	6,276	
Military expenditures		2,880	
	31,603	26,118	+5,485
Unilateral transfers:			
Remittances and pensions		812	
United States government grants and capital flow (net) excluding advance debt repayments†		3,789	
		4,601	−4,601
2. Private long-term capital:			
United States direct investment and other United States long-term capital		3,440	
Foreign long-term investments	387		
	387	3,440	−3,053
"Basic" balance (Items 1 + 2 + 5)			−1,485
3. Private short-term capital:			
United States short-term capital		642	
Foreign short-term capital other than liquid assets in U.S.	5		
	5	642	−637
4. Errors and omissions		495	
		495	−495
Balance on "regular" transactions (Items 1 + 2 + 3 + 4)			−3,301

SOURCE OF DATA: U.S. Department of Commerce.

* Excludes military transfers under grants.

** Includes such things as current interest and dividends, insurance, and military transactions.

† Includes also very small amounts of changes in "miscellaneous government nonliquid liabilities."

Table 21-1 (continued).

Items	Credit (Receipts of funds for exports)	Debits (Payments of funds for imports)	Net Credits (+'s) or Debits (−'s)
5. Special United States government transactions:			
Nonscheduled receipts on government loans	325		
Advances on military exports (net)	359		
Sale of nonmarketable, nonconvertible, medium-term securities		43	
	684	43	+641
Over-all surplus or deficit (−) (Items 1 + 2 + 3 + 4 + 5)			−2,660
6. Financing the over-all surplus or deficit:			
Liquid liabilities	2,282		
United States monetary reserve assets			
IMF position	30		
Convertible currencies		113	
Gold	461		
	2,773	113	+2,660

SOURCE OF DATA: U.S. Department of Commerce.

privately held. The foreign short-term capital under item 3, moreover, has been of nominal economic significance as contrasted with the liquid United States liabilities in item 6, Table 21-1.

As for long-term funds, securities or claims against foreigners are recorded as imports when dollars are made available to foreigners. Such funds flow into the United States when foreign firms or individuals exchange funds for the security issues or liabilities of American firms and individuals. The receipt of securities from abroad, looked upon as an import, is recorded as a debit to the United States in Table 21-1. The giving up of securities, looked upon as an export, is recorded as a credit to the United States. The funds exchanged for the securities in both instances may or may not be used to purchase equipment and other capital goods.

Errors and omissions. The fourth item in Table 21-1 is errors and omissions. It corresponds to errors in data and transactions omitted from the balance of payments statement. Usually the errors and omissions are small compared with the size of the recorded transactions. The account for them, however, varies over time, and there is support for the view that the account reflects unrecorded movements in short-term capital.[2]

Special United States government transactions. Item 5, special United States government transactions, came about in response to this country's balance of payments difficulties in the early 1960's. For the most part, the credit entries under item 5 represent payments to the United States in advance of the time at which they would otherwise have been due.

Financing the over-all surplus (or deficit). Item 6 reflects the financing of the net deficit on all other accounts in Table 21-1. Note that the deficit was paid by the extension of United State liabilities and to a lesser extent on export of gold (Sect. 10.3). Other small changes in accounts—namely, the United States IMF position and convertible currencies—also appear. These come up later.

The effect of changes in the balance of payments in GNP. In outlining the composition of expenditures for the current output of goods and services (Sect. 15.1), net exports of goods and services were mentioned. These include some portion of the net export of goods and services under item 1.[3] And, although "net exports of goods and services" (Sect. 15.1) is small in relation to GNP, in the United States, changes in the net exports in question will have a multiplier effect on the level of income and on employment (and/or prices)—all as set forth earlier (Sect. 5.2). In some countries, where foreign investment is a more important part of the economy, changes in net foreign investment can of course have extremely unstabilizing effects on output, employment, and the general functioning of the economy. The extent of these unstabilizing effects will in part depend upon the slope of the consumption function.

Equilibrium in the balance of payments. Equilibrium in a country's balance of payments exists when the country is not experiencing sustained unemployment (or over-full employment), and when the net credit (+) or debit (−) balance resulting from transactions in goods and services, and unilateral transfers, are exactly offset by a net debit or credit balance in the long-term capital account. In fact, some emphasize this equilibrium by referring to the balance between the exports of goods and services and imports of goods and services (including unilateral transfers) and net long-term capital movements as the "basic" balance of payments position. This position is shown in Table 21-1 as the sum of net credit and debit balances for items 1, 2, and 5.

Balances on "regular" transactions. The balance on "regular" transactions is the sum of the net credit and debit balances for items 1, 2, 3, and 4 in Table 21-1. It has been viewed as an indicator of the extent of the correction that is required in the balance of payments. It does not include the acceleration of payments before their due date as appropriate balancing items, and it implies a treatment of errors and omissions and transactions under item 3 that is analogous to the treatment of private long-term capital.

Over-all surplus (or deficit). The over-all payments surplus (or deficit) differs from that on "regular" transactions only by the inclusion of item 5. As a measure of a payments surplus (or deficit), it recognizes efforts to accelerate payments before their due dates as a means of meeting a deficit even though the effects of these efforts may be only transitory and small in magnitude.

From the American point of view, an over-all payments deficit is the balance that must be financed, mainly and in effect, by an increase in liquid liabilities and/or a sale of gold. A payments surplus is likely to be met by an inflow of gold. Here, the peculiar role of the short-term liabilities of such a country as the United States is implied. Its internationally held liquid liabilities serve as a substitute for gold for many foreign institutions, including governments, central banks, and others. Indeed, over the post-World War II years, such claims against the United States came to constitute a large portion of the free world's monetary reserves.

The latter role of the United States as a supplier of monetary reserves is later (Sect. 23.3) described as that of a key currency country. It has many additional implications for both domestic and international monetary goals. But, for the present, we simply wish to anticipate subsequent emphasis on changes in liquid United States liabilities to the rest of the world as a means of financing United States deficits, as a substitute for gold flows in this respect, and as a substitute for gold as a monetary reserve asset in some instances.

21.3. Foreign Exchange Rates, Interest Arbitrage, and Flows of Short-term Capital

The above discussion of exchange rates (Sect. 21.1) dealt with the spot rate, but rates for the currencies traded may be quoted for both spot and forward exchange. The spot rate is that for exchange to be delivered immediately or within a few days. The spot rate for cable transfers is the basic rate in the market, and rates for other spot transactions, such as mail transfers, will vary from this one depending upon the length of time required to receive payment in the foreign currency. The rate for forward exchange, on the other hand, is that for currency for future delivery. The rate at which the forward transaction is to take place is fixed at the time of sale, but payment is not made until the exchange is delivered by the seller. The main rates in the market are for one, three, and six months' future delivery. Banks quote the rates on an outright basis to their customers; in the interbank market, they are usually quoted on the basis of a discount (or premium) under (or over) the spot rate. For example, if spot sterling is quoted at $2.80 and the one-month forward rate at $2.79½, the forward rate may be quoted as a one-half discount.

The existence of trading in and rates for both spot and forward exchange complicates the setting of international finance. In doing so, it enlarges upon the number of different ways to speculate in foreign exchange, introduces a way of conducting foreign exchange arbitrage over time, and gives rise to covered interest arbitrage in an international setting by permitting one to cover the possibility of losses from exchange rate fluctuations. At the same time, the more complicated setting also opens up new possibilities for the exercise of indirect control by monetary authorities over movements of short-term financial claims and gold flows.

Speculation in foreign exchange and arbitrage. Trading in foreign exchange may involve dealers, other traders, and brokers. The dealers, of course, trade on their own account and carry inventories for customers, and the brokers effect transactions for others for a fee. Some dealers may simply maintain inventories of currencies for their customers and base customer rates on buying and selling rates quoted in the interdealer market. The dealers, however, must keep an eye on their inventory position with respect to the rates prevailing in the foreign exchange markets, and some dealers tend to speculate in their inventory position to a greater extent than others. Anticipating a decline in the value of a particular currency, they may reduce their stock of that currency. Also, in the latter instance, they may sell a currency short—i.e., borrow a currency for sale in the spot market with the view that the currency may be purchased for repayment at a lower price in the future. And, anticipating appreciation in the value of a particular currency, they may purchase a larger amount of it.

The existence of a forward market, however, opens up two possibilities for carrying out transactions that may serve the same purposes as the last two transactions above. A dealer or another party anticipating a decline in the value of a currency, for example, may contract to sell forward exchange. At the time for the delivery of the currency he purchases and gains or loses, depending on whether the rate is below that for the exchange he sold. On the other hand, anticipating appreciation in the value of a currency, he may buy forward exchange for future delivery and sale in the spot market at the future time. If he buys forward exchange at a rate below his selling rate, then he profits; if he buys at a higher price, he loses.

What these latter type of transactions do is to make forward rates reflect more nearly the rates the markets expect to prevail in the future. Expecting a decline in the value of the pound, dealers and others engaging in speculation will contract to sell pounds in the forward market. By doing so they will tend to lower the rate on pounds in the forward market. Expecting a rise in the value of the pound, they will contract to buy forward pounds for future delivery. They will bid up the forward rate in the present market. Of course, the spot rates, too, reflect expectations about the future since the demands for currencies for inventories reflect expectations, but the maintenance of an excess of inventories ties up funds, and short sales involve an interest cost on the borrowed funds. Consequently, these differences in the cost of speculation in the spot and forward markets and some occasional market imperfections contribute to the difference between the spot rate and the forward rate on a particular type of currency. Furthermore, the stronger the prospect of a rise in the value of a particular currency, the greater will be the discrepancy, in view of the extra cost of acquiring larger inventories of currencies or of effecting a larger volume of short sales.

The existence of forward markets is not for the purpose of speculation. Their existence permits an importer to enter into a contract for the delivery of goods and to avoid any risk of appreciation in the value of the currency with which he agrees to make payment. In this respect, he may elect to buy forward exchange for use at the time of payment and at the time he settled upon the cost of the goods. Thus the importers may shift the risk of possible changes in the values of the currencies they need to professional speculators.

Their existence also broadens the alternatives open to investors in securities without their assuming the risk of changes in the values of particular currencies. A portfolio manager may, for example, be confronted with the opportunity to purchase ninety-one-day Treasury bills in London or New York. If the rate is higher in London than in New York on these bills, then the manager may get a greater return without additional risk by buying the bills in London, provided he can be assured of converting pounds into dollars at the maturity date of the bills at a given rate. This sort of thing then leads to another type of arbitrage —covered interest arbitrage—and provides foreign exchange dealers with additional opportunity for arbitrage transactions in forward exchange. For example, dealers may now buy dollars in the spot market to sell them in the forward market until the difference between the spot and forward exchange rate on dollars is no larger than the difference between interest cost of borrowing funds to carry dollars as contrasted with pounds. This sort of arbitrage across time emphasizes a tie between the spread between interest rates in the various markets and the spread between spot and forward rates.

Covered interest arbitrage. Transactions resulting in the movement of short-term funds between international financial centers as one tries to take advantage of a yield differential on short-term investments between the respective centers are called interest arbitrage. Such transactions are called covered interest arbitrage when the possibility of a loss from exchange rate changes over the time to maturity of the investment is covered by a purchase of forward exchange.

The profitability of moving funds from one financial center to another depends (1) on the yield spread between investments of relatively comparable risk and maturity in the respective centers and (2) on the relation of the two currencies in the spot and forward exchange markets. An American investor switching from United States Treasury bills to British Treasury bills, because of the yield spread, must first purchase sterling in order to buy British Treasury bills in London. At the same time, he must execute a forward sale of sterling to coincide with the maturity of the investment in order to assure some extra return from the yield differential and avoid the effect of any possible depreciation of sterling that might offset the gain. There is zero interest arbitrage incentive when the gain (loss) from the interest differential is just offset by the discount (premium) on forward exchange.

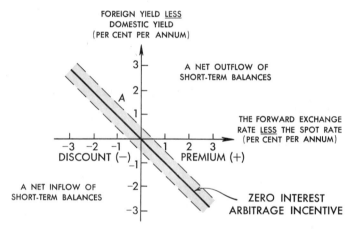

Fig. 21-2. *Interest Arbitrage Incentive: Foreign Yields Less Domestic Yields, Plus the Discount (—) or Premium (+) on Forward Exchange. Source: Alan R. Holmes, The New York Foreign Exchange Market (Federal Reserve Bank of New York, 1959).*

The incentive and the tendency toward parity between the yield differential and the discount (or premium) may be simply illustrated, as in Fig. 21-2. In that diagram the interest differential in per cent per annum between the yield on a particular type of security in the domestic market and the yield on a comparable type of security of the foreign country is shown on the vertical axis. There, a plus differential indicates a higher interest rate in the foreign country and a negative differential indicates a lower interest rate in the foreign country. On the other axis, the discount (minus) or premium (plus) on the forward exchange of the foreign country is shown as a per cent per annum. The interest parity line is the diagonal that intersects the lines representing zero interest differential and zero discount or premium. Any point on the interest parity line represents an equilibrium for the yield spread between rates in the respective countries and the discount or premium on forward exchange. For instance, a point on the interest parity line corresponding to a 2 per cent interest differential also corresponds to a 2 per cent discount on the forward exchange axis. Now, when the discount or premium on forward exchange gets out of line with the zero interest arbitrage incentive (or so-called interest parity), a positive (or negative) incentive emerges and the switching of funds from one financial center to the other becomes profitable, without the need to incur additional risk. This may be illustrated by reference to point A in the illustration. At that spot, the yield in the foreign country is 1½ per cent higher than the yield on a similar type security in the domestic economy, and the forward discount is only one-half per cent. Under such conditions, a switching of short-term investments from the domestic to the foreign center would add an additional yield of one per cent at no additional risk. However, it should be noted that, as indicated by the broken lines in the diagram, as a general consideration the additional yield must be in excess of one-half per cent per annum before it becomes worthwhile to move funds from one market to another because of transaction costs.

In the illustration, the above movement of short-term funds abroad through the switching transaction by those engaging in the covered interest arbitrage would tend to restore the parity between the yield spread and the discount (or premium) on forward exchange. The movement would do this in two ways:

(1) It would increase the forward discount by way of a price-rising force in the market for spot exchange and a price-reducing force in the forward market.

(2) It would lower the interest rate differential as funds were transferred from one market to another. In other words, the tendency in effect would be for any arbitrarily selected point, such as A, to get sent into the locus of points corresponding to zero incentive by setting in motion adjustments in interest rates in the respective countries and in the spot and forward exchange markets.

As an exercise, the reader may wish to select another point and trace out the tendency from the selected point toward zero incentive.

Exchange rates and interest rates: some interrelationships. The latter discussion of zero interest arbitrage incentive and incentives for net outflows and inflows of short-term financial claims provides the framework for examining the effect of speculation in foreign exchange on the movement of short-term balances. It also emphasizes an interrelationship between yields in the financial markets of one country and those in the financial markets of other countries. Further, it provides the framework for considering the possibilities for indirect monetary controls over the movement of short-term balances between financial centers.

To illustrate some of the possible effects of speculation in exchange rates, let us suppose that speculators in foreign exchange anticipate depreciation in the exchange value of the dollar. They may anticipate this change for a number of reasons, including the prospect that the excess of American exports of merchandise over imports will be substantially altered by an improvement of cost and price conditions abroad relative to those in the United States for merchandise of comparable quality. In such a case the dollar exchange rate on pounds, as an example, would rise. The forward rate would move to a premium, a point, such as A in Fig. 21-2, would move to the right, parallel to the horizontal axis. There would be greater incentive for a net outflow of short-term capital balances as the point A, for example, moved away from the locus of points for zero interest arbitrage. As time passed, the spot rate too may rise, the purchase of short-term securities in London would contribute to a reduction in interest rates there, and the sale of such securities in the United States would raise rates. This narrowing of the yield spread would contribute to the movement toward zero incentive by the point A in Fig. 21-2.

Paralleling these developments, however, the rise in the spot rate would, in turn, lessen the incentive for the outflow of short-term funds, but (by way of the mechanics implied in Fig. 21-1) there would be at the same time an increase in the demand for pounds. As the rate on pounds moved above the gold export points in Fig. 21-1, the Bank of England would supply pounds in exchange for dollars. Soon, with their large supply of dollars, they may wish to purchase gold from the United States Treasury, giving us an outflow of gold. By this time, the speculators' prospects may very well be fulfilled, both with respect to the prospect of a rise in the dollar rate on pounds in the spot market and with respect to a weakening of the United States trade position as shown in the balance of payments.

Of course, the converse set of prospects could be held by speculations. In this case, the flows and rate changes would be the reverse of those above.

Exchange rates, interest rates, and central bank operations. Now, there are two possibilities for indirect monetary control over the movement of short-term balances as just outlined. One of these is very old and traditional, although it fell out of prominence with the decline in the importance of the international gold standard in the early 1930's.[4] It would involve an increase in the rate on short-term funds on the domestic side. Clearly, from Fig. 21-2, this would narrow the yield differential between the domestic and foreign financial centers. In doing so, it would also reduce the incentive for an outflow of short-term balances. If the differential were narrow enough (or negative), depending on the discount (or premium) on forward exchange, a rise in the domestic rate may even provide the incentive for a net inflow of short-term balances. Of course, the rise in the rate in the domestic market may not be consistent with the use of monetary controls called for by the conditions of output, employment, and prices on the domestic side. There are complications (Sect. 23.2).

The other possibility for monetary intervention involves open market transactions in foreign currencies. As early as March 1961, the Treasury conducted forward operations in German marks, and, in February 1962, the Federal Open Market Committee authorized open market operations in foreign currencies. Under the latter authorization, the New York bank may "purchase and sell foreign currencies in the form of cable transfers through spot or forward transactions in the open market at home and abroad, including transactions with the stabilization fund of the Secretary of the Treasury. . . ." [5]

The broader range of possible currency operations may involve the purchase or sale of currencies in either the spot or forward markets for a wide range of currencies. In the above framework, however, a sale of British pounds in the forward market would exert a price depressing effect on the forward exchange rate. This (through the mechanics outlined in Fig. 21-2) would tend to increase the discount on forward exchange, or to offset speculative forces operating in the other direction. By doing so it would tend to reduce the incentive for effecting a net outflow of short-term balances, or it may even provide the incentive for effecting a net inflow of such balances.

Obviously, there are other possibilities in the use of purchases and sales of foreign exchange to influence short-term financial movements by way of the framework corresponding to Fig. 21-2. There are also possibilities to influence gold flows by way of the framework corresponding to Fig. 21-1. As an exercise, the reader may wish to reflect upon these.

21.4. Free Gold Markets, Speculation in Gold, and Gold Flows

Speculation over the dollar price of gold is another possible factor giving risk to gold flows, particularly with respect to the United States. This possibility arises as a result of the presence of free gold markets outside of the United States, the United States position with respect to the dollar price of gold (Sect. 10.1), and the presence of those who are prone to speculate over the possibility of changes in the price of gold. In the world around us, with some exceptions including the United States, gold coins and metals may still serve as a store of value (Sect. 2.1). They may still be held and traded as a hedge against monetary schemes and inflation.

Free gold markets. There are free gold markets in London and Zurich, as well as some smaller markets in other centers. In those markets, gold and gold for future delivery are bought and sold freely, and contracts for future delivery can be purchased in both markets in hard currencies. Trading in the London market is open to private interest other than those of nonsterling countries, and a Swiss resident or a foreigner can usually buy, sell, import, or store gold in Switzerland without formality. Further, the purchase of gold abroad is illegal under United States law, but there is nothing in Swiss law to limit such transactions.

Speculation against the dollar price of gold. The United States Treasury, as the principal holder of the free world's gold, stands ready to buy and sell gold for official monetary purposes at $35 per ounce, after allowance for the transactions cost. This is done along the lines set forth earlier (Sect. 10.1). In doing it, the Treasury gives a world value to the dollar (Sect. 6.2) and permits the dollar to have a par value in terms of the currencies of other countries whose monetary units are tied to gold. From time to time, however, the prospect may arise over whether the United States will change the value of gold. This may be done by increasing the dollar price of gold (i.e., depreciating the value of the dollar in terms of gold), but the prospect of its being done may lead to speculation over the dollar price of gold and hence to gold flows.

As noted earlier (Sect. 6.3), price level changes are the principal means of bringing about adjustments in the balance of payments, where the countries involved have their monetary units tied to gold. A payments deficit, for example, may be corrected by a country's effecting a declining or less rapidly rising price level in relation to the price levels of other countries. But a payments deficit may also be corrected by the devaluation of the deficit country's currency. This will make its currency less costly in terms of other currencies, and it will, without actually changing prices, effectively make prices lower for other countries. Consequently, when a country in the position of the United States faces a serious payments deficit, some uncertainty may arise as to how that country will react. There are serious problems involved in devaluation, and we shall deal with these subsequently (Sect. 23.2). But, given some prospect of devaluation and the commitment to purchase gold at $35 per ounce, speculators may buy gold or gold for future delivery in free gold markets at a prevailing dollar price per ounce on gold for future delivery. They may do this with the view to selling the gold at the new higher price at the future delivery date.

Under the given arrangements for trading and exchanging gold for dollars, this speculation will result in an outflow of gold from the United States. It may occur by way of several routes. The first of these needs no elaborate explanation, since the mechanics of it are no different from those associated with Fig. 21-1. Private holders of short-term liabilities of the United States and its nationals may liquidate their securities and exchange their dollar balances for other currencies. As a foreign exchange rate rises above gold export points, the foreign country exchanges its currency for dollars, and the foreign monetary authorities may, in turn, purchase gold from the United States Treasury. In other instances the dollar balances may be used to purchase gold directly, and they soon may be added to the dollar balances of banks supplying gold to the market (principally, the Bank of England). As dollars accumulate, the bank finds its gold reserve diminished, and, then, it may convert some dollar balances by purchasing gold from the United States Treasury. In still other instances, the Bank of England as an official institution, may elect to obtain gold from the United States in order to stabilize the price of gold in the London market. An example of speculation in gold and bank support operations is given below.

An example of speculation in gold. An example may be based on market practice, as described by one world expert in the field of gold and foreign exchange operation,* in the early 1960's. Accordingly,** payment for future delivery under future gold contracts takes place on the day the future operations fall due. In order to enter into such a contract, funds need not necessarily be put up, but this may depend on the credit standing of the customer. The forward price depends upon the spot price and is invariably at a premium. The premium, or positive spread between the spot price and future price in turn, corresponds roughly to the interest on dollars for the length of the future period.

Thus, to provide a specific and simplified example, let the speculator enter into a futures contract to buy 10 bars (400 ounces per bar) of gold at the end of 3 months, where

$35.65 per ounce is the price of gold for present delivery, and

$1,782.50 is the cost of the futures contract (i.e., 1.25 per cent per annum premium on a 3-month contract for 4,000 ounces at 35.65 per ounce).

An outline of the speculators cost and a net gain after a devaluation of 50 per cent is as follows:

	Use of Funds ($-$), *and Source of Funds* ($+$)
Cost of futures contract	$-$$1,782.50
Return from the sale of 4,000 ounces of gold at $70 per ounce	$+$280,000.00
Cost from purchase of 4,000 ounces of gold at $35.65 under futures contract	$-$142,600.00
Net gain	$+$$135,617.50

* Dr. K. Thiersch, Head of Foreign Exchange Section, Bank for International Settlements (Sect. 23.5).

** Letter from K. Thiersch (Basle, February 12, 1963) to Ralph Young, Adviser to the Board of Governors of the Federal Reserve System.

After a rise in the dollar price of gold, the speculator would have gained $135,617.50. On the other hand, had the price not risen, the speculator would have lost no more than the 1.25 per cent premium cost of the futures contract and $2,600 (i.e., the difference between his buying price of gold under the futures contract and the selling price to the United States Treasury).

Now, if speculation against the dollar in the free gold markets became a reality, apart from any offsetting effects, a gold outflow from the United States would follow. The speculation would drive the dollar price of gold upward, possibly to a level of about $41 per ounce as it did in mid-October 1960. The rise in the price of gold may reach a point where, in the case of the London gold market, the Bank of England sells gold to stabilize the price. The Bank of England, then, may use dollars to replenish its supply of gold through purchases from the United States Treasury with a decline in the United States gold stock as the result.[6]

21.5. Summary

The balance of payments is a record of international receipts (and payments) in the form of an accounting statement. It records claims and counterclaims between one country and others that arise from the flow of trade, financial claims, gifts, gold, and so on for a given period. The original sources of the data entering into the construction of the statement are somewhat independent of one another in some countries (including the United States). Nevertheless, the presentation of the statement in the form of flows within the framework of the fundamental accounting identity facilitates the recording of transactions.

The accounts appearing on the statement for the balance of payments may be arbitrarily broken down in many different ways. Among the items that we wish to emphasize, however, are (1) goods and services and unilateral transfers, (2) private long-term capital, (3) private short-term capital, (4) errors and omissions, (5) special United States government transactions, and (6) the financing of the over-all surplus (or deficit). In terms of this breakdown, the net balance on items (1), (2), and (5) constitutes the "basic balance"; the net balance on items (1), (2), (3), and (4) constitutes the balance on "regular" transactions; and the net balance on items (1), (2), (3), (4), and (5) constitutes the over-all surplus or deficit. From the United States point of view, then, an over-all deficit becomes the amount to be financed, mainly through the sale to foreign governments and central banks of gold or liquid liabilities.

The above items are also fundamentally related to the definition of a balance of payments equilibrium. Such an equilibrium is defined as the absence of a net credit or debit balance in the combined accounts under items (1), (2), and (5), all at a time when the country in question is not experiencing sustained unemployment or over-full employment.

In using the balance of payments in the analysis of the effects of the rest of the world expenditures on a country's domestic income and level of employment, we are concerned with net balances on the combined accounts for goods, services, and unilateral transfers. For one thing, changes in net foreign investment (as indicated by changes in the balance on goods and services and unilateral transfers) may have multiple effects on the level of domestic expenditure. Through the national income multiplier a positive change in flows for net foreign investment may cause domestic income to increase by a multiple amount depending upon the slope of the consumption function. These changes may have the desirable effect of expanding output and employment (net of induced increases in import expenditures associated with higher incomes) or they may have inflationary consequences, depending upon the level of employment, that may in turn cause a decline in the flows for net foreign investment. A negative change in net foreign investment, then, may cause a decline in domestic income and employment, and these declines may be some multiple of the decline in net foreign investment, depending upon the slope of the consumption function. These sets of changes will be more or less significant for a country, too, depending on their magnitude relative to a country's total domestic expenditure and output. The countries that are most dependent upon international trade are more vulnerable to unstabilizing shifts in net foreign investment.

International payments (receipts) are made in exchange for imports (exports), but the primary means of payment is a transfer of bank balances. Moreover, the balances themselves may be exported or imported. The conversion and purchase (and sale) of currencies by banks for their own account or for others give rise to foreign exchange rates. A foreign exchange rate is the price of one currency in terms of another. At any given time it may be viewed as determined by the supply of the given type of currency offered for exchange and the quantity sought at the prevailing rate.

Viewing foreign exchange as a means of effecting transactions alone and thinking only of two countries (or one country and the rest of the world), we note that there is a tendency for a country experiencing a payment's surplus to have an excess accumulation of a deficit country's currency. This in turn may cause the exchange rate of the country with the surplus of foreign currency to rise. As the rate goes above the gold export points from the point of view of the country experiencing the deficit, a government fund or central bank of the country with a surplus would probably supply its own currency to the market. The currency of the country with the deficit would then face the prospect of having to exchange gold for that part of its currency acquired by the central bank. An outflow of gold would probably be the result.

Gold is a basic means of payment for a payments deficit. But net flows of short-term securities and currency balances are also means of off-setting surpluses and deficits within the framework of the balance of payments. For some countries with heavy foreign commitments and the responsibility for financial leadership, the behavior of the gold and short-term capital accounts are of particular importance, even when the country in question is experiencing a "basic balance" in its balance of payments. This particular importance results, in part, from the use of the country's short-term liabilities by other countries as monetary reserves. It also results from the fact that an increase in short-term liabilities and an inflow of gold by an equal amount may not affect one country's payments position, but it can substantially affect the world's supply of monetary reserves (i.e., gold plus liquid claims against key currency countries).

The primary factor contributing to an imbalance in a country's payments position and to any subsequent adjustment is a change in the relationship between the price levels of the country in question and the rest of the world, respectively. A declining price level or a less rapidly rising one in relationship to other price levels tends to bring about an increase in the exports of goods and services in such a way as to overcome a payments deficit or effect a payments surplus, in a world experiencing some relative amount of freedom with respect to trade and the movement of short-term capital. Conversely, a rising or a less rapidly declining price level would have the reverse effects in such a world.

In the post-World War II years, exchange rates have come to fluctuate rather freely within limits agreed upon with the International Monetary Fund. Under this arrangement for international cooperation, most rates have a par value in terms of the dollar, and the rates with such a value have a fixed relationship to a certain amount of gold. However, the official exchange rate of a country may be changed under certain conditions to be discussed (Sect. 22.1).

A decrease in the par value of a country's currency in terms of other currencies and in terms of its relationship to gold has the same effect as decreasing the domestic price level for foreign buyers and increasing foreign price levels for domestic buyers. An increase in the par value of a country's currency has the reverse set of effects. Consequently, the prospect of such exchange rate changes brings about considerable speculation in currencies and gold in a world where free gold markets exist and where the United States Treasury stands ready to buy and sell gold under specified conditions. The anticipation of devaluation of the dollar by United States Treasury officials, for example, may cause some to purchase gold at approximately $35 per ounce in the free markets with the view to selling gold at a later date to the United States Treasury at a much higher price. The prospect of such a devaluation may develop when a country's price and cost conditions for a given quality of merchandise appear to be rising faster than those elsewhere in the world. The speculative activity, furthermore, may lead to an outflow of short-term balances and gold. The prospect of such developments may cause a withdrawal of dollar balances, and their use in the purchase of gold or other currencies. The increased demand for gold may then contribute to a rise in its price, and efforts to stabilize the price by foreign monetary authorities may lead to the subsequent acquisition of gold from the United States. Similarly, an increase in the demand for a foreign currency may tend to drive its price beyond the gold points. If the currency with the rising price is supplied in exchange for dollars by stabilization officials, then the dollar balances held by them increase. In such a case, the foreign monetary authority may soon wish to exchange dollars for gold at the United States Treasury. Hence, an outflow of gold.

Foreign exchange rates are quoted in the foreign exchange markets for both spot and forward exchange. The existence of trading in and rates on both forward and spot exchange complicates the setting of international finance. On the one hand, it increases the number of ways in which speculators may speculate. On the other, it permits exporters and buyers of foreign securities to transfer the risk of possible losses from exchange rate fluctuations to professional speculators. Investors in securities, for example, may compare the relationship between yields on securities of the same quality in two different financial centers in the process of preparing to purchase or switch into higher yielding securities. Then, in the event of foreign purchases of securities, the investors may cover the risk of converting one currency into another at the maturity of the securities by buying currency balances of their own country for delivery at the maturity dates for the securities. This is called covered interest arbitrage.

The incentive for engaging in covered interest arbitrage, however, depends upon the foreign yield on the type of security in question, less the domestic yield, plus the discount or premium on forward exchange —all in per cent per annum. When the sum of these rates is positive, this is an incentive to purchase abroad and thus contribute to a net outflow of short-term balances from the domestic point of view. When the sum of the rates is negative, there is the incentive for foreigners to purchase securities and thus contribute to an inflow of short-term funds.

This latter framework emphasizes two things: the interrelationships between the yields and exchange rates of the respective countries operating within an international setting of the type envisaged, and the possibilities for indirect monetary controls over short-term capital movements. In the framework, as outlined, open market operations may be conducted in foreign exchange in both spot and forward markets with the view to altering the incentive for inflows or outflows of short-term capital. Also some monetary control may be exercised by the various central banks in their own economies by way of the short-term securities. At times, however, from a given country's point of view, there may be a conflict over the need to raise yields in the market to restrain a capital outflow and the need to lower the yields in the process of stimulating a fuller utilization of resources on the domestic side. We shall deal later (Sect. 23.2 and 23.3) with this potential conflict in the demands upon the use of monetary controls.

References

1. For a discussion of the problems of measurement and classification with respect to the balance of payments, see Walter Lederer, "Measuring the Balance of Payments," *Factors Affecting the United States Balance of Payments* (Washington, D.C.: U.S. Government Printing Office, 1962), pp. 75-85.

2. See Philip W. Bell, "Private Capital Movements and the U.S. Balance-of-Payments Position," *Factors Affecting the United States Balance of Payments* (Washington, D.C.: U.S. Government Printing Office, 1962), pp. 450-457.

3. See *U.S. Income and Output: A Supplement to the Survey of Current Business* (Washington, D.C.: U.S. Department of Commerce, 1959), pp. 57-58.

4. With respect to monetary policy, international considerations affected Federal Reserve actions at an earlier date (Sect. 7.5). In particular, the Bank of England had at one time considered the bank (or discount rate) a device primarily for attracting short-term loans from other financial centers and for bringing about domestic adjustments to strengthen the flow of exports.

See R. S. Sayers, "Bank Rate in the Twentieth Century," *Central Banking After Bagehot* (London: Oxford University Press, 1956), pp. 60-63. Also, on the working of discount rate policy in the period before 1941 and its influence on the international flow of short-term funds to and from England, see Arthur I. Bloomfield, *Monetary Policy Under the International Gold Standard: 1880-1914* (New York: Federal Reserve Bank of New York, 1959), pp. 40-46.

5. For a discussion of these operations and the authorization regarding open market transactions in foreign currencies see Charles A. Coombs, "Treasury and Federal Reserve Foreign Exchange Operations," *Monthly Review,* Federal Reserve Bank of New York, October 1962, pp. 131-140. For one of the later progress reports, see Charles A. Coombs, "Treasury and Federal Reserve Foreign Exchange Operations and the Gold Pool," *Monthly Review,* Federal Reserve Bank of New York, March 1964, pp. 47-53.

6. Henry C. Wallich, "Government Action," *The Dollar in Crisis* (Seymour E. Harris, ed.) (New York: Harcourt, Brace and World, Inc., 1961), pp. 110-111.

22

The International Monetary Fund, Other Matters, and the World Bank (and Its Affiliates)

At the conference of 1892, the German economist, Julius Wolf, proffered a new idea, namely, that an international gold reserve be deposited in a neutral country and that international bank notes be issued on the basis of this reserve—the idea that, though in an entirely different form, was to be partly realized by the International Funds of Bretton Woods fame (Joseph A. Schumpeter, *History of Economic Analysis* [1954]).

In the 1920's, great effort was made to put the gold standard into order again for the purpose of establishing a workable system of international monetary organization. It was natural, in this effort, that both those responsible for monetary policy and the general public should look back to the pre-World War I days when the international gold standard had worked so well in providing the appropriate setting for a remarkable increase in production and trade. The attempt failed, however, because of changes in the underlying conditions. Certain problems were confronted, and a solution was not provided by adherence to the old ideas (Sect. 7.5). In the 1930's, the countries in the so-called sterling area* kept together as effectively as possible; on the Continent of Europe,

---

* The term "sterling area" refers to a group of countries who are mostly members of the British Commonwealth and who follow generally comparable policies in their overseas financial transactions. The sterling area system had its beginning in 1931 when Britain went off the gold standard and certain dominions and countries outside of the British Empire with close financial ties to London decided it was of great importance for their currencies to remain stable in terms of one another. Its essential features have been (1) the use of sterling as a reserve currency by area countries other than Britain, (2) the freedom of capital movements within the area, and (3) the widespread use of sterling by area countries and others for trading purposes. The fundamental structure of the system has remained through post-World War

501

exchange restrictions became more and more common; and there was a flight of capital to the United States (Sect. 10.3), largely as a result of political fears abroad. The state of affairs in the 1920's and 1930's was politically and economically unappealing. Therefore, during World War II some imaginative individuals began to plan for the future. Their plans, reflecting the necessity for a new arrangement for international cooperation, were directed toward the establishment of an organization to provide sufficient flexibility through international assistance. At the same time, a substitute would be provided for the monetary discipline formerly imposed by the international gold standard.

Experts from forty-four nations, meeting at Bretton Woods, New Hampshire, in July 1944, called for the establishment of two new international financial institutions: the International Monetary Fund, with certain regulatory powers and resources for short-term assistance to the various member countries, and the International Bank for Reconstruction and Development, an agency to provide long-term capital under government guarantee for specific projects. In large part, the philosophy underlying the establishment and operations of these institutions, and the Fund in particular, was concerned with the maintenance of the regulatory and freedom of trade aspects of the gold standard. It reflected an attempt to maintain these products of the gold standard arrangement while avoiding the harsher discipline of the fully automatic gold standard.

Since the inception of the Bretton Woods institutions, their membership and resources have been vastly enlarged. In 1956 and 1960, respectively, two new institutions—the International Finance Corporation and the International Development Association—began operations as affiliates and as a supplement to the resources of the World Bank. Also, in October 1962, the resources of the International Monetary Fund as well as its tools were augmented by the establishment of stand-by borrowing facilities within the framework of the International Monetary Fund itself. The establishment of the latter was in response to the special need for additional resources and a new tool as a result of the widespread convertibility of currencies at year-end 1958 and the greater freedom of short-term capital movements.

The objectives of these international institutions were broad, though they may not have always fulfilled them to the desired degree. The institutions, nevertheless, have provided special arrangements for cooperation in monetary matters of mutual concern to the participating members, and the degree of the success of the functioning of the international

---

II years. For discussions of it, see A. R. Conan, *The Rationale of the Sterling Area* (New York: St. Martin's Press, 1961); and Judd Polk, *Sterling—Its Meaning in World Finance* (New York: Harper and Brothers, 1956).

monetary system by the early 1960's was in striking contrast to its functioning at any time in over a half century. Thus, as a means of better understanding these international institutions and their contribution to the functioning of the international monetary economy, this chapter deals with their purposes and functions. It also treats the subject of the par value system of exchange rates as it relates to the Bretton Woods agreements. It then deals with instances of assistance by the IMF and the stand-by borrowing facilities of the IMF, since the operations of the latter are so largely related to short-run financial phenomena as emphasized in the last chapter.

22.1. The International Monetary Fund

The International Monetary Fund (IMF) is a specialized agency within the meaning of the charter of the United Nations. It is independent of the United Nations, however, and its headquarters are in Washington, D.C. Its purposes pertain to international monetary matters, and its structure, organization, and functions are designed with the view of the fulfillment of these purposes.

This section contains a list of the purposes of the IMF. It also describes the structure and organization of the institution and reviews the functions as they relate to the various purposes to be served by the organization.

The purposes of the IMF. The purposes of the IMF, as stated in the often quoted Article I of the Bretton Woods agreements, are:

(1) To promote international monetary cooperation through a permanent institution which provides the machinery for consultation and collaboration on international monetary problems.

(2) To facilitate the expansion and balanced growth of international trade, and to contribute thereby to the promotion and maintenance of high levels of employment and real income and to the development of the productive resources of all members as primary objectives of economic policy.

(3) To promote exchange stability, to maintain orderly exchange arrangements among members, and to avoid competitive exchange depreciation.

(4) To assist in the establishment of a multilateral system of payments in respect of current transactions between members and in the elimination of foreign exchange restrictions which hamper the growth of world trade.

(5) To give confidence to members by making the Fund's resources available to them under adequate safeguards, thus providing them with opportunity to correct maladjustments in their balance of payments without resorting to measures destructive of national or international prosperity.

(6) In accordance with the above, to shorten the duration and lessen the degree of disequilibrium in the international balances of payments of members.

The structure and organization. Membership in the IMF numbered thirty-five national governments at the outset, and since that time the number has grown by more than 100 per cent. Each member is allotted a quota roughly proportioned to its share of world trade. The quota then determines the financial contribution of the member to the Fund's assets. It is also important, however, in relation to the voting right of members, and, as shall be noted presently, the right to make use of the Fund's resources.

The quotas and votes for the respective member countries are reported regularly in the Fund's annual reports. While the quotas of most countries, including the United States and the United Kingdom, were increased by 50 per cent in 1958, the quotas of the three countries experiencing exceptional postwar growth—Canada, Germany, and Japan— were increased more substantially. The very small quotas of some countries were adjusted to bring them up to a reasonable level. These increases reflected the first approach to member governments for additional resources since the Fund began operation.

The voting power is vested in the Board of Governors and the twelve executive directors. Each nation appoints a governor, and each governor has 250 votes plus one additional vote for each $100,000 of his nation's quota. The number of votes, however, is increased by one vote for each $100,000 of a nation's currency sold by the Fund and decreased by one vote for $100,000 of foreign money purchased from the Fund by the member nations. Each executive director—one from each of the five nations with the largest quotas and seven elected by the other nations—is, in turn, entitled to cast a number of votes equal to the number of votes possessed by the country or countries to which he owes his selection. The Board of Governors may delegate all but the most important of its functions to the executive directors. There is also a managing director.

Specific functions of the IMF. The main functions performed by the IMF may include the following:

(1) The administration of the foreign exchange policy set forth in the Articles of Agreement,

(2) The extension of technical advice to members concerning economic and financial measures to achieve internal stability and external balance,

(3) The approval (or disapproval) of changes in par values and official exchange rates of member-nation currencies, and the

regular consultation with members concerning the restrictions imposed by the member countries on international payments,

(4) The extension of short-term advances in foreign currencies to members from the Fund's pool of currencies, and

(5) The borrowing and lending of currencies among the more industrialized countries.

The first four of these functions are more traditional with respect to the Fund. The fifth is more recent and comes under authority extended to the Fund in October 1962. In effect, it represents a new tool for use in fulfilling the purposes of the Fund. Since this fifth function adds a new dimension to the Fund, and since operations with respect to it are limited to a small group of countries from among the Fund's total membership, we shall consider it below (Sect. 22.4), after some further consideration of the first four functions.

Foreign exchange policy. The first function concerns the foreign exchange policy that member countries have pledged themselves to carry out. The policy provides that each country agree with the Fund on a par value for its currency and that each country maintain exchange rates for its currency, free from restrictions on current transactions, within one per cent of that par value.

The Fund favors a realistic par value or one that provides a satisfactory link between the cost and prices of a member country and those of the important trading countries with which a member deals, but the Fund is prevented by the Articles of Agreement from proposing changes in par value. The problem must be approached from the side of the general health of the economy. If an exchange rate overvalues the currency of a country, the consequences are likely to be an unfavorable balance of trade (Sect. 21.2), whereby the demand for a country's merchandise exports declines and the demand for merchandise imports increases. Under such circumstances, and the resulting pressures of unemployment, sooner or later the country must depreciate its exchange rate, take some combination of actions with respect to foreign exchange and domestic policies, or intensify restrictions on payments. A country wishing to change its exchange rate, however, must consult with the Fund. A proposed change not exceeding 10 per cent, together with previous changes, may not be objected to by the Fund. A large change may be agreed upon or objected to by the Fund. Generally, if the charge is directed toward correcting a fundamental disequilibrium it will be approved by the Fund.*

* In giving approval or in deciding to devalue or revalue a currency as a means of correcting a payments disequilibrium, there are complication factors. One of these is the elasticity of the foreign demand for the deficit country's exports. As noted, a decrease in the exchange rate in effect reduces the general price level of the deficit

As a rule, the Fund itself favors stable exchange rates. It encourages countries to follow the internal monetary and fiscal policies that will contribute to the achievement of stability in exchange rates. There are, nevertheless, circumstances which lead some countries to put exchange rates on a fluctuating basis rather than on a par value basis with the Fund's approval. They may do so as a means of ultimately arriving at a realistic par value with the aid of the market forces of supply and demand. Several revaluations of the par value of a country's currency may also be effected for the same reason.

The advisory function. The second function of the Fund is to advise countries. In addition to technical assistance, the Fund may suggest to countries where inflation has been excessive, government spending has exceeded government revenues, or credit expansion has been excessive that certain financial measures be adopted. These measures may include a tightening of credit policy, a strengthening of the monetary tools and independence of the central bank, an overhaul of fiscal affairs to reduce expenditures and improve revenues, and a re-examination of the operations of state agencies designed to eliminate a source of drain on the public finances. In some instances, the measures called for may be a new, more depreciated, fixed rate of exchange, or, as indicated above,

---

country from the point of view of foreign buyers. The question then is whether the devaluation or, more generally, a revaluation will increase the total revenue from exports. The answer is that the devaluation—in effect, a decrease in the price level of the deficit country from the point of view of the rest of the world—calls forth an increase in the quantity of exports sufficient to increase total revenue where the proportional change in the price level confronting foreigners is less than the proportional change in exports. This we call the elasticity of demand (η, eta) and denote an elastic demand $\eta \approx (\Delta Q/Q)/(\Delta P/P) > 1$,

where P is the general price level in the deficit country from the point of view of the
     rest of the world, and
     Q is total quantity demanded (in constant prices) or

$$\sum_{i=1}^{n} (q)_i,$$

where $(q)_i$ is the ith commodity. Otherwise, foreign demand is inelastic (i.e., $\eta < 1$) or unity (i.e., $\eta = 1$), and devaluation would decrease or not change the volume of foreign sales in monetary units. In any case, where devaluation would possibly decrease foreign sales, an upward revaluation of the rate may be called for.

Other complicating factors are the elasticity of the demand for imports by the deficit country, and the inelasticity of supply in the rest of the world. In the first of these instances, the question may be whether the effective increase in the price levels abroad from the domestic point of view will curb expenditures on imports. In the other, it may be whether the rest of the world will find difficulty in cutting the output of commodities competing with the deficit country's exports or in diverting productive resources to domestic or other markets. In the short run, the domestic demand for foreign goods and services may be inelastic primarily because producers cannot adjust their purchasing habits to a change in relative prices, while, in the long run, the possibilities of substitution between domestic and foreign products or raw materials is considerably greater.

the rate may be allowed to fluctuate until a decision can be reached on a new fixed rate. In other instances, the measure called for may be a dual exchange market, one for most types of trade and one for other selected types of transactions. When a country agrees on a program to deal with any internal inflation and external imbalance, then the Fund is prepared to give its financial support.

The approval of changes in par values. The third function of the Fund is to approve (or disapprove) changes in par values of official exchange rates and to consult regularly with member countries concerning the restrictions they have imposed on international payments. In carrying out this function the Fund must do two things: (1) decide whether changes are justified and whether restrictions on payments are permissible and (2) analyze the basic internal and external economic conditions of the member countries involved in order to recommend an appropriate line of action to facilitate a reduction or elimination of restrictions.

In this latter respect, the scope of the Fund's activities changed radically in February 1961. At that time, practically all of the currencies used to finance international trade became convertible; in addition to Western Hemisphere currencies already convertible, nine member countries from Western Europe—Belgium, France, Germany, Ireland, Italy, Luxembourg, the Netherlands, Sweden, and the United Kingdom—and Peru accepted obligations of convertibility under Article VIII of the Fund's Articles of Agreement. The Article requires member countries subject to its provisions to avoid restrictions on currency payments, multiple exchange rates, and discriminatory currency practices.

Short-term advances. The fourth function of the Fund is to make short-term advances to member countries whose balance of payments difficulties are considered to be temporary. In this instance, a short term is considered to be from three to five years. Moreover, the attitude of the Fund toward requests for drawings depends upon the size of the drawings in proportion to the country's quota and the Fund's holdings of the member's currency. Requests for drawings amounting to the first 25 per cent of the quota net of the Fund's holdings of the member's currency (i.e., request amounting to the "gold tranche") are virtually given automatic approval. Requests for drawings amounting to the second 25 per cent of the quota (the so-called "first-credit tranche") are liberally permitted. To receive the first-credit tranche the member is required only to demonstrate that it is making a reasonable effort to deal with the difficulties that have caused the balance of payments deficit. Requests for drawing beyond the first 50 per cent of a country's quota, however, are granted only after substantial justification is shown. There must be convincing evidence "that the drawings are in support of a sound program likely to ensure enduring stability at realistic rates of exchange."

In addition to the drawings referred to, the Fund may enter into stand-by arrangements with a member country. These arrangements, similar to lines of credit, entitle a country to draw up to a stated amount within a period of six months to a year; some of the arrangements may be extended for subsequent periods. In granting stand-by arrangements, the Fund may require that a "declaration of intent" be incorporated into the provisions of the agreements themselves.

22.2. The Par Value System and Fluctuating Exchange Rates

The par value system is one involving the establishment of par values for currencies (e.g., Fig. 21-1), the practice of stabilizing fluctuations in exchange rates within agreed-upon limits (i.e., one per cent above and below par value), and the practice of permitting a par value to be changed from time to time to help correct fundamental balance of payments disequilibria (Sect. 21.2). It is the system that was written into the articles set for under the Bretton Woods Agreements of 1944. As system of fluctuating exchange, on the other hand, is one whereby the currency values of major countries would be free to fluctuate without definite limits in relation to one another. Instead of relying upon occasional changes in par values and price level changes in the various countries as a means of facilitating economic adjustments and correcting payments disequilibria, the system of freely fluctuating exchange rates would call for even larger and more frequent exchange rate changes as a means of bringing about economic adjustments and correcting payments disequilibria. Under this system, fluctuations beyond the present gold points can be relied upon as a means of adjustments since a more extreme decline in the value of a country's currency is, in its effect, the same thing as a decline in its price level, from the point of view of the purchasing power of foreign countries.

The arguments for and against a system of fluctuating exchange rates and for and against a system of fixed rates (i.e., par values and agreed-upon limits) are numerous. (The literature on this is prolific.[1]) But the IMF position is that the best system, as judged from the experience of the world over many years, is their system of fixed rates with occasional adjustments to correct fundamental disequilibria, and with the occasional use of a fluctuating rate for a particular country in order to help arrive at the most satisfactory par value. The usual arguments against a system of fluctuating exchange rates have to do with one's views of the real world and real-world experience, as contrasted with the logic of the system itself.

The economics professors who specialize in the area of exchange rates vary in their advocacy of the system of fluctuating exchange rates, and practitioners in the field are solidly against any proposal to effect such rates. As one spokesman said, the proposal "has probably through the years fascinated 'more professors and frustrated more practitioners than any other tool in the kit of international financial machinery." [2] Also the experience with fluctuating exchange rates has been confined to only a few of the countries at a time as contrasted with a group of several major industrial countries operating under such rates at one time. In any event, there are practical barriers to effecting such a system as the following dialogue indicates:

> REPRESENTATIVE REUSS: Well, flexible rates would require a radical reformation of the IMF charter, would it not?
> MR. VANEK: Yes.
> REPRESENTATIVE REUSS: So you are assuming that there is a big Bretton Woods-type monetary conference, and we all agree to abrogate Bretton Woods and start in with new flexible rates.
> MR. VANEK: Also, there could be a U.S. action, a floating of the dollar against all the other currencies.
> REPRESENTATIVE REUSS: This, under Bretton Woods, would require the consent of our partners, would it not?
> MR. VANEK: Yes.
> REPRESENTATIVE REUSS: So, however it is done, whether by a universal acceptance of flexible rates or by a unilateral U.S. devaluation, it would require the consent of other members of the Monetary Fund. But let us assume that, somehow or other, that consent is obtained. Otherwise, you never get to your thesis.
> MR. VANEK: Yes.[3]

With this background in mind, then, and without providing a complete list of the pros and cons of either system of exchange rates, we introduce only two of the topics that arise in controversy over the most desirable system of rates—that pertaining to an exchange rate as a market price, and that pertaining to a domestic monetary policy, independent of international considerations.

The foreign exchange rate as a price. The foreign exchange rate is a price of one currency in terms of another. The various rates reveal what a unit of one money will buy in other countries, given the prices of the various goods and services in the respective countries, and they serve as a link between national price systems. Thus, viewing the rate as a price, one may argue that the price should be as free as any other price in a market system to vary with shifting supply and demand conditions until it finds a natural level. As one professorial critic notes:

> People who believe in the market system thoroughly would auction off the places in every trolly car as it went by to try to get full utilization of capacity. . . . But the lady going shopping would like to know what the price of trolly cars is going to be that day and what it is going to be the next day and the day after that. Trolly car rates may acquire changes from time to

time . . . but the notion of auctioning off the seats in each and having every price fully flexible goes too far, it seems to me, in support of the free enterprise system, which we all support.[4]

Against the proposal for fully flexible exchange rates, one may also argue that a fixed rate provides more time for producers, sellers, and buyers to adjust to new price and cost relationships. The IMF, for example, takes the following position:

> There is no such thing as a "natural" level for the rate of exchange of a currency. The proper rate will, in each case, depend upon the economic, financial and monetary policies followed by the country concerned and by other countries with whom it has important economic relationships. If the economy of a country is to adapt itself to a given exchange rate, there must be time for the producers, sellers and buyers of goods and services to respond to the new set of price and cost relationships to which the rate gives rise. This means that in the short run changes in the exchange rate are either no test or a very poor test of basic economic inter-relationships. It also means that whether a given exchange rate is at the correct level can be determined only after there has been time to observe the course of the balance of payments in response to that rate.[5]

It might be noted, however, that most of the proponents of flexible exchange rates accept price level stability (Sect. 8.1) as a desirable national economic goal. One states that "the defense of price stability ought at least to be given credit for the strengthening of the exchange-rate stability it implies." [6]

The independence of domestic monetary policy. Under the postwar system of fixed exchange rates, we have noted an interrelationship between a country's domestic monetary policy, payments position (Sect. 21.3), and movements of short-term capital. A higher interest rate, for example, may attract capital balances, serve as a constraint on domestic prices, and tend to correct payments deficits, depending upon the changes in the price level in other countries. Such a restrictive policy, however, may also temporarily contribute to a rise in unemployment in the domestic economy.

Consequently, one may argue that, given the nature of policy-makers on the national level, the policy objective of full employment for the domestic economy will receive priority over the policy called for by a payments deficit. Thus, to get around this nationalistic view of the policy-maker and his supporters, one could argue for a system of fluctuating exchange rates. It could provide a mechanism of adjustment through market processes without the need for an adjustment in domestic prices.

As a rebuttal to this latter argument, one might observe that there is a loss of discipline from having to check price increases by organized groups in selected industries (Sect. 16.3). In the view of the IMF directors:

> If, as in most countries at present, wages are not equally flexible in both directions, fluctuations in the exchange rate may create inflationary pressures. Any circumstances leading to a temporary depreciation of the rate will raise the domestic currency cost of imports and will directly and indirectly lead to price increases. These increases will encourage demands for higher money wages, at least some of which may be met. Hence, depreciations are likely to encourage increases in domestic costs. By contrast, institutional rigidities limit reductions in money wages, so that exchange appreciations are unlikely to lead to significant decreases in domestic costs. Therefore, a fluctuating rate may be expected to encourage a rising trend in domestic costs. In turn, increases in costs exert a downward pressure on the rate.[7]

To this, one may add that the better organized workers (Sect. 16.3) and those without relatively fixed incomes (Sect. 5.3) would be the primary beneficiaries. Those who operate more as individuals and those whose incomes are relatively fixed would not have the recourse of the balance of payments discipline.

With respect to the need to effect the discipline of a satisfactory monetary policy, the IMF directors would also add the following from their experience: "The experience of the postwar period . . . suggests that if a country does not clearly and quickly adopt a monetary policy aimed at stability, the movements of its fluctuating rate are likely to be oscillations not around a stable value but around a declining trend. It is an illusion to expect the fluctuating rate to ease the problems facing the monetary authorities. . . ."[8]

Continuing, the directors may add the following:

> Suggestions that a fluctuating rate serves to maintain an equilibrium relation between an economy following an inflationary policy and the rest of the world are based on the belief that any variations in the rate will be fairly closely associated with changes in the relation between domestic and foreign prices. In practice, however, countries that have sought protection by adopting a fluctuating rate have often pegged the rate rather quickly, even though internal stability and external equilibrium were not assured. Consequently, if the rate was an appropriate one initially, it soon became inappropriate. Recent experience covers quite a few cases where "fluctuating rates" were kept pegged in the face of large losses in reserves and sharp increases in domestic prices. In these circumstances, the fall in reserves convinced importers, exporters, and foreign and domestic holders of liquid assets that a depreciation was inevitable. The demand for imports rose and exports were held back, while capital flight was fostered. All the basic pressures on the rate were aggravated. If the rate had been left to fluctuate freely, its immediate depreciation would have reduced the possible

gains to be obtained by capital flight, discouraged imports, and encouraged exports. . . .

The use of fluctuating rates in the last decade has been limited to a relatively small number of countries, of which only one, Canada, accounts for a substantial proportion of world trade; and Canada, which introduced a fluctuating rate in 1950, adopted, with the approval of the Fund, a new par value after the end of the [fiscal year 1962]. . . .[9]

22.3. Instances of Assistance by the IMF

The Fund effected exchange transactions with forty-four members—some on several occasions—from the beginning of its operations until the end of the fiscal year 1962. Three other members were extended assistance in the form of stand-by arrangements over that same period, but they did not draw on the available funds. Of the forty-seven members, nineteen were from Latin America, twelve from Europe, five from the Middle East, seven from the Far East, and four from Africa.

To give a clearer understanding of the Fund's loan and stand-by arrangement policies, the instances of assistance may be classified in several groups. Some examples of the assistance are given also, but those given represent some unusual instances of the largest amounts of assistance.

Emergency needs. Assistance has been granted to meet emergency needs, such as in response to the 1956 Suez Crisis, when the Egyptians moved to take over the Suez Canal from the British. At that time there suddenly arose some speculation against the pound sterling because of the fear that the position of the United Kingdom would be seriously impaired by a decline in oil supplies and for other reasons, although the British had a surplus in the current account of their balance of payments. It was believed to be in the general interest to safeguard the value of the pound sterling against the wave of speculation opposing it and the accompanying drain on Britain's gold and dollar reserves. Assistance was granted to the United Kingdom in December 1956, when a 561 million dollar drawing was provided along with a stand-by arrangement amounting to 739 million dollars. The crisis was weathered by the pring of 1957, and additional controls on trade and payments were avoided.

It may be noted, however, that at the time of the assistance the British government declared its intention to avoid the reimposition of external controls and to follow monetary and fiscal measures designed to strengthen its economy both internally and externally. In fact, in the wake of the Suez Crisis, the discount rate (i.e., "the Bank rate") at the Bank of England was moved to 7 per cent for the first time since 1921.

Deterioration in the current account. Assistance has been granted to countries experiencing an increasing strain in the current account of their balance of payments. The circumstances have varied considerably, but the strain in the current account was most often caused by inflation; in one specific case, the support was to maintain the strength of sterling in the face of large speculative flows of funds. Generally, the circumstances were such that equilibrium could be restored only if steps were taken to reduce the volume of spending or to temporarily prevent its expansion. Some special difficulties arose where countries adopted rather ambitious development plans that required financing during a period of increasing capital shortage. In these, as in other instances, the Fund gave only temporary support while adjustments were made to void the inflationary dangers.

In the specific case referred to, the United Kingdom was granted assistance totaling the equivalent of 2,000 million dollars—1,500 million in nine currencies and 500 million under a stand-by arrangement. The assistance by the Fund was also combined with informal support from a number of central banks as a means of helping the British government in its effort to maintain the strength of sterling.

The circumstances leading to the support involved a construction boom in England, high interest rates there, and a withdrawal of funds from the United States and other centers despite deterioration in the current account of the United Kingdom; in addition, there was a revaluation of the deutsche mark and the Dutch guilder by 5 per cent in March 1961. With the large inflow of short-term capital and the deterioration, the revaluation of the deutsche mark and the Dutch guilder proved very damaging to confidence and led to a massive outflow of capital. Then came the defenses—the Bank of England adopted a 7 per cent rate on July 25, and there was the IMF and other assistance. As one source said, in reviving an old adage: "Seven per cent will bring gold from the moon." It was a striking test of power in some ways; a British bond that originally sold at 100—the Dalton $2\frac{1}{2}$'s—traded as low as $36\frac{1}{2}$. Money market rates rose, the exchange rate on the pound improved, funds were again attracted to London. By October 5, the Bank rate was lowered somewhat, and by year-end Britain was repaying a record level of assistance.

Seasonal difficulties. Assistance has been granted to meet temporary balance of payments difficulties caused by seasonal factors. Countries, in such instances, are largely dependent on a single export crop, and seasonal difficulties may arise before the export crop is sold. In granting such assistance, arrangements to liquidate the credit have been made to correspond to a strengthening of the exchange position by the inflow of export proceeds.

Assistance to stabilization programs. Assistance has been granted for the definite purpose of backing stabilization programs. The Fund, for example, has agreed to accept fluctuating exchange rates and has agreed on the use of its resources to carry out stabilization operations in free-exchange markets. In these instances, also, fiscal and monetary reforms have been a part of the stabilization program, and it has been understood that the respective currencies would be stabilized at a fixed rate as soon as practicable.°

22.4. Stand-by Borrowing Facilities for the IMF

A proposal to increase the IMF's resources by means of stand-by borrowing facilities grew out of a meeting of finance ministers and central bankers in Vienna in September 1961. The occasion was the sixteenth annual meeting of the IMF and the World Bank, and one of the main themes of the meeting was international liquidity—the adequacy and ease of conversion of international balances for international transactions and trade. The proposal itself, however, was in response to this particular need as it related to the presence of a greater freedom of capital movements between the free world countries and the increase in the convertibility of the currencies of the major industrial nations of the free world.

Following the Vienna meeting, the more industrialized countries pledged supplementary resources. These became available to the IMF in October 1962, following the formal adherence of the United States government to the Fund's proposal. At the time the proposal took effect, the size of these additional resources was only in excess of one-third of the total of the quotas of the members of the IMF, but the philosophical implications of the addition to the Fund's resources was quite significant. In this respect, it indicated some capacity on the part of the IMF to evolve and respond to the needs of the international monetary system. In doing so, it lessened the need for an essentially new international or-

---

° In the instances referred to, the assistance granted by the Fund has been combined with credits from other sources, such as the United States Treasury and the Export-Import Bank. The latter, it may be noted, is strictly an American lending agency. It primarily assists economic development which, presumably, may take account of political realities at home and abroad.

Another special agency, outside of the United Nations Charter and serving its function in the field of development rather than that of short-term finance is the Inter-American Development Bank. This institution takes account of the special political, economic, and financial interrelationships of the Americas. It is designed to supplement other sources of credit, to assist the countries of Latin America in mobilizing their own resources, and, in encouraging domestic and foreign private capital, to undertake desirable investments to promote the economic development of these countries. Both the capital and the management of this institution are shared by the Latin American countries, and its financial structure involves paid-in capital and a guarantee fund for securities issued by the bank. This feature makes the financing of the Bank somewhat similar to the World Bank.

ganization to cope with the problems relating to international liquidity (Sect. 23.6).

The provision of the facilities for borrowing enlarges upon the IMF's function as a financial intermediary as contrasted with a warehouse of world moneys. Under the arrangement and subject to safeguards, the IMF may borrow currencies from some nations and lend to others as the need arises. In principle, the IMF may obtain funds from one of the participating members with a payments surplus and loan them to a member with a temporary payments deficit. For example, suppose there were speculation against the dollar in London, and the need arose for the Bank of England to exchange pounds for dollars as the exchange rate approached gold export points (Fig. 21-1). In such a case, the IMF could borrow pounds and lend them to the United States, wherein the United States could exchange the borrowed pound rather than gold for dollars. In this way also, an outflow of gold could be averted temporarily, at least, and there would likely be less uncertainty (and, therefore, less loss of liquidity) over the liquidity of short-term liabilities of the United States to foreigners and foreign governments.

The stand-by borrowing facilities of the Fund make it possible to mobilize quickly a large amount of additional resources in defense of international liquidity. The plan has general applicability, and any large industrial country, under the conditions of widespread convertibility and free movements of short-term capital, may find its payments position temporarily under pressure. The delegates at Vienna in September 1961, however, had in mind the possibility of a large supply of dollar balances in foreign hands that might under some circumstances be withdrawn from the United States and reduce international liquidity. Such a withdrawal could result in losses of United States gold reserves and international liquidity along the lines introduced in the earlier discussion of the gold and short-term capital accounts (Sect. 21.2).

Requests for borrowed funds under the stand-by borrowing arrangements are assessed according to the funds established policies and practices in the use of its resources. The actual funds for loans are put up by the countries participating in the special arrangements as the need may arise, and the funds are repayable when a borrower's problem is solved and, in any event, within three to five years. The repayment is made to the IMF, and the IMF repays the country (countries) that made the supplementary resources available. A country that has made resources available, however, may receive an earlier repayment if its own payments position deteriorates.

Interest on the loans to the fund is based on a formula, plus a charge of one-half of one per cent on each borrowing transaction. At the outset for the stand-by arrangements for borrowing, the formula yielded a rate of $1\frac{1}{2}$ per cent per annum. Further, rights to repayment are backed by all the assets of the IMF, and this provision, too, emphasizes the liquidity of the claims of the lending country against the IMF.

The borrowing arrangements are scheduled to remain in effect until October 1966, and there are provisions for the extension of the arrangements. Also the amounts in the provision for the supplementary resources may be reviewed from time to time with the thought to effecting changes in the light of developing circumstances and with the agreement of the participating countries and the IMF.

22.5. The International Bank for Reconstruction and Development and Its Affiliates

The organization of the International Bank for Reconstruction and Development (IBRD, popularly known as the World Bank)[10] is similar to that of the IMF. The World Bank is also a specialized agency within the meaning of the charter of the United Nations, and, as such, it is required to function as an independent international organization. Furthermore, the membership of both the World Bank and the IMF consists of the same countries. The primary differences between the two international financial institutions are in the loan programs and the method of financing. Loans of the World Bank are intermediate and long term, whereas the loans of the IMF are short term. And the bank finances loans through the sale of its own bonds in the world capital markets and in other ways, whereas the IMF is primarily a "revolving fund" and independent of outside financing. Further, in those instances where safeguards against lending by the bank limit its effectiveness, the bank's operations are supplemented by those of two affiliates—the International Finance Corporation and the International Development Association.

This section describes briefly the structure and organization of the World Bank and the provisions governing loans, as well as the financial operations of the Bank, the International Finance Corporation, and the International Development Association.

The structure and organization. The World Bank, like the Fund, is located in Washington, D.C. It has a Board of Governors, sixteen executive directors (one each being appointed by the five largest stockholders and eleven being elected by the remaining members), and a president (elected by the executive directors). The bank is a corporate form of organization, all of whose capital stock is owned by its member governments. The election of officials, as well as other voting privileges, are commensurate with the capital stock subscribed to by the respective members. Each member of the bank has 250 votes, plus one additional vote for each share of capital stock subscribed to. Data concerning subscriptions to the Bank's capital and the member's voting strength are readily obtained from the Bank's annual reports.

A December 1958 proposal of the directors of the Bank resulted in an increase in the Bank's authorized capital and the subscriptions of the members. The first part of the effected proposal increased the Bank's authorized capital to 21 billion dollars, and the second part increased the subscriptions of the present members by 100 per cent. The increase in the capital under the first part of the proposal actually provided room for some additional shares to take care of the admission of new members and adjustments in subscriptions. Also the 100 per cent increase in capital was quite generally subscribed to, and increases in the subscriptions of some countries were intended to bring their liability more in keeping with their current standing in the world economy.

Only a part of the subscriptions are paid in. The subscriptions are divided into three parts to provide the Bank with loan resources from both its own paid-in capital and from a sizable guaranty fund designed to enable the Bank to mobilize capital for international investment:

> 1. Two per cent of each subscription is payable in gold or United States dollars, which may be used freely by the Bank in any of its operations.
> 2. Eighteen per cent of each subscription is payable in the currency of the subscribing member. These funds may be lent only with the consent of the member whose currency is lent.
> 3. The remaining 80% of each subscription is not available to the Bank for lending but is subject to call only if required by the Bank to meet its obligations on borrowing or on loans guaranteed by it. Payments on any such call may be made either in gold, U.S. dollars, or the currency required to discharge the obligations of the Bank for which the call is made.[11]

The 2 per cent and the 18 per cent comprising the first and second parts, respectively, provided the Bank directly with loan resources. The 80 per cent, on the other hand, provided the Bank with its guaranty fund. It enabled the Bank to mobilize private capital for international investment, either through reducing the risk to investors or through bank guarantees of private international credits. Also it put the risk on an international basis with each of the members sharing responsibility, whether borrower or lender, up to the amount of its capital subscription. The 80 per cent subscription reflected an emphasis upon the concept of the Bank as a "safe bridge" over which private capital may move into the international economy in comparison with the smaller proportion of paid-in capital from which the Bank may lend directly. Now, this division of the subscription still was continued, after the increase in subscriptions, but none of the newly subscribed capital was called. It was simply added to the contingent obligations of the members, so that the guaranty fund became about 90 per cent of the Bank's capital. This latter portion of capital, then, is subject to call to meet the Bank's own obligations in the event it could not meet them from other resources.

Provisions governing bank loans. The Bank's charter contains a number of provisions governing loans to be made or guaranteed and the character of bank lending from which the Bank's operating policies have been derived. The protective provisions governing loans to be made or guaranteed by the Bank are partly intended as criteria for the purpose of avoiding the errors of the past and assures the success of the program in the future. First, the loans must be for productive purposes and, except in special circumstances, for financing the foreign exchange requirements of specific project. This provision requires a clear agreement upon the use of the proceeds of the loan and on what the loan is to achieve. It also limits the use of bank loans to cover only the direct import needs of the borrower. Second, the merits of all projects to be financed must be studied carefully, and arrangements must be made to assure that the most useful and urgent projects are dealt with first. In carrying out this provision, the bank may seek to investigate the over-all economic position of the borrowing country to determine whether a proposed project is of the highest priority or whether lower-priority projects have been submitted. It may emphasize the project's contribution to internal production, and its ultimate benefit to the balance of payments. Third, the loan must be guaranteed by the member government or central bank in whose territories the project to be financed is located if the borrower is other than the government. In practice, the Bank has always obtained a government as distinct from a central bank guarantee. Fourth, the Bank must act "prudently" in making loans, with due regard to the prospect of repayment by the borrower and/or guarantor. In this regard, the Bank has urged public utility rates that would ensure the amortization of public utility loans. And, if dollars must be repaid, the Bank may limit its financing to a project that indirectly at least yields the dollars required for financing. For example, it may encourage the development of power and transportation facilities, on the assumption that these will yield a larger output of exportable commodities and reduce imports. Further, it may avoid the financing of projects, say, to exploit copper mines from which the resultant flow of dollars may be squandered on increased imports of luxuries. Also, though the Bank must accept special risk (risk not acceptable in the existing financial markets), judgment must be exercised in considering such factors as the effectiveness of the government administration and of the business community, the availability of managerial and technical skills, the availability of natural resources and existing productive plant, the scale and character of investment, and the likely economic and financial policies, particularly those affecting the level of domestic saving and the flow of foreign private capital. Fifth, the Bank must ensure that the proceeds of each loan are used only for the purposes for which the loan was granted. It must also pay due attention to considerations of economy and efficiency. To do these things the Bank keeps in touch with the progress of the project.

The character of Bank lending is governed by two provisions. Tied loans are prohibited. The Bank consequently is enjoined from tying the use of the proceeds of a loan to a particular source of supply; borrowers are free to use the proceeds to make purchases in any member country and in Switzerland, in recognition of that country's cooperative role in financial matters. Next, the Bank must be satisfied, before making or guaranteeing any loan, that the prospective borrower will otherwise be unable to obtain the loan under reasonable conditions in the prevailing market.

The total and distribution of the Bank's loans. Under the Bank's loan operations alone, they had extended 321 loans for assistance to sixty countries or territories for about 700 projects by mid-1962. These loans totaled over 6,500 million dollars and were distributed among the regions of the world as follows:

Region	Amount in Millions of Dollars	Per Cent of Total
Africa	885	13.38
Asia and the Middle East	2,185	33.39
Australia	418	6.38
Europe	1,443	22.05
Western Hemisphere	1,613	24.80
	6,544	100.00

SOURCE: International Bank for Reconstruction and Development.

Financial operations. The sources of funds for lending operations generally are several. The first source, and the one used most during the early years of bank operations, is the 2 per cent subscription of member countries in the form of gold or United States dollars and the released portions of the 18 per cent local currency subscription. The second source, and the largest over an extended period, is borrowings by the Bank through the issuance of its direct obligations in the various capital markets of the world. The third source of funds is from the sale of a portion of the Bank's portfolio, sometimes with and at other times without the guarantee of the Bank, to other institutions and the principal repayments to the Bank. The fourth source of loanable funds is the net earnings of the Bank.

In marketing its own obligations, the Bank relies heavily upon public issues, though private placements are frequently made. The public issues may be marketed through both the agency and competitive bidding methods (Sect. 14.1).* The market for the Bank's issues has broadened considerably since it began operations, and, although the American capital market has been an important supplier of borrowed funds, the Bank has sought and developed sources of funds in other capital markets. In the beginning of its operations in the United States, the financial community distrusted international lending, and many institutional investors could not legally purchase its bonds. Since that time, however, the Bank's bonds have become a legal investment, subject to statutory and administrative qualifications, for commercial banks, savings banks, insurance companies, and trust funds in a large majority of states. Federal action has broadened the market for the Bank's bonds[12] by authorizing them for investments for national banks, insurance companies in the District of Columbia, and state member banks of the Federal Reserve. Several states have passed legislation specifically authorizing the investment of public funds in the Bank's obligations.

The Bank, on the uses of funds side, employs its funds in the form of intermediate- and long-term loans, apart from working capital in the form of cash and short-term investments. It is the Bank's policy to tailor the terms of loans to suit the anticipated life of the equipment to be financed. For example, loans for such heavy equipment as power installations may be extended for a twenty- to twenty-five-year period, and loans for less durable equipment may cover a period of around seven years. In addition to the outright extension of its own funds, however, the Bank lends its credit by participating with private institutions in the financing of a loan. In most such instances, the private institutions take the short maturity portion of the loan.

The interest cost of funds to the Bank is, in effect, passed on to the ultimate borrower at a more favorable rate than could otherwise be obtained, as a result of the reduced risk involved in the Bank's bonds. The Bank, in addition to a rate commensurate with the estimated cost of market funds to the Bank, however, charges a one per cent commission on all loans. Out of the one per cent is paid an administrative cost (about one-fourth of one per cent) and a contribution to reserves (the remainder of the one per cent). The total interest rate on each bank loan, therefore, is made up of three components—the cost of borrowing to the Bank, the fraction for administrative cost, and the fraction for a contribution to reserves. From a different point of view, the commission may be said to encourage recourse to the private capital markets directly whenever possible at reasonable rates.

International Finance Corporation. The International Finance Corpora-

---

* It may be noted that the Federal Reserve Bank of New York is fiscal agent for the World Bank in connection with its bond issues in the United States. As such, the New York bank handles payments of principal and interest, registration, transfer and exchange of bonds, and other miscellaneous fiscal functions.

tion (IFC), an affiliate of the Bank, came into existence in June 1956. Most of the members of the Bank are also members of the IFC. The corporation, nevertheless, is a legal entity. The voting power of members, as with the Bank, is in proportion to the capital subscription, although, in the case of the corporation, subscriptions are payable in full in gold and United States dollars at the time of joining. The executive directors of the Bank, insofar as they represent countries that have joined the corporation, constitute the IFC's board of directors, and the president of the Bank is the ex officio chairman of the IFC's board; since October 1961, he has also been its president.

The corporation has operated on only 100 million dollars of total authorized capital, but additional funds amounting to about 20.7 million dollars had been generated from such sources as earnings and sales of investments by mid-1962. Moreover, its purpose is somewhat different from the Bank. In the first place, no restriction stands between the operations of the IFC and the borrowing governments, and the corporation enjoys greater freedom in choosing its investments. The restrictions, insofar as they exist, limit the corporation from investing in such "social overhead" as housing, hospitals, and schools; also, it is prohibited from engaging in refunding or refinancing activities, and from investing in government-owned and -operated or government-managed undertakings. In the second place, its primary aim is to make only moderate size investments in association with private capital. Its main criterion in selecting investments is the extent to which it can promote the investment of additional private capital in the less developed countries. It may do this by demonstrating the profitability of its investments so as to attract new capital and, as the enterprises mature, by revolving its portfolio.

The investments of the corporation are best classified as being intermediate between conventional loan capital and share capital, although during the fiscal year ended June 30, 1962, a former restriction on equity investment was removed. A new amendment to the articles of agreement, at that time, extended to the IFC the authority to make investments in the form of stock with the restriction that the investment would not project the IFC into a management position in the firms receiving the funds. The IFC, too, may seek to increase the attractiveness of its investments to a subsequent purchaser by acquiring rights, the exercise of which will permit the conversion of the investment into equities. Moreover, in addition to a feature which makes the basic yield on all loans uniform to all borrowers at any particular time, the IFC's investment pattern permits the corporation to negotiate a further yield with each borrower in the light of risk and expected return.

International Development Association. The International Development Association (IDA) has been an affiliate of the World Bank since the IDA came into being in September 1960. Still, its relationship to the World Bank is similar to that of the IFC. The Board of Governors, Executive Directors, and President of the World Bank serve ex officio the same positions in IDA, and the governors delegate the same broad powers to the Executive Director. The membership is about the same as that for the World Bank, and, as of mid-1962, the subscriptions to IDA's initially proposed capital of one billion dollars were roughly of the same proportions as those to the World Bank's capital. IDA, however, is designed to supplement the Bank's activities by financing development in the less developed member countries and in the less developed dependent and associated territories of the member countries, as well as to further the development objectives of the Bank.

In addition to member's subscriptions to the initially proposed one billion dollars of capital, on the sources of funds side, the IDA may receive, without altering the voting rights, supplementary resources from any member in the currency of another member when the latter member approves. This provision, for example, provides administrative machinery for a strong currency country to return balances obtained from weaker currency countries, as occurred in the disposition by the United States of American food supplies resulting from the government's postwar price support program. And, on the uses of funds side, the funds obtained from the IDA for use in the less developed areas may be used, in contrast with those from the IFC, for projects of high development priority in the light of the needs of the areas. The funds may also be used to provide financing to a member government. Such projects, consequently, as those pertaining to water supply, sanitation, and pilot housing are eligible, as well as projects of the type financed by the Bank.

22.6. Summary

The IMF and the IBRD are both independent international agencies with certain common ties, though with somewhat specialized functions. They have roughly a common membership; members of the IBRD must also be members of the IMF. And their respective boards of governors meet jointly under a common chairman. Both provide a means of international cooperation and a source of technical advice in the solution to exchange development and balance of payments problems. The efforts of both agencies have been directed toward overcoming or reducing balance of payments difficulties and providing a climate within which international trade may develop and private capital flow freely.

The IMF specializes in facilitating adjustments through the use of short-term credits. The instances of assistance through the granting of such credits may be classified as those to meet emergency needs, to support temporary deterioration in the current account, to lessen the impact of difficulties arising from seasonal factors, and to help expedite stabilization programs. Most of these instances have been rather routine. Others have been dramatic, such as those involving the United Kingdom. On one occasion the IMF helped the United Kingdom with its temporary financial needs that arose in response to the Suez Crisis in 1956; on another, in the era of the greater mobility of short-term balances, the IMF helped them cope with a large withdrawal of short-term balances in response to revaluation and the prospect of further revaluation of strong European currencies. In both of these instances, strong defensive measures were taken on the domestic side—the bank rate went to 7 per cent —and the assistance helped to avoid any extreme loss of international liquidity, such as would have resulted from a loss of British gold reserves and a further contraction of short-term liabilities.

The IMF also helps member countries establish realistic exchange rates, and they approve of large adjustments in the par value of exchange rates when the adjustments are directed toward correcting payments disequilibria. In general, the par value system of exchange rates underlies the Bretton Woods Agreements of 1944, and the IMF favors such a system with stable exchange rates. They believe it is the best system as judged from the experience of the world over many years, but, within this framework, they may still support fluctuating exchange rates as a means of arriving at realistic par values.

The IBRD, along with its affiliate, the IFC, specializes in facilitating the flow of private capital for economic development. The Bank makes its contribution through extending its own funds outright, through marketing its own issues and extending the proceeds to member countries, and through the use of bank guarantees. The IFC supplements the Bank's activities by facilitating the flow of private capital for private development projects in some instances where the Bank is restricted by its governing provisions. And the IDA, another affiliate of the IBRD, in part supplements the activities of the IBRD by expediting the flow of funds to the less developed countries. The IDA, in particular, offers the opportunity for industrialized countries of the free world to jointly contribute to the growth of the less developed areas.

In extending their services, both the IMF and the IBRD must deal with the realities of the interrelated problems of foreign exchange, development, and balance of payments. In doing so, they must also, at times, concern themselves with the domestic conditions of the borrowing country and they may recommend and encourage by the use of their facilities the pursuit of economic, monetary and fiscal policies designed to foster balanced growth within a world of expanding trade, free from restrictions and regulations. In a sense, therefore, the institutions referred to have restored some measure of the international monetary discipline previously provided by the gold standard in its day.

The degree of freedom from exchange restriction has steadily improved in the post-World War II world through the aid of the Fund, and despite occasional unsettling international incidences. The Bank, too, has made material contributions, first to reconstruction and increasingly to development. The contribution of the Bank, however, cannot be judged solely by the size of its loans relative to the alleged capital needs of the less developed countries of the world. Among its objectives has been the fostering of the flow of private funds, and the Bank has stimulated this by broadening the market for its own bonds, by stimulating the acceptance of its guarantee of other issues, and by the dissemination of the knowledge and technical skill resulting from its study of the problems confronting the less developed countries.

Somewhat in recognition of the usefulness of the Bretton Woods institutions, the member-country officials approved in 1958 increases in the Fund quotas and the Bank subscriptions. Also, a new tool for the IMF grew out of a meeting of finance ministers and central bankers in Vienna in September 1961. The development of this new tool for the IMF indicates some capacity on the part of that institution to evolve in response to changing conditions. In particular, there was the widespread convertibility of currencies following 1958, the increased freedom of capital movements between the market-oriented economies of the world, the need to provide greater liquidity for the short-term balances that were more subject to temporary movements in response to speculative developments, and the new tool to cope with these developments that took the form of standby borrowing facilities for the IMF. These were provided by the more industrialized countries for use by the group of countries pledging the supplementary resources. There are safeguards surrounding the use of the facilities. However, subject to these, a country facing downward pressures on its exchange rate, the prospect of a temporary withdrawal of foreign balances, and the prospect of a loss of gold reserves in response to speculative pressures may obtain the currency that is needed through the IMF facility to supply to the foreign exchange market as a means of mitigating the downward pressure on its own currency. In utilizing such stand-by facilities, the more industrialized countries can avoid some losses of gold reserves and the withdrawal and reduced liquidity of short-term liabilities to foreigners that might otherwise follow in response to speculative developments in the foreign exchange and international financial markets. In this way, in turn, the industrialized countries in cooperation with the IMF can assure the world of a supply of more liquid balances with which to support transactions arising from foreign trade.

References

1. See the references in footnote 2 (Chap. 6) and the references in Halm, "Fixed or Flexible Exchange Rates?" as cited in that footnote.

See also "Exchange Rates and Payments Restrictions," *Annual Report of the Executive Directors for the Fiscal Year Ended April 30, 1962* (Washington, D.C.: International Monetary Fund, 1962), pp. 55-69; and *Hearings: Outlook for United States Balance of Payments* (Washington, D.C.: U.S. Government Printing Office, 1963), pp. 116-121 and 174-198.

2. See the statement of Hon. Robert V. Roosa, Undersecretary of the Treasury for Monetary Affairs, in *Hearings* . . . (cited in footnote 1), p. 118.

3. See dialogue in *Hearings* . . . (cited in footnote 1), pp. 184-185.

4. See dialogue in *Hearings* . . . (cited in footnote 1), p. 182.

5. See *Annual Report* (cited in footnote 1), p. 59-60.

6. Egon Sohmen, *International Monetary Policy and the Foreign Exchanges*, Special Papers in International Economics, No. 4 (Princeton University: International Finance Section, Department of Economics, 1963), p. 5.

7. *Annual Report* (cited in reference 1), pp. 63-64.

8. *Ibid.*, p. 63.

9. *Ibid.*, pp. 64-66.

10. See *The World Bank: Policies and Operations* (Washington, D.C.: International Bank for Reconstruction and Development, 1957). See also Geoffrey M. Wilson, "World Bank Operations," *The Fund and Bank Review: Finance and Development*, June 1964, pp. 15-25.

11. *The World Bank: Policies and Operations* (Washington, D.C.: International Bank for Reconstruction and Development, 1957), p. 22.

12. It may be noted that Congressional action in 1949 amended the National Banking Act and the Bretton Woods Agreements Act in order to facilitate the Bank's marketing activities:

"The amendment to the National Bank Act permits national banks and state member banks of the Federal Reserve System to deal in and underwrite securities issued by the Bank up to 10% of their unimpaired paid-in capital stock and unimpaired surplus, provided those securities are at the time eligible for purchase by national banks for their own account. Pursuant to a ruling by the U.S. Comptroller of the Currency, Bank bonds are eligible for purchase by national banks for their own account up to 10% of their capital and surplus and are also eligible as security for U.S. Government deposits. The amendment to the Bretton Woods Agreements Act exempts securities issued or guaranteed by the Bank from certain provisions of the Securities Act of 1933 and the Securities Exchange Act of 1934, in effect according them the same general treatment under these Acts as United States Government, state and municipal bonds" (*Ibid.*, pp. 94-95).

23

United States Payments Deficits (Surpluses) and International Liquidity

> Nobody could ever have conceived of a more absurd waste of human resources than to dig gold in distant corners of the earth for the sole purpose of transporting it and reburying it immediately afterwards in other deep holes, especially excavated to receive it and heavily guarded to protect it. The history of human institutions, however, has a logic of its own (Robert Triffin, *Gold and the Dollar Crisis* [Yale University Press, 1960]).

The balance of payments and short-term capital and gold flows played a prominent role in the history and theory of central banking prior to the 1930's. Following the 1920's and the breakdown of the particular monetary arrangements of that decade, however, there was a predominating tendency for central bankers, in cooperating with national treasuries and governments, to focus almost solely on purely domestic economic goals, and later on the problem of war finance. They did this in almost complete isolation from any consideration of the monetary problems and economic conditions of other countries. In the World War II years there was the problem of planning for the future, but the plans, their implementation in early postwar years, and world conditions still permitted a routine consideration of the national goals of monetary policy in isolation from problems of gold flows and short-term capital movements among nations.

The later post-World War II years, however, revealed a fulfillment in some degree of the plans made for the future. The discipline imposed by the presence of convertible currencies and gold flows, and the need to consider balance of payments conditions in attempting to achieve national economic goals, all came to more nearly resemble the conditions of the mid-1920's or pre-World War I days than those of the 1930's and years of post-World War II adjustment.

Still, there were important differences in the payments mechanism and the arrangements for monetary cooperation and trade in the world of the late 1950's and early 1960's as contrasted with that of the 1920's, or even earlier. The resulting monetary mechanism of post-World War II years was viewed as being somewhat less than fully automatic. Nonetheless, in these later post-World War II years, currencies became more fully convertible, short-term capital and gold flows showed a responsiveness to interest rate differentials in respective countries, and exports and imports showed a greater sensitivity to changes in price level differentials between respective countries. The old disciplines once imposed by the gold standard mechanism on domestic policies with respect to price level and interest rate changes returned in varying degrees.

The pressure of these latter restraints, on the framework within which domestic monetary and fiscal policies could be considered, became especially evident to the United States in the late 1950's and early 1960's, paralleling a series of payments deficits and gold losses, and some occasional speculation against the strength of the dollar. The problems with respect to United States payments deficits were compounded by the role of the United States as a world banker, the rising competition for exports by Japan and some countries of Western Europe, and the prospect for further growth in the capacity of Western Europe to sell in competitive markets through the development of a common European market and the like. In particular, there was the need for the United States to reconsider the prospects of a combination of domestic goals and those concerning the United States balance of payments. There was also a need to examine clearly the implications of the United States' role as a world banker, to improve the functioning of the payments mechanism, to develop and reconstruct central banking arrangements for dealing with unstabilizing gold and short-term capital flows, and to examine the prospect of adequate growth in international liquidity in relationship to a growing volume of world trade.

As anticipated by these remarks, this chapter outlines the developments in the United States balance of payments over the post-World War II years (Sect. 23.1) to indicate the problems relating to United States deficits over the years 1958-1963, in particular, and sets forth a list of the theraputic measures advanced as possible solutions to the problems (Sect. 23.2). Beyond this, the chapter deals with specific aspects of the problems and their solutions under several additional topics: payments deficits, a key currency, and the dollar (Sect. 23.3); payments deficits, the United States competitive position, and the role of monetary policy (Sect. 23.4); central banking and the means of stabilizing short-term capital and gold flows (Sect. 23.5); and the long-run problem of maintaining adequate international liquidity (Scct. 23.6).

Payments deficits have a way of effecting discipline that result in payments surpluses, under reasonably well-functioning international trade and financial arrangements. The portions of the present chapter emphasizing problems concerning a payments deficit, consequently, should be viewed as a case—a case about how a modern industrial economy (and a key currency country, in particular) faces a series of deficits. Knowledge of the mechanics for dealing with a deficit, with special allowance for the special role of a key currency country, should be educational even when a given country is no longer facing a deficit. The present chapter should be read with this latter point of view in mind.

23.1. United States Balance of Payments: Postwar Developments

The United States has experienced several distinct periods of disequilibria in the postwar years 1946-1963. These are the periods 1946-1949, 1950-1956, 1957, 1958-1960, and 1961-1963, inclusively. They are presently viewed in terms of the over-all balance (and the financing of the over-all surplus or deficit) as set forth in Table 21-1. The periods encompassing the years in question are reflected in Table 23-1 in terms of the over-all surplus or deficit and the financing involved.

Payments surpluses, 1946-1949. In the years 1946-1949, most of the more highly industrialized nations were attempting to rebuild a wartorn world. The United States was the only major nation in this world with sufficient industrial capacity to supply essential domestic needs and at the same time facilitate recovery elsewhere. The net export of goods and services by the United States over the four-year period was considerable. Nonmilitary grants, such as those under the European Recovery Program (i.e., the Marshall Plan), and long-term loans by the United States government facilitated the purchase of over two-thirds of the net exports of goods and services. After the allowance for minor sources of funds and apart from the American IMF position, a net payments surplus of 7,010 million dollars was financed by the inflow of foreign gold amounting to 4,479 million dollars and a net reduction in United States liquid liabilities of 1,059 million. This meant that the rest of the world had given up gold, short-term securities, and bank balances in order to acquire needed dollars for purchases from the United States. The net acquisition of gold also meant that the United States had further enlarged the monetary reserves with which to support an increased volume of short-term liabilities to foreigners in the future.

Payments deficits, 1950-1956. The United States balance of payments revealed an extremely large deficit of 3,580 million dollars in 1950, and such deficits continued in varying and smaller amounts throughout the seven-year period of 1950-1956. The deficit in 1950 largely reflected a

Table 23-1. United States Balance of Payments Over the Post-World War II Years

(In millions of dollars)

			Financing		
		Changes in Liquid	*Changes in United States Monetary Reserve Assets (Decrease −)*		
Year	*Over-All Surplus or Deficit (−)* *	*United States Liabilities (Increase −)*	*Gold*	*Convertible Currencies*	*IMF Position* **
1946	1,261	638	623	0	(†)
1947	4,567	1,252	2,162	0	1,153
1948	1,005	−731	1,530	0	206
1949	175	−91	164	0	102
1950	−3,580	−1,822	−1,743	0	−15
1951	−301	−338	53	0	−20
1952	−1,046	−1,461	379	0	36
1953	−2,152	−896	−1,161	0	−95
1954	−1,550	−1,070	−298	0	−182
1955	−1,145	−963	−41	0	−141
1956	−935	−1,804	306	0	563
1957	520	−645	798	0	367
1958	−3,529	−1,237	−2,275	0	−17
1959	−3,743	−2,708	−1,075	0	40
1960	−3,881	−1,738	−1,702	0	−441
1961	−2,370	−1,764	−857	0	135
1962	−2,186	−653	−890	−17	−626
1963	−2,666	−2,282	−461	113	−30

* Over-all surplus or deficit (−) is defined in Table 21-1.

** The IMF position is the net position of the United States at the IMF. It measures the amount the United States may draw essentially automatically from the Fund (Sect. 22.1), after allowing for the IMF's holdings of dollars.

† Not applicable.

SOURCE OF DATA: U.S. Department of Commerce.

drop in the flow of merchandise exports and a rise in merchandise imports. These extreme changes were in response to two major events: (1) currency devaluations in the fall of 1949 effected by foreign governments—most by 30 per cent—and (2) the outbreak of the Korean War in the summer of 1950.

The first event had effects that caused both a rise in merchandise imports and a decline in merchandise exports. The currency devaluations in effect made foreign goods less expensive to domestic buyers and the United States goods more expensive to foreign buyers. The second event, on the other hand, contributed initially to a speculative rush for materials by the United States. The foreign governments also needed American materials, but they were more restricted by foreign import and exchange controls effected earlier by the foreign governments.

The effects of the Korean War were to diminish. Those of the currency devaluations were to persist in helping the foreign governments achieve more favorable payments positions. Furthermore, there had been some improvement in the productive capacities of the foreign economies, in a world full of cold war tensions United States military expenditures abroad rose in 1950, and the average of the net flows of private long-term investment expenditures abroad more than doubled over the seven-year period. The net effects of these events on the United States payments position was deficits as shown in Table 23-1. These deficits were financed mainly by an increase in United States liquid liabilities and some reduction in gold. The increase in United States liquid liabilities provided a means of payment for effecting a growing volume of trade; the gold losses, too, added to the monetary reserves of other countries.

A year of surplus, 1957. The year 1957 resulted in the only United States payments surplus for a single year in the 1950's. This was ultimately the result of the Suez Canal Crisis and the ensuing foreign purchases from the United States, in the first part of the year, of crude oil, petroleum products, and other basic commodities. The foreign countries more than offset this payments surplus of 520 million dollars with gold sales to the United States amounting to 798 million. The extra funds resulting from the gold sales were used to acquire liquid claims against the United States, including dollar balances.

High deficit years, 1958-1960. American exports of goods and services dropped in 1958, which was the main component contributing to a United States payments deficit amounting to 3,529 million dollars for 1958. The decline in exports was the result of a damping of an industrial boom abroad and a return to the usual sources of supply for fuel following a settlement of the Suez Crisis. The exports of goods and services, nevertheless, continued in 1959. In that year, however, imports of goods and services rose in response to a rise in domestic income, an increase in the purchases of foreign steel in anticipation of a steel strike in the United States, and some apparent increase in competition from Europe and Japan from suppliers of automobiles, textiles, and finished manufactured goods generally.

This decline in the United States competitive position is reflected in the following data for exports of manufactured goods as percentages of the total exports for seven countries:[1]

Year	United States	Belgium and Luxem- bourg	France	Ger- many	Italy	Japan	United King- dom	Total of Seven Coun- tries
1957	30.3	7.1	9.4	20.6	4.5	7.0	21.2	100
1958	27.6	7.0	10.2	22.0	4.9	7.1	21.2	100
1959	25.3	7.2	10.9	22.8	5.3	7.9	20.6	100
1960	25.5	7.0	11.4	22.8	6.1	8.2	18.9	100
1961	24.4	6.9	11.2	24.1	6.7	8.1	18.6	100

SOURCE OF DATA: *Foreign Trade Statistics,* Organization for Economic Co-operation and Development.

Here we view the simplest and most commonly used indicator of change in a country's competitive position—the change in a country's share of the export market. The data show a sharp drop in the United States share of the export market after 1957, and increases throughout the period for Germany, Japan, and Italy, in particular.

All of the major changes contributing to United States deficits combined to bring about a deficit in 1959 amounting to 3,743 million dollars and a deficit in 1960 amounting to 3,881 million. In 1960, in addition, there were sharp increases in net exports of goods and services. This was partly as a result of a transitory increase in the average rate of United States government loans per annum [partly in the form of the increase in subscription to the IMF (Sect. 22.1) and the World Bank (Sect. 22.5)], partly as a result of relaxation in discriminatory restrictions on the import of American goods abroad, and partly as a result of the United States national export expansion program on American selling efforts. Throughout the three-year period of 1958-1960, the annual average flows for United States grants and long-term capital exerted relatively constant effects.

On the financial side, the deficits for the three-year period were financed by net exports of gold and net increases in dollar liabilities. The changes reflected an older institutional pattern in 1958, and later a new feature of the postwar scene. The strong preference for gold in payment for the 1958 deficit was in response to United States transactions with industrial and nonindustrial countries, at a time when the nonindustrial countries used their balances for purchases in the industrial countries that traditionally hold their reserves in the form of gold. The relative strength of the preference for gold on the part of these countries was apparently reinforced by the less favorable yield on United States short-term securities in the 1957-1958 recession. Then in 1959 there was a strengthened preference abroad for the United States liquid liabilities relative to gold, probably in response to the altered yield differentials shown in Fig. 23-1.

In 1960, the new feature clearly revealed itself. There was a relative weakening in the preference for short-dated United States securities abroad and a relatively stronger preference for gold and foreign short-dated investments. These conditions occurred (1) partly in response to the more favorable terms on foreign securities, (2) partly in response to the widespread convertibility of foreign currencies at year-end 1958 and the formal recognition of this convertibility in February 1961 (Sect.

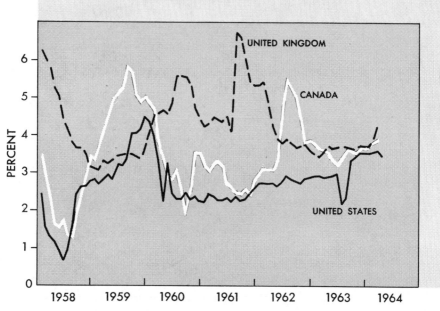

Fig. 23-1. Yields on Three-Month Treasury Bills: United Kingdom, Canada, and the United States.

22.1), and (3) partly in response to the feeling abroad that the United States may, in the face of rising domestic prices and foreign competition, devalue the dollar. The yield spread between British and United States Treasury bill rates almost continuously exceeded 3 per cent, from June through October 1960. After the allowance for the cost of covering the exchange risk (Sect. 21.3) there was a net incentive in favor of the British bills averaging in excess of one per cent. This feature, in combination with the others referred to, evidenced new ability for the international financial system to experience large movements of short-term capital.

Continued deficits, 1961-1963. Concerned over continued deficits, the United States took a number of actions in 1961 and 1962 to improve the United States payments position. Some arrangements were provided to stabilize the speculative movements of short-term funds and to assure a greater liquidity of bank balances and short-term securities held by foreigners and foreign central banks and governments in the major industrial countries. We deal with some of these arrangements in subsequent sections and with the speculative episodes engendered by United States deficits as a part of the United States reaction to the over-all problem of payments deficits. We might note, however, that the data in Table 23-1 do not reflect much of an improvement in the payments deficits in response to any of the actions taken. Indeed, if allowance is made for special government transactions (Sect. 21.2), no decisive improvement was evident.

The deficit position was even worse in the first half of 1963. This brought about some additional United States action and some improvement in the second half of the year, but the deficit for the year was still large, as the data in Table 23-1 show. The actions taken included the following:

(1) An increase in the discount rate and an increase in the maximum interest rate permitted on major categories of time and savings deposits under the Federal's Regulation Q (see, for example, the July 1963 actions outlined in the Appendix to Chapter 24),

(2) A special proposal by the President to enact a temporary "interest equilization tax" on purchases by Americans of the securities with three or more years to maturity of foreign industrial nations, and

(3) An announcement that the United States had arranged a 500 million dollar stand-by facility with the IMF (Sect. 22.1).

The mid-July increase in market yields is shown in Fig. 23-1. There was apparently some "announcement" effect of the tax proposal in the form of a decline in the volume of new foreign security issues. The proposed tax was to increase the cost to foreigners of financing in the United States.

Evidence cited in the 1963 situation as being indicative of future improvement in the United States payments position was a slight increase in the second half of the year in merchandise exports in excess of an increase in imports. This, too, apparently reflected several developments:

(1) Some disciplinary effects of payments deficits on prices and wages in the United States at a time when several major competitor countries faced inflationary pressures, and

(2) The promotion of United States exports and improvements in export financing facilities.

However, deficits continued in 1964 and 1965.

23.2. United States Payments Deficits: Problems and Solutions

The postwar developments in the United States balance of payments revealed contrasting sets of problems. At the outset there were those concerning payments surpluses. The large amounts of United States net exports of goods and services facilitated reconstruction and development in a wartorn world. These were in part necessarily financed by large reductions in foreign gold stocks—as well as American aid—but despite the aid the gold losses precipitated a wave of foreign currency devaluations and the imposition of exchange restrictions on foreign balances in 1948. These latter changes in turn and in combination with the United States demand for merchandise at the outset of the Korean War brought about a sharp reversal of the United States payments position in 1950. Then increases in productive capacity in Western Europe and Japan and rising United States income combined with earlier developments to contribute to persistent United States payments deficits until 1957. In late 1956 the Suez Canal Crisis caused fuel shortages and speculative buying that temporarily brought about a United States payments surplus in 1957. After 1957, however, deficits averaged 3,718 million dollars per annum for the years 1958 through 1960. The 1958 deficit apparently contributed to the removal of restrictions by the leading countries of Western Europe on dollar purchases and exchange balances. The international money market was beginning to reflect a freer interplay of market forces, and the deficits in general brought about a recognition in the United States of the need to enter more aggressively into international economic competition.

The impact of the early postwar developments on many minds was so intense that one frequently heard and saw the words "dollar shortage" and "dollar gap" long after the United States payments deficits become chronic and persistent. The words gave way to "dollar glut" only in the latter phase of the 1958-1960 developments. These brought with them the recognition of new problems.

The problems. The problems relating to the developments in the system of international payments and financial arrangements in the period 1958-1960 were both international and domestic in their nature. The international problems themselves could be set forth in broad outline as concerning (1) the adequacy of the payments mechanism to deal with the greater mobility of short-term balances and the widespread convertibility of currencies (Sect. 22.4) and (2) the adequacy of the supply of liquid balances (and their reserve base) for effecting the growing volume of international trade. The special and related problems for the United States, on the other hand, were due mainly to its special role with respect to the supply of liquid balances for effecting international transactions. The problems centered around the United States ability to compete with other industrialized countries and maintain its share of the growing volume of international trade (Sect. 23.1), and the confidence of others in the ability and willingness of the United States to adequately fulfill its role as a world banker.

Therapy: a list of suggestions. As the current and prospective problems became more obvious in the post-1958-1960 period of deficits, listing the remedies for their solution became almost a pastime.[2] Some of the therapeutic measures suggested, as one may expect, were entirely academic (e.g., see Sect. 22.2) in their failure to allow for the constraints within which proposals could be effected in the real world. Nevertheless, a list of some of the suggestions should provide a perspective on the breadth of their range. Many of the suggestions, moreover, are related to others, and they may be related to several alternative ways. In the present listing we simply distinguish between those that relate primarily to the United States and those that relate primarily to the IMF member nations as a group. The lists of suggestions are followed by a list of the items contained in President Johnson's message of February 10, 1965, concerning his program to improve the United States balance of payments.

Suggestions relating to the United States position in particular:

(1) A use of monetary and fiscal measures to increase exports and restrain the flow of imports (Sect. 23.4).

(2) Restriction of wage increases effected by other than market means to conform to increases in productivity in general (Sect. 23.4).

(3) Restraint on price changes for particular products of firms with monopoly power (Sect. 23.4).

(4) Increases in short-term interest rates as opposed to long-term ones in the United States in order to restrain the withdrawal of short-term balances from the United States without restraining the level of capital outlays in the United States (Sect. 23.4).

(5) Revaluation upward of exchange rates for countries with persistent payments surpluses (Sect. 22.4).

(6) Reductions in defense expenditures and foreign aid (Sect. 23.4).

(7) Reductions in barriers abroad on the purchase of exports from the United States (Sect. 23.4).

(8) Improvements in the marketing techniques for expanding exports (Sect. 23.4).

(9) Faster increase in productivity in the United States (Sect. 23.4).

(10) Stimulation of tourist travel to the United States (Sect. 23.4).

(11) Tie funds for foreign aid and defense to purchases in the United States whenever possible (Sect. 23.4).

(12) Tax reforms to restrain the flow of capital expenditures abroad in response to special tax favors or tax loopholes (Sect. 23.4).

(13) Reductions in the purchases by United States military personnel abroad (Sect. 23.4).

(14) Abandoning the minimum gold certificate reserve requirements of the Federal act (Sect. 23.4).

(15) Strengthening of the United States liquidity position by drawing on the IMF (Sect. 23.4).

(16) A guarantee by the United States government against losses from dollar holdings by some or all foreign holders in the event of a devaluation of the dollar (Sect. 23.3).

(17) Devaluation of the dollar (Sect. 23.3 and 23.6).

(18) A widening of the spread between the gold points (Sect. 23.3).

(19) Reductions in foreign interest rates to reduce the withdrawal of short-term balances from the United States.

(20) Persuading foreign countries with payments surpluses to restrict price level changes by means other than general credit controls (and, therefore, interest rates).

(21) Exemptions from taxes on United States government securities for foreign governments investing in such securities.

The following are suggestions relating more generally to IMF member countries:

(1) A transformation of the IMF into a supercentral bank [e.g., the Triffin Plan (Sect. 23.6)].

(2) A greater use of currencies other than the dollar by the IMF (for example, Sect. 22.4).

(3) An adaptation of key currencies other than the dollar and the pound, such as the German mark, the French franc, and the Swiss frank (Sect. 23.2).

(4) Mutual assistance, among central banks (Sect. 23.5).

(5) Freely fluctuating rates (Sect. 22.2).

Some of the items in the lists have come up as a part of previous discussions, but most of them are dealt with below.

President Johnson's early-1965 program. President Johnson's message to Congress early in 1965 on the balance of payments stressed domestic costs and prices and called for the following (as outlined by the presidents of the Federal Reserve banks):

(1) Legislation to continue the Interest Equalization Tax through December 31, 1967;

(2) Immediate action under the existing statute to impose the Interest Equalization Tax on bank loans with maturity of one year or more;

(3) Legislation to apply the Interest Equalization Tax, retroactive to February 10, 1965, to nonbank credits to foreigners if such credits have a maturity of one year or more;

(4) A call on the Federal Reserve System—in cooperation with the Treasury—to work with all banks to limit lending to foreigners;

(5) Legislation to provide immunity from anti-trust laws for specified voluntary programs, if needed, with respect to foreign loans by banks.

(6) A call on the Department of Commerce to work with corporations with business interests abroad to effectuate a reduction of their capital outflows;

(7) A more vigorous export promotion drive;

(8) Encouragement of foreign investment in the U.S. through appropriate tax legislation;

(9) Legislation to reduce from $100 to $50 the duty-free allowance of tourists returning from abroad, and a "See the USA First" program designed to increase tourism in the U.S.;

(10) An intensified effort to reduce military expenditures abroad;

(11) Continued action to minimize adverse balance of payments effects of the foreign aid program.

23.3. Payments Deficits, a Key Currency, and the Dollar

The term "currency" carries a broad meaning in the literature of international finance: it refers to money balances including deposits. A "key currency" is the currency of a country (1) whose unit of account serves as a unit of account in international matters; (2) whose money balances serve as a widely accepted means of effecting international payments (Sect. 22.2); and (3) whose liquid liabilities, including money balances, serve as monetary reserves for the currency and deposit liabilities of other countries.

The pound and the United States dollar to an increasing extent have predominantly served as such currencies, but the currency of any country could serve as a key currency in some degree, depending upon the extent of such a country's leadership in international financial matters. As one may say:

> The emergence of the dollar as a key currency was not an event planned by governments or by the financial community or by international experts. It was the natural response to a real and obvious need—particularly in the earlier post-World War II period

—for a source of international liquidity that would supplement the limited availability of gold and for a means of international exchange. . . .[3]

Thus, to shed light upon these matters and the special problem of payments deficits with respect to a key currency country and the United States in particular, this section describes the position of a key currency country and deals with the relationship between a key currency, confidence, and gold reserves. The section also deals with the question of the devaluation of the dollar, the question of a gold guarantee for United States short-term liabilities, and related questions, since these have arisen in discussions concerning payments deficits as they relate to the unique position of a key currency country and the United States dollar in particular. The question of devaluation may also arise in the context of the long-run problem of adequate international liquidity. Monetary devices, too, play a role in dealing with various aspects of payments deficits. But these latter subjects are covered separately (Sect. 23.5 and 23.6) following a discussion of the broad alternatives the United States faced when confronted with a series of payments deficits (Sect. 23.4).

The position of a key currency country. A country whose currency achieves the role of a key currency is somewhat in the position of an international banker to the rest of the world. The country has international liabilities subject to withdrawal and in effect backed by its gold stock, but there is no international lender of last resort and an ultimate source of liquidity that is comparable, to a central bank, on the domestic side. The position as a world banker and key currency country, therefore, carries with it quite special responsibilities, which may be classified as short run and long run. This is because one set of responsibilities has to do with financial crises and the other with providing the free world with adequate media of exchange for an increasing volume of free world exports over the long run. In line with this distinction and the relevance of the short run to monetary crises, this subsection deals with the responsibilities of a key currency country, such as the United States, in the short run, and the related need to contribute to the supply of foreign exchange reserves.

Gold and foreign exchange reserves and the volume of trade. From the international side, we may view the quantity of gold and foreign exchange reserves demanded as some increasing function of the volume of free world trade [as measured by exports (= imports)]. Thus, given the stock of gold and foreign exchange reserves (including deposits and other liquid liabilities of key currency countries) as being independent of the volume of trade, a model could be constructed along the lines of our earlier one (Sect. 1.2) dealing with the domestic demand for money balances and the determination of national income. The analogy is not perfect,[4] however, since changes in clearing systems may affect the slope of the demand function over time, and, under current institutional arrangements, the international transactions involving trade in commodities and services are effected in national currencies. Our main point, then, is that the domestic money stocks are affected by foreign exchange reserves; these, in turn, affect the level of domestic expenditure (and income) and expenditures on imports (usually viewed as some increasing function of income). Other points are that a payments crisis for a key currency country results in a downward shift in the supply function for gold and foreign exchange reserves, and that the potential magnitude for such shifts varies directly with the stock of foreign exchange reserves and the volume of trade.

To illustrate the above points, suppose there is speculation against the dollar, possibly in anticipation of its being devalued. What then? Foreign central banks would wish to exchange liquid liabilities of the United States for gold. Thus the free world's total stock of gold is unchanged, but the stock of monetary reserves (i.e., gold plus foreign exchange reserves) is reduced. The key currency country's money stock, as in the case of the United States, may not depend upon gold, but its capacity to support liquid liabilities by some multiple amount of a given quantity of gold is affected. A possibly smaller international reserve base, consequently, would affect national money stocks, expenditures on imports, and so on. This, of course, would be the case of a strengthened demand for gold and a weakening of the demand for liquid liabilities and money balances of one or more key currency countries. In other cases, there could occur simply a switching of investments and gold from one financial center to another, without a general hoarding of gold. This, however, need not cause a general shift in the speculative demand for gold and short-term investments.

As the above implies, a key currency country has some responsibility for resisting sustained outflows from its gold stock and withdrawals of liquid foreign balances. In the long run, it should likely help to provide a supply of foreign exchange balances that is consistent with the free world demand for such balances and a volume of trade corresponding to a relatively full utilization of the free world's resources.

A key currency, confidence, and gold reserves. In fulfilling the responsibilities of a banker, a key currency country must maintain adequate reserves and given assurance of the liquidity of its liquid liabilities. The mechanics for withdrawing gold and the type of crises that may give rise to a run (i.e., a run to exchange liabilities for gold) on a key currency country has been outlined (Sect. 21.3 and 21.4). However, the increase in the mobility of short-term capital in the late 1950's and early 1960's has re-emphasized the special need for a key currency country to minimize unstabilizing movements of these short-term funds by providing confidence in the conduct of its political and economic affairs. This increased response of short-term balances to changes in confidence is why public officials must, in times of crises and change, reaffirm publicly their determination to maintain the integrity of the currency, and why they must on other occasions support their words with reassuring actions.

Such reassuring words, were, for example, needed from the new United States President at the time of the London gold episode of late 1960, following the 1960 Presidential campaign. At that time unsettling words had aggravated other sources of strain on the market so as to contribute to a withdrawal of funds from the United States, and because the expected possibility of United States currency depreciation and possible increases in domestic prices had kept the price of gold bullion in the London market as hedge against such things at more than one per cent above the United States dollar parity from mid-October 1960 to the end of January. In fact, the free gold price rose to the unusual high of $41 per fine ounce—approximately $6 above the United States selling price—on October 20. The market finally closed on that Thursday at a price of $38 —with a spread between the bid and ask price of $37 to $39—only after some profit taking, and partly in response to the following United States Treasury statement: "The United States will continue its policy of buying gold from and selling gold to foreign governments, central banks and, under certain conditions, to international institutions for the settlement of international balances or for other legitimate monetary purposes at the established rate of $35 per fine troy ounce exclusive of handling charges." [5]

Devaluation of the dollar. The question of the devaluation of the dollar arises with respect to both payments deficits on the part of the United States and the long-run problem of international liquidity (Sect. 23.6). Here we deal only with the question of devaluation as a solution to United States payments deficits. Such a means of correcting persistent payments deficits is a familiar one to governments, international institutions, and others. The IMF recognizes it as such, in carrying out its foreign exchange policy (Sect. 22.1). Only there, the question is one of depreciating the par value of a currency. Such changes, together with previous changes of no more than 10 per cent, are readily approved of by the Fund; changes beyond this magnitude require the approval of the Fund.

Such a policy was written into the Fund's Articles of Agreement because the world had on other historical occasions, notably in the 1930's, experienced much competitive devaluation. Under competitive devaluation, one country devalues, and then another, so that the relative values of the respective currencies are unchanged and the country experiencing the deficit to begin with still faces the same pressures on its balance of payments. Nothing is gained in terms of payments equilibria; in addition, the devaluations have contributed to instability in the foreign exchange markets.

The IMF was to avoid competitive devaluation through its assistance to member countries and cooperation among its members. Prior to the IMF, however, and even where such devaluations may take place, the problem is an acute one for a key currency country. The central bankers were keenly aware of this problem in the 1920's (Sect. 7.5) when they exercised a cooperative effort to support the British pound, even though it was overvalued. The complication results because others may devalue when the key currency country devalues, and, according to some, the key currency country should exercise the responsibility of providing an anchor or a rallying point for others to adjust to.

This question of whether there is a need for a rallying point at all comes up in the discussion of fixed versus freely fluctuating exchange rates (Sect. 22.2). If all rates are left free to fluctuate beyond gold points, some natural and presumably realistic set of exchange rates will come to exist. There should be, in this case, no need for leadership. The need for responsible key currency countries would be eliminated.

The spread between gold points. The suggestion is sometimes advanced that the spread between the gold points for the dollar sterling exchange rate (Fig. 21-1) should be widened. This suggestion is viewed as a compromise between a policy of freely fluctuating exchange rates and the policy of fixed rates with gold points at one per cent on either side of parity, in accordance with the IMF agreement (Sect. 22.1).*

One spokesman for this view is quoted as follows:

> I see no sufficient reason why the gold points for the dollar should not be allowed to vary a few per cent in all up and down as allowed in the International Monetary Fund charter. The result would be a greater discouragement of short-term capital movements, one of the most disturbing factors accounting for the gyrations in the balance of payments. A widening of the gold points would introduce an element of uncertainty which would greatly cut these capital movements.[6]

And, we might add, the greater uncertainty would reduce the liquidity of short-term liabilities.

Abandoning the key currency position. As a result of such problems and the complications involved in being a key currency country, some have questioned whether the United States should abandon its position. Others have responded, however, that "the question on abandoning our role as world banker suggests the Wordsworthian nostalgia of an adult wishing he could be a child again." They have suggested instead that "there is

---

* Actually, some central banks maintain exchange rates at more or less than the one per cent margin. Such rates were reported for major foreign currencies in the *Monthly Review,* Federal Reserve Bank of St. Louis, September 1962.

much that can be done through a sharing of our responsibilities with others who are growing up to a stature capable of bearing some of them." They note that "that is what happened as the dollar moved up alongside sterling during the interwar period." [7]

A gold guarantee. The suggestion has been made that the United States could support the dollar as an international currency by giving a gold value guarantee[8] to foreign holders of dollars against devaluation. To do this, the necessary act of Congress would effect directly or through the IMF a guarantee to some or all foreign holders of liquid dollar assets against losses from such holdings in the event of a devaluation of the dollar in terms of gold. In other words, the United States would, for example, promise to pay foreigners and/or their governments and central banks one extra dollar for every predevaluation dollar held in the event of a rise in the dollar price of gold from $35 to $70 per ounce. To the extent that the liquid dollar balances were interest earning assets, the guarantee would be actually better than gold in some respects; it would be "a kind of interest bearing gold."

The suggestion, however, has been criticized on several grounds. For one, the proposal to give a guarantee, and public discussions of such a proposal would seem to admit the possibility of a rise in the dollar price of gold. For another, foreign holders should not trust the guarantee if they did not believe the repeated statements that we would not devalue the dollar to begin with.

23.4. Payments Deficits, the United States Competitive Position, and the Role of Monetary Policy

In the decade of the 1950's the economic strength of such foreign countries as Japan and those of Western Europe grew steadily. Production in the Western European countries grew at an annual rate of about 5 per cent per annum as contrasted with a rate of about 3 per cent for the United States. The growth in these foreign countries was desirable from the United States point of view. Still there were complications. The increased competitive strength of such countries as Japan, Germany, and Italy began to reflect itself in United States payments deficits (Sect. 23.1).

Moreover, there were further prospects of continuing industrial growth in these countries and Western Europe in particular, as revealed by the emergence of two economic groups in Europe. One of these—the European Economic Community (EEC), better known as the Common Market—was an outgrowth of the Rome Treaty at year-end 1957. The membership initially included six countries—West Germany, France, Italy, the Netherlands, Belgium, and Luxembourg—and there have been prospects of others joining. The objectives of the Common Market have been to integrate these respective economies with a target date of 1970 by effecting freer trade, increasing the mobility of resources, forming larger-scale productive units, reducing tariffs and other barriers to trade within the group, and confronting the rest of the world with common external tariffs.

In Europe, too, the European Free Trade Association (EFTA)—the "little trade area"—came into existence in May 1960. It included Britain, Switzerland, Sweden, Norway, Denmark, Austria, and Portugal. This group's main objective has been freer trade among the members in industrial goods, and there was the prospect of continued integrating of Europe with respect to both the EFTA and EEC.

Thus, faced with the sort of competition arising abroad, the problem of payments deficits was compounded. For not only must the United States exert effort to reduce the deficits as they did by moderate amounts of 1961-1962, but there was still the prospect of continuing payments pressures from the growing ability of other industrialized countries to sell in their own and in world markets. Among other things, at that time, the United States effected a temporary reduction of the duty-free exemptions for American tourists and undertook export promotion programs: steps to encourage the use of the proceeds of United States government credit in the United States, steps to reduce military expenditures overseas wherever possible, and steps to encourage foreign travel in the United States.

Competition, restrictions, and the sharing of foreign aid and defense. To deal with this problem, the United States faced three broad alternatives, apart from those pertaining directly to central banking, the role of a key currency country, and means of improving the payments mechanism:

(1) It could get other countries to take over a larger proportion of the free world's burden of foreign aid and defense.

(2) It could effect trade and exchange restrictions, such as high tariffs, and exchange controls with the view to directly controlling the volume of foreign trade and the movement of capital and money balances.

(3) It could pursue policies designed to strengthen its competitive position through the production of quality products at competitive costs and prices.

With respect to the first of these alternatives, the growing industrialized nations would probably continue to cooperate in taking over a larger proportion of aid and defense expenditures. However, due to the prospects of the need to accelerate the absolute level of outlays for economic development and defense, the United States would probably have to enlarge its aid and defense outlays even in the event of a balanced sharing of the total amount by such countries as Britain, Germany, France, Italy, and Japan.

With respect to the other two alternatives, there was actually but one choice. The United States has throughout the postwar years actively encouraged the removal of restrictions upon foreign exchange and trade as well as the pursuit of monetary and fiscal policies to achieve strong competitive economies. It would then be ironical indeed for America to adopt restrictive practices at the time when other countries are contributing to a pattern of free international trade and payments.

In the case of making the American economy more competitive, there have been economic problems concerning the wage and price structure (Sect. 16.3). Possibly these will persist for some time in the future. But, of present importance, there is the view that competitive American wages, in relating to those abroad, would mean a standard of living for the American worker equivalent to that for foreign workers. Those who hold this view may argue for protective tariffs as well as import quotas and other restrictions of United States purchases, but these arguments are advanced on logically inconsistent grounds, if we accept two widely held assumptions: (1) as in elementary economics, mutually advantageous free trade can take place among low- and high-wage countries, when the comparative advantages of the countries are different and (2) the United States has some comparative advantage as a result of the state of its technology and the availability of education. In this case, the validity of the above view depends upon the acceptance of assumption (1) and the implicit assumption of the absence of any comparative advantage for the United States. This implicit assumption, then, is inconsistent with assumption (2), and the view in question is invalid. The full meaning of assumption (2), however, is that the American worker is not a comparable worker, but that he is, on the contrary, a superior technological worker with a greater capacity to add to a firm's production and revenue and with at least a temporary monopoly on the superior capacity. The economic goal then comes to be one of making the latter assumption true of the American worker through education, if he is to enjoy a superior standard of living.

In support of the decision to attempt to compete in a free market, the United States Congress passed the Trade Expansion Act of 1962, which gave the President vast powers to negotiate the reductions on tariffs on broad categories of goods and to eliminate tariffs on many products. The implication of this action and the growing foreign competition are profound. Meeting the competition successfully could result in changes in labor skills and widespread migration of workers, engineers, and so on as they move from less productive to more productive jobs. Possibly, too, monetary devices will have to be used to help achieve domestic goals, such as equilibrium in the balance of payments in the long run, and the stabilization of gold and short-term capital flows.

The role of monetary policy. Apart from earlier suggestions (Sect. 22.3) about the par value of the dollar and the sterling dollar gold points, monetary operation should be conducted with the view to attaining both domestic goals and certain international goals as long as the United States plays its post-World War II role. Foreign competition must be met, and, in so doing, monetary and fiscal policy will have to be directed toward encouraging the mobility of workers, developing the necessary skills, and restraining the outflow of gold and liquid balances at times. The implication is that domestic resources should be fully utilized, and that the level of prices effected must allow for price developments abroad.

In this context, the monetary officials must guard against the danger of an excessive availability of credit and interest rates that would encourage capital outflows. At other times, it must assure the availability of credit and interest rates that would encourage capital outflows. At other times, it must assure the availability of credit for growth. It must also allow for the prospect of rising domestic prices that would produce speculation, curtail exports, and overstimulate imports. Even after maintaining prices at a level consistent with the payments objectives, however, some prices may still be out of line with those abroad, and in this case international competition may help bring about the necessary adjustments.

One important monetary spokesman viewed monetary operations as being somewhat passive in this context, from the point of view of a fuller utilization of resources.[9] There was the view that tax policy (e.g., Sect. 19.4) may provide the stimulus for growth. The faster growth would put prices under pressure, but it would utilize resources more fully, and the prices under the most severe pressure would be those where "grievous competitive problems exist." The logic is that the net result would be a relative improvement in wages and salaries in the employments contributing the most to productiveness.

23.5. Central Banking and the Means of Stabilizing Short-term Capital and Gold Flows

Over most of the postwar period, monetary operations were conducted mainly with consideration for their impact on the domestic economy (Sect. 24.3), and only in the latter part of the postwar period was there consideration for their direct effect on international short-term capital movements and gold flows. At that time, there was some concern over the excessive liquidation of foreign holdings of short-term United States investments and a withdrawal of gold (Sect. 23.1). In particular, at the time of the 1960-1961 United States recession, yields in the American financial markets were below those in some foreign centers (Fig. 23-1). On the one hand, lower yields were called for to combat the recession, and, on the other, higher domestic yields were called for to restrain the flow of investible funds from the United States to other financial centers. In fact, the apparent dilemma confronting monetary officials reflected a combination of modern notions about the effects of the cost and availability of credit (Part VI), the goals (Sect. 8.1) of the Federal Reserve, and the greater mobility of short-term capital among financial centers. Monetary operations had, since the 1930's, come to be conducted more aggressively in the official's attempts to stabilize economic activity and attain the high-priority goal of full employment. There were obvious questions, then, over the apparent choice between full employment and a reduction in payments deficits.

There was the prospect of an inconsistency in the need simultaneously to confront domestic borrowers with low rates and foreign lenders with high rates. To some extent this could be attempted by open market purchases at the long end of the yield curve (Sect. 4.5) and sales at the short end with the objective of facing domestic borrowers with lower long-term rates and foreign lenders with higher short-term rates. But, in the end, some broader notion about the phasing of operations to achieve both international and domestic goals was called for. For one thing, there was the need for the acceptance of at least temporary movements of funds in response to interest rate differentials and the cost of covering the exchange risk. For another, there was the need to utilize means of strengthening the United States payments position, since the United States could withstand temporary withdrawals of short-term funds, if its balance of payments was in equilibrium over a period of years and on the average. For still another, there was the need to develop new tools and arrangements whereby the Federal Reserve and other central banks could cope more adequately with the movement of funds for temporary employment from one financial center to another.

The increased mobility of short-term capital caused the United States and others to focus on an entire kit of techniques to restrain the movements of short-term funds and reinforce the international payments system. These included the working out of arrangements to engage in open market operations in foreign currencies, arrangements for swapping of dollars for other currencies on an activated or stand-by basis, the outright acquisition of foreign currencies to be held alongside gold as a part of United States monetary reserves, and arrangements for a central banks' gold pool. In addition to these arrangements, too, there were other suggestions—the suggestion that the minimum gold certificate reserve requirements of the Federal Reserve Act be abandoned, and the suggestion that the United States draw upon the IMF to lessen the impact of payments deficits.

Open market operations in forward exchange. The entry of the Federal Reserve into foreign exchange transactions was a noteworthy development. The governments and central banks of other countries had been active in foreign exchange markets, but the Federal Reserve did not find this necessary until early 1962. The United States, for its part, had simply relied upon the fixed relationship between gold and the dollar and the foreign exchange operations of others to stabilize the dollar exchange rate (Sect. 21.1). However, with the advent of the greater mobility of speculative balances, the Federal Reserve was given cause to begin such operations in both spot and forward exchange markets (Sect. 21.3). By these means, they may contribute to a reduction in the incentive for an outflow of short-term balances by buying dollars in the forward market, and, conversely, they could contribute to an increase in the incentive by selling dollars.

If the Federal Reserve was to purchase dollars and not lose gold, they needed an inventory of foreign currencies and/or arrangements for acquiring the currencies when they are needed. To this end, foreign currencies were acquired and swap arrangements were worked out—mostly on a stand-by basis—with the cooperation of leading foreign central banks and the Bank for International Settlements in Basle, Switzerland.*

Swap arrangements. Under swap arrangements the Federal Reserve may acquire, or arrange to acquire on call, specified amounts of foreign currencies against a contractual agreement to sell the currency back. At the same time, the foreign central bank acquires or can acquire on call an equivalent amount of dollars against a resale contract for the same period.

The details of swap arrangements have varied somewhat, but on the basis of early practices certain general principles stood out. These were summarized by the Open Market Committee's Special Manager for Foreign Economic Operations as follows:

> 1. A swap constitutes a reciprocal credit facility under which a central bank agrees to exchange on request its own currency for the currency of the other party up to a maximum amount over a limited period of time, such as three months or six months.
> 2. If such a stand-by swap between the Federal Reserve and the Bank of England, for example, were to be drawn upon by the Federal Reserve, the Federal Reserve would credit the dollar ac-

* The Bank for International Settlements was an outgrowth of the financial turbulence of the 1920's and cooperative arrangements developing between central banks over and prior to those years. The Bank was established in the 1930's in Basle, Switzerland, under a charter from the Swiss government, which provides for exemption from Swiss laws, in view of the Bank's international character. The purposes of the bank include (1) the promotion of cooperation among central banks and (2) the provision of additional facilities for international financial settlements.

It is essentially a European institution, and with the re-emergence of the importance of central banking in international matters it should continue to provide services and arrangements for cooperation among central banks. See Henry H. Schloss, *The Bank for International Settlements* (Amsterdam: North-Holland Publishing Company, 1958).

count of the Bank of England with $50 million at a rate of, say, $2.80 to the pound, while obtaining in exchange a credit on the books of the Bank of England of about £18 million. Both parties would agree to reserve the transaction on a specified date, say, within three months, at the same rate of exchange, thus providing each with forward cover against the remote risk of a devaluation of either currency.

3. The foreign currency obtained by each party as a result of such cross credits to each other's accounts would, unless disbursed in exchange operations, be invested in a time deposit or other investment instrument, earning an identical rate of interest of, say, 2 per cent and subject to call on two days' notice.

4. After consultation with the other, each party would be free to draw upon the foreign currency acquired under the swap to conduct spot transactions or meet forward exchange obligations.

5. Each swap arrangement is renewable upon agreement of both parties.[10]

As of early 1964, the swap network included eleven foreign central banks, plus the Bank for International Settlements.[11] The list of central banks, at that time, included the Bank of France, the Bank of England, the Netherlands Bank, the National Bank of Belgium, the Bank of Canada, the Swiss National Bank, the German Federal Bank, the Bank of Italy, the Austrian National Bank, and the Bank of Sweden and the Bank of Japan.

Central banks' gold pool. An example of speculation in gold against its dollar price and the mechanics of an outflow of gold was set forth earlier (Sect. 21.4). They were set forth independently of possibly offsetting effects from any direct market intervention. One potential source of direct intervention, however, is the central banks' gold pool [12] that was set up in December 1961.

The pool was set up with each of the participating countries being given a quota for the amount of gold it was willing to provide against dollars. But it also came to involve supplementary arrangements for the purchase of gold, and both sales and purchases of gold in the London gold market (Sect. 21.4) have been made with the view to moderating fluctuations in gold prices.

The pool is managed by the Bank of England, and its members have included the United States, the Federal Republic of Germany, the United Kingdom, France, Italy, Switzerland, Belgium, and the Netherlands. The participating members initially agreed upon quotas, but the United States made a special contribution of 35 million dollars of gold in July 1962, at the time of the Cuban Crisis, when there was speculation against the dollar. This was made in line with the arrangement that the pool should not bear the whole strain of a general wave of speculation against the dollar.

The elimination of the gold certificate reserve requirements. Under the

Federal Reserve Act, the Federal Reserve banks have been required to maintain a minimum ratio of gold certificates of 25 per cent both against Federal Reserve bank deposits and against Federal Reserve notes (Sect. 9.2). The question has arisen of whether the requirements may cause some to suspect that the United States would not pay out its gold in exchange for its liabilities when the minimum requirements were reached. And the consideration of this question has caused some to recommend the permanent elimination of the requirements.[13] It has caused a minority of others to note that "mounting liabilities against a shrinking gold stock" exert a desirable influence on American policy by calling forth corrective measurres to avoid the restraint on our freedom of action.[14]

In either case the Board of Governors has had the authority to temporarily suspend the requirement; and the requirement for deposit liabilities, as distinct from Federal Reserve notes, was repealed in March 1965. With respect to the board's authority, it has provided for a suspension of gold reserve requirements for a period of 30 days and for the renewal of such suspension for 15-day periods thereafter. There are some technicalities and penalties involved in running deficits, but it seems clear that temporary suspension is not meant to provide a solution to a national problem of more than temporary import.[15]

The repeal of the requirement against deposit liabilities was mainly a response to continued deficits and the need to free gold certificate holdings for the expansion of the note issue, rather than to the need to avert a crisis over confidence in the convertibility of the dollar. Gold certificate reserves had reached a postwar peak of over 23 billion dollars in September 1949 and thereafter had declined to 15 billion by year-end 1964. The Federal Reserve note issue, on the other hand, increased from about 23 billion to 35 billion over the same period, while reserve bank deposits increased only from $17\frac{1}{2}$ billion to $19\frac{1}{2}$ billion. The net effect of these changes on the ratio of gold certificate reserves to deposit and note-issue liabilities was a ratio (as a percentage) of 27.5 by year-end 1964,* as against a requirement of 25 per cent.

* The ratio of gold certificate reserves to note-issue and deposit liabilities for year-end dates, 1949-1964, follows:

Year-end	Ratio (as a percentage)	Year-end	Ratio (as a percentage)
1949	54.7	1957	46.3
1950	49.4	1958	42.1
1951	46.4	1959	39.9
1952	46.2	1960	37.4
1953	44.5	1961	34.8
1954	45.1	1962	31.8
1955	44.4	1963	29.7
1956	44.6	1964	27.5

SOURCE OF DATA: Board of Governors of the Federal Reserve System.

The suspension of the deposit liability requirement dealt temporarily with the restraint on the expansion of the note issue, and at the same time it partially carried out the recommendation of some that the entire requirement be eliminated. The retention of the note-issue reserve requirement, however, satisfied proponents of such a requirement and avoided the need to deal with the question of abolishing the gold cover entirely. The tie between circulating currency and gold is symbolic. Most central banks in the major market economies maintain some sort of cover against their note issue, and they expect others to do so. The note-issue requirement can still be temporarily suspended to deal with crises.

The use of IMF resources by the United States. The question was raised about why the United States should not simply draw upon the IMF to lessen the impact of a temporary payments disequilibrium.[16] After all, the Fund makes its resources available for dealing with temporary disequilibria, and if the subscriptions to the Fund are inadequate they may be enlarged as they were in 1959 (Sect. 22.1). The United States, moreover, should be eligible to draw other currencies in exchange for dollars up to an amount consistent with the Fund's rules.

As matters evolved, the United States entered into a stand-by arrangement (Sect. 22.1) with the IMF in 1963 (Sect. 23.1), and on July 28, 1965, total United States drawings from the Fund had been equivalent to 900 million dollars. On the latter date the United States quota in the Fund was 4,125 million, of which 1,031.25 million was paid in gold.

23.6. The Maintenance of Adequate International Liquidity

The need for international liquidity (as indicated by the aggregate of the monetary gold stock and foreign exchange reserves) is seen as an increasing function of the volume of free world trade. The need for obtaining additional liquidity arises, however, in the context of an earlier model (Sect. 23.3), if the projected growth in liquidity is less than the projected or desired growth in the volume of trade. In such a context, there would be an inadequate supply of liquid balances to accommodate the transactions called for by the volume of trade, and there would be the accompanying and depressing effects on the volume of trade. The inadequate supply of funds for expanding trade may also contribute to a rise in world interest rates and a decline in income and imports. Such a rise in rates would result where the key currency country attempts to raise the rates on short-term liabilities, other than those payable on demand, as a means of increasing the supply of foreign exchange reserves. There, higher rates would in turn influence long-term rates and exert an additionally depressing effect on the level of domestic expenditures, income, employment, and imports.

In support of the projected imbalance between the two rates of growth —that for trade and that for liquid funds—two explanations may be offered. One explanation would be the inability of the United States as a key currency country to continue supplying an increasing volume of foreign exchange reserves, even with a growing use of other currencies as foreign exchange reserves. The other explanation would be an inadequate flow of newly mined gold for monetary purposes and as a means of broadening the base for the growth of short-term liabilities. Thus, to shed light upon these matters, this section considers the United States as a source of foreign exchange reserves and the free world production of gold. It also deals with other questions pertaining to the solution of any prospective problem of inadequate international liquidity. These include the proposal to devalue gold and to transform the IMF into a supercentral bank.

Foreign exchange reserves. An increase in the supply of foreign exchange reserves could result from the growth of the deposit and liquid liabilities of the key currency countries, mainly the United States, to the rest of the world, and from a more widespread use of other currencies, such as those of Common Market nations. Any growth in the volume of United States deposit and short-term liabilities, however, depends in part on the growth of the United States international reserves to support such liabilities. Traditionally, these reserves have depended entirely on the United States stock of gold; since 1960, they have depended on the gold stock and modest amounts of convertible foreign currencies. Convertible foreign currencies help expand the reserve base some, and cooperative arrangements between other central banks and the IMF have become a source of additional international liquidity. But, in the long run, the rate of the production of new gold and its accumulation as a part of monetary gold stocks imposes one form of constraint on the growth of international liquidity.

In the case where the United States may be expected to supply an increasing volume of foreign exchange reserves, there are elements of inconsistency limiting them from doing so. To begin with, the United States received large sums of gold from abroad in the politically unstable 1930's, and in the years of a United States payments surplus after World War II. They achieved a position of unquestioned monetary strength, and, on the basis of this, they were able for most of the 1950's to afford payments deficits and supply the free world with an increasing supply of foreign exchange reserves. At the end of the 1950's and in the early 1960's, however, there was the question of how long the United States could maintain confidence in the dollar as a key currency and continue to experience payments deficits and a reduction in the United States gold stock.

The hypothetical problem envisioned as a result of an increasing gap between some index for the volume of potential trade and some index of liquidity would vanish, if the monetary gold supply would increase at a sufficient rate and/or if foreign exchange balances could expand without an expanding gold base. To some extent, the increased convertibility of currencies means more liquidity, but, to some extent, this has also affected the volume of United States short-term liabilities to foreigners and foreign central banks and governments. Other strong currencies may arise, but, over the long run, the ability of the free world to supply adequate liquidity is restricted by the supply of monetary gold and the institutional framework for effecting international transactions.

Gold production: private and official stocks. The tendency for progress in the discovery and production of gold to keep. pace with progress in other directions in the nineteenth century fascinated Keynes (Sect. 6.3). Since that century, moreover, the world has experienced more than the usual sequence of unique and unsettling events. With the rise of nationalism in the 1930's and the tendency for powerful governments to consider themselves in isolation from others, interest in gold production declined. In any event, gold production was at a peak in 1940, following the universal currency devaluations of the Great Depression (Sect. 7.5). In the late 1950's and the early 1960's, however, the question of the relationship between progress in the production of gold and progress in other things was with us again[17] as a part of the rise in the volume of free trade and the growth of nations whose nationals have a tradition of appreciation for gold.

Gold as a store of value is still valued as a hedge against inflation, devaluation, and paper money schemes. During the years 1948-1963, increased flows of gold into industrial uses and private stocks occurred in four waves.[18] The first dates back to the Korean inflation, the second paralleled the Suez Crisis, the third increase paralleled the speculation over the devaluation of the dollar and the London gold episode in 1960, and the 1962 increase paralleled price increases in Europe and some trading in gold at the time of the Cuban Crisis.

All in all, uses of gold in the arts and industry have been expanding, as one would expect, as over-all operations of society increase in scale. Some of these uses, however, are new industrial applications—the spacecraft Mariner II was gold and silver plated—and the net consumption of the United States in 1961 was reported to have increased by about 100 per cent from five years earlier. As a rule, United States uses exceed United States production so as to serve as a constant drain on the United States gold stock.

The amount of gold that is left in monetary reserves depends upon the amount required to satisfy the speculative and industrial demands, and the level of production. The level of production, in turn, depends upon new discoveries, new economies in production, subsidies, and the price of gold. Large increases in the world gold output (excluding Russia, Mainland China, and so on) in 1962 and 1963, in fact, were attributed to (1) rich new discoveries, (2) improvements in techniques of production, and (3) production in association with uranium. Some of these factors, moreover, contributed to increased production in 1964. The estimates for gold production in 1964 and the percentage changes in production in 1964 and 1963, as well as those from the 1940 peak year to year-end 1963 and from 1953—the year when the post-World War II rise in production began—to year-end 1963 are shown below, as publicized by the First National City Bank:

	1964 Gold Production in Millions of Dollars	Per Cent Change in Production			
		1963 to 1964	1962 to 1963	1953 to 1963	1940 to 1963
South Africa	1,025	+7	+8	+131	+96
Canada	131	−6	−5	−3	−26
United States	51	—	−6	−26	−70
Australia	34	−6	−2	−2	−36
Ghana	32	—	+2	+25	+3
Southern Rhodesia	20	—	+3	+14	−31
Philippines	15	+14	−32	−40	−74
All others*	107	+4	+4	−12	−59
Total*	1,415	+4	+5	+60	+8

* Excluding U.S.S.R., other Eastern European countries, Mainland China and North Korea, for which figures are not reported.

A revaluation of gold. The production of gold depends in part on its price, and this is one reason why the question of revaluation of gold (or devaluation of a currency such as the dollar) occasionally arises at times of a short supply of monetary gold. Gold was last revalued in the United States in 1934 for other reasons than its short supply (Sect. 7.5), but its monetary value has remained unchanged since that time, despite substantial increases in the levels of other prices throughout the world.

In the late 1950's the interest in revaluing gold was in response to doubts about the adequacy of international liquidity. The proponents of such an act of revaluation would argue that a higher price would stimulate the mining of new gold. They would also argue that an increase in the price of gold would automatically raise the dollar or pound sterling value of the gold held by monetary authorities and would at the same time increase international liquidity. The opponents of any action to revalue gold, on the other hand, would point out that the change called for to stimulate production would be large, while the change called for to provide adequate liquidity should be gradual. Perhaps, most persuasively, it would be correctly pointed out that the Union of South Africa and the Soviet Union—the major suppliers of new gold—would be the major beneficiaries of a rise in the dollar price of gold.

The transformation of the IMF. J. M. Keynes said that the IMF should have been referred to as a bank, and that the World Bank (Sect. 22.5) should have been referred to as a fund. Perhaps he had in mind the similarity between the role of banks in granting short-term loans and the role of the IMF in granting credits for drawings and in providing stand-by arrangements as contrasted with the role of the World Bank as a source of long-term capital. Keynes, nevertheless, was a participant in the establishment of these institutions. He originally offered in 1943 a competing proposal to the synthesis of plans resulting in the IMF, as did an American, Harry Dexter White.[19]

Keynes' proposal has been viewed, in fact, as one of the categories of proposals for a supernational bank[20]—a simple extension of central banking within a national credit system to the international scene. Such proposals have been made in more recent years as one means, among others, of economizing gold and providing the world with the liquidity that is necessary for the growth of foreign trade. Among the best known of these is the Triffin Plan.[21] It arose in response to United States gold losses in the late 1950's and the prospect of inadequate international liquidity in the years ahead.

In essence, the original Triffin Plan would internationalize gross monetary reserves (i.e., gold plus foreign exchange reserves). Initially, the parties to the agreement would turn over to the IMF a minimum of 20 per cent of their gross monetary reserves, and would accept instead gold-convertible deposits at the IMF. The members would then be entitled to convert into gold any deposits accruing to their account in excess of an agreed minimum at a guaranteed exchange rate. An excess may accrue, for example, because countries would now use the deposits to settle balance of payments deficits. But excesses may also result from the desirability of keeping a larger portion of gross monetary reserves with the Fund, since the IMF would pay interest on all of the deposits just as countries receive from less liquid short-term investments. Furthermore, the IMF would be empowered to extend loans and thus increase their assets and create new deposits just as a national bank would. They would even purchase obligations of the World Bank and conduct open market investments in the financial markets of member countries. They could, for example, through a purchase of securities, cause a particular member-country's deposits to increase, and thus provide the means for meeting a member-country's payments deficit. In fact, the inflationary danger of an overexpansion of deposits would be limited by placing a ceiling on their expansion of 3 to 5 per cent annually, depending in practice upon the compromise between divergent national viewpoints and the anticipated growth in the transactions demand for deposits.

Under the original Triffin Plan, the IMF would have the essential attributes of an international central bank. Its depositors would be national central banks, but through negotiation this feature could be broadened. It would have a specific legal cover, or limit on deposit expansion, such as that provided by the legal reserve requirement for the Federal Reserve. It could create gold-convertible deposits, through both loans and open market operations, and the earnings from its operations would be available to pay operating expenses and interest on deposits, as the Federal Reserve would to its stockholders. The analogy to a national central bank would seem meaningful.

There would be a number of advantages to the original plan, and some reservations about it as well.[22] The key currency countries—namely, the United States and the United Kingdom—would no longer have to court the dangers or have the responsibilities of having the dollar and the pound, respectively, serve as international currencies. These responsibilities would instead be shared by other countries through processes of decision-making similar to those in the present IMF, only voting power under the new system would be in proportion to the reserves on deposit. And another possible advantage to the United States would be access to drawings on the IMF that have not been permitted as a practical matter.

Most of the reservations about putting the plan into effect would be political rather than purely financial. Some governments would give up some of their responsibilities, but they would in the process give up some of their national sovereignty. Almost for certain the international central bank would be in a position to affect the net foreign investment of particular countries, and they would be in a position to exercise some influence on monetary and fiscal policies as well. Moreover, the IMF would have to substitute some additional form of discipline upon member countries for that provided by the mechanics of gold flows and foreign exchange reserves. Also, under the new plan, the IMF would be empowered to liquidate some of the holdings they would inherit. The bulk of these would be in the form of bank deposits, commercial paper, and Treasury bills previously held in New York and London, but presumably these could be liquidated in some undisturbing manner consistent with the super-IMF's own operations.

23.7. Summary

The United States emerged from the aftermath of World War II with the industrial strength to perform as a net exporter of goods and services for reconstruction and development abroad. The financing of these exports was in the form of foreign aid, mainly under the European Recovery Program, loans, and large inflows of gold. The drain on financial strength abroad, however, led to widespread currency devaluations and restrictions on purchases. These latter changes, in combination with increased industrial capacity abroad and United States expenditures abroad at the outset of the Korean War, led to a substantial United States payments deficit in 1950. United States deficits continued in lesser amounts until the Suez Crisis. That crisis in late 1956 caused scare buying and fuel shortages abroad that contributed to the 1957 payments surplus—the only United States surplus in the decade of the 1950's. This single surplus position brought with it some renewed discussion of the myth of a dollar shortage. To dispel the myth, substantial United States deficits and critical gold losses were required. These accrued in the three years of 1958 to 1960, and continued at somewhat lower levels in 1961-1963. To dispel any doubt about the meaning of the deficits, there was, as early as year-end 1958, a reduction in restrictions on foreign currencies and widespread convertibility.

The deficits during 1958-1960 and the continued deficits in 1961-1963 meant an end to the notion of a dollar shortage as that notion had abounded in early post-World War II years. The deficits exposed, in addition, a need for the United States to re-examine its competitive position in the international economy. This need was even more urgent in view of the likely effects of the Common Market and European Free Trade Association on the competitive strength of the countries of Western Europe. The deficits, furthermore, contributed to a re-examination of the United States position as a key currency country and stimulated evaluations of the present and probable future adequacy of international liquidity to support the present volume of trade and the probable growth of trade.

The United States could have done a number of things to restrain gold losses and the flows of short-term funds abroad. Among others, it could have imposed widespread restrictions on American purchases abroad and on the convertibility of the dollar, and possibly it could have devalued the dollar. It could have reduced military expenditures and those for economic development abroad. The first set of actions by the United States would have been ironical, however, for the United States had over the postwar years advocated for others a removal of restrictions and the pursuit of monetary and fiscal policies to achieve sound economies and increased output. The second set may have resulted in a substantial setback for the cause of freedom.

Consequently, instead of these latter things, the United States Congress passed the Trade Expansion Act of 1962, and there were other expressions of the need for the United States to compete more aggressively in international markets. Public officials affirmed the United States determination to maintain the integrity of the dollar. They also accepted as well the burden to be shared with other industrialized countries in the free world of maintaining military strength and continuing support of economic development in the less industrialized countries.

The changes in the decade of the 1950's were evolutionary, but the return to widespread convertibility at year-end 1958, and the evidence of increased mobility of short-term funds in the early 1960's to achieve better earnings and to be used for speculative purposes, appeared revolutionary. They symbolized phenomena with which the free world had lost some familiarity since the 1920's. The policies of the Federal Reserve, on the domestic side, could be considered no longer in isolation from their international effect in the new setting, and techniques for monetary cooperation were explored. The cooperation and explorations resulted in new stand-by borrowing facilities for the IMF, the entry of the Federal Reserve into foreign exchange transactions, arrangements among the central banks of the more industrialized countries for swapping currencies for use in support of foreign exchange rates, and a central banks' gold pool for use in moderating swings in gold prices in free markets.

The long-run problem ahead was suggested as being one of assuring adequate international liquidity to accommodate increasing growth in the volume of trade. The impact of temporary shifts in the payments position for most countries could be lessened by the use of the facilities of the IMF in its present form, and these IMF facilities could be expanded as the need arose. Beyond this, however, was the long-run need to satisfy the transactions demand for currency balances. The United States, a key currency country and a major source of foreign exchange reserves in the 1950's, was in the inconsistent position at the close of the decade of having to supply balances and at the same time strengthen its payments position. Changing the world price of gold to broaden the reserve base for more currency reserves appeared to be an unacceptable approach, since the primary beneficiaries would be the Soviet Union and the Union of South Africa. But there were other possibilities—new gold discoveries, economies in mining operations, and subsidies to gold producers—and there was the prospect of other currencies sharing the role of key currency countries. In addition, there was the idea of transforming the IMF into a supranational bank with the power to expand the supply of international currency in the form of gold-convertible deposits. It is an idea for possible consideration in the future. However, one would wish to consider it in terms of its effect on individual liberty, national sovereignty, regional and sectional interest, and the efficiency of the free world economies, as well as its being a possible solution to any likely shortage of international liquidity.

References

1. Bela Balassa, "Recent Developments in the Competitiveness of American Industry and Prospects for the Future," *Factors Affecting the United States Balance of Payments* (Washington, D.C.: U.S. Government Printing Office, 1962), p. 31.

2. For such lists, see Fritz Machlup, "Proposals for Reform of the International Monetary System," *Factors Affecting the United States Balance of Payments* (Washington, D.C.: U.S. Government Printing Office, 1962), pp. 216 ff; Jaroslav Vanek, "Overevaluation of the Dollar: Causes, Effects, and Remedies," *Factors Affecting the United States Balance of Payments* (Washington, D.C.: U.S. Government Printing Office, 1962), pp. 275-284; Seymour E. Harris (ed.) "Introduction," *The Dollar in Crisis* (New York: Harcourt, Brace and World, 1961), pp. 2-3.

3. See statement by Alan R. Holmes, *Hearings: Outlook for United States Balance of Payments* (Washington, D.C.: U.S. Government Printing Office, 1963), p. 153.

4. Fritz Machlup, *Plans for Reform of the International Monetary System,* Special Papers in International Economics, No. 3 (Princeton University: International Finance Section, Dept. of Economics, rev. ed., 1964), pp. 16-17; and Egon Sohmen, *International Monetary Problems and the Foreign Exchanges,* Special Papers in International Economics, No. 4 (Princeton University: International Finance Section, Department of Economics, 1963), pp. 18-19.

5. The statement was widely discussed. See *The Times* and *The Financial Times,* London, October 21, 1960; *The Wall Street Journal,* October 21, and 24, 1960, and *The Journal of Commerce,* October 25, 26, and 27, 1960, New York; and Henry C. Wallich, "Government Action," *The Dollar in Crisis* (New York: Harcourt, Brace and World, 1961), pp.110-111.

6. See Seymour E. Harris, *op.cit.,* p. 24.

7. See statement by Robert V. Roosa, *Hearings* . . . (cited in footnote 3), pp. 118-120.

8. For a discussion of the gold guarantee and gold guarantees in general, see "The Question of Gold Guarantees," *Monthly Economic Letter,* National City Bank of New York, October 1962.

9. See William McChesney Martin, Jr., "Monetary Policy and International Payments," *Monthly Review,* Federal Reserve Bank of New York, January 1963, pp. 9-14.

10. See Charles A. Coombs, "Treasury and Federal Reserve Foreign Exchange Operations," *Monthly Review,* Federal Reserve Bank of New York, October 1962, p. 137.

11. See Charles A. Coombs, "Treasury and Federal Reserve Foreign Exchange Operations," *Monthly Review,* Federal Reserve Bank of New York, March 1963, pp. 39-45; and "Ministerial Statement of The Group of Ten and Annex Prepared by Deputies," August 1964 (reprinted in the *Federal Reserve Bulletin,* August 1964, pp. 975-999), pp. 6-8.

12. See *The Economist,* London, November 17 and 24, 1962; and Charles A. Coombs, "Treasury and Federal Reserve Foreign Exchange Operations, and the Gold Pool," *Monthly Review,* Federal Reserve Bank of New York, March 1964, pp. 53-56.

13. See *The International Position of the Dollar* (New York: Committee for

Economic Development, 1961), p. 65; Commission on Money and Credit, *Money and Credit: Their Influence on Jobs, Prices, and Growth* (Englewood Cliffs, N.J.: Prentice-Hall, Inc., 1961), pp. 233-234; and Report of the Joint Economic Committee, Congress of the United States, *The United States Balance of Payments* (Washington, D.C.: U.S. Government Printing Office, 1964), pp. 13-14.

14. See Report of Joint Economic Committee, *op. cit.*, p. 7.

15. For a discussion of the authority and the gold-cover requirement by Chairman Martin, see Martin *op. cit.*, p. 11 and Martin's statement on gold reserve requirements before both the Senate and House Committees on Banking and Currency as reprinted in the *Federal Reserve Bulletin*, February 1965, pp. 226-230.

16. *The International Position of the Dollar* (New York: Committee for Economic Development, 1961), pp. 66-67.

17. See "Annual Gold Review," *Monthly Economic Letter*, National City Bank of New York, January 1963, pp. 5-8; and "Annual Gold Review," *Monthly Economic Letter*, National City Bank of New York, January 1964, pp. 6-11.

18. *Ibid.*, p. 8.

19. See R. F. Harrod, *The Life of John Maynard Keynes* (New York: Harcourt, Brace and Company, 1951), pp. 525-585.

20. See George N. Halm, "Special Problems of a Key Currency in Balance-of-Payments Deficits," *Factors Affecting the United States Balance of Payments* (Washington, D.C.: U.S. Government Printing Office, 1962), pp. 543-556; and Machlup, *Plans for Reform of the International Monetary System*, Special Papers in International Economics, No. 3 (Princeton University: International Finance Section, Department of Economics, revised edition, 1964), 39-45.

21. See Robert Triffin, *Gold and the Dollar Crisis*, revised edition (New Haven: Yale University Press, 1961), pp. 87-120; and especially *Hearings Before the Joint Economic Committee, Congress of the United States*, October 26-30, 1959 (Washington, D.C.: U.S. Government Printing Office, 1959), pp. 2905-2954. See also, Machlup, *op. cit.*, in footnote 20, pp. 45-47.

22. See Fred Hirsch, "Development Aid and World Reserves: A Rejoinder to Professor Triffin," *The Banker*, March 1960, pp. 144-152.

part eight

United States Monetary Policy

24

Monetary Policy: A Historical Perspective of the Post-World War II Years

> The central bank is generally regarded, in some sense, as the conscience or the guardian of a nation's financial responsibility; so that a unique position is found for it within each governmental structure. . . . [Central bankers] must use what powers they have, within the framework of each country's financial markets, to keep the flow of money and credit adequate for the productive use and expansion of resources, capacity, and employment opportunities. They must also give full practicable assistance to the necessitous financing of government. But they must keep the total of money and credit generated for all of these purposes within limits . . . (Robert V. Roosa, "Monetary and Credit Policy," in *Economics and the Policy Maker* [1959]).

This chapter includes an outline of changes in indicators of credit conditions (Sect. 24.3)—all as effected by the monetary officials and against the background of changes in general economic conditions. It also includes a discussion (Sect. 24.2) on the rationale underlying the use of selected indicators of changes in credit conditions as effected by the actions and inactions of the monetary officials. Of course, changes in credit conditions imply changes in the stock of money, given changes in loans and investments, and time deposit and cash drains (Sect. 3.3). But the present emphasis is on the changes in credit conditions that are preliminary to changes in the stock of money or other intermediate or ultimate targets. The present chapter, nevertheless, contains (Sect. 24.1) some reference to the sequence of relationships ranging from Federal Reserve credit to the national economic goals (Sect. 8.1). These are in anticipation of the subsequent chapters concerning monetary policy.

The changes in credit conditions as viewed against the background of cyclical changes reveal a unique economic problem confronting the monetary officials in each of four postwar periods of cyclical change. There is of course a good bit of regularity and repetition reflected in the indicators of economic recession and recovery, but, of equal significance for one's view of monetary problems, there is considerable irregularity.

The present point of view is that of an outsider (as contrasted with that of an official in the Federal Reserve System). It abstracts from the particular problems confronting monetary officials in their search for the right principles relating their use of the monetary tools to their goals. In the subsequent chapter, on the other hand, we attempt to achieve the point of view of officials and others who are confronted with the responsibility of conducting monetary operations on the basis of the right principles for achieving the goals and with the occasional need to defend the principles they enunciate as being the right ones.

24.1. Some Definitions and Relationships

The term "policy" refers to objectives. These may apply to several levels—central bank operations, the money stock, the aggregate for goods and services, and so on. In this section, consequently, we review some of the uses of the term "policy" and outline some relationships concerning credit controls and monetary goals.

Some uses of the term "policy." "Credit policy" or "monetary policy" may refer to credit or monetary ease or tightness, and so on, while "discount policy" may refer to the even narrower objectives, such as discount rate changes or the amount of member-bank borrowing through the discount window (Sect. 8.2). In any case, implementing a policy requires a course of deliberate action or inaction (Sect. 10.2), and by implementation of a "monetary policy," has been meant the actions (and inactions) of the Federal Reserve officials with respect to the use of the tools for controlling such variables as the stock of money and the rate of interest (Sect. 4.4). Often, references to the effects of monetary policy refer to the effects of the cost and availability of credit on total expenditures.

The control over the cost of credit and the money supply operates primarily through the Federal Reserve System's continuous control over the reserve position of commercial banks and the System's capacity to influence the supply of bank credit. Sometimes this exercise of control over the supply of bank credit is termed "credit policy," but clearly credit policy is essential to monetary policy under our fractional-reserve banking system (Chap. 3).

Operational		Intermediate		Ultimate	
Instruments	*Targets*	*Instruments*	*Targets*	*Instruments*	*Targets*
1. Federal Reserve credit	1. Free reserves	1. Free reserves	1. Tone	1. Tone	1. Specified change in demand
2. Discount rates	2. Discount rate—Federal funds rate spread	2. Discount rate—Federal funds rate spread	2. Volume of bank earning asset (deposit) expansion	2. Volume of bank earning asset (deposit) expansion	2. Price stability
3. Reserve requirements	3. Member-bank earning asset potential	3. Member-bank earning asset potential	3. Bank interest rates and security yields	3. Bank interest rates and security yields	3. Specified growth in production capacity

Credit controls and monetary goals. Clearly, from the references to the term "policy" in its general and narrower uses, the relationship between the general credit controls (Sect. 8.2) and the ultimate goals such as maximum employment, production, and so on (Sect. 8.1) may involve other intermediate objectives, such as a given money supply, a given level of interest rates, or a given tone in the money and credit markets. In fact, we may distinguish three levels of relationships in setting forth the relationships between the general credit controls and the ultimate goals as described in the chart on the preceding page (p. 565). Here we denote the goals as targets and view an initial relationship at the level of day-by-day central banking operations[1] between the instruments of credit policy as they operate, and some of the initial set of targets, such as a particular spread between the discount rate (Sect. 8.2) and the Federal funds rate (Sect. 14.2), or a particular level of free reserves (i.e., the level of excess reserves less member-bank borrowings from the Federal Reserve) as dealt with later (Sect. 24.2). We then view these targets as becoming instruments at the intermediate stage for achieving an intermediate set of targets including the tone (Sect. 10.2) of the money and credit markets.[2] Finally, these intermediate targets become the ultimate instruments for achieving the ultimate targets. In the latter instance, for example, the tone may parallel changes in the money supply and give rise to a greater or lesser use of credit by borrowers, and changes in the flows for investment and consumption expenditures, and the level of output and employment, and so on.

24.2. Indicators of Changes in Credit Conditions

The selection of indicators of credit ease (or tightness) is not without complication. Some works imply that we should simply observe the use of the tools of monetary control—the discount rate, changes in reserve requirements, and open market transactions (Sect. 8.2). We have, however, observed that other factors, such as gold flows, may affect the level of bank reserves independently of changes in any of the instruments of monetary policy (Sect. 10.1). We have also observed that the demand side of the market for bank credit may shift so as to decrease the availability of additional funds and raise their cost, and that shifts in the speculative demand for money balances may influence both their cost and availability (Sect. 4.4). We are then left with the alternative of selecting those indicators that reflect the influence of the monetary authorities in the short run, and that reflect developments on the demand side of the market.

As we suggest, the selection of indicators is no simple task, since we are not particularly aided by a chronological statement of the uses of the basic instruments for carrying out monetary policy. Even so, the large amount of detail with respect to the uses of these basic tools and the explanations for their use are of general interest. A chronological account of the actions taken over the postwar years and the explanations given for the actions are set forth in an appendix to this chapter.

Our concern below is with the most objective criteria of changes in credit ease or tightness rather than with the ultimate targets confronting the policy-makers. They may quite likely set their intermediate objective in terms of a magnitude for one of our indicators, such as the Treasury bill rate.[3]

Short-term security yields and free reserves. As matters have evolved, widely accepted indicators of credit ease or tightness have been free reserves[4] and short-term security yields (Sect. 14.2). Free reserves are the excess reserves of member banks less borrowings from the Federal Reserve banks. They are sometimes referred to as "net" free reserves, and negative "net" free reserves are sometimes redundantly referred to as "net" borrowed reserves.

Free reserves may also be viewed as the reserve balances of member banks less the sum of required reserves and borrowings from the Federal Reserve System, and some adjustments may be made in the various measures.[5]

Neither measures of reserves after the above adjustments nor the Treasury bill rate, however, is a sufficiently general indicator to be independent of the need for allowances for changes in some other conditions.[6] As we shall see, changes in short-term interest rates served very well from early 1951 to 1960, but, in the postwar year prior to March 1951, the rates were pegged. In those years prior to March 1951, interest rates tended to reflect a policy of constant ease (or tightness) in both expansion and recession phases of the cycle. And, since 1960, occasional efforts were made to vary the yield spread between short- and long-term rates with the view to achieving balance in the system of international payments (Sect. 23.5). With respect to free reserves as an indicator, furthermore, a somewhat obvious shortcoming may be emphasized.* That is, the stock of free reserves actually held may not be the desired stock under some conditions, such as a given rate of interest and the prospect of a rise in that rate (and, therefore, a decline in the value of assets) by portfolio managers (Sect. 4.5). The analysis is analogous to the early

* An even greater departure is made by a Commission on Money and Credit task force, which completely rejects a free reserve-type concept on statistical grounds. It views the excessive number of degrees of freedom lurking behind the determination of the level of free reserves and substitutes a concept of the maximum earning assets which member banks in the aggregate can hold. See E. C. Brown, R. M. Solow, A. Ando, and J. Kareken, "Lags in Fiscal and Monetary Policy," in Commission on Money and Credit, *Stabilization Policies* (Englewood Cliffs, N.J.: Prentice-Hall, Inc., 1963), Appendix to Part I.

liquidity preference demand for money (Sect. 4.4). There, the relationship between the actual stock of money and the desired stock may vary with the result that the interest rate changes so as to re-establish a balance between the existing stock and the strength of the preference for that stock.

The changes in so-called free reserves, however, may be taken for our purposes as a reasonably good and supplementary indicator of changes in credit policy, and monetary policy as well—after allowances for shifts between time and demand deposits (Sect. 3.3) and such changes as those in the distribution of excess reserves among different size banks and in the level of reserves desired by bankers themselves. Thus, viewing free reserves as an indicator of changes in credit and to a lesser extent monetary policy, a rise (decline) in free reserves tends to indicate a policy in support of greater (less) credit and monetary ease. A decline in free reserves to include even a negative level, of course, may lead us to refer to a tight credit policy—one possibly in support of less credit and monetary expansion. And a constant level of free reserves with the stocks for credit and money constantly rising or constantly expanding may lead us to refer to a constant policy of ease or tightness, depending upon the level of free reserves.

Underlying conditions and an elementary model. In emphasizing some of the underlying conditions that may affect the meaning of a given level of free reserves and the relationship between free reserves as an indicator and money-market yields (Sect. 14.2) as an indicator, we may construct a simple supply-demand model. Thus

(1) $$F_s = \gamma, \gamma \rightarrow -\infty \text{ at } i^*,$$

(2) $$F_d = \alpha + \frac{\beta}{i}, \quad 0 < i \leqq i^*, \quad \text{and} \quad \beta \rightarrow -\infty \text{ at } i^*, \text{ and}$$

(3) $$F_s = F_d,$$

where F_s is the supply of free reserves [or Federal funds (Sect. 3.2)] as determined by the Federal Reserve;[7]

i^* is the discount rate;

F_d is the demand for Federal funds (or free reserves) as some function of the Federal funds rate (i);

α is that portion of the demand for reserves, net of borrowings from the Federal Reserve in excess of the required reserves that varies proportionally with the scale of operations; and

β corresponds to the condition underlying the speculative demand for reserves, net of borrowed reserves, in excess of the required reserves.

Equation (1) says that the supply of free reserves is some constant function of the rate on free reserves (or Federal funds) up to the discount rate. According to the function, the discount window is wide open at $i = i^*$, and the supply of free reserves would become negative as $i \to i > i^*$, although the Federal Reserve presumably would soon effect some constraint over the use of the discount privilege (Sect. 8.1).* Equation (2) defines a demand schedule for Federal funds. The function specifies that the quantity demanded quickly drops off when the Federal funds rate exceeds the discount rate. The real-world behavior of the Federal funds rate in its relationship to the discount rate supports this point (Sect. 14.2). Equation (3) is simply the condition for a solution. The model and its solution are sketched in Fig. 24-1.

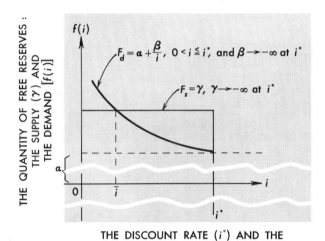

THE DISCOUNT RATE (i^*) AND THE
RATE ON FREE RESERVES (i)

Fig. 24-1. The Determination of the Rate on Free Reserves.

With reference to Fig. 24-1, suppose there is an increase in the supply of free reserves, as may be effected through open market operations. This would indicate an easier credit policy. Also the equilibrium rate on Federal funds i would decline. As this rate declined, we may expect other rates in the money market (Sect. 4.2) to decline. Thus the change in the level of free reserves indicates a change in policy, along with the change in such money market rates as those applied to Federal funds and Treasury bills. Still viewing the changes from the supply side, we see that a decrease in the supply of free reserves brings about changes toward credit tightness. If this decrease is carried far enough, the Federal funds rate is pushed up to the discount rate. Beyond that level, expansion in reserves must be effected through borrowing at the discount window, the demand for Federal funds drops off sharply, and

---

* Indeed, to be strictly formal and avoid the possible criticism of our having defined a multivalued function at i^*, we may simply wish to note that the functions are defined only over the domain $0 < i \leq i^*$.

borrowing through the discount window sharply decreases the supply of free reserves.

"Desired free reserves." Now, discussion has evolved about whether we should view the level of free reserves or the level of "desired free reserves" as the indicator of change in credit and monetary policy.[8] As we

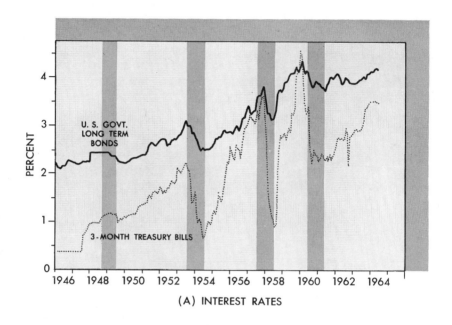

(A) INTEREST RATES

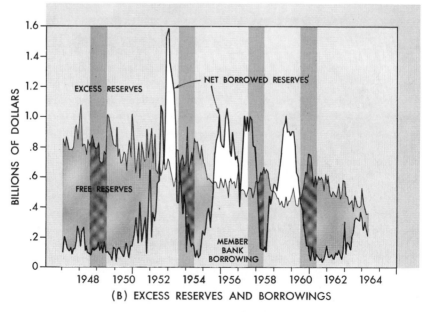

(B) EXCESS RESERVES AND BORROWINGS

see in the diagram, however, the Federal funds rate adjusts so as to relate the desired level with the level of free reserves. If there is a strengthened desire for free reserves (an increase in β) in anticipation of a rise in rates on loans and investments, then the Federal funds rate rises so as to relate the "desired level" to the effective level. The level of free reserves, in this instance, will not reflect a change in credit policy. The Federal funds rate and presumably other money market rates (Sect. 14.2), nevertheless, will reflect this change.

A change in the distribution of free reserves among country and city banks could cause a shift in the desired level of free reserves (a change in α). For example, if country banks tend to hold more excess reserves in relationship to asset size and in anticipation of currency drains and unfavorable clearing balances, then a redistribution favoring the country banks would cause a small increase in the constant factor (α) for bank cash. This redistribution would in turn have the effect of raising the demand for free reserves and the rate on Federal funds. Such a redistribution would not be a frequent or routine occurrence, but some anticipated such a possibility as a result of the inclusion of vault cash as a part of legal reserves in 1960 (Sect. 8.2). Others questioned the significance of the hypothesis that small banks tended to hold a larger cushion against a cash drain in relationship to their asset size. In any event, one clearly notes the manner in which changes in underlying conditions may alter the extent to which a change in free reserves indicates the degree of ease or tightness in monetary policy. One also observes in Fig. 24-1 the interaction between changes in the level of free reserves, the desired level of free reserves, and the use of money market rates of interest as indicators of credit and monetary policy.

The indicators: an empirical illustration. This interrelationship between the money market rates and the level of free reserves is illustrated empirically in Fig. 24-2. There, one observes changes over the postwar years in the level of excess reserves, borrowings from the Federal Reserve, excess reserves less borrowings (i.e., free reserves), and the Treasury bill rate. Note, when free reserves are positive, that the bill rate is

---

Fig. 24-2. Excess Reserves, Borrowing, and Interest Rates: Indicators of Changes in Monetary Policy. The shaded areas in the illustration correspond to the reference dates for cyclical change as reported by the National Bureau of Economic Research. The series are based on average yields. For three-month bills (taxable), the yields are averages of yields on new issues during monthly periods. For long-term bonds (taxable), they are averages of daily figures for marketable $2\frac{1}{2}$ per cent bonds as follows: prior to April 1952, those due or callable after 15 years; from April 1952 through September 1955, first callable after 12 years; and from October 1955 through November 1957, those due or callable in 10 to 20 years. Beginning December 1957, the long-term yields are averages of daily figures for bonds (taxable) maturing or callable in ten years or more. Source of data: Board of Governors of the Federal Reserve System.

down; when free reserves are negative, the bill rate is up; and, when free reserves remain unchanged, the bill rate tends to move about a constant level. Thus—with reference to these indicators of changes in credit conditions, an outline of domestic economic conditions (Sect. 24.3), and balance of payments conditions (Sect. 23.1)—the next section (Sect. 24.3) describes post-World War II credit policy and the special problems confronting the monetary officials.

24.3. Credit Policy: Experiences Since 1946

Changes in credit policy may now be briefly described with reference to changes in the postwar setting of economic conditions as shown below. The description of the changes with respect to credit ease or tightness proceeds in terms of the variables pertaining to the vertical and horizontal axes in Fig. 24-1. The use of these variables as general indicators of changes in credit policy facilitates abstraction from the detailed uses of the more basic instruments of monetary policy, the purpose behind their use, and the timing of the actions taken.

The background of postwar developments against which we wish to view policy changes has included an early postwar expansion, the 1948-1949 recession, the upturn preceding and including the period of the Korean episode, the 1953-1954 recession, the substantial boom succeeding the 1953-1954 recession, the 1957-1958 recession, the succeeding recovery, the mild and brief recession of 1960-1961, and the weak boom immediately succeeding the 1960-1961 recession. These changes are all reflected in the selected economic indicators and the National Bureau reference dates for cyclical change as shown in Fig. 24-3. The particular indicators shown are those that would correspond in varying degrees to the key variables focused upon in earlier national income analysis (Sect. 15.2)—namely GNP, employment, production, and purchasing power. Any smooth and strictly repetitious sets of cyclical changes in the data, as may be expected from a highly abstract analysis of such changes, however, are marred by the varying degrees of correspondence between the job qualifications of the unemployed and the qualifications sought to fill job openings (Sect. 15.1), changes in the spread between domestic and foreign price levels (Sect. 6.3), military events, irregular shifts in underlying expectations, and institutional practices with respect to the use of credit controls, restrictions on the proper wage and price behavior in the labor and product markets, and the settlement of wage-price disputes (Sect. 16.3). These would include a whole host of special developments, such as the entry of the United States in the Korean War in June 1950, as reflected in the advance in prices in the second half of 1950, and the lengthy steel strike from mid-June to early November 1959,

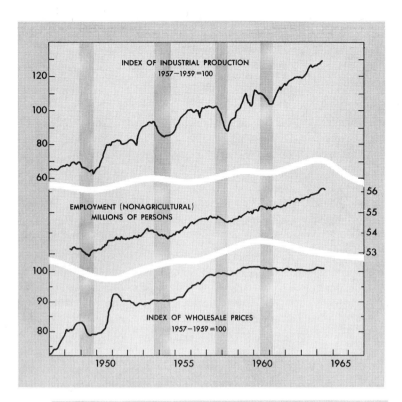

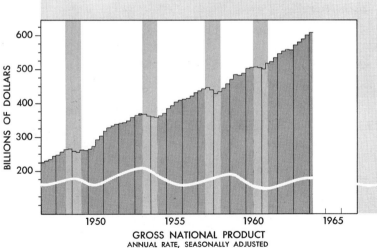

GROSS NATIONAL PRODUCT
ANNUAL RATE, SEASONALLY ADJUSTED

Fig. 24-3. Selected Indicators of Cyclical Change. The shaded areas correspond to recession according to the reference dates for cyclical change as reported by the National Bureau of Economic Research. Peaks: November 1948, July 1953, July 1957, and May 1960. Troughs: October 1949, August 1954, April 1958, and February 1961. All series are seasonally adjusted except wholesale prices. Source of data: In the descending order of their appearance, the series are those of the Board of Governors of the Federal Reserve System, the Bureau of Labor Statistics, and the U.S. Department of Commerce.

as reflected in the decline in industrial production over the intervening months.

The policy changes effected over each of the succeeding postwar periods of expansion, recession, and recovery reflect a unique problem in each period. In their way, these problems proved to be more dramatic than the routine and recurring problem of providing for the day-to-day needs of the banking system. In the period including the 1948-1949 recession, the problem was one of supporting Federal financing by pegging the yields on government bonds. The problem then became one of freeing the marketable debt from pegged rates and effecting the transition to a flexible monetary policy. In the period including the 1957-1958 recession, the problem was one of conflicting objectives relating to diverse changes in prices and the level of employment. Then, in the period including the 1960-1961 recession and its recovery, the uppermost problem became one of achieving a balanced United States position in the international payments mechanism and, at the same time, providing stimulus for a fuller utilization of productive resources.

The period of pegged interest rates, 1946-1950. In the period 1946-1950, general credit policy was subordinated to the role of supporting the government securities market. This support was effected by maintaining relatively fixed rates on the marketable Federal debt, in large measure, through open market operations. These rates were referred to as pegged rates, and there was the view that a transition to a successful peace-time economy called for such support. At times, however, the relationships between the Federal Reserve and the Treasury were strained over the lack of agreement about the support policy. At the close of the period this underlying tension erupted into open discord. There was no longer uncertainty about postwar recovery to strengthen the argument favoring such a policy. At that time the support of the government securities market was withdrawn under renewed inflationary pressures.

The attempts to control the inflation of the immediate postwar years were, for the most part, limited to fiscal actions, combined, at times, with selective controls over credit (Sect. 8.3). The authority to control consumer credit was temporarily reinstated in 1948, and in September of that year selective regulations on installment credit and loans reimposed minimum downpayments and maximum maturities. The more stringent requirements were relaxed from March to April 1949, but this form of control was again temporarily reinstated after the outbreak of the Korean Conflict. At that time, a new temporary credit control applied to real estate credit (Sect. 8.3) was introduced.

The inflexibility of general credit policy over the period in question is reflected in Fig. 24-2. In terms of the above model (Sect. 24.2) and the series in the illustration showing, roughly, constant yields and levels of free reserves over the expansion and recession phases of the first postwar cycle relative to later cycles, a set of preferences are revealed that indicate an effective and relatively unchanging credit policy. This consistency of credit policy we attribute to the policy of pegged interest rates.

At the outset of this period of pegged interest rates, both the Treasury and the Federal Reserve agreed to the support action. There was the general view that future economic developments were unclear.[9] The authorities as a group apparently placed equal probability weights on the deflationary and the inflationary possibilities in the changeover from war to peace. The prevailing view was that the maintenance of orderly conditions in the government securities market, as well as low interest rates, were called for, although the support policy was said to have been over emphasized at times in the very early postwar years.[10]

In 1947, the Treasury officials, less annoyed over the possibility of "transition unemployment," [11] joined with the Federal Reserve to raise interest rates. In the absence of long-term bonds in the Federal open market account, the Treasury sold long-term taxable government securities from government investment accounts (Sect. 13.5). The Secretary reported, for instance, "About $\frac{1}{4}$ billion had been sold in the last half of 1946. Then in 1947 we sold $1\frac{1}{2}$ billion of such bonds from April into October." [12] The result of the selling program—combined with additional securities that had come on the market to further weaken it—was a marked weakness in the government bond market beginning in October.[13] Thus the monetary authorities reversed their position in these latter months. In the last quarter the Federal Reserve increased its holdings of medium-term bonds by about 2.1 billion dollars and its holdings of notes by about one billion dollars, and the Treasury purchased long-term bonds for its trust accounts. The net effect of these actions and pronouncements was an upward shift in yields in the summer of 1947.

At mid-1948, a special session of Congress was called to survey the problem of inflation as shown by price level changes in Fig. 24-3. This development, combined with the fear that the Federal Reserve's support of the government securities market would be removed, contributed to a rise in rates in July. Throughout this whole period, nevertheless, security prices were supported. And, looking back, the Chairman of the Board of Governors described the action as the right one.[14] Even after the 1948-1949 recession set in, a change in the direction of monetary policy was not aggressively pursued. Margin requirements (Sect. 8.3) were reduced from 75 per cent to 50 per cent on March 30, and there was a reduction in reserve requirements (Sect. 8.2) in three steps beginning in May. In the attempt to prevent any change in the pattern of interest rates, however, the System reduced its government security holding by 5.8 billion dollars between December 1948 and August 1949. A formal redirection of monetary policy to permit interest rates to decline did not occur until June 28. At that time the Open Market Committee issued this often quoted statement:

> The Federal Open Market Committee, after consultation with the Treasury, announced today that with a view to increasing the supply of funds available in the market to meet the needs of commerce, business, and agriculture it will be the policy of the Committee to direct purchases, sales, and exchanges of Government securities by the Federal Reserve Banks with primary regard to the general business and credit situation. The policy of maintaining orderly conditions in the Government security market, and the confidence of investors in Government bonds will be continued. Under present conditions the maintenance of a relatively fixed pattern of rates has the undesirable effect of absorbing reserves from the market at a time when the availability of credit should be increased.

After the announcement, the rate on the longest-term government bonds declined from an average in June of 2.38 per cent to 2.24 per cent for August—a decline of 14 basis points.

As recovery proceeded in 1950, the concern over "transition unemployment" lessened even more, and the recurring problem of inflation tended to accentuate conflicting views between the Federal Reserve and the Treasury over the support policy. The central bankers strengthened their preference for general monetary controls.[15] In August, underlying discord erupted openly. On August 18 the Federal Open Market Committee announced that ". . . in the light of current and prospective economic conditions and the general credit situation of the country, open market operations should be carried on with a view to increasing restraint upon inflationary developments. . . ."[16] The time proved too crucial. On the same date the Treasury announced plans for marketing an issue of securities that required support.[17] The Open Market Committee, on the other hand, allowed short-term rates to rise to a level inconsistent with the rate on the refunding offering, and subsequently they permitted rates to go higher. The events during the fall of the year were referred to as a "fiasco," and the discord remained to be settled.[18] Short- and medium-term issues of government securities were primarily affected, although there was also, as well as in other areas of the rate structure, a rise at the long end of the Treasury yield curve (Sect. 4.5).

The transition to a flexible monetary policy, 1951-1954. Monetary policy underwent a redirection during the period 1951-1954. It grew out of the persistent efforts of the Federal Reserve authorities to implement a disinflationary monetary policy under inflationary conditions, and the discord that erupted openly over the failure of the Federal Open Market Committee to provide support for Treasury financing during August 1950. The discord was not settled until after it was widely discussed, in the press, the Congress and the White House.

The statement of accord was issued on March 4, 1951.[19] It symbolized an end to the era of "pegged rates," as the support operations of the Federal Open Market Committee had been called.[20] Shortly afterward, the Treasury officials themselves initiated a clear countercyclical monetary policy.[21] In reference to Treasury 1953-1954 actions, one observer said, "The Treasury proposed to push out long securities, at relatively high rates of interest, when excess liquidity is contributing to cyclical boom. It will borrow short, at low rates of interest, when more liquidity may soften a cyclical recession. Debt management is stepping into the market arena from which the Federal Reserve has withdrawn." [22] In any event, a high degree of flexibility came to characterize monetary policy in the period 1951-1954.

The selective controls imposed upon consumer and real estate credit early in the Korean Conflict were allowed to expire in 1952. The general credit controls over credit were the primary ones used during the 1952-1953 boom—and the accompanying speculation in inventories following a steel strike at mid-1952—and subsequently used to cope with the recession. Changes in credit policy in this period are reflected in Fig. 24-2. There, one may observe the rise in the yields on government securities and the decline in the level of free reserves in the expansion phases, and the early movement toward the converse set of changes in the recession phase.

The events underlying the distinctive changes in credit policy during 1953-1954 call for further description. To begin with, the new Secretary of the Treasury moved early in 1953 to, in his words, "stop the depreciation of the dollar." As events proceeded, he was especially concerned with "anticipated inflation" as a result of the inventory speculation following a mid-1952 steel strike,[23] and the removal of direct controls over credit. Upon entering office he took steps to raise interest rates, in addition to subjecting the market to pronouncements regarding future financial policy. The most significant of the steps taken was a billion dollar offering of twenty-five- to thirty-year $3\frac{1}{4}$ per cent bonds for cash subscription. This occurred on April 13 and reached the market on May 1. The issue was oversubscribed. The bidding was attributed to speculators, and the market subsequently became disorderly as speculators sold bonds.[24] The $3\frac{1}{4}$ per cent bonds went to a discount.

On May 6, the Federal Reserve reversed its policy which had been one of restraint. It purchased Treasury bills in the open market, after having previously left the market without even token support. Finally, as the Treasury's last refunding for the fiscal year (ended June 30) approached, they backed away from the long end of the yield curve, and certificates were offered in exchange for certificates and bonds. These actions were reflected throughout the term structure of interest rates.

In 1954 monetary operations continued to be directed toward stimulating recovery from the recession that set in at mid-1953. The Treasury was moderate in its efforts to lengthen the maturity of the debt, and central bank actions directed toward stimulating recovery consisted of reductions in the discount rate in February and again in April. Reductions in reserve requirements over a period of several weeks ended on August 1. The latter actions were taken along with appropriate open market operations to smooth out their effects. As time passed, the low yield on bonds, some earlier tax changes, and 50 per cent margin requirements contributed to a rise in stock market prices.[25]

The period 1955-1958 and divergent changes in prices and the level of employment. In the period 1955-1958 the Treasury acquiesced to monetary policy, and monetary policy continued to exhibit the capacity for flexibility achieved in the years immediately following the Federal Reserve-Treasury accord of 1951. In this period, encompassing this third postwar business cycle, prices moved upward in the latter phase of expansion, and they continued to move upward even after output and employment declined as shown in Fig. 24-3. The monetary authorities were faced with the dilemma of declining output and rising prices, and they continued a policy of credit tightness even after the downturn. Credit policy was only slowly redirected toward credit ease in November 1957, and then it was directed toward credit tightness as the economy began another phase of expansion in the second half of 1958.

The broad changes in credit policy are dramatically reflected in Fig. 24-2. In terms of earlier analysis (Sect. 24.2) and from the series showing rising yields and a reduced volume of free reserves in the latter illustration, a set of preferences are revealed that indicate an effective policy of tighter credit prior to the 1957-1958 recession and during the earlier part of the recession. Credit policy then shifts to one of ease and later tightness as reflected by the series in the diagram.

With respect to a defense of the continuation of policy of tighter credit, on into the recession, there was the view that "once the business investor became convinced that selling prices next year could always be moved up above present levels, and that investment cost next year would always be higher, the fundamental basis for discipline, and for an orderly selection among alternative investment projects by the action of market forces, would be lost." [26] As late in the year as August, discount rates at all Reserve banks were raised from 3 to $3\frac{1}{3}$ per cent to bring them in line with other rates (Sect. 8.2). Open market transactions continued to meet changing reserve needs and, at the same time, maintain continuing pressure on bank reserves. Then by mid-November 1957 a decisive change in credit policy occurred. The August increase of one-half per cent in the discount rate was reversed at all Reserve banks. The Board's first overt action in the new year to facilitate the adjustment was a reduction in margin requirements from 70 to 50 per cent on January 16. Between late January and early May there occurred three rounds of reductions in discount rates; the rates at all Reserve banks reached 1¾. Also, in mid-February, mid-March, and mid-April, reductions in reserve requirements were announced. Open market operations were conducted alongside of these moves; they kept the Federal Reserve System's portfolio steady or rising during a season when small reductions would otherwise have been in order. Treasury bills were trading at rates of interest below one per cent by mid-year.

In addition to the broad changes in credit policy, however, the monetary authorities were faced with a series of unusual problems connected with Treasury financing operations, as the end of the 1957-1958 recession approached.* With respect to one of these, the Treasury announced near the end of May an offering of one billion dollars of long-term bonds for cash subscription on June 3, along with an announcement about a 9½ billion dollar refunding. Coming at the end of sequence of successful Treasury offerings in the long- and intermediate-term range and at a time when the initial reception of the financing was good, the announcement of the success confirmed the market's suspicions of speculative interest in the financing, however, and deteriorations began in the government securities market before the new securities were physically delivered.

With respect to another monetary problem pertaining to Treasury financing, the turn in the market outlook toward one of a tighter credit policy at mid-June 1958 paralleled a sharp drop in yields, and the initial result was disorderly market conditions. In the first phase of this disorder, late June and early July 1958, the Treasury purchased 600 million dollars of newly issued seven-year bonds partly as a support action. In the second phase of the disorder—corresponding to the July 15 announcement of the landing of American troops in Lebanon, and by another scheduled refinancing operation of the Treasury—the Federal Open Market Committee announced its intention to support the market with purchases other than those of short maturity, and the Treasury switched to the

---

* The magnitude of these problems were dramatized by a subsequent Treasury-Federal Reserve study, in three parts, of the government securities market:

Part I of the study was a report on whether an organized exchange or a dealer market (Chap. 14) might better serve the public interest in effecting transactions in government securities. See *Treasury-Federal Reserve Study of the Government Securities Market*, Part I (Washington, D.C.: Board of Governors, 1959).

Part II of the study was a report on the build-up in market speculation prior to mid-1958 and its liquidation during the subsequent months of declining security prices and rising interest rates. See *Treasury-Federal Reserve Study of the Government Securities Market*, Part II (Washington, D.C.: Board of Governors of the Federal Reserve System, 1960).

Part III of the study was a report on major lenders to, and participants in, the government securities market. See *Treasury-Federal Reserve Study of the Government Securities Market*, Part III (Washington, D.C.: Board of Governors of the Federal Reserve System, 1960).

short end of the market for its financing. Throughout the mid-year interval of disorderly market conditions the Federal Reserve System purchased more than $1\frac{1}{4}$ billion dollars of securities.

However, as the policy of tighter credit continued, in August 1958, the Board raised margin requirements to 70 per cent. This use of margin

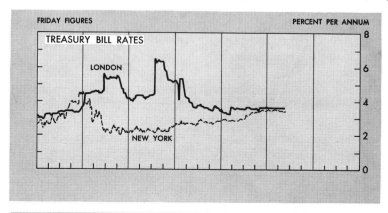

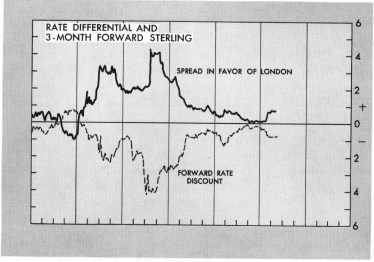

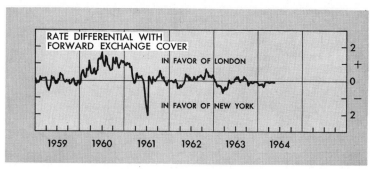

requirements as a supplementary tool in support of a general policy of credit tightness was reinforced by a further advance from 70 to 90 per cent in October.

The quest for balance of payments equilibrium, 1959-1963. Large balance of payments deficits occurred in 1958 and in varying amounts subsequent to that time (Sect. 23.1). These events along with the increase in the convertibility of European currencies and the speculative activity in the European gold markets in 1960 (Sect. 21.3) shocked economists, government officials, and others into the realization of the rising importance of the international economy, and the trend toward freer trade. On the domestic side, on the other hand, the economy had shown a tendency toward structural unemployment and a decline in the utilization of labor resources and productive capacity (as defined by the potential output per unit of time from constant amounts of labor, plant, equipment, and material).

The two sets of developments—the foreign and the domestic—were not unrelated. The increased foreign competition served as a constraint on increases in the prices of domestic goods, and this doubtlessly contributed to some of the underutilization of resources through a squeeze on profits. Furthermore, the monetary and other United States officials were committed to confronting the problem of the payments deficit and the sluggish domestic economy, and the solution to one problem did not appear as a solution to the other. The dilemma facing the monetary officials at this time is emphasized by the spread between United States and London bill rates, as shown in Fig. 24-4, and the arbitrage incentive favoring London, as well as the tendency for the percentage of unemployed labor force in the United States to rise in each succeeding postwar period of recession and recovery, as shown in Fig. 24-5.* The bill rate differential called for an increase in the Treasury bill rate, and the domestic problem of unemployment called for greater credit ease.

---

* The official unemployment data are based on a sampling technique, and hence contain some sampling error. Nevertheless, the data are thought to be adequate as an indicator of a trend toward the underutilization of available labor. See *Fiscal and Monetary Policy for High Employment* (Committee for Economic Development, 1961), pp. 38-42.

Fig. 24-4. The Bill Rates and Interest Arbitrage. "Friday figures. Bill rates, three-month Treasury, for U.S. (New York) computed from closing bid prices, and for U.K. (London) average yield at tender. Forward exchange margin: New York closing quotations on three-month forward sterling, discount (favor of New York) or premium (favor of London). . . . Solid line in middle grid is the difference between the two bill rates and measures the incentive to move funds from one market to the other without cover of foreign exchange risk. Line in bottom grid is the difference between the bill rate differential and the forward exchange margin (sum of the two when both favor the same center) and measures incentive to move with cover of foreign exchange risk."
Source of data: Board of Governors of the Federal Reserve System.

In the period 1959-1963, the monetary officials adjusted to the circumstances. Throughout 1959 they effected a constraint on credit, as indicated by the series showing a rising bill rate and the excess of borrowings over excess reserves. The rising bill rate served to constrain outflows of short-term funds. However, in early 1960, and prior to the 1960-1961 recession, the policy shifted toward one of greater ease. At this time the policy changes called for by the domestic conditions began to move out of phase with those changes called for on the international side. Consequently, in August 1960, the monetary officials instructed the man-

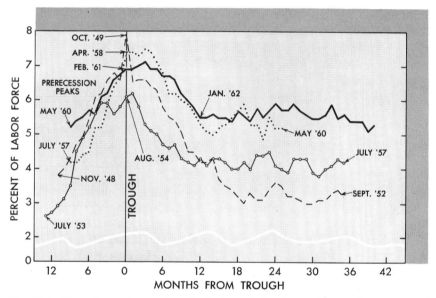

Fig. 24-5. *Unemployment as a Per Cent of the Labor Force in Four Recessions and Recoveries. Source of data: Bureau of Labor Statistics.*

ager of the open market account to conduct operations so as to encourage bank credit without exerting undue downward pressure on the bill rate. Subsequently, they took other actions to facilitate the adaptation of operating techniques to changing circumstances.

In early 1961 the Federal Open Market Committee authorized the manager of the open market account to engage in transactions outside the short-term maturity sector, and in March 1961 they discontinued statements of operating policies necessitating the special authorization for the transactions.[27] The purpose of the authorization was simply to permit the purchase of longer-term maturities and the sale of short-term securities with the view to encouraging bank credit expansion through a net purchase of securities and, at the same time, through the "swap transactions," to raising short-term yields in order to lessen the outflow of short-term funds attracted by higher interest rates abroad. There was the feeling, too, that the resulting action to raise the short-term rate would not lessen domestic expenditures, since domestic expenditures on plant and equipment were more largely affected by changes in the long-term rate of interest. The discontinuance of the earlier statements of operating policies, the authorization, and the market actions taken, however, renewed old anxieties over a return to pegged interest rates. Ever since 1953 and the early post-accord period, the Federal Reserve had confined open market operations to purchases and sales of Treasury bills and other securities in the short-term maturity sector, except to correct such disorderly market conditions as existed in July 1958. This policy with respect to open market transactions had come to be referred to as a "bills-only" policy or one of minimum direct intervention in the government securities market. Under the policy, the Federal Reserve System tended to confine transactions in government securities to short-term maturities, preferably bills, and to avoid direct support for a particular Treasury issue.

The main arguments in support of the bills-only policy were (1) that the principal effect of open market operations was through bank liquidity, the multiple effect on the credit granting capacity of the banks, and through bank transactions in securities, rather than directly upon security prices; and (2) that operations outside the short-maturity section impaired the usefulness of the market as an indicator of market expectations (Sect. 14.2) and economic and financial movements. The main arguments against the policy were (1) that the arbitrage mechanism (Sect. 4.2) failed to operate well enough to transmit effects to the long end of the curve and (2) that there should be on occasions operations in the long-maturity sector to correct incipient disorder in the market.[28]

The purpose of discontinuing the old statements of operating policies associated with the bills-only policy, however, was simply that more frequent departures from the old policies would be needed for adapting operating techniques to changing circumstances. There was the majority view of members of the Federal Open Market Committee that the policy statements had already achieved some purpose in aiding in the re-establishment of a free market and that there was no intention to change the basic position of the Federal Reserve in relation to the government securities market.[29] The old type of policy directive to the Federal Reserve Bank of New York was replaced in December 1961 with two new directives: a continuing authority directive and a current economic policy directive. The new continuing authority directive replaced the previous single directive, except for economic policy instructions, and the continuing authority directive restricted the purchase of government securities to maturities of twenty-four months or less at the time of purchase, rather than fifteen months, as under the old directive.* The current economic policy directive, on the other hand, was to provide a more detailed set of instructions to the Federal Reserve Bank of New York, as may be called for at the regular meetings of the Committee.

With respect to the twin objectives of raising short-term rates and lowering long ones, the evidence in Fig. 24.2 would indicate that operations in the short-maturity sector in 1960 achieved a smaller than usual decline in short-term interest rates, and that the rise of free reserves during the 1960-1961 recession gave some support to credit ease. Even after the 1961 recovery, excess reserves remained relatively high and borrowings from the Federal Reserve relatively low.

Further, in early 1962, the Federal Open Market Committee formally associated itself with the actions by the Treasury to reduce temporary incentives for interest arbitrage (Sect. 21.3) and to engage in transactions in foreign currencies for the first time in a generation. In February the committee authorized the Federal Reserve Bank of New York to undertake transactions in foreign currencies. They were to be effected in the spot and forward exchange markets with several objectives in view:[30] the offsetting of temporarily disequilibrating forces, the smoothing out of abrupt changes in spot exchange rates and forward premiums and discounts, the supplementing of other international exchange arrangements, and the contribution toward meeting the needs of international liquidity.

The Treasury's debt operations also contributed to a partial solution to the dilemma, and they even managed to maintain the average maturity of the marketable debt in 1961. Over that year, short-term maturities increased by 10.6 billion dollars, one- to five-year maturities decreased, and securities in the maturity range of over twenty years increased. The means for maintaining the average maturity when long-term rates were rising was found in reliance upon the technique of advanced refunding (Sect. 13.4).[31]

24.4. Summary

An outline of postwar changes in the policies of monetary officials and the accompanying problems confronting the monetary officials was facilitated, in part, by the use of selected indicators of the tone of the money and credit markets, and, in part, by various incidental references. The indicators, in particular, include money market rates of interest or the

* Another important change was to include in the continuing authority directive any authorization to the Federal Reserve Bank of New York to enter into repurchase agreements with United States government security dealers or to buy or sell bankers' acceptances (outright or under repurchase agreements). Such authorizations used to be granted separately and on an annual basis.

rate on Treasury bills and the level of free reserves. However, one must rely upon these indicators in combination with one another, since the preference of commercial bankers for a given level of free reserves may influence the ease (or availability) and tightness (or lack of availability) of credit.

As shown by our outline of postwar problems, the monetary officials were faced with problems pertaining to the achievement of the usual goals of stability and maximum employment, output, and purchasing power, and these problems were enlarged by the need to achieve other goals with respect to Treasury financing, faster economic growth, and payments equilibria. At one time, there was an apparent choice between stable prices and excess unemployment, and, at another, there was an apparent choice between a payments deficit and the desirable effects of credit ease on the domestic side.

In the immediate postwar years, the economy experienced rising production and prices with the emphasis increasingly being shifted to prices. This was followed by a recession in the latter part of 1948, and then by an expansion of economic activity and renewed inflationary pressures. In this setting, monetary policy was relatively inflexible. The use of general controls throughout the period was largely subordinated to the role of supporting the government securities market. The main controls used to limit excessive expansion and stimulate recovery were those over margin requirements and consumer credit. The monetary authorities, outwardly in accord with the Treasury officials, were able to effect only limited changes in the tone of general credit conditions. The transition from war to peace was successful, but the monetary authorities and their supporters became increasingly dissatisfied with the subordinate role of monetary policy as prices rose in 1950. Consequently, the monetary officials openly acted in discord with the Treasury officials. They effected an upward shift in yields at a crucial moment for Treasury financing, and the events in the fall of the year were a "fiasco."

In the next period from 1951 to 1954, credit policy exhibited a high degree of flexibility. A policy of credit tightness was directed toward mitigating the speculation with respect to inventories accompanying the 1952-1953 boom and following the expiration of the authority to control consumer and real estate credit. The Treasury, for its part, contributed to the increased tightness of credit by lengthening the maturity of its debt and pushing long-term rates higher. The Federal Reserve's policy of credit tightness was then speedily reversed to counter the 1953-1954 recession and contribute to recovery. The Treasury, for its part, backed away from its efforts to lengthen the maturity distribution of the debt and, instead, supplied the more liquid short-term securities.

Credit policy continued to exhibit flexibility in the period 1955-1958. In the expansion phase prior to the 1957 peak there was upward pressure on prices. The monetary authorities pursued a persistent policy of credit restraint. As the expansion phase ended, and the rate of output declined, prices continued their upward movement. Faced with this dilemma, the change to a policy of credit ease came late in the recession. Subsequently, moreover, the expectation on the part of the market of a change to a more restrictive credit policy contributed to the change itself. The initial effect of this expectation was a period of disorderly market conditions with repercussions upon Treasury financing operations. Treasury purchases and purchases for the Federal Reserve System's open market account were both directed to smoothing out the change to a policy of credit tightness.

Moving into the 1959-1962 period of expansion, recession, and recovery there were increasing downward pressures on prices from foreign competition. Also there was a trend toward a decrease in the utilization of productive capacity and an increase in unemployment as a per cent of the labor force, on the domestic side, and there was a trend toward freer trade and increasing mobility of short-term balances, on the international side. In fact, the decline in the utilization of resources and a recurring outflow of short-term currency balances posed another dilemma for the monetary authorities. This they attempted to meet by actions designed to sustain or raise the level of short-term interest rates and provide, at times simultaneously, a reserve position inducive to credit expansion. These actions were also supported by the debt operations of the Treasury. The monetary authorities, further, undertook fundamental changes to meet the developments in the international field. In this respect, they revised directives pertaining to the so-called bills-only policy so as to facilitate the adaptation of operating techniques to changing circumstances, and they authorized the Federal Reserve Bank of New York to undertake transactions in foreign currencies in order to counter temporary shifts in the incentive for disruptive movements of short-term balances, among other things.

The rising importance of freer international trade, flexible financial arrangements, and the outcome of the need to achieve faster growth and a fuller utilization of resources in the United States pose interesting challenges for the monetary officials as well as for policies concerning the debt and fiscal management of government. There is always, too, the extreme likelihood of new and unique challenges arising to confront the American people and their policy-making officials. Those who would like to keep abreast of all of these developments may like to do so by reading the financial press, the economic reports of the President, the monthly reviews of the various Federal Reserve banks, the annual reports of the Federal Reserve Bank of New York and the Board of Governors of the Federal Reserve System, and the frequent hearings before the Congress of the United States on financial, monetary, and economic subjects, generally. The skillful reader will keep in mind, however, the need for judgment and analysis in interpreting the content of these documents. The meaning they convey is often between the lines rather than in the lines themselves.

References

1. See Robert V. Roosa, "Monetary and Credit Policy," in *Economics and the Policy Maker, Brookings Lectures 1958-1959* (Washington, D.C.: The Brookings Institution, 1959), p. 99. The present relationship and the others with respect to instruments and targets follow Mr. Roosa's discussion.

2. "Tone" is synonymous with relative "ease" or "tightness." Roosa (see reference 1), pp. 104-105, prefers the term "pressure" and emphasizes pressure on bank reserves.

3. *Annual Report of the Board of Governors of the Federal Reserve System for the Year 1961* (Washington, D.C.: Board of Governors of the Federal Reserve System, 1962), p. 89.

4. See "The Significance and Limitations of Free Reserves," *Monthly Review*, Federal Reserve Bank of New York, November 1958, pp. 162-167. And see also such later uses as in "Monetary Developments," *Review*, Federal Reserve Bank of St. Louis, June 1962, pp. 4-5; "Monetary Policy, Bank Credit, and Money," *Federal Reserve Bulletin*, July 1962, pp. 790-791; and Edward R. Fry, "Measures of Member Bank Reserves," *Federal Reserve Bulletin*, July 1963, pp. 890-903. The standard reference work on free reserve literature before 1962 is A. James Meigs, *Free Reserves and the Money Supply* (Chicago: University of Chicago Press, 1962).

5. For a list of reserve measures and their definitions see "Reserves: Definitions," *Review*, Federal Reserve Bank of St. Louis, September 1963, p. 6. The various measures are frequently reported on in this publication.

6. See *ibid.;* Milton Friedman, "Vault Cash and Free Reserves," *The Journal of Political Economy*, April 1961, pp. 181-182; and "Free Reserves and Bank Reserve Management," *Monthly Review*, Federal Reserve Bank of Kansas City, November 1961, pp. 10-16.

7. For a use of the Federal funds rate as a rate on excess reserve balances, see *Annual Report of the Board of Governors of the Federal Reserve System for the Year 1961* (Washington, D.C.: Board of Governors of the Federal Reserve System, 1962), p. 5.

8. See Milton Friedman, *A Program for Monetary Stability* (New York: Fordham University Press, 1959), pp. 41-42.

9. See statement by the Secretary of the Treasury, *Monetary Policy and the Management of the Public Debt*, Part I (Washington, D.C.: U.S. Government Printing Office, 1952), p. 53.

10. Henry C. Murphy, *The National Debt in War and Transition* (New York: McGraw-Hill Book Company, 1951), p. 223. See also *United States Government Securities and the Money Market* (New York: Bankers Trust Company, 1946) pp. 11-12.

11. See *Monetary Policy and the Management of the Public Debt*, Part I (Washington, D.C.: U.S. Government Printing Office, 1952), p. 61.

12. *Ibid.*, p. 62.   13. See Murphy, *op.cit.*, pp. 242-243.

14. See *Monetary Policy and the Management of the Public Debt*, Part I (Washington, D.C.: U.S. Government Printing Office, 1952), p. 360.

15. *Ibid.*, pp. 68-69.

16. *See Annual Report of the Board of Governors of the Federal Reserve System for the Year 1950* (Washington, D.C.: Board of Governors, 1951), pp. 70-79.

17. See *Monetary Policy and the Management of the Public Debt,* Part I (Washington, D.C.: U.S. Government Printing Office, 1952), p. 61.

18. *Ibid.*, p. 70.

19. See *Annual Report of the Board of Governors of the Federal Reserve System for the Year 1951* (Washington, D.C.: Board of Governors, 1952), p. 98.

20. See, for example, address by William McChesney Martin, Jr., *Federal Reserve Bulletin,* April 1953, p. 330; Richard Youngdahl, "Monetary Policy in Recent Years," *American Economic Review,* May 1955, p. 402; and Charles Cortez Abbott, *The Federal Debt* (New York: The Twentieth Century Fund, 1953), p. 108.

21. Attempts at a literal definition of a "free market" became academic. The market for Treasury securities was defined as not a "free market," in the sense of the term. It was thought it should be an adequate one to enjoy the "freedom to reflect fully, into market prices and yields, the transactions of the public." See *Annual Report, Board of Governors of the Federal Reserve System,* pp. 84-85; and *United States Monetary Policy: Recent Thinking and Experience* (Washington, D.C.: U.S. Government Printing Office, 1954), pp. 15-17, 83, 109, and 117.

22. *Ibid.*, p. 74. See also *The Economic Report of the President* (Washington, D.C.: U.S. Government Printing Office, January 1956), p. 32.

23. See *U.S. Monetary Policy: Recent Thinking and Experience* (Washington, D.C.: U.S. Government Printing Office, 1954), pp. 208-210. For similar views by monetary authorities, *ibid.*, p. 246.

24. One definition of a disorderly market states that "a market is disorderly when rapid price reductions tend to feed on themselves, inducing further offerings instead of bids, and an element of panic is present." See *Treasury-Federal Reserve Study of the Government Securities Market,* Part I (Washington, D.C.: Board of Governors of the Federal Reserve System, 1959), p. 15. For a longer list of attempts at defining such a market, see Joint Economic Committee, *Hearings, Study of Employment, Growth and Price Levels,* Part 6C (Washington, D.C.: U.S. Government Printing Office, 1959), pp. 1927-1931.

25. See *Factors Affecting the Stock Market* (Washington, D.C.: U.S. Government Printing Office, 1955).

26. *Annual Report of the Federal Reserve Bank of New York,* December 1957, p. 9.

27. *Annual Report of the Board of Governors of the Federal Reserve System for 1961* (Washington, D.C.: Board of Governors of the Federal Reserve System, 1962), pp. 94-95.

28. For longer lists of the pros and cons, see the following:
Money and Credit: The Reports of the Commission on Money and Credit (Englewood Cliffs, N.J.: Prentice-Hall, Inc., 1961), pp. 62-64; Otto Eckstein and John Kareken, "The Bills Only Policy: A Summary of the Issues," *Readings in Money and Banking,* 2nd ed., Lawrence S. Ritter (ed.), (Boston: Houghton Mifflin Company, 1961), pp. 274-277; and *Annual Report of the Board of Governors of the Federal Reserve System for the Year 1961* (Washington, D.C.: Board of Governors of the Federal Reserve System, 1962), pp.

95-99. See also Winfield Riefler, "Open Market Operations in Long-Term Securities," *Federal Reserve Bulletin*, November 1958, pp. 1260-1274; and Ralph A. Young and Charles A. Yager, "The Economics of 'Bills Preferably'," *The Quarterly Journal of Economics*, August 1960, pp. 341-373. The Riefler article is a "classic" Federal Reserve defense, and Young and Yager discuss pros and cons.

29. See *Annual Report* (cited in reference 27), pp. 96-97.

Presumably the Committee statements in this *1961 Annual Report* clarified the bills-only policy further so as to reflect the spirit of the content of a recommendation by the Commission on Money and Credit with respect to the bills-only policy. See Commission on Money and Credit, *op.cit.*, p. 64.

30. See "Treasury and Federal Foreign Exchange Operations," *Monthly Review*, Federal Reserve Bank of New York, October 1962, p. 139. This article (pp. 131-140) includes as an appendix the complete text of the Federal Open Market Committee authorization.

31. See *Annual Report of the Joint Economic Committee on the January 1962 Economic Report of the President* (Washington, D.C.: U.S. Government Printing Office, 1962), pp. 22-24.

Appendix to Chapter 24

Principal Federal Reserve Actions Since 1946[*]

Date	Action	Basis for Action
February 1945 to January 1946	Margin requirements raised from 40 to 50 per cent of market value in February; to 75 per cent in July; and to 100 per cent in January 1946.	Continued upward trend of stock prices, volume of trading, and stock market credit.
April to May 1946	Removal of preferential discount rate of one-half per cent on advances secured by short-term government securities.	Required borrowing banks to pay regular discount rate of one per cent and thereby made it less easy for member banks to obtain Federal Reserve credit on the basis of which to expand loans. Indicated that the Federal Reserve System did not favor a further decline in interest rates in the circumstances then prevailing.
January 1946 to October 1947	Reduced total holdings of government securities by more than 2 billion dollars. Retirements of about 7 billion dollars of maturing securities offset in part by 5 billion dollars net purchases of other short-term securities. Buying rate on bankers' acceptances raised (July-August 1946).	Restrained growth in member-bank reserves (due chiefly to gold inflow) by redeeming maturing United States securities as Treasury retired securities using accumulated balances in war loan accounts and budget surplus. Business active; inflationary pressures were strong.

[*] Source: Board of Governors of the Federal Reserve System.

Date	Action	Basis for Action
December 1946	Removed noninstallment credit from regulation; list of articles under credit control curtailed.	For purpose of simplifying the regulation, making it administratively more workable, and narrowing its scope to a minimum that is consistent with the exercising of a stabilizing influence on the economy. Amended regulation covered approximately 70 per cent of installment credit.
February 1947	Margin requirements reduced from 100 to 75 per cent of market value.	Stock prices and the volume of credit in the stock market had been reduced to levels at or below those prevailing at the time of the previous increase in requirements.
July 1947 to October 1947	Discontinued buying rate on three-eighths per cent on Treasury bills and support of certificates at seven-eighths per cent.	Relieved Federal Reserve System of necessity of continuing to buy short-term securities at the extremely low wartime rates and thereby of providing the basis for further monetary expansion. Business activity at very high levels; inflationary pressures strong. Coupon rates on new issues of certificates raised by Treasury to one per cent.
November 1947 to March 1948	Bought 5 billion dollars of Treasury bonds.	Bought large amounts of Treasury bonds in November and December to stem decline in bond prices. Dropped buying prices in late December to levels slightly above par. Bought bonds thereafter to maintain these price levels.
	Sold or redeemed over 6 billion dollars of short-term government securities. Buying rate on bankers' acceptances raised (December 1947—January 1948).	Sold or redeemed short-term Treasury securities, partly to offset effect on bank reserves of bond purchases and continued gold inflow, in the effort to restrain the growth in bank credit. Inflationary pressures continued strong. Short-term rates rose further.

Date	Action	Basis for Action
November 1947	Joint statement by bank supervisory authorities.	Urged banks to avoid making nonessential loans in view of inflationary conditions. Statement was followed by action by American Bankers Association to arrange bankers' meetings in various parts of the country early in 1948 to urge avoidance of unnecessary or undesirable extension of credit.
January 1948 to August 1948	Buying rate on bankers' acceptances raised (August). Raised discount rate from one to 1½ per cent at all banks.	Part of an antiinflationary program designed to keep pressure on member-bank reserves and thereby to restrain expansion of bank credit and at the same time continue the policy of stabilizing the long-term rate on government bonds.
February 1948 to September 1948	Bought 2 billion dollars of government securities in September including 1.5 billion dollars of bonds and .5 billion dollars of bills, certificates, and notes. Raised reserve requirements on demand deposits from 20 to 26 per cent at central Reserve city banks; 20 to 22 per cent at Reserve city; and 14 to 16 per cent at country banks; on time deposits from 6 to 7½ per cent at all banks.	Reserve requirement action to help absorb additional reserves made available by gold inflow and by Federal Reserve purchases in support of the market for government securities. Congress provided authority (until June 30, 1949) for increases in reserve requirements above those otherwise authorized. Securities purchased in open market to maintain the stability of the market and to assist temporarily in the adjustment of member banks to increased reserve requirements.
September 1948	On installment credit for a list of consumer durable goods reimposed downpayment of 20 to 33⅓ per cent; maximum maturity fifteen to eighteen months; same maturity on installment loans.	Congress restored (until June 30, 1949) board's authority to regulate consumer credit, which it had terminated in November 1947. Consumer installment credit was expanding at a rate of 2 billion dollars a year; this growth was contributing to inflationary pressures. Regulation as re-established af-

Date	*Action*	*Basis for Action*
		fected about 70 per cent of consumer installment credit.
March 1949	Margin requirements reduced from 75 to 50 per cent of market value.	Stock market credit outstanding was close to the lowest level on record. Stock prices declining and volume of trading low. Equity financing of business small.
March 1949 to April 1949	On consumer installment credit reduced downpayment to 10 per cent (except on autos); increased maturity to twenty-four months on all listed articles.	Consumer buying pressures had moderated significantly many commodities covered by regulation in larger supply; consumer installment credit expanding less rapidly than formerly; general inflationary pressures had abated somewhat.
May 1949 to September 1949	Reduced reserve requirements on demand deposits by 4 percentage points; on time deposits by $2\frac{1}{2}$ percentage points. Changes in several steps.	Recession in business and prices. Credit policy aimed at encouraging a high level of business activity, but avoiding conditions of such ease as would prevent needed adjustments or encourage undue expansion.
January 1949 to September 1949	Reduced holdings of government securities by more than 5 billion dollars. Sold over 3 billion dollars of bonds from January through June; sold or redeemed 2 billion dollars of bills, certificates, and notes.	To prevent prices of long-term bonds from rising sharply and to meet heavy demands for short-term United States securities arising out of reduced member-bank reserve requirements, net government disbursements, reduced currency circulation, gold inflow, and other factors. More flexible credit policy announced June 28 determining operations on basis of the needs of general business and credit situation and of maintaining orderly conditions in the government security market, rather than a fixed pattern of rates on United States government securities. Open market operations throughout the period consistent with easier credit

Date	*Action*	*Basis for Action*
		conditions, while recession lasted.
November 1949 to June 1950	Sold 1.5 billion dollars of long-term Treasury bonds.	Sales of bonds to meet market demand for long-term securities and discourage overextension of private long-term financing.
	Bought a net of 1.6 billion dollars of short-term government securities. Little change in total portfolio.	Operations designed to allow money market to firm moderately in response to increased demand for funds, as business recovery gained momentum and signs of inflationary pressures reappeared, and, at same time, to aid Treasury refunding. Slight rise in yields on both short-term and long-term securities.
August 1950	Buying rate on bankers' acceptances raised. Raised discount rate from $1\frac{1}{2}$ to $1\frac{3}{4}$ per cent at all banks. Request by bank supervisory agencies for voluntary cooperation of lenders in restraining credit.	Output and employment close to peacetime record levels; accelerated expansion of credit; prices rising; prospective increases in government expenditures for military purposes. System announced it was prepared to use all means at its command to restrain further bank credit expansion consistent with policy of maintaining orderly conditions in government securities market.
August 1950 to December 1950	Bought 8 billion dollars of maturing government securities (August), one billion dollars of restricted bonds (September-December), and 1.4 billion dollars of short-term securities (December).	Purchases to aid Treasury refundings and prevent decline in long-term bonds below par.
	Sold 7 billion dollars of short-term government securities (August).	Sales of short-term securities at lower prices (higher yields) to offset effect of purchases. *Note:* The above-mentioned sales did not completely offset purchases so that the actual net effect

Date	*Action*	*Basis for Action*
		of operations for this period was expansionary.
September 1950 to October 1950	On installment credit for list of consumer durable goods down payment 10 to 33⅓ per cent; maximum maturity fifteen months, except home improvements, thirty months; maximum maturity of fifteen months on installment loans. On real estate credit down payments 10 to 50 per cent of value of residential property; maximum maturity twenty years with certain exceptions.	Unprecedented rate of expansion of consumer installment of real estate credit. Regulations are parts of fiscal, monetary, and credit measures to restrain inflationary pressures and facilitate diversion of critical material and manpower to production of defense needs, under authority of Defense Production Act of 1950. For reasons of administrative and regulative efficiency consumer credit regulation confined to installment credit and scope set to affect about 75 per cent of such business.
November 1950	Banks again requested to restrain unnecessary credit expansion.	Unprecedented expansion in bank loans from mid-year to mid-November. Continued expansion in credit put upward pressure on prices, impairing purchasing power of dollar and adding to cost of defense program.
January 1951 to February 1951	Bought 8 billion dollars of long-term Treasury bonds. Raised reserve requirements by 2 per cent on demand deposits; maximum limits except at central Reserve city banks.	To maintain prices of long-term government securities. Continued expansion of bank credit. Action taken to absorb about 2 billion dollars of funds, largely from seasonal return of currency and Reserve System purchases of bonds, and generally to reduce the ability of banks to expand credit that would add to inflationary pressures. At central Reserve city banks requirements were raised to a level considerably above those that prevailed during most of the war period. To facilitate adjustment to reserve requirement increase.
	Bought a net of 300 million dollars of short-term government securities.	

Date	Action	Basis for Action
January 1951	Margin requirements raised from 50 to 75 per cent of market value.	Continued upward trend of stock prices, volume of trading, and stock market credit.
January to February 1951	Real estate credit control extended to cover multi-family and certain nonresidential properties.	To add further restraints on inflation by limiting the credit available for the financing of nonresidential construction and to bring about a decrease in building to provide materials and labor for the defense program.
February to May 1951	All financing institutions requested to participate in program of voluntary credit restraint.	Program formulated by representatives of banks, investment bankers, and life insurance companies, in consultation with Federal Reserve representatives, for organized effort by all types of financing institutions to restrain unnecessary credit expansion in accordance with the Defense Production Act of 1950.
March to mid-April 1951	Lowered buying prices on government securities.	Action taken, under Treasury-Federal Reserve accord, to terminate support of government securities market at fixed prices, with a view to promoting a self-sustaining market and discouraging sales of government securities to Federal Reserve System to obtain funds with which to extend credit to private borrowers.
	Bought 1.1 billion dollars of Treasury bonds and 100 million dollars of bills.	Interim purchases taken to maintain orderly market conditions in transition of self-sustaining market and to facilitate exchange of long-term marketable bonds into nonmarketable bonds with longer-term and higher-interest coupon.
April 1951	Ceased purchases of government securities except primarily to maintain orderly market conditions.	To minimize monetization of public debt without jeopardizing necessary government financing; to enable

Date	*Action*	*Basis for Action*
		the Federal Reserve System to regain greater control over its extensions of Federal Reserve credit through security operations, and thereby more effectively to restrain inflationary expansion of credit.
Mid-April 1951 to November 1951	Bought 300 million dollars of long-term bonds through June, and 1.5 billion dollars of short-term securities during refunding periods.	Purchased restricted bonds to aid in readjustment of bond market; purchased short-term securities to aid in Treasury refundings.
	Sold or redeemed 1.7 billion dollars of short-term government securities at other times.	Sales to absorb reserves created by above purchases.
July 1951	On installment credit for list of consumer durable goods and for installment loans increased maximum maturity to eighteen months (home improvements, thirty-six months); down payment on appliances reduced to 15 per cent cash or cash and trade-in.	Action taken to bring Regulation W into conformity with the provisions of the Defense Production Act amendments of 1951.
September 1951	Increased maximum maturity to twenty-five years for houses up to $12,000; raised maximum value per family unit for specified down payment requirements; suspended credit restrictions for programed housing in critical defense housing areas.	Action taken to bring Regulation X into conformity with the provisions of the Defense Housing and Community Facilities and Services Act of 1951.
December 1951	Increased holdings of securities in late December by about 600 million dollars net.	To meet seasonal reserve needs.
January 1952	Reduced holdings of securities by 1.1 billion dollars net.	To offset currency inflow and the effects of other seasonal factors on bank reserves.
February to June 1952	Increased holdings by about 200 million dollars net.	Large purchases of securities made in February and June to facilitate market

Date	*Action*	*Basis for Action*
		adjustments to Treasury financings. Most of those purchases were offset by sales of other securities.
September 1952	Suspension of regulation of real estate credit.	To conform with the terms of the Defense Production Act, as amended, requiring suspension of regulation if housing starts in each of three consecutive months fell short of an annual rate of 1.2 million units, seasonally adjusted.
July to December 1952	Limited net purchases of United States government securities in open market to 1.8 billion dollars.	To meet seasonal and other reserve drains only in part, requiring banks to borrow some of the deposit expansion at a time when credit demand was very large and the economy was fully employed. Purchases in August and September were made primarily at times of Treasury refunding operations and were offset in part by subsequent sales.
January to April 1953	Sold in open market or redeemed 800 million dollars net of United States government securities.	To offset seasonal changes in factors affecting reserves and thus to maintain pressure on member-bank reserve positions.
January 1953	Raised discount rates from $1\frac{3}{4}$ to 2 per cent and buying rates on ninety-day bankers' acceptances from $1\frac{7}{8}$ to $2\frac{1}{8}$ per cent.	To bring discount rates as well as buying rates on acceptances into closer alignment with open market money rates and to provide an additional deterrent to member-bank borrowing from the Reserve banks.
February 1953	Reduced margin requirements on loans for purchasing or carrying listed securities from 75 to 50 per cent of market value of securities.	To reduce margin requirements from the high level imposed early in 1951, in the judgment that the lower requirement would be adequate to prevent excessive use of credit for purchasing and carrying stocks.
May to June 1953	Purchased in open market about 900 million dollars of	To provide banks with reserves and to permit a re-

Date	*Action*	*Basis for Action*
	United States government securities.	duction of member-bank borrowing from the Reserve banks at a time when such borrowing was high, credit and capital markets were showing strain, and seasonal needs for funds were imminent.
July 1953	Reduced reserve requirements on net demand deposits by 2 percentage points at central Reserve city banks and by one percentage point at Reserve city and country banks, thus freeing an estimated 1.2 billion dollars of reserves.	To free additional bank reserves for meeting expected seasonal and growth credit demands, including Treasury financing needs, and to further reduce the pressure on member-bank reserve positions.
July to December 1953	Made net purchases in open market of United States government securities totaling 1.7 billion dollars.	To provide banks with reserves to meet seasonal and growth needs and to offset continuing gold outflow with little or no additional recourse to borrowing. This action and the one below were taken in pursuance of a policy of active ease adopted in view of the business downturn.
January to June 1954	Limited net sales to about 900 million dollars of United States government securities in open market.	To absorb only part of the reserves made available by seasonal deposit contraction and return flow of currency thereby further easing bank reserve positions.
February 1954	Reduced discount rates from $1\frac{3}{4}$ per cent and buying rates on ninety-day bankers' acceptances from $2\frac{1}{8}$ to $1\frac{3}{4}$ per cent.	To bring discount rates as well as buying rates on bankers' acceptances into closer alignment with market rates of interest and to eliminate any undue deterrent to bank borrowing from the Reserve banks for making temporary reserve adjustments.
April to May 1954	Reduced discount rates from $1\frac{3}{4}$ to $1\frac{1}{2}$ per cent and buying rates on ninety-day bankers' acceptances from $1\frac{3}{4}$ to $1\frac{1}{2}$.	

Date	*Action*	*Basis for Action*
June to August 1954	Reduced reserve requirements on net demand deposits by 2 percentage points at central Reserve city banks and by one percentage point at Reserve city and country banks, and requirements on time deposits by one percentage point at all member banks, thus freeing about 1.5 billion dollars of reserves in the period June 16 to August 1. Sold in open market or redeemed United States government securities totaling about one billion dollars in July and August.	To supply the banking system with reserves to meet expected growth and seasonal demands for credit and money, including Treasury financing needs. Reductions in reserve requirements were offset in part by temporary sales of securities in order to prevent excess reserves from increasing unduly at the time, but security purchases were resumed as need for funds developed.
September to November 1954	Made net purchases in open market of approximately 850 million dollars.	To supply the banking system with reserves to meet expected growth and seasonal demands for credit and money.
December 1954	Made net purchases of United States government securities in open market of less than 50 million dollars, all under repurchase agreements with dealers and brokers. Member-bank borrowing increased to an average of 250 million dollars in December.	To meet part of the temporary end-of-year needs of banks for reserve funds, but, in view of rising credit demands, to permit these needs to be reflected in part in slightly less easy reserve positions.
January to June 1955	Sold in the open market or redeemed United States government securities totaling 1.3 billion dollars. Member-bank borrowing increased to an average of more than 400 million dollars in the second quarter.	To offset effects of seasonal factors affecting bank reserve positions, and, in view of strong credit demands, to bring about somewhat greater member-bank borrowing from Federal Reserve banks.
January 1955	Raised margin requirements on loans for purchasing or carrying listed securities from 50 to 60 per cent of market value of securities.	To help prevent an excessive use of credit for purchasing or carrying securities in a period of increasing use of credit for carrying securities.
April 1955	Raised margin requirements on loans for purchasing or carrying listed securities from 60 to 70 per cent	

Date	Action	Basis for Action
	of market value of securities.	
April 1955	Raised discount rates from $1\frac{1}{2}$ to $1\frac{3}{4}$ per cent.	To bring discount rates into closer alignment with open market money rates and make borrowing by individual banks more expensive.
March to December 1955	Made net purchase of bankers' acceptances in open market totaling 28 million dollars.	To recognize increased use of bankers' acceptances by business as a means of financing international trade.
July to December 1955	Made outright purchases of Treasury bills in the open market totaling 700 million dollars net and increased repurchase agreements with dealers and brokers by 300 million dollars. Member-bank borrowing increased to an average of about 850 million dollars in September and more than one billion dollars in November but declined to about 850 million dollars in December.	To meet part of reserve needs associated with seasonal factors, thus requiring banking system to meet needs in part by further increasing indebtedness. This action was taken with a view to providing for seasonal needs while limiting undue expansion of bank credit.
November to December 1955	Purchased when issued Treasury certificates of indebtedness totaling 167 million dollars.	To facilitate Treasury refunding in period of money market stringency. Supply of reserve was consistent with over-all open market policy at time.
August to September 1955	Increased discount rates from $1\frac{3}{4}$ to $2\frac{1}{4}$ per cent. This increase was made in two steps at all Reserve banks except Cleveland.	To keep discount rates in an appropriate relationship with market rates of interest and thus maintain a deterrent on excessive borrowing by individual banks at the Reserve banks.
November 1955	Increased discount rates from $2\frac{1}{4}$ to $2\frac{1}{2}$ per cent.	
January 1956	Reduced Reserve System holdings of United States government securities by over 1.4 billion dollars through sales in the market redemption of maturing bills, and termination of repurchase agreements.	To offset seasonal return flow of currency and reduction in reserve needs and restore degree of restraint prevailing before December action to moderate restraint temporarily.

Date	*Action*	*Basis for Action*
	Member-bank borrowings increased to weekly averages of 900 million dollars in late January.	
February to March 1956	Bought small amounts of government securities at times. Member-bank borrowings declined somewhat in February but increased substantially in March as result of sharp increase in required reserves.	To meet changing reserve needs and avoid an increasing degree of credit restraint in view of growing tone of uncertainty as to economic prospects.
April to May 1956	Discount rates raised from 2½ per cent to 2¾ per cent at ten Reserve banks and to 3 per cent at two banks around middle of April; Reserve System holdings of United States government securities reduced by 350 million dollars. Member-bank borrowings at Reserve banks rose to over one billion dollars.	To increase restraint on credit expansion, in view of sharp increase in bank credit in March and indications of broad increase in spending, growing demands for credit, and upward pressures on prices and costs.
Late May to early August 1956	Increased Federal Reserve System holdings of United States government securities around end of May and end of June and maintained holdings at higher level than in previous period.	To meet currency needs around holidays, to cover added demands for reserves around tax payment and mid-year settlement periods, and to avoid increasing the degree of restraint in view of uncertainties in economic situation.
August to November 1956	Discount rates raised late in August to 3 per cent at the ten Reserve banks with rates of 2¾ per cent. System holdings of United States government securities increased by nearly one billion dollars; member-bank borrowings at Reserve banks rose to average of 900 million dollars in August and averaged between 700 million dollars and 800 million dollars in other months.	Discount rates increased in conformity with rise in market rates resulting from vigorous credit demands. Policies designed to increase and maintain restraint on undue credit expansion while covering seasonal and other temporary variations in reserve needs, including effects of frequent Treasury financing operations.
December 1956	Reserve System holdings of United States government	To supply reserve funds in recognition of additional

Date	Action	Basis for Action
	securities and bankers' acceptances increased by over 550 million dollars, including substantial repurchase agreements with dealers. Member-bank borrowings declined to weekly averages of around 600 million dollars, except in last week of year, and at times were less than excess reserves.	pressures in money, credit, and capital markets resulting from seasonal factors and international conditions, at a time when lower liquidity ratios of banks were themselves exerting restraint on bank lending.
January to June 1957	Reduced holdings of government securities by about 1.8 billion dollars. Member-bank borrowings increased from an average of 400 million dollars in January to one billion dollars in June.	To offset the effect on reserves of seasonal factors and the sale of 600 million dollars of gold to the United States Treasury by the International Monetary Fund, and to exert pressure on bank reserve positions by bringing about a higher level of member-bank borrowings.
August 1957	Raised discount rates from 3 to 3½ per cent at all Reserve banks.	To bring discount rates into closer alignment with open market money rates and maintain the restrictive effect of member-bank borrowing.
July-mid-October 1957	Bought and subsequently sold small amounts of United States government securities at various times. Member-bank borrowings remained at or near average of one billion dollars.	To meet changing reserve needs and at the same time maintain continuing pressure on bank reserve positions.
Mid-October-December 1957	Reserve System holdings of United States government securities increased by one billion dollars, including substantial amounts of securities held under repurchase agreement. Member-bank borrowings declined to an average of less than 750 million dollars.	To increase the availability of bank reserves and thereby cushion adjustments and mitigate recessionary tendencies in the economy.
November-December 1957	Deduced discount rates from 3½ to 3 per cent at all Reserve banks.	To reduce the cost of borrowing from the Reserve banks and eliminate any undue restraint on bank borrowing in view of the decline in business activity

Date	*Action*	*Basis for Action*
		and evidences of economic recession.
January 1958	Limited net reduction in holdings of United States government securities to 900 million dollars, more than half of which represented securities held under repurchase agreement at end of year. Member-bank borrowings declined to an average of 450 million dollars.	To ease reserve positions by absorbing only part of the reserves made available by seasonal factors affecting bank reserve positions.
January	Reduced margin requireing or carrying listed securities from 70 to 50 per cent of market value of securities.	To recognize that dangers of excessive use of credit for stock market speculation had subsided, since stock prices and the volume of credit in the stock market had declined to levels near or below those prevailing at the time of the previous increase in requirements.
January-February	Reduced discount rates from 3 to $2\frac{3}{4}$ per cent at eleven Reserve banks.	
February	Reduced reserve requirements on demand deposits from 20 to $19\frac{1}{2}$ per cent at central Reserve city banks; from 18 to $17\frac{1}{2}$ per cent at Reserve city banks; and from 12 to $11\frac{1}{2}$ per cent at country banks, thus freeing an estimated 500 million dollars of reserves.	To reduce further the cost of borrowing from the Reserve banks and increase further the availability of bank reserves in order to encourage bank credit and monetary expansion conducive to resumed growth in economic activity.
March	Reduced discount rates from $2\frac{3}{4}$ to $2\frac{1}{4}$ per cent at eleven Reserve banks and from 3 to $2\frac{1}{4}$ per cent at one Reserve bank.	
March	Reduced reserve requirements on demand deposits from $19\frac{1}{2}$ to 19 per cent at central Reserve city banks; from $17\frac{1}{2}$ to 17 per cent at Reserve city banks; and from $11\frac{1}{2}$ to 11 per cent at country banks, thus freeing an additional 500 million dollars of reserves.	

Date	Action	Basis for Action
February- mid-April 1958	Purchased about 450 million dollars of United States government securities. Member-bank borrowings declined further to an average of about 180 million dollars.	To supplement reserve requirement actions in further increasing the availability of bank reserves.
April 1958	Reduced reserve requirements on demand deposits from 19 to 18 per cent (in two stages) at central Reserve city banks and from 17 to $16\frac{1}{2}$ per cent at Reserve city banks, thus freeing a total of about 450 million dollars of reserves.	To supplement previous actions to encourage bank credit and monetary expansion and resumed growth in economic activity and to offset current gold outflow.
April-May 1958	Reduced discount rates from $2\frac{1}{4}$ to $1\frac{3}{4}$ per cent at all Reserve banks.	
Mid-April-June 1958	Purchased outright about 1.7 billion dollars net of United States government securities. Member-bank borrowings declined further to an average of 100 million dollars at the end of June.	
July-early August 1958	Bought a small volume of United States government securities other than short-term issues and a large amount of securities involved in a Treasury refinancing. Promptly thereafter reduced Treasury bill holdings substantially.	To correct disorderly conditions in the government securities market, to facilitate the Treasury refinancing, and then to recapture the bank reserves created by the earlier securities purchases.
August 1958	Raised margin requirements on loans for purchasing or carrying listed securities from 50 to 70 per cent of market value of securities.	To help prevent an excessive use of credit for purchasing or carrying securities. The volume of credit in the stock market and stock prices were advancing sharply and were at or near the highest levels since World War II.
August-early September 1958	Made little change in holdings of United States government securities. Member-bank borrowings, increased to an average of	Open market action not taken to offset drains on reserve funds reflecting bank credit and monetary expansion resulting from

Date	*Action*	*Basis for Action*
	more than 400 million dollars in early September.	seasonal factors and the sharp upturn in economic activity.
August-September 1958	Raised discount rates from $1\frac{3}{4}$ to 2 per cent at all Reserve banks.	To keep discount rates in an appropriate relationship with market rates and to increase the cost of borrowing by individual banks from the Reserve banks in case of increasing demands for bank credit.
October 1958	Raised margin requirements on loans for purchasing or carrying listed securities from 70 to 90 per cent of market value of securities.	To help prevent an excessive use of credit for purchasing or carrying securities.
Late October-early November 1958	Raised discount rates from 2 to $2\frac{1}{2}$ per cent at all Reserve banks.	To bring discount rates into closer alignment with open market rates.
Mid-November-December 1958	Increased system holdings of United States government securities about 900 million dollars, including securities held under repurchase agreement. Member-bank borrowings rose to average of 560 million dollars in December.	To meet part of reserve needs associated with seasonal factors and a further moderate outflow of gold.
January-February 1959	Reduced holdings of United States government securities in January by about one billion dollars. Member-bank borrowings at the Federal Reserve banks continued at an average of 500 million dollars or more.	To offset the seasonal inflow of reserve funds resulting mainly from the postholiday return flow of currency from circulation and thus maintain restraint on credit expansion.
March-mid-July 1959	Increased Reserve System holdings of United States government securities by about 1.1 billion dollars. Member-bank borrowings rose further to an average of one billion dollars in mid-July.	To offset partially the absorption of reserves due mainly to a decline of 780 million dollars in gold stock and an increase of about one billion dollars in currency in circulation and to keep credit expansion under restraint.

Date	Action	Basis for Action
March 1959	Raised discount rates from $2\frac{1}{2}$ to 3 per cent at all Reserve banks.	To keep discount rates in an appropriate relationship with the rise in market rates resulting from vigorous credit demands and to restrain undue credit expansion.
May-June 1959	Raised discount rates from 3 to $3\frac{1}{2}$ per cent at all Reserve banks.	
Mid-July-October 1959	Bought and subsequently sold small amounts of United States government securities around periods of Treasury financing and the third quarter tax date. Member-bank borrowings averaged about 900 million dollars with temporary increases above one billion dollars around Treasury financing and tax payment dates.	To supply special reserve needs for only limited periods in recognition of pressures in money, credit, and capital markets resulting from vigorous public and private demand for credit.
September 1959	Raised discount rates from $3\frac{1}{2}$ to 4 per cent at all Reserve banks.	To keep discount rates in an appropriate relationship with the rise in market rates resulting from vigorous credit demands and to restrain undue credit expansion.
November-December 1959	Increased Federal Reserve System holdings of United States government securities by about 800 million dollars through mid-December and then reduced holdings somewhat. Authorized member banks to count about 300 million dollars of their vault cash as required reserves through amendment to Regulation D, effective December 1, under new legislation. Average borrowings rose to about one billion dollars in the last half of December.	To meet part of the temporary end-of-year needs of banks for reserve funds but at the same time to keep bank reserve positions under pressure.
January-March 1960	Reduced Federal Reserve System holdings of United States government securities by about 1.6 billion dollars. Member-bank borrowings	To offset the seasonal inflow of reserve funds, mainly from the postholiday return of currency from circulation, while permit-

Date	Action	Basis for Action
	at the Federal Reserve banks dropped from an average of 900 million dollars in December to 635 million dollars in March.	ting some reduction in borrowed reserves.
Late March-July 1960	Increased Reserve System holdings of government securities by nearly 1.4 billion dollars. Member-bank borrowings at Reserve banks declined to an average of less than 400 million dollars in July.	To promote further reduction in the net borrowed reserve positions of member banks and, beginning in May, to provide reserves needed for moderate bank credit and monetary expansion.
June 1960	Reduced discount rates from 4 to 3½ per cent at all Reserve banks.	To reduce the cost of borrowed reserves for member banks and to bring the discount rate closer to market interest rates.
July 1960	Reduced margin requirements on loans for purchasing or carrying listed securities from 90 to 70 per cent of market value of securities.	To lower margin requirements from the high level in effect since October 1958 in recognition of decline in volume of stock market credit outstanding and lessened danger of excessive speculative activity in the market.
August 1960	Authorized member banks to count about 500 million dollars of their vault cash as required reserves, effective for country banks August 25 and for central Reserve and Reserve city banks September 1. Reduced reserve requirements against net demand deposits at central Reserve city banks from 18 to 17½ per cent, effective September 1, thereby releasing about 125 million dollars of reserves.	To provide mainly for seasonal needs for reserve funds, and to implement 1959 legislation directed in part toward equalization of reserve requirements of central Reserve and Reserve city banks.
August-September 1960	Reduced discount rates from 3½ to 3 per cent at all Reserve banks.	To reduce further the cost of borrowing from the Reserve banks and reduce the differential between the discount rate and market rates of interest.

Date	*Action*	*Basis for Action*
August- November 1960	Bought or sold at different times varying amounts of goverment securities with a net increase in System holdings of about one billion dollars, including securities held under repurchase agreement and issues with short maturities other than Treasury bills. Member-bank borrowing declined further to average below 150 million dollars in October and November.	To encourage bank credit and monetary expansion by meeting changing reserve needs and offsetting the impact of a large gold outflow without exerting undue downward pressure on short-term Treasury bill rates that might stimulate further outflow of funds.
Late November- December 1960	Authorized member banks to count all their vault cash in meeting their reserve requirements and increased reserve requirements against net demand deposits for country banks from 11 to 12 per cent. The net effect of these two actions, effective November 24, was to make available about 1,050 million dollars of reserves. Reduced reserve requirements against net demand deposits at central Reserve city banks from 17½ to 16½ per cent, effective December 1, thereby releasing about 250 million dollars of reserves. Sold United States government securities except for seasonal purchases in last week of December. Member-bank borrowings at the Reserve banks averaged less than 90 million dollars in December.	To provide, on a liberal basis, for seasonal reserve needs, to complete implementation of legislation directed in part toward equalization of reserve requirements of central Reserve and Reserve city banks, and to offset the effect of continued gold outflow, while avoiding direct impact on short-term rates that might stimulate further outflow of funds.
January 1961	Limited net sales of United States government securities from Federal Reserve portfolio to about 500 million dollars. Member-bank borrowing at Reserve banks averaged only 50 million dollars.	To encourage bank credit and monetary expansion by absorbing only part of seasonal inflow of reserve funds not otherwise offset by a large gold outflow.

Date	Action	Basis for Action
February-August 1961	Bought substantial amounts of United States government securities with maturities over one year, following February 20 announcement that Federal Reserve System open market operations would include securities outside the short-term area. These purchases were partly offset by net sales of short-term securities. Total System holdings of governments increased about 700 million dollars. Member-bank borrowings averaged 75 million dollars.	To encourage bank credit and monetary expansion while avoiding direct downward pressure on short-term interest rates, thereby moderating pressures on the United States balance of payments from outflow of short-term capital attracted by higher interest rates abroad.
September-December 1961	Bought or sold at different times varying amounts of United States government securities, including securities with longer maturities. Total System holdings of government securities increased about 1.6 billion dollars. Member-bank borrowings at Reserve banks remained generally low.	To continue to encourage bank credit and monetary expansion while allowing for changing reserve needs due to seasonal and other factors, including a large gold outflow, and while continuing to give consideration to the balance of payments problem.
December 1961	Raised, effective January 1, 1962, maximum interest rates payable by member banks on any savings deposit from 3 to $3\frac{1}{2}$ per cent, and 4 per cent on those left in the bank for one year or more; also raised maximum rates on time deposits with a maturity of six months to one year from 3 to $3\frac{1}{2}$ per cent, and to 4 per cent on those deposits with a maturity of a year or longer.	To enable banks to compete more effectively for savings and other time deposits, including foreign time deposits, thus moderating pressures on the United States balance of payments, and, over the long run, to offer additional incentive for the accumulation of savings required for financing future economic growth.
January-February 1962	Reduced Federal Reserve System holdings of United States government securities by about 500 million dollars through net sales and redemptions. Member-	To permit further bank credit and monetary expansion by absorbing only part of seasonal inflow of reserve funds, mainly from post-holiday return to currency

Date	Action	Basis for Action
	bank borrowings from the Reserve banks averaged less than 100 million dollars.	from circulation, while minimizing downward pressures on short-term interest rates.
February 1962	Authorized open market transactions in foreign currencies.	To moderate and offset short-term pressures on the dollar in the foreign exchange market.
March– mid-June 1962	Increased System holdings of United States government securities by about 1.3 billion dollars, of which half represented purchases of securities with maturities of more than one year. Member-bank borrowings from Reserve banks continued to average less than 100 million dollars.	To promote further bank credit and monetary expansion while avoiding sustained downward pressures on short-term interest rates.
Mid-June– late October 1962	Increased System holdings of United States government securities by about 200 million dollars with net sales and redemptions of Treasury bills of about 700 million dollars being more than offset by purchases of coupon issues, of which two-thirds were issues maturing in more than one year. Member-bank borrowings from Reserve banks averaged less than 100 million dollars.	To permit moderate increase in bank credit and money supply while avoiding redundant bank reserves that would encourage capital outflows, taking into account gradual improvement in domestic economy and possibilities for further advance, while recognizing the bank credit growth of past year and continuing adverse balance of payments.
July 1962	Reduced margin requirements on loans for purchasing or carrying listed securities from 70 to 50 per cent of market value of securities.	To take into account the recent sharp reduction in stock market credit and the abatement in speculative psychology in the stock market.
October 1962	Reduced reserve requirements against time deposits from 5 to 4 per cent, effective October 25 for Reserve city banks and November 1 for other member banks, thereby releasing about 780 million dollars of reserves.	To help meet seasonal needs for reserves, while minimizing downward pressures on short-term interest rates, and to provide for the longer-term growth in bank deposits needed to facilitate the expansion in economic activity and trade.

Date	*Action*	*Basis for Action*
Late October– December 1962	Increased Federal Reserve System holdings of United States government securities by about one billion dollars, with more than half of the net increase in issues maturing in more than one year. Member-bank borrowing from the Reserve banks rose gradually over period, but only to an average of about 200 million dollars.	To help further in meeting seasonal needs for reserve funds while encouraging moderate further increase in bank credit and the money supply and avoiding money market conditions unduly favorable to capital outflows internationally. In mid-December open market operations were modified to provide a somewhat firmer tone in money markets and to offset the anticipated seasonal easing in Treasury bill rates.
January– mid-May 1963	Reduced System holdings of United States government securities and then increased them in line with seasonal and moderate growth needs of the economy. Total holdings rose about 470 million dollars on balance, owing mainly to net purchases of issues maturing in more than one year. Member-bank borrowing rose slightly to a level of about 150 million dollars in the first half of May.	To offset seasonal downward pressures on short-term interest rates early in the period and to provide for growth in bank credit and the money supply at a rate consistent with minimizing capital outflows in accordance with the policy of slightly reduced reserve availability adopted at the December 18, 1962, meeting of the Federal Open Market Committee.
Mid-May– late-July 1963	Reduced the degree of reserve availability slightly further. System holdings of United States government securities increased nearly 1.2 billion dollars, about one-fifth representing net purchases of issues maturing in more than one year. Member-bank borrowing increased further, averaging 275 million dollars over the period.	To achieve a slightly greater degree of firmness in the money market in order to minimize the outflow of capital while continuing to provide reserves for moderate monetary and credit growth.
Mid-July 1963	Raised the discount rate from 3 to 3½ per cent. Raised maximum interest rates payable by member banks on time deposits (other than savings) and	To help reduce short-term capital outflows by firming United States short-term money market rates and permitting member banks to compete more effectively

Date	Action	Basis for Action
	certificates of deposit with maturities of ninety days to six months from 2½ to 4 per cent and with maturities of six months to one year from 3½ to 4 per cent.	for foreign and domestic funds.
Late-July-December 1963	Reduced a little further the degree of reserve availability. Federal Reserve System holdings of United States government securities increased about 1.1 billion dollars, of which more than one-half represented purchases of securities with maturities of more than one year. Member-bank borrowing averaged about 325 million dollars over the period.	To attain slightly more firmness in the money market, in the context of a higher discount rate with a view to minimizing the outflow of funds abroad while offsetting seasonal reserve drains and providing for growth needs of the domestic economy.
November 1963	Raised margin requirements on loans for purchasing or carrying listed securities from 50 to 70 per cent of market value of securities. Also increased retention requirements on proceeds of sales from undermargined accounts from 50 to 70 per cent.	To help prevent excessive use of stock market credit, which had increased sharply since July 1962, when margin requirements were lowered from 70 to 50 per cent.
January-mid-August 1964	Increased the System's holdings of U.S. Government securities, after having reduced them seasonally early in the year. On balance, total holdings rose about $1.1 billion, $300 million of which represented net purchases of securities with maturities of over 1 year. Member bank borrowings averaged about $275 million.	To provide for moderate growth in the reverse base, bank credit, and the money supply for the purpose of facilitating continued expansion of the economy while fostering improvement in the capital account of U.S. international payments, after offsetting seasonal downward pressures on short-term interest rates early in the period.
Mid-August-late November 1964	Increased the System's holdings of U.S. Government securities by about $1.5 billion, of which $600 million represented net purchases of securities with maturities of more than 1 year. Mem-	To maintain slightly firmer conditions in the money market with a view to minimizing the outflow of funds attracted by higher short-term interest rates abroad while offsetting reserve

Date	*Action*	*Basis for Action*
	ber bank borrowings averaged about $350 million.	drains and providing for growth needs of the domestic economy.
Late November 1964	Raised discount rates from 3½ to 4 per cent. Raised maximum interest rates payable on savings deposits held for less than 1 year from 3½ to 4 per cent and those on other time deposits from 4 to 4½ per cent for maturities of 90 days or more and from 1 to 4 per cent for maturities of 30-89 days.	To counter possible capital outflows that might be prompted by any widening spread between money market rates in this country and the higher rates abroad, following a rise in official and market rates in London, while at the same time ensuring that the flow of savings to commercial banks remains ample for the financing of domestic investment.
Late November-December 1964	Increased the System's holdings of U.S. Government securities by about $765 million, part of which represented securities acquired under repurchase agreements. Member bank borrowings averaged about $275 million.	To offset seasonal reserve drains and to accommodate further moderate expansion in aggregate bank reserves while ensuring that the rise in money market rates following the discount rate actions did not restrict the availability of domestic credit.

25

Monetary Policy (continued):
Some Principles and Problems

> The orthodox picture of the financial system rather resembles a concertina: if you squeeze the monetary end the whole thing sooner or later contracts, and *vice versa*. . . .
>
> The Radcliffe analogy* is not the concertina but the balloon: squeeze one end (sufficiently gently to prevent a total collapse— the image is apt!) and the other end merely bulges to compensate (A. B. Cramp, "Two Views on Money," *Lloyds Bank Review* [July 1962], p. 5).

The previous chapter set forth the indicators of changes in credit and monetary policy (Sect. 24.2). It was concerned with interpreting the actions and inactions of the monetary officials in their conduct of monetary policy at the operational level, and it was subsequently concerned with providing some perspective of the postwar years (Sect. 24.3) with respect to the operations of, and problems confronting, the monetary officials.

In the present chapter, however, we concern ourselves with the role of monetary officials, who control the use of the instruments for achieving policy targets, and present general principles and problems pertaining to monetary policy. Our concern with the role of the policy-makers leads us to consider a quantitative monetary policy (Sect. 25.1). Later, in reviewing details with respect to the general instruments for influencing both qualitative and quantitative targets (Sect. 25.1), we bring together under a single heading the orthodox view of monetary policy (Sect. 25.2). We then deal with problem areas pertaining to the effectiveness of the instruments of monetary policy. This leads to the presentation of the avail-

* Committee on the Working of the Monetary System, *Report,* Command Paper No. 827 (London: Her Majesty's Stationery Office, 1959). The document is commonly called the "Radcliffe Report," after the committee's chairman, Lord Radcliffe.

ability doctrine (Sect. 25.3) and discussions of induced changes in income velocity (Sect. 25.4).

25.1 A Quantitative Monetary Policy

An approach for dealing quantitatively with the instruments and targets of monetary policy (Sect. 24.1) and their interrelationships was set forth in a succession of books from 1952 by a Dutch economist—Jan Tinbergen of the Netherlands School of Economics.[1] The approach and terminology used by Professor Tinbergen, moreover, has gained wide acceptance,[2] exclusive of his controversial conclusions. Indeed, his writings have influenced the techniques of econometric model building and other areas of economics (namely, welfare economics) as well as a quantitative approach to monetary policy. Thus, as a means of introducing the reader to the essentials pertaining to the notions of a quantitative monetary policy, we summarize the principal propositions pertaining to Tinbergen's approach, introduce some terminology, and present two illustrations of policy models with quantitative target variables.

The principal propositions. We wish to state some definitions and then prove Tinbergen's principal propositions by referring to these definitions and earlier analysis. The following are our definitions:

(1) Quantitative variables are those that are concerned with measurable quantities. They may be expressed in units of measurement in the sense that they obey the usual axioms of algebra.

(2) Qualitative variables are not measurable. However, one may seek artificial units of measure based on statistical information, specify boundary conditions, and apply the axioms of order (i.e., axioms concerned with concepts of "more than" and "less than"). The "tone" of the credit market is an example of such a variable. "Satisfaction," "preference" (Sect. 4.1), "desire" (Sect. 24.2), and—in the case of the Federal Reserve's "bills only" policy—minimum interference with the free market's orderly determination of government securities prices and yields (Sect. 24.3) are also examples.

(3) Dependent goals (or target variables) are those that can be attained if and only if some other related target variable is attained. Dependent in this case means uniquely dependent, and it does not exactly follow the mathematical meaning of the term (Sect. 1.2). For example, a broad goal, such as the full utilization of resources, would be dependent on the goal of full employment, since the former implies the latter.

(4) Independent goals are those that are not dependent.

(5) Conflicting goals (or target variables) are those whereby the attainment of one requires a compromise of the other.

(6) Consistent goals (or target variables) are nondependent goals that may be achieved simultaneously.

The following propositions are deduced from the above definitions, other propositions, or earlier analysis:[3]

Proposition 1: *Goals are expressed in qualitative and quantitative terms.* Viewing the range of goals (or target variables) set forth over the operational, intermediate, and ultimate levels outlined earlier (Sect. 24.1), we note that some, such as the volume of bank earning assets and interest rates, are quantitative by definition (1) and others, such as the "tone" of the credit market, are qualitative by definition (2). Thus the proposition follows.

Furthermore, quantitative targets may be stated in terms of numerical value or in terms of constraints in the form of weak inequalities—i.e., inequalities including boundary conditions. To distinguish between the alternative methods of statement, however, a numerical target, such as a given change in the money supply, is sometimes called a "fixed target"; others pertaining to more than (less than) or easier (tighter) are sometimes called "flexible targets."

Proposition 2: *Goals are dependent or independent.* The maximum utilization of resources within the context of a free society is a goal that is uniquely dependent upon the attainment of full employment and utilization of capacity, since the labor force and capacity are resources. The attainment of full utilization of plant capacity, however, is not necessarily dependent on the attainment of full employment and vice versa.

Proposition 3: *Independent goals may be consistent or conflicting.* Assuming that some nonuniquely dependent goals, such as price stability (i.e., changes in GNP deflator = 0) and increased employment, cannot always be achieved simultaneously and others, such as a larger volume of deposits and lower interest rates, can, then by definitions (4) and (5) this proposition holds. An analysis dealing with cost-push inflation (Sect. 16.3) and the 1957-1958 recession (Sect. 24.3) would tend to support the former assumption; an analysis dealing with the liquidity-preference demand for money balances (4) would tend to support the latter.

Proposition 4: Part I. *The number of nonredundant policy instruments* (i.e., instruments whereby two or more do not influence precisely the same targets*) *available to the policy-maker must be at least equal to the number of independent targets.* Part II. *If the number of policy instruments exceeds the number of nonredundant policy instruments, then the*

---

* If we regard the instruments of orthodox monetary policy as Federal Reserve credit, reserve requirements, and discount rates (Sect. 24.1), and if each of these instruments operates only through its influence on the money supply, then the instruments are redundant by the definition of redundancy. We could just as well choose arbitrary values for two of the instrumental variables, and concentrate on one variable to achieve the target.

number of policy instruments exceeds the number of target variables, but a solution to the model may still exist. With respect to Part I, a solution to a model may be assumed to exist if the model consists of N independent variables and N nonredundant equations. Thus let

    I be the number of instrumental variables,
    E be the number of exogenous variables other than the instrumental
       variables,
    T be the number of target variables, and
    K be the number of other endogenous "irrelevant" variables.

Then, given values for I and E, in a determinate system:

(1) $N = T + K$, and, given values for T and E,
(2) $N = I + K$.

Therefore, from equations (1) and (2), $I = T$, and the first part of the proposition is true. Next, if the number of instrument variables exceeds the number of nonredundant instrumental variables, the excess variables may be treated as constants and a unique solution to the policy model still exists.

Proposition 5: *Every independent target must be influenced by at least one policy instrument.* In order for a solution to the policy model to exist, the number of nonredundant instruments must equal the number of independent targets by proposition (4). In order for policy instruments to be effective, each of the targets must somehow be linked to one or more instruments. Put differently, the condition specified by proposition (4) is a necessary but insufficient condition for a solution to exist.

In this instance, the relationship we have in mind is a functional one whereby the target variable is some function of an instrumental variable. The instrumental variable consequently has a domain of the definition and the target variable a range; as we note below, the domain may be restricted by institutional considerations. Moreover, since the relationship between an instrument and a target is a functional one, it involves a composite function, where we view the operational, intermediate, and ultimate sets of relationships between instruments and variables (Sect. 24.1). For example, from the earlier schema (Sect. 24.1), it is feasible to denote the following:

price index $= f$ (money supply)
           money supply $= g$ (free reserves)
                   free reserves $= f$ (Fed. Res. credit),

and the sequence of causation is ΔFed. Res. credit $\rightarrow$ Δfree reserves $\rightarrow$ Δmoney supply $\rightarrow$ Δprice index. In composite form, we could write price index $= f$ (money supply) $= g\ [f$ (Fed. Res. credit)].

Proposition 6: *Instrumental variables may be restricted by various eco-*

nomic or institutional considerations, called boundary conditions." Assuming that institutional considerations prohibit the assignment of values,
such as negative ones, to instrumental variables, such as discount rates,
Federal Reserve credit, and member-bank reserves (Sect. 24.1), then
instrumental variables are said to be restricted by such prohibitions.

Proposition 7: Part I. *The achievement of just any preassigned values
to independent target variables depends upon the restrictions on the use
of instrumental variables by the monetary authorities.* Part II. *The
achievement also depends on their willingness to vary the instrumental
variables.* Clearly, restrictions on the use of instrumental variables affect
the range of control over target variables. Thus by proposition (6), the
use of instrumental variables may be restricted, and, therefore, the feasi-
bility of achieving just any values for the target variables is restricted.
Assuming that the predominant view among the monetary authorities is
an unwillingness to vary the instruments of monetary and credit control
even over their formally restricted domain, the range of feasible values
for target variables is even smaller than would result from the formal
restrictions alone. Ignorance and unawareness may also be factors contributing to the restriction in the use of instrumental variables.

Classes of variables. In Tinbergen's approach to a quantitative monetary policy there are four classes of variables. Two of these were set
forth earlier (Sect. 1.2)—endogenous variables and exogenous variables
or variable parameters. In the earlier setting, given a determinant model
of N equations and N unknown variables (e.g., Sect. 3.3, and 5.2), the
unknowns could be found in terms of the parameters. The unknowns in
such a case were said to be determined within the equation system (i.e.,
endogenously) or within an economic system, and the parameters were
said to correspond to conditions outside of the system.

Tinbergen, however, refers to endogenous and exogenous variables
and their corresponding subsets:

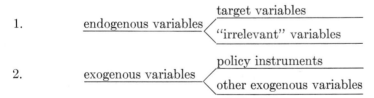

1.   endogenous variables ⟨ target variables / "irrelevant" variables

2.   exogenous variables ⟨ policy instruments / other exogenous variables

A target variable in this case could be a given level of income (for example, Sect. 1.2 and 5.4), and any other variables in the model would
simply be irrelevant for the purpose at hand, in the sense that we are not
directly concerned with them. A policy instrument, on the other hand,
could simply be the money supply (for example, in an earlier model,
Sect. 1.2 or 5.4), and "other exogenous variables" would simply refer to
the other variable parameters.

In the earlier models parameters were usually given or viewed as corresponding to some time series, and the variables, such as income and the present targets, were determined, though they too may be viewed as corresponding to some empirical measure in the real world. Now, however, we may wish to think of matters as somewhat reversed. In this case, we could, for example, view income as a given quantitative target and ask what the parameter corresponding to the money supply should be to achieve the target or goal. If the policy model were a determinate one in accordance with proposition (4), and if the conditions of proposition (5) were met, then any preassigned values for the target variables could be achieved, subject only to the restrictions set by institutional considerations [propositions (6) and (7)].

A simple quantity theory model. Some of Tinbergen's principal propositions may be illustrated, first with a simple quantity theory model (Sect. 5.1).

Recall that an income version of the equation of exchange type of identity may be stated as

(1) $M V_y = P O$, where

M is the average stock of money of a period,

V_y is the income velocity of money,

P is the price index of output for the same period, and

O is the value of output in constant prices for the period.

We, thus, begin with one equation in four variables. Two of these variables we shall regard as exogenously determined:

(2) $$V_y = V_{yo}, \text{ and}$$

(3) $$O = O_0$$

Now, after plugging in these known values for velocity and output in the first equation, we are left with one equation in two unknowns—M and P. Thus, in the above quantity theory model, we can treat money (or changes in money) as an exogenously determined variable, i.e.,

(4) $$M = M_0,$$

and we can solve for the variable P, since we now have reduced the problem to one equation in one unknown:

(5) $$P = (V_{yo}/O_0) \cdot M_0$$

As a policy problem, on the other hand, we set some price level, denoted as $\overline{P}$, as a target, i.e.,

(6) $$P = \overline{P}$$

Then instead of treating the money supply as given, we treat it as an instrumental variable and solve for the necessary money supply:

(7) $$M = (O_0/V_{y_0}) \cdot \overline{P}$$

The necessary equality of instruments and targets (one each) is apparent here.

We can make the above model a little more complicated by regarding the money supply as an intermediate target (or an "irrelevant variable," depending on terminological preferences) instead of an instrumental variable. To do this, assume that the Federal Reserve has three policy instruments—the volume of Federal Reserve credit (F), the level of member-bank reserve requirements (R), and the level of discount rates (D), —that these three instruments directly affect only the money supply (M), and that the effects on M may, over a narrow range of values of M, be adequately expressed by a linear approximation:

(8) $$M = m_1F - m_2R - m_3D, \quad (m_1, m_2, m_3 \geq 0)$$

Combining equations (7) and (8), we now have as our policy solution:

(9) $$m_1F - m_2R - m_3D = (O_0/V_{y_0}) \cdot \overline{P}$$

It is apparent that we have too many instruments for our lone price level target. Thus we can choose arbitrary values for any two instrument variables (subject, perhaps, to "boundary conditions," discussed earlier) and solve for the required value of the third.

Since we have so many instruments, the question might arise as to whether we could set forth more independent targets instead of throwing away instruments. In this model, however, the instruments all work through one intermediate target—the money supply—and hence two of these are always redundant, regardless of the number of ultimate targets.

A two-instrument, two-target model. The present two-instrument, two-target model illustrates the meaning of independent targets [propositions (2) and (3)] and nonredundant policy instruments [proposition (4)] in particular. The targets with which the model is concerned were introduced earlier (see payments equilibrium and utilization of resources, Sect. 24.3)—a given level of domestic employment and a limited or specified amount of gold outflow. The key policy instruments, in the present instance, are Federal Reserve credit and the Federal Reserve's capacity to buy dollars abroad in exchange for foreign currencies with its foreign exchange reserves (Sect. 23.5).

Written in its most expanded form, the model is as follows:

(1) $Y = C + I$

(2) $C = cY$

(3) $I = -ir$

(4) $N = nY$

(5) $M_d = l_1Y \quad -l_2r \qquad\qquad l_3$

(6) $M =$ $M_0 + m_1 \Delta F - m_2 \Delta R - m_3 \Delta D$

(7) $M_d =$ M

(8) $A =$ $a_1 r_x \quad - a_1 r$ $- a_2 E$

(9) $r_x =$ r_{x_0}

(10) $N =$ $\overline{N}$

(11) $A =$ $\overline{A}$

There are eleven equations and fourteen variables, as the system presently stands. But, as matters turn out, we shall treat some of the variables as constant, and there is the prospect of redundancy in the instrument variables, as in the above example.

The variables, according to the four types set forth earlier, are as follows:

Instrumental variables:

ΔF is the the change in Federal Reserve credit,
ΔR is the change in reserve requirements,
ΔD is the change in the level of discount rates, and
E is net Federal Reserve sales of foreign exchange per period.

Other exogenous variables:

r_x is the level of interest rates in foreign countries and
M_0 is the initial supply of money.

Target variables:

N is the level of employment and
A is the net gold outflow from the United States.

Irrelevant variables:

Y is the flow of aggregate income in current prices per period,
C is the flow of consumption expenditures per period,
I is the flow of domestic investment expenditures per period,
r is the level of domestic interest rates,
M_d is the demand for money, and
M is the total stock of money.

The parameters—c, i, n, l_1, l_2, l_3, m_1, m_2, m_3, a_1, and a_2—are all assumed to be nonnegative. This is in order to permit the direction of their influence on the variables of the model to be easily ascertained from the signs attached to the parameters.

Equations (1) to (3), (5), and (7) are more or less standard ingredients of a linear version of a static "Keynesian" model (Sect. 15.2 and 20.1). Equation (4) states that the level of employment is a simple linear function of aggregate demand. This is reasonable, of course, only for a fairly narrow range of values for aggregate demand, and the model would be made more complex if we introduced a separate target variable for the GNP deflator and made allowance for special features pertaining to the structure of the labor market.

Equation (6) states that the total money supply results from some initial amount M_0 plus (or minus) a net increment (or decrement) due to charges in the Federal Reserve's instrument variables. Just as in the quantity theory example, there is a redundancy of instrument variables affecting the money supply, so, in order to reduce the system to a determinate policy situation, we need to select arbitrary values for any two of the three instrument variables. Assume, for simplicity, then, that

$$\Delta R = 0 \quad \text{and} \quad \Delta D = 0,$$

so that equation (6) reduces to

(6')
$$M = m_1 \Delta F + M_0$$

Equation (8) asserts that the magnitude of the net gold outflow from the United States per period is positively related to the excess of foreign over domestic interest rates and negatively related to the Federal Reserve's net sales of foreign exchange. ("Net" here means over and above the Federal Reserve's purchase of foreign exchange and other central banks' net sales of short-term dollar assets.) Note that we are here implicitly assuming the current account (21.2) to be continually in balance, so that no net export item appears in equation (1). This means that the gold outflow in this model is evidently related to disturbances in the long-term and short-term capital accounts (Sect. 21.2).

Equations (10) and (11) set forth the target levels of employment $(\overline{N})$ and the gold outflow $(\overline{A})$. The latter in the present case is positive as implied, but it could be zero or negative (i.e., a net inflow).

If we plug in the exogenously determined initial money supply M_0, the level of foreign interest rates r_{x_0}, and the targets $\overline{N}$ and $\overline{A}$ and hold Federal Reserve discount rates and member-bank reserve requirements constant, then the system reduces to eight equations in the two instrument variables ΔF and E and the six "irrelevant variables" Y, C, I, r, M_d, and M. If we solve for each of the instrument variables, we obtain:

(12)
$$\Delta F = \frac{1}{m_1 n} \left[l_1 + \frac{l_2(1 - c)}{i} \right] \overline{N} + \frac{l_3 - M_0}{m_1}$$

and

(13)
$$E = \frac{a_1(1 - c)}{a_2 i n} \overline{N} - \frac{1}{a_2} \overline{A} + \frac{a_1}{a_2} r_{x_0}$$

These two equations comprise what is called the "simplified version" or "inverted reduced form" of the model. It is "simplified" or "reduced" in these equations to just the relationships between the instrument variables and the exogenous and target variables, together with the parameters of the system (i.e., "irrelevant variables" are eliminated). It is "inverted" because it is backwards so far as aggregative income determination models are normally solved, i.e., it is inverted because the instrument variables are regarded as unknowns and employment and the gold outflow as known.

Equations (12) and (13) illustrate an important distinction between "dependence" in a mathematical sense and "dependence" (or "independence") where policy targets are concerned, as in definitions (3) and (4). The level of employment is clearly an independent policy goal, because its attainment is not at all dependent in the model on the gold outflow target; in other words, it appears by itself in equation (12). The gold outflow target, however, does not appear by itself. According to equation (13), the larger the employment target, the greater must be the magnitude of the Federal Reserve's net sales of foreign exchange in order to reduce the gold outflow. (This is because higher employment targets require greater money supply increases and lower domestic interest rates, which increases the gold outflow unless offset by Federal Reserve sales of foreign exchange.) The gold outflow target, however, is not *uniquely* dependent on the employment target, since the Federal Reserve can still in principle attain the gold outflow target, even if it has to work harder with a higher employment target. Hence, the gold outflow target is also properly conceived as an independent policy goal.

Of course, the Federal Reserve could not persistently sell foreign exchange to restrain gold outflows, as may be implied in this simplified short-run model. A gold outflow in response to temporary speculation against the dollar could be handled in this way, but if the inducements for the outflow persisted, the supply of foreign exchange reserves would be depleted. Proposition (6) would come into play.

Moreover, there are other possible complications. Proposition (5) tells us that each independent target must be influenced by at least one instrument variable, and there are all sorts of reasons in this illustration why this might not be true and, thus, why monetary policy would be "ineffective." To avoid problems of dividing by zero, it is better to go back to the original equations, instead of using equations (12) and (13) as the basis for discussion. To cite a few examples, if employment is unrelated to income (i.e., $n = 0$), then it would be impossible to influence employment by working through the stock of money, interest rates, investment, and income. If investment is unrelated to interest rates (i.e., $i = 0$), an employment target would be impossible, since income would be unaffected by monetary policy. Similarly, if either interest rates are insensitive to money supply changes (because l_2 is infinitely large) or if the money supply is insensitive to changes in the Federal Reserve's instrument variables (i.e., m_1, m_2, $m_3 = 0$), then an employment target would be impossible to attain through the use of the instruments of monetary policy.

25.2. Orthodox Monetary Policy: Its Ideal Operation

Below we review details with respect to the general instruments for influencing both quantitative and qualitative intermediate targets (Sect. 25.1) within the financial system, including financial institutions other than member banks. In reviewing the relationships between these instruments and the intermediate targets at the level of day-to-day central banking operations, moreover, we are at the same time bringing together under a single heading the orthodox view of monetary policy as it developed in the post-World War II years. It is the so-called "concertina" view of the financial system. Squeeze the monetary end and the whole instrument contracts, everywhere emitting consistent changes in interest rates and credit conditions. In considering later (Sect. 25.4) some of the major obstacles to the effectiveness of monetary policy, we shall be dealing with arguments in support of the view that only the monetary end of the concertina is subject to constraint by the monetary officials. The other end, for practical purposes, remains unaffected; that is, the financial system is more like a balloon—constrain or squeeze the monetary portion and the balloon bulges somewhere else.

The orthodox instruments of monetary policy. We have dealt at some lengths and in numerous places (for example, Sect. 8.2) with the mechanics of the traditional instruments of monetary policy. We can divide these up in at least two ways:

(1) Federal Reserve credit (including open market purchases and sales and lending to member banks), the level of reserve requirements of member banks, and the level of discount rates charged member banks by the twelve Federal Reserve banks; or

(2) Open market operations, reserve requirements, and discount policy (including both discount rates and lending to member banks).

For purposes of illustrating general policy models, it was useful above (Sect. 25.1) to apply the former classification, so as to separate total lending and credit extended through open market purchases by the Federal Reserve from discount rates. Now, however, we shall return to the latter classification.

Open market operations. The open market purchase and sale of United States government securities by the Federal Reserve ideally works in three ways.[4] First and foremost in the minds of Federal Reserve officials, open market operations influence the level of member-bank reserves and thus encourage such banks to increase their earning assets and deposits at different rates or to contract them and, by these actions, to change market yields and customer rates.

Secondly, open market operations directly add to or subtract from the stock of government securities available to trade in the open market. Substantial Federal Reserve purchases add initially to the demand for this stock, directly bidding up prices and lowering yields; the Federal Reserve's purchases withdraw from the market a portion of the stock of securities available for subsequent private trading, thus tending to maintain higher prices and lower yields. Even though the Federal Reserve confines its purchases to only a narrow range of maturities of United States government securities, the effect will soon pervade all maturities in all types of open market instruments through phenomena known as switching and arbitrage (Sect. 4.3). Federal Reserve sales of securities, of course, work in the opposite direction in each of these respects.

Closely related to the arbitrage and switching responses of investors to open market purchases or sales is the third way open market operations work. The third way pertains to the effect on the expectations of financial investors about the future prices and yields of open market instruments. This is one instance of what are often called "announcement effects." Federal Reserve purchases of Treasury bills, for example, may cause investors to anticipate rising prices and falling yields in other maturities, which induces them to buy these maturities in the hope of capital gains. This, of course, would tend to reinforce the effects of arbitrage and, perhaps even to speed up the process of transmitting price and yield changes. During the "bills-only" era (Sect. 24.3), a major defense of the practice was the argument that it avoided the kind of speculative activity in intermediate and long-term markets based on guesses about the timing and magnitude of direct Federal Reserve operations, in these markets. If the market was certain there would be no such operations, the incentive for such disruptive speculation would thus be removed.[5] Further, it is a simple arithmetical phenomenon that the yields on short-term securities tend to fluctuate much more than yields on long-term securities, while at the same time the prices (or capitalized values) of short-term securities tend to be more stable than the prices (or capitalized values) of long-term securities (Sect. 4.2 and 4.3). Hence, by confining its open market operations to short-term securities and by convincing the market that it would continue to do so except under unusual circumstances, the Federal Reserve can in principle effect substantial yield changes without directly causing either large capital gains or losses in short-term securities or capital gains speculation in longer-term securities due to the anticipation of Federal Reserve operations in these maturities.

Changes in reserve requirements. Changes in reserve requirements for demand deposits are in principle, "double-barrelled" in their effect on intermediate money, interest rate, or market "tone" targets. They immediately affect the volume of excess reserves of member banks, as well as alter the magnitude of money and credit multipliers (Sect. 3.2). Changes in reserve requirements for time deposits, while quite infrequent, similarly affect excess reserves; if time deposits participate in processes of expansion and contraction of demand deposits and bank credit, then money and credit multipliers will also be influenced by changes in reserve requirements for time deposits (Sect. 3.3).

Open market sales and increases in reserve requirements both absorb bank reserves, and open market purchases and reductions in reserve requirements both release reserves. There may be, however, an important difference in the effects of the two instruments on the earning assets and on the liquidity of the total structure of bank assets. A use of linear programing techniques, for example, could be shown to generate such differences, and Professor Aschheim[6] has emphasized a slightly different approach. The latter's basic argument is simply that the use of both instruments leads to changes in total bank assets, but that there are differences in the way they affect the composition of bank assets. Open market operations tend to leave unchanged the relative composition of assets as between earning and liquid assets, while changes in reserve requirements tend to decrease or increase liquid assets relative to earning assets, depending on whether the requirements are lowered or raised. According to Aschheim, increases in reserve requirements force banks to be more liquid, and this intensifies their desire to dump government securities to replenish earnings. (Note the assumption here that required reserves are liquid.)

The discount rate and discounts and advances. Discount policy refers both to changes in discount rates and changes in the volume of lending to member banks not attributable to the price-rationing effect of rate changes. Discount policy, as with any policy instrument, may assume one of three roles relative to other policy instruments as we illustrate below. These roles are reinforcement, substitute, or compensation.[7] As we will point out after some discussion of each of these rules, the actual role of discount policy in the United States is a compromise of reinforcement and compensation.

Prior to illustrating these various roles of discount policy and giving some explanation of discount policy in America, however, let us recall the money supply equation [i.e., equation (6)] from the two-target model presented earlier (Sect. 25.1): $M = m_1 \Delta F - m_2 \Delta R - m_3 \Delta D + M_0$. Assume the change in Federal Reserve credit (ΔF) may be broken down into net open market purchases or sales (ΔF_{om}) and net lending to member banks (ΔF_l), other than those already expressed in the $m_3 \Delta D$ term,

$$\Delta F = \Delta F_{om} + \Delta F_l$$

We can rearrange the equation as follows:

$$\underbrace{M - M_0}_{} = \underbrace{m_1 \Delta F_{om}}_{} - \underbrace{m_2 \Delta R}_{} + \underbrace{m_1 \Delta F_l - m_3 \Delta D}_{}$$

| Change in money supply | Open market operations (net) | Changes in reserve requirements | Changes in discount policy |

Thus the equation now indicates the contribution to a change in the money supply from the use of the three policy instruments.

Moreover, to indicate the possibility of a reinforcement role of discount policy, note the two elements of a change in discount policy, i.e., volume of lending and rates, in the latter equation. There, an increase in open market purchases could be accompanied by a deliberate increase in lending to member banks $(m_1 \Delta F_l)$, apart from discount rate changes, and/or a reduction in discount rates $(m_3 \Delta D)$, which presumably stimulates member-bank borrowing from the Federal Reserve and adds to the money supply. In this case, discount policy reinforces open market operations and contributes to larger money supply changes than would otherwise result with a given amount of open market purchases.

Another possibility is that changes in discount policy could be used as a substitute for open market operations to achieve a policy target expressed in terms of a certain money supply change. In the two-target models (Sect. (25.1), we treated changes in both discount policy and reserve requirements in such a fashion. Under certain circumstances, this might require substantial changes in discount rates and/or lending to member banks.

A final possibility is that changes in discount policy are used to offset or compensate for changes in open market operations. In terms of the above equation, a positive or negative ΔF_{om} would be accompanied by a ΔF_l with opposite sign and/or a ΔD with the same sign. Such actions would presumably be intended to provide some relief from pressures stemming from other actions (or provide pressures to offset relief from other actions).

Now in the United States, discount policy has tended to be a compromise of the first and third of the above possibilities. Rate changes generally reinforce other policy actions and, as with other actions, may carry expectational or "announcement" effects as well (Sect. 8.2). But, what is important, the Federal Reserve has never chosen over the early post-World War II decades very substantial discount rate changes nor have the rates themselves been very high relative to central bank discount rates in other countries.[*] The point is that the Federal Reserve

---

[*] Since the debacle of 1929 and 1930 when the Federal Reserve Bank of New York discount rate, at one point, reached 6 per cent (Sect. 7.5), discount rates have never exceeded 4 per cent. The all-time historical high was 7 per cent in 1920 and 1921.

has chosen not to use discount rates as "penalty rates" ** (Sect. 8.2), in contrast to the practices of many other central banks, in particular the Bank of England and the Bank of Canada.

The reason for not wanting to discourage banks very strongly from borrowing from the Federal Reserve is to be found mainly in the role of such borrowing as a partial and necessary offset to open market sales and increased reserve requirements. This is the function of the discount mechanism as a "safety valve" to help compensate for the differential effects of other actions on a system of banks of greatly varying size, location, and nature of business. It is here that the Federal Reserve still serves in a limited sense as a passive "lender of last resort." How is it, one may ask, that the "safety valve" does not become an "escape route" for banks seeking reserves, especially if discount rates are not very high? In principle, there are two constraining forces supposedly at work, one on each side of the "discount window." [8] On the lender's side is the presumption that discounting is a "privilege" rather than a "right" of member banks; a privilege, unlike a right, is subject to the will of the grantor.

On the borrower's side of the window the constraint against abuse of discounting is the alleged "reluctance" of banks to borrow and remain in debt to the Federal Reserve. The need to do so is supposedly an admission of poor bank management, and the subsequent scrutiny of a bank's affairs is humiliating.[9] This basis for reluctance, though, tends to diminish as banks become larger and their management more impersonal. Further, any eagerness by banks to repay indebtedness to the Federal Reserve may account for some of the delay which tends to prolong the attainment of intermediate policy targets at times of reserve decreases (Sect. 26.2).

Orthodox monetary policy and nonmember financial institutions. If the financial system is, ideally, more like a concertina than a balloon, then there must be some explanation for how the effects of Federal Reserve actions are either, at best, transmitted beyond the confines of member banks in such ways as to reinforce the effects on member banks or, at least, are not systematically offset by reactions elsewhere in the financial system. There are basically four reasons why this might be forthcoming.[10] All four of these reasons logically apply just as well to nonmember commercial banks (Sect. 11.5) as to many other types of financial institutions, although the specific details may differ.

First of all, nonmember commercial banks and other financial institutions have important business connections with member banks. The nonmember banks generally use member banks as correspondents (Sect.

** A penalty discount rate has been generally defined as a rate above "the rate on the pivotal assets through which the commercial banks adjust their portfolios; these are the assets (most often Treasury bills . . .) that the banks would sell first during periods of reserve pressure." See Peter G. Fousek, *Foreign Central Banking: The Instruments of Monetary Policy* (Federal Reserve Bank of New York, 1957), p. 18.

3.2, 7.4, and 7.5), and many other financial institutions rely on commercial banks as sources of short-term funds. The latter would especially include those institutions specializing in short-term lending, such as business "factors" (Sect. 17.5), or institutions engaged in the temporary carrying of loan and investment portfolios, such as mortgage companies (Sect. 18.3) and security brokers and dealers (Sect. 14.1).* Presumably, member-banks' interest rate and credit availability changes directly affect these other institutions through the member-bank advisory services as well as through their loan departments.

Second, even small interest rate increases resulting from Federal Reserve actions may have substantial effects on the capitalized values of long-term assets (for example, Sect. 4.3 and 17.3). The rise in rates reduces the liquidity of financial assets with fixed flows of returns (Sect. 5.4) in particular and causes the financial institutions in effect to "lock in" their holdings until prices rise and yields fall again, until the returns on alternative assets rise sufficiently to compensate for the paper losses, or until there are capital gains to offset the losses. Conversely, even slight decreases in interest rates would cause financial institutions to release some loans and investments in exchange for newer higher yielding ones.

Third, to the extent that nonbank financial institutions regularly remain "loaned-up" in long-term assets over the business cycle, these institutions would not have an excess of liquid funds. Consequently, they could not expand the flow of funds into new loans and investments to the nonfinancial sector during periods of restrictive Federal Reserve policy nor could they buy old debt instruments from banks so that banks may do the new lending and investing.

Fourth, the ability of nonbank financial institutions to bid away the deposits of member banks by offering higher interest returns and thus to secure funds for expanding their own earning assets in the face of a restrictive monetary policy is limited by at least three factors: (1) the feasible differential between the interest rates they pay depositors or shareholders and the rates paid by member banks after allowances for differences in risk, (2) the differential between the rates they earn on their loans and investments and the rates they pay depositors or shareholders, and (3) the willingness of their depositors or shareholders to substitute successive increments of deposits or shares in such institutions for deposits in member banks. The first two factors, however, are partly related. With respect to the first factor, payments by member banks are limited by the Federal Reserve's interest ceilings and by the extent of competitive pressures to approach the ceilings, and, with respect to the

* In 1959 the Federal Reserve began publishing separate figures for bank loans to other banks and to nonbank financial institutions. On June 30, 1964, for example, member banks accounted for almost 95 per cent of the 2.9 billion dollars of loans to banks and about 95 per cent of the 10.5 billion dollars of loans to nonbank financial institutions.

first and second factors, the same interest ceilings apply to nonmember commercial and mutual savings banks whose deposits are insured by the Federal Deposit Insurance Corporation. Nearly all of the nonmember commercial banks and two-thirds of the mutual savings banks are so insured, so these institutions have little leeway for engaging in "price competition" with member banks for deposits.

While not legally constrained by interest ceilings, all other financial institutions no longer have much latitude for paying higher interest rates to savers. In 1962, interest ceilings were raised and the long-standing reserve requirement against time deposits was reduced in order to make member banks both more able and willing to compete for savings deposits.. With lower account turnover and higher yielding, less-liquid earning assets, nonbank financial institutions can presumably afford to pay higher savings interest. At the same time, though, they *need* to pay higher savings interest for the same reasons, i.e., less favorable deposit contracts and somewhat riskier loans and investments. Further, nonbank financial institutions and commercial banks have, in the post-World War II period, become substantial competitors in installment and mortgage lending and the government securities markets. Also many institutions are heavily dependent on FHA- and VA-insured mortgages, which at least in principle carry fixed interest returns. Thus, as a result of the competition and the duplication of efforts to extend loans in somewhat similar markets, one should not expect the nonbank financial institutions to cover increased savings interest by raising rates to borrowers.

Even if nonmember financial institutions were not constrained in their competition for deposits by effective limits on interest rates to savers and from borrowers, they would still be limited in their ability to attract deposits from member banks on other grounds. For example, the more money that households, governmental units, and business firms exchange for savings accounts, the less willing they become to make further exchanges because of the particular attributes of money for making transactions, other things being equal in the partial derivative sense.[11]

25.3 A Reformulation of Orthodox Monetary Policy: The Availability Doctrine

In the 1950's some writers and monetary officials effected a revival of an old doctrine—the availability doctrine. It attempts to explain the effectiveness of monetary policy on private expenditures and thus the ultimate target levels of income, employment, and so on, while at the same time avoiding the conclusions of certain critics about the ineffectiveness of monetary policy in other respects. The latters' conclusions were (1) that the instruments of monetary policy have little influence on interest rates, and, still worse, (2) that the private demand for bank credit is interest inelastic anyway.*

This alternative explanation of the effectiveness of monetary policy is variously known as "the 'new' theory of credit control," the "availability" doctrine, and the "credit rationing doctrine." [12] The word "new" is used with quotation marks to indicate that the basic notion is not really very new, and "availability" and "credit rationing" both refer to fundamental aspects of the doctrine. What is, perhaps, most important about the doctrine is that it provides a rationale for the successful conduct of monetary policy under the very circumstances where the opposite would seem to be the case, i.e., where the central bank is not able or willing to bring about very substantial interest rate changes and where the private demand for bank credit is thought to be generally interest rate inelastic. It is not surprising, then, that the theory has its most ardent advocates from among central bankers.

A statement of the doctrine: the availability of funds and credit rationing. As with most doctrines, the availability one is relatively simple in its abstract form, but extremely complex in a particular real-world setting.

Essentially the proponents of the doctrine assert that a rise in interest rates reduces the availability of bank credit, consequently widens the margin of unsatisfied borrowers, and results in the rationing** of the limited supply of credit to customers by the credit-granting institutions.[13] The rise in the rates reduces the supply of available credit by decreasing long-term security values and by "locking in" the holdings of financial institutions and by decreasing private purchases of securities. Given the quantity (q_s) of available credit as an increasing function of the rate of interest (i), and the quantity demanded (q_a) as a decreasing function of the rate, we in effect have a leftward shift in the supply function due mainly to the locking-in effect as shown in Fig. 25-1. Also, due to the sluggishness of the market and the tendency for rates at banks to be sticky in their adjustment to other rates, we notice a tendency toward unsatisfied demand at the old equilibrium rate ($\bar{i}$) and a larger unsatisfied demand at the old effective rate (i_0) as indicated by the horizontal arrows in the diagram. The demand function is shown, too, to reflect the assumptions of the relatively insensitivity of demand to interest rate changes over the relevant domain of the definition of the function.

---

* The reader will recall the definition of the inelasticity of demand as a percentage change in the rate of interest (i) that calls forth a smaller percentage change in the quantity (q) demanded, i.e., $|dq/di|(i/q) < 1$. Quantity, of course, is expressed as a dollar amount. (See Appendix to Chapter 17.)

** In a properly functioning market system, resources are usually allocated by prices (or rates of return, Sect. 4.1). This allocation is a form of rationing, but in the present context "rationing" refers to nonprice rationing. This may take the form of rationing on a first-come-first-served basis, on the use of some priority or waiting list, or rationing with price controls and ration coupons.

Leftward shifts in the demand for credit of a somewhat smaller magnitude than the shifts in the supply schedule are further introduced as a part of the availability doctrine, and the explanation for them is more complicated than the explanation for shifts in the supply schedule. In Lindbeck's fairly simple model [14] the demand function for private credit is viewed as varying inversely with the interest rates on private credit, directly with investment expenditures, and inversely with yields on government securities—all to cause this demand to shift to the left (decrease). Investment expenditures are regarded as

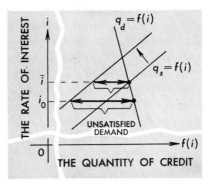

Fig. 25-1. The Rate of Interest and the Availability of Credit.

depending on interest rates on private credit, the quantity of private credit supplied, and yields on government securities. When these yields rise and when the credit supplied decreases, investment as a downward sloping function of interest rates on private credit shifts to the left, inducing a further leftward shift in the demand for private credit. The reasons for linking investment expenditures and the total demand for private credit inversely to government security yields are to be found in a variety of somewhat tenuous arguments concerning borrowers' demands for liquidity over future market conditions, and changes in the eligibility to apply for loans.

The effect of all this on aggregate demand and, thus, on equilibrium levels of income, output, and employment depends on the magnitude of the change in investment expenditures, the marginal propensities to spend out of increased income, and the magnitude of any additional induced effects on consumption (saving) caused by the rise in government securities yields and accompanying effects on the value for accumulated savings and on savers' expectations about the future.

In the scheme of things envisaged by the proponents of the availability doctrine, the central bank concentrates on securities as the instrument variable in order to bring about target changes successively in government security yields and, regardless of the effects on private interest rates, in the availability of private credit. It hopes thereby to influence directly or indirectly private expenditures and thus ultimate target levels of income, employment, and so forth. Note that what is "orthodox" about the theory is the policy instrument used and the ultimate results presumably obtained. What is "unorthodox" is the substitution of credit rationing phenomena for any sort of market supply-and-demand determination of interest rates and credit allocation. The chief reasons for the doctrine's decline in popularity were (1) the gradual decline in the bond component of the Federal government's debt, diminishing the quantitative basis of "locking-in" effects, and (2) the increasing evidence that financial institutions, particularly commercial banks, may not be reluctant to realize losses on government security holdings when more profitable alternatives exist in other types of earning assets.

Quasi-credit rationing. In more recent years some new life was given to the credit rationing doctrine in the works of Donald R. Hodgman,[15] although the particular phenomenon he uncovered in an extensive survey of commercial bankers would be more properly called quasi-credit rationing. It ought to be so called because implicit rather than explicit price rationing of credit lies at the heart of the Hodgman thesis.

Briefly Professor Hodgman argues that, for quite rational reasons of wanting to maximize long-run profits, bankers give preferential treatment in lending to their deposit customers. Customer deposits, depending on average size and turnover, grant net earning power to banks. This is particularly true of the seasonal balances of large business depositor-borrowers. Thus, in a setting where banks cannot compete for deposits through explicit interest payments as a result of the interest prohibition or demand deposits and interest ceilings on insured time and savings deposits, there are good reasons to reduce loans to nondepositor borrowers in favor of depositor-borrowers during periods of credit tightness.

The Hodgman thesis also presents the rationale for both the "prime rate" (i.e., the interest rate on business loans to a bank's best customers) and the compensating balance requirements (Sect. 14.2) imposed at times on prime business depositor-borrowers.

The exclusion of nondepositor-borrowers at times when credit is tight and the prime rate and compensating balance requirements are raised really amounts to implicit price rationing. This is clear when one realizes that banks would have to quote an inordinately high contract interest rate to nondepositor-borrowers in order to equalize the net gain from loans to depositor-borrowers. In fact, the rate may be thought of as being so high that banks do not bother to quote it and, instead, refuse the loans.[16]

25.4. Induced Changes in Velocity and the Effectiveness of Monetary Policy

It has long been asserted that a fundamental weakness in using orthodox monetary measures to influence aggregate demand is the inability to control the rate at which money is spent in various sorts or transactions. Up until now, we have not specifically considered this question. Even so, it was lurking in the background in a number of places, particularly in the discussions of income velocity (Sect. 5.1), the financing of increases in aggregate demand (Sect. 15.2), and nonbank financial institutions.

Now, however, we want to examine the behavior of velocity against this earlier background, but we wish to do so from a slightly different point of view. Namely, we wish to deal with the question of how movements in velocity might be related to the actions of the monetary authorities, and whether such movements constitute a serious weakness in the operation of orthodox monetary policy (Sect. 25.2). In handling this question, we review some of the earlier background, outline alternative views on the subject in question, and deal especially with the relationship between velocity changes and switching between demand and other types deposits and changes in the composition of portfolios (or total assets). Deposit shifts and portfolio shifts, as the latter changes are called, relate to changes in the demand for money balances, and, therefore, velocity—as our review of earlier background reveals. Consequently, these shifts need to be allowed for in selecting the bank reserve and money supply change called for in order to achieve a given ultimate target, such as a specific change in demand.

Some previous considerations. Earlier we set forth the motives for holding money (Sect. 4.4). There was the implication that a strengthening of the speculative and precautionary motives, relative to the transactions motive, pulled balances out of the sphere of active balances, and that a weakening of the motive contributed to an increase in the activation of money balances. Later (Sect. 5.4), in illustrating this, we saw why (money supply-const.) changes in income velocity tend to parallel changes in the flow of income. Obviously, the money supply is not likely to be constant over such short cycles of income change, but we wished to illustrate the forces at work. As a logical matter, velocity and the flow of income could still change in accordance with the earlier pattern, after allowances for changes in the money supply. This phenomenon we demonstrate below as a basis for the support of orthodox monetary policy.

Earlier discussion (Sect. 17.1 and 20.2), furthermore, indicated the usefulness of explicit statements of the money demand function in the traditional theory of money and macroeconomics. This function assumes that the demand for money, as with other financial assets, changes at the same rate as total assets (i.e., that the various financial assets remain constant proportions of the total)[17] provided other things are constant, such as underlying conditions, and the various claims against assets as proportions of assets. This implies a rather restrictive approach, but it helps in the analysis of factors giving rise to secular changes in velocity. For example, in terms of the demand function for money, an increase over a period of years in the proportion of assets held in such forms as deposits at savings intermediaries or such near-money forms as government securities and a decrease in the proportion held in money balances lead us to expect a secular rise in income velocity, other things being equal. In effect, one form of liquid assets other than money balances may be substituted for money balances for some purposes, such as to satisfy the precautionary motive, with the result that only balances held for more active uses are left. In such a case, a target variable for the money supply could be lower than otherwise called for to achieve a given ultimate target for expenditures. In considering secular trends other things must be considered, however, such as changes in the illiquidity of the liability structure (Sect. 4.1 and 17.1) for households and firms. In the short run, shifts in deposits and portfolios may less likely be affected by changes in these other things, but our failure to consider them as a part of deposit and portfolio shifts should be kept in mind.

Changes in income velocity, in the above framework, could result from a growth rate of savings intermediaries in excess of the growth rate for the money supply. They could also result from the substitution of one form of liquid assets, such as savings deposits, where in the short run the holders of the assets regarded them as near-perfect substitutes and consequently wished to dispose of the excess of money balances over the desired amount.

Later we consider changes in the composition of assets and changes in the relative importance of different types of deposits.

Alternative views of the effectiveness of monetary policy. On those occasions where the monetary authorities attempt to effect a policy of monetary ease or tightness through changes in the level of reserves and the money supply, velocity may behave in one of three possible ways: (1) it might remain constant, (2) it might move "concertina-like" so as to reinforce the effects of actions affecting bank reserves and the money supply, or (3) it might move "balloon-like" so as to offset the effect of these actions to some extent.

An earlier model (Sect. 1.2 and 5.4) implied an orthodox view of monetary policy. Therefore, let us re-examine Fig. 1-1 and the definition of income velocity. Recall, to begin with, that the equation defining the demand for money (i.e., $M_d = \alpha Y + \beta$) gives the effective demand for money at the equilibrium income value Y at a given time and the "desired" level of money balances at other hypothetical income values. Now in this framework, velocity rises when the actual money supply (γ) exceeds the desired amount of balances at the old equilibrium, and it declines when the money supply is less than the desired amount.

As the expansion phase of business activity proceeds (i.e., excess of supply over desired amount of balances), income rises as from the initial time (t) to a subsequent time $(t + 1)$ in the illustration. This results from the effort to dispose of balances in excess of the desired amount, but, as income rises, the level of desired balances for effecting transactions rises $(\alpha > 0)$ and a new equilibrium is approached [e.g., $(Y_{t+1},$

M_s)]. In this setting, the monetary authorities may expand the money supply as they usually have in the initial expansion phase of post-World War II cycles. The result will be a continued rise in income and in velocity as long as the supply of balances exceeds the desired level of balances, and until a new equilibrium level of velocity is reached.

In terms of the earlier definition of velocity (Sect. 5.4),

$$V_y = \frac{1 - \beta/\gamma}{\alpha}, \quad \alpha > 0, \text{ and}$$

$$\beta < 0, \text{ in expansion phase, and}$$

$$\beta > 0, \text{ in contraction phase.}$$

Moreover,

$$\frac{dV_y}{d\gamma} = \frac{\beta/\gamma^2}{\alpha}, \text{ and}$$

velocity is a decreasing function of the money supply in the expansion phase ($\beta < 0$), and an increasing function of the money supply in the contraction phase ($\beta > 0$). The latter are true statements, once new levels of velocity are attained in response to the changes in β.

What this means—in the expansion phase, $\beta = \text{const.} < 0$—is that a contraction of the money supply increases velocity. This fact seems to imply that velocity moves "balloon-like" and as an offset to the effects of a contraction in bank credit and the stock of money. Of course, contractions in the stock of money are rare in an expansion phase (see Table 2-1). In any event, we would still view changes in the credit and the stock of money as operating on the level of aggregate expenditures and β through the rate of interest vis-à-vis the rate of return (for example, Sect. 5.4 and 17.2).

Our view of velocity and changes in the stock of money would not appear too unusual, if one realizes that an increase in the money stock depends on the effective demand for active balances at the banks, as we emphasize in subsequent discussions of deposit shifts and velocity changes. However, we have shown decreases in the money supply to have a constraining effect on velocity and on increases in the average of prices for current output, in the expansion phase, if and only if it has a constraining effect on expenditures. To attempt to control rises in velocity by increasing the money supply, as would be called for by the above exposition, would be inconsistent with the achievement of other targets. The increase in the money supply would further increase the excess of balances over the desired level when β is moving in the negative direction, and it would contribute to a rise in velocity expenditures, and so on at a time when the objective may be to restrain expenditures, and so on. A quantitative target for velocity could only be a dependent target, in the sense that velocity can be controlled only by controlling expenditures, and so on, via shifts in β, for example. But velocity may not be "uniquely dependent" in the real world in the sense that it may possibly be attained by control over expenditures. A target for velocity is implied (i.e., $V_y =$ const.) by a policy of rigidly tying the rate of change in the money supply to the rate of change in income [i.e., $Y(Y = PO)$] or output at constant prices. [Compare "An appraisal of the fixed rule proposal" (Sect. 26.5).]

Deposit shifts (in general). When the Federal Reserve acts to reduce bank excess reserves (Sect. 24.2) and the money supply and raise interest rates, their efforts will be hampered if the public can be induced to shift from liquid assets that absorb bank reserves at a higher rate to those that absorb bank reserves at a lower rate. All sorts of such shifts are conceivable, for example, from currency to demand deposits, from demand deposits to time deposits, from time deposits to savings-and-loan shares, or from any asset earlier in the list to a later one. The first two examples would cause excess reserves to be generated, since, in the first, a cash inflow constitutes a primary deposit for the banking system, and, in the second, time deposits carry lower reserve requirements than demand deposits. A shift from bank deposits (demand or time) to a nonbank financial institution, on the other hand, increases the lending power of the nonbank financial institution without decreasing that of banks; stated differently, the same volume of bank reserves comes to support a larger volume of deposits and deposit-type claims. This is merely one instance of a long recognized phenomenon known as the increased "pyramiding" of reserves.*

Let us consider below numerical examples of two types of deposit shifts: Case 1, a shift from demand deposits to time deposits (Sect. 3.3), and, Case 2, a shift from demand deposits to savings-and-loan shares (Sect. 15.2).

A shift from demand to time deposits (Case 1). In Case 1, the public decides to shift $10 from demand deposits to time deposits in commercial banks. If reserve requirements for demand deposits are 15 per cent and for time deposits 4 per cent, banks are initially loaned up, and they have initial demand deposits of $100 and time deposits of $50, their reserve and deposit accounts just before and just after the shift will appear as follows:

---

* That banks need only to maintain fractional reserves for their deposit liabilities is the basis for the simplest sort of reserve pyramid. Additional layers are added to the pyramid when other financial institutions maintain their own fractional reserves in the form of balances in banks. Other examples of pyramiding are the present-day role of United States gold reserves relative to the money supply (Sect. 9.2), and the place of gold reserves when a number of countries adopt gold exchange standards (Sect. 6.1 and 23.3).

All Commercial Banks

Before	Required reserves	$17.00	Demand deposits	$100.00
	Excess reserves	0.00	Time deposits	50.00
			Total	$150.00

All Commercial Banks

After	Required reserves	$15.90	Demand deposits	$ 90.00
	Excess reserves	1.10	Time deposits	60.00
			Total	$150.00

Banks now have excess reserves of $1.10, which they can use as the basis for a multiple expansion of earning assets and deposits (Sect. 3.2). The outcome depends on the ability and willingness of banks to "use up" the excess reserves to support increased deposits or to meet any induced cash drain.*

A shift from demand deposits to savings-and-loan shares (Case 2). In Case 2, we assume that the nonfinancial public shifts $10 of demand deposits to savings-and-loan shares instead of to time deposits, that savings-and-loan associations keep their cash "reserves" in the form of demand deposits in commercial banks (which, by the way, are counted as part of the money supply in the money supply accounts), and that these "reserves" are kept at 4 per cent of savings shares. If savings-and-loan associations have initial shares of $50 and are loaned up at the beginning, and if the beginning reserve and deposit accounts for commercial banks are the same as in Case 1, then the balance sheets for both sets of financial institutions just before and just after the shift will appear as follows:

All Commercial Banks

Required reserves	$17.00	Demand deposits of savings-and-loan associations	$ 2.00
Excess reserves	0.00	Demand deposits of nonfinancial public	98.00
		Time deposits	50.00
		Total	$150.00

Savings-and-Loan Associations

Demand deposits in commercial banks	$ 2.00	Savings shares	$ 50.00

Before {

---

* Actually, there are a number of possible families of "claims shift multipliers," depending on the nature of the original shift and the nature of induced reserve drains. Such multipliers are merely special cases of the financial multipliers discussed earlier (Chap. 3). See William P. Yohe, "The Derivation of Certain Financial Multipliers," *Southern Economic Journal*, July 1962, pp. 26-32.

All Commercial Banks

Required reserves	$17.00	Demand deposits of savings-and-loan associations	$ 12.00
Excess reserves	0.00	Demand deposits of nonfinancial public	88.00
		Time deposits	50.00
		Total	$150.00

After

Savings-and-Loan Associations

Demand deposits in commercial banks	$12.00	Savings shares	$60.00

Note that an increase has occurred in the liquid asset holdings of the nonbank public. Further, savings-and-loan associations now have "excess reserves" of $9.60 which they can use to expand their own loans and investments, paying the proceeds with checks drawn against their bank accounts. If savings-and-loan associations do expand, the balance sheets will then be as follows:*

All Commercial Banks

Required reserves	$17.00	Demand deposits of savings-and-loan associations	$ 2.40
Excess reserves	0.00	Demand deposits of nonfinancial public	97.60
		Time Deposits	50.00
		Total	$150.00

Savings-and-Loan Associations

Demand deposits in commercial banks	$ 2.40	Savings shares	$ 60.00
Increased loans and investments	9.60		

Now banks and savings-and-loan associations are again loaned up, and there has been an increase in both liquid assets and "credit."

Deposit shifts (timing and effect on velocity). Cases 1 and 2 above raise some questions: (1) Under what circumstances might such shifts occur? (2) How is velocity affected in each case?

With respect to the first question, the shifts would most likely occur when the rates on time and savings deposits were rising relative to the

---

* This assumes that the checks drawn on the demand deposits of savings-and-loan associations are redeposited to demand deposit accounts. In actual practice, a savings-and-loan association, in, for example, making a mortgage loan, usually makes the check payable to both the borrower and the seller of the property; the borrower, in turn, endorses the check and gives it to the seller, who deposits it to his own account.

structure of rates and when there was general strengthening of the demand for assets with a fixed flow of returns (Sect. 5.4). The former type would be most serious to the effectiveness of a restrictive monetary policy, as evidenced by rising interest rates, because it would contribute most to a rise in velocity as outlined below. Although such a shift is not apt to occur frequently, it did occur in the first half of 1962, when the ceiling on time and savings deposits at insured banks was raised.[18] The increase in the rate at that time precipitated a shift from demand to time deposits, so as to contribute to excess reserves.

Since nonbank financial institutions do not have interest ceilings imposed on their savings liabilities, they are less likely to find their rates out of line at a time of rising interest rates. Even so, in principle, they may be able to bid deposits away from banks at times when their rates of returns on loans and investments are rising. We have already seen, however, that their ability to do this is self-limiting (Sect. 24.2). Further, there has evidently been a gradual decrease in the postwar period in the margin between their savings interest rates and commercial bank rates on savings.[19] This would seem to reflect, despite generally rising interest rates, a relative improvement of the competitive position of commercial banks for savings.

With respect to the other question, velocity would tend to rise in each of the kinds of deposit shifts depicted in the above illustrations. In Case 1, it would presumably be a relatively idle demand deposit that a customer could be induced to hold in the form of a time deposit. His shift releases reserves, which makes it possible to restore a fairly large portion of the "lost" demand deposit through multiple expansion of deposits and bank "credit." In any event, the new demand deposits are created for borrowers, who spend them, very probably for new goods and services. These deposits then enter the income stream and will be respent. The result is a greater rate of turnover of money. Similar reasoning would hold for Case 2. The relatively idle bank deposit is lured to a savings-and-loan association, which transfers most of the old demand deposit to borrower-spenders.

Proposals to stabilize deposit shifts. If deposit or claims shifts are truly systematically disturbing to Federal Reserve policy (the evidence is not in favor of such an interpretation), then remedies might be in order. Several will be mentioned, but it will be left to the reader to work out the logic behind these proposals. One suggestion is to equalize the reserve requirement for demand and time deposits.* Another is to extend reserve requirements to all financial institutions.

Portfolio shifts. Substantially more credence may be placed in the sec-

---

* "One hundred per cent reserve banking" is really an extreme case of this proposal. Note, however, that "100 per cent" reserves for the banking system would not eliminate the effects of shifts to nonbank financial institutions.

ond major type of velocity offset to actions by the central bank—the so-called "portfolio shifts." This could be quite a pervasive phenomenon, although the evidence points mainly to commercial banks as the villains, so we shall proceed with an illustration involving banks.

Suppose that commercial banks, facing demand deposit reserve requirements of 15 per cent and time deposit requirements of 4 per cent, are loaned up and that a greatly simplified version of their consolidated balance sheet appears as follows:

All Commercial Banks

Required reserves	$ 17.00	Demand deposits:	
Excess reserves	0.00	Customers A	$ 10.00
United States govern-		Customers B	90.00
ment securities	33.00	Time deposits	50.00
Loans	100.00	Total	$150.00
Total	$150.00		

Note that demand deposit customers are divided into two groups—A and B. Group A customers, for reasons to be explored below, hold idle balances.

Next, assume that banks are deluged with loan applications. If they could sell some of their government securities to group A customers, they would be able to grant an equal amount of loan requests without any need for additional reserves. Suppose first of all that banks sell $10 of their government securities to group A customers. Their consolidated balance sheet then will be:

All Commercial Banks

Required reserves	$ 15.50	Demand deposits:	
Excess reserves	1.50	Customers A	$ 0.00
United States govern-		Customers B	90.00
ment securities	23.00	Time deposits	50.00
Loans	100.00	Total	$140.00
Total	$140.00		

Observe that group A's deposits are simply extinguished as some of banks' debt is "demonetized." Now banks can expand their loans by $10, so their balance sheet will end up as follows:

All Commercial Banks

Required reserves	$ 17.00	Demand deposits:	
Excess reserves	0.00	Customers B	$ 90.00
United States govern-		New deposits	10.00
ment securities	23.00	Time deposits	50.00
Loans	110.00	Total	$150.00
Total	$150.00		

Of course, as borrowers spend the newly created deposits, they will wind up in the hands of group A or B customers, but this is not specifically shown. Note, and this is important, that (1) the demand deposit component of the money supply is back to its initial level, $100, and (2) the velocity of money has risen, since idle balance holders were induced to exchange their deposit "slot" for government securities and the vacancy was filled through increased loans to borrower-spenders.

These customers A were partly identified earlier (Sec. 17.2). There we noted that nonfinancial corporations, particularly large manufacturing corporations, were net purchasers of liquid assets in the early phase of cyclical expansion. These securities were acquired partly in anticipation of subsequent expenditures. Also there is some support for the view that households, too, enter as net purchasers at times,[20] and in 1959, a year of cyclical expansion, that foreign and international investors were net purchasers.[21]

Portfolio shifts (timing and effects). Once again, questions arise: (1) Under what circumstances and at which times would banks want to sell and customers A want to buy government securities? (2) What are some of the effects of the shifts?

With respect to the first question, the banks would be willing to sell securities to the above buyers in order to make loans when loan rates are rising so as to compensate them for any losses they might incur from "unlocking" their government securities portfolio. As noted earlier (Sect. 4.5), banks may be expected to acquire short-dated securities in the contraction phase of economic activity in order to increase their loan portfolios in the expansion phase and avoid losses from depreciation at times of rising interest rates.

The banks appear to be among the leading initiators of portfolio shifts among financial institutions, at least. For one thing, banks have a decided preference among financial institutions for short-term government securities, which are the least likely securities to be locked in when interest rates are rising.

The effect of this shift out of short-dated securities is, of course, a more rapid credit expansion at times of a rising loan demand. The presence of the shift at such a time provides one argument against countercyclical management of the Federal debt (Sect. 13.3)—shortening the maturity structure in recessions and lengthening in the boom. The policy encourages banks to load up on short-dated securities at a time when loan demand is limited, and it provides them with liquid securities to unload during the boom.

A proposal for stabilizing portfolio shifts. There is, in principle, a simple remedy for the unstabilizing portfolio shifts by banks. In practice, however, the problems would be formidable. Some sort of secondary reserve requirement would have to be imposed, whereby banks would be required to hold, in addition to cash reserves, reserves chiefly in the form of government securities, thus "freezing" at least part of their securities holdings.

A great many specific proposals have been made for stabilizing portfolio shifts, but most of these are resuscitated proposals from the era of Federal Reserve "pegging" of the government securities market (Sect. 24.3). At that time, banks unloaded their wartime accumulation of such securities at the Federal Reserve.[22]

25.5. Summary

To implement a rational and effective monetary policy with a given set of instruments, the monetary officials should know certain formal relationships involving its policy instruments and policy targets. Tinbergen's notion of a quantitative economic policy suggests a framework in which to assess the adequacy of instruments relative to the number of targets, the redundancy of instruments, the dependence or independence of targets, the conflicts among independent targets, and the constraints within which policy actions are conducted. These constraints include the willingness and/or ability of the central bankers to employ a sufficient number of instruments to a sufficient extent to achieve all of their targets.

Two simple models illustrate Tinbergen's notion of a quantitative economic policy, the uses of some propositions, and the meaning of terms. Using an oversimplified quantity-theory equation, we noted four variables and one equation. Two variables, velocity and output, were viewed as being determined outside of the system, and a given price level was chosen as a target variable. The money stock, or value of the single remaining variable for achieving the target, was then defined by the single equation. Thus, there was one target variable (= number of policy variables), with other variables and conditions constant. The system became a determinant one. The money stock was then defined as a function of Federal Reserve credit, the level of member bank reserves, and the level of the discount rate. The excessive number of instruments was manifest, and the need to treat two of them as being given was apparent as a means of determining the magnitude of the remaining instrument. Here we illustrated the proposition that a solution may still exist when the number of policy instruments exceeds the number of non-redundant policy instruments.

A two-instrument, two-target model was introduced in the form of eleven equations and fourteen variables, and through processes similar to those just summarized, the system was reduced to two equations—one defining a change in Federal Reserve Credit and one defining net Federal Reserve sales of foreign exchange. The latter quantities were those required to achieve two targets—the level of employment and the net gold outflow from the United States—within the context of the larger model. The level of employment in the model was an example of an independent policy goal, in the sense that its attainment did not depend on the gold outflow target. The gold outflow target, on the other hand, was dependent on the level of employment, but it was not "uniquely dependent," since it could still be attained.

According to the orthodox view of monetary policy, monetary actions involving the instruments of monetary policy at the level of day-to-day operations induce responses in interest rates, bank reserves, and expectations. These responses, in turn, may affect ultimate targets, such as given levels for income, employment, and prices. The orthodox view has also been alternatively formulated in terms of the availability doctrine. This doctrine attempts to provide an argument for the effectiveness of monetary policy under certain assumed conditions under which the instruments of monetary policy appear ineffective. These conditions are mainly an interest inelastic demand for bank credit and pegged interest rates in the government securities market. The doctrine attempts to explain, under these conditions, the restrictive effects of an increase in the demand for credit on the nonprice rationing of credit and thus on the entire financial system.

Doctrine concerning credit rationing has also been somewhat broadened to include an implicit form of price rationing—one in which credit is rationed on a nonprice basis to large depositor-borrowers during periods of reduced availability of credit. The compensation to the banks for extending loans to depositor-borrowers rather than others is in the form of compensating balances and so on. A reduction in the availability of credit may then apparently have some effect via the reduced availability of credit to nondepositor borrowers.

There are other arguments pertaining to the ineffectiveness of monetary policy, and there are also major research and central banking problems pertaining to time lags (Chapter 26). In the present chapter, views have been expressed to the effect that credit tightness and a contraction of the money supply simply result in certain escapes from the intended effects through an increase in income velocity. Given that shifts in the demand for money are constant as in the expansion phase of a cycle (e.g., $\beta = \text{const.} < 0$), then a contraction in the money supply increases velocity. Velocity is viewed as moving "balloon" fashion in response to a tight money policy, in contrast to the orthodox view. Shifts in the demand for money, however, give rise to imbalances in the desired level of balances and the stock of existing balances. In such a case, when the desired level of balances exceeds the stock of balances, velocity rises, and a contraction in the supply would reduce velocity in accord with the orthodox view. Conversely, when the desired balances exceed the stock of balances, velocity declines, and an expansion of balances would increase velocity. In this context, too, according to Tinbergen's definitions, velocity could only be a dependent target, since it could be controlled only by controlling shifts in the demand for money. But velocity need not necessarily be "uniquely dependent" in the appropriate real-world setting.

Views have been expressed, too, that rising interest rates result in an increase in the velocity of money, via a transfer of money balances from the holders of idle balances to borrower-spenders. Higher rates may also cause a shift to time deposits, and this releases reserves for credit expansion. There are, further, portfolio shifts to be dealt with, as when a bank shifts out of short-dated securities to satisfy a rising loan demand, and there are also potential problems arising from the prospect of a growth rate for nonbank financial intermediaries and money substitutes in excess of the growth rate for total assets. Despite the above—the possible causes for an ineffective monetary policy and the possible problems—however, there is considerable logic with reasonably satisfactory hypothetical foundations to supporting the orthodox view of the effects of intermediate targets (such as tone, volume of bank earning assets and deposits, and interest rates) on the ultimate targets (such as specified changes in demand and price stability) after proper allowances for inhibiting institutional patterns.

References

1. On the Theory of Economic Policy (1952), Centralization and Decentralization in Economic Policy (1954), and Economic Policy: Principles and Design (1956). All three books are part of the series, Contributions to Economic Analysis, published by the North-Holland Publishing Co., Amsterdam.

2. Professor Arthur Smithies of Harvard even views Tinbergen's influence as having extended to the Commission on Money and Credit, at least with respect to their use of the terms "instruments" and "targets." See Arthur Smithies, "The Commission on Money and Credit," The Quarterly Journal of Economics, November 1961, pp. 547 ff.

Approaches somewhat similar to Tinbergen's were pioneered in the 1930's by Ragnar Frisch in Norway and Erik Lindahl, among others, in Sweden, and some of Bent Hansen's work in Sweden in the 1950's paralleled that of Tinbergen.

3. The enumeration of the propositions follows Smithies, op.cit., pp. 548-549.

4. See Winfield W. Riefler, "Open Market Operations in Long-Term Securities," Federal Reserve Bulletin, November 1958, pp. 1262-1264.

5. Ibid.

6. See Joseph Aschheim, Techniques of Monetary Control (Baltimore, Md.: Johns Hopkins Press, 1961), pp. 19-32; Joseph Ascheim, "Restrictive

Open-Market Operations versus Reserve-Requirement Increases: A Reformulation," *Economic Journal,* June 1963, pp. 254-266.

7. See Carl E. Parry, "Selective Instruments of National Credit Policy," in *Federal Reserve Policy,* Postwar Economic Studies, No. 8 (Washington, D.C.: Board of Governors of the Federal Reserve System, 1947), pp. 65-87.

8. For an extensive discussion and criticism of these forces, see Charles R. Whittlesey, "Credit Policy at the Discount Window," *Quarterly Journal of Economics,* May 1959, pp. 207-216. The same issue contains a reply by Robert V. Roosa.

9. See Whittlesey, *op.cit.,* pp. 212-214.

10. Stephen H. Axilrod, "Liquidity and Public Policy," *Federal Reserve Bulletin,* October 1961, pp. 1175-1176.

11. See Donald Shelby, "Some Implications of the Growth of Financial Intermediaries," *Journal of Finance,* December 1958, p. 539.

12. The standard work on this subject is Assar Lindbeck, "The 'New' Theory of Credit Control in the United States," *Stockholm Economic Studies,* Pamphlet Series, No. 1, 2nd ed. (Stockholm: Almqvist & Wiksell, 1962). The doctrine is most closely associated with Robert V. Roosa, who was associated for many years with the Federal Reserve Bank of New York.

13. The simplest statement of this prediction was given by J. M. Keynes. See J. M. Keynes, *A Treatise on Money,* Vol. II (London: The Macmillan Company, Ltd., 1930), esp. pp. 364-367.

14. Lindbeck, *op.cit.,* pp. 40-47.

15. See especially *Commercial Bank Loan and Investment Policy* (Champaign, Ill.: Bureau of Economic and Business Research, University of Illinois, 1963), pp. 146-158.

16. *Ibid.,* pp. 150-151.

17. Here we are assuming that the money demand function is homogeneous of degree one in prices with respect to financial assets. For some discussion about the homogeneous function of degree one, see David S. Huang, *Introduction to the Use of Mathematics in Economic Analysis* (New York: John Wiley and Sons, Inc., 1964), pp. 83 ff.

18. "Interest Rates on Time Deposits, Mid-January 1962," *Federal Reserve Bulletin,* February 1962, pp. 147-151. In the sample of 1,016 banks, over half raised their maximum rate to the 4 per cent ceiling and two-thirds to at least 3.5 per cent. Most of the banks not responding already had their maximum rate at the old 3 per cent ceiling.

19. See "Growth in Institutional Savings," *Federal Reserve Bulletin,* May 1962, p. 515. *The Savings and Loan Fact Book,* published annually by the United States Savings and Loan League since 1930, regularly contains a tabulation of effective rates for savings-and-loan associations, savings banks, and commercial banks.

20. See W. L. Smith, "Financial Intermediaries and the Effectiveness of Monetary Controls," *Quarterly Journal of Economics,* November 1959, p. 547.

21. See United States Treasury and flow of funds data, *Federal Reserve Bulletin.*

22. These proposals are also known as "differential asset classes reserves" and "supplementary reserves." The most extensive discussion is contained in the famous "Patman Report" (U.S. Congress, Joint Committee on the Economic Report, *Monetary Policy and the Management of the Public Debt* [Washington, D.C.: U.S. Government Printing Office, 1952], pp. 123-129, 477-484, 426-429, and 1176-1184).

Appendix to Chapter 25

Causal Ordering and the Logical Structure of Monetary Policy Problems

Earlier (Sect. 25.1), a simple two-target, two-instrument model was used to demonstrate many of the propositions underlying the pure theory of quantitative monetary policy. In that instance, there was little or no difficulty to reduce the model to its simplified version, i.e., two equations containing only target variables, instrumental variables, parameters, and other exogenous variables. Carrying out such a task, however, is not always so easy in policy problems. Yet our knowing something about the logical structure of the problem and the existence of a solution is important, even when it is not feasible to attempt a solution. Thus this appendix introduces the subject of causal ordering. The latter is merely a way of rearranging the equations of a model as a means of shedding light on the structure and solubility of the model.[1] In so rearranging the equations, furthermore, the construction of diagrams illustrating the role of the four kinds of variables in monetary policy problems (Sect. 25.1) becomes possible.

At the outset, let us make two observations about causal ordering:

(1) Such ordering does not necessarily imply the direction of causation. Indeed, in static policy models, the instrumental and irrelevant variables must be regarded as interdependent, since they are all, in effect, simultaneously determined.

(2) The causal ordering of a policy problem is not the same as for a "normal" problem of economic analysis because of the inverted structure of the former relative to the latter.

Causal ordering involves, first, finding all instrumental and irrelevant variables in the model which solely depend on target or other exogenous variables. Such instrumental and irrelevant variables are given the order or rank of zero. In turn, first order variables are those instrument and irrelevant variables which can be determined solely from zero order variables and from target and other exogenous variables, and so on. This consecutive ordering or ranking is shown in the row opposite the row denoted "ordering" in Fig. 25-A. It also determines the order of the equation numbers set forth in the following row.

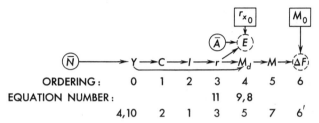

ORDERING: 0   1   2   3   4   5   6

EQUATION NUMBER: 11   9,8

                        4,10 2   1   3   5   7   6'

Fig. 25-A. The Logical Structure of the Two-Target, Two-Instrument Model. For simplicity some of the equations have been combined in the diagram. Target variables are enclosed in solid circles, instrumental variables are enclosed in broken circles, irrelevant variables are unenclosed, and other exogenous variables are enclosed in squares.

Now, we proceed to illustrate causal ordering in terms of our earlier (Sect. 25.1) two-target, two-instrument model. In that model, we know what the level of income must be to achieve the employment target, given the target level of employment $\overline{N}$, and a simple linear relationship between income and employment in equation (4). With this requisite level of income, we know from equation (2) what consumption expenditures must be. Then, through equation (1), we know what investment expenditures must be. Given this level of investment, we know what the level of domestic interest rates must be for such investment to be forthcoming, and so on, all as set forth in Fig. 25-A.

That diagram makes clear the nature of several distinctions that Professor Tinbergen sets forth among targets and among instrumental variables.[2] Namely, a model may be either partitionable or consecutive in the targets (i.e., the variables in solid circles in the illustration) and in the instruments (i.e., variables in broken circle). The two-target, two-instrument example happens to be consecutive in the instruments and partitionable in the targets. This means that the magnitudes of the targets do not depend on each other. In other words, the particular gold flow target $\overline{A}$ is presumably chosen independently of the employment target and is neither flexible with respect to, nor conflicting with, the employment target. On the other hand, the instruments are consecutive, which means that they are not entirely independent of each other (see Sect. 25.1). This absence of a strict independence is shown in the diagram by the fact that the chain of arrows emanating from $\overline{N}$ splits into two branches beyond r. The branches indicate that the magnitude of E (i.e., the sales of foreign exchange instrument) is partly dependent on the magnitude of the change in Federal Reserve credit ΔF needed to achieve the employment target $\overline{N}$. The absence of a strict independence, moreover, suggests the need for coordination in the use of the two instruments. Indeed, the need for coordination is an important reason for Tinbergen's making the distinction. Only when both targets and instruments are partitionable is there no particular need for coordination of policy-making. In that case, separate authorities could pursue separate targets with separate instruments and not have to bother about any interdependence.

The uses of causal ordering may also be illustrated with matrices and determinants. In fact, through the use of the ordering the equations given in Fig. 25-A, the system of equations for the two-target, two-instrument model may be written in matrix form as follows:

$$
\begin{pmatrix}
n & 0 & 0 & 0 & 0 & 0 & 0 & 0 \\
c & -1 & 0 & 0 & 0 & 0 & 0 & 0 \\
1 & -1 & -1 & 0 & 0 & 0 & 0 & 0 \\
0 & 0 & 1 & i & 0 & 0 & 0 & 0 \\
0 & 0 & 0 & -a_1 & -a_2 & 0 & 0 & 0 \\
-l_1 & 0 & 0 & l_2 & 0 & 1 & 0 & 0 \\
0 & 0 & 0 & 0 & 0 & 1 & -1 & 0 \\
0 & 0 & 0 & 0 & 0 & 0 & 1 & -m_1
\end{pmatrix}
\begin{pmatrix}
Y \\ C \\ I \\ r \\ E \\ M_d \\ M \\ \Delta F
\end{pmatrix}
=
\begin{pmatrix}
\overline{N} \\ 0 \\ 0 \\ 0 \\ \overline{A} - a_1 r_{x_0} \\ l_3 \\ 0 \\ M_0
\end{pmatrix}
$$

Note that arranging the equations in this particular order (and, at the same time, rearranging the terms in each equation so as to get the instrumental and irrelevant variables and their coefficients on the left and the constant terms in the vector of constants on the right) yields a square coefficient matrix. This suggests the prospect of a determinate model and, therefore, the existence of a solution depending on whether the determinant corresponding to the matrix is different from zero. Further, the matrix is triangular (i.e., all coefficients to the right of the main diagonal are zeros), and this reflects the causal ordering of a determinate model with partitionable targets.

From the shape and composition of the coefficient matrix, such as that above, many properties of a model are revealed including whether a solution exists.[3] The illustration here may, of course, be reduced and solved through the use of determinants.

References

1. See Herbert A. Simon, "Causal Ordering and Identifiability," in W. C. Hood and T. C. Koopmans (eds.), *Studies in Econometric Method* (New York: John Wiley and Sons, Inc., 1953); and Jan Tinbergen, *Economic Policy: Principles and Design* (Amsterdam: North-Holland Publishing Co., 1956), pp.

31 and 118-129. The exposition in this appendix is based on Tinbergen's work. Not all systems of equations may be causally ordered. For a discussion of systems which may be so ordered, see Franklin M. Fisher, "On the Cost of Appropriate Specification in Simultaneous Equation Estimation, "*Econometrica,* April 1961, pp. 111-138.

2. Jan Tinbergen, *On the Theory of Economic Policy* (Amsterdam: North-Holland Publishing Co., 1952), pp. 29-32.

3. See Simon, *op.cit.;* and Tinbergen, *op.cit.* Causal ordering is useful in constructing econometric models, as well as purely theoretical models.

A volume containing reprints of the above papers by Simon and Fisher, as well as other related collaborative works with Albert Ando, is their *Essays on the Structure of Social Science Models* (Cambridge, Mass.: M.I.T. Press, 1963).

26

Monetary Policy (continued): Time Lag Problems

> . . . One polar view is that, while monetary policy is extremely powerful, it operates with a very long and irregular lag . . . and that this converts a powerful tool into a weapon much too dangerous to be used. The opposite view is that, while monetary policy is extremely powerful, it is also very quick-acting, easily reversed, and delicately manipulated. Our conclusion is that it works neither so slowly as Friedman thinks, nor as quickly and surely as the Federal Reserve itself seems to believe (E. Cary Brown *et al.*, "Lags in Fiscal and Monetary Policy," in *Stabilization Policies* [1963]).

There are a number of features about economic policy measures that are relevant to a discussion of time lags. For one, the measures may be conceived, formulated, carried out, and exert their varied influences in a dimension of time. For another, policy actions may be taken at irregular times and have their effects over varying intervals of time. And, for still another, the actions are likely to be based on imperfect knowledge about the future. This imperfect knowledge would be in terms of precisely what would have happened in the absence of a given set of actions, on the basis of a different timing of actions, or on the basis of the use of a different set of alternative measures for carrying out the actions. It would also be in terms of precisely what would be the effects of taking a particular set of actions.

Insofar as monetary policy in particular is concerned, the above are all features of a central problem facing the central bank—that of time lags—but our knowledge of these is very primitive. Still, we introduce the subject in this chapter. In the presentation, moreover, two crucial questions are continuously lurking in the background: (1) Are the time lags in question impracticably long? (2) Are the time lags significantly irregular? Proposals for moderate or extensive reform or even abandonment of monetary policy have their foundations in the answers to these questions. We proceed by first examining the basic types of lagged relationships among economic variables (Sect. 26.1), by discussing monetary policy and the time lag complex (Sect. 26.2), by discussing a diagram and the measurement of some time lags (Sect. 26.3), by discussing time lags and "composition of demand" effects (Sect. 26.4), and, finally, by considering time lags with respect to the arguments in favor of fixed monetary rules (Sect. 26.5).

26.1 Time Lags in Economic Models

It is customary to recognize the existence of two kinds of lagged responses in economic models.[1] The simplest is a "fixed-time delay" or "discrete" lag, which means that one event occurs after another event with a definite time lapse between events. The time link between many pairs of events are adequately described by such lags. For example, a business man deposits a customer's check in a bank; a definite amount of time elapses until, all at once, the customer's own account in another bank is debited. For another example, the average of prices (Sect. 5.3) rises one month; when the computations have been made and published in the following month, wage rates in labor contracts with "escalator clauses" (Sect. 16.3) are increased.

The second type of lagged response is the so-called "distributed" lag. The term "distributed" simply suggests that the effects of an event may be spread out over time. When the Federal Reserve buys securities in the open market (Sect. 8.2), for example, it does not expect total bank reserves to increase by the full amount all at once. This would require impossibly synchronous behavior by banks, security dealers, investors, and the United States Post Office Department, among others. Rather, the total increase in bank reserves might be the result of smaller changes at first, larger changes a week or two later, and negligible changes thereafter. To cite another example, the reasoning behind the 1964 tax cut (Sect. 19.3) and the notion that the cut would contribute to an actual increase in tax revenues was based on the belief that the tax cut would successively increase tax revenues in subsequent years because of its expansionary effect on aggregate demand and economic growth.

One of the most frequently encountered examples of distributed lags in economics is the case of "geometrically distributed" lags, where the dependent variable follows the path of a geometric progression over time. We have already dealt with several of these: expansion and contraction in money and credit in response to initial changes in bank reserves (Sect. 3.2) and multiplier models of income determination (Sect. 15.2). In each of these models an initial "shock" causes a new equilibrium value of some important variable to be approached by successively smaller amounts over an infinite number of time periods. The reason is that in each there is a certain ratio, less than one in absolute value; this ratio is raised to ever higher powers and multiplied by the same constant "shock" to yield successive increments.

Unfortunately, many responses to actions by the monetary officials neither in principle nor in reality can be described by simple geometric progressions over time. For one thing, the initial stimulus may not be maintained at a constant rate. It may deliberately be greater in earlier periods in order to speed up the response of the target, or it may be subject to "feedback" from changes in the target, particularly when the policy stimulus is used on a trial-and-error basis. Further, the response may well not proceed very rapidly in early periods but, rather, gain momentum, reach a peak in rate of change, and decline rapidly or gradually in rate of change thereafter. There are all sorts of reasons for such a pattern or response. There may be certain "slippage" in the early stages of a process, whereby it is possible temporarily to avoid or subvert the effects of a policy action, or the nature of the lag distribution may be such that a number of periods are required before significant effects on behavior occur. In the instance of "slippage," for example, a net purchase of securities for the Federal open market account (Sect. 8.2) could be effected with the view to attaining given increases in excess reserves, net ("free") reserves, and loans and investments. Then, in the process of implementing the policy, there may be some "slippage" in the effect of open market purchase on excess reserves, since banks may use some of the increase in excess reserves to repay borrowed reserves. The effect on the free reserve target may be attained, but the ultimate effect on loans and investments will be less than the product of the reserve multiplier (Sect. 3.2) and the net purchase of securities for the open market account.

There are at least two ways to deal with the problem of simulating and (ultimately) measuring time lags that involve neither fixed-time delays nor purely geometrical lag distributions. The simpler method is associated with the Dutch economist, Leendert Koyck, who was one of the first to deal extensively with the statistical measurement of distributed lags.[2] Koyck's procedure is to initiate the actual "decay" of the terms in a lag distribution, not in the initial period when a policy disturbance occurs, but after a small number of periods has elapsed. This he accomplishes by including in the lag equation a sequence of terms whose value increases for several periods at a sufficiently great enough rate to offset any geometrical decay in the first few periods. After the lapse of these early periods the extra terms become a constant, and geometrical decay takes over. This technique can be shown to pose serious statistical determinacy problems.

The other method for simulating lagged responses which build up and eventually taper off is to make use of mathematical probability distributions. One of the simplest varieties of these is a binomial distribution. The use of a broader class of mathematical probability distributions than binomial distributions has been suggested by Professor Robert Solow for the simulation of distributed lags.[3] They are the so-called Pascal distributions. Like binomials, they are unimodal (single-peaked) but offer a much greater variety of shapes, although they are mathematically much more complex.

Why all the concern about the time-shape of responses to policy actions? As we shall see, those who believe that the nature of "true" monetary policy lags is best depicted in terms of "fixed-time delays" generally conclude that monetary policy actions are subject to long and irregular response lags. Their view leads them to look elsewhere for effective policy instruments and to call for extensive reforms in the conduct of monetary policy. Those who believe that reactions to the use of monetary policy instruments are distributed over time, however, tend toward a much more sympathetic view of orthodox monetary policy. Thus our interest is in seeking out the true nature of the lag distributions as a means of supporting the actions called for by the reformers or as a defense for orthodoxy.

Thus far, we have only dealt with single isolated lag response patterns and in rather abstract terms, at that. It is well for us to have some appreciation of the complexity of the time lag problems facing the monetary authorities, as well as to see some of the other problems which arise from the existence of lagged responses.

26.2 Monetary Policy and the Time Lag Complex

It is customary, in discussing various broad categories of time lags in economic policy questions, to distinguish three basic lags: the recognition lag, the decision lag, and the operation lag. In monetary policy discussions, however, the recognition and decision lags have come to be grouped together as inside lags vis-à-vis the operations lags. In contrast with the other lags in the whole lag complex, the recognition and decision lags tend to be of the fixed-time delay variety. The operation lag, on the other hand, is commonly discussed as the intermediate lag and the outside lag, and it is particularly complex. This complexity results from the large number of independent component lags and the tendency for the component lags to be of the distributed rather than of the fixed-time period or discrete lag variety. Later we introduce some of the specific features contributing to the complexity of the outside lag in particular.

The recognition lag. The recognition lag pertains to the time lapse between the need for some sort of policy action and the recognition of this need by the appropriate policy-making authorities. Such things as the speed and accuracy of economic forecasting and the process of assembling and transmitting information within the organizational structures of policy-making agencies are important determinants of this lag.

The decision lag. The decision lag relates to the lapse from the time when policy-makers realize they ought to take some kind of action until they actually do take action. There are many factors influencing this lag, not nearly all of which are economic in nature.

When action depends on the decisions of a discretionary body, such as the United States Congress or the Federal Open Market Committee, we may well need the help of political scientists, sociologists, and psychologists, among others, in order to understand both the length and the outcome of the decision-making process.[4] An often heard defense of monetary policy is its shorter decision lag as contrasted with that for discretionary fiscal policy (Sect. 19.1). The Board of Governors and the Open Market Committee are small groups, meet frequently, and are able to reach a consensus with relative ease. This contrasts strongly with the time involved in initiation, study, debate, and compromise, however justified in most instances, where passage of Congressional legislation is concerned.

Another determinant of the length of the decision lag is the philosophy of the policy-making body regarding the advisability of using *quick and dirty solutions,* as opposed to long and careful deliberations over policy measures, with the risk of actions that are *too little and too late.*

The operation lag. The operation lag concerns the elapsed time between the taking of action and significant effects, somehow defined and measured, on particular ultimate target variables. In monetary policy discussions it is divided into the intermediate lag and the outside lag for analytical convenience.

The intermediate lag. The intermediate lag is the time elapsing between the taking of action and, because this is a distributed lag, the accumulation of some desired level of total effects on an intermediate target variable. For example, the Federal Reserve may engage in open market operations, using an operational target (Sect. 24.2) of net ("free") reserves and aiming toward an intermediate target change in gross reserves, bank interest rates on loans to customers, bank earning assets, demand deposits, and so on. Note that these representative intermediate targets do not necessarily change simultaneously. For example, changes in gross reserves would be a relatively early intermediate target, while changes in the money supply would be quite a late intermediate target. This merely indicates that the line between intermediate and outside lags is not an absolute one but depends on the choice of intermediate targets.

The outside lag. "Outside" in "outside lag" means outside the banking system or, more properly, the outside lag relates to the time involved for the effects on ultimate target variables of changes in intermediate targets to build up to certain levels. This is where the time lag structure really becomes complicated, and there are some very good reasons why it should.

(1) Outside the financial system, there are three rather heterogenous groups of behavioral units whose expenditure decisions may be influenced by changes in the intermediate targets and whose expenditures, in turn, influence the ultimate targets. These three include governments, business firms, and consumer households.

(2) These expenditure decisions may be influenced through a number of direct or indirect routes (although what is direct or indirect depends in part on the nature of intermediate targets). "Direct routes" implies that changes in the intermediate targets directly bear on decisions to spend or not to spend. For example, if the intermediate target is changes in interest rates on bank loans to customers, then bank customers find themselves immediately faced with quantitatively different terms for financing expenditures with bank loans. If the intermediate target changes affect other variables, which, in turn, influence expenditure decisions, then the effects are indirect. The intermediate targets, for example, might work through other financial variables, such as bond yields or interest rates on loans from nonbank financial institutions. Or, even more difficult to trace, the intermediate targets may operate, at least for a time, through their effects on the expectations of spending units.

(3) The decisions of behavioral units involve expenditures for all sorts of consumption goods, capital goods, and factor services (Chap. 17-19).

(4) Expenditure changes may involve various feedbacks. Consumption changes, for example, may induce changes in investment expenditures (Sect. 15.3). Or changes in expenditures may induce monetary authorities to adjust the use of policy instruments.

(5) Finally, responses occur in a far from frictionless setting. Resource immobilities, technical delays in production, and the tying of decisions to conventional accounting periods, to cite just a few examples, all contribute to lengthened response time.[5]

26.3. Monetary Policy: The Measurement of Some Time Lags

The various kinds of time lags pertaining to monetary policy have been outlined and defined. But now we wish to introduce time measurements for some particular lags. To do this, we primarily consider examples of the outside lag, following the presentation of a diagram of the main lags under consideration. The others are more simply disposed of by simple statements about estimates. The average inside lag, for instance, has been estimated as being about three months in length, and the intermediate lag—using a net reserves operational target and a gross reserves intermediate target—has been found by several independent studies to average about a month in length.

A diagram of some time lags. The three types of time lags—inside, intermediate, and outside—may be set out in a highly simplified illustration as shown in Fig. 26-1.[6] There the three types are denoted along the right-hand margin of the illustration and, roughly, the order in which the events occur may be read from top to bottom. Initially, in our further consideration of these lags below, we are interested in focusing attention on the first of two phases or portions of the outside lag as shown in the diagram: (1) that phase spanning from the response in the intermediate target(s) to the multiplier time period and (2) that one involving the multiplier time period (or period in which changes in expenditures affect the ultimate targets, such as output and employment), as set forth earlier (Sect. 15.2). Note, too, with respect to the diagram that the expectational effects, mostly resulting from changes in the intermediate target variables, simply fan out in indefinite ways and in several directions.

The first portion of the outside lag, as set forth, shows four columns: (1) pertains to the consumption of consumer durable goods and the production of these goods; (2) pertains to orders for producer's durables and changes in output; (3) pertains to residential construction; and (4) pertains to debt-financed construction of capital goods by state and local governments (where the latter might be expanded to cover, as well, investment in new plant and equipment by government-owned public utilities). With respect to each of these, we review immediately below the approximate time magnitudes according to some investigators, but one should recall that there is a considerable difference of opinion over some of the findings.[7] We then consider some estimates of the duration of the multiplier time period as it would relate to one intermediate target variable—namely, the money supply. This is not exactly the multiplier time period pertaining to a shift in expenditures and the resulting multiple changes in the flow variable for income and so on, as suggested by our diagram. Nevertheless, it is one such period in which monetary analysts show an interest.

The outside lag (capital expenditures lags). As for the outside lag, we need to distinguish the capital expenditures lags from the multiplier time period. If, by default, we use short-term bank loan rates as the intermediate target, the effects on capital expenditures depends both on the interest elasticities of such expenditures and the nature of the distributed

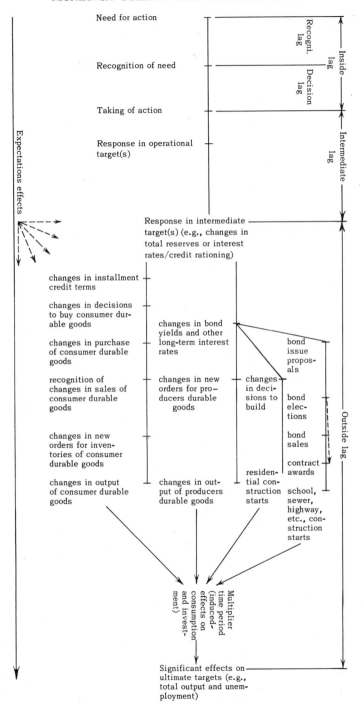

Fig. 26-1. Monetary Policy: Some Time Lags.

responses. The study by Brown, Solow, Ando, and Kareken finds that a one per cent change in bank interest rates will eventually cause a change in the level of inventory investment by about four to five billion dollars, one-fourth of which occurs in the first three months, two-fifths within six months, and about two-thirds within a year. We should expect investment in fixed capital goods to respond somewhat more slowly, both because of its connection with long-term interest rates and because of the greater technological problems involved in planning, constructing, and backlogging orders of such goods. Brown *et al.* actually studied the electrical machinery industry; the steps they found to be important in the lag pattern are shown in the producers durable goods column in Fig. 26-1. They found the new orders for electrical machinery to respond nearly twice as fast as the above inventory investment, but the subsequent response in actual output of machinery was found to be very slow, with only about half of the total effect achieved within a year after a change in orders.

Where residential construction starts are concerned, only fragmentary evidence is also available. Even so, the custom has been to speak of roughly a four- to six-month lag between Federal Reserve actions and a change in housing starts, or roughly a three- to five-month outside lag.[8] The reasons are partly behavioral, mostly technical (involving such things as FHA and VA interest ceilings, loan and loan insurance applications, processing, and commitments). In addition, there has been evidence of an important mechanism operative in mortgage lending and accounting for a fairly high interest rate sensitivity of expenditures for new housing, as we shall note later. The beginning of construction, moreover, is still not the time when the bulk of expenditures for it occur; consequently, a few additional months should be added to get the average elapsed time before the income stream is significantly affected.

As with private investment, capital expenditures by state and local governments respond, if at all, according to their interest rate elasticities (or sensitiveness to changes in some other policy target) and their distributed lag patterns. Brown *et al.* do not treat this problem at all, but there have been a number of studies. Most of these have dealt with aggregates, and a major portion of them has dealt with the period of 1955-1958, when apparently substantial influences on such expenditures by the Federal Reserve's policy of tight money were observed. In some respects, the analysis of time lags in capital expenditures by state and local governments is even more difficult than private capital expenditures. This is due to the large number of independent units involved, as well as the importance of so many noneconomic considerations. There is, however, some agreement that the interest elasticities are small and that the lags are distributed over a fairly long period, with an average outside lag of perhaps a year.

The multiplier time period (examples pertaining to the money supply variable). There are serious problems in identifying a multiplier time period empirically, even apart from any agreement on how such a period ought to be measured. Even so, two somewhat extreme possibilities might be mentioned. One is merely to measure the average time that elapses between the turning point in either an instrument or some intermediate series and the turning point in an ultimate target series. This method tends (with qualifications) to yield fairly short lags. The other extreme is to accumulate the time it takes for the entire effect of a sustained change in an instrument variable or intermediate target to work itself out. This method tends to yield rather long lags since it allows for various feedbacks in expenditures, as well as the working off and accumulation of stocks of goods.

Consider an illustration of each. There have been several studies of the time lags between money supply changes and changes in the Federal Reserve index of industrial production. Brown *et al.*, for example, found an average lag between cyclical turning points in changes in the stock of money (i.e., turning points in ΔM) and in changes in the flow variable for industrial production (i.e., turning points in ΔO, where O is the flow of industrial production) of almost three months.[9] But whether one relates stocks and flows as changes in stocks and changes in flows depends on the model, possibly implicit, behind the study in question.

Milton Friedman, in contrast to Brown *et al.*, for example, argues that the relevant lag is between a turning point in a cyclical series for changes in the stock of money (i.e., ΔM) and the next turning point in the flow variable for output[10] (i.e., O) rather than in the series for changes in the flow variable (i.e., ΔO). He finds that, over the long historical period 1870-1960, money supply changes (including time deposits) have reached peaks an average of about sixteen months before the upper turning point in business activity, although this lag in industrial activity has, since 1908, been as short as nine months (1953) and as long as twenty-one months (1956-1957). Money supply changes over the same period have, according to Friedman, reached troughs on an average of about twelve months ahead of business activity, with a range since 1908 from five (1908) to twenty-one months (1910-1912); the range for 1949-1960 is from eight months (1957-1958) to sixteen months (1959-1961). Note the variability in the length of the lag, because it is crucial to Friedman's policy proposals (Sect. 26.5).

Three criticisms that Friedman has received illustrate some of the problems in implying the multiplier time period portion of the outside lag from turning points in statistical series.[11] One is the simple mathematical phenomenon that, if two series (money and income, in this case) move roughly synchronously, then the rate of change in one will necessarily lead the absolute of the other. We have already seen how this works in examining a simple accelerator model (Sect. 15.3) in an earlier illustration (Fig. 15-5). In that diagram, investment expenditures which depend on the rate of change in aggregate sales will naturally peak before the peak in sales and trough before the trough in sales, since investment will be greatest or least at the inflection points of the sales flow. Thus, if money and income move together, then we should expect the rate of change of money to peak before the level of income, for the simple reason that the rate of change of income peaks before the level of income, and similarly for troughs. That this lag is long and irregular is merely a reflection that the cycle itself in income (or some other measure of business activity) is long and irregular.

A second criticism pertains to whether it is unfair to measure the success or failure of monetary policy by measuring the whole time lapse from, say, the peak change (e.g., max. ΔM) in an intermediate target variable to the upper turning point in an ultimate target (i.e., just before a recession), since a significant response to the variable may well have been achieved much earlier.

The third and final criticism is that such lag measures cannot ordinarily indicate anything about the effectiveness of monetary measures, since, to do so, it would be necessary to show what would have happened to business activity if the monetary measures had not been taken. Brown *et al.* use a simple illustration to make their point. Suppose, through cyclical changes in the money supply, the monetary authorities were able to eliminate cycles in business activity. Friedman, finding no relation between the change in money and in business activity, would conclude that, in this case, monetary policy is not perverse but, rather, completely impotent, which would be opposite to the truth.

The other extreme is to measure the total time for all effects to work themselves out, i.e., the time elapsing between a change in an intermediate target and, in the absence of any other outside shocks (including other policy measures), the attainment of a new equilibrium in the ultimate target. Since we can never actually observe such an adjustment in the real world, about the only way to measure the outside lag in this way is to feed a sustained intermediate target change into an econometric model and observe the successive values of the ultimate target as the model simulates the adjustment process in the absence of any other shocks. Little work has yet been done with monetary policy lags with this approach. Where fiscal policy is concerned, Professor Suits, for example, shows that in the Klein-Goldberger-Suits model a permanent increase in government purchases of goods and services reaches a peak in effect on the GNP during the year after the increase and subsequently declines, due to feedbacks on derived demand and the accumulation of producers and consumers durable goods, until it reaches a constant level of effect about the fifth year.[12] This, however, is an annual model and, moreover, contains few monetary variables.

26.4. Time Lags and Composition of Demand Effects

The monetary authorities face a certain bundle of problems which can logically be traced in some measure to time lags. These are the so-called "composition of demand" effects associated with the working out of orthodox monetary measures (Sect. 25.2). These effects draw attention to an important characteristic of general monetary controls, namely, their inherent selectivity.

The selectivity of general credit controls. It may initially come as a surprise to find that general monetary controls are expected to be selective, when there has been so much opposition to the restoration of selective credit controls per se (Sect. 8.3). After a moment's reflection, this is not in the least surprising. After all, interest rates are merely a particular set of prices and, as such, are an important part of a competitive economy's mechanism for allocating resources. Just as we would not expect each individual's demand for a consumer good to be equally sensitive to price changes nor the market demand for one consumer good to be just as sensitive to price changes as the market demand for another consumer good, we expect widely varying interest rate elasticities of demand for expenditures with borrowed funds. When interest rates rise, the "price rationing" that occurs ideally will reflect a greater restriction of credit to less productive than to more productive uses. The terms "more" and "less productive" involve value judgments—in competitive markets these have to do with such things as the relative strength of consumer preferences for products and the comparative productivity of additional resources. Thus, for example, when interest rates rise, we might expect the quantity of funds demanded to finance the expansion of equipment to produce custom auto bodies to decrease relatively more than funds demanded to expand hospital facilities, given certain assumptions. These are, of course, that the demand for custom auto bodies is relatively more price elastic than the demand for hospital services and that it is relatively easier to substitute labor for capital goods in producing custom auto bodies than in providing hospital services.

It is sometimes argued that the automatic selectivity associated with price rationing in private credit markets is perverse. The charge of perversity stems from two basic sources: (1) imperfections in the money and credit markets which interfere with the operation of the allocation mechanism and (2) interference with the attainment of certain objectives beyond the reach of free market forces and possibly in conflict with them.

To make matters worse, we cannot always isolate these sources in particular cases of alleged discrimination. Tight money and high interest rates have specifically been blamed for discriminating perversely against, among others: (1) certain types of private expenditures and (2) certain types of government expenditures. Let us briefly examine each of these and see how time lags might be involved. These are known more euphemistically as "composition of demand effects." [13]

Selectivity and private expenditures. Monetary restriction has been accused of perversely affecting both residential construction and loan-financed expenditures for capital goods by small businesses. The mechanism in the case of the former is a very subtle one and was discussed in detail earlier (Sect. 18.2). The alleged perversity in that case is said to be the result of market imperfections, and it is criticized as discouraging the social objective of widespread home ownership. We refer to the tendency for the supply of funds, because of FHA and VA ceiling rates, to be diverted away from mortgages during periods of rising interest rates and toward more profitable lending alternatives.

The argument that tight money discriminates against small business borrowers has many facets. If, in certain industries, small businesses are suboptimal in size or narrowly specialized, their borrowing may well decline by relatively more than large firms as the result of automatic market rationing. Further, their size and legal form of organization may effectively deprive them of access both to internal funds and to many sectors of the national money and capital markets and, perhaps, make them dependent on local bank financing. It has even been asserted that many large business borrowers are in collusion with large banks to provide a continuous source of financing at preferential rates, with the alleged result that small businesses are always charged relatively higher interest rates and are the first to be excluded when credit is tight. However persuasive these arguments might be, they were instrumental in the passage of the Small Business Act of 1953 and the Small Business Investment Act of 1958. The latter provides for the establishment of small business investment companies to serve as the source of equity capital and long-term loans to small businesses at favorable interest rates.

Selectivity and government expenditures. The second category of discriminatory effects of tight money is the debt financing of capital improvements by state, county, and municipal governments. Included here are such things as highways, school buildings, and water and sewer facilities. There are two main aspects to the argument. One is that private markets may be myopic so far as the adequate provision for long-run social needs is concerned, i.e., from a short-range, coldly economic point of view, such projects would represent inefficient uses of scarce funds and ought to be frozen out when interest rates rise. Yet to prevent this is to create serious long-run problems (note that conservation programs are defended on similar grounds). The other aspect of the argument again involves market imperfections. Governmental units in many states are faced with ceilings on the interest rates they are permitted to pay (Sect. 19.1), which causes sharp "kinks" in their demands for funds at the statutory maxim. Many local governments are faced with a combination of tax rate ceilings and sluggishly responsive tax bases, which makes them loathe to commit larger portions of their tax revenue to debt service if, by postponing projects, they can incur a lower interest burden.

A somewhat related argument is that about the discriminatory effects on purchases of capital equipment by public utilities—both government-owned and privately owned—whose rates are regulated by state and Federal government commissions. Since the process of gaining approval of rate changes is frequently long and costly, significant changes in the cost of funds to utilities may cause them to postpone construction.[14]

26.5. Time Lags and Fixed Monetary Rules

Those who believe that monetary policy actions and their effects are subject to long and irregular lags as a result of the inadequacies of the policy-makers and the monetary instruments are often led to search for rules to be followed by the officials. Such a group would usually express the view that the sum of the lengths of the recognition, decision, and operational lags would be reduced by the use of rules. This would seem to imply that those who formulate the rules understand the system better than the monetary officials, as they well might (Sect. 11.1), but fixed rules are also advocated for other reasons. In particular, there has been the tradition (Sect. 6.3 and 7.5) and libertarian desire to subject the government and monetary officials to the discipline of automatic forces, somewhat as individuals, households, and businesses are subjected to market forces.

Even today we have Professors Milton Friedman and Edward S. Shaw as advocates for the use of a fixed formula for increases in the money supply.[15] The modern formulas would have the Federal Reserve supply the necessary reserves so that the money supply would vary at the same rate as the average rate of growth in GNP in constant prices (Sect. 5.3) at full employment. This could be interpreted in various ways, depending on whether money included savings deposits or just currency outside of banks and demand deposits, on the concept of the full employment level of GNP, the length of the averaging period, and the frequency of possible lagged adjustments permitted in the rate of growth of the money supply.

Below we examine one such simple rule and present an appraisal of it. **A rule for determining the money supply.** The rule is as follows: *The* *money supply should grow at a fixed rate per annum, roughly the rate for the growth in the full employment level of output at constant prices.*

Now, this rule follows from a simple formula and a series of adjustments. The initial formula is

$$\Delta M_t / M_{t-1} = m_t$$

where ΔM is the change in the money supply,

      M is the stock of money,

      m is the rate of growth in the money supply per time period, and

$t = 1, 2, \ldots$ are successive time periods.

Here, m may be specified as a fixed rate each period (which, however, compounds over time) or it may be subject to an adjustment, e.g.,

$$m_t = \frac{\sum\limits_{i=1}^{t} \left(\frac{\Delta O_i}{O_{i-1}} \right)}{t}$$

where ΔO is the change in the full employment level of real GNP, and O is the full employment level of real GNP.

If t covers a large number of periods and the period-to-period changes in full employment GNP are neither large nor greatly variable, then m may still be taken as a constant.

By this time, several questions will have arisen in the reader's mind. For one thing, what is the point in tying the rate of growth of money to the full employment level in GNP constant prices? Apparently, the purpose would be to stabilize the price level at full employment. Consider the two identities (Sect. 5.2 and 25.1):

$$M_t V_t = P_t O_t, \text{ and}$$
$$M_{t-1} V_{t-1} = P_{t-1} O_{t-1}, \text{ where}$$

in addition to M and O,

      V is the rate (velocity) at which money would be spent at full employment, and

      P is the price level at full employment.

(Note that we are applying the identities to the potential, not the actual, GNP.) Subtracting the second equation from the first and dividing the result by the second equation, we get:

$$\frac{M_t V_t - M_{t-1} V_{t-1}}{M_{t-1} V_{t-1}} = \frac{P_t O_t - P_{t-1} O_{t-1}}{P_{t-1} O_{t-1}}$$

Next, for the moment, let us assume that V has the same value in t and $t - 1$ in the latter equation. In that case, the V's cancel out and the left side of the equation becomes

$$\frac{M_t - M_{t-1}}{M_{t-1}} \quad \text{or} \quad \frac{\Delta M_t}{M_{t-1}}$$

Then, let us specify a constant price level as a monetary target, i.e., $P_t = P_{t-1}$ (or $\Delta P_t = 0$) so that the right side of the above equation becomes

$$\frac{O_t - O_{t-1}}{O_{t-1}} \quad \text{or} \quad \frac{\Delta O_t}{O_{t-1}}$$

Thus combining the identities and adjustments yields

$$\frac{\Delta M_t}{M_{t-1}} = \frac{\Delta O_t}{O_{t-1}}$$

This means that stabilizing the full employment price level requires the same rate of growth in the money supply as in real output, if velocity (V) is constant, and it is the rationale for the Friedman rule above.

Professor Friedman suggests a 3 per cent growth rate for the money supply and an alternative 4 per cent rate. The smaller rate is roughly the rate at which the full employment level of output in constant prices was growing in the United States in the early post-World War II decades. The alternative rate—the 4 rate—would allow for a more optimistic growth in GNP and provide a slight offset to Professor Friedman's anticipated secular decline in velocity in response to rising income and the accumulation of wealth.* It should be noted, too, that he includes demand, time, and savings deposits in his concept of money, and thereby eliminates one source of the short-run instability in the velocity of conventionally defined money (i.e., shifts back and forth between currency and demand deposits, on the one hand, and time and savings deposits, on the other).

Another obvious question is whether such money changes are only to

---

* Friedman has argued that money is a luxury good, the demand for which is income elastic, i.e., $(dM_d/dY)Y/M > 1$, analogous to the demand for such things as yachts and sports cars.

However, this view would not be supported by the data for the demand by business firms for a large portion of the money supply. In fact, tests of data have supported the likely truth of the statement that cash as a percentage of assets varies inversely with firm size and presumably income or sales. See William J. Frazer, Jr., *The Financial Structure of Firms and Monetary Economics* (Gainesville, Fla.: University of Florida Press, 1965), Chap. 7.

Some of Meltzer's findings, too, are of present interest. Studying long-run demand functions for money (defined, respectively, as M_1, the sum of currency plus demand deposits, and M_2, currency plus demand deposits plus time deposits at commercial banks) for the society as a whole, and with the rate of interest and non-human wealth as the major independent variables, he finds the following. Demand for both M_1 and M_2 are stable, the demand to hold M_1 is at least as stable as the demand for M_2, the demand for M_1 is approximately unit elastic with respect to wealth, the elasticity of the demand for M_2 is greater than the elasticity of the demand for M_1, and the demand for M_1 is more unstable in the short run than the demand for M_2. See Allan H. Meltzer, "The Demand for Money: The Evidence from Time Series," *Journal of Political Economy*, June 1963, pp. 219-231.

be achieved over a whole time period (a year, to Friedman), permitting the central bank to engage in seasonal ("defensive") operations, or whether the rule is to be rigidly applied to shorter intervals as well. Friedman recommends the latter:

> . . . I see no objection to seasonal variation in the stock of money, provided it is regular so that the public can adapt to it. On the other hand, neither do I see any objection to seasonal fluctuations in short-term interest rates. While the kind of pegging involved in eliminating seasonal fluctuations in interest rates has some special justifications, it is by no means free from the defects of other kinds of pegging. Moreover, there is no way to determine at all precisely what seasonal movement is required in the stock of money to eliminate a seasonal in interest rates. . . .[17]

Contrary to frequent assumption, moreover, Friedman does not regard his rule of an annual rate of increase in the money stock of from 3 to 5 per cent "as a rule which is somehow to be written in tablets of gold and enshrined for all future time." On the contrary, economists may persuade each other and others of a better rule at a future date.[17]

An appraisal of the fixed rule proposal. The major objection to the Friedman-type of proposal is straightforward: We do not know whether the acceptance of any particular fixed rule would generate better results than the intelligent exercise of discretionary monetary authority. Some proponents of fixed rules may argue that intelligent exercise of authority is impossible, but for others the solution to the problem of an unintelligent exercise of discretion could be a change in the composition of the Board of Governors (Sect. 11.1) and a more intelligent exercise of authority rather than the use of fixed rules.

One professor—Martin Bronfenbrenner—made a study to compare the performance of several fixed rules since 1900, including the "judgment" or actual historical rule.[18] On the whole, he found the 3 per cent rule to have performed most satisfactorily over the nearly sixty-year interval of the study, but he found the rule to have had a considerable inflationary bias in the post-World War II period. It is an interesting exercise to compare the result of applying the 3 per cent rule to the latter period with the money supply change that actually occurred. Using the 1946 money supply as base, we would get from the 3 per cent rule a money supply (i.e., currency outside banks plus demand deposits adjusted) of 183.2 billion dollars by the end of 1964, while the actual (seasonally adjusted) amount was 159.3 billion dollars. If time deposits are also included, the rule would have resulted in a money supply of 275.1 billion dollars, compared with the actual 335.2 billion dollars.* These last two amounts

---

* This kind of calculation is simple to make. In this case we merely consult a compound interest table for the value of 1.03^{18}, which is 1.7024 or about a 70 per cent increase over the base amounts (the base amounts were 107.6 billion and 161.6 billion dollars, respectively). The 4 per cent rule, however, would have given us a 102.6 per cent increase in the money supply (i.e., $1.04^{18} = 2.258$).

would have been much closer had it not been for the substantial increase in time deposits in 1962-1964.

There is no coincidence that the data generated by an application of the rule and the actual data are as close as they are over the whole 1946-1964 period. Indeed, growth in the money supply at approximately the same rate as the growth in GNP was an important intermediate target (Sect. 24.1) of the Federal Reserve in the pursuit of their ultimate price stability objective. However, to have abandoned all seasonal ("defensive") considerations in favor of absolutely steady money supply changes would have been of questionable benefit (Sect. 25.4).*

Another economist, Franco Modigliani,[19] testing some fixed rules in relation to the goals of full employment and price stability and comparing the results of the rules with the actual results over the postwar years found varying results. Viewing the authorities as being free to pursue wholeheartedly the goals only over the years of 1952 through the first half of 1960, he finds that the authorities outperformed the conventional rules, though not a more sophisticated rule tested by him. By his tests, however, the record of the authorities over the entire stretch from 1947 to 1962 looks considerably poorer, but Modigliani excuses the authorities because they were not "wholeheartedly" free (see Sect. 24.3) to pursue the goals in question. Of course, one of Friedman's points in emphasizing the need for rules is probably that he would restrict the freedom to pursue any goals other than those officially set, such as maximum employment, production, and purchasing power (Sect. 8.1).

26.6 Summary

Recognition, decision, and operation (including intermediate and outside) lags are present in discussions of money policy. The recognition and decisions lags tend to be of a fixed-time delay variety, and the operation lags tend to be of the distributed lag variety. Some of the latter are geometrically distributed lags and others are more irregularly distributed. These are the more complex distributions.

The study of time lags, however, is important. Some who believe that the recognition, decision, and operation lags are both excessively and unpredictably long advocate fixed monetary rules as a basis for monetary actions. Others, as well as some of the latter advocates, favor fixed rules as a course of control over the authority of monetary officials.

* A cartoon accompanying an article in *Business Week,* "Free Enterprise—Without Any Strings," October 6, 1962, pp. 76-79, describes "Friedman's dream" and "The Fed in chains and the money supply growing slowly and steadily, come what may." The Chairman of the Board of Governors is shown manacled to the wall and kicking furiously at, though out of the reach of, the "automatic money-maker," which calmly grinds out money at a 3 to 5 per cent rate.

One monetary rule states that the money supply should grow at a fixed rate per annum, roughly the rate for the growth in the full employment level of output at constant prices. Simple calculations show, however, that the money supply changes generated by the application of the rule over the period 1946-1962 would not be substantially different from the actual money supply changes. Still, there is the additional question of the benefits to be gained or lost from abandoning all seasonal ("defensive") operations in favor of absolutely steady money supply changes. There is also the prospect that the decision-makers will become more sensitive and accurate forecasters, as well as more courageous, intelligent, and astute men, and thereby negate the need for fixed monetary rules.

References

1. See R. G. D. Allen, *Mathematical Economics,* 2nd ed. (London: The Macmillan Company, Ltd., 1959), pp. 23-30, and references cited there; and Robert M. Solow, "On a Family of Lag Distributions," *Econometrica,* April 1960, pp. 393-406.

2. L. Koyck, *Distributed Lags and Investment Analysis* (Amsterdam: North-Holland Publishing Co., 1954); see also Solow, *op.cit.,* pp. 393-394; Lawrence R. Klein, "The Estimation of Distributed Lags," *Econometrica,* October 1958, pp. 553-565; and Frank de Leeuw, "The Demand for Capital Goods by Manufacturers: A Study of Quarterly Time Series," *Econometrica,* July 1962, pp. 407-423. The last contains a summary of distributed lags in investment literature.

3. Solow, *op.cit.* Of course, other conventional distributions used in mathematical statistics could also be used.

4. For a simple account of the factors affecting monetary policy deliberations, see William P. Yohe, "The Open Market Committee Decision Process and the 1964 Patman *Hearings," National Banking Review,* March 1965.

5. For an enumeration of all the separate lags that may be involved just between the time that sellers meet an unforeseen increase in sales by drawing down their inventories and the time that production (and income) is affected, see Gardner Ackley, "The Multiplier Time Period: Money, Inventories, and Flexibility," *American Economic Review,* June 1951, esp. pp. 357-363.

6. This was constructed from various sources, chiefly C. Brown, R. Solow, A. Ando, and J. Kareken, *op.cit,* and Ackley, *op.cit.* The portion dealing with state and local government bond issues to finance construction projects owes its origin to W. O. Shropshire.

The trichotomy for the basic time lags originated in Milton Friedman, "A Monetary and Fiscal Framework for Economic Stability," *American Economic Review,* June 1948, pp. 245-264 (reprinted in F. A. Lutz and L. W. Mints [eds.], *Readings in Monetary Theory* [Philadelphia: The Blakiston Co., 1951], pp. 369-393).

7. There are really two camps: a long-lag camp and a short-lag one. In between are numerous economists working on particular components in the lag structure. Federal Reserve economists have concentrated particular attention on the intermediate lag. Most of the findings described here are from

C. Brown, R. Solow, A. Ando, and J. Kareken, *op.cit.* This study generally supports the short-lag view.

8. Brown *et al.* affirm, on the basis of admittedly cursory observations, an average lag of about three and one-half months between Federal Reserve actions and changes in building plans, as indicated by requests for FHA and VA mortgage insurance (Sect. 18.3).

9. Do not forget that money supply changes should be closely related to expenditure changes (Sect. 2.3). John Culbertson estimates the average lag between cyclical turning points in the stock of money (*M*) and the flow of income (*Y*) to be five months (see "The Lag in Effect of Monetary Policy: Reply," *Journal of Political Economy,* October 1961, p. 468).

10. Friedman has reported the results of his statistical lag studies in many places, in particular in two studies with Anna J. Schwartz for the National Bureau of Economic Research: *A Monetary History of the United States, 1867-1960* (Princeton, N.J.: Princeton University Press, 1963); and "Money and Business Cycles" (1963). The data reported in the text are from the latter study.

11. The first two are from Culbertson, *op.cit.,* and "Friedman on the Lag in Effect of Monetary Policy," *Journal of Political Economy,* December 1960, pp. 617-621; the third stems from C. Brown, R. Solow, A. Ando, and J. Kareken, *op.cit.*

12. D. B. Suits, "Forecasting and Analysis with an Econometric Model," *American Economic Review,* March 1962, pp. 104-132.

Two preliminary attempts at monetary policy simulation are contained in the following: Ta-Chung Liu, "An Explanatory Quarterly Econometric Model of Effective Demand in the Postwar U.S. Economy," *Econometrica,* July 1963, esp. pp. 331-345; and Frank de Leeuw, "Financial Markets in Business Cycles: A Simulation Study," *American Economic Review,* May 1964, pp. 309-323.

13. See Report of the Commission on Money and Credit, *Money and Credit: Their Influence on Jobs, Prices, and Growth* (Englewood Cliffs, N.J.: Prentice-Hall, Inc., 1961), pp. 246-247. See also W. L. Smith, "The Effects of Monetary Policy on the Major Sectors of the Economy," in L. S. Ritter (ed.), *Money and Economic Activity* (Boston: Houghton Mifflin Company, 1961), pp. 178-195. A somewhat extreme statement of the case is contained in Conference on Economic Progress (Leon H. Keyserling, Pres.), *Tight Money and Rising Interest Rates . . . and the Damage They Are Doing* (Washington, D.C.: Conference, 1960).

14. Much of the available evidence is summarized in J. R. Meyer and E. Kuh, *The Investment Decision* (Cambridge, Mass.: Harvard University Press, 1957). Interest rate changes are reputed to be significant influences on investment in new railroad and electric power facilities.

15. Milton Friedman, *A Program for Monetary Stability* (New York: Fordham University Press, 1960), pp. 84-99; and Edward S. Shaw, "Money Supply and Stable Economic Growth," in *United States Monetary Policy,* revised edition (New York: The American Assembly, Columbia University and Frederick A. Praeger, 1964), pp. 83-91.

16. Milton Friedman, *A Program for Monetary Stability,* p. 92.

17. See Milton Friedman, *Capitalism and Freedom* (Chicago: University of Chicago Press, 1962), pp. 54-55.

18. "Statistical Tests of Rival Monetary Rules," *Journal of Political Economy,* February 1961, pp. 1-14. Bronfenbrenner distinguishes between the "judgment" rule, which was the actual historical "rule," the 3 and 4 per cent

versions of the Friedman-Shaw "inflexible" rule, and his own "lag" rule, whereby the rate of growth of the money supply in one period is geared positively to the previous period's rate of growth in employment and man-hour productivity and negatively to the previous period's rate of growth in velocity.

19. See his "Some Empirical Tests of Monetary Management and of Rules versus Discretion," *Journal of Political Economy*, June 1964, pp. 211-245.

Index